CYPHER SYSTEM RULEBOOK

CREDITS

Designers	Monte Cook, Bruce R. Cordell, Sean K. Reynolds
Additional Designers	Shanna Germain, Robert J. Schwalb
Creative Director	Monte Cook
Managing Editor	Shanna Germain
Editor/Proofreader	Ray Vallese
Art Director	Bear Weiter
Cover Artist	Roberto Pitturru

Artists

Eren Arik, Jacob Atienza, Bruce Brenneise, Marco Caradonna, chrom, Vincent Coviello, Biagio D'Alessandro, Sarah Dahlinger, Florian Devos, Jason Engle, Felipe Escobar, David Hueso, Baldi Konijn, Guido Kuip, Kezrek Laczin, Katerina Ladon, Brandon Leach, Eric Lofgren, Raph Lomotan, Anton Kagounkin Magdalina, Patrick McEvoy, Jeremy McHugh, Brynn Metheney, Giorgio De Michele (Erebus), Reiko Murakami, Federico Musetti, Irina Nordsol, Mirco Paganessi, Grzegorz Pedrycz, Angelo Peluso, Mike Perry, John Petersen, Roberto Pitturru, Scott Purdy, Aaron Riley, Riccardo Rullo, Nick Russell, Seth Rutledge, Martin de Diego Sádaba, Sam Santala, Lie Setiawan, Joe Slucher, Lee Smith, Kim Sokol, Matt Stawicki, Cyril Terpent, Cory Trego-Erdner, Tiffany Turrill, Shane Tyree, Jordan K. Walker, Chris Waller, Cathy Wilkins, Ben Wootten, Kieran Yanner

© 2019 Monte Cook Games, LLC. **CYPHER SYSTEM** and its logo are trademarks of Monte Cook Games, LLC in the U.S.A. and other countries. All Monte Cook Games characters and character names, and the distinctive likenesses thereof, are trademarks of Monte Cook Games, LLC.

Printed in Canada

TABLE OF CONTENTS

THE CYPHER SYSTEM — 4
- Chapter 1: WORLDS OF ADVENTURE — 4
- Chapter 2: ANYTHING GOES — 5
- Chapter 3: HOW TO PLAY THE CYPHER SYSTEM — 7

PART 1: CHARACTERS — 13
- Chapter 4: CREATING YOUR CHARACTER — 14
- Chapter 5: TYPE — 20
- Chapter 6: FLAVOR — 34
- Chapter 7: DESCRIPTOR — 38
- Chapter 8: FOCUS — 60
- Chapter 9: ABILITIES — 95
- Chapter 10: EQUIPMENT — 201

PART 2: RULES — 205
- Chapter 11: RULES OF THE GAME — 206
- Chapter 12: EXPERIENCE POINTS — 237

PART 3: GENRES — 251
- Chapter 13: FANTASY — 252
- Chapter 14: MODERN — 261
- Chapter 15: SCIENCE FICTION — 270
- Chapter 16: HORROR — 280
- Chapter 17: ROMANCE — 286
- Chapter 18: SUPERHEROES — 289
- Chapter 19: POST-APOCALYPTIC — 295
- Chapter 20: FAIRY TALE — 302
- Chapter 21: HISTORICAL — 307

PART 4: GAME MASTERING — 311
- Chapter 22: CREATURES — 312
- Chapter 23: NPCs — 372
- Chapter 24: CYPHERS — 377
- Chapter 25: RUNNING THE CYPHER SYSTEM — 402

PART 5: BACK MATTER — 443
- INDEX — 444
- CAMPAIGN DESIGN WORKSHEET — 446
- CHARACTER SHEET — 447

Chapter 1

WORLDS OF ADVENTURE

Ultimately, what we all want is to play precisely the game we want to play. Game masters all have a perfect setting in the back of their brain. Players have that one character idea that would be their best character ever, if they could just have the chance to make and play them.

Those dreams of playing exactly what you want to play are why this book exists.

This is a revised version of the original *Cypher System Rulebook*. I pulled the contents of that book together from the Cypher System games that existed at the time—Numenera and The Strange. It was basically a compilation of all that game material, plus a lot of suggestions for how to use it in any way you wished. Players and GMs told us that it served those needs well.

We've learned a lot since then, though. Not so much about the system rules themselves—which remain essentially untouched—but about how we want to use this kind of book, and therefore how to present the information in it. It's really challenging to make something that's usable by anyone for anything and present it in a truly user-friendly way. But I think we did just that with this book. The innovations you'll find in these pages—the way all the abilities have been cataloged so you can use them however you need, the focus on subtle cyphers, the breadth of the genres presented—make this material easier to use and easier to customize. The brand-new content, like the character arc system, the crafting system, the additional genre information, and so on, will hopefully make your games more fun and your stories richer.

But let me reiterate: we haven't changed the way the game works. You can use this book alongside the old *Cypher System Rulebook* without much issue at all.

In some ways, this book is a companion volume to a book that I wrote called *Your Best Game Ever*. That book is a system-agnostic guide to understanding and enjoying roleplaying games. This book takes the ideas and suggestions presented there and gives them a set of rules that empowers them. It's my goal to give you the tools to have your best game ever. And that, I believe, involves getting to play in the setting and with the characters that you've always wanted. Now, hopefully, you can do just that.

Have fun!

Monte Cook
March 2019

Chapter 2
ANYTHING GOES

For just a moment, we're talking directly to the game masters out there. Both players and GMs will use this book, but more than likely the GM will look at it first.

What you hold in your hands is a guidebook. A how-to. You can't just sit down and start playing, because the *Cypher System Rulebook* is not meant to be used that way. You have to put something of your own into it first. There is no setting or world here. The system is designed to help you portray any world or setting you can dream up.

Think of this book as a chest of toys. You can pull out whatever you want and play with it however you want. You won't use everything in it, at least not all at once. You'll use parts of it to build the game you want to play. Pull out some pieces and give them a try. Put back the ones that don't suit you, and try different ones. Use some now and save others for your next game. You have all the freedom in the world (many worlds, actually).

> Think of this book as a chest of toys. You can pull out whatever you want and play with it however you want.

Speaking of worlds, you get to decide what setting to use, based on what genre you want. It can be anything. Pick your favorite book or movie, or design something from scratch.

GENRES

Take a look at Part 3: Genres, which has a number of chapters devoted to genres. These are broad categories, and we use them in this book as a starting point. Those categories are: fantasy, modern, science fiction, horror, romance, superheroes, post-apocalyptic, fairy tale, and historical.

With those broad strokes, we cover most (but probably not all) of the kinds of games you can run with the Cypher System. Some of these genres require unique equipment, artifacts, or descriptors. Some need new rules to convey the experience you're after.

We say "experience" because in many ways, that's what a genre is. If you want to capture the experience of being terrified by zombies swarming around a character's home, you want horror. If you want to convey the experience of being extremely powerful and using those powers to protect the world from aliens, you want superheroes (maybe with a dash of science fiction).

Part 3: Genres, page 251

> *Genre categories are difficult. Sometimes they can be constricting when they should be liberating. Don't worry too much about being a genre purist. Just have a fun game.*

So, really, what you're choosing here is the experience you want to have—and that you want the players to have. This is such a fundamental decision that perhaps the whole group should be in on it. Ask the other players what genre they like and what kinds of experiences they want to have. This is vital because it ensures that everyone gets what they want out of the game.

Of course, not everything in this book is suitable for every genre. You, the GM, will need to read through it once you've chosen a genre and pick types, foci, and so forth. Then tell your players what material you've chosen to be available so they can create characters that fit the genre.

Flavor, page 34
Chapter 5: Type, page 20

SETTINGS

While genres are useful categories to organize your thoughts, what you're actually going to create is a setting. Labels like "science fiction" or "space opera" are fine, but in the end, what is important is the specific setting.

Your setting—whether it's your original creation or adapted from something else—is yours to do with as you will. Don't worry about what anyone else might think is appropriate for the genre. Once you start putting together the setting, you might want to go through the character creation material in this book again. Just because something is appropriate for the fantasy genre, it might not work for your fantasy setting. For example, you might have designed it such that fire magic is always evil and in the hands of demon-possessed priests, and thus Bears a Halo of Fire is not an appropriate focus

Chapter 7: Descriptor, page 38
Chapter 8: Focus, page 60
Bears a Halo of Fire, page 64

> If you like the Cypher System but don't want to create your own setting, check out the games Numenera or The Strange, or the books *Gods of the Fall*, *Predation*, and *Unmasked*, as well as the upcoming titles *The Stars Are Fire*, *Stay Alive!*, *Godforsaken*, and *We Are All Mad Here*. All of these offer complete settings with predetermined genres, foci, types, and more. None require customization if you don't want to do that.

Chapter 25: Running the Cypher System, page 402

for your PCs, even though it's fine in other fantasy games.

The more specific details you have about your setting, the easier this is to do. And the more distinct your setting is from genre tropes, the more you'll have to do it. But that's okay. Specific, distinct settings are usually the most fun, the most memorable, and the most likely to engage your players. They're worth the extra work.

TAILORING THE RULES

Sometimes you have to alter things to make them into what you need and want. Take, for example, the magic flavor that you can give to any of the types in chapter 5. It's called "magic" and has a lot of the trappings of magic, but it would be simple to change the name to "psionics," "mutant powers," or whatever your setting needs.

In other words, picking and choosing material from this book might not be enough. You might have to tweak things here and there. Fortunately, most of the material is made to be changed or manipulated. In fact, because the core mechanics of the Cypher System are so simple, tweaking things here and there is a breeze. This is not the kind of game where changing one thing creates a domino effect that has a lot of unintended consequences.

In chapter 7, you'll find guidelines for creating new descriptors. In chapter 8, you'll find an entire section dedicated to helping you create brand-new foci specific to your own games. And the character types in chapter 5 are designed to be tailored and reshaped.

When making alterations, worry less about game balance and more about telling the stories you want to tell and allowing the players to create and play the characters they want to play. If you do both of those things successfully, everyone will be happy. And that's really what game balance is all about.

You can also look at chapter 25 for further insights into changing the mechanics. But mostly, that chapter will tell you the same thing that you're reading now: it's your game to do with as you will.

Chapter 3
HOW TO PLAY THE CYPHER SYSTEM

The rules of the Cypher System are quite straightforward at their heart, as all of gameplay is based around a few core concepts. This chapter provides a brief explanation of how to play the game, and it's useful for learning the game. Once you understand the basic concepts, you'll likely want to reference Chapter 11: Rules of the Game, for a more in-depth treatment.

The Cypher System uses a twenty-sided die (1d20) to determine the results of most actions. Whenever a roll of any kind is called for and no die is specified, roll a d20.

The game master sets a difficulty for any given task. There are ten degrees of difficulty. Thus, the difficulty of a task can be rated on a scale of 1 to 10.

Each difficulty has a target number associated with it. The target number is always three times the task's difficulty, so a difficulty 1 task has a target number of 3, but a difficulty 4 task has a target number of 12. To succeed at the task, you must roll the target number or higher. See the Task Difficulty table (page 8) for guidance in how this works.

Character skills, favorable circumstances, or excellent equipment can decrease the difficulty of a task. For example, if a character is trained in climbing, they turn a difficulty 6 climb into a difficulty 5 climb. This is called *easing the difficulty by one step* (or just *easing the difficulty*, which assumes it's eased by one step). If they are specialized in climbing, they turn a difficulty 6 climb into a difficulty 4 climb. This is called *easing the difficulty by two steps*. Decreasing the difficulty of a task can also be called *easing a task*. Some situations increase, or *hinder*, the difficulty of a task. If a task is hindered, it increases the difficulty by one step.

A skill is a category of knowledge, ability, or activity relating to a task, such as climbing, geography, or persuasiveness. A character who has a skill is better at completing related tasks than a character who lacks the skill. A character's level of skill is either trained (reasonably skilled) or specialized (very skilled).

If you are trained in a skill relating to a task, you ease the difficulty of that task by one step. If you are specialized, you ease the difficulty by two steps. A skill can never decrease a task's difficulty by more than two steps.

Anything else that reduces difficulty (help from an ally, a particular piece of equipment, or some other advantage) is referred to as an *asset*. Assets can never decrease a task's difficulty by more than two steps.

You can also decrease the difficulty of a given task by applying Effort. (Effort is described in more detail in chapter 11.)

Hinder, page 207
Chapter 11: Rules of the Game, page 206
Skill, page 19

Difficulty, page 207

Trained, page 207
Specialized, page 207

Asset, page 209

Effort, page 15
Ease, page 207

TASK DIFFICULTY

Task Difficulty	Description	Target No.	Guidance
0	Routine	0	Anyone can do this basically every time.
1	Simple	3	Most people can do this most of the time.
2	Standard	6	Typical task requiring focus, but most people can usually do this.
3	Demanding	9	Requires full attention; most people have a 50/50 chance to succeed.
4	Difficult	12	Trained people have a 50/50 chance to succeed.
5	Challenging	15	Even trained people often fail.
6	Intimidating	18	Normal people almost never succeed.
7	Formidable	21	Impossible without skills or great effort.
8	Heroic	24	A task worthy of tales told for years afterward.
9	Immortal	27	A task worthy of legends that last lifetimes.
10	Impossible	30	A task that normal humans couldn't consider (but one that doesn't break the laws of physics).

To sum up, three things can decrease a task's difficulty: skills, assets, and Effort.

If you can ease a task so its difficulty is reduced to 0, you automatically succeed and don't need to make a roll.

WHEN DO YOU ROLL?

Any time your character attempts a task, the GM assigns a difficulty to that task, and you roll a d20 against the associated target number.

When you jump from a burning vehicle, swing an axe at a mutant beast, swim across a raging river, identify a strange device, convince a merchant to give you a lower price, craft an object, use a power to control a foe's mind, or use a blaster rifle to carve a hole in a wall, you make a d20 roll.

However, if you attempt something that has a difficulty of 0, no roll is needed—you automatically succeed. Many actions have a difficulty of 0. Examples include walking across the room and opening a door, using a special ability to negate gravity so you can fly, using an ability to protect your friend from radiation, or activating a device (that you already understand) to erect a force field. These are all routine actions and don't require rolls.

Armor, page 202

Using skill, assets, and Effort, you can ease the difficulty of potentially any task to 0 and thus negate the need for a roll. Walking across a narrow wooden beam is tricky for most people, but for an experienced gymnast, it's routine. You can even ease the difficulty of an attack on a foe to 0 and succeed without rolling.

Special rolls, page 9

If there's no roll, there's no chance for failure. However, there's also no chance for remarkable success (in the Cypher System, that usually means rolling a 19 or 20, which are called special rolls; chapter 11 also discusses special rolls).

COMBAT

Making an attack in combat works the same way as any other roll: the GM assigns a difficulty to the task, and you roll a d20 against the associated target number.

The difficulty of your attack roll depends on how powerful your opponent is. Just as tasks have a difficulty from 1 to 10, creatures have a level from 1 to 10. Most of the time, the difficulty of your attack roll is the same as the creature's level. For example, if you attack a level 2 bandit, it's a level 2 task, so your target number is 6.

It's worth noting that players make all die rolls. If a character attacks a creature, the player makes an attack roll. If a creature attacks a character, the player makes a defense roll.

The damage dealt by an attack is not determined by a roll—it's a flat number based on the weapon or attack used. For example, a spear always does 4 points of damage.

Your Armor characteristic reduces the damage you take from attacks directed at you. You get Armor from wearing physical armor (such as a leather jacket in a modern game or chainmail in a fantasy setting) or from special abilities. Like weapon damage, Armor is a flat number, not a roll. If you're attacked, subtract your Armor from the damage you take. For example, a leather jacket gives you +1 to Armor, meaning that you take 1 less point of damage from attacks. If a mugger hits you with a knife for 2 points of damage while you're wearing a leather jacket, you take only 1 point of damage. If your Armor reduces the damage from an attack to 0, you take no damage from that attack.

When you see the word "Armor" capitalized in the game rules (other than in the name of a special ability), it refers to your Armor characteristic—the number you subtract from

How to Play the Cypher System

> **GLOSSARY**
>
> **Game master (GM):** The player who doesn't run a character, but instead guides the flow of the story and runs all the NPCs.
>
> **Nonplayer character (NPC):** Characters run by the GM. Think of them as the minor characters in the story, or the villains or opponents. This includes any kind of creature as well as people.
>
> **Party:** A group of player characters (and perhaps some NPC allies).
>
> **Player character (PC):** A character run by a player rather than the GM. Think of the PCs as the main characters in the story.
>
> **Player:** The players who run characters in the game.
>
> **Session:** A single play experience. Usually lasts a few hours. Sometimes one adventure can be accomplished in a session. More often, one adventure is multiple sessions.
>
> **Adventure:** A single portion of the campaign with a beginning and an end. Usually defined at the beginning by a goal put forth by the PCs and at the end by whether or not they achieve that goal.
>
> **Campaign:** A series of sessions strung together with an overarching story (or linked stories) with the same player characters. Often, but not always, a campaign involves a number of adventures.
>
> **Character:** Anything that can act in the game. Although this includes PCs and human NPCs, it also technically includes creatures, aliens, mutants, automatons, animate plants, and so on. The word "creature" is usually synonymous.

incoming damage. When you see the word "armor" with a lowercase "a," it refers to any physical armor you might wear.

Typical physical weapons come in three categories: light, medium and heavy.

Light weapons inflict only 2 points of damage, but they ease attack rolls because they are fast and easy to use. Light weapons are punches, kicks, clubs, knives, handaxes, rapiers, small pistols, and so on. Weapons that are particularly small are light weapons.

Medium weapons inflict 4 points of damage. Medium weapons include swords, battleaxes, maces, crossbows, spears, pistols, blasters, and so on. Most weapons are medium. Anything that could be used in one hand (even if it's often used in two hands, such as a quarterstaff or spear) is a medium weapon.

Heavy weapons inflict 6 points of damage, and you must use two hands to attack with them. Heavy weapons are huge swords, great hammers, massive axes, halberds, heavy crossbows, blaster rifles, and so on. Anything that must be used in two hands is a heavy weapon.

SPECIAL ROLLS

When you roll a natural 19 (the d20 shows "19") and the roll is a success, you also have a minor effect. In combat, a minor effect inflicts 3 additional points of damage with your attack, or, if you'd prefer a special result, you could decide instead that you knock the foe back, distract them, or something similar. When not in combat, a minor effect could mean that you perform the action with particular grace. For example, when jumping down from a ledge, you land smoothly on your feet, or when trying to persuade someone, you convince them that you're smarter than you really are. In other words, you not only succeed but also go a bit further.

When you roll a natural 20 (the d20 shows "20") and the roll is a success, you also have a major effect. This is similar to a minor effect, but the results are more remarkable. In combat, a major effect inflicts 4 additional points of damage with your attack, but again, you can choose instead to introduce a dramatic event

For more on the types of weapons that characters can use, see Chapter 10: Equipment.

For some people, combat will be an important part of the Cypher System. However, it's your choice; a Cypher System game doesn't have to be about combat.

In the Cypher System, players make all die rolls. If a character attacks a creature, the player makes an attack roll. If a creature attacks a character, the player makes a defense roll.

such as knocking down your foe, stunning them, or taking an extra action. Outside of combat, a major effect means that something beneficial happens based on the circumstance. For example, when climbing up a cliff wall, you make the ascent twice as fast. When a roll grants you a major effect, you can choose to use a minor effect instead if you prefer.

In combat (and only in combat), if you roll a natural 17 or 18 on your attack roll, you add 1 or 2 additional points of damage, respectively. Neither roll has any special effect options—just the extra damage.

Rolling a natural 1 is always bad. It means that the GM introduces a new complication into the encounter.

RANGE AND SPEED

Distance is simplified into four categories: immediate, short, long, and very long.

Immediate distance from a character is within reach or within a few steps. If a character stands in a small room, everything in the room is within immediate distance. At most, immediate distance is 10 feet (3 m).

Short distance is anything greater than immediate distance but less than 50 feet (15 m) or so.

Long distance is anything greater than short distance but less than 100 feet (30 m) or so.

Very long distance is anything greater than long distance but less than 500 feet (150 m) or so. Beyond that range, distances are always specified—1,000 feet (300 m), a mile (1.5 km), and so on.

The idea is that it's not necessary to measure precise distances. Immediate distance is right there, practically next to the character. Short distance is nearby. Long distance is farther off. Very long distance is really far off.

All weapons and special abilities use these terms for ranges. For example, all melee weapons have immediate range—they are close-combat weapons, and you can use them to attack anyone within immediate distance. A thrown knife (and most other thrown weapons) has short range. A bow has long range. An Adept's Onslaught ability also has short range.

For more information on special rolls and how they affect combat and other interactions, see page 210.

Distance, page 213

Adept, page 24
Onslaught, page 167

How to Play the Cypher System

A character can move an immediate distance as part of another action. In other words, they can take a few steps over to the control panel and activate a switch. They can lunge across a small room to attack a foe. They can open a door and step through.

A character can move a short distance as their entire action for a turn. They can also try to move a long distance as their entire action, but the player might have to roll to see if the character slips, trips, or stumbles as the result of moving so far so quickly.

For example, if the PCs are fighting a group of cultists, any character can likely attack any cultist in the general melee—they're all within immediate range. Exact positions aren't important. Creatures in a fight are always moving, shifting, and jostling, anyway. However, if one cultist stayed back to fire a pistol, a character might have to use their entire action to move the short distance required to attack that foe. It doesn't matter if the cultist is 20 feet (6 m) or 40 feet (12 m) away—it's simply considered short distance. It does matter if the cultist is more than 50 feet (15 m) away because that distance would require a long or very long move.

EXPERIENCE POINTS

Experience points (XP) are rewards given to players when the GM intrudes on the story (this is called GM intrusion) with a new and unexpected challenge. For example, in the middle of combat, the GM might inform the player that they drop their weapon. However, to intrude in this manner, the GM must award the player 2 XP. The rewarded player, in turn, must immediately give one of those XP to another player and justify the gift (perhaps the other player had a good idea, told a funny joke, performed an action that saved a life, and so on).

Alternatively, the player can refuse the GM intrusion. If they do so, they don't get the 2 XP from the GM, and they must also spend 1 XP that they already have. If the player has no XP to spend, they can't refuse the intrusion.

The GM can also give players XP between sessions as a reward for making discoveries during an adventure. Discoveries are interesting facts, wondrous secrets, powerful artifacts, answers to mysteries, or solutions to problems (such as where the kidnappers are keeping their victim or how the PCs repair the starship). You don't earn XP for killing foes or overcoming standard challenges in the course of play. Discovery is the soul of the Cypher System.

Experience points, page 237

GM intrusion, page 408

Many rules in this system avoid the cumbersome need for precision. Does it really matter if the ghost is 13 feet away from you or 18? Probably not. That kind of needless specificity only slows things down and draws away from, rather than contributes to, the story.

11

> You don't earn XP for killing foes or overcoming standard challenges in the course of play. Discovery is the soul of the Cypher System.

Chapter 4: Creating Your Character, page 14

Experience points are used primarily for character advancement (for details, see Chapter 4: Creating Your Character), but a player can also spend 1 XP to reroll any die roll and take the better of the two rolls.

CYPHERS

Cypher, page 377

Cyphers are abilities that have a single use. In many campaigns, cyphers aren't physical objects—they might be a spell cast upon a character, a blessing from a god, or just a quirk of fate that gives them a momentary advantage. In some campaigns, cyphers are physical objects that characters can carry. Whether or not cyphers are physical objects, they are part of the character (like equipment or a special ability) and are things characters can use during the game. The form that physical cyphers take depends on the setting. In a fantasy world they might be wands or potions, but in a science fiction game they could be alien crystals or prototype devices.

Characters will find new cyphers frequently in the course of play, so players shouldn't hesitate to use their cypher abilities. Because cyphers are always different, the characters will always have new special powers to try.

OTHER DICE

A d6 is used most often for recovery rolls (page 218) and to determine the level of cyphers (page 377).

In addition to a d20, you'll need a d6 (a six-sided die). Rarely, you'll need to roll a number between 1 and 100 (often called a d100 or d% roll), which you can do by rolling a d20 twice, using the last digit of the first roll as the "tens" place and the last digit of the second roll as the "ones" place. For example, rolling a 17 and a 9 gives you 79, rolling a 3 and an 18 gives you 38, and rolling a 20 and a 10 gives you 00 (also known as 100). If you have a d10 (a ten-sided die), you can use it instead of the d20 to roll numbers between 1 and 100.

Part 1
CHARACTERS

Chapter 4: CREATING YOUR CHARACTER	14
Chapter 5: TYPE	20
Chapter 6: FLAVOR	34
Chapter 7: DESCRIPTOR	38
Chapter 8: FOCUS	60
Chapter 9: ABILITIES	95
Chapter 10: EQUIPMENT	201

Chapter 4
CREATING YOUR CHARACTER

This chapter explains how to create characters to play in a Cypher System game. This involves a series of decisions that will shape your character, so the more you understand what kind of character you want to play, the easier character creation will be. The process involves understanding the values of three game statistics and choosing three aspects that determine your character's capabilities.

CHARACTER STATS

Every player character has three defining characteristics, which are typically called "statistics" or "stats." These stats are Might, Speed, and Intellect. They are broad categories that cover many different but related aspects of a character.

MIGHT

Might defines how strong and durable your character is. The concepts of strength, endurance, constitution, hardiness, and physical prowess are all folded into this one stat. Might isn't relative to size; instead, it's an absolute measurement. An elephant has more Might than the mightiest tiger, which has more Might than the mightiest rat, which has more Might than the mightiest spider.

Might governs actions from forcing doors open to walking for days without food to resisting disease. It's also the primary means of determining how much damage your character can sustain in a dangerous situation. Physical characters, tough characters, and characters interested in fighting should focus on Might.

SPEED

Speed describes how fast and physically coordinated your character is. The stat embodies quickness, movement, dexterity, and reflexes. Speed governs such divergent actions as dodging attacks, sneaking around quietly, and throwing a ball accurately. It helps determine whether you can move farther on your turn. Nimble, fast, or sneaky characters will want good Speed stats, as will those interested in ranged combat.

INTELLECT

This stat determines how smart, knowledgeable, and likable your character is. It includes intelligence, wisdom, charisma, education, reasoning, wit, willpower, and charm. Intellect governs solving puzzles, remembering facts, telling convincing lies, and using mental powers. Characters interested in communicating effectively, being learned scholars, or wielding supernatural powers should stress their Intellect stat.

Speed could be thought of as Speed/Agility because it governs your overall swiftness and reflexes.

Might could be thought of as Might/Health because it governs how strong you are and how much physical punishment you can take.

Intellect could be thought of as Intellect/Personality because it governs both intelligence and charisma.

POOL, EDGE, AND EFFORT

Each of the three stats has two components: Pool and Edge. Your Pool represents your raw, innate ability, and your Edge represents knowing how to use what you have. A third element ties into this concept: Effort. When your character really needs to accomplish a task, you apply Effort.

POOL

Your Pool is the most basic measurement of a stat. Comparing the Pools of two creatures will give you a general sense of which creature is superior in that stat. For example, a character who has a Might Pool of 16 is stronger (in a basic sense) than a character who has a Might Pool of 12. Most characters start with a Pool of 9 to 12 in most stats—that's the average range.

When your character is injured, sickened, or attacked, you temporarily lose points from one of your stat Pools. The nature of the attack determines which Pool loses points. For example, physical damage from a sword reduces your Might Pool, a poison that makes you clumsy reduces your Speed Pool, and a psionic blast reduces your Intellect Pool. You can also spend points from one of your stat Pools to decrease a task's difficulty (see Effort, below). You can rest to recover lost points from a stat Pool, and some special abilities or cyphers might allow you to recover lost points quickly.

EDGE

Although your Pool is the basic measurement of a stat, your Edge is also important. When something requires you to spend points from a stat Pool, your Edge for that stat reduces the cost. It also reduces the cost of applying Effort to a roll.

For example, let's say you have a mental blast ability, and activating it costs 1 point from your Intellect Pool. Subtract your Intellect Edge from the activation cost, and the result is how many points you must spend to use the mental blast. If using your Edge reduces the cost to 0, you can use the ability for free.

Your Edge can be different for each stat. For example, you could have a Might Edge of 1, a Speed Edge of 1, and an Intellect Edge of 0. You'll always have an Edge of at least 1 in one stat. Your Edge for a stat reduces the cost of spending points from that stat Pool, but not from other Pools. Your Might Edge reduces the cost of spending points from your Might Pool, but it doesn't affect your Speed Pool or Intellect Pool. Once a stat's Edge reaches 3, you can apply one level of Effort for free.

> ### CREATING YOUR CHARACTER IN 5 EASY STEPS
> 1. Grab a pen and blank piece of paper (or a character sheet) to record all your choices. Choose from one of four types in chapter 5. Follow the instructions provided for finishing your stats, abilities, equipment, and cyphers. A walk-through example of a player creating a character (Warrior Example, Adept Example, Explorer Example, and Speaker Example) accompanies each type. Each example showcases a player following all the steps presented here.
> 2. Choose a descriptor in chapter 7.
> 3. Choose a focus in chapter 8.
> 4. Choose a character arc in chapter 12.
> 5. Begin your adventure!

A character who has a low Might Pool but a high Might Edge has the potential to perform Might actions consistently better than a character who has a Might Edge of 0. The high Edge will let them reduce the cost of spending points from the Pool, which means they'll have more points available to spend on applying Effort.

EFFORT

When your character really needs to accomplish a task, you can apply Effort. For a beginning character, applying Effort requires spending 3 points from the stat Pool appropriate to the action. Thus, if your character tries to dodge an attack (a Speed roll) and wants to increase the chance for success, you can apply Effort by spending 3 points from your Speed Pool. Effort eases the task by one step. This is called applying one level of Effort.

You don't have to apply Effort if you don't want to. If you choose to apply Effort to a task, you must do it before you attempt the roll—you can't roll first and then decide to apply Effort if you rolled poorly.

Applying more Effort can lower a task's difficulty further: each additional level of Effort eases the task by another step. Applying one level of Effort eases the task by one step, applying two levels eases the task by two steps, and so on. However, each level of Effort after the first costs only 2 points from the stat Pool instead of 3. So applying two levels of Effort costs 5 points (3 for the first level plus 2 for the second level), applying three levels costs 7 points (3 plus 2 plus 2), and so on.

Chapter 5: Type, page 20

Warrior Example, page 23
Adept Example, page 26
Explorer Example, page 29
Speaker Example, page 32

Chapter 7: Descriptor, page 38
Chapter 8: Focus, page 60
Chapter 12: Experience Points, page 237

Recovering points in a Pool, page 218

Your stat Pools, as well as your Effort and Edge, are determined by the character type, descriptor, and focus that you choose. Within those guidelines, however, you have a lot of flexibility in how you develop your character.

Every character has an Effort score, which indicates the maximum number of levels of Effort that can be applied to a roll. A beginning (first-tier) character has an Effort of 1, meaning you can apply only one level of Effort to a roll. A more experienced character has a higher Effort score and can apply more levels of Effort to a roll. For example, a character who has an Effort of 3 can apply up to three levels of Effort to reduce a task's difficulty.

When you apply Effort, subtract your relevant Edge from the total cost of applying Effort. For example, let's say you need to make a Speed roll. To increase your chance for success, you decide to apply one level of Effort, which will ease the task. Normally, that would cost 3 points from your Speed Pool. However, you have a Speed Edge of 2, so you subtract that from the cost. Thus, applying Effort to the roll costs only 1 point from your Speed Pool.

What if you applied two levels of Effort to the Speed roll instead of just one? That would ease the task by two steps. Normally, it would cost 5 points from your Speed Pool, but after subtracting your Speed Edge of 2, it costs only 3 points.

Once a stat's Edge reaches 3, you can apply one level of Effort for free. For example, if you have a Speed Edge of 3 and you apply one level of Effort to a Speed roll, it costs you 0 points from your Speed Pool. (Normally, applying one level of Effort would cost 3 points, but you subtract your Speed Edge from that cost, reducing it to 0.)

Skills and other advantages also ease a task, and you can use them in conjunction with Effort. In addition, your character might have special abilities or equipment that allow you to apply Effort to accomplish a special effect, such as knocking down a foe with an attack or affecting multiple targets with a power that normally affects only one.

EFFORT AND DAMAGE

Instead of applying Effort to ease your attack, you can apply Effort to increase the amount of damage you inflict with an attack. For each level of Effort you apply in this way, you inflict 3 additional points of damage. This works for any kind of attack that inflicts damage, whether a sword, a crossbow, a mind blast, or something else.

When using Effort to increase the damage of an area attack, such as the explosion created by an Adept's Concussion ability, you inflict 2 additional points of damage instead of 3 points. However, the additional points are dealt to all targets in the area. Further, even if one or more of the targets resist the attack, they still take 1 point of damage.

MULTIPLE USES OF EFFORT AND EDGE

If your Effort is 2 or higher, you can apply Effort to multiple aspects of a single action. For example, if you make an attack, you can apply Effort to your attack roll and apply Effort to increase the damage.

The total amount of Effort you apply can't be higher than your Effort score. For example, if your Effort is 2, you can apply up to two levels of Effort. You could apply one level to an attack roll and one level to its damage, two levels to the attack and no levels to the damage, or no levels to the attack and two levels to the damage.

You can use Edge for a particular stat only once per action. For example, if you apply Effort to a Might attack roll and to your damage, you can use your Might Edge to reduce the cost of one of those uses of Effort, not both. If you spend 1 Intellect point to activate your mind blast and one level of Effort to ease the attack roll, you can use your Intellect Edge to reduce the cost of one of those things, not both.

STAT EXAMPLES

A beginning character is fighting a giant rat. The PC stabs their spear at the rat, which is a level 2 creature and thus has a target number of 6. The character stands atop a boulder and strikes downward at the beast, and the GM rules that this helpful tactic is an asset that eases the attack by one step (to difficulty 1). That lowers the target number to 3. Attacking with a spear is a Might action; the character has a Might Pool of 11 and a Might Edge of 0. Before making the roll, they decide to apply a level of Effort to ease the attack. That costs 3 points from their Might Pool, reducing the Pool to 8. But the points are well spent. Applying the Effort lowers the difficulty from 1 to 0, so no roll is needed—the attack automatically succeeds.

Another character is attempting to convince a guard to let them into a private office to speak to an influential noble. The GM rules that this is an Intellect action. The character is third tier and has an Effort of 3, an Intellect Pool of 13, and an Intellect Edge of 1. Before making the roll, they must decide whether to apply Effort. They can choose to apply one, two, or three levels of Effort, or apply none at all. This action is important to them, so they decide to apply two levels of Effort, easing the task by two steps. Thanks to their Intellect Edge, applying the Effort costs only 4 points from their Intellect Pool (3 points for the first level of Effort plus 2 points for the second level minus 1 point for their Edge). Spending those points reduces their Intellect

---

When applying Effort to melee attacks, you have the option of spending points from either your Might Pool or your Speed Pool. When making ranged attacks, you may spend points only from your Speed Pool. This reflects that with melee you sometimes use brute force and sometimes use finesse, but with ranged attacks, it's always about careful targeting.

For information on additional types of damage, see Damage Track, page 218, and Special Damage, page 219.

Concussion, page 121

Creating Your Character

Pool to 9. The GM decides that convincing the guard is a difficulty 3 (demanding) task with a target number of 9; applying two levels of Effort reduces the difficulty to 1 (simple) and the target number to 3. The player rolls a d20 and gets an 8. Because this result is at least equal to the target number of the task, they succeed. However, if they had not applied some Effort, they would have failed because their roll (8) would have been less than the task's original target number (9).

CHARACTER TIERS

Every character starts the game at the first tier. Tier is a measurement of power, toughness, and ability. Characters can advance up to the sixth tier. As your character advances to higher tiers, you gain more abilities, increase your Effort, and can improve a stat's Edge or increase a stat. Generally speaking, even first-tier characters are already quite capable. It's safe to assume that they've already got some experience under their belt. This is not a "zero to hero" progression, but rather an instance of competent people refining and honing their capabilities and knowledge. Advancing to higher tiers is not really the goal of Cypher System characters, but rather a representation of how characters progress in a story.

To progress to the next tier, characters earn experience points (XP) by pursuing character arcs, going on adventures, and discovering new things—the system is about both discovery and exploration, as well as achieving personal goals. Experience points have many uses, and one use is to purchase character benefits. After your character purchases four character benefits, they advance to the next tier. Each benefit costs 4 XP, and you can purchase them in any order, but you must purchase one of each kind of benefit (and then advance to the next tier) before you can purchase the same benefit again. The four character benefits are as follows.

Increasing Capabilities: You gain 4 points to add to your stat Pools. You can allocate the points among the Pools however you wish.

Moving Toward Perfection: You add 1 to your Might Edge, your Speed Edge, or your Intellect Edge (your choice).

Extra Effort: Your Effort score increases by 1.

Skills: You become trained in one skill of your choice, other than attacks or defense. As described in Chapter 11: Rules of the Game, a character trained in a skill treats the difficulty

Skills are a broad category of things your character can learn and accomplish. For a list of sample skills, see the Skills sidebar on page 19.

17

of a related task as one step lower than normal. The skill you choose for this benefit can be anything you wish, such as climbing, jumping, persuading, or sneaking. You can also choose to be knowledgeable in a certain area of lore, such as history or geology. You can even choose a skill based on your character's special abilities. For example, if your character can make an Intellect roll to blast an enemy with mental force, you can become trained in using that ability, easing the task of using it. If you choose a skill that you are already trained in, you become specialized in that skill, easing related tasks by two steps instead of one.

Other Options: Players can also spend 4 XP to purchase other special options in lieu of gaining a new skill. Selecting any of these options counts as the skill benefit necessary to advance to the next tier. The special options are as follows:

- Reduce the cost for wearing armor. This option lowers the Speed cost for wearing armor by 1.
- Add 2 to your recovery rolls.
- Select a new type-based ability from your tier or a lower tier.

You can use flavors (chapter 6) to slightly modify character types to customize them for different genres.

Descriptor, page 38
Type, page 20
Focus, page 60

Recovery roll, page 218

Warrior, page 20
Adept, page 24
Explorer, page 27
Speaker, page 30

CHARACTER DESCRIPTOR, TYPE, AND FOCUS

To create your character, you build a simple statement that describes them. The statement takes this form: "I am a [fill in an adjective here] [fill in a noun here] who [fill in a verb here]."

Thus: "I am an *adjective noun* who *verbs*." For example, you might say, "I am a Rugged Warrior who Controls Beasts" or "I am a Charming Explorer who Focuses Mind Over Matter."

In this sentence, the adjective is called your descriptor.

The noun is your character type.

The verb is called your focus.

Even though character type is in the middle of the sentence, that's where we'll start this discussion. (Just as in a sentence, the noun provides the foundation.)

Your character type is the core of your character. In some roleplaying games, it might be called your character class. Your type helps determine your character's place in the world and relationship with other people in the setting. It's the noun of the sentence "I am an *adjective noun* who *verbs*."

You can choose from four character types in chapter 5: Warriors, Adepts, Explorers, and Speakers.

Your descriptor defines your character—it colors everything you do. Your descriptor places your character in the situation (the first adventure, which starts the campaign) and helps provide motivation. It's the adjective of the sentence "I am an *adjective noun* who *verbs*."

Unless your GM says otherwise, you can choose from any of the character descriptors in chapter 7.

Focus is what your character does best. Focus gives your character specificity and provides interesting new abilities that might come in handy. Your focus also helps you understand how you relate with the other player characters in your group. It's the verb of the sentence "I am an *adjective noun* who *verbs*."

There are many character foci in chapter 8. The ones you choose from will probably depend on the setting and genre of your game.

SPECIAL ABILITIES

Character types and foci grant PCs special abilities at each new tier. Using these abilities usually costs points from your stat Pools; the cost is listed in parentheses after the ability name. Your Edge in the appropriate stat can reduce the cost of the ability, but remember that you can apply Edge only once per action. For example, let's say an Adept with an Intellect Edge of 2 wants to use their Onslaught ability to create a bolt of force, which costs 1 Intellect point. They also want to increase the damage from the attack by using a level of Effort, which costs 3 Intellect points. The total cost for their action is 2 points from their Intellect Pool (1 point for the bolt of force, plus 3 points for using Effort, minus 2 points from their Edge).

Sometimes the point cost for an ability has a + sign after the number. For example, the cost might be given as "2+ Intellect points." That means you can spend more points or more levels of Effort to improve the ability further, as explained in the ability description.

Many special abilities grant a character the option to perform an action that they couldn't normally do, such as projecting rays of cold or attacking multiple foes at once. Using one of these abilities is an action unto itself, and the end of the ability's description says "Action" to remind you. It also might provide more information about when or how you perform the action.

Some special abilities allow you to perform a familiar action—one that you can already do—in a different way. For example, an ability might let you wear heavy armor, reduce the difficulty of Speed defense rolls, or add 2 points of fire damage to your weapon damage. These abilities are called enablers. Using one of these abilities is not considered an action. Enablers either function constantly (such as being able to wear heavy armor, which isn't an action) or happen as part of another action (such as adding fire damage to your weapon damage, which happens as part of your attack action). If a special ability is an enabler, the end of the ability's description says "Enabler" to remind you.

Some abilities specify a duration, but you can always end one of your own abilities anytime you wish.

Onslaught, page 167

Because this book covers so many genres, not all of the descriptors, types, and foci might be available for players. The GM will decide what's available in their particular game and whether anything is modified, and they'll let the players know.

SKILLS

Sometimes your character gains training in a specific skill or task. For example, your focus might mean that you're trained in sneaking, in climbing and jumping, or in social interactions. Other times, your character can choose a skill to become trained in, and you can pick a skill that relates to any task you think you might face.

The Cypher System has no definitive list of skills. However, the following list offers ideas:

Astronomy	Healing	Philosophy
Balancing	History	Physics
Biology	Identifying	Pickpocketing
Botany	Initiative	Piloting
Carrying	Intimidation	Repairing
Climbing	Jumping	Riding
Computers	Leatherworking	Smashing
Deceiving	Lockpicking	Sneaking
Disguise	Machinery	Stealth
Escaping	Metalworking	Swimming
Geography	Perception	Vehicle driving
Geology	Persuasion	Woodworking

You could choose a skill that incorporates more than one of these areas (interacting might include deceiving, intimidation, and persuasion) or that is a more specific version of one (hiding might be sneaking when you're not moving). You could also make up more general professional skills, such as baker, sailor, or lumberjack. If you want to choose a skill that's not on this list, it's probably best to run it past the GM first, but in general, the most important thing is to choose skills that are appropriate to your character.

Remember that if you gain a skill that you're already trained in, you become specialized in that skill. Because skill descriptions can be nebulous, determining whether you're trained or specialized might take some thinking. For example, if you're trained in lying and later gain an ability that grants you skill with all social interactions, you become specialized in lying and trained in all other types of interactions. Being trained three times in a skill is no better than being trained twice (in other words, specialized is as good as it gets).

Only skills gained through character type abilities or other rare instances allow you to become skilled with attack or defense tasks.

If you gain a special ability through your type, your focus, or some other aspect of your character, you can choose it in place of a skill and become trained or specialized in that ability. For example, if you have a mind blast, when it's time to choose a skill to be trained in, you can select your mind blast as your skill. That would ease the attack every time you used it. Each ability you have counts as a separate skill for this purpose. You can't select "all mind powers" or "all spells" as one skill and become trained or specialized in such a broad category.

In most campaigns, fluency in a language is considered a skill. So if you want to speak French, that's the same as being trained in biology or swimming.

Chapter 5
TYPE

Character type is the core of your character. Your type helps determine your character's place in the world and relationship with other people in the setting. It's the noun of the sentence "I am an *adjective noun* who *verbs*."

You can choose from four character types: Warrior, Adept, Explorer, and Speaker. However, you may not want to use these generic names for them. This chapter offers a few more specific names for each type that might be more appropriate to various genres. You'll find that names like "Warrior" or "Explorer" don't always feel right, particularly in games set in modern times. As always, you're free to do as you wish.

Since the type is the basis upon which your whole character is built, it's important to consider how the type relates to the chosen setting. To help with this, types are actually general archetypes. A Warrior, for example, might be anyone from a knight in shining armor to a cop on the streets to a grizzled cybernetic veteran of a thousand futuristic wars.

To further massage the four types for better use in various settings, different methods called flavors are presented in chapter 6 to help slightly tailor the types toward fantasy, science fiction, or other genres (or to address different character concepts).

Finally, more fundamental options for further customization are provided at the end of this chapter.

In some roleplaying games, your character type might be called your character class.

Most Cypher System games, like Numenera, The Strange, and Predation, have highly specific types designed to fit those settings perfectly.

Flavor, page 34

Further Customization, page 33

WARRIOR

Fantasy/Fairy tale: Warrior, fighter, swordsman, knight, barbarian, soldier, myrmidon, valkyrie
Modern/Horror/Romance: police officer, soldier, watchman, detective, guard, brawler, tough, athlete
Science fiction: security officer, warrior, trooper, soldier, merc
Superhero/Post-Apocalyptic: hero, brick, bruiser

You're a good ally to have in a fight. You know how to use weapons and defend yourself. Depending on the genre and setting in question, this might mean wielding a sword and shield in the gladiatorial arena, an AK-47 and a bandolier of grenades in a savage firefight, or a blaster rifle and powered armor when exploring an alien planet.

Individual Role: Warriors are physical, action-oriented people. They're more likely to overcome a challenge using force than by other means, and they often take the most straightforward path toward their goals.

Group Role: Warriors usually take and deal the most punishment in a dangerous situation. Often it falls on them to protect the other group members from threats. This sometimes means that warriors take on leadership roles as well, at least in combat and other times of danger.

PLAYER INTRUSION

A player intrusion is the player choosing to alter something in the campaign, making things easier for a player character. Conceptually, it is the reverse of a GM intrusion: instead of the GM giving the player XP and introducing an unexpected complication for a character, the player spends 1 XP and presents a solution to a problem or complication. What a player intrusion can do usually introduces a change to the world or current circumstances rather than directly changing the character. For instance, an intrusion indicating that the cypher just used still has an additional use would be appropriate, but an intrusion that heals the character would not. If a player has no XP to spend, they can't use a player intrusion.

A few player intrusion examples are provided under each type. That said, not every player intrusion listed there is appropriate for all situations. The GM may allow players to come up with other player intrusion suggestions, but the GM is the final arbiter of whether the suggested intrusion is appropriate for the character's type and suitable for the situation. If the GM refuses the intrusion, the player doesn't spend the 1 XP, and the intrusion doesn't occur.

Using an intrusion does not require a character to use an action to trigger it. A player intrusion just happens.

Societal Role: Warriors aren't always soldiers or mercenaries. Anyone who is ready for violence, or even potential violence, might be a Warrior in the general sense. This includes guards, watchmen, police officers, sailors, or people in other roles or professions who know how to defend themselves with skill.

Advanced Warriors: As warriors advance, their skill in battle—whether defending themselves or dishing out damage—increases to impressive levels. At higher tiers, they can often take on groups of foes by themselves or stand toe to toe with anyone.

WARRIOR PLAYER INTRUSIONS

You can spend 1 XP to use one of the following player intrusions, provided the situation is appropriate and the GM agrees.

Perfect Setup: You're fighting at least three foes and each one is standing in exactly the right spot for you to use a move you trained in long ago, allowing you to attack all three as a single action. Make a separate attack roll for each foe. You remain limited by the amount of Effort you can apply on one action.

Old Friend: A comrade in arms from your past shows up unexpectedly and provides aid in whatever you're doing. They are on a mission of their own and can't stay longer than it takes to help out, chat for a while after, and perhaps share a quick meal.

Weapon Break: Your foe's weapon has a weak spot. In the course of the combat, it quickly becomes damaged and moves two steps down the object damage track.

WARRIOR STAT POOLS

Stat	Pool Starting Value
Might	10
Speed	10
Intellect	8

You get 6 additional points to divide among your stat Pools however you wish.

FIRST-TIER WARRIOR

First-tier warriors have the following abilities:

Effort: Your Effort is 1.

Physical Nature: You have a Might Edge of 1 and a Speed Edge of 0, or you have a Might Edge of 0 and a Speed Edge of 1. Either way, you have an Intellect Edge of 0.

Cypher Use: You can bear two cyphers at a time.

Weapons: You become practiced with light, medium, and heavy weapons and suffer no penalty when using any kind of weapon. Enabler.

Starting Equipment: Appropriate clothing and two weapons of your choice, plus one expensive item, two moderately priced items, and up to four inexpensive items.

Special Abilities: Choose four of the abilities listed below. You can't choose the same ability more than once unless its description says otherwise. The full description for each listed ability can be found in chapter 9, which also has descriptions for flavor and focus abilities in a single vast catalog.

○ Bash (112)
○ Combat Prowess (120)
○ Control the Field (121)
○ Improved Edge (151)
○ No Need for Weapons (166)
○ Overwatch (168)
○ Physical Skills (170)
○ Practiced in Armor (171)
○ Quick Throw (174)
○ Swipe (188)
○ Trained Without Armor (193)

GM intrusion, page 408

Player intrusions should be limited to no more than one per player per session.

Object damage track, page 116

Your type is who your character is. You should use whatever name you want for your type, as long as it fits both your character and the setting.

Practiced, page 207

Your character's starting equipment is as important as their starting skills. Learn more about what you carry and how it's used in Chapter 10: Equipment.

Chapter 9: Abilities, page 95

The small numbers you see after abilities throughout this book are page numbers for easy reference.

SECOND-TIER WARRIOR
Choose two of the abilities listed below (or from a lower tier) to add to your repertoire. In addition, you can replace one of your lower-tier abilities with a different one from a lower tier.
○ Crushing Blow (123)
○ Hemorrhage (149)
○ Reload (176)
○ Skill With Attacks (183)
○ Skill With Defense (183)
○ Successive Attack (187)

A character can't apply Effort or other abilities to any task they accomplish using Tough As Nails.

THIRD-TIER WARRIOR
Choose three of the abilities listed below (or from a lower tier) to add to your repertoire. In addition, you can replace one of your lower-tier abilities with a different one from a lower tier.
○ Deadly Aim (125)
○ Energy Resistance (134)
○ Experienced in Armor (136)
○ Expert Cypher Use (137)
○ Fury (144)
○ Lunge (159)
○ Reaction (174)
○ Seize the Moment (181)
○ Slice (183)
○ Spray (185)
○ Trick Shot (194)
○ Vigilance (196)

FOURTH-TIER WARRIOR
Choose two of the abilities listed below (or from a lower tier) to add to your repertoire. In addition, you can replace one of your lower-tier abilities with a different one from a lower tier.
○ Amazing Effort (109)
○ Capable Warrior (118)
○ Experienced Defender (136)
○ Feint (139)
○ Increased Effects (153)
○ Momentum (164)
○ Pry Open (172)
○ Snipe (183)
○ Tough As Nails (192)

WARRIOR BACKGROUND CONNECTION
Your type helps determine the connection you have to the setting. Roll a d20 or choose from the following list to determine a specific fact about your background that provides a connection to the rest of the world. You can also create your own fact.

d20	Background
1	You were in the military and have friends who still serve. Your former commander remembers you well.
2	You were the bodyguard of a wealthy woman who accused you of theft. You left her service in disgrace.
3	You were the bouncer in a local bar for a while, and the patrons there remember you.
4	You trained with a highly respected mentor. They regard you well, but they have many enemies.
5	You trained in an isolated monastery. The monks think of you as a brother, but you're a stranger to all others.
6	You have no formal training. Your abilities come to you naturally (or unnaturally).
7	You spent time on the streets and were in prison for a while.
8	You were conscripted into military service, but you deserted before long.
9	You served as a bodyguard to a powerful criminal who now owes you their life.
10	You worked as a police officer or constable of some kind. Everyone knows you, but their opinions of you vary.
11	Your older sibling is an infamous character who has been disgraced.
12	You served as a guard for someone who traveled extensively. You know a smattering of people in many locations.
13	Your best friend is a teacher or scholar. They are a great source of knowledge.
14	You and a friend both smoke the same kind of rare, expensive tobacco. The two of you get together weekly to chat and smoke.
15	Your uncle runs a theater in town. You know all the actors and watch all the shows for free.
16	Your craftsman friend sometimes calls on you for help. However, they pay you well.
17	Your mentor wrote a book on martial arts. Sometimes people seek you out to ask about its stranger passages.
18	Someone you fought alongside in the military is now the mayor of a nearby town.
19	You saved the lives of a family when their house burned down. They're indebted to you, and their neighbors regard you as a hero.
20	Your old trainer still expects you to come back and clean up after their classes; when you do, they occasionally share interesting rumors.

FIFTH-TIER WARRIOR

Choose three of the abilities listed below (or from a lower tier) to add to your repertoire. In addition, you can replace one of your lower-tier abilities with a different one from a lower tier.

- Adroit Cypher Use (108)
- Arc Spray (110)
- Improved Success (152)
- Jump Attack (156)
- Mastery in Armor (161)
- Mastery With Attacks (161)
- Mastery With Defense (161)
- Parry (168)

SIXTH-TIER WARRIOR

Choose two of the abilities listed below (or from a lower tier) to add to your repertoire. In addition, you can replace one of your lower-tier abilities with a different one from a lower tier.

- Again and Again (109)
- Finishing Blow (140)
- Magnificent Moment (159)
- Murderer (165)
- Spin Attack (185)
- Weapon and Body (196)

WARRIOR EXAMPLE

Ray wants to create a Warrior character for a modern campaign. He decides that the character is an ex-military fellow who is fast and strong. He puts 3 of his additional points into his Might Pool and 3 into his Speed Pool; his stat Pools are now Might 13, Speed 13, and Intellect 8. As a first-tier character, his Effort is 1, his Might Edge is 1, and his Speed Edge and Intellect Edge are both 0. His character is not particularly smart or charismatic.

He wants to use a large combat knife (a medium weapon that inflicts 4 points of damage) and a .357 Magnum (a heavy pistol that inflicts 6 points of damage but requires the use of both hands). Ray decides not to wear armor, as it's not really appropriate to the setting, so for his first ability, he chooses Trained Without Armor so he eases Speed defense actions. For his second ability, he chooses Combat Prowess so he can inflict extra damage with his big knife.

Ray wants to be fast as well as tough, so he selects Improved Edge. This gives him a Speed Edge of 1. He rounds out his character with Physical Skills and chooses swimming and running.

The Warrior can bear two cyphers. The GM decides that Ray's first cypher is a pill that restores 6 points of Might when swallowed, and his second is a small, easily concealed grenade that explodes like a firebomb when thrown, inflicting 3 points of damage to all within immediate range.

Ray still needs to choose a descriptor and a focus. Looking ahead to the descriptor rules, Ray chooses Strong, which increases his Might Pool to 17. He also becomes trained in jumping and breaking inanimate objects. (If he had chosen jumping as one of his physical skills, the Strong descriptor would have made him specialized in jumping instead of trained.) Being Strong also gives Ray an extra medium or heavy weapon. He chooses a baseball bat that he'll use in a pinch. He keeps it in the trunk of his car.

For his focus, Ray chooses Masters Weaponry. This gives him yet another weapon of high quality. He chooses another combat knife and asks the GM if he could use it in his left hand—not to make attacks, but as a shield. This will ease his Speed defense rolls if he has both knives out (the "shield" counts as an asset). The GM agrees. During the game, Ray's Warrior will be hard to hit—he is trained in Speed defense rolls, and his extra knife eases his defense rolls by another step.

Thanks to his focus, he also inflicts 1 additional point of damage with his chosen weapon. Now he inflicts 6 points of damage with his blade. Ray's character is a deadly combatant, likely starting the game with a reputation as a knife fighter.

For his character arc, Ray chooses Defeat a Foe. That foe, he decides, is none other than someone in his company who was once a friend but went rogue.

> **DEFENSE TASKS**
> Defense tasks are when a player makes a roll to keep something undesirable from happening to their PC. The type of defense task matters when using Effort.
>
> **Might defense:** Used for resisting poison, disease, and anything else that can be overcome with strength and health.
>
> **Speed defense:** Used for dodging attacks and escaping danger. This is by far the most commonly used defense task.
>
> **Intellect defense:** Used for fending off mental attacks or anything that might affect or influence one's mind.

Remember that at higher tiers, you can choose special abilities from lower tiers. This is sometimes the best way to ensure that you have exactly the character you want. This is particularly true with abilities that grant skills, which can usually be taken multiple times.

Strong, page 56

Masters Weaponry, page 72

Trained Without Armor, page 193

Combat Prowess, page 120

Improved Edge, page 151

Defeat a Foe, page 244

Physical Skills, page 170

"Magic" here is a term used very loosely. It's a catch-all for the kinds of wondrous, possibly supernatural things that your character can do that others cannot. It might actually be an expression of technological devices, channeling spirits, mutations, psionics, nanotechnology, or any number of other sources.

ADEPT

Fantasy/Fairy tale: wizard, mage, sorcerer, cleric, druid, seer, diabolist, fey-touched
Modern/Horror/Romance: psychic, occultist, witch, practitioner, medium, fringe scientist
Science fiction: psion, psionicist, telepath, seeker, master, scanner, ESPer, abomination
Superhero/Post-Apocalyptic: mage, sorcerer, power-wielder, master, psion, telepath

You master powers or abilities outside the experience, understanding, and sometimes belief of others. They might be magic, psychic powers, mutant abilities, or just a wide variety of intricate devices, depending on the setting.

Individual Role: Adepts are usually thoughtful, intelligent types. They often think carefully before acting and rely heavily on their supernatural abilities.

Group Role: Adepts are not powerful in straightforward combat, although they often wield abilities that provide excellent combat support, both offensively and defensively. They sometimes possess abilities that facilitate overcoming challenges. For example, if the group must get through a locked door, an Adept might be able to destroy it or teleport everyone to the other side.

Societal Role: In settings where the supernatural is rare, strange, or feared, Adepts are likely rare and feared as well. They remain hidden, shadowy figures. When this is not the case, Adepts are more likely to be common and forthright. They might even take leadership roles.

Advanced Adepts: Even at low tiers, Adept powers are impressive. Higher-tier Adepts can accomplish amazing deeds that can reshape matter and the environment around them.

ADEPT PLAYER INTRUSIONS

When playing an Adept, you can spend 1 XP to use one of the following player intrusions, provided the situation is appropriate and the GM agrees.

Advantageous Malfunction: A device being used against you malfunctions. It might harm the user or one of their allies for a round, or activate a dramatic and distracting side effect for a few rounds.

Convenient Idea: A flash of insight provides you with a clear answer or suggests a course of action with regard to an urgent question, problem, or obstacle you're facing.

Inexplicably Unbroken: An inactive, ruined, or presumed-destroyed device temporarily activates and performs a useful function relevant to the situation. This is enough to buy you some time for a better solution, alleviate a complication that was interfering with your abilities, or just get you one more use out of a depleted cypher or artifact.

Player intrusions, page 21

Adepts are almost always emblematic of the paranormal or superhuman in some way—wizards, psychics, or something similar. If the game you're playing has none of that, an Adept could be a charlatan mimicking such abilities with tricks and hidden devices, or a gadgeteer character with a "utility belt" full of oddments. Or a game like that might not have Adepts. That's okay too.

ADEPT STAT POOLS

Stat	Pool Starting Value
Might	7
Speed	9
Intellect	12

You get 6 additional points to divide among your stat Pools however you wish.

ADEPT BACKGROUND CONNECTION

Your type helps determine the connection you have to the setting. Roll a d20 or choose from the following list to determine a specific fact about your background that provides a connection to the rest of the world. You can also create your own fact.

d20	Background
1	You served as an apprentice for an Adept respected and feared by many people. Now you bear their mark.
2	You studied in a school infamous for its dark, brooding instructors and graduates.
3	You learned your abilities in the temple of an obscure god. Its priests and worshippers, although small in number, respect and admire your talents and potential.
4	While traveling alone, you saved the life of a powerful person. They remain indebted to you.
5	Your mother was a powerful Adept while she lived, helpful to many locals. They look upon you kindly, but they also expect much from you.
6	You owe money to a number of people and don't have the funds to pay your debts.
7	You failed disgracefully at your initial studies with your teacher and now proceed on your own.
8	You learned your skills faster than your teachers had ever seen before. The powers that be took notice and are paying close attention.
9	You killed a well-known criminal in self-defense, earning the respect of many and the enmity of a dangerous few.
10	You trained as a Warrior, but your Adept predilections eventually led you down a different path. Your former comrades don't understand you, but they respect you.
11	While studying to be an Adept, you worked as an assistant for a bank, making friends with the owner and the clientele.
12	Your family owns a large vineyard nearby known to all for its fine wine and fair business dealings.
13	You trained for a time with a group of influential Adepts, and they still look upon you with fondness.
14	You worked the gardens in the palace of an influential noble or person of wealth. They wouldn't remember you, but you made friends with their young daughter.
15	An experiment you conducted in the past went horribly awry. The locals remember you as a dangerous and foolhardy individual.
16	You hail from a distant place where you were well known and regarded, but people here treat you with suspicion.
17	People you meet seem put off by the strange birthmark on your face.
18	Your best friend is also an Adept. You and your friend share discoveries and secrets readily.
19	You know a local merchant very well. Since you give them so much business, they offer you discounts and special treatment.
20	You belong to a secretive social club that gathers monthly to drink and talk.

FIRST-TIER ADEPT

First-tier Adepts have the following abilities:

Effort: Your Effort is 1.

Genius: You have an Intellect Edge of 1, a Might Edge of 0, and a Speed Edge of 0.

Expert Cypher Use: You can bear three cyphers at a time.

Starting Equipment: Appropriate clothing, plus two expensive items, two moderately priced items, and up to four inexpensive items of your choice.

Weapons: You can use light weapons without penalty. You have an inability with medium weapons and heavy weapons; your attacks with medium and heavy weapons are hindered.

Special Abilities: Choose four of the abilities listed below. You can't choose the same ability more than once unless its description says otherwise. The full description for each listed ability can be found in chapter 9, which also has descriptions for flavor and focus abilities in a single vast catalog.

O Distortion (130)
O Erase Memories (136)
O Far Step (138)
O Hedge Magic (149)
O Magic Training (159)
O Onslaught (167)
O Push (173)
O Resonance Field (176)
O Scan (179)
O Shatter (182)
O Ward (196)

Your character's starting equipment is as important as their starting skills. Learn more about what you carry and how it's used in Chapter 10: Equipment.

Chapter 9: Abilities, page 95

Cautious Adepts rely on Ward. Depending on what you work out with your GM, the energy shield might be completely invisible, visible only when you are attacked, always visible as a faint glimmer surrounding you, or something else.

Adept abilities require at least one free hand unless the GM says otherwise.

GMs are always free to pre-select a type's special abilities at a given tier to reinforce the setting. In the fantasy setting of Jen's sorcerer, the GM might have said that all sorcerers (Adepts) start with Magic Training as one of their tier 1 abilities. This doesn't make the character any less powerful or special, but it says something about her role in the world and expectations in the game.

Onslaught, page 167
Ward, page 196
Magic Training, page 159
Scan, page 179

Graceful, page 46

Leads, page 71

SECOND-TIER ADEPT

Choose one of the abilities listed below (or from a lower tier) to add to your repertoire. In addition, you can replace one of your lower-tier abilities with a different one from a lower tier.

- Adaptation (108)
- Cutting Light (123)
- Hover (149)
- Mind Reading (162)
- Retrieve Memories (177)
- Reveal (178)
- Stasis (186)

THIRD-TIER ADEPT

Choose two of the abilities listed below (or from a lower tier) to add to your repertoire. In addition, you can replace one of your lower-tier abilities with a different one from a lower tier.

- Adroit Cypher Use (108)
- Countermeasures (122)
- Energy Protection (134)
- Fire and Ice (140)
- Force Field Barrier (143)
- Sensor (181)
- Targeting Eye (189)

FOURTH-TIER ADEPT

Choose one of the abilities listed below (or from a lower tier) to add to your repertoire. In addition, you can replace one of your lower-tier abilities with a different one from a lower tier.

- Death Touch (125)
- Exile (136)
- Invisibility (155)
- Matter Cloud (161)
- Mind Control (162)
- Projection (172)
- Rapid Processing (174)
- Regeneration (175)
- Reshape (176)
- Wormhole (200)

FIFTH-TIER ADEPT

Choose two of the abilities listed below (or from a lower tier) to add to your repertoire. In addition, you can replace one of your lower-tier abilities with a different one from a lower tier.

- Absorb Energy (108)
- Concussion (121)
- Conjuration (121)
- Create (122)
- Dust to Dust (133)
- Knowing the Unknown (156)
- Master Cypher Use (160)
- Teleportation (190)
- True Senses (194)

SIXTH-TIER ADEPT

Choose one of the abilities listed below (or from a lower tier) to add to your repertoire. In addition, you can replace one of your lower-tier abilities with a different one from a lower tier.

- Control Weather (122)
- Earthquake (133)
- Move Mountains (164)
- Traverse the Worlds (194)
- Usurp Cypher (195)

ADEPT EXAMPLE

Jen wants to create an Adept—a sorcerer for a fantasy campaign. She decides to be somewhat well rounded, so she puts 2 of her additional points into each stat Pool, giving her a Might Pool of 9, a Speed Pool of 11, and an Intellect Pool of 14. Her Adept is smart and quick. She has an Intellect Edge of 1, a Might Edge of 0, and a Speed Edge of 0. As a first-tier character, her Effort is 1. As her initial abilities, she chooses Onslaught and Ward, giving her a strong offense and defense. She also chooses Magic Training and rounds out her character with Scan, which she hopes will be useful in gaining insight and information. For this character, Onslaught, Ward, and Scan are all spells she has mastered through years of training and study.

She can bear three cyphers. The GM gives her a potion that acts as a short-range teleporter, a small charm that restores 5 points to her Intellect Pool, and a fluid-filled flask that explodes like a fiery bomb. Jen's sorcerer is skilled with light weapons, so she chooses a dagger.

For her descriptor, Jen chooses Graceful, which adds 2 points to her Speed Pool, bringing it to 13. That descriptor means she is trained in balancing and anything requiring careful movements, physical performing arts, and Speed defense tasks. Perhaps she is a dancer. In fact, she begins to develop a backstory that involves graceful, lithe movements that she incorporates into her spells.

For her focus, she chooses Leads. This gives her training in social interactions, which again helps round her out—she's good in all kinds of situations. Moreover, she has the Good Advice ability, which enables her to be a focal point of her group.

Her spells and focus abilities cost Intellect points to activate, so she's glad to have a lot of points in her Intellect Pool. In addition, her Intellect Edge will help reduce those costs. If she uses her Onslaught force blast without applying Effort, it costs 0 Intellect points and deals 4 points of damage. Her Intellect Edge will allow her to save points to devote toward applying Effort for other purposes, perhaps to boost the accuracy of Onslaught.

For her character arc, Jen chooses Aid a Friend. She decides that when her sorcerer character was young, she had a magical mentor. That mentor was later taken prisoner by a demon, so her character is always looking for clues on how to find the demon and release her friend from bondage.

EXPLORER

Fantasy/Fairy tale: Explorer, adventurer, delver, mystery seeker
Modern/Horror/Romance: athlete, explorer, adventurer, drifter, detective, scholar, spelunker, trailblazer, investigative reporter
Science fiction: Explorer, adventurer, wanderer, planetary specialist, xenobiologist
Superhero/Post-Apocalyptic: adventurer, crimefighter

You are a person of action and physical ability, fearlessly facing the unknown. You travel to strange, exotic, and dangerous places, and discover new things. This means you're physical but also probably knowledgeable.

Individual Role: Although Explorers can be academics or well studied, they are first and foremost interested in action. They face grave dangers and terrible obstacles as a routine part of life.

Group Role: Explorers sometimes work alone, but far more often they operate in teams with other characters. The Explorer frequently leads the way, blazing the trail. However, they're also likely to stop and investigate anything intriguing they stumble upon.

Societal Role: Not all Explorers are out traipsing through the wilderness or poking about an old ruin. Sometimes, an Explorer is a teacher, a scientist, a detective, or an investigative reporter. In any event, an Explorer bravely faces new challenges and gathers knowledge to share with others.

Advanced Explorers: Higher-tier Explorers gain more skills, some combat abilities, and a number of abilities that allow them to deal with danger. In short, they become more and more well-rounded, able to deal with any challenge.

EXPLORER PLAYER INTRUSIONS

When playing an Explorer, you can spend 1 XP to use one of the following player intrusions, provided the situation is appropriate and the GM agrees.

Fortuitous Malfunction: A trap or a dangerous device malfunctions before it can affect you.

Serendipitous Landmark: Just when it seems like the path is lost (or you are), a trail marker, a landmark, or simply the way the terrain or corridor bends, rises, or falls away suggests to you the best path forward, at least from this point.

Weak Strain: The poison or disease turns out not to be as debilitating or deadly as it first seemed, and inflicts only half the damage that it would have otherwise.

Player intrusions, page 21

Aid a Friend, page 242

EXPLORER BACKGROUND CONNECTION

Your type helps determine the connection you have to the setting. Roll a d20 or choose from the following list to determine a specific fact about your background that provides a connection to the rest of the world. You can also create your own fact.

d20	Background
1	You were a star high school athlete. You're still in great shape, but those were the glory days, man.
2	Your brother is the lead singer in a really popular band.
3	You have made a number of discoveries in your explorations, but not all opportunities to capitalize on them have panned out yet.
4	You were a cop, but you gave it up after encountering corruption on the force.
5	Your parents were missionaries, so you spent much of your young life traveling to exotic places.
6	You served in the military with honor.
7	You received assistance from a secretive organization, which paid for your schooling. Now they seem to want a lot more from you.
8	You went to a prestigious university on an athletic scholarship, but you excelled in class as well as on the field.
9	Your best friend from your youth is now an influential member of the government.
10	You used to be a teacher. Your students remember you fondly.
11	You worked as a small-time criminal operative until you were caught and served some time in jail, after which you tried to go straight.
12	Your greatest discovery to date was stolen by your arch-rival.
13	You belong to an exclusive organization of Explorers whose existence is not widely known.
14	You were kidnapped as a small child under mysterious circumstances, although you were recovered safely. The case still has some notoriety.
15	When you were young, you were addicted to narcotics, and now you are a recovering addict.
16	While exploring a remote location, you saw something strange you've never been able to explain.
17	You own a small bar or restaurant.
18	You published a book about some of your exploits and discoveries, and it has achieved some acclaim.
19	Your sister owns a store and gives you a hefty discount.
20	Your father is a high-ranking officer in the military with many connections.

EXPLORER STAT POOLS

Stat	Pool Starting Value
Might	10
Speed	9
Intellect	9

You get 6 additional points to divide among your stat Pools however you wish.

FIRST-TIER EXPLORER

First-tier Explorers have the following abilities:

Effort: Your Effort is 1.

Physical Nature: You have a Might Edge of 1, a Speed Edge of 0, and an Intellect Edge of 0.

Cypher Use: You can bear two cyphers at a time.

Starting Equipment: Appropriate clothing and a weapon of your choice, plus two expensive items, two moderately priced items, and up to four inexpensive items.

Weapons: You can use light and medium weapons without penalty. You have an inability with heavy weapons; your attacks with heavy weapons are hindered.

Special Abilities: Choose four of the abilities listed below. You can't choose the same ability more than once unless its description says otherwise. The full description for each listed ability can be found in chapter 9, which also has descriptions for flavor and focus abilities in a single vast catalog.

O Block (115)
O Danger Sense (124)
O Decipher (126)
O Endurance (134)
O Find the Way (140)
O Fleet of Foot (141)
O Improved Edge (151)
O Knowledge Skills (157)
O Muscles of Iron (165)
O No Need for Weapons (166)
O Physical Skills (170)

Chapter 9: Abilities, page 95

Your character's starting equipment is as important as their starting skills. Learn more about what you carry and how it's used in Chapter 10: Equipment.

- ○ Practiced in Armor (171)
- ○ Practiced With All Weapons (171)
- ○ Surging Confidence (188)
- ○ Trained Without Armor (193)

SECOND-TIER EXPLORER

Choose four of the abilities listed below (or from a lower tier) to add to your repertoire. In addition, you can replace one of your lower-tier abilities with a different one from a lower tier.

- ○ Curious (123)
- ○ Danger Instinct (124)
- ○ Enable Others (133)
- ○ Escape (136)
- ○ Eye for Detail (138)
- ○ Foil Danger (142)
- ○ Hand to Eye (148)
- ○ Investigative Skills (155)
- ○ Quick Recovery (173)
- ○ Range Increase (174)
- ○ Skill With Defense (183)
- ○ Stand Watch (186)
- ○ Travel Skills (193)
- ○ Wreck (200)

THIRD-TIER EXPLORER

Choose three of the abilities listed below (or from a lower tier) to add to your repertoire. In addition, you can replace one of your lower-tier abilities with a different one from a lower tier.

- ○ Controlled Fall (122)
- ○ Experienced in Armor (136)
- ○ Expert Cypher Use (137)
- ○ Ignore the Pain (150)
- ○ Obstacle Running (167)
- ○ Resilience (176)
- ○ Run and Fight (179)
- ○ Seize the Moment (181)
- ○ Skill With Attacks (183)
- ○ Stone Breaker (186)
- ○ Think Your Way Out (191)
- ○ Trapfinder (193)
- ○ Wrest From Chance (200)

FOURTH-TIER EXPLORER

Choose two of the abilities listed below (or from a lower tier) to add to your repertoire. In addition, you can replace one of your lower-tier abilities with a different one from a lower tier.

- ○ Capable Warrior (118)
- ○ Expert Skill (137)
- ○ Increased Effects (153)
- ○ Read the Signs (174)
- ○ Runner (179)
- ○ Subtle Steps (187)
- ○ Tough As Nails (192)

FIFTH-TIER EXPLORER

Choose three of the abilities listed below (or from a lower tier) to add to your repertoire. In addition, you can replace one of your lower-tier abilities with a different one from a lower tier.

- ○ Adroit Cypher Use (108)
- ○ Free to Move (143)
- ○ Group Friendship (147)
- ○ Hard to Kill (148)
- ○ Jump Attack (156)
- ○ Mastery With Defense (161)
- ○ Parry (168)
- ○ Physically Gifted (170)
- ○ Take Command (188)
- ○ Vigilant (196)

SIXTH-TIER EXPLORER

Choose three of the abilities listed below (or from a lower tier) to add to your repertoire. In addition, you can replace one of your lower-tier abilities with a different one from a lower tier.

- ○ Again and Again (109)
- ○ Inspire Coordinated Actions (154)
- ○ Mastery in Armor (161)
- ○ Mastery With Attacks (161)
- ○ Negate Danger (165)
- ○ Share Defense (181)
- ○ Spin Attack (185)
- ○ Wild Vitality (198)

EXPLORER EXAMPLE

Sam decides to create an Explorer character for a science fiction campaign. This character will be a hardy soul who explores alien worlds. They put 3 additional points into their Might Pool, 2 into their Speed Pool, and 1 into their Intellect Pool; their stat Pools are now Might 13, Speed 11, and Intellect 10. As a first-tier character, their Effort is 1, their Might Edge is 1, and their Speed Edge and Intellect Edge are 0. Their character is fairly well-rounded so far.

Sam immediately leaps in and starts choosing abilities. They pick Danger Sense and Surging Confidence, thinking those abilities will be generally useful. They also choose Practiced in Armor, reasoning that the character wears high-tech medium armor when exploring. Last, they choose Knowledge Skills and select geology and biology to help during interplanetary explorations.

Sam's Explorer can bear two cyphers, which in this setting involve nanotechnology. The GM decides that one is a nanite injector that grants a +1 bonus to Might Edge when used, and the other is a device that can create one simple handheld object the user wishes.

The small numbers you see after abilities throughout this book are page numbers for easy reference.

Danger Sense, page 124

Surging Confidence, page 188

Practiced in Armor, page 171

Knowledge Skills, page 157

A character can't apply Effort or other abilities to any task they accomplish using Expert Skill or Tough As Nails.

Sam's Explorer is not really geared toward fighting, but sometimes the universe is a dangerous place, so they note that they're carrying a medium blaster as well.

Sam still needs a descriptor and a focus. Looking to the descriptor chapter, they choose Hardy, which increases their Might Pool to 17. They also heal more quickly and can operate better when injured. They're trained in Might defense but have an inability with initiative; however, it's effectively canceled out by their Danger Sense (and vice versa). Sam could go back and select something else instead of Danger Sense, but they like it and decide to keep it. Overall, the descriptor ends up making the character tough but a little slow.

For their focus, Sam chooses Explores Dark Places (in this case, weird ruins of alien civilizations). This gives the character a bunch of additional skills: searching, listening, climbing, balancing, and jumping. They're quite the capable Explorer.

For their character arc, Sam chooses Enterprise. Exploring alien places sometimes turns up strange relics, and Sam figures they might be able to set up a service to reliably transport these items to responsible third parties, rather than allow them to fall into the hands of pirates and rich private collectors. For a small fee, of course.

Explores Dark Places, page 68
Hardy, page 47

Inability, page 207
Enterprise, page 245

SPEAKER

Fantasy/Fairy tale: bard, speaker, skald, emissary, priest, advocate

Modern/Horror/Romance: diplomat, charmer, face, spinner, manipulator, minister, mediator, lawyer

Science fiction: diplomat, empath, glam, consul, legate

Superhero/Post-Apocalyptic: charmer, mesmerist, puppet master

You're good with words and good with people. You talk your way past challenges and out of jams, and you get people to do what you want.

Individual Role: Speakers are smart and charismatic. They like people and, more important, they understand them. This helps speakers get others to do what needs to be done.

Group Role: The Speaker is often the face of the group, serving as the person who speaks for all and negotiates with others. Combat and action are not a Speaker's strong suits, so other characters sometimes have to defend the Speaker in times of danger.

Societal Role: Speakers are frequently political or religious leaders. Just as often, however, they are con artists or criminals.

Advanced Speakers: Higher-tier speakers use their abilities to control and manipulate people as well as aid and nurture their friends. They can talk their way out of danger and even use their words as weapons.

SPEAKER BACKGROUND CONNECTION

Your type helps determine the connection you have to the setting. Roll a d20 or choose from the following list to determine a specific fact about your background that provides a connection to the rest of the world. You can also create your own fact.

d20	Background
1	One of your parents was a famous entertainer in their early years and hoped you would excel in the same medium.
2	When you were a teenager, one of your siblings went missing and is presumed dead. The shock rent your family, and it's something you've never gotten over.
3	You were inducted into a secret society that claims to hold and protect esoteric knowledge opposing the forces of evil.
4	You lost one of your parents to alcoholism. They may still be alive, but you'd be hard pressed to find forgiveness.
5	You have no memory of anything that happened to you before the age of 18.
6	Your grandparents raised you on a farm far from bustling urban centers. You like to think the instruction they gave you prepared you for anything.
7	As an orphan, you had a difficult childhood, and your entry into adulthood was challenging.
8	You grew up in extreme poverty, among criminals. You still have some connections with the old neighborhood.
9	You served as an envoy for a powerful and influential person in the past, and they still look upon you with favor.
10	You have an annoying rival who always seems to get in your way or foil your plans.
11	You've worked yourself into the position of spokesperson for an organization or company of some importance.
12	Your neighbors were murdered, and the mystery remains unsolved.
13	You have traveled extensively, and during that time you accumulated quite a collection of strange souvenirs.
14	Your childhood sweetheart ended up with your best friend (now your ex-best friend).
15	You are part of a maligned minority, but you work to bring the injustice of your status to public attention.
16	You're part owner of a local bar, where you're something of a whiz in creating specialty cocktails.
17	You once ran a con that cheated important people out of money, and they want revenge.
18	You used to act in a traveling theater, and they remember you fondly (as do people in the places you visited).
19	You are in a close romantic relationship with someone in local politics.
20	Someone out there tries to pose as you, using your identity, often for nefarious ends. You've never met the culprit, but you'd certainly like to.

SPEAKER PLAYER INTRUSIONS

When playing a Speaker, you can spend 1 XP to use one of the following player intrusions, provided the situation is appropriate and the GM agrees.

Friendly NPC: An NPC you don't know, someone you don't know that well, or someone you know but who hasn't been particularly friendly in the past chooses to help you, though doesn't necessarily explain why. Maybe they'll ask you for a favor in return afterward, depending on how much trouble they go to.

Perfect Suggestion: A follower or other already-friendly NPC suggests a course of action with regard to an urgent question, problem, or obstacle you're facing.

Unexpected Gift: An NPC hands you a physical gift you were not expecting, one that helps put the situation at ease if things seem strained, or provides you with a new insight for understanding the context of the situation if there's something you're failing to understand or grasp.

SPEAKER STAT POOLS

Stat	Pool Starting Value
Might	8
Speed	9
Intellect	11

You get 6 additional points to divide among your stat Pools however you wish.

FIRST-TIER SPEAKER

First-tier speakers have the following abilities:

Effort: Your Effort is 1.

Genius: You have an Intellect Edge of 1, a Might Edge of 0, and a Speed Edge of 0.

Cypher Use: You can bear two cyphers at a time.

Weapons: You can use light weapons without penalty. You have an inability with medium and heavy weapons; your attacks with medium and heavy weapons are hindered.

Starting Equipment: Appropriate clothing and a light weapon of your choice, plus two expensive

Player intrusions, page 21

Your character's starting equipment is as important as their starting skills. Learn more about what you carry and how it's used in Chapter 10: Equipment.

items, two moderately priced items, and up to four inexpensive items.

Special Abilities: Choose four of the abilities listed below. You can't choose the same ability more than once unless its description says otherwise. The full description for each listed ability can be found in chapter 9, which also has descriptions for flavor and focus abilities in a single vast catalog.

- Anecdote (109)
- Babel (112)
- Demeanor of Command (127)
- Encouragement (134)
- Enthrall (136)
- Erase Memories (136)
- Fast Talk (138)
- Inspire Aggression (154)
- Interaction Skills (155)
- Practiced With Medium Weapons (171)
- Spin Identity (185)
- Terrifying Presence (190)
- Understanding (194)

SECOND-TIER SPEAKER

Choose two of the abilities listed below (or from a lower tier) to add to your repertoire. In addition, you can replace one of your lower-tier abilities with a different one from a lower tier.

- Basic Follower (112)
- Calm Stranger (118)
- Disincentivize (129)
- Gather Intelligence (144)
- Impart Ideal (151)
- Inspiring Ease (154)
- Interaction Skills (155)
- Practiced in Armor (171)
- Skill With Defense (183)
- Speedy Recovery (185)
- Unexpected Betrayal (195)

THIRD-TIER SPEAKER

Choose three of the abilities listed below (or from a lower tier) to add to your repertoire. In addition, you can replace one of your lower-tier abilities with a different one from a lower tier.

- Accelerate (108)
- Blend In (113)
- Discerning Mind (129)
- Expert Cypher Use (137)
- Expert Follower (137)
- Grand Deception (146)
- Lead by Inquiry (157)
- Mind Reading (162)
- Oratory (167)
- Perfect Stranger (169)
- Quick Wits (174)
- Telling (190)

FOURTH-TIER SPEAKER

Choose two of the abilities listed below (or from a lower tier) to add to your repertoire. In addition, you can replace one of your lower-tier abilities with a different one from a lower tier.

- Anticipate Attack (110)
- Confounding Banter (121)
- Feint (139)
- Heightened Skills (149)
- Psychosis (172)
- Read the Signs (174)
- Spur Effort (186)
- Strategize (187)
- Suggestion (188)

FIFTH-TIER SPEAKER

Choose three of the abilities listed below (or from a lower tier) to add to your repertoire. In addition, you can replace one of your lower-tier abilities with a different one from a lower tier.

- Adroit Cypher Use (108)
- Discipline of Watchfulness (129)
- Experienced in Armor (136)
- Flee (141)
- Foul Aura (143)
- Knowing the Unknown (156)
- Regeneration (175)
- Skill With Attacks (183)
- Stimulate (186)

SIXTH-TIER SPEAKER

Choose two of the abilities listed below (or from a lower tier) to add to your repertoire. In addition, you can replace one of your lower-tier abilities with a different one from a lower tier.

- Assume Control (111)
- Battle Management (112)
- Crowd Control (123)
- Inspiring Success (154)
- Recruit Deputy (175)
- Shatter Mind (182)
- True Senses (194)
- Word of Command (199)

SPEAKER EXAMPLE

Mary wants to create a Speaker for a Lovecraftian horror campaign. She puts 3 of her additional stat points into her Intellect Pool and 3 into her Speed Pool; her stat Pools are now Might 8, Speed 12, and Intellect 14. As a first-tier character, her Effort is 1, her Might Edge and Speed Edge are 0, and her Intellect Edge is 1. She's smart and charismatic but not particularly tough.

Mary chooses Fast Talk and Spin Identity to help get into places and learn things she

---

Chapter 9: Abilities, page 95

Some Speaker abilities, like Mind Reading or True Senses, imply a supernatural element. If this is inappropriate to the character or the setting, these abilities can be replaced with something from the stealth flavor, or the GM can slightly modify them so they are based in extraordinary talents and insight rather than the supernatural.

Stealth flavor, page 34

Followers, page 233

The small numbers you see after abilities throughout this book are page numbers for easy reference.

The vegetative state created by Shatter Mind can be healed by advanced magic or science, or by a condition remover cypher that cures psychosis.

A Speaker with Discerning Mind has practiced swaying the minds of others so much that they've gained a measure of protection against others attempting the same on them.

Fast Talk, page 138
Spin Identity, page 185

wants to know. She's a bit of a con artist. She's good to her friends, however, and chooses Encouragement as well. Mary rounds out her first-tier abilities with Interaction Skills (deceiving and persuasion).

A Speaker normally starts with two cyphers, but the GM rules that characters in this campaign start with only one—something creepy relating to their background. Mary's cypher is an odd pocket watch given to her by her grandfather. She doesn't know how or why, but when activated, the watch allows her to take twice as many actions for three rounds.

Mary's character carries a small knife hidden in her bag in case of trouble. As a light weapon, it inflicts 2 points of damage, but attacks with it are eased.

Mary chooses Resilient for her descriptor and decides that she can probably learn the truth behind some of the strange things that she's heard about without feeling too much trauma if it's horrible. Resilient increases her Might Pool to 10 and her Intellect Pool to 16. She's trained in Might and Intellect defense actions and gains an extra recovery roll each day. At first, Mary is sad that her descriptor gives her an inability in knowledge and puzzle tasks, but then she realizes that the flaw fits her character well—she's better at getting people to tell her what she needs to know than at figuring out the information herself.

For her focus, Mary chooses Moves Like a Cat, granting her a final Speed Pool of 18 and training in balance. In the end, she's graceful and quick, charismatic, and hardier than she initially thought thanks to her drive. She's ready to investigate the weird.

For her character arc, Mary chooses Fall From Grace. She decides she's had an obsession with a strange tome that's been in her family for generations, and her character is drawn to its strange languages and rituals.

FURTHER CUSTOMIZATION

The rules in this section are more advanced and always involve the GM. They can be used by the GM to tailor a type to better fit the genre or setting, or by a player and a GM to tweak a character to fit a concept.

MODIFYING TYPE ASPECTS

The following aspects of the four character types can be modified at character creation. Other abilities should not be changed.

Stat Pools: Each character type has a starting stat Pool value. A player can exchange points between their Pools on a one-for-one basis. For example, they can trade 2 points of Might for 2 points of Speed. However, no starting stat Pool should be higher than 20.

Edge: A player can start with an Edge of 1 in whichever stat they wish.

Cypher Use: If a character gives up the ability to bear one cypher, they gain an additional skill of their choice.

Weapons: Some types have static first-tier abilities that let them use light, medium, and/or heavy weapons without a penalty. Warriors can use all weapons, Explorers can use light and medium weapons, and Adepts and Speakers can use light weapons. Any one of these weapon abilities can be sacrificed to gain training in a different skill of the player's choice.

DRAWBACKS AND PENALTIES

In addition to other customization options, a player can choose to take drawbacks or penalties to gain further advantages.

Weakness: A weakness is, essentially, the opposite of Edge. If you have a weakness of 1 in Speed, all Speed actions that require you to spend points cost 1 additional point from your Pool. At any time, a player can give their character a weakness in one stat and, in exchange, gain +1 to their Edge in one of the other two stats. So a PC can take a weakness of 1 in Speed to gain +1 to their Might Edge.

Normally, you can have a weakness only in a stat in which you have an Edge of 0. Further, you can't have more than one weakness, and you can't have a weakness greater than 1 unless the additional weakness comes from another source (such as a disease or disability arising from actions or conditions in the game).

Inabilities: Inabilities are like negative skills. They make one type of task harder by hindering it. If a character chooses to take an inability, they gain a skill of their choice. Normally, a character can have only one inability unless the additional inability comes from another source (such as a descriptor or a disease or disability arising from actions or conditions in the game).

Encouragement, page 134
Interaction Skills, page 155

Resilient, page 54

Inability, page 207

Moves Like a Cat, page 73

Fall From Grace, page 245

Chapter 6
FLAVOR

Flavors are groups of special abilities the GM and players can use to alter a character type to make it more to their liking or more appropriate to the genre or setting. For example, if a player wants to create a magic-using thief character, she could play an Adept with stealth flavoring. In a science fiction setting, a Warrior might also have knowledge of machinery, so the character could be flavored with technology.

At a given tier, abilities from a flavor are traded one for one with standard abilities from a type. So to add the Danger Sense stealth flavor ability to a Warrior, something else—perhaps Bash—must be sacrificed. Now that character can choose Danger Sense as they would any other first-tier warrior ability, but they can never choose Bash.

The GM should always be involved in flavoring a type. For example, they might know that for their science fiction game, they want a type called a "Glam," which is a Speaker flavored with certain technology abilities—specifically those that make the character a flamboyant starship pilot. Thus, they exchange the first-tier abilities Spin Identity and Inspire Aggression for the technology flavor abilities Datajack and Tech Skills so the character can plug into the ship directly and can take piloting and computers as skills.

In the end, flavor is mostly a tool for the GM to easily create campaign-specific types by making a few slight alterations to the four base types. Although players may wish to use flavors to get the characters they want, remember that they can also shape their PCs with descriptors and foci very nicely.

The flavors available are stealth, technology, magic, combat, and skills and knowledge.

The full description for each listed ability can be found in chapter 9, which also contains descriptions for type and focus abilities in a single vast catalog.

STEALTH FLAVOR

Characters with the stealth flavor are good at sneaking around, infiltrating places they don't belong, and deceiving others. They use these abilities in a variety of ways, including combat. An Explorer with stealth flavor might be a thief, while a Warrior with stealth flavor might be an assassin. An Explorer with stealth flavor in a superhero setting might be a crimefighter who stalks the streets at night.

Chapter 9: Abilities, page 95

Unless otherwise noted, you cannot choose the same ability twice, even if you get it from both your type and a flavor.

FIRST-TIER STEALTH ABILITIES
- Danger Sense (124)
- Goad (145)
- Legerdemain (157)
- Opportunist (167)
- Stealth Skills (186)

SECOND-TIER STEALTH ABILITIES
- Contortionist (121)
- Find an Opening (139)
- Get Away (145)
- Sense Ambush (181)
- Surprise Attack (188)

THIRD-TIER STEALTH ABILITIES
- Evanesce (136)
- From the Shadows (144)
- Gambler (144)
- Inner Defense (154)
- Misdirect (163)
- Run and Fight (179)
- Seize the Moment (181)

FOURTH-TIER STEALTH ABILITIES
- Ambusher (109)
- Debilitating Strike (126)
- Outwit (168)
- Preternatural Senses (171)
- Tumbling Moves (194)

FIFTH-TIER STEALTH ABILITIES
- Assassin Strike (110)
- Mask (160)
- Return to Sender (177)
- Uncanny Luck (194)

SIXTH-TIER STEALTH ABILITIES
- Exploit Advantage (137)
- Spring Away (186)
- Thief's Luck (191)
- Twist of Fate (194)

TECHNOLOGY FLAVOR

Characters with a flavor of technology typically are from science fiction or at least modern-day settings (although anything is possible). They excel at using, dealing with, and building machines. An Explorer with technology flavor might be a starship pilot, and a Speaker flavored with technology could be a techno-priest.

Some of the less computer-oriented abilities might be appropriate for a steampunk character, while a modern-day character could use some of the abilities that don't involve starships or ultratech.

FIRST-TIER TECHNOLOGY ABILITIES
- Datajack (124)
- Hacker (147)
- Machine Interface (159)
- Scramble Machine (179)
- Tech Skills (189)
- Tinker (192)

SECOND-TIER TECHNOLOGY ABILITIES
- Distant Interface (130)
- Machine Efficiency (159)
- Overload Machine (168)
- Serv-0 (181)
- Serv-0 Defender (181)
- Serv-0 Repair (181)
- Tool Mastery (192)

THIRD-TIER TECHNOLOGY ABILITIES
- Mechanical Telepathy (161)
- Serv-0 Scanner (181)
- Ship Footing (182)
- Shipspeak (183)
- Spray (185)

FOURTH-TIER TECHNOLOGY ABILITIES
- Machine Bond (159)
- Robot Fighter (178)
- Serv-0 Aim (181)
- Serv-0 Brawler (181)
- Serv-0 Spy (181)

FIFTH-TIER TECHNOLOGY ABILITIES
- Control Machine (121)
- Jury-Rig (156)
- Machine Companion (159)

SIXTH-TIER TECHNOLOGY ABILITIES
- Information Gathering (153)
- Master Machine (160)

The small numbers you see after abilities throughout this book are page numbers for easy reference.

Of course, you can "flavor" a character in the Cypher System in many ways. To make a character more stealthy, for example, you can choose the Stealthy descriptor or any number of foci, including Works the Back Alleys.

Stealthy, page 56

Works the Back Alleys, page 79

MAGIC FLAVOR

You know a little about magic. You might not be a wizard, but you know the basics—how it works, and how to accomplish a few wondrous things. Of course, in your setting, "magic" might actually mean psychic powers, mutant abilities, weird alien tech, or anything else that produces interesting and useful effects.

An Explorer flavored with magic might be a wizard-hunter, and a Speaker with magical flavor might be a sorcerer-bard. Although an Adept flavored with magic is still an Adept, you might find that swapping some of the type's basic abilities with those given here tailors the character in desirable ways.

Giant spider, page 335

FIRST-TIER MAGIC ABILITIES
- Blessing of the Gods (114)
- Closed Mind (119)
- Entangling Force (136)
- Hedge Magic (149)
- Magic Training (159)
- Mental Link (161)
- Premonition (171)

SECOND-TIER MAGIC ABILITIES
- Concussive Blast (121)
- Fetch (139)
- Force Field (143)
- Lock (159)
- Repair Flesh (176)

THIRD-TIER MAGIC ABILITIES
- Distance Viewing (130)
- Fire Bloom (140)
- Fling (141)
- Force at Distance (142)
- Summon Giant Spider (188)

FOURTH-TIER MAGIC ABILITIES
- Elemental Protection (133)
- Ignition (150)
- Pry Open (172)

FIFTH-TIER MAGIC ABILITIES
- Create (122)
- Divine Intervention (130)
- Dragon's Maw (131)
- Fast Travel (139)
- True Senses (194)

SIXTH-TIER MAGIC ABILITIES
- Relocate (176)
- Summon Demon (188)
- Traverse the Worlds (194)
- Word of Death (200)

COMBAT FLAVOR

Combat flavor makes a character more martial. A Speaker with combat flavor in a fantasy setting would be a battle bard. An Explorer with combat flavor in a historical game might be a pirate. An Adept flavored with combat in a science fiction setting could be a veteran of a thousand psychic wars.

There's very little to gain by flavoring a Warrior with combat.

FIRST-TIER COMBAT ABILITIES
- Danger Sense (124)
- Practiced in Armor (171)
- Practiced With Medium Weapons (171)

SECOND-TIER COMBAT ABILITIES
- Bloodlust (115)
- Combat Prowess (120)
- Trained Without Armor (193)

THIRD-TIER COMBAT ABILITIES
- Practiced With All Weapons (171)
- Skill With Attacks (183)
- Skill With Defense (183)
- Successive Attack (187)

FLAVOR

FOURTH-TIER COMBAT ABILITIES
- Capable Warrior (118)
- Deadly Aim (125)
- Fury (144)
- Misdirect (163)
- Spray (185)

FIFTH-TIER COMBAT ABILITIES
- Experienced Defender (136)
- Hard Target (148)
- Parry (168)

SIXTH-TIER COMBAT ABILITIES
- Greater Skill With Attacks (147)
- Mastery in Armor (161)
- Mastery With Defense (161)

FOURTH-TIER SKILLS AND KNOWLEDGE ABILITIES
- Multiple Skills (165)
- Quick Wits (174)
- Task Specialization (189)

FIFTH-TIER SKILLS AND KNOWLEDGE ABILITIES
- Practiced With Medium Weapons (171)
- Read the Signs (174)

SIXTH-TIER SKILLS AND KNOWLEDGE ABILITIES
- Skill With Attacks (183)
- Skill With Defense (183)

The skills and knowledge flavor is particularly useful in shaping character types to fit modern and futuristic science fiction settings, where characters are more likely to be defined by what they know more than anything else. This flavor can distinguish a scientist and a medical doctor, for example, who both might be Explorers at their core.

SKILLS AND KNOWLEDGE FLAVOR

This flavor is for characters in roles that call for more knowledge and more real-world application of talent. It's less flashy and dramatic than supernatural powers or the ability to hack apart multiple foes, but sometimes expertise or know-how is the real solution to a problem.

A Warrior flavored with skills and knowledge might be a military engineer. An Explorer flavored with skills and knowledge could be a field scientist. A Speaker with this flavor might be a teacher.

FIRST-TIER SKILLS AND KNOWLEDGE ABILITIES
- Interaction Skills (155)
- Investigative Skills (155)
- Knowledge Skills (157)
- Physical Skills (170)
- Travel Skills (193)

SECOND-TIER SKILLS AND KNOWLEDGE ABILITIES
- Extra Skill (138)
- Tool Mastery (192)
- Understanding (194)

THIRD-TIER SKILLS AND KNOWLEDGE ABILITIES
- Flex Skill (141)
- Improvise (152)

Chapter 7

DESCRIPTOR

Charming, page 41
Explorer, page 27
Vicious, page 58
Customizing Descriptors, page 59
Species as Descriptor, page 59

Inability, page 207

Your descriptor defines your character—it flavors everything you do. The differences between a Charming Explorer and a Vicious Explorer are considerable. The descriptor changes the way those characters go about every action. Your descriptor places your character in the situation (the first adventure, which starts the campaign) and helps provide motivation. It is the adjective of the sentence "I am an *adjective noun* who *verbs*."

Descriptors offer a one-time package of extra abilities, skills, or modifications to your stat Pools. Not all of a descriptor's offerings are positive character modifications. For example, some descriptors have inabilities—tasks that a character isn't good at. You can think of inabilities as negative skills—instead of being one step better at that kind of task, you're one step worse. If you become skilled at a task that you have an inability with, they cancel out. Remember that characters are defined as much by what they're *not* good at as by what they *are* good at.

Descriptors also offer a few brief suggestions for how your character got involved with the rest of the group on their first adventure. You can use these, or not, as you wish.

This section details fifty descriptors. Choose one of them for your character. You can pick any descriptor you wish regardless of your type. At the end of this chapter, a few options are provided for Customizing Descriptors, including making a character's species their descriptor.

APPEALING

You're attractive to others, but perhaps more important, you are likeable and charismatic. You've got that "special something" that draws others to you. You often know just the right thing to say to make someone laugh, put them at ease, or spur them to action. People like you, want to help you, and want to be your friend.

You gain the following characteristics:

Charismatic: +2 to your Intellect Pool.

Skill: You are trained in pleasant social interactions.

Resistant to Charms: You're aware of how others can manipulate and charm people, and you notice when those tactics are used on you. Because of this awareness, you are trained in resisting any kind of persuasion or seduction if you wish it.

Initial Link to the Starting Adventure: From the following list of options, choose how you became involved in the first adventure.

1. You met a total stranger (one of the other PCs) and charmed them so much that they invited you along.

DESCRIPTORS

Appealing	Cruel	Hideous	Mad	Skeptical
Beneficent	Dishonorable	Honorable	Mechanical	Stealthy
Brash	Doomed	Impulsive	Mysterious	Strong
Calm	Empathic	Inquisitive	Mystical	Strong-Willed
Chaotic	Exiled	Intelligent	Naive	Swift
Charming	Fast	Intuitive	Perceptive	Tongue-Tied
Clever	Foolish	Jovial	Resilient	Tough
Clumsy	Graceful	Kind	Risk-Taking	Vicious
Craven	Guarded	Learned	Rugged	Virtuous
Creative	Hardy	Lucky	Sharp-Eyed	Weird

2. The PCs were looking for someone else, but you convinced them that you were perfect instead.

3. Pure happenstance—because you just go along with the flow of things and everything usually works out.

4. Your charismatic ways helped get one of the PCs out of a difficult spot a long time ago, and they always ask you to join them on new adventures.

BENEFICENT

Helping others is your calling. It's why you're here. Others delight in your outgoing and charitable nature, and you delight in their happiness. You're at your best when you're aiding people, either by explaining how they can best overcome a challenge or by demonstrating how to do so yourself.

You gain the following characteristics:
Generous: Allies who have spent the last day with you add +1 to their recovery rolls.
Altruistic: If you're standing next to a creature that takes damage, you can intercede and take 1 point of that damage yourself (reducing the damage inflicted on the creature by 1 point). If you have Armor, it does not provide a benefit when you use this ability.
Skill: You're trained in all tasks related to pleasant social interaction, putting other people at ease, and gaining trust.
Helpful: Whenever you help another character, that character gains the benefit as if you were trained even if you are not trained or specialized in the attempted task.
Inability: While you are alone, all Intellect and Speed tasks are hindered.
Initial Link to the Starting Adventure: From the following list of options, choose how you became involved in the first adventure.

1. Even though you didn't know most of the other PCs beforehand, you invited yourself along on their quest.

2. You saw the PCs struggling to overcome a problem and selflessly joined them to help.

3. You're nearly certain the PCs will fail without you.

4. The choice was between your tattered life and helping others. You haven't looked back since.

BRASH

You're a self-assertive sort, confident in your abilities, energetic, and perhaps a bit irreverent toward ideas that you don't agree with. Some people call you bold and brave, but those you've put in their place might call you puffed up and arrogant. Whatever. It's not in your nature to care what other people think about you, unless those people are your friends or family. Even someone as brash as you knows that friends sometimes have to come first.

You gain the following characteristics:
Energetic: +2 to your Speed Pool.
Skill: You are trained in initiative.
Bold: You are trained in all actions that involve overcoming or ignoring the effects of fear or intimidation.
Initial Link to the Starting Adventure: From the following list of options, choose how you became involved in the first adventure.

1. You noticed something weird going on, and without much thought, you jumped in with both feet.

2. You showed up when and where you did on a dare because, hey, you don't back down from dares.

3. Someone called you out, but instead of walking into a fight, you walked into your current situation.

4. You told your friend that nothing could scare you, and nothing you saw would change your mind. They brought you to your current point.

Initiative, page 214

Helping, page 226

CALM

Calm is a great descriptor for characters who never intended to have adventures but were thrust into them, a trope that occurs often in modern games and particularly in horror games.

You've spent most of your life in sedentary pursuits—books, movies, hobbies, and so on—rather than active ones. You're well versed in all manner of academia or other intellectual pursuits, but nothing physical. You're not weak or feeble, necessarily (although this is a good descriptor for characters who are elderly), but you have no experience in more physical activities.

You gain the following characteristics:

Bookish: +2 to your Intellect Pool.

Skills: You are trained in four nonphysical skills of your choice.

Trivia: You can come up with a random fact pertinent to the current situation when you wish it. This is always a matter of fact, not conjecture or supposition, and must be something you could have logically read or seen in the past. You can do this one time, although the ability is renewed each time you make a recovery roll.

Inability: You're just not a fighter. All physical attacks are hindered.

Inability: You're not the outdoorsy type. All climbing, running, jumping, and swimming tasks are hindered.

Initial Link to the Starting Adventure: From the following list of options, choose how you became involved in the first adventure.

1. You read about the current situation somewhere and decided to check it out for yourself.

2. You were in the right (wrong?) place at the right (wrong?) time.

3. While avoiding an entirely different situation, you walked into your current situation.

4. One of the other PCs dragged you into it.

CHAOTIC

Danger doesn't mean much to you, mainly because you don't think much about repercussions. In fact, you enjoy sowing surprises, just to see what will happen. The more unexpected the result, the happier you are. Sometimes you are particularly manic, and for the sake of your companions, you restrain yourself from taking actions that you know will lead to disaster.

You gain the following characteristics:

Tumultuous: +4 to your Speed Pool.

Skill: You are trained in Intellect defense actions.

Chaotic: Once after each ten-hour recovery roll, if you don't like the first result, you can reroll a die roll of your choice. If you do, and regardless of the outcome, the GM presents you with a GM intrusion.

Inability: Your body is a bit worn from occasional excesses. Might defense tasks are hindered.

Initial Link to the Starting Adventure: From the following list of options, choose how you became involved in the first adventure.

1. Another PC recruited you while you were on your best behavior, before realizing how chaotic you were.

2. You have reason to believe that being with the other PCs will help you gain control over your erratic behavior.

3. Another PC released you from captivity, and to thank them, you volunteered to help.

4. You have no idea how you joined the PCs. You're just going along with it for now until answers present themselves.

DESCRIPTOR

CHARMING

You're a smooth talker and a charmer. Whether through seemingly supernatural means or just a way with words, you can convince others to do as you wish. Most likely, you're physically attractive or at least highly charismatic, and others enjoy listening to your voice. You probably pay attention to your appearance, keeping yourself well groomed. You make friends easily. You play up the personality facet of your Intellect stat; intelligence is not your strong suit. You're personable, but not necessarily studious or strong-willed.

You gain the following characteristics:

Personable: +2 to your Intellect Pool.

Skill: You're trained in all tasks involving positive or pleasant social interaction.

Skill: You're trained when using special abilities that influence the minds of others.

Contact: You have an important contact who is in an influential position, such as a minor noble, the captain of the town guard/police, or the head of a large gang of thieves. You and the GM should work out the details together.

Inability: You were never good at studying or retaining facts. Any task involving lore, knowledge, or understanding is hindered.

Inability: Your willpower is not one of your strong points. Defense actions to resist mental attacks are hindered.

Additional Equipment: You've managed to talk your way into some decent discounts and bonuses in recent weeks. As a result, you have enough cash jangling in your pocket to purchase a moderately priced item.

Initial Link to the Starting Adventure: From the following list of options, choose how you became involved in the first adventure.

1. You convinced one of the other PCs to tell you what they were doing.

2. You instigated the whole thing and convinced the others to join you.

3. One of the other PCs did a favor for you, and now you're repaying that obligation by helping them with the task at hand.

4. There is a reward involved, and you need the money.

CLEVER

You're quick-witted, thinking well on your feet. You understand people, so you can fool them but are rarely fooled. Because you easily see things for what they are, you get the lay of the land swiftly, size up threats and allies, and assess situations with accuracy. Perhaps you're physically attractive, or maybe you use your wit to overcome any physical or mental imperfections.

You gain the following characteristics:

Smart: +2 to your Intellect Pool.

Skill: You're trained in all interactions involving lies or trickery.

Skill: You're trained in defense rolls to resist mental effects.

Skill: You're trained in all tasks involving identifying or assessing danger, lies, quality, importance, function, or power.

Inability: You were never good at studying or retaining trivial knowledge. Any task involving lore, knowledge, or understanding is hindered.

Additional Equipment: You see through the schemes of others and occasionally convince them to believe you—even when, perhaps, they should not. Thanks to your clever behavior, you have an additional expensive item.

Initial Link to the Starting Adventure: From the following list of options, choose how you became involved in the first adventure.

1. You convinced one of the other PCs to tell you what they were doing.

2. From afar, you observed that something interesting was going on.

3. You talked your way into the situation because you thought it might earn some money.

4. You suspect that the other PCs won't succeed without you.

CLUMSY

Graceless and awkward, you were told that you'd grow out of it, but you never did. You often drop things, trip over your own feet, or knock things (or people) over. Some people get frustrated by this quality, but most find it funny and even a little charming.

You gain the following characteristics:

Butterfingers: –2 to your Speed Pool.

Thick-Muscled: +2 to your Might Pool.

Inelegant: You have a certain lovable charm. You are trained in all pleasant social interactions when you express a lighthearted, self-deprecating manner.

Dumb Luck: The GM can introduce a GM intrusion on you, based on your clumsiness, without awarding you any XP (as if you had rolled a 1 on a d20 roll). However, if this happens, 50% of the time, your clumsiness works to your advantage. Rather than hurting you (much), it helps you, or it hurts your enemies. You slip, but it's just in time to duck an attack. You fall down, but you trip your enemies as you crash into their legs. You turn around too quickly, but you end up knocking the weapon from your foe's hand. You

Some players may not want to be defined by a "negative" quality like Clumsy, but in truth, even this kind of descriptor has enough advantages that it makes for capable and talented characters. What negative descriptors really do is make more interesting and complex characters that are often great fun to play.

GM intrusions, page 408

and the GM should work together to determine the details. If the GM wishes, they can use GM intrusions based on your clumsiness normally (awarding XP).

Skill: You've got a certain bull-like quality. You are trained in tasks involving breaking things.

Inability: Any task that involves balance, grace, or hand-to-eye coordination is hindered.

Initial Link to the Starting Adventure: From the following list of options, choose how you became involved in the first adventure.

1. You were in the right place at the right time.
2. You had a piece of information that the other PCs needed to make their plans.
3. A sibling recommended you to the other PCs.
4. You stumbled into the PCs as they were discussing their mission, and they took a liking to you.

CRAVEN

Courage fails you at every turn. You lack the willpower and resolve to stand fast in the face of danger. Fear gnaws at your heart, chewing away at your mind, driving you to distraction until you cannot bear it. Most times, you back down from confrontations. You flee from threats and vacillate when faced with difficult decisions.

Yet for all that fear dogs you and possibly shames you, your cowardly nature proves to be a useful ally from time to time. Listening to your fears has helped you escape danger and avoid taking unnecessary risks. Others may have suffered in your place, and you might be the first to admit this fact, but secretly you feel intense relief from having avoided an unthinkable and terrible fate.

You gain the following characteristics:

Furtive: +2 to your Speed Pool.
Skill: You're trained in stealth-based tasks.
Skill: You're trained in running actions.
Skill: You're trained in any action taken to escape danger, flee from a dangerous situation, or wheedle your way out of trouble.

Inability: You do not willingly enter dangerous situations. Any initiative actions (to determine who goes first in combat) are hindered.

Inability: You fall to pieces when you have to undertake a potentially dangerous task alone. Any such task (such as attacking a creature by yourself) is hindered.

Additional Equipment: You have a good luck charm or protective device to keep you out of harm's way.

Initial Link to the Starting Adventure: From the following list of options, choose how you became involved in the first adventure.

1. You believe that you're being hunted, and you have hired one of the other PCs as your protector.
2. You seek to escape your shame and take up with capable individuals in the hopes of repairing your reputation.
3. One of the other PCs bullied you into coming along.
4. The group answered your cries for help when you were in trouble.

CREATIVE

Maybe you have a notebook where you write down ideas so you can develop them later. Perhaps you email yourself ideas that strike you out of the blue so you can sort them in an electronic document. Or maybe you just sit down, stare at your screen and, by indomitable force of will, produce something from nothing. However your gift works, you're creative—you code, write, compose, sculpt, design, direct, or otherwise create narratives that enthrall other people with your vision.

You gain the following characteristics:

Inventive: +2 to your Intellect Pool.

Original: You're always coming up with something new. You're trained in any task related to creating a narrative (such as a story, play, or scenario). This includes deception, if the deception involves a narrative you're able to tell.

Skill: You are naturally inventive. You are trained in one specific creative skill of your choice: writing, computer coding, composing music, painting, drawing, and so on.

Skill: You love solving riddles and the like. You are trained in puzzle-solving tasks.

Skill: To be creative requires that you always be learning. You are trained in any task that involves finding out something new, such as when you're digging through a library, data bank, news archive, or similar collection of knowledge.

Inability: You're inventive but not charming. All tasks related to pleasant social interaction are hindered.

Initial Link to the Starting Adventure: From the following list of options, choose how you became involved in the first adventure.

1. You were doing research for a project and convinced the PCs to bring you along.
2. You're looking for new markets for the results of your creative output.
3. You fell in with the wrong crowd, but they grew on you.
4. A creative life is often one beset with financial hurdles. You joined the PCs because you hoped it would be profitable.

Descriptors like Craven, Cruel, and Dishonorable might not be appropriate for every group. These are villainous traits and some people want their PCs to be entirely heroic. But others don't mind a little moral greyness thrown into the mix. Still others see things like Craven and Cruel as traits to overcome as their characters develop (probably earning them different descriptors).

CRUEL

Misfortune and suffering do not move you. When another endures hardship, you find it hard to care, and you may even enjoy the pain and difficulty the person experiences if they've done you wrong in the past. Your cruel streak may derive from bitterness brought about by your own struggles and disappointments. You might be a hard pragmatist, doing what you feel you must even if others are worse for it. Or you could be a sadist, delighting in the pain you inflict.

Being cruel does not necessarily make you a villain. Your cruelty may be reserved for those who cross you or other people useful to you. You might have become cruel as the result of an intensely awful experience. Abuse and torture, for example, can strip away compassion for other living beings.

As well, you need not be cruel in every situation. In fact, others might see you as personable, friendly, and even helpful. But when angered or frustrated, your dual nature reveals itself, and those who have earned your scorn are likely to suffer for it.

You gain the following characteristics:

Cunning: +2 to your Intellect Pool.

Cruelty: When you use force, you can choose to maim or deliver painful injuries to draw out your foe's suffering. Whenever you inflict damage, you can choose to inflict 2 fewer points of damage to ease your next attack against that foe.

Skill: You're trained in tasks related to deception, intimidation, and persuasion when you interact with characters experiencing physical or emotional pain.

Inability: You have a hard time connecting with others, understanding their motives, or sharing their feelings. Any task to ascertain another character's motives, feelings, or disposition is hindered.

Additional Equipment: You have a valuable memento from the last person you destroyed. The memento is moderately priced, and you can sell it or trade it for an item of equal or lesser value.

Initial Link to the Starting Adventure: From the following list of options, choose how you became involved in the first adventure.

1. You suspect that you might gain a long-term advantage from helping the other PCs and may be able to use that advantage against your enemies.

2. By joining the PCs, you see an opportunity to grow your personal power and status at the expense of others.

3. You hope to make another PC's life more difficult by joining the group.

4. Joining the PCs gives you an opportunity to escape justice for a crime you committed.

DISHONORABLE

There is no honor among thieves—or betrayers, backstabbers, liars, or cheats. You are all of these things, and either you don't lose any sleep over it, or you deny the truth to others or to yourself. Regardless, you are willing to do whatever it takes to get your own way. Honor, ethics, and principles are merely words. In your estimation, they have no place in the real world.

You gain the following characteristics:

Sneaky: +4 to your Speed Pool.

Just Desserts: When the GM gives another player an experience point to award to someone for a GM intrusion, that player cannot give it to you.

Skill: You are trained in deception.

Skill: You are trained in stealth.

Skill: You are trained in intimidation.

Inability: People don't like or trust you. Pleasant social interactions are hindered.

Initial Link to the Starting Adventure: From the following list of options, choose how you became involved in the first adventure.

1. You are interested in what the PCs are doing, so you lied to them to get into their group.

2. While skulking about, you overheard the PCs' plans and realized that you wanted in.

3. One of the other PCs invited you, having no idea of what you're truly like.

4. You bullied your way in with intimidation and bluster.

GM intrusions, page 408

DOOMED

You are quite certain that your fate is leading you, inextricably, toward a terrible end. This fate might be yours alone, or you might be dragging along the people closest to you.

You gain the following characteristics:

Jumpy: +2 to your Speed Pool.

Skill: Always on the lookout for danger, you are trained in perception-related tasks.

Skill: You are defense minded, so you are trained in Speed defense tasks.

Skill: You are cynical and expect the worst. Thus, you are resistant to mental shocks. You are trained in Intellect defense tasks having to do with losing your sanity or equanimity.

Doom: Every other time the GM uses GM intrusion on your character, you cannot refuse it and do not get an XP for it (you still get an XP to award to another player). This is because you are doomed. The universe is a cold, uncaring place, and your efforts are futile at best.

Initial Link to the Starting Adventure: From the following list of options, choose how you became involved in the first adventure.

1. You attempted to avoid it, but events seemed to conspire to draw you to where you are.

2. Why not? It doesn't matter. You're doomed no matter what you do.

3. One of the other PCs saved your life, and now you're repaying that obligation by helping them with the task at hand.

4. You suspect that the only hope you have of avoiding your fate might lie on this path.

EMPATHIC

Other people are open books to you. You may have a knack for reading a person's tells, those subtle movements that convey an individual's mood and disposition. Or you may receive information in a more direct way, feeling a person's emotions as if they were tangible things, sensations that lightly brush against your mind. Your gift for empathy helps you navigate social situations and control them to avoid misunderstandings and prevent useless conflicts from erupting.

The constant bombardment of emotions from those around you likely takes a toll. You might move with the prevailing mood, swinging from giddy happiness to bitter sorrow with little warning. Or you might close yourself off and remain inscrutable to others out of a sense of self-preservation or an unconscious fear that everyone else might learn how you truly feel.

You gain the following characteristics:

Open Mind: +4 to your Intellect Pool.

Skill: You're trained in tasks involving sensing other emotions, discerning dispositions, and getting a hunch about people around you.

Skill: You're trained in all tasks involving social interaction, pleasant or otherwise.

Inability: Being so receptive to others' thoughts and moods makes you vulnerable to anything that attacks your mind. Intellect defense rolls are hindered.

Initial Link to the Starting Adventure: From the following list of options, choose how you became involved in the first adventure.

1. You sensed the commitment to the task the other PCs have and felt moved to help them.

2. You established a close bond with another PC and can't bear to be parted from them.

3. You sensed something strange in one of the PCs and decided to join the group to see if you can sense it again and uncover the truth.

4. You joined the PCs to escape an unpleasant relationship or negative environment.

DESCRIPTOR

EXILED

You have walked a long and lonely road, leaving your home and your life behind. You might have committed a heinous crime, something so awful that your people forced you out, and if you dare return, you face death. You might have been accused of a crime you didn't commit and now must pay the price for someone else's wicked deed. Your exile might be the result of a social gaffe—perhaps you shamed your family or a friend, or you embarrassed yourself in front of your peers, an authority, or someone you respect. Whatever the reason, you have left your old life behind and now strive to make a new one.

You gain the following characteristics:

Self-Reliant: +2 to your Might Pool.

Loner: You gain no benefit when you get help with a task from another character who is trained or specialized in that task.

Skill: You're trained in all tasks involving sneaking.

Skill: You're trained in all tasks involving foraging, hunting, and finding safe places to rest or hide.

Inability: Living on your own for as long as you have makes you slow to trust others and awkward in social situations. Any task involving social interaction is hindered.

Additional Equipment: You have a memento from your past—an old picture, a locket with a few strands of hair inside, or a lighter given to you by someone important. You keep the object close at hand and pull it out to help you remember better times.

Initial Link to the Starting Adventure: From the following list of options, choose how you became involved in the first adventure.

1. The other PCs earned your trust by helping you when you needed it. You accompany them to repay them.

2. While exploring on your own, you discovered something strange. When you traveled to a settlement, the PCs were the only ones who believed you, and they have accompanied you to help you deal with the problem.

3. One of the other PCs reminds you of someone you used to know.

4. You have grown weary of your isolation. Joining the other PCs gives you a chance to belong.

FAST

You're fleet of foot. Because you're quick, you can accomplish tasks more rapidly than others can. You're not just quick on your feet, however—you're quick with your hands, and you think and react quickly. You even talk quickly.

You gain the following characteristics:

Energetic: +2 to your Speed Pool.

Skill: You are trained in running.

Fast: You can move a short distance and still take another action in the same round, or you can move a long distance as your action without needing to make any kind of roll.

Inability: You're a sprinter, not a long-distance runner. You don't have a lot of stamina. Might defense rolls are hindered.

Initial Link to the Starting Adventure: From the following list of options, choose how you became involved in the first adventure.

1. You jumped in to save one of the other PCs who was in dire need.

2. One of the other PCs recruited you for your unique talents.

3. You're impulsive, and it seemed like a good idea at the time.

4. This mission ties in with a personal goal of your own.

Helping, page 226

It can be liberating and really fun to play a foolish character. In some ways, the pressure to always do the right, smart thing is off. On the other hand, if you play such a character as a bumbling moron in every situation, that can become annoying to everyone else at the table. As with everything, moderation is the key.

FOOLISH

Not everyone can be brilliant. Oh, you don't think of yourself as stupid, and you're not. It's just that others might have a bit more . . . wisdom. Insight. You prefer to barrel along headfirst through life and let other people worry about things. Worrying's never helped you, so why bother? You take things at face value and don't fret about what tomorrow might bring.

People call you "idiot" or "numbskull," but it doesn't faze you much.

You gain the following characteristics:

Unwise: −4 to your Intellect Pool.

Carefree: You succeed more on luck than anything. Every time you roll for a task, roll twice and take the higher result.

Intellect Weakness: Any time you spend points from your Intellect Pool, it costs you 1 more point than usual.

Inability: Any Intellect defense task is hindered.

Inability: Any task that involves seeing through a deception, an illusion, or a trap is hindered.

Initial Link to the Starting Adventure: From the following list of options, choose how you became involved in the first adventure.

1. Who knows? Seemed like a good idea at the time.

2. Someone asked you to join up with the other PCs. They told you not to ask too many questions, and that seemed fine to you.

3. Your parent (or a parental/mentor figure) got you involved to give you something to do and maybe "teach you some sense."

4. The other PCs needed some muscle who wouldn't overthink things.

GRACEFUL

You have a perfect sense of balance, moving and speaking with grace and beauty. You're quick, lithe, flexible, and dexterous. Your body is perfectly suited to dance, and you use that advantage in combat to dodge blows. You might wear garments that enhance your agile movement and sense of style.

You gain the following characteristics:

Agile: +2 to your Speed Pool.

Skill: You're trained in all tasks involving balance and careful movement.

Skill: You're trained in all tasks involving physical performing arts.

Skill: You're trained in all Speed defense tasks.

Initial Link to the Starting Adventure: From the following list of options, choose how you became involved in the first adventure.

1. Against your better judgment, you joined the other PCs because you saw that they were in danger.

2. One of the other PCs convinced you that joining the group would be in your best interests.

3. You're afraid of what might happen if the other PCs fail.

4. There is reward involved, and you need the money.

DESCRIPTOR

GUARDED

You conceal your true nature behind a mask and are loath to let anyone see who you really are. Protecting yourself, physically and emotionally, is what you care about most, and you prefer to keep everyone else at a safe distance. You may be suspicious of everyone you meet, expecting the worst from people so you won't be surprised when they prove you right. Or you might just be a bit reserved, careful about letting people through your gruff exterior to the person you really are.

No one can be as reserved as you are and make many friends. Most likely, you have an abrasive personality and tend to be pessimistic in your outlook. You probably nurse an old hurt and find that the only way you can cope is to keep it and your personality locked down.

You gain the following characteristics:

Suspicious: +2 to your Intellect Pool.

Skill: You are trained in all Intellect defense tasks.

Skill: You are trained in all tasks involving discerning the truth, piercing disguises, and recognizing falsehoods and other deceptions.

Inability: Your suspicious nature makes you unlikeable. Any task involving deception or persuasion is hindered.

Initial Link to the Starting Adventure: From the following list of options, choose how you became involved in the first adventure.

1. One of the PCs managed to overcome your defenses and befriend you.

2. You want to see what the PCs are up to, so you accompany them to catch them in the act of some wrongdoing.

3. You have made a few enemies and take up with the PCs for protection.

4. The PCs are the only people who will put up with you.

HARDY

Your body was built to take abuse. Whether you're pounding down stiff drinks while holding up a bar in your favorite watering hole or trading blows with a thug in a back alley, you keep going, shrugging off hurts and injuries that might slow or incapacitate a lesser person. Neither hunger nor thirst, cut flesh nor broken bone can stop you. You just press on through the pain and continue.

As fit and healthy as you are, the signs of wear show in the myriad scars crisscrossing your body, your thrice-broken nose, your cauliflower ears, and any number of other disfigurements you wear with pride.

You gain the following characteristics:

Mighty: +4 to your Might Pool.

Fast Healer: You halve the time it takes to make a recovery roll (minimum one action).

Almost Unstoppable: While you are impaired on the damage track, you function as if you were hale. While you are debilitated, you function as if you were impaired. In other words, you don't suffer the effects of being impaired until you become debilitated, and you never suffer the effects of being debilitated. You still die if all your stat Pools are 0.

Skill: You are trained in Might defense actions.

Inability: Your big, strong body is slow to react. Any task involving initiative is hindered.

Ponderous: When you apply Effort when making a Speed roll, you must spend 1 extra point from your Speed Pool.

Initial Link to the Starting Adventure: From the following list of options, choose how you became involved in the first adventure.

1. The PCs recruited you after learning about your reputation as a survivor.

2. You joined the PCs because you want or need the money.

3. The PCs offered you a challenge equal to your physical power.

4. You believe the only way the PCs will succeed is if you are along to protect them.

Damage track, page 218

47

HIDEOUS

You are physically repugnant by almost any human standard. You might have had a serious accident, a harmful mutation, or just poor genetic luck, but you are incontrovertibly ugly.

You've more than made up for your appearance in other ways, however. Because you have to hide your appearance, you excel at sneaking about unnoticed or disguising yourself. But perhaps most important, being ostracized while others socialized, you took the time growing up to develop yourself as you saw fit—you grew strong or quick, or you honed your mind.

You gain the following characteristics:

Versatile: You get 4 additional points to divide among your stat Pools.

Skill: You are trained in intimidation and any other fear-based interactions, if you show your true face.

Skill: You are trained in disguise and stealth tasks.

Inability: All tasks relating to pleasant social interaction are hindered.

Initial Link to the Starting Adventure: From the following list of options, choose how you became involved in the first adventure.

1. One of the other PCs approached you while you were in disguise, recruiting you while believing you were someone else.

2. While skulking about, you overheard the other PCs' plans and realized you wanted in.

3. One of the other PCs invited you, but you wonder if it was out of pity.

4. You bullied your way in with intimidation and bluster.

HONORABLE

You are trustworthy, fair, and forthright. You try to do what is right, to help others, and to treat them well. Lying and cheating are no way to get ahead—these things are for the weak, the lazy, or the despicable. You probably spend a lot of time thinking about your personal honor, how best to maintain it, and how to defend it if challenged. In combat, you are straightforward and offer quarter to any foe.

You were likely instilled with this sense of honor by a parent or a mentor. Sometimes the distinction between what is and isn't honorable varies with different schools of thought, but in broad strokes, honorable people can agree on most aspects of what honor means.

You gain the following characteristics:

Stalwart: +2 to your Might Pool.

Skill: You are trained in pleasant social interactions.

Skill: You are trained in discerning people's true motives or seeing through lies.

Initial Link to the Starting Adventure: From the following list of options, choose how you became involved in the first adventure.

1. The PCs' goals appear to be honorable and commendable.

2. You see that what the other PCs are about to do is dangerous, and you'd like to help protect them.

3. One of the other PCs invited you, hearing of your trustworthiness.

4. You asked politely if you could join the other PCs in their mission.

IMPULSIVE

You have a hard time tamping down your enthusiasm. Why wait when you can just do it (whatever it is) and get it done? You deal with problems when they arise rather than plan ahead. Putting out the small fires now prevents them from becoming one big fire later. You are the first to take risks, to jump in and lend a hand, to step into dark passages, and to find danger.

Your impulsiveness likely gets you into trouble. While others might take time to study the items they discover, you use such items without hesitation. After all, the best way to learn what something can do is to use it. When a cautious explorer might look around and check for danger nearby, you have to physically stop yourself from bulling on ahead. Why fuss around when the exciting thing is just ahead?

You gain the following characteristics:

Reckless: +2 to your Speed Pool.

Skill: You're trained in initiative actions (to determine who goes first in combat).

Skill: You're trained in Speed defense actions.

Inability: You'll try anything once, but quickly grow bored after that. Any task that involves patience, willpower, or discipline is hindered.

Initial Link to the Starting Adventure: From the following list of options, choose how you became involved in the first adventure.

1. You heard what the other PCs were up to and suddenly decided to join them.

2. You pulled everyone together after you heard rumors about something interesting you want to see or do.

3. You blew all of your money and now find yourself strapped for cash.

4. You're in trouble for acting recklessly. You join the other PCs because they offer a way out of your problem.

Impulsive characters get into trouble. That's their thing, and that's fine. But if you're constantly dragging your fellow PCs into trouble (or worse, getting them seriously hurt or killed), that will be annoying, to say the least. A good rule of thumb is that impulsiveness doesn't always mean a predilection for doing the wrong thing. Sometimes it's the urge to do the right thing.

DESCRIPTOR

INQUISITIVE

The world is vast and mysterious, with wonders and secrets to keep you amazed for several lifetimes. You feel the tugging on your heart, the call to explore the wreckage of past civilizations, to discover new peoples, new places, and whatever bizarre wonders you might find along the way. However, as strongly as you feel the pull to roam the world, you know there is danger aplenty, and you take precautions to ensure that you are prepared for any eventuality. Research, preparation, and readiness will help you live long enough to see everything you want to see and do everything you want to do.

You probably have a dozen books and travelogues about the world on you at any time. When not hitting the road and looking around, you spend your time with your nose in a book, learning everything you can about the place you're going so you know what to expect when you get there.

You gain the following characteristics:

Smart: +4 to your Intellect Pool.

Skill: You are eager to learn. You are trained in any task that involves learning something new, whether you're talking to a local to get information or digging through old books to find lore.

Skill: You have made a study of the world. You are trained in any task involving geography or history.

Inability: You tend to fixate on the details, making you somewhat oblivious to what's going on around you. Any task to hear or notice dangers around you is hindered.

Inability: When you see something interesting, you hesitate as you take in all the details. Initiative actions (to determine who goes first in combat) are hindered.

Additional Equipment: You have three books on whatever subjects you choose.

Initial Link to the Starting Adventure: From the following list of options, choose how you became involved in the first adventure.

1. One of the PCs approached you to learn information related to the mission, having heard you were an expert.

2. You have always wanted to see the place where the other PCs are going.

3. You were interested in what the other PCs were up to and decided to go along with them.

4. One of the PCs fascinates you, perhaps due to a special or weird ability they have.

INTELLIGENT

You're quite smart. Your memory is sharp, and you easily grasp concepts that others might struggle with. This aptitude doesn't necessarily mean that you've had years of formal education, but you have learned a great deal in your life, primarily because you pick things up quickly and retain so much.

You gain the following characteristics:

Smart: +2 to your Intellect Pool.

Skill: You're trained in an area of knowledge of your choice.

Skill: You're trained in all actions that involve remembering or memorizing things you experience directly. For example, instead of being good at recalling details of geography that you read about in a book, you can remember a path through a set of tunnels that you've explored before.

Initial Link to the Starting Adventure: From the following list of options, choose how you became involved in the first adventure.

1. One of the other PCs asked your opinion of the mission, knowing that if you thought it was a good idea, it probably was.

2. You saw value in what the other PCs were doing.

3. You believed that the task might lead to important and interesting discoveries.

4. A colleague requested that you take part in the mission as a favor.

INTUITIVE

You are often tickled by a sense of knowing what someone will say, how they will react, or how events might unfold. Maybe you have a mutant sense, maybe you can see just a few moments ahead through time, or maybe you're just good at reading people and extrapolating a situation. Whatever the case, many who look into your eyes immediately glance away, as if afraid of what you might see in their expression.

You gain the following characteristics:

Innate: +2 to your Intellect Pool.

Skill: You are trained in perception tasks.

Know What to Do: You can act immediately, even if it's not your turn. Afterward, on your next regular turn, any action you take is hindered. You can do this one time, although the ability is renewed each time you make a recovery roll.

Initial Link to the Starting Adventure: From the following list of options, choose how you became involved in the first adventure.

1. You just knew you had to come along.

2. You convinced one of the other PCs that your intuition is invaluable.

3. You felt that something terrible would happen if you didn't go.

4. You're confident the reason you arrived at this point will soon become clear.

Your descriptor matters most when you are a beginning character. The benefits (and perhaps drawbacks) that come from your descriptor will eventually be overshadowed by the growing importance of your type and focus. However, the influence of your descriptor will remain at least somewhat important throughout your character's life.

JOVIAL

You're cheerful, friendly, and outgoing. You put others at ease with a big smile and a joke, possibly one at your own expense, though lightly ribbing your companions who can take it is also one of your favorite pastimes. Sometimes people say you never take anything seriously. That's not true, of course, but you have learned that to dwell on the bad too long quickly robs the world of joy. You've always got a new joke in your back pocket because you collect them like some people collect bottles of wine.

You gain the following characteristics:

Witty: +2 to your Intellect Pool.

Skill: You're convivial and set most people at ease with your attitude. You are trained in all tasks related to pleasant social interaction.

Skill: You have an advantage in figuring out the punch lines of jokes you've never heard before. You are trained in all tasks related to solving puzzles and riddles.

Initial Link to the Starting Adventure: From the following list of options, choose how you became involved in the first adventure.

1. You solved a riddle before realizing that answering it would launch you into the adventure.

2. The other PCs thought you'd bring some much-needed levity to the team.

3. You decided that all fun and no work was not the best way to get through life, so you joined up with the PCs.

4. It was either go with the PCs or face up to a circumstance that was anything but jovial.

KIND

It's always been easy for you to see things from the point of view of other people. That ability has made you sympathetic to what they really want or need. From your perspective, you're just applying the old proverb that "it's easier to catch flies with honey than with vinegar," but others simply see your behavior as kindness. Of course, being kind takes time, and yours is limited. You've learned that a small fraction of people don't deserve your time or kindness—true sadists, narcissists, and similar folk will only waste your energy. So you deal with them swiftly, saving your kindness for those who deserve it and can benefit from your attention.

You gain the following characteristics:

Emotionally Intuitive: +2 to your Intellect Pool.

Skill: You know what it's like to go a mile in someone else's shoes. You're trained in all tasks related to pleasant social interaction and discerning the dispositions of others.

Karma: Sometimes, strangers just help you out. To gain the aid of a stranger, you must use a one action, ten-minute, or one-hour recovery roll (without gaining its healing benefit), and the GM determines the nature of the aid you gain. Usually, the act of kindness isn't enough to turn a bad situation completely around, but it may moderate a bad situation and lead to new opportunities. For example, if you are captured, a guard loosens your bonds slightly, brings you water, or delivers a message.

Inability: Being kind comes with a few risks. All tasks related to detecting falsehoods are hindered.

Initial Link to the Starting Adventure: From the following list of options, choose how you became involved in the first adventure.

1. A PC needed your help, and you agreed to come along as a kindness.

2. You gave the wrong person access to your money, and now you need to make some back.

3. You're ready to take your benevolence on the road and help more people than you could if you didn't join the PCs.

4. Your job, which seemed like it would be personally rewarding, is the opposite. You join the PCs to escape the drudgery.

LEARNED

You have studied, either on your own or with an instructor. You know many things and are an expert on a few topics, such as history, biology, geography, mythology, nature, or any other area of study. Learned characters typically carry a few books around with them and spend their spare time reading.

You gain the following characteristics:

Smart: +2 to your Intellect Pool.

Skill: You're trained in three areas of knowledge of your choice.

Inability: You have few social graces. Any task involving charm, persuasion, or etiquette is hindered.

Additional Equipment: You have two additional books on topics of your choice.

Initial Link to the Starting Adventure: From the following list of options, choose how you became involved in the first adventure.

1. One of the other PCs asked you to come along because of your knowledge.
2. You need money to fund your studies.
3. You believed that the task might lead to important and interesting discoveries.
4. A colleague requested that you take part in the mission as a favor.

LUCKY

You rely on chance and timely good luck to get you through many situations. When people say that someone was born under a lucky star, they mean you. When you try your hand at something new, no matter how unfamiliar the task is, as often as not you find a measure of success. Even when disaster strikes, it's rarely as bad as it could be. More often, small things seem to go your way, you win contests, and you're often in the right place at the right time.

You gain the following characteristics:

Luck Pool: You have one additional Pool called Luck that begins with 3 points, and it has a maximum value of 3 points. When spending points from any other Pool, you can take one, some, or all of the points from your Luck Pool first. When you make a recovery roll to recover points to any other Pool, your Luck Pool is also refreshed by the same number of points. When your Luck Pool is at 0 points, it does not count against your damage track. Enabler.

Advantage: When you use 1 XP to reroll a d20 for any roll that affects only you, add 3 to the reroll.

Initial Link to the Starting Adventure: From the following list of options, choose how you became involved in the first adventure.

1. Knowing that lucky people notice and take active advantage of opportunities, you became involved in your first adventure by choice.

2. You literally bumped into someone else on this adventure through sheer luck.
3. You found a briefcase lying alongside the road. It was battered, but inside you found a lot of strange documents that led you here.
4. Your luck saved you when you avoided a speeding vehicle by a fortuitous fall through an opening in the ground (a manhole, if in a modern setting). Beneath the ground, you found something you couldn't ignore.

MAD

You have delved too deeply into subjects people were not meant to know. You are knowledgeable in things beyond the scope of most, but this knowledge has come at a terrible price. You are likely in questionable physical shape and occasionally shake with nervous tics. You sometimes mutter to yourself without realizing it.

You gain the following characteristics:

Knowledgeable: +4 to your Intellect Pool.

Fits of Insight: Whenever such knowledge is appropriate, the GM feeds you information although there is no clear explanation as to how you could know such a thing. This is up to the GM's discretion, but it should happen as often as once each session.

Erratic Behavior: You are prone to acting erratically or irrationally. When you are in the presence of a major discovery or subjected to great stress (such as a serious physical threat), the GM can introduce a GM intrusion that directs your next action without awarding XP. You can still pay 1 XP to refuse the intrusion. The GM's influence is the manifestation of your madness and thus is always something you would not likely do otherwise, but it is not directly, obviously harmful to you unless there are extenuating circumstances. (For example, if a foe suddenly leaps out of the darkness, you might spend the first round babbling incoherently or screaming the name of your first true love.)

Skill: You are trained in one area of knowledge (probably something weird or esoteric).

Inability: Your mind is quite fragile. Tasks to resist mental attacks are hindered.

Initial Link to the Starting Adventure: From the following list of options, choose how you became involved in the first adventure.

1. Voices in your head told you to go.
2. You instigated the whole thing and convinced the others to join you.
3. One of the other PCs obtained a book of knowledge for you, and now you're repaying that favor by helping them with the task at hand.
4. You feel compelled by inexplicable intuition.

GM intrusions, page 408

Damage track, page 218

MECHANICAL

You have a special talent with machines of all kinds, and you're adept at understanding and, if need be, repairing them. Perhaps you're a bit of an inventor, creating new machines from time to time. You get called "techie," "tech," "mech," "gear-head," "motor-head," or any of a number of other nicknames. Mechanics usually wear practical work clothes and carry around a lot of tools.

You gain the following characteristics:

Smart: +2 to your Intellect Pool.

Skill: You're trained in all actions involving identifying or understanding machines.

Skill: You're trained in all actions involving using, repairing, or crafting machines.

Additional Equipment: You start with a variety of machine tools.

Initial Link to the Starting Adventure: From the following list of options, choose how you became involved in the first adventure.

1. While repairing a nearby machine, you overheard the other PCs talking.

2. You need money to buy tools and parts.

3. It was clear that the mission couldn't succeed without your skills and knowledge.

4. Another PC asked you to join them.

MYSTERIOUS

The dark figure lurking silently in the corner? That's you. No one really knows where you came from or what your motives are—you play things close to the vest. Your manner perplexes and confounds others, but that doesn't make you a poor friend or ally. You're just good at keeping things to yourself, moving about unseen, and concealing your presence and identity.

You gain the following characteristics:

Skill: You are trained in all stealth tasks.

Skill: You are trained in resisting interrogation or tricks to get you to talk.

Confounding: You pull talents and abilities seemingly out of nowhere. You can attempt one task in which you have no training as if you were trained, attempt a task that you are trained in as if specialized, or gain a free level of Effort with a task that you are specialized in. This ability refreshes every time you make a recovery roll, but the uses never accumulate.

Inability: People never know where they stand with you. Any task involving getting people to believe or trust you is hindered.

Initial Link to the Starting Adventure: From the following list of options, choose how you became involved in the first adventure.

1. You just showed up one day.

2. You convinced one of the other PCs that you had invaluable skills.

Free level of Effort, page 209

3. Some equally mysterious figure told you where to be and when (but not why) to join the group.

4. Something—a feeling, a dream—told you where to be and when to join the group.

MYSTICAL

You think of yourself as mystical, attuned with the mysterious and the paranormal. Your true talents lie with the supernatural. You likely have experience with ancient lore, and you can sense and wield the supernatural—though whether that means "magic," "psychic phenomena," or something else is up to you (and probably up to those around you as well). Mystical characters often wear jewelry, such as a ring or an amulet, or have tattoos or other marks that show their interests.

You gain the following characteristics:
Smart: +2 to your Intellect Pool.
Skill: You're trained in all actions involving identifying or understanding the supernatural.
Sense Magic: You can sense whether the supernatural is active in situations where its presence is not obvious. You must study an object or location closely for a minute to get a feel for whether a mystical touch is at work.
Spell: You can perform Hedge Magic as a spell when you have a free hand and can pay the Intellect point cost.
Inability: You have a manner or an aura that others find a bit unnerving. Any task involving charm, persuasion, or deception is hindered.
Initial Link to the Starting Adventure: From the following list of options, choose how you became involved in the first adventure.

1. A dream guided you to this point.
2. You need money to fund your studies.
3. You believed the mission would be a great way to learn more about the supernatural.
4. Various signs and portents led you here.

NAIVE

You've lived a sheltered life. Your childhood was safe and secure, so you didn't get a chance to learn much about the world—and even less chance to experience it. Whether you were training for something, had your nose in a book, or just were sequestered in a secluded place, you haven't done much, met many people, or seen many interesting things so far. That's probably going to change soon, but as you go forward into a larger world, you do so without some of the understanding that others possess about how it all works.

You gain the following characteristics:
Fresh: You add +1 to your recovery rolls.
Incorruptible: You are trained in Intellect defense tasks and all tasks that involve resisting temptation.
Skill: You're wide-eyed. You are trained in perception tasks.
Inability: Any task that involves seeing through deceptions or determining someone's secret motive is hindered.
Initial Link to the Starting Adventure: From the following list of options, choose how you became involved in the first adventure.

1. Someone told you that you should get involved.
2. You needed money, and this seemed like a good way to earn some.
3. You believed that you could learn a lot by joining the other PCs.
4. Sounded like fun.

Hedge Magic, page 149

Is there really much difference between a character who is Hardy, one who is Resilient, and another who is Tough? The descriptors are indeed close, but the differences will become apparent in play. Players should choose the one they like best.

PERCEPTIVE

You miss little. You pick out the small details in the world around you and are skilled at making deductions from the information you find. Your talents make you an exceptional sleuth, a formidable scientist, or a talented scout.

As adept as you are at finding clues, you have no skill at picking up on social cues. You overlook an offense that your deductions give or how uncomfortable your scrutiny can make the people around you. You tend to dismiss others as being intellectual dwarfs compared to you, which avails you little when you need a favor.

You gain the following characteristics:

Smart: +2 to your Intellect Pool.

Skill: You have an eye for detail. You are trained in any task that involves finding or noticing small details.

Skill: You know a little about everything. You are trained in any task that involves identifying objects or calling to mind a minor detail or bit of trivia.

Skill: Your skill at making deductions can be imposing. You are trained in any task that involves intimidating another creature.

Inability: Your confidence comes off as arrogance to people who don't know you. Any task involving positive social interactions is hindered.

Additional Equipment: You have a bag of light tools.

Initial Link to the Starting Adventure: From the following list of options, choose how you became involved in the first adventure.

1. You overheard the other PCs discussing their mission and volunteered your services.
2. One of the PCs asked you to come along, believing that your talents would be invaluable to the mission.
3. You believe that the PCs' mission is somehow related to one of your investigations.
4. A third party recruited you to follow the PCs and see what they were up to.

RESILIENT

You can take a lot of punishment, both physically and mentally, and still come back for more. It takes a lot to put you down. Neither physical nor mental shocks or damage have a lasting effect. You're tough to faze. Unflappable. Unstoppable.

You gain the following characteristics:

Resistant: +2 to your Might Pool, and +2 to your Intellect Pool.

Recover: You can make an extra recovery roll each day. This roll is just one action. So you can make two recovery rolls that each take one action, one roll that takes ten minutes, a fourth roll that takes one hour, and a fifth roll that requires ten hours of rest.

Skill: You are trained in Might defense tasks.

Skill: You are trained in Intellect defense tasks.

Inability: You're hardy but not necessarily strong. Any task involving moving, bending, or breaking things is hindered.

Inability: You have a lot of willpower and mental fortitude, but you're not necessarily smart. Any task involving knowledge or figuring out problems or puzzles is hindered.

Initial Link to the Starting Adventure: From the following list of options, choose how you became involved in the first adventure.

1. You saw that the PCs clearly need someone like you to help them out.
2. Someone asked you to watch over one of the PCs in particular, and you agreed.
3. You are bored and desperately in need of a challenge.
4. You lost a bet—unfairly, you think—and had to take someone's place on this mission.

RISK-TAKING

It's part of your nature to question what others think can't or shouldn't be done. You're not insane, of course—you wouldn't attempt to leap across a mile-wide chasm just because you were dared. There's impossible and then there's the just barely possible. You like to push the latter further than others, because it gives you a rush of satisfaction and pleasure when you succeed. The more you succeed, the more you find yourself looking for that next risky challenge to try yourself against.

You gain the following characteristics:

Nimble: +4 to your Speed Pool.

Skill: You're adept at leveraging risk, and you are trained in tasks that involve some element of chance, such as playing games or choosing between two or three apparently equal options.

Pressing Your Luck: You can choose to automatically succeed on one task without

rolling, as long as the task's difficulty is no higher than 6. When you do so, however, you also trigger a GM intrusion as if you had rolled a 1. The intrusion doesn't invalidate the success, but it probably qualifies it in some fashion. You can do this one time, although the ability renews each time you make a ten-hour recovery roll.

Inability: You may be nimble, but you're not sneaky. Tasks related to sneaking and staying quiet are hindered.

Initial Link to the Starting Adventure: From the following list of options, choose how you became involved in the first adventure.

1. It seemed like there were equal odds that the other PCs wouldn't succeed, which sounded good to you.

2. You think the tasks ahead will present you with unique and fulfilling challenges.

3. One of your biggest risks failed to go your way, and you need money to help pay that debt.

4. You bragged that you never saw a risk you didn't like, which is how you reached your current point.

RUGGED

You're a nature lover accustomed to living rough, pitting your wits against the elements. Most likely, you're a skilled hunter, gatherer, or naturalist. Years of living in the wild have left their mark with a worn countenance, wild hair, or scars. Your clothing is probably much less refined than the garments worn by city dwellers.

You gain the following characteristics:

Skill: You're trained in all tasks involving climbing, jumping, running, and swimming.

Skill: You're trained in all tasks involving training, riding, or placating natural animals.

Skill: You're trained in all tasks involving identifying or using natural plants.

Inability: You have no social graces and prefer animals to people. Any task involving charm, persuasion, etiquette, or deception is hindered.

Additional Equipment: You carry an explorer's pack with rope, two days' rations, a bedroll, and other tools needed for outdoor survival.

Initial Link to the Starting Adventure: From the following list of options, choose how you became involved in the first adventure.

1. Against your better judgment, you joined the other PCs because you saw that they were in danger.

2. One of the other PCs convinced you that joining the group would be in your best interests.

3. You're afraid of what might happen if the other PCs fail.

4. There is reward involved, and you need the money.

SHARP-EYED

You're perceptive and well aware of your surroundings. You notice the little details and remember them. You can be difficult to surprise.

You gain the following characteristics:

Skill: You're trained in initiative actions.

Skill: You're trained in perception actions.

Find the Flaw: If an opponent has a straightforward weakness (takes extra damage from fire, can't see out of their left eye, and so on), the GM will tell you what it is.

Initial Link to the Starting Adventure: From the following list of options, choose how you became involved in the first adventure.

1. You heard about what was going on, saw a flaw in the other PCs' plan, and joined up to help them out.

2. You noticed that the PCs have a foe (or at least a tail) they weren't aware of.

3. You saw that the other PCs were up to something interesting and got involved.

4. You've been noticing some strange things going on, and this all appears related.

SKEPTICAL

You possess a questioning attitude regarding claims that are often taken for granted by others. You're not necessarily a "doubting Thomas" (a skeptic who refuses to believe anything without direct personal experience), but you've often benefited from questioning the statements, opinions, and received knowledge presented to you by others.

You gain the following characteristics:

Insightful: +2 to your Intellect Pool.

Skill: You're trained in identifying.

Skill: You're trained in all actions that involve seeing through a trick, an illusion, a rhetorical ruse designed to evade the issue, or a lie. For example, you're better at keeping your eye on the cup containing the hidden ball, sensing an illusion, or realizing if someone is lying to you (but only if you specifically concentrate and use this skill).

Initial Link to the Starting Adventure: From the following list of options, choose how you became involved in the first adventure.

1. You overheard other PCs holding forth on a topic with an opinion you were quite skeptical about, so you decided to approach the group and ask for proof.

2. You were following one of the other PCs because you were suspicious of him, which brought you into the action.

3. Your theory about the nonexistence of the supernatural can be invalidated only by your own senses, so you came along.

4. You need money to fund your research.

STEALTHY

You're sneaky, slippery, and fast. These talents help you hide, move quietly, and pull off tricks that require sleight of hand. Most likely, you're wiry and small. However, you're not much of a sprinter—you're more dexterous than fleet of foot.

You gain the following characteristics:

Quick: +2 to your Speed Pool.

Skill: You're trained in all stealth tasks.

Skill: You're trained in all interactions involving lies or trickery.

Skill: You're trained in all special abilities involving illusions or trickery.

Inability: You're sneaky but not fast. All movement-related tasks are hindered.

Initial Link to the Starting Adventure: From the following list of options, choose how you became involved in the first adventure.

1. You attempted to steal from one of the other PCs. That character caught you and forced you to come along with them.

2. You were tailing one of the other PCs for reasons of your own, which brought you into the action.

3. An NPC employer secretly paid you to get involved.

4. You overheard the other PCs talking about a topic that interested you, so you decided to approach the group.

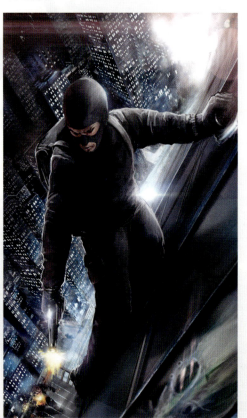

STRONG

You're extremely strong and physically powerful, and you use these qualities well, whether through violence or feats of prowess. You likely have a brawny build and impressive muscles.

You gain the following characteristics:

Very Powerful: +4 to your Might Pool.

Skill: You're trained in all actions involving breaking inanimate objects.

Skill: You're trained in all jumping actions.

Additional Equipment: You have an extra medium weapon or heavy weapon.

Initial Link to the Starting Adventure: From the following list of options, choose how you became involved in the first adventure.

1. Against your better judgment, you joined the other PCs because you saw that they were in danger.

2. One of the other PCs convinced you that joining the group would be in your best interests.

3. You're afraid of what might happen if the other PCs fail.

4. There is reward involved, and you need the money.

STRONG-WILLED

You're tough-minded, willful, and independent. No one can talk you into anything or change your mind when you don't want it changed. This quality doesn't necessarily make you smart, but it does make you a bastion of willpower and resolve. You likely dress and act with unique style and flair, not caring what others think.

You gain the following characteristics:

Willful: +4 to your Intellect Pool.

Skill: You're trained in resisting mental effects.

Skill: You're trained in tasks requiring incredible focus or concentration.

Inability: Willful doesn't mean brilliant. Any task that involves figuring out puzzles or problems, memorizing things, or using lore is hindered.

Initial Link to the Starting Adventure: From the following list of options, choose how you became involved in the first adventure.

1. Against your better judgment, you joined the other PCs because you saw that they were in danger.

2. One of the other PCs convinced you that joining the group would be in your best interests.

3. You're afraid of what might happen if the other PCs fail.

4. There is reward involved, and you need the money.

DESCRIPTOR

SWIFT

You move quickly, able to sprint in short bursts and work with your hands with dexterity. You're great at crossing distances quickly but not always smoothly. You are likely slim and muscular.

You gain the following characteristics:
Fast: +4 to your Speed Pool.
Skill: You're trained in initiative actions (to determine who goes first in combat).
Skill: You're trained in running actions.
Inability: You're fast but not necessarily graceful. Any task involving balance is hindered.
Initial Link to the Starting Adventure: From the following list of options, choose how you became involved in the first adventure.

1. Against your better judgment, you joined the other PCs because you saw that they were in danger.
2. One of the other PCs convinced you that joining the group would be in your best interests.
3. You're afraid of what might happen if the other PCs fail.
4. There is reward involved, and you need the money.

TONGUE-TIED

You've never been much of a talker. When forced to interact with others, you never think of the right thing to say—words fail you entirely, or they come out all wrong. You often end up saying precisely the wrong thing and insult someone unintentionally. Most of the time, you just keep mum. This makes you a listener instead—a careful observer. It also means that you're better at doing things than talking about them. You're quick to take action.

You gain the following characteristics:
Actions, Not Words: +2 to your Might Pool, and +2 to your Speed Pool.
Skill: You are trained in perception.
Skill: You are trained in initiative (unless it's a social situation).
Inability: All tasks relating to social interaction are hindered.
Inability: All tasks involving verbal communication or relaying information are hindered.
Initial Link to the Starting Adventure: From the following list of options, choose how you became involved in the first adventure.

1. You just tagged along and no one told you to leave.
2. You saw something important the other PCs did not and (with some effort) managed to relate it to them.
3. You intervened to save one of the other PCs when they were in danger.
4. One of the other PCs recruited you for your talents.

TOUGH

You're strong and can take a lot of physical punishment. You might have a large frame and a square jaw. Tough characters frequently have visible scars.

You gain the following characteristics:
Resilient: +1 to Armor.
Healthy: Add 1 to the points you regain when you make a recovery roll.
Skill: You're trained in Might defense actions.
Additional Equipment: You have an extra light weapon.
Initial Link to the Starting Adventure: From the following list of options, choose how you became involved in the first adventure.

1. You're acting as a bodyguard for one of the other PCs.
2. One of the PCs is your sibling, and you came along to watch out for them.
3. You need money because your family is in debt.
4. You stepped in to defend one of the PCs when that character was threatened. While talking to them afterward, you heard about the group's task.

57

A vicious ally is a good thing to have, until it isn't.

VICIOUS

You try to hide what's inside, fold it into yourself when everything inside you screams to let go, make them pay, make them hurt, and make them bleed. Sometimes you succeed for your friends—smiling like they smile, laughing when they laugh, and sometimes even having other emotions of your own. But it's always there, that feeling of frantic glee mixed with hate that sometimes leaps out of you when you confront a foe. Violence your friends can tolerate, but you sometimes worry they will also learn that you are cruel.

You gain the following characteristics:

Skill: You are trained in tracking creatures. If a creature has wronged you, the tracking task is eased.

Bloodthirsty: Once you begin fighting, you see only red. You inflict 2 additional points of damage with any attack.

Berserk: Once you begin fighting, it's hard for you to stop. In fact, it's a difficulty 2 Intellect task to do so, even if your foe surrenders or you've run out of foes. If the latter occurs and you fail to stop, you attack the nearest ally within short range.

Additional Equipment: You have a record that you use to list those who've wronged you.

Initial Link to the Starting Adventure: From the following list of options, choose how you became involved in the first adventure.

1. Another PC saw you take down a mean drunk in a tavern, not realizing you were the one who started the fight.

2. You wanted to get away from a bad situation, so you went with the other PCs.

3. You want to change, and you hope that being with the other PCs will help you calm yourself.

4. One of the other PCs asked you to come along, believing that your viciousness could be harnessed for the benefit of the mission.

VIRTUOUS

Doing the right thing is a way of life. You live by a code, and that code is something you attend to every day. Whenever you slip, you reproach yourself for your weakness and then get right back on track. Your code probably includes moderation, respect for others, cleanliness, and other characteristics that most people would agree are virtues, while you eschew their opposites: sloth, greed, gluttony, and so on.

You gain the following characteristics:

Dauntless: +2 to your Might Pool.

Skill: You are trained in discerning people's true motives or seeing through lies.

Skill: Your adherence to a strict moral code has hardened your mind against fear, doubt, and outside influence. You are trained in Intellect defense tasks.

Initial Link to the Starting Adventure: From the following list of options, choose how you became involved in the first adventure.

1. The PCs are doing something virtuous, and you're all about that.

2. The PCs are on the road to perdition, and you see it as your task to set them on the proper moral route.

3. One of the other PCs invited you, hearing of your virtuous ways.

4. You put virtue before sense and defended someone's honor in the face of an organization or power far greater than you. You joined the PCs because they offered aid and friendship when, out of fear of reprisals, no one else would.

WEIRD

You aren't like anyone else, and that's fine with you. People don't seem to understand you—they even seem put off by you—but who cares? You understand the world better than they do because you're weird, and so is the world you live in. The concept of "the weird" is well known to you. Strange devices, ancient locales, bizarre creatures, storms that can transform you, living energy fields, conspiracies, aliens, and things most people can't even name populate the world, and you thrive on them. You have a special attachment to it all, and the more you discover about the weirdness in the world, the more you might discover about yourself.

Weird characters might be mutants or people born with strange qualities, but sometimes they started out "normal" and adopted the weird by choice.

You gain the following characteristics:

Inner Light: +2 to your Intellect Pool.

Distinctive Physical Quirk: You have a unique physical aspect that is, well, bizarre. Depending on the setting, this can vary greatly. You might have purple hair or metal spikes on your head. Perhaps your hands don't connect to your arms, although they move as if they do. Maybe a third eye stares out from the side of your head, or superfluous tendrils grow from your back. Whatever it is, your quirk might be a mutation, a supernatural trait (a blessing or curse), a feature with no explanation, or just a really wild tattoo that draws a lot of attention.

A Sense for the Weird: Sometimes—at the GM's discretion—weird things relating to the supernatural or its effects on the world seem to call out to you. You can sense them from afar, and if you get within long range of such a thing, you can sense whether it is overtly dangerous or not.

Skill: You are trained in supernatural knowledge.

Inability: People find you unnerving. All tasks relating to pleasant social interaction are hindered.

Initial Link to the Starting Adventure: From the following list of options, choose how you became involved in the first adventure.

1. It seemed weird, so why not?
2. Whether the other PCs realize it or not, their mission has to do with something weird that you know about, so you got involved.
3. As an expert in the weird, you were specifically recruited by the other PCs.
4. You felt drawn to join the other PCs, but you don't know why.

CUSTOMIZING DESCRIPTORS

Under the normal rules, each descriptor is based on some modification of the following guidelines:

- Some descriptors offer +4 to one stat Pool and either two narrow skills or one broad skill.
- Other descriptors offer +2 to one stat Pool and either three narrow skills or one narrow skill and one broad skill.
- A broad skill covers many areas (such as all interactions). A narrow skill covers fewer areas (such as deceptive interactions). Combat-related skills, such as defense or initiative, are considered broad skills in this sense.
- Regardless, you can add an additional skill if it is balanced by an inability.
- You can add other non-skill abilities by eyeballing them and trying to equate them to the value of a skill, if possible. If the descriptor seems lacking, add a moderately priced item as additional equipment to balance things out.

With this general information, you can customize a descriptor, but keep in mind that a heavily customized descriptor isn't a descriptor if it no longer says one thing about a character. It's better to use this information to create a new descriptor that fits exactly how the player wants to portray the character.

SPECIES AS DESCRIPTOR

Sometimes, in settings that have alien or fantasy species, players want to play a member of that species rather than the default (which is usually "human"). Most of the time, this choice is one of flavor rather than game mechanics. If you're a 7-foot-tall furry Rigellian with three eyes, that's great, but it doesn't change your stats or skills (though it may have roleplaying challenges).

However, sometimes being a nonhuman results in more substantive changes. A PC ogre in a fantasy setting might have the Strong or Tough descriptor, or perhaps it has a descriptor simply called Ogre, which is similar to Strong or Tough but more pronounced (with greater Might but even greater drawbacks). This would mean that instead of being a Tough Warrior who Controls Beasts, the character is an Ogre Warrior who Controls Beasts.

The genre chapters in part 3 offer a few species descriptors, but many GMs will want to create their own as suits their setting. It can't be stressed enough, however, that nine times out of ten, in most genres, species differences aren't significant enough to warrant this treatment. The differences between a Mysterious character and a Virtuous one are probably greater than those between an Alpha Centauran and an Earthling.

Chapter 8

FOCUS

Pilots Starcraft, page 74

Focus is what makes a character unique. No two PCs in a group should have the same focus. A focus gives a character benefits when they create their character and each time they ascend to the next tier. It's the verb of the sentence "I am an *adjective noun* who *verbs*."

This chapter contains nearly a hundred sample foci, such as Bears a Halo of Fire, Would Rather Be Reading, and Pilots Starcraft. These foci can be chosen and used as presented by a player, or by the GM who adds them to a list of available foci for their players in their next campaign.

In addition, the latter half of this chapter provides tools for the GM or an enterprising player to create their own custom foci that perfectly match the needs of a given game or campaign, as presented in Creating New Foci.

Creating New Foci, page 80

Part 3: Genres, page 251

Commands Mental Powers, page 65

Howls at the Moon, page 69

Loves the Void, page 71

Have Spacesuit, Will Travel, page 148

CHOOSING FOCI

Not all foci are appropriate for every genre. The genre chapters in part 3 provide guidance, but this section offers some broad generalizations. Obviously, the GM can include whatever foci are available in their setting. Foci end up being an important distinction in this case, because Commands Mental Powers, for example, makes it clear that psychic abilities exist in the setting, just as Howls at the Moon implies the existence of lycanthropes like werewolves, and Pilots Starcraft, of course, requires starships available to pilot.

When a focus is chosen for a character, they get a special connection to one or more of their fellow PCs, a first-tier ability, and perhaps additional starting equipment: one or two pieces of equipment that might be required for the character to use their ability, or that might pair well with the focus. For instance, a character that can build things needs a set of tools. A character that's constantly on fire needs a set of clothes that are immune to flame. A character that draws runes to cast spells needs writing implements. A character that slays monsters with a sword needs a sword. And so on. That said, many foci don't require additional equipment.

Each focus also offers one or more suggestions—GM intrusions—for possible effects or consequences of really good or really bad die rolls.

A couple of foci presented in this chapter provide a "type swap option" that allows a player to swap an ability that would otherwise be gained from their type for the indicated ability instead. A player doesn't have to make the swap; they merely have the option. For instance, the focus Loves the Void provides the option to gain the ability Have Spacesuit, Will Travel instead of a type ability.

As a character progresses to a new tier, a focus grants more abilities. Each tier's benefit is usually labeled Action or Enabler. If an ability is labeled Action, a character must take an action to use it. If an ability is labeled Enabler, it makes other actions better or gives some other benefit, but it's not an action. An ability that allows a character to blast foes with lasers is an action. An ability that grants additional damage when an attack is made is an enabler. An enabler is used in the same turn as another action, and often as part of another action.

Each tier's benefits are independent of and cumulative with benefits from other tiers (unless indicated otherwise). So if a first-tier ability grants +1 to Armor and a fourth-tier ability also grants +1 to Armor, when the character reaches fourth tier, a total of +2 to Armor is granted.

At tier 3 and tier 6, the character is asked to choose one ability from the two options provided.

Finally, you can choose whether you want to expand the story behind the focus (though that's not mandatory).

FOCUS CONNECTIONS

Choose a connection that goes well with the focus. If you're a GM choosing (or creating) one or more foci for your players, choose up to four of the following connections.

1. Pick one other PC. For reasons unknown to you, that character is completely immune to your focus abilities, whether you use them for help or for harm.
2. Pick one other PC. You knew of that character years ago, but you don't think they knew you.
3. Pick one other PC. You're always trying to impress them, but you're not sure why.
4. Pick one other PC. That character has a habit that annoys you, but you're otherwise quite impressed with their abilities.
5. Pick one other PC. That character shows potential in appreciating your particular paradigm, fighting style, or other focus-provided attribute. You would like to train them, but you're not necessarily qualified to teach (that's up to you), and they might not be interested (that's up to them).
6. Pick one other PC. If they are within immediate range when you're in a fight, sometimes they provide an asset, and sometimes they accidentally hinder your attack rolls (50% chance either way, determined per fight).
7. Pick one other PC. You once saved their life, and they clearly feel indebted to you. You wish they didn't; it's just part of the job.
8. Pick one other PC. That character recently mocked you in some fashion that really hurt your feelings. How you deal with this (if at all) is up to you.
9. Pick one other PC. That character knows you have suffered at the hands of robotic entities in the past. Whether you hate robots now is up to you, which may affect your relationship with the character if they are friendly with robots or have robotic parts.
10. Pick one other PC. That character comes from the same place you do, and you knew each other as children.
11. Pick one other PC. In the past, they taught you a few tricks to use in a fight.
12. Pick one other PC. That character doesn't seem to approve of your methods.
13. Pick one other PC. Long ago, the two of you were on opposite sides of a fight. You won, though you "cheated" in their eyes (but from your perspective, all's fair in a fight). They may be ready for a rematch, though that's up to them.
14. Pick one other PC. You are always trying to impress that character with your skill, wit, appearance, or bravado. Perhaps they are a rival, perhaps you need their respect, or perhaps you're romantically interested in them.
15. Pick one other PC. You fear that character is jealous of your abilities and worry that it might lead to problems.
16. Pick one other PC. You accidentally caught them in a trap you set, and they had to get free on their own.
17. Pick one other PC. You were once hired to track down someone who was close to that character.
18. Pick two PCs (preferably ones who are likely to get in the way of your attacks). When you miss with an attack and the GM rules that you struck someone other than your target, you hit one of these two characters.
19. Pick one other PC. You're not sure how or from where, but that character has a line on bottles of rare alcohol and can get them for you for half price.
20. Pick one other PC. You recently had a possession go missing, and you're becoming convinced that they took it. Whether or not they did is up to them.
21. Pick one other PC. They always seem to know where you are, or at least in what direction you are in relation to them.
22. Pick one other PC. Seeing you use your focus abilities seems to trigger an unpleasant

Story Behind the Focus, page 63

memory in that character. That memory is up to the other PC, although they may not be able to consciously recall it.

23. Pick one other PC. Something about them interferes with your abilities. When they stand next to you, your focus abilities cost 1 additional point.
24. Pick one other PC. Something about them complements your abilities. When they stand next to you, the first focus ability you use in any 24-hour period costs 2 fewer points.
25. Pick one other PC. You have known that character for a while, and they helped you gain control of your focus-related abilities.
26. Pick one other PC. Sometime in that character's past, they had a devastating experience while attempting something that you do as a matter of course thanks to your focus. Whether they choose to tell you about it is up to them.
27. Pick one other PC. Their occasional clumsiness and loud behavior irritate you.
28. Pick one other PC. In the recent past, while practicing, you accidentally hit them with an attack, wounding them badly. It is up to them to decide whether they resent or forgive you.
29. Pick one other PC. They owe you a significant amount of money.
30. Pick one other PC. In the recent past, while escaping a threat, you accidentally left that character to fend for themselves. They survived, but just barely. It is up to the player of that character to decide whether they resent you or have decided to forgive you.
31. Pick one other PC. Recently, they accidentally (or perhaps intentionally) put you in a position of danger. You're fine now, but you're wary around them.
32. Pick one other PC. From your perspective, they seem nervous around a specific idea, person, or situation. You would like to teach them how to be more comfortable with their fears (if they will let you).
33. Pick one other PC. They called you a coward once.
34. Pick one other PC. That character always recognizes you or your handiwork, whether you're in disguise or are long gone when they arrive on the scene.
35. Pick one other PC. You inadvertently caused an accident that put them into a sleep so deep they didn't wake for three days. Whether they forgive you or not is up to them.
36. Pick one other PC. You are pretty sure you are related in some fashion.
37. Pick one other PC. You accidentally learned something they were trying to keep a secret.
38. Pick one other PC. They are especially sensitive to the use of your flashier focus abilities, and occasionally they become dazzled for a few rounds, which hinders their actions.
39. Pick one other PC. They appear to have a treasured item that was once yours, but that you lost in a game of chance years ago.
40. Pick one other PC. If it wasn't for you, that character would have failed a past test of mental achievement.
41. Pick one other PC. Based on a couple of comments you've overheard, you suspect that they don't hold your area of training or favorite hobby in the highest regard.
42. Pick one other PC whose focus intertwines with yours. This odd connection affects them in some way. For example, if the character uses a weapon, your focus ability sometimes improves their attack in some fashion.
43. Pick one other PC. They are deathly afraid of heights. You would like to teach them how to be more comfortable with their feet off the ground. They must decide whether or not to take you up on your offer.
44. Pick one other PC. They are skeptical of your claims about something momentous that happened in your past. They might even attempt to discredit you or discover the "secret" behind your story, though that's up to them.
45. Pick one other PC. They have a knack for being able to recognize where your plans or schemes have a weak spot.
46. Pick one other PC. That character's face is so intriguing to you in a way you don't understand that you sometimes find yourself sketching their likeness in the dirt or using some other medium you have access to.
47. Pick one other PC. That character has an extra item of regular equipment you gave them, either something you made or an item you just wanted to give them. (They choose the item.)
48. Pick one other PC. They commissioned you to do a job for them. You've already been paid but haven't yet completed the job.
49. Pick one other PC. You worked together in the past, and the job ended badly.
50. Pick one other PC. While they stand next to you and use their action to concentrate on helping you, one of your focus ability's ranges is doubled.

STORY BEHIND THE FOCUS

The foci in this book have been purposely stripped down to basics so they have the widest possible application across multiple genres. A single descriptive sentence or two summarizes each one. After you choose a focus, you have the option to expand its presentation by adding more story and description relevant to the world or to the character.

For instance, if you choose Operates Undercover, the summarizing description is "Under the guise of someone else, you seek to find answers the powerful do not want divulged." If you choose Conducts Weird Science, the summary is "Your preternatural insight and ability make you a scientist capable of amazing feats." These descriptions provide what you need to know to use the focus.

However, if you wish (and *only* if you wish; there is no requirement to do so), you can add more to those descriptions in a fashion that's relevant for your game. For example, if you choose both Operates Undercover and Conducts Weird Science for use in a modern genre such as horror, urban fantasy, espionage, or something similar, you might expand the descriptions as shown in the following examples.

Operates Undercover: Espionage is not something you know anything about. At least, that's what you want everyone to believe, because in truth, you've been trained as a spy or covert agent. You might work for a government or for yourself. You might be a police detective or a criminal. You could even be an investigative reporter.

Regardless, you learn information that others attempt to keep secret. You collect rumors and whispers, stories and hard-won evidence, and you use that knowledge to aid your own endeavors and, if appropriate, provide your employers with the information they desire. Alternatively, you might sell what you have learned to those willing to pay a premium.

You probably wear dark colors—black, charcoal grey, or midnight blue—to help blend into the shadows, unless the cover you've chosen requires you to look like someone else.

Conducts Weird Science: You could be a respected scientist, having been published in several peer-reviewed journals. Or you might be considered a crank by your contemporaries, pursuing fringe theories on what others consider to be scant evidence. Truth is, you have a particular gift for sifting the edges of what's possible. You can find new insights and unlock odd phenomena with your experiments. Where others see a crackpot cornucopia, you sift the conspiracy theories for revelation. Whether you conduct your enquiries as a government contractor, a university researcher, a corporate scientist, or an indulger of curiosity in your own garage lab following your muse, you push the boundaries of what's possible.

You probably care more about your work than trivialities such as your appearance, polite or proper behavior, or social norms, but then again, an eccentric like you might turn the tables on that stereotype too.

If you want to go even further, you could determine where a character's focus abilities come from. Depending on the genre, they could derive those abilities from advanced and persistent training, via magical runes, through cybernetic parts, from their genetic heritage, or because of their access to advanced technology. For instance, a character might be able to blast targets with lightning because they got zapped by strange radiation or because they picked up a lightning gun. On the other hand, it might be because their intense training allowed them to learn lightning magic. The possibilities are nearly endless, and up to you to include or forgo. Because however a focus's abilities were gained, it's also enough that they just work.

Operates Undercover, page 73

Conducts Weird Science, page 65

Chapter 9: Abilities, page 95

Some creatures are a mixture of machine and biology. Your GM decides whether such creatures can be treated as biological, machine, or both in some cases. Often, if a creature is part machine, it qualifies.

For more abilities that improve your physical attacks, see the attack skill and meta ability categories in chapter 9.

Attack Skill, page 96
Meta, page 100

Bears a Halo of Fire is perfect for a superhero setting, but in a fantasy game, the same focus could just as easily represent a fire mage.

For more abilities relating to defense and altering your body, see the protection and transform ability categories in chapter 9.

Protection, page 102
Transform, page 107

FOCI

The full description for each focus ability listed in this section is found in chapter 9, which has descriptions for type, flavor, and focus abilities in a single vast catalog. The numbers listed after the abilities are page numbers for easy reference.

ABIDES IN STONE

Your flesh is made of hard mineral, making you a hulking, difficult-to-harm humanoid.
- Tier 1: Golem Body (145)
- Tier 1: Golem Healing (145)
- Tier 2: Golem Grip (145)
- Tier 3: Trained Basher (193)
- Tier 3: Golem Stomp (145) or Weaponization (197)
- Tier 4: Deep Reserves (126)
- Tier 5: Specialized Basher (185)
- Tier 5: Still As a Statue (186)
- Tier 6: Ultra Enhancement (194) or Mind Surge (162)

GM Intrusions: Creatures of stone sometimes forget their own strength or weight. A walking statue can terrify common folk.

ABSORBS ENERGY

You can harness kinetic energy and transform it into other kinds of energy.
- Tier 1: Absorb Kinetic Energy (108)
- Tier 1: Release Energy (175)
- Tier 2: Energize Object (134)
- Tier 3: Absorb Pure Energy (108) or Improved Absorb Kinetic Energy (151)
- Tier 4: Overcharge Energy (168)
- Tier 5: Energize Creature (134)
- Tier 6: Energize Crowd (134) or Overcharge Device (168)

GM Intrusions: Energy goes to ground in a destructive way. Some predators feed directly on energy. An unintended item is drained of energy.

AWAKENS DREAMS

You can pull images from dreams and bring them to life in the waking world.
- Tier 1: Dreamcraft (132)
- Tier 1: Oneirochemy (167)
- Tier 2: Dream Thief (132)
- Tier 3: Dream Becomes Reality (132) or Enhanced Intellect (135)
- Tier 4: Daydream (124)
- Tier 5: Nightmare (165)
- Tier 6: Chamber of Dreams (119) or Reactive Field (174)

GM Intrusions: An unexpected sleepwalking episode puts the character into a dangerous situation. A nightmare breaks free of a dream.

BATTLES ROBOTS

You excel in battling robots, automatons, and machine entities.
- Tier 1: Machine Vulnerabilities (159)
- Tier 1: Tech Skills (189)
- Tier 2: Defense Against Robots (126)
- Tier 2: Machine Hunting (159)
- Tier 3: Disable Mechanisms (128) or Surprise Attack (188)
- Tier 4: Robot Fighter (178)
- Tier 5: Drain Power (131)
- Tier 6: Deactivate Mechanisms (125) or Lethal Damage (158)

GM Intrusions: The robot explodes upon defeat. Other robots come after the character for revenge.

BEARS A HALO OF FIRE

You can sheath your body in flames, which protects you and harms your foes.
- Tier 1: Shroud of Flame (183)
- Tier 2: Hurl Flame (149)
- Tier 3: Wings of Fire (199) or Fiery Hand of Doom (139)
- Tier 4: Flameblade (140)
- Tier 5: Fire Tendrils (140)
- Tier 6: Fire Servant (140) or Inferno Trail (153)

GM Intrusions: Fire burns flammable material. Fire spreads out of control. Primitive creatures fear fire and often attack what they fear.

BLAZES WITH RADIANCE

You can create light, sculpt it, bend it away from you, or gather it to use as a weapon.
- Tier 1: Enlightened (136)
- Tier 1: Illuminating Touch (150)
- Tier 2: Dazzling Sunburst (125)
- Tier 3: Burning Light (116) or Skill With Defense (183)
- Tier 4: Sunlight (188)
- Tier 5: Disappear (128)
- Tier 6: Living Light (158) or Defensive Field (127)

GM Intrusions: Allies are accidentally dazzled or blinded. Bright flashes draw guards.

BRANDISHES AN EXOTIC SHIELD

You deploy an amazing shield of pure force that provides protection and some offensive options.
- Tier 1: Force Field Shield (143)
- Tier 1: Force Bash (142)
- Tier 2: Enveloping Shield (136)
- Tier 3: Healing Pulse (148) or Throw Force Shield (191)
- Tier 4: Energized Shield (134)
- Tier 5: Force Wall (143)
- Tier 6: Bouncing Shield (115) or Shield Burst (182)

GM Intrusions: The shield is temporarily lost. A foe temporarily ends up with the shield.

BUILDS ROBOTS
Your robotic creations do as they are commanded.
- Tier 1: Robot Assistant (178)
- Tier 1: Robot Builder (178)
- Tier 2: Robot Control (178)
- Tier 3: Expert Follower (137) or Skill With Defense (183)
- Tier 4: Robot Upgrade (179)
- Tier 5: Robot Fleet (179)
- Tier 6: Robot Evolution (178) or Robot Upgrade (179)

GM Intrusions: The robot is hacked, gains a mind of its own, or unexpectedly detonates.

CALCULATES THE INCALCULABLE
Awesome mathematical ability allows you to model the world in real time, giving you an edge over everyone.
- Tier 1: Predictive Equation (171)
- Tier 1: Higher Mathematics (149)
- Tier 2: Predictive Model (171)
- Tier 3: Subconscious Defense (187) or Enhanced Intellect (135)
- Tier 4: Cognizant Offense (119)
- Tier 5: Greater Enhanced Intellect (146)
- Tier 5: Further Mathematics (144)
- Tier 6: Knowing the Unknown (156) or Greater Enhanced Intellect (146)

GM Intrusions: Too many predicted results threaten to overwhelm and stun the character. A result points to imminent disaster.

CHANNELS DIVINE BLESSINGS
A devout follower of a divine being, you channel some of your deity's power to achieve wonders.
- Tier 1: Blessing of the Gods (114)
- Tier 2: Enhanced Intellect (135)
- Tier 3: Divine Radiance (130) or Fire Bloom (140)
- Tier 4: Overawe (168)
- Tier 5: Divine Intervention (130)
- Tier 6: Divine Symbol (131) or Summon Demon (188)

GM Intrusions: A demon investigates divine magic use. A rival cult has issues with the character's teachings.

COMMANDS MENTAL POWERS
You can pull images from dreams and bring them to life in the waking world.
- Tier 1: Telepathic (189)
- Tier 2: Mind Reading (162)
- Tier 3: Psychic Burst (172) or Psychic Suggestion (172)
- Tier 4: Use Senses of Others (195)
- Tier 5: Precognition (171)
- Tier 6: Mind Control (162) or Telepathic Network (190)

GM Intrusions: Something glimpsed in the target's mind is horrifying. A feedback loop allows the target to read the character's mind.

CONDUCTS WEIRD SCIENCE
Your preternatural insight and ability make you a scientist capable of amazing feats.
- Tier 1: Lab Analysis (157)
- Tier 1: Knowledge Skills (157)
- Tier 2: Modify Device (164)
- Tier 3: Better Living Through Chemistry (113) or Incredible Health (153)
- Tier 4: Knowledge Skills (157)
- Tier 4: Just a Bit Mad (156)
- Tier 5: Weird Science Breakthrough (197)
- Tier 6: Incredible Feat of Science (153)
- Tier 6: Inventor (155) or Defensive Field (127)

GM Intrusions: Creations get out of control. Side effects cannot always be predicted. Weird science terrifies people and can draw the media. When a device created or modified by weird science is depleted, it detonates.

CONSORTS WITH THE DEAD
The dead answer your questions, and their reanimated corpses serve you.
- Tier 1: Speaker for the Dead (184)
- Tier 2: Necromancy (165)
- Tier 3: Reading the Room (175) or Repair Flesh (176)
- Tier 4: Greater Necromancy (147)
- Tier 5: Terrifying Gaze (190)
- Tier 6: True Necromancy (194) or Word of Death (200)

GM Intrusions: The character's necromantic reputation precedes them. A corpse seeks revenge for being reanimated.

CONTROLS BEASTS
Your ability to communicate and lead beasts is uncanny.
- Tier 1: Beast Companion (112)
- Tier 2: Soothe the Savage (184)
- Tier 2: Communication (121)
- Tier 3: Mount (164) or Stronger Together (187)
- Tier 4: Beast Eyes (112)
- Tier 4: Improved Companion (151)
- Tier 5: Beast Call (112)
- Tier 6: As If One Creature (110) or Control the Savage (122)

GM Intrusions: The community is reluctant to welcome dangerous animals. Out-of-control beasts become a real hazard.

The word "robot" is used globally in this focus, though the robot you create might look very different from one created by someone else, depending on the genre. Steampunk robots, organic robots, or even magical golems are all feasible "robots."

For more abilities relating to crafting and repairing objects and structures, see the craft ability category in chapter 9.

Craft, page 97

For more abilities relating to controlling and influencing minds, see the control ability category in chapter 9.

Control, page 97

As someone who Conducts Weird Science, a PC in a modern-day setting could be given the "mad scientist" label by the media if news of their exploits becomes public. Whether they conduct their science ethically or with disregard for the safety of others (or whether they really are insane) is the only true measure of how "mad" they are.

For more abilities relating to companions and followers, see the companion ability category in chapter 9.

Companion, page 96

A creature's level determines its target number, health, and damage, unless otherwise stated. So a level 2 beast companion has a target number of 6 and a health of 6, and it inflicts 2 points of damage. A level 4 beast companion has a target number of 12 and a health of 12, and it inflicts 4 points of damage. And so on.

Cyphersmith works only in a setting where the cyphers are physical objects. If this isn't the case, this ability should probably be replaced with something akin to Weird Science Breakthrough from the Conducts Weird Science focus.

For more abilities relating to crafting objects, see the craft ability category in chapter 9.

Craft, page 97

For more abilities relating to defense, see the protection ability category in chapter 9.

Protection, page 102

CONTROLS GRAVITY
You can sway the attraction of gravity itself.
- Type Swap Option: Weighty (197)
- Tier 1: Hover (149)
- Tier 2: Enhanced Speed Edge (135)
- Tier 3: Define Down (127) or Gravity Cleave (146)
- Tier 4: Field of Gravity (139)
- Tier 5: Flight (141)
- Tier 6: Improved Gravity Cleave (151) or Weight of the World (197)

GM Intrusions: Onlookers react with unreasoning fear. A weird interaction sends an ally or object careening into the sky.

CRAFTS ILLUSIONS
You fashion images from light that are so perfect they seem real.
- Tier 1: Minor Illusion (162)
- Tier 2: Illusory Disguise (150)
- Tier 3: Cast Illusion (118) or Major Illusion (160)
- Tier 4: Illusory Selves (150)
- Tier 5: Terrifying Image (190)
- Tier 6: Grandiose Illusion (146) or Permanent Illusion (169)

GM Intrusions: The illusion isn't believable. The illusion is pierced at just the wrong moment.

CRAFTS UNIQUE OBJECTS
You're an inventor of strange and useful objects.
- Tier 1: Crafter (122)
- Tier 1: Master Identifier (160)
- Tier 2: Artifact Tinkerer (110)
- Tier 2: Quick Work (174)
- Tier 3: Master Crafter (160) or Built-In Weaponry (116)
- Tier 4: Cyphersmith (124)
- Tier 5: Innovator (154)
- Tier 6: Inventor (155) or Fusion Armor (144)

GM Intrusions: The object malfunctions, breaks, or suffers catastrophic or unexpected failure.

DANCES WITH DARK MATTER
You can manipulate shadow and "dark" matter.
- Tier 1: Ribbons of Dark Matter (178)
- Tier 2: Void Wings (196)
- Tier 3: Dark Matter Shroud (124) or Dark Matter Strike (124)
- Tier 4: Dark Matter Shell (124)
- Tier 5: Windwracked Traveler (199)
- Tier 6: Dark Matter Structure (124) or Embrace the Night (133)

GM Intrusions: Dark matter skulks away as if possessed by a mind of its own.

DEFENDS THE GATE
Everyone wants you on their side when it comes to a fight because nothing gets by you.
- Tier 1: Fortified Position (143)
- Tier 1: Rally to Me (174)
- Tier 2: Mind for Might (162)
- Tier 3: Fortification Builder (143) or Divert Attacks (130)
- Tier 4: Greater Enhanced Might (146)
- Tier 5: Reinforcing Field (175)
- Tier 6: Generate Force Field (145) or Stun Attack (187)

GM Intrusions: A strategically important structure collapses. The enemy attacks from an unexpected direction.

DEFENDS THE WEAK
You stand up for the helpless, the weak, and the unprotected.
- Tier 1: Courageous (122)
- Tier 1: Warding Shield (196)
- Tier 2: Devoted Defender (128)
- Tier 2: Insight (154)
- Tier 3: Dual Wards (132) or True Guardian (194)
- Tier 4: Combat Challenge (120)
- Tier 5: Willing Sacrifice (199)
- Tier 6: Resuscitate (177) or True Defender (194)

GM Intrusions: A character focused on protecting others may periodically leave themselves vulnerable to attacks.

DESCENDS FROM NOBILITY
A descendent of wealth and power, you carry a noble title and the abilities granted by a privileged upbringing.
○ Type Swap Option: Retinue (177)
○ Tier 1: Privileged Nobility (172)
○ Tier 2: Trained Interlocutor (193)
○ Tier 3: Advanced Command (108) or Noble's Courage (166)
○ Tier 4: Expert Follower (137)
○ Tier 5: Asserting Your Privilege (110)
○ Tier 6: Able Assistance (108) or Mind of a Leader (162)

GM Intrusions: Debts incurred by a family are owed by the character. A long-lost sibling seeks to disinherit rivals. An assassin finds the character.

DOESN'T DO MUCH
You're a slacker, but you know a little about a lot of things.
○ Tier 1: Life Lessons (158)
○ Tier 2: Totally Chill (192)
○ Tier 3: Skill With Attacks (183) or Improvise (152)
○ Tier 4: Life Lessons (158)
○ Tier 4: Greater Skill With Defense (147)
○ Tier 5: Greater Enhanced Potential (146)
○ Tier 6 Drawing on Life's Experiences (131) or Quick Wits (174)

GM Intrusions: New situations are confounding and stressful. Past actions (or inactions) come back to haunt the character.

DRIVES LIKE A MANIAC
Whether balancing on two wheels, jumping another vehicle, or driving head-on toward an oncoming enemy car, you don't think about the risks when you're behind the wheel.
○ Tier 1: Driver (132)
○ Tier 1: Driving on the Edge (132)
○ Tier 2: Car Surfer (118)
○ Tier 2: Stare Them Down (186)
○ Tier 3: Expert Driver (137) or Enhanced Speed Edge (135)
○ Tier 4: Sharp-Eyed (182)
○ Tier 4: Enhanced Speed (135)
○ Tier 5: Something in the Road (184)
○ Tier 6: Trick Driver (194) or Lethal Damage (158)

GM Intrusions: The engine develops a knock. The bridge on the road ahead is out. The windshield shatters. Someone unexpectedly runs in front of the vehicle.

EMERGED FROM THE OBELISK
Your body, hard as crystal, gives you a suite of unique abilities, gained after an interaction with a floating crystalline obelisk.
○ Tier 1: Crystalline Body (123)
○ Tier 2: Hover (149)
○ Tier 3: Inhabit Crystal (154) or Immovable (150)
○ Tier 4: Crystal Lens (123)
○ Tier 5: Resonant Frequency (177)
○ Tier 6: Resonant Quake (177) or Return to the Obelisk (177)

GM Intrusions: Cyphers and artifacts react unexpectedly in the character's hands.

EMPLOYS MAGNETISM
You command metal and the power of magnetism.
○ Tier 1: Move Metal (164)
○ Tier 2: Repel Metal (176)
○ Tier 3: Destroy Metal (127) or Guide Bolt (147)
○ Tier 4: Magnetic Field (159)
○ Tier 5: Command Metal (120)
○ Tier 6: Diamagnetism (128) or Iron Punch (155)

GM Intrusions: The metal twists, bends, or produces shrapnel. A lapse in concentration might cause something to slip or drop at just the wrong time.

ENTERTAINS
You perform, mostly for the benefit of others.
○ Tier 1: Levity (158)
○ Tier 2: Inspiration (154)
○ Tier 3: Knowledge Skills (157) or Greater Enhanced Potential (146)
○ Tier 4: Calm (118)
○ Tier 5: Able Assistance (108)
○ Tier 6: Master Entertainer (160) or Vindictive Performance (196)

GM Intrusions: The audience is annoyed or offended. Musical instruments break. Paints dry in their pots. The words to a poem or song are forgotten.

EXISTS IN TWO PLACES AT ONCE
You exist in two places at once.
○ Tier 1: Duplicate (132)
○ Tier 2: Share Senses (182)
○ Tier 3: Superior Duplicate (188) or Resilient Duplicate (176)
○ Tier 4: Damage Transference (124)
○ Tier 5: Coordinated Effort (122)
○ Tier 6: Multiplicity (165) or Resilient Duplicate (176)

GM Intrusions: Perceiving the world from two different places disorients the character, causing momentary vertigo, nausea, or confusion.

For more abilities relating to general social activities and interacting with NPCs, see the social ability category in chapter 9.

Social, page 103

Weird creatures are something that explorers might expect to see on a regular basis, and someone who has emerged from an obelisk qualifies. However, normal people are likely to be highly suspicious and perhaps even afraid of such a character, at least initially.

For more abilities relating to manipulating the environment or things in it, see the environment ability category in chapter 9.

Environment, page 99

As is true for other foci in this chapter, Entertains and Helps Their Friends are examples of foci suitable for non-fantastic campaigns.

Someone who Drives Like a Maniac needs access to a car or motorcycle.

For more abilities relating to movement, see the movement ability category in chapter 9.

Movement, page 101

EXISTS PARTIALLY OUT OF PHASE

A bit translucent, you're slightly out of phase and can move through solid objects.
- Tier 1: Walk Through Walls (196)
- Tier 2: Defensive Phasing (127)
- Tier 3: Phased Attack (170) or Phase Door (170)
- Tier 4: Ghost (145)
- Tier 5: Untouchable (195)
- Tier 6: Enhanced Phased Attack (135) or Phase Foe (170)

GM Intrusions: The character is sent phasing into an unexpected dimension. The character becomes lost in a large solid.

EXPLORES DARK PLACES

You're the archetypal treasure hunter, scavenger, and finder of lost things.
- Tier 1: Superb Explorer (188)
- Tier 2: Superb Infiltrator (188)
- Tier 2: Eyes Adjusted (138)
- Tier 3: Nightstrike (166) or Slippery Customer (183)
- Tier 4: Hard-Won Resilience (148)
- Tier 5: Dark Explorer (124)
- Tier 6: Blinding Attack (115) or Embraced by Darkness (133)

GM Intrusions: Possessions fall out of pockets or bags in the dark; maps get lost; information gained fails to include an important detail.

FIGHTS DIRTY

You'll do anything to win a fight: bite, scratch, kick, trick, and worse.
- Tier 1: Tracker (193)
- Tier 1: Stalker (186)
- Tier 2: Sneak (183)
- Tier 2: Quarry (173)
- Tier 3: Betrayal (113) or Surprise Attack (188)
- Tier 4: Mind Games (162)
- Tier 4: Capable Warrior (118)
- Tier 5: Using the Environment (195)
- Tier 6: Twisting the Knife (194) or Murderer (165)

GM Intrusions: People look poorly upon those who cheat or fight without honor. Sometimes a dirty trick backfires.

FIGHTS WITH PANACHE

You're a swashbuckling daredevil who fights with flamboyant style that's entertaining to watch.
- Tier 1: Attack Flourish (111)
- Tier 2: Quick Block (173)
- Tier 3: Acrobatic Attack (108) or Flamboyant Boast (140)
- Tier 4: Block for Another (115)
- Tier 4: Fast Kill (138)
- Tier 5: Using the Environment (195)
- Tier 6: Agile Wit (109) or Return to Sender (177)

GM Intrusions: The display comes off looking silly, clumsy, or unattractive.

FLIES FASTER THAN A BULLET

You can fly, and you're superstrong, hard to hurt, and fast too. Is there anything you can't do?
- Tier 1: Hover (149)
- Tier 2: Greater Enhanced Potential (146)
- Tier 3: Hidden Reserves (149) or See Through Matter (180)
- Tier 4: Blink of an Eye (115)
- Tier 4: Up to Speed (195)
- Tier 5: Not Dead Yet (166)
- Tier 6: Burning Light (116) or Ignore Affliction (150)

GM Intrusions: A nemesis finds the character. A strange material is found to nullify the character's abilities.

FOCUSES MIND OVER MATTER

You can telekinetically move objects with your mind without physically touching them.
- Tier 1: Divert Attacks (130)
- Tier 2: Telekinesis (189)
- Tier 3: Cloak of Opportunity (119) or Enhance Strength (134)
- Tier 4: Apportation (110)
- Tier 5: Psychokinetic Attack (172)
- Tier 6: Improved Apportation (151) or Reshape (176)

GM Intrusions: One mental slip, and moving objects drop or fragile objects break. Sometimes the wrong item moves, falls, or breaks.

Psychokinesis doesn't necessarily mean "mental powers." Someone who uses it might be accessing a mechanical or bioengineered portion of their brain to direct nanites that move or change matter.

For more abilities relating to manipulating the environment or things in it, see the environment ability category in chapter 9.

Environment, page 99

For more abilities that improve your physical attacks, see the attack skill and meta ability categories in chapter 9.

Attack Skill, page 96
Meta, page 100

> "A friend is someone that you'd do anything for. You lend them your cool stuff, like comic books and trading cards. And they never break a promise."
> ~Stranger Things

FUSES FLESH AND STEEL
Your body is part machine.
- Tier 1: Enhanced Body (134)
- Tier 2: Interface (155)
- Tier 3: Sensing Package (181) or Weaponization (197)
- Tier 4: Fusion (144)
- Tier 5: Deep Reserves (126)
- Tier 6: Mind Surge (162) or Ultra Enhancement (194)

   GM Intrusions: People in most societies are afraid of someone who is revealed to have mechanical parts.

FUSES MIND AND MACHINE
Electronic aids implanted in your brain make you a mental powerhouse.
- Tier 1: Enhanced Intellect (135)
- Tier 1: Knowledge Skills (157)
- Tier 2: Network Tap (165)
- Tier 3: Action Processor (108) or Machine Telepathy (159)
- Tier 4: Greater Enhanced Intellect (146)
- Tier 4: Knowledge Skills (157)
- Tier 5: See the Future (180)
- Tier 6: Machine Enhancement (159) or Mind Surge (162)

   GM Intrusions: Machines malfunction and shut down. Powerful machine intelligences can take control of lesser thinking machines. Some people don't trust a person who isn't fully organic.

GROWS TO TOWERING HEIGHTS
For brief periods, you can grow larger and, with enough experience, to towering heights.
- Tier 1: Enlarge (135)
- Tier 1: Freakishly Large (143)
- Tier 2: Bigger (113)
- Tier 2: Advantages of Being Big (109)
- Tier 3: Huge (149) or Throw (191)
- Tier 4: Grab (146)
- Tier 5: Gargantuan (144)
- Tier 6: Colossal (120) or Lethal Damage (158)

   GM Intrusions: Rapid growth knocks over furnishings or smashes through ceilings or hanging lights. An enlarged character breaks through the floor.

HELPS THEIR FRIENDS
You love your friends and help them out of any difficulty, no matter what.
- Type Swap Option: Advice From a Friend (109)
- Tier 1: Friendly Help (143)
- Tier 1: Courageous (122)
- Tier 2: Weather the Vicissitudes (197)
- Tier 3: Buddy System (116) or Skill With Attacks (183)
- Tier 4: In Harm's Way (152)
- Tier 4: Enhanced Physique (135)
- Tier 5: Inspire Action (154)
- Tier 6: Deep Consideration (126) or Skill With Defense (183)

   GM Intrusions: Others sometimes have ulterior motives. The law takes an undue interest. Even when everything goes right, repercussions follow.

HOWLS AT THE MOON
For brief periods, you become a fearsome and powerful creature with control issues.
- Tier 1: Beast Form (112)
- Tier 2: Controlled Change (122)
- Tier 3: Bigger Beast Form (113) or Greater Beast Form (146)
- Tier 4: Greater Controlled Change (146)
- Tier 5: Enhanced Beast Form (134)
- Tier 6: Lethal Damage (158) or Perfect Control (169)

   GM Intrusions: The change happens in an uncontrolled fashion. People are terrified of monsters.

HUNTS
You are a stalking hunter who excels at bringing down your selected quarry.
- Tier 1: Attack Flourish (111)
- Tier 1: Tracker (193)
- Tier 2: Quarry (173)
- Tier 2: Sneak (183)
- Tier 3: Horde Fighting (149) or Sprint and Grab (186)
- Tier 4: Surprise Attack (188)
- Tier 5: Hunter's Drive (149)
- Tier 6: Greater Skill With Attacks (147) or Multiple Quarry (164)

   GM Intrusions: The quarry notices the character. The quarry isn't as vulnerable as it seemed.

For more abilities relating to altering or improving your body, see the transform ability category in chapter 9.

Transform, page 107

For more abilities relating to assisting your allies, see the support ability category in chapter 9.

Support, page 105

For more abilities relating to common skills such as stealth and tracking, see the task ability category in chapter 9.

Task, page 106

For more abilities relating to general social activities and interacting with NPCs, see the social ability category in chapter 9.

Social, page 103

INFILTRATES
Subtlety, guile, and stealth allow you to get in where others can't.
- Tier 1: Stealth Skills (186)
- Tier 1: Sense Attitudes (181)
- Tier 2: Impersonate (151)
- Tier 2: Flight Not Fight (141)
- Tier 3: Awareness (111) or Skill With Attacks (183)
- Tier 4: Invisibility (155)
- Tier 5: Evasion (136)
- Tier 6: Brainwashing (116) or Spring Away (186)

GM Intrusions: Spies are treated harshly when caught. Allies disavow infiltrators who get caught. Some secrets are better left unknown.

INTERPRETS THE LAW
You excel at winning others over to your views.
- Tier 1: Opening Statement (167)
- Tier 1: Knowledge of the Law (156)
- Tier 2: Debate (126)
- Tier 3: Able Assistance (108) or Enhanced Intellect Edge (135)
- Tier 4: Castigate (118)
- Tier 5: No One Knows Better (166)
- Tier 6: Greater Enhanced Potential (146) or Legal Intern (157)

GM Intrusions: Onlookers react badly to a know-it-all. A distraction or interruption throws the character's argument off the rails.

Although Is Licensed to Carry is designed with modern firearms in mind, it could apply to flintlock weapons, futuristic laser blasters, or other ranged weapons.

For more abilities that improve your physical attacks, see the attack skill and meta ability categories in chapter 9.

Attack Skill, page 96
Meta, page 100

IS IDOLIZED BY MILLIONS
You're a celebrity and most people adore you.
- Tier 1: Entourage (136)
- Tier 1: Celebrity Talent (119)
- Tier 2: Perks of Stardom (169)
- Tier 3: Incredible Health (153) or Skill With Attacks (183)
- Tier 4: Captivate With Starshine (118)
- Tier 4: Expert Follower (137)
- Tier 5: Do You Know Who I Am? (131)
- Tier 6: Transcend the Script (193) or Improved Companion (151)

GM Intrusions: Fans are endangered or hurt on your behalf. Someone in your entourage betrays you. Your show, tour, contract, or other event is canceled. The media posts photos of you in an embarrassing situation.

IS LICENSED TO CARRY
You carry a gun and you know how to use it in a fight.
- Tier 1: Gunner (147)
- Tier 1: Practiced With Guns (171)
- Tier 2: Careful Shot (118)
- Tier 3: Trained Gunner (193) or Damage Dealer (124)
- Tier 4: Snap Shot (183)
- Tier 5: Arc Spray (110)
- Tier 6: Special Shot (184) or Lethal Damage (158)

GM Intrusions: Misfire or jam! The attack fails and the action is lost, plus an additional action is needed to fix the problem.

IS WANTED BY THE LAW
"WANTED, DEAD OR ALIVE" posters (or their equivalent) have appeared featuring your face. It's up to you whether it's a mistake that snowballed out of control or you actually would kill someone just for looking at you.
- Tier 1: Enhanced Speed (135)
- Tier 1: Danger Sense (124)
- Tier 2: Surprise Attack (188)
- Tier 3: Outlaw Reputation (168) or Successive Attack (187)
- Tier 4: Fast Kill (138)
- Tier 5: Band of Desperados (112)
- Tier 6: Not Dead Yet (166) or Lethal Damage (158)

GM Intrusions: Most people do not take well to discovering a wanted outlaw in their midst.

KEEPS A MAGIC ALLY

An allied magic creature bound to an object (such as a minor djinn in a lamp, or a ghost in a pipe) is your friend, protector, and weapon.
- Tier 1: Bound Magic Creature (115)
- Tier 2: Object Bond (167)
- Tier 2: Hidden Closet (149)
- Tier 3: Minor Wish (162) or Mount (164)
- Tier 4: Improved Object Bond (152)
- Tier 5: Moderate Wish (163)
- Tier 6: Object Bond Mastery (167) or Trust to Luck (194)

GM Intrusions: The creature unexpectedly disappears into its bound object. The bound object cracks. The creature disagrees and doesn't do as asked. The creature says it's leaving unless a task is performed for it.

LEADS

Your natural leadership capability allows you to command others, including a loyal band of followers.
- Tier 1: Natural Charisma (165)
- Tier 1: Good Advice (145)
- Tier 2: Enhanced Potential (135)
- Tier 2: Basic Follower (112)
- Tier 3: Advanced Command (108) or Expert Follower (137)
- Tier 4: Captivate or Inspire (118)
- Tier 5: Greater Enhanced Potential (146)
- Tier 6: Band of Followers (112) or Mind of a Leader (162)

GM Intrusions: Followers fail, betray, lie, become corrupted, get kidnapped, or die.

LEARNS QUICKLY

You deal with bad situations as they arise, learning new lessons each time.
- Tier 1: Enhanced Intellect (135)
- Tier 1: There's Your Problem (190)
- Tier 2: Quick Study (174)
- Tier 3: Hard to Distract (148)
- Tier 3: Enhanced Intellect Edge (135) or Flex Skill (141)
- Tier 4: Pay It Forward (168)
- Tier 5: Enhanced Intellect (135)
- Tier 5: Learned a Few Things (157)
- Tier 6: Two Things at Once (194) or Skill With Defense (183)

GM Intrusions: Accidents and mistakes are great teachers.

LIVES IN THE WILDERNESS

You can survive in badlands where others perish.
- Tier 1: Wilderness Life (199)
- Tier 1: Enhanced Might (135)
- Tier 2: Living Off the Land (158)
- Tier 2: Wilderness Explorer (199)
- Tier 3: Animal Senses and Sensibilities (109) or Wilderness Encouragement (198)
- Tier 4: Wilderness Awareness (198)
- Tier 5: The Wild Is on Your Side (198)
- Tier 6: One With the Wild (167) or Wild Camouflage (198)

GM Intrusions: People in cities and towns sometimes disparage those who look (and smell) like they live in the wilds, as if they were ignorant or barbaric.

LOOKS FOR TROUBLE

You're a scrapper and love a good fight.
- Tier 1: Fists of Fury (140)
- Tier 1: Wound Tender (200)
- Tier 2: Protector (172)
- Tier 2: Straightforward (187)
- Tier 3: Skill With Attacks (183) or Greater Enhanced Potential (146)
- Tier 4: Knock Out (156)
- Tier 5: Mastery With Attacks (161)
- Tier 6: Greater Enhanced Might (146) or Lethal Damage (158)

GM Intrusions: Weapons break or fly from even the strongest grip. Brawlers trip and fall. Even the battlefield can work against you with things falling or collapsing.

LOVES THE VOID

When it's just you, your spacesuit, and the panorama of stars wheeling out forever and always, you are at peace.
- Type Swap Option: Have Spacesuit, Will Travel (148)
- Tier 1: Vacuum Skilled (196)
- Tier 1: Microgravity Adept (162)
- Tier 2: Enhanced Speed Edge (135)
- Tier 2: Enhanced Physique (135)
- Tier 3: Space Fighting (184) or Fusion Armor (144)
- Tier 4: Silent As Space (183)
- Tier 4: Push Off and Throw (173)
- Tier 5: Microgravity Avoidance (162)
- Tier 6: Weightless Shot (197) or Reactive Field (174)

GM Intrusions: Spacesuits develop glitches. Air refill cartridges sometimes misreport capacity. Micrometeorites are common in space.

A bound magic creature requires a fair bit of attention and energy to keep happy and satisfied, but it's usually worth it.

For more abilities relating to common skills like hunting and searching, see the task ability category in chapter 9.

Task, page 106

For more abilities relating to followers, see the companion ability category in chapter 9.

Companion, page 96

For more abilities relating to learning information, see the information ability category in chapter 9.

Information, page 99

For more abilities relating to defense, see the protection ability category in chapter 9.

Protection, page 102

MASTERS DEFENSE
You use protective equipment and practiced techniques to avoid becoming hurt in a fight.
O Tier 1: Shield Master (182)
O Tier 2: Sturdy (187)
O Tier 2: Practiced in Armor (171)
O Tier 3: Dodge and Resist (131) or Dodge and Respond (131)
O Tier 4: Tower of Will (193)
O Tier 4: Experienced in Armor (136)
O Tier 5: Nothing but Defend (166)
O Tier 6: Defense Master (127) or Wear It Well (197)

GM Intrusions: Shields break when hit, as do weapons used to parry. Armor straps break.

Spellcasting, page 259

Those who specialize in spellcasting carry a spellbook or some other aid such as pouches filled with a variety of odd dusts, scales of strange beasts, oils of suspicious origin, and related materials that allow them to cast spells quickly or without an extreme effort of will. Others can learn basic spellcasting, and they get by without these trappings, but their spells require more effort to cast.

MASTERS SPELLS
By specializing in spellcasting and keeping a spellbook, you can quickly cast spells of arcing lightning, rolling fire, creeping shadow, and summoning.
O Tier 1: Arcane Flare (110)
O Tier 2: Ray of Confusion (174)
O Tier 3: Fire Bloom (140) or Summon Giant Spider (188)
O Tier 4: Soul Interrogation (184)
O Tier 5: Granite Wall (146)
O Tier 6: Summon Demon (188) or Word of Death (200)

GM Intrusions: The spell goes wrong. The summoned creature turns on the caster. A rival spellcaster is drawn to the magic use.

MASTERS THE SWARM
Insects. Rats. Bats. Even birds. You master one type of small creature that obeys you.
O Tier 1: Influence Swarm (153)
O Tier 2: Control Swarm (122)
O Tier 3: Living Armor (158) or Skill With Attacks (183)
O Tier 4: Call Swarm (118)
O Tier 5: Gain Unusual Companion (144)
O Tier 6: Deadly Swarm (125) or Skill With Defense (183)

For more abilities relating to companion creatures, see the companion ability category in chapter 9.

Companion, page 96

GM Intrusions: A command is misunderstood. Control is erratic or is lost. Bites and stings are not uncommon for masters of the swarm.

Someone who Masters Weaponry might have additional equipment, including a high-quality weapon.

For more abilities that improve your physical attacks, see the attack skill and meta ability categories in chapter 9.

Attack Skill, page 96
Meta, page 100

MASTERS WEAPONRY
You are a master user of a particular type of weapon, be it a sword, whip, dagger, gun, or something else.
O Tier 1: Weapon Master (197)
O Tier 1: Weapon Crafter (197)
O Tier 2: Weapon Defense (197)
O Tier 3: Rapid Attack (174) or Disarming Strike (129)
O Tier 4: Never Fumble (165)
O Tier 5: Extreme Mastery (138)
O Tier 6: Murderer (165) or Deadly Strike (125)

GM Intrusions: Weapons break. Weapons can be stolen. Weapons can be dropped or forced out of your hand.

METES OUT JUSTICE
You right wrongs, protect the innocent, and punish the guilty.
O Tier 1: Make Judgment (160)
O Tier 1: Designation (127)
O Tier 2: Defend the Innocent (126)
O Tier 2: Improved Designation (151)
O Tier 3: Defend All the Innocent (126) or Punish the Guilty (173)
O Tier 4: Find the Guilty (139)
O Tier 4: Greater Designation (146)
O Tier 5: Punish All the Guilty (173)
O Tier 6: Damn the Guilty (124) or Inspire the Innocent (154)

GM Intrusions: Guilt or innocence can be complicated. Some people resent the presumption of a self-appointed judge. Passing judgment makes enemies.

MOVES LIKE A CAT
Lithe, flexible, and graceful, you move quickly and smoothly, and never seem to be where danger is.
- Tier 1: Greater Enhanced Speed (146)
- Tier 1: Balance (112)
- Tier 2: Movement Skills (164)
- Tier 2: Safe Fall (179)
- Tier 3: Hard to Hit (148)
- Tier 3: Enhanced Speed Edge (135) or Greater Enhanced Speed (146)
- Tier 4: Quick Strike (174)
- Tier 5: Slippery (183)
- Tier 6: Perfect Speed Burst (169) or Greater Enhanced Speed (146)

GM Intrusions: Even a cat can be clumsy. A jump isn't quite as easy as it looks. An escape move is so overzealous that it sends the character right into harm's way.

MOVES LIKE THE WIND
You can move so fast that you become a blur.
- Tier 1: Greater Enhanced Speed (146)
- Tier 1: Fleet of Foot (141)
- Tier 2: Hard to Hit (148)
- Tier 3: Speed Burst (185) or Greater Enhanced Speed (146)
- Tier 4: Blink of an Eye (115)
- Tier 5: Hard to See (148)
- Tier 6: Perfect Speed Burst (169) or Incredible Running Speed (153)

GM Intrusions: Surfaces can be slick or offer hidden obstacles. The movement of other creatures can be unpredictable, and the character might run into them.

MURDERS
You're an assassin, whether by trade, by inclination, or because it was that or be killed yourself.
- Tier 1: Surprise Attack (188)
- Tier 1: Assassin Skills (110)
- Tier 2: Quick Death (173)
- Tier 2: Infiltrator (153)
- Tier 3: Awareness (111) or Poison Crafter (170)
- Tier 4: Better Surprise Attack (113)
- Tier 5: Damage Dealer (124)
- Tier 6: Escape Plan (136) or Murderer (165)

GM Intrusions: Most people do not react well to a professional killer.

NEEDS NO WEAPON
Powerful punches, kicks, elbows, knees, and full body movements are all the weapons you need.
- Tier 1: Fists of Fury (140)
- Tier 1: Flesh of Stone (141)
- Tier 2: Advantage to Disadvantage (109)
- Tier 2: Unarmed Fighting Style (194)
- Tier 3: Moving Like Water (164) or Greater Enhanced Potential (146)
- Tier 4: Divert Attacks (130)
- Tier 5: Stun Attack (187)
- Tier 6: Master of Unarmed Fighting Style (160) or Lethal Damage (158)

GM Intrusions: Striking certain foes hurts you as much as it hurts them. Opponents with weapons have greater reach. Complicated martial arts moves can knock you off balance.

NEVER SAYS DIE
You never quit, can shrug off a beating, and always come back for more.
- Tier 1: Improved Recovery (152)
- Tier 1: Push on Through (173)
- Tier 2: Ignore the Pain (150)
- Tier 3: Blood Fever (115) or Hidden Reserves (149)
- Tier 4: Increasing Determination (153) or Outlast the Foe (167)
- Tier 5: Not Dead Yet (166)
- Tier 6: Final Defiance (139) or Ignore Affliction (150)

GM Intrusions: Sometimes, it's equipment or weapons that give out.

OPERATES UNDERCOVER
Under the guise of someone else, you seek to find answers the powerful do not want divulged.
- Tier 1: Investigate (155)
- Tier 2: Disguise (129)
- Tier 3: Agent Provocateur (109) or Run and Fight (179)
- Tier 4: Pull a Fast One (173)
- Tier 5: Using What's Available (195)
- Tier 6: Trust to Luck (194) or Deadly Strike (125)

GM Intrusions: Bad luck can ruin the best plans. Disguises fail. Allies are revealed to be agents, too.

PERFORMS FEATS OF STRENGTH
A muscled prodigy, you can haul incredible weight, hurl your body through the air, and punch through doors.
- Tier 1: Athlete (111)
- Tier 1: Enhanced Might Edge (135)
- Tier 2: Feat of Strength (139)
- Tier 3: Iron Fist (155) or Throw (191)
- Tier 4: Greater Enhanced Might (146)
- Tier 5: Brute Strike (116)
- Tier 6: Greater Enhanced Might (146) or Jump Attack (156)

GM Intrusions: It's easy to break delicate things or hurt someone accidentally.

For more abilities relating to movement, see the movement ability category in chapter 9.

Movement, page 101

For more abilities relating to common skills like climbing and sneaking, see the task ability category in chapter 9.

Task, page 106

Someone who Operates Undercover might have additional equipment that includes a disguise kit.

Disguise kit, page 265

Someone who Murders might have additional equipment, including three doses of a level 2 blade poison that inflicts 5 points of damage.

For more abilities that make you better at doing the things you do, see the meta ability category in chapter 9.

Meta, page 100

PILOTS STARCRAFT
You're a crack starship pilot.
- Tier 1: Pilot (170)
- Tier 1: Flex Lore (141)
- Tier 2: Salvage and Comfort (179)
- Tier 2: Mentally Tough (162)
- Tier 3: Expert Pilot (137)
- Tier 3: Ship Footing (182) or Machine Companion (159)
- Tier 4: Sensor Array (181)
- Tier 4: Enhanced Speed (135)
- Tier 5: Like the Back of Your Hand (158)
- Tier 6: Incomparable Pilot (152)
- Tier 6: Remote Control (176) or Skill With Attacks (183)

GM Intrusions: Starcraft get lost, break down, and are attacked in space. An alien stowaway is found.

PLAYS TOO MANY GAMES
Lessons, reflexes, and strategies you've learned by playing too many games have applications in the real world, where people who don't play enough toil and live their dreary lives.
- Tier 1: Game Lessons (144)
- Tier 1: Gamer (144)
- Tier 2: Zero Dark Eyes (200)
- Tier 2: Resist Tricks (176)
- Tier 3: Sniper's Aim (184) or Enhanced Speed Edge (135)
- Tier 4: Mind Games (162)
- Tier 4: Enhanced Intellect (135)
- Tier 5: Gamer's Fortitude (144)
- Tier 6: Mind Surge (162) or Gaming God (144)

GM Intrusions: Missed attacks strike the wrong target. Equipment breaks. Sometimes people react negatively to someone who has lived most of their life in imaginary game worlds.

RAGES
When you go berserk, everyone fears you.
- Tier 1: Frenzy (143)
- Tier 2: Greater Enhanced Might (146)
- Tier 2: Movement Skills (164)
- Tier 3: Power Strike (171) or Unarmored Fighter (194)
- Tier 4: Greater Frenzy (146)
- Tier 5: Attack and Attack Again (111)
- Tier 6: Greater Enhanced Potential (146) or Lethal Damage (158)

GM Intrusions: It's easy for a berserker to lose control and attack friend as well as foe.

RIDES THE LIGHTNING
You create and discharge electrical power.
- Tier 1: Shock (183)
- Tier 1: Charge (119)
- Tier 2: Bolt Rider (115)
- Tier 3: Electric Armor (133) or Drain Charge (131)
- Tier 4: Bolts of Power (115)
- Tier 5: Electrical Flight (133)
- Tier 6: Flash Across the Miles (141) or Wall of Lightning (196)

GM Intrusions: Targets other than those intended are shocked. Objects explode.

RUNS AWAY
Your first instinct is to run from danger, and you've gotten very good at it.
- Tier 1: Go Defensive (145)
- Tier 2: Enhanced Speed (135)
- Tier 2: Quick to Flee (174)
- Tier 3: Incredible Running Speed (153) or Greater Enhanced Speed (146)
- Tier 4: Increasing Determination (153)
- Tier 4: Quick Wits (174)
- Tier 5: Go to Ground (145)
- Tier 6: Burst of Escape (116) or Skill With Defense (183)

GM Intrusions: Quick movements sometimes lead to dropped items, slipping on uneven ground, or going the wrong way by accident.

SAILED BENEATH THE JOLLY ROGER
You sailed with a crew of dread pirates, but you've decided to end your days as a pirate and join some other cause. The question is, will your past let you go so easily?
- Tier 1: Ignore the Pain (150)
- Tier 1: Sailor (179)
- Tier 2: Taking Advantage (188)
- Tier 2: Fearsome Reputation (139)
- Tier 3: Skill With Attacks (183) or Skill With Defense (183)
- Tier 4: Sea Legs (180)
- Tier 4: Movement Skills (164)
- Tier 5: Lost in the Chaos (159)
- Tier 6: Duel to the Death (132) or Successive Attack (187)

GM Intrusions: The dangers of the high seas are many, including severe storms and disease. Other pirates sometimes get ahead through betrayal. A pirate tracks down former sailing mates to find hidden treasure.

For more abilities relating to getting away safely, see the movement ability category in chapter 9.

Movement, page 101

Characters who are still pirates, rather than former pirates, have a slightly renamed focus: Sails Beneath the Jolly Roger.

For more abilities that improve your physical attacks, see the attack skill and meta ability categories in chapter 9.

Attack Skill, page 96
Meta, page 100

Before a player chooses Pilots Starcraft, they should work with the GM to be sure that they'll have the opportunity to access a starcraft.

Focus

Characters who See Beyond or Separate Mind From Body know that there's far more to the world than the obvious material universe around them. Either or both could be seen as visionaries. Perhaps coincidentally, they would make extremely good spies.

SCAVENGES
When not running and hiding, you sift the ruins of civilization for useful remnants to ensure your survival.
- Tier 1: Post-Apocalyptic Survivor (170)
- Tier 1: Ruin Lore (179)
- Tier 2: Junkmonger (156)
- Tier 3: Taking Advantage (188) or Incredible Health (153)
- Tier 4: Know Where to Look (156)
- Tier 5: Recycled Cyphers (175)
- Tier 6: Artifact Scavenger (110) or Reactive Field (174)

GM Intrusions: An item made with recycled junk breaks. Someone shows up claiming that the useful item or piece of junk scavenged belongs to them. A recycled cypher explodes.

SEES BEYOND
You have a psychic sense that allows you to see what others cannot.
- Tier 1: See the Unseen (180)
- Tier 2: See Through Matter (180)
- Tier 3: Find the Hidden (140) or Sensor (181)
- Tier 4: Remote Viewing (176)
- Tier 5: See Through Time (181)
- Tier 6: Mental Projection (161) or Total Awareness (192)

GM Intrusions: Some secrets are too terrible to know.

SEPARATES MIND FROM BODY
You can project your mind out of your body to see faraway places and learn secrets that would otherwise remain hidden.
- Tier 1: Third Eye (191)
- Tier 2: Open Mind (167)
- Tier 2: Sharp Senses (182)
- Tier 3: Roaming Third Eye (178) or Find the Hidden (140)
- Tier 4: Sensor (181)
- Tier 5: Psychic Passenger (172)
- Tier 6: Mental Projection (161) or Improved Sensor (152)

GM Intrusions: Reuniting mind and body can sometimes be disorienting and require a character to spend a few moments to get their bearings.

SHEPHERDS THE COMMUNITY
You keep the place where you live safe from all danger.
- Tier 1: Community Knowledge (121)
- Tier 1: Community Activist (121)
- Tier 2: Skill With Attacks (183)
- Tier 3: Shepherd's Fury (182) or Skill With Defense (183)
- Tier 4: Greater Enhanced Potential (146)
- Tier 5: Evasion (136)
- Tier 6: Greater Skill With Attacks (147) or Protective Wall (172)

GM Intrusions: People in the community misunderstand the character's motives. Rivals try to oust the character.

Scavenging, page 296

Crafting, Building, and Repairing, page 227

For more abilities relating to crafting and repairing objects, or survival in general, see the craft and protection ability categories in chapter 9.

Craft, page 97
Protection, page 102

For more abilities relating to general social activities and interacting with NPCs, see the social ability category in chapter 9.

Social, page 103

For more abilities relating to enhancing your senses, see the senses ability category in chapter 9.

Senses, page 103

75

In some settings, the Shepherds Spirits focus applies to only one kind of spirit, such as spirits of the deceased, nature spirits, and so on.

Robots and other living machines should be treated as creatures, not machines, for the purposes of siphoning power from them.

Although wielding a sword in a setting where people usually do not carry such weapons is fine, you can change the Slays Monsters sword-related abilities to use a different weapon, such as a gun with silver bullets.

For more abilities that improve your physical attacks, or make you better at what you already can do, see the attack skill and meta ability categories in chapter 9.
Attack Skill, page 96
Meta, page 100

SHEPHERDS SPIRITS

Wandering souls, nature spirits, and elemental beings aid and support you.
- Tier 1: Question the Spirits (173)
- Tier 2: Spirit Accomplice (185)
- Tier 3: Command Spirit (121) or Preternatural Senses (171)
- Tier 4: Wraith Cloak (200)
- Tier 5: Call Dead Spirit (117)
- Tier 6: Call Otherworldly Spirit (117) or Infuse Spirit (153)

GM Intrusions: Some people don't trust those who deal with spirits. The dead sometimes don't want shepherding.

SHREDS THE WALLS OF THE WORLD

Speed plus phasing gives you a unique ability to evade danger and simultaneously inflict damage.
- Tier 1: Phase Sprint (170)
- Tier 1: Disrupting Touch (129)
- Tier 2: Scratch Existence (180)
- Tier 3: Invisible Phasing (155) or Walk Through Walls (196)
- Tier 4: Phase Detonation (169)
- Tier 5: Very Long Sprinting (196)
- Tier 6: Shred Existence (183) or Untouchable While Moving (195)

GM Intrusions: Moving so quickly while sprinting sometimes leads to stumbles on unexpected, exotic obstacles.

SIPHONS POWER

You suck power out of machines and creatures alike in order to empower yourself.
- Tier 1: Drain Machine (131)
- Tier 2: Drain Creature (131)
- Tier 3: Drain at a Distance (131) or Unraveling Consumption (195)
- Tier 4: Store Energy (186)
- Tier 5: Share the Power (182)
- Tier 6: Explosive Release (138) or Sun Siphon (188)

GM Intrusions: Drained power also transmits something unwanted—compulsions, afflictions, or alien thoughts. Siphoned power can overload the character, causing feedback.

SLAYS MONSTERS

You kill monsters.
- Tier 1: Practiced With Swords (171)
- Tier 1: Monster Bane (164)
- Tier 1: Monster Lore (164)
- Tier 2: Will of Legend (199)
- Tier 3: Trained Slayer (193)
- Tier 3: Improved Monster Bane (152) or Misdirect (163)
- Tier 4: Fight On (139)
- Tier 5: Greater Skill With Attacks (swords) (147)
- Tier 6: Murderer (165) or Heroic Monster Bane (149)

GM Intrusions: The monster laid a trap or set an ambush. The monster has previously undisclosed abilities. The monster's mother vows revenge.

SOLVES MYSTERIES
You're a master of deduction, using evidence to find the answer.
- Tier 1: Investigator (155)
- Tier 1: Sleuth (183)
- Tier 2: Out of Harm's Way (167)
- Tier 3: You Studied (200) or Skill With Attacks (183)
- Tier 4: Draw Conclusion (131)
- Tier 5: Defuse Situation (127)
- Tier 6: Seize the Initiative (181) or Greater Skill With Defense (147)

GM Intrusions: Evidence disappears, red herrings confuse, and witnesses lie. Initial research can be faulty.

SPEAKS FOR THE LAND
Your spiritual connection to nature and the environment grants you mystical abilities.
- Tier 1: Seeds of Fury (181)
- Tier 1: Wilderness Lore (199)
- Tier 2: Grasping Foliage (146)
- Tier 3: Soothe the Savage (184) or Communication (121)
- Tier 4: Moon Shape (164)
- Tier 5: Insect Eruption (154)
- Tier 6: Call the Storm (117) or Earthquake (133)

GM Intrusions: An injured natural (but dangerous) creature is discovered. Someone's poaching wildlife for their skins, leaving the carcasses to rot. A tree falls in the forest, one of the last elder trees.

STANDS LIKE A BASTION
Your armor, along with your size, strength, incredible training, or machine enhancement, makes you difficult to move or hurt.
- Tier 1: Practiced in Armor (171)
- Tier 1: Experienced Defender (136)
- Tier 2: Resist the Elements (176)
- Tier 3: Unmovable (195)
- Tier 3: Greater Enhanced Might (146) or Practiced With All Weapons (171)
- Tier 4: Living Wall (158)
- Tier 5: Hardiness (148)
- Tier 5: Mastery in Armor (161)
- Tier 6: Lethal Damage (158) or Shield Training (182)

GM Intrusions: Armor is damaged. Small foes conspire in ingenious ways.

TALKS TO MACHINES
You use your organic brain like a computer, interfacing "wirelessly" with any electronic device. You can control and influence them in ways that others can't.
- Tier 1: Machine Affinity (159)
- Tier 1: Distant Interface (130)
- Tier 2: Coaxing Power (119)
- Tier 2: Charm Machine (119)
- Tier 3: Intelligent Interface (155) or Command Machine (120)
- Tier 4: Machine Companion (159)
- Tier 4: Robot Fighter (178)
- Tier 5: Information Gathering (153)
- Tier 6: Control Machine (121) or Improved Machine Companion (152)

GM Intrusions: The machine malfunctions or acts unpredictably.

THROWS WITH DEADLY ACCURACY
Everything that leaves your hand goes exactly where you'd like it to go and at the range and speed to make the perfect impact.
- Tier 1: Precision (171)
- Tier 2: Careful Aim (118)
- Tier 3: Quick Throw (174) or Skill With Defense (183)
- Tier 4: Everything Is a Weapon (136)
- Tier 4: Specialized Throwing (185)
- Tier 5: Whirlwind of Throws (198)
- Tier 6: Lethal Damage (158) or Mastery With Defense (161)

GM Intrusions: Missed attacks strike the wrong target. Ricochets can be dangerous. Improvised weapons break.

THUNDERS
You emit destructive sound and manipulate soundscapes.
- Tier 1: Thunder Beam (191)
- Tier 2: Sound Conversion Barrier (184)
- Tier 3: Nullify Sound (166) or Echolocation (133)
- Tier 4: Shattering Shout (182)
- Tier 5: Subsonic Rumble (187)
- Tier 5: Amplify Sounds (109)
- Tier 6: Earthquake (133) or Lethal Vibration (158)

GM Intrusions: Loud noises attract attention.

TRAVELS THROUGH TIME
You can see through time, try to reach through it, and eventually even travel through it.
- Tier 1: Anticipation (110)
- Tier 2: See History (180)
- Tier 3: Temporal Acceleration (190) or Time Loop (192)
- Tier 4: Temporal Dislocation (190)
- Tier 5: Time Doppelganger (191)
- Tier 6: Call Through Time (118) or Time Travel (192)

GM Intrusions: Paradoxes are created. Others remember past events differently.

For more abilities relating to acquiring information or common skills like interrogation and searching, see the information and task ability categories in chapter 9.

Information, page 99
Task, page 106

For more abilities relating to manipulating the environment or things in it, see the environment ability category in chapter 9.

Environment, page 99

For more abilities that improve your physical attacks, see the attack skill and meta ability categories in chapter 9.

Attack Skill, page 96
Meta, page 100

Some characters who Stand Like a Bastion might already be experts in armor. They can choose a different tier 1 ability instead of Practiced in Armor.

For more abilities relating to defense, see the protection ability category in chapter 9.

Protection, page 102

Although all character choices are subject to GM approval, Travels Through Time is a focus that the GM and player should probably have a long conversation about ahead of time, so the player knows the rules of time travel (if any) that exist in the GM's setting. A character with this focus can drastically alter a setting, if the rules of time travel allow it.

For more abilities relating to influencing people and interacting with NPCs, see the control and social ability categories in chapter 9.

Control, page 97
Social, page 103

For more abilities that improve your physical attacks, see the attack skill and meta ability categories in chapter 9.

Attack Skill, page 96
Meta, page 100

For more abilities relating to crafting and common skills like fixing things, see the craft and task ability categories in chapter 9.

Craft, page 97
Task, page 106

WAS FORETOLD

You are the "chosen one," and prophecy, prediction, prognostication, or some other method of determination expects great things of you one day.

- Tier 1: Interaction Skills (155)
- Tier 1: Knowing (156)
- Tier 2: Destined for Greatness (127)
- Tier 3: Overcome All Obstacles (168) or Hard-Won Resilience (148)
- Tier 4: Center of Attention (119)
- Tier 5: Show Them the Way (183)
- Tier 6: As Foretold in Prophecy (110) or Greater Enhanced Potential (146)

GM Intrusions: An enemy described in prophecy appears. Unbelievers threaten to ruin the moment. The character gains a reputation in outside circles as a fraud.

WEARS A SHEEN OF ICE

You command the wintery power of cold and ice.

- Tier 1: Ice Armor (150)
- Tier 2: Frost Touch (144)
- Tier 3: Freezing Touch (143) or Ice Creation (150)
- Tier 4: Resilient Ice Armor (176)
- Tier 5: Cold Burst (119)
- Tier 6: Ice Storm (150) or Winter Gauntlets (199)

GM Intrusions: Ice makes surfaces slippery. Extreme cold causes objects to crack and break.

WEARS POWER ARMOR

- Tier 1: Powered Armor (171)
- Tier 1: Enhanced Might (135)
- Tier 2: Heads-Up Display (148)
- Tier 3: Fusion Armor (144) or Incredible Health (153)
- Tier 4: Force Blast (142)
- Tier 5: Field-Reinforced Armor (139)
- Tier 6: Masterful Armor Modification (Jet Assisted Flight) (160) or Masterful Armor Modification (Cypher Pod) (160)

GM Intrusions: The armor won't come off. The armor acts under its own power. The armor suffers a momentary power loss. NPCs are scared by the power armor.

WIELDS TWO WEAPONS AT ONCE

You bear steel with both hands, ready to take on any foe.

- Tier 1: Dual Light Wield (132)
- Tier 2: Double Strike (131)
- Tier 2: Infiltrator (153)
- Tier 3: Dual Medium Wield (132) or Precise Cut (171)
- Tier 4: Dual Defense (132)
- Tier 5: Dual Distraction (132)
- Tier 6: Disarming Attack (129) or Spin Attack (185)

GM Intrusions: A blade snaps in two or a weapon flies loose from its bearer's grip.

WORKS FOR A LIVING

You take great satisfaction in a job well done, whether it's coding, building houses, or mining asteroids.

- Tier 1: Handy (148)
- Tier 2: Muscles of Iron (165)
- Tier 3: Eye for Detail (138) or Improvise (152)
- Tier 4: Enhanced Might (135)
- Tier 4: Tough It Out (193)
- Tier 5: Expert Skill (137)
- Tier 6: Greater Enhanced Potential (146) or Hard-Won Resilience (148)

GM Intrusions: Repairs sometimes fail. Wiring can be tricky to decipher and still carry an electrical charge. Some people are rude to those who work for a living.

A character in a setting without magic or gods who Works Miracles might—knowingly or unknowingly—be using nanites to heal, directing and speeding up the cells' mitotic phase or even the migration of cells in the system.

WORKS MIRACLES

You can heal others with a touch, alter time to help others, and are generally beloved by everyone.
- Tier 1: Healing Touch (149)
- Tier 2: Alleviate (109)
- Tier 3: Font of Healing (142) or Miraculous Health (163)
- Tier 4: Inspire Action (154)
- Tier 5: Undo (195)
- Tier 6: Greater Healing Touch (147) or Restore Life (177)

GM Intrusions: Attempts to heal might cause harm instead. A community or individual needs a healer so desperately that they hold one against their will.

WORKS THE BACK ALLEYS

You make your way unseen, stealing from the wealthy to achieve your ends.
- Tier 1: Stealth Skills (186)
- Tier 2: Underworld Contacts (195)
- Tier 3: Pull a Fast One (173) or Guild Training (147)
- Tier 4: Master Thief (160)
- Tier 5: Dirty Fighter (128)
- Tier 6: Alley Rat (109) or All-Out Con (109)

GM Intrusions: Thieves are thrown in jail. Powerful enemies are made.

WORKS THE SYSTEM

You can exploit flaws in artificial systems, including but not limited to computer code.
- Tier 1: Hack the Impossible (147)
- Tier 1: Computer Programming (121)
- Tier 2: Connected (121)
- Tier 3: Confidence Artist (121) or Skill With Attacks (183)
- Tier 4: Confuse Enemy (121)
- Tier 5: Work the Friendship (200)
- Tier 6: Call in Favor (117) or Greater Enhanced Potential (146)

GM Intrusions: Contacts sometimes have ulterior motives. Devices sometimes have failsafes or even traps.

WOULD RATHER BE READING

Books are your friends. What's more important than knowledge? Nothing.
- Tier 1: Knowledge Is Power (156)
- Tier 2: Greater Enhanced Intellect (146)
- Tier 3: Applying Your Knowledge (110) or Flex Skill (141)
- Tier 4: Knowledge Is Power (156)
- Tier 4: Knowing the Unknown (156)
- Tier 5: Greater Enhanced Intellect (146)
- Tier 6: Knowledge Is Power (156)
- Tier 6: Tower of Intellect (193) or Read the Signs (174)

GM Intrusions: Books burn, get wet, or get lost. Computers break or lose power. Glasses break.

For more abilities relating to healing, see the cure ability category in chapter 9.

Cure, page 98

For more abilities relating to learning information, see the information ability category in chapter 9.

Information, page 99

For more abilities relating to combat and common skills like sneaking and lying, see the attack skill and task ability categories in chapter 9.

Attack Skill, page 96

Task, page 106

FOCUS CATEGORIES
- Ally use
- Basic
- Energy manipulation
- Environment manipulation
- Exploration
- Influence
- Irregular
- Movement expertise
- Striker combat
- Support
- Tank combat

Chapter 9: Abilities, page 95

Bears a Halo of Fire, page 64

Feel free to build Stokes the Flames of the Apocalypse and Lights Fires With a Thought for your own use, or as an exercise in using this chapter.

Ability Categories and Relative Power, page 95

CREATING NEW FOCI

This section provides everything you need to create your own foci.

Every focus has an overarching style, whether that's exploration, energy manipulation, or simply dealing a lot of damage in combat. These broad classifications are called focus categories.

Each focus category has an overarching theme, followed by selection guidelines that describe how to choose abilities from chapter 9 at each tier, from tier 1 to tier 6.

The newly created focus should be named in the form of a verb, like Controls Beasts or Abides in Stone. For instance, a fire-using focus created by following the guidelines in the energy manipulation focus category might be called Bears a Halo of Fire (one of the sample foci in this chapter). Alternatively, a new fire-using focus should get an all-new name like Stokes the Flames of the Apocalypse or Lights Fires With a Thought.

CHOOSING ABILITIES BY RELATIVE POWER

The ability selection guidelines invite you to choose an ability from one of three ranges: low tier, mid tier, and high tier. These ranges correspond with the power "grades" given for every ability. These abilities are further sorted into ability categories based on the kinds of things they do—abilities that improve physical attacks are in the attack skill category, abilities that assist allies are in the support category, and so on. Look for the grades and categories in the Ability Categories and Relative Power section of chapter 9.

Low-tier abilities are best suited for focus options at tiers 1 and 2. Mid-tier abilities are best suited for focus options at tiers 3 and 4. High-tier abilities are best suited for focus options at tiers 5 and 6.

That said, sometimes you'll find it appropriate to assign a low-tier ability at tier 3 or 4, or maybe a mid-tier ability at tier 1 or 2. Do so sparingly, but don't rule it out. It might be the only way to get all the abilities you want for the focus you're building. Higher-tier abilities usually cost more Pool points to use. So if a mid-tier ability is made available at tier 1 or 2, or a high-tier ability is made available at tier 3 or 4, the higher cost will be a balancing factor.

BALANCING ABILITIES

The guidelines within each category go a long way toward ensuring that the focus you build will be balanced. Sometimes it might be appropriate to grant a low-power ability along with a regular ability at a given tier, depending on the needs of the focus. A "low-power ability" is deliberately open for GM interpretation, but generally speaking, should be no more potent than a low-tier ability (that is, an ability that is normally available at tier 1 or 2).

For instance, someone who uses cold might be able to create small snow sculptures in addition to emitting a cold ray. Someone who uses electricity might be able to charge a depleted artifact or have an asset for dealing with electrical systems. And so on.

Often, the focus guidelines note this as a possibility. However, you have great leeway in deciding if a focus needs an additional ability, even if the guidelines for that tier don't indicate one. If you do add an ability, or there is a higher-power ability at a tier that normally shouldn't have it, it might mean that the choice given at the next tier, or the previous tier, isn't quite as good. Balancing a focus is a bit of an art. Resist the urge to overpower the focus, but don't underpower it, either.

ABILITY GUIDELINES ARE NOT PRESCRIPTIVE

Each focus category provides a guideline for what kind of ability you should select at every tier. But don't regard the guidelines as something that you can't vary. They're not prescriptive; they're just a place to start. You might want to vary the kind of ability at a particular tier that isn't indicated in the guidelines. As long as the chosen ability falls within the expected power curve for that tier, it's fine. The guideline isn't meant to be a straitjacket.

For example, if you're building a cold-using focus for a game set in a fantasy genre, you may decide that an ability that calls up a demon is a better choice at a particular tier than an ability that does damage in an area, which is what the tier 5 guideline for energy manipulation calls for. Making the change is probably especially valid if you call your new focus something like Channels the Ninth Circle.

ABILITY SWAP

If you're creating a focus and you think it should provide a suite of abilities at first tier that would mechanically overload it, you have the option to add one as a "swap" ability. Doing so is as easy as allowing a character to swap out one of their type abilities for an indicated low-tier focus ability. The ability is gained instead of one of the abilities normally granted by the character's type.

CONCEPT AND CATEGORY

Choosing to create a focus that uses a particular concept—say, creating illusions—doesn't lock you into creating a focus within a particular category—in this case, environment manipulation. A focus can be constructed in a variety of ways using a particular energy, tool, or concept, each ultimately leading to a focus that provides different results. It all depends on your ends. In this case, creating illusions might be used to sway others, which argues for a focus built using the influence category guidelines.

In the same way, if a focus grants a character the ability to call some kind of force or energy, that doesn't mean the focus should automatically be built using the energy manipulation category guidelines (though of course it *could*, if attacking and protecting yourself with that energy is the point). But a focus could be built that grants abilities to call energy or force that is primarily focused on durability, suggesting a tank combat focus (someone who can take a lot of punishment in a fight); or blasting away with a main concern for maximizing damage, thus suggesting a striker combat focus; or creating a follower composed of that energy or force, suggesting an ally use focus (that is, someone who uses helping creatures, NPCs, or even duplicate versions of themselves to give them a leg up).

Here's another example: the focus Controls Gravity could conceivably be an environment manipulation focus or an energy manipulation focus. It depends on whether the focus is more concerned with crushing and holding things in place (environment manipulation) or on blasting things and protecting yourself with gravity (energy manipulation).

The same malleability of concept holds true in other realms. For instance, if someone is able to call up and mold raw earth, they might use it to transform themselves into a being of stone (tank combat), to batter foes (striker combat), or to create walls, barricades, and shields to protect their allies (support).

ABILITIES THAT REFERENCE OTHER ABILITIES

Some abilities in chapter 9 reference other abilities. If you select an ability for your focus or type that refers to or modifies a lower-tier ability, also include that lower-tier ability in your type or focus as a selection a PC can make at a lower tier.

MODIFYING ABILITIES TO FIT A CONCEPT

If you're looking for an ability and can't seem to find the right one in the vast catalog in chapter 9, consider reskinning one to make it seem new (and to accomplish what you need). Reskinning means that you use the underlying mechanics of an ability as written but change the flavor in some fashion. For instance, maybe you're creating a new earth-moving focus but can't find enough earth-related abilities to meet your need. It's easy enough to change up other abilities so they use earth instead of fire, cold, or magnetism. For instance, Wings of Fire might become Wings of Earth, Ice Armor could become Earth Armor, and so on. These alterations change nothing except the type of damage and any knock-on effects (for instance, Wings of Earth might generate clouds of dust in their wake).

Wings of Fire, page 199
Ice Armor, page 150

CREATING BRAND-NEW ABILITIES

You can go further than reskinning and create one or more brand-new abilities. When doing this, try to find something as close as possible to the effect you want, then use it as a template. In any case, deciding how much an ability should cost when it comes to a character's Pool is one of the most important aspects of getting an ability right.

You may notice that higher-tier abilities are more expensive. This is partly because they do more, but it's also because higher-tier characters have more Edge than lower-tier characters, which means they pay fewer points from their relevant Pools. A third-tier character with 3 Edge in a relevant Pool pays no cost for abilities that cost 3 or fewer points. That's great for lower-tier abilities, but you'll usually want a character to think a little bit about how often to use their most powerful abilities. That means they should cost at least 1 point more than the Edge the character is likely to have at that tier. (Often, a character will have an Edge in their relevant Pool equal to their tier.)

Controls Gravity, page 66
Edge, page 15

As a good rule of thumb, a typical ability should cost points equal to its tier.

CHOOSE GM INTRUSIONS

Think about the kinds of things that might surprise, alarm, or go catastrophically wrong for someone with the new focus being created, and assign it as a GM intrusion for that focus. Of course, this often is done on the fly during the game. But giving the topic some thought while the focus is being constructed and the ideas are fresh in your head is likely to yield some particularly devilish options.

GM intrusions, page 408

ALLY USE FOCI
The following are examples and not meant to provide a complete list of all possible foci in this category.
- Builds Robots
- Consorts With the Dead
- Controls Beasts
- Exists in Two Places at Once
- Leads
- Masters the Swarm
- Shepherds Spirits

Focus connections, page 61

Follower, page 233

FOCUS CATEGORIES

ALLY USE
Foci that prioritize providing NPC followers to the character are ally use foci. The followers give aid to the PC in a variety of ways, but at base they usually provide an asset to the character's actions.

Multiple potential themes exist within the ally use category, from abilities that allow a character to summon or craft allies to those that allow them to attract allies through fame, magic, or essential authority or charisma.

Connection: Choose four relevant connections from the Focus Connections list.

Additional Equipment: Any object necessary for the character to keep an ally. For instance, someone with a focus that uses super-science to create robot allies would require tools to build and repair those allies. Some foci in this category don't require anything to gain or retain their benefits.

Minor Effect Suggestions: The NPC ally's tasks are eased on its next turn.

Major Effect Suggestions: The NPC ally gains an immediate extra action.

ABILITY SELECTION GUIDELINES
Tier 1: Choose a low-tier ability that grants a level 2 NPC follower to the character, or gives a similar benefit provided by an NPC. Alternatively, lay the groundwork for gaining such NPC allies at higher tiers by choosing an ability that gives the character influence over others.

Sometimes an additional low-power ability is appropriate, depending on the focus. Often, this is an ability that grants skill training in a related area of knowledge or a related skill. For instance, training in a skill related to the kind of NPC follower the character gains would be appropriate.

Tier 2: Choose a low-tier ability that grants influence over similar kinds of NPCs as the follower gained at the previous tier. If no follower was gained at the previous tier, this ability should provide that benefit now.

Sometimes a secondary ability might be appropriate in addition to the ability provided above, perhaps a low-power ability that grants 2 or 3 points to a Pool.

Tier 3: Choose two mid-tier abilities. Give both of them as options for the focus; a PC will choose one or the other.

One option should be a mid-tier ability that improves the NPC follower previously provided (usually from level 2 to level 3) or grants an additional follower.

The other option should be something that benefits the character—perhaps an offensive or defensive ability, or something that broadens their influence over their followers (or potential followers).

Tier 4: Choose a mid-tier ability that gives the character an offensive or defensive capability if they haven't previously gained one, preferably within the theme of the focus. For instance, if the character gains followers because of their charisma, this ability might let them command foes for brief periods. If the character gains followers by building or calling them, this ability might let them affect entities of the same type that are not already their followers.

Alternatively, this ability might further improve a previously gained follower from level 3 to level 4, or grant an additional follower.

Tier 5: Choose an ability that improves the character by providing a defense, an improved stat Pool, or another kind of protection.

Alternatively, this ability could open a new front in influencing and calling NPC allies related to the focus's theme. For instance, someone who keeps beast allies might gain an ability to call a horde of lesser beasts. Someone who builds robots might gain an ability to build several lesser robot helpers. And so on.

Finally, this ability might improve a previously gained follower to level 5.

Tier 6: Choose two high-tier abilities. Give both of them as options for the focus; a PC will choose one or the other.

One of the abilities should improve a previously gained follower to level 5, if that wasn't already provided at tier 5. If that's the case, this ability might be provided *in addition* to two other related abilities.

Another high-tier option could provide a handful of level 3 followers to the character.

The last high-tier ability could open a new front in influencing and calling NPC allies related to the focus's theme. For instance, someone who gains followers through high charisma and training might gain an ability to learn otherwise impossible-to-glean information.

BASIC

Foci that rely mostly on providing skill training, assets to tasks, and bumps to stat Pools and Edge in order to improve a character fall within the basic category. An overarching theme is also included, as with most of the other categories, that makes sense of the various basic abilities provided.

In addition, because the benefits provided by such foci are mostly straightforward (usually with a few exceptions), most basic foci would also be appropriate for non-fantastic campaigns where magic, super-science, or psychic abilities normally don't come into play. That said, just because the abilities granted by basic foci are straightforward doesn't mean they are not potent when combined with the abilities granted by type, descriptor, cyphers, and other character aspects.

Connection: Choose four relevant connections from the Focus Connections list.

Additional Equipment: Any object necessary to fulfill the overarching theme of the focus. For instance, a focus called Would Rather Be Reading should grant a handful of books to the character. A focus called Works for a Living should provide a set of tools.

Minor Effect Suggestions: Next action is eased.

Major Effect Suggestions: Make a free, no-action recovery roll that doesn't count against daily recovery rolls.

ABILITY SELECTION GUIDELINES

Tier 1: Choose an ability that grants training or an asset to skills associated with the focus's theme, or that grants 5 or 6 points to a particular Pool.

Alternatively, choose an ability that grants only 2 or 3 points to a particular Pool and an ability that provides training or an asset to just one task.

Tier 2: Choose whichever kind of ability wasn't chosen at tier 1.

Tier 3: Choose two mid-tier abilities. Give both of them as options for the focus; a PC will choose one or the other.

One option should be a non-fantastic ability that improves the character's abilities within the focus's theme. For instance, if the theme involves paying attention in some fashion, an information-gathering ability might be appropriate.

The other option should be something that either improves the character's Edge in an appropriate stat or provides the character with some kind of defense.

Tier 4: Choose another ability that grants additional training or an asset to skills associated with the focus's theme, or that grants 5 or 6 points to a particular Pool best suited to the focus. Or choose two abilities that provide only 2 or 3 points plus another tier 4 ability that improves a single task or skill.

Alternatively, provide a branch-out ability suggested at tier 5.

Finally, if the focus has yet to grant some kind of defense, a defensive ability could be provided here.

Tier 5: Choose an ability that allows the character to branch out slightly—perhaps one like Expert Skill that allows them to automatically succeed on a task they're trained in.

Alternatively, if a nonstandard benefit was provided at tier 4, provide the benefits suggested at tier 4 here.

Tier 6: Choose two high-tier abilities. Give both of them as options for the focus; a PC will choose one or the other.

One option should be an ability that provides another 5 or 6 points to a particular Pool best suited to the focus, or that the character can divide up as they wish. Alternatively, training in offense or defense would also be appropriate.

The other tier 6 option should give the character a brand-new ability within their theme, but not one that strays into the realm of the fantastic. For instance, an ability that allows a character to take two actions instead of one would be reasonable. Granting additional training, assets, or Edge would also be fine.

> **BASIC FOCI**
> The following are examples and not meant to provide a complete list of all possible foci in this category.
> - Doesn't Do Much
> - Interprets the Law
> - Learns Quickly
> - Works for a Living
> - Would Rather Be Reading

Expert Skill, page 137

ENERGY MANIPULATION FOCI

The following are examples and not meant to provide a complete list of all possible foci in this category.

- Absorbs Energy
- Bears a Halo of Fire
- Dances With Dark Matter
- Rides the Lightning
- Thunders
- Wears a Sheen of Ice

Focus connections, page 61

Follower, page 233

ENERGY MANIPULATION

Energy manipulation foci offer abilities that can call fire, electricity, force, magnetism, or nonstandard forms of energy such as cold, stone, or something stranger like "void" or "shadow." These abilities usually give a character a way to achieve something of a balance between attacking enemies and granting themselves or allies additional protection. The focus usually also offers abilities that provide other ways to use specific energy for things like transportation, creating large concentrations of energy that can affect multiple targets, or creating a temporary object or barrier of energy.

Connection: Choose four relevant connections from the Focus Connections list.

Additional Equipment: One or more pieces of equipment immune to the energy manipulated, which might be a set of clothes. Alternatively, something related to the energy being generated. Some foci in this category don't require additional equipment.

Energy Abilities: If a character type grants special abilities that normally use some other kind of energy, they now produce the kind used by this focus. For example, if a character uses this focus to manipulate electricity, their force blasts become blasts of electricity. These alterations change nothing except the type of damage and any knock-on effects (for instance, electricity might temporarily short out electronic systems).

Minor Effect Suggestions: The target or something near the target is hindered because of residual energy.

Major Effect Suggestions: An important item on the target's person is destroyed.

ABILITY SELECTION GUIDELINES

Tier 1: Choose a low-tier ability that either inflicts damage or provides protection using the appropriate energy type in some fashion.

Sometimes an additional low-power ability is appropriate, depending on the energy type. For instance, a focus that manipulates cold might grant an ability to create snow sculptures. A focus that manipulates electricity might grant an ability to charge a depleted artifact or have an asset for dealing with electrical systems. A focus that absorbs energy might grant an ability to release it as a basic attack. And so on.

Tier 2: Choose whichever kind of ability wasn't chosen at tier 1.

Tier 3: Choose two mid-tier abilities. Give both of them as options for the focus; a PC will choose one or the other.

One option should be an ability that inflicts damage using the appropriate energy type (and possibly a related effect).

The other should grant enhanced movement by use of the appropriate energy type, give additional protection provided by the preferred energy, or use the energy in a completely new way, such as by draining the energy from a machine (if using electricity), entombing a victim in a layer of ice (if using cold), creating perfect silence (if using sound), creating a dazzling blast of illumination (if using light), and so on.

Tier 4: Choose whichever kind of ability wasn't chosen at tier 3.

Tier 5: Choose a high-tier ability that inflicts damage (and possibly a related effect) that can affect more than one target using the appropriate energy type, or an ability that uses the energy in some fashion not previously used, as described in tiers 3 and 6.

Tier 6: Choose two high-tier abilities. Give both of them as options for the focus; a PC will choose one or the other.

One of the high-tier abilities should use the preferred energy to inflict a lot of damage to a single target or to several.

The other option should use the appropriate energy type to accomplish a task not previously provided by lower-tier abilities, such as fashioning a fiery follower (if using fire), teleporting a great distance as a blast of lightning (if using electricity), creating solid objects out of the energy, and so on.

ENVIRONMENT MANIPULATION

Foci that allow a character to move objects, affect gravity, create objects (or illusions of objects), and so on are environment manipulation foci. Given that, in many cases, energy is used as part of this process, this category and energy manipulation overlap to some extent. Environment manipulation foci prioritize abilities that indirectly affect enemies and allies via objects, forces, and alterations of the surroundings; energy manipulation foci prioritize directly damaging targets with the chosen energy or force.

For example, rather than blasting a foe with a gravity pulse that does damage, a character using an environment manipulation focus based on gravity is more likely to have abilities that hold a target in place, use gravity to throw heavy objects as an attack, or lower gravity in a particular area or even on a particular object.

Connection: Choose four relevant connections from the Focus Connections list.

Additional Equipment: Any object necessary to manipulate the surrounding environment. For instance, someone with a focus that grants the ability to craft objects would require basic tools. Some foci in this category don't require anything to gain or retain their benefits.

Environment Manipulation Abilities: Foci themes that involve imagery or visible energies can affect the look of your type abilities. Such alterations, if any, do nothing but change the appearance of effects. If gravity is manipulated, perhaps a telltale bluish glow permeates all ability uses, including type abilities. If illusion is generated, perhaps flamboyant visual and auditory qualities accompany type abilities, such as the appearance of a tentacled beast holding a target in place when Stasis is used. And so on.

Minor Effect Suggestions: The target gets turned around, and its next attack is hindered.

Major Effect Suggestions: The character is refreshed and recovers 4 points to one Pool.

ABILITY SELECTION GUIDELINES

Tier 1: Choose a low-tier ability that grants a basic use of an ability that alters the environment (or predicts it) using the focus's theme. For instance, a gravity-affecting focus might provide an ability that makes a target lighter or heavier. An illusion-crafting focus might grant an ability that allows the creation of an image. An object-making focus might grant a basic proficiency in creating a particular kind of object. A predictive focus might calculate outcomes and provide the character with the benefits of that foreknowledge. And so on.

Sometimes an additional low-power ability is appropriate, depending on the focus. Often, this is an ability that grants skill training in a related area of knowledge.

Tier 2: Choose a low-tier ability that provides a new defensive or offensive capability related to the focus's theme.

Alternatively, this ability might provide an additional or brand-new capability to manipulate the environment related to the focus's theme.

Tier 3: Choose two mid-tier abilities. Give both of them as options for the focus; a PC will choose one or the other.

One option should be a mid-tier ability related to the focus's theme that provides an additional environment manipulation capacity or further improves the basic environment manipulation ability previously granted. This ability isn't directly offensive or defensive, but provides either an all-new ability related to the basic ability, or one that increases the strength, range, or some other extension of the previously unlocked basic ability.

The other mid-tier option should provide an offensive or defensive ability related to the specific form of movement the focus provides, if possible.

Tier 4: Choose a mid-tier ability that is either an offensive or a defensive use of the ability, whichever one wasn't chosen as an option in the previous tier.

Tier 5: Choose a high-tier penultimate use of the environment-manipulation ability. For instance, if the focus-granted manipulation is illusory, this ability might haunt a target with terrifying images. If the focus is gravity based, it might unlock flight. If magnetic, it might allow the user to reshape metal. If the focus grants telekinetic powers, this ability could allow a character to hurl massive objects at foes. And so on.

Tier 6: Choose two high-tier abilities. Give both of them as options for the focus; a PC will choose one or the other.

One of the abilities should provide either an offensive or a defensive ability, opposite the ability provided at tier 4 (though high tier rather than mid tier).

The other option should be something that further explores the use of the basic environment manipulation capability. If the tier 5 choice was the penultimate ability, this might be an even better ultimate ability related to the kind of manipulation offered, or a different way of using that ability to unlock an as-yet-unexplored facet of the ability.

ENVIRONMENT MANIPULATION FOCI

The following are examples and not meant to provide a complete list of all possible foci in this category.
- Awakens Dreams
- Blazes With Radiance
- Calculates the Incalculable
- Controls Gravity
- Crafts Illusions
- Crafts Unique Objects
- Employs Magnetism
- Focuses Mind Over Matter

Stasis, page 186

EXPLORATION FOCI
The following are examples and not meant to provide a complete list of all possible foci in this category.
- Explores Dark Places
- Infiltrates
- Operates Undercover
- Pilots Starcraft
- Sees Beyond
- Separates Mind From Body

Focus connections, page 61

EXPLORATION
Foci that allow a character to gather information, survive in unfamiliar environments, and find their way to new locations or track down particular creatures and foes are exploration foci. Surviving in unfamiliar environments requires a reasonable selection of defensive options; however, abilities that allow a character to find and learn are prioritized.

Exploration foci rely on a variety of methods, though training and expertise are the mainstays. Some methods require specific tools (such as a vehicle) to grant the benefits provided, while others might rely on the supernatural or super-science to learn new things and explore strange places from afar.

Connection: Choose four relevant connections from the Focus Connections list.

Additional Equipment: Any object necessary to explore. For instance, starting maps and/or a compass would be basic equipment, while someone who uses psychic abilities might require a mirror or crystal sphere to gaze into. Equipment might also include access to a vehicle required for exploration, as previously noted.

Minor Effect Suggestions: You have an asset on any action that involves using your senses, such as perceiving or attacking, until the end of the next round.

Major Effect Suggestions: Your Intellect Edge increases by 1 until the end of the next round.

ABILITY SELECTION GUIDELINES
Tier 1: Choose a low-tier ability that grants the character basic exploratory, survival, or information-gathering capabilities within the focus's theme.

Sometimes an additional low-power ability is appropriate, depending on the focus. Often, this is an ability that grants skill training in a related area of knowledge or a related skill (though this may already be covered in the main ability). Alternatively, it might offer a simple bonus of 2 or 3 points to the Might Pool.

Tier 2: Choose another low-tier ability that grants an additional capability related to exploration, survival, or information gathering.

For instance, a focus dedicated to surviving savage conditions might offer an ability (or two) that makes it easier to avoid natural hazards, poisons, difficult terrain, and so on. A focus dedicated to exploration of a particular area might grant abilities to gain access to that area, or a capability that others normally lack (like the ability to see in the dark).

Tier 3: Choose two mid-tier abilities. Give both of them as options for the focus; a PC will choose one or the other.

One option should further improve the basic exploration ability granted, or give a new exploratory, survival, or information-gathering ability.

The other option should be something that benefits the character, either an offensive or defensive ability (especially if this focus hasn't already granted that) or something that further broadens the character's ability to explore in the focus's chosen realm.

Tier 4: Choose a mid-tier offensive or defensive ability (whichever wasn't offered at tier 3) that benefits the character. Alternatively, if offensive and defensive abilities are already well represented, choose a different mid-tier ability that broadens the character's ability to explore, survive, or gather information.

Tier 5: Choose a high-tier ability that alleviates some of the penalties for exploring, surviving, or gathering information in a normally inhospitable place.

Tier 6: Choose two high-tier abilities. Give both of them as options for the focus; a PC will choose one or the other.

One option should further improve the basic exploration-themed ability previously granted, or give a brand-new exploratory, survival, or information-gathering ability.

The other option should be something that benefits the character, either an offensive or defensive ability, or yet another ability that further broadens their capacity to explore in the focus's chosen realm.

INFLUENCE

Foci that prioritize authority and influence—whether that's to make people or machines do as commanded, to help others, or to rise to some other prestigious and significant position—fall within the influence category.

These foci grant influence through training and persuasion, by direct mental manipulation, by using fame to get people's attention and influence their actions, or simply by knowing and learning things that affect later decisions. In this sense, the concept of influence is broad.

Connection: Choose four relevant connections from the Focus Connections list.

Additional Equipment: Any object necessary to achieve the influence suggested should be granted as additional equipment. Some influence foci don't require anything to gain or retain their benefits.

Minor Effect Suggestions: The range or duration of the influencing ability is doubled.

Major Effect Suggestions: An ally or indicated target can take an additional action.

ABILITY SELECTION GUIDELINES

Tier 1: Choose a low-tier ability that allows the character to learn something significant enough that they can choose a smart course of action (or use that knowledge to persuade or intimidate). How the character learns the information varies by the specifics of the focus. One character might do experiments to learn answers, another might open a telepathic link with others to trade information secretly and quickly, and still another might simply be trained in interaction tasks.

Sometimes an additional low-power ability is appropriate, depending on the focus. Often, this is an ability that grants skill training in a related area of knowledge.

Tier 2: Choose a low-tier ability that improves the character's ability to apply influence. This might open an additional front on the focus's basic theme or simply further enhance the basic ability already provided. For instance, this tier 2 ability could ease influence-related tasks by a few steps, allow a telepath to read the minds of others who have secrets they'd otherwise not reveal, or grant influence over physical objects (either to improve them or to learn more about them). And so on.

Tier 3: Choose two mid-tier abilities. Give both of them as options for the focus; a PC will choose one or the other.

One option should provide an offensive or defensive capability related to the focus's specific kind of influence, if possible. For instance, an inventor might create a serum that gives them increased abilities (which could be used for offense or defense), a telepath might have some method of blasting foes with mental energy, and someone with only the basic skills of debate and influence through fame might have to rely on weapon training or their entourage.

The other mid-tier option should provide an additional ability to influence in the theme of the focus, or further improve the basic influence ability previously granted. This option isn't directly offensive or defensive, but provides either an all-new ability related to the basic ability, or increases the strength, range, or some other extension of the previously unlocked basic ability. For instance, a telepath might have a psychic suggestion ability.

Tier 4: Choose a mid-tier ability that is either an offensive or a defensive use of the influence ability, whichever one wasn't chosen as an option in the previous tier.

Alternatively, this ability could grant an additional capability related to the kind of influence the focus provides.

Tier 5: Choose a high-tier penultimate use of the specific influence ability granted at lower tiers.

Alternatively, choose an ability not previously gained at a lower tier, one that opens a new front on the particular influence capability. For instance, if the focus-granted influence is telepathic, the tier 5 ability might allow a character to see into the future to gain assets for dealing with enemies (and allies).

Tier 6: Choose two high-tier abilities. Give both of them as options for the focus; a PC will choose one or the other.

One of the options should provide either an offensive or a defensive ability, opposite the ability provided at tier 4 (though high tier rather than mid tier).

The other option should be something that further explores the use of the basic influence ability provided by the focus. If the tier 5 choice was the penultimate ability, this might be an even better ultimate ability related to the kind of influence used, or a different way of using that ability to unlock an as-yet-unexplored facet of the ability.

> **INFLUENCE FOCI**
> The following are examples and not meant to provide a complete list of all possible foci in this category.
> - Commands Mental Powers
> - Conducts Weird Science
> - Fuses Mind and Machine
> - Is Idolized by Millions
> - Solves Mysteries
> - Talks to Machines
> - Works the System

IRREGULAR FOCI

The following are examples and not meant to provide a complete list of all possible foci in this category.

- Channels Divine Blessings
- Descends From Nobility
- Emerged From the Obelisk
- Flies Faster Than a Bullet
- Masters Spells
- Speaks for the Land

Power shifts, page 292
Spellcasting, page 259

Focus connections, page 61

IRREGULAR

Most foci have a basic theme, a "character story" that logically leads to a series of related abilities. However, certain foci themes are so wide that they don't fit into any other category except an irregular one of their own.

Irregular foci provide a basket of disparate abilities. Usually that's because the overarching theme is one that demands variability and access to several different kinds of abilities. Often, these foci are found in genres that suggest additional rule tweaks to leverage their use even further, such as power shifts in the superhero genre and spellcasting in the fantasy genre. However, other irregular foci are possible.

Connection: Choose four relevant connections from the Focus Connections list.

Additional Equipment: Any object necessary to the focus's theme. For instance, a superhero-themed focus might grant a superhero costume.

Minor Effect Suggestions: The target is also dazed for one round, during which time all of its tasks are hindered.

Major Effect Suggestions: The target is stunned and loses its next turn.

ABILITY SELECTION GUIDELINES

Tier 1: Choose a low-tier ability that grants one of the benefits the focus theme promises, one that a first-tier character should have.

Sometimes an additional low-power ability is appropriate, depending on the focus. Often, this is an ability that grants skill training in a related area of knowledge or a related skill. Alternatively, it might offer a simple bonus of 2 or 3 points to a Pool.

Tier 2: Choose a low-tier ability that grants one of the benefits the focus theme promises, one that's presumably not immediately related to the one provided at tier 1. That said, if a defense wasn't provided at tier 1, tier 2 is a good place to add it.

Tier 3: Choose two mid-tier abilities. Give both of them as options for the focus; a PC will choose one or the other.

One option should provide one of the benefits the focus theme promises, one that may not be immediately related to those provided at earlier tiers.

The other option should include a method of attack if none has previously been granted. Alternatively, if the lower-tier abilities don't quite get the character where they need to be, this option might further increase a capability unlocked at a lower tier.

Tier 4: Choose a mid-tier ability that grants one of the benefits the focus theme promises, one that may not be immediately related to those provided at earlier tiers.

Tier 5: Choose a high-tier ability that grants one of the benefits the focus theme promises, one that may not be immediately related to those provided at earlier tiers.

Tier 6: Choose two high-tier abilities. Give both of them as options for the focus; a PC will choose one or the other.

One option should grant one of the benefits the focus theme promises, one that may not be immediately related to those provided at earlier tiers. However, this ability might also provide an ultimate version of a lower-tier ability if a mid-tier or low-tier option wasn't quite sufficient.

The other option should provide an alternate method to round out the character in a way that doesn't replicate the first tier 6 option. For instance, if the first option provided some kind of attack, this one might be an interaction, information-gathering, or healing ability, depending on the focus's overarching theme.

MOVEMENT EXPERTISE

Foci that prioritize novel forms of movement—in order to excel in combat, escape situations most others can't, move with stealth for purposes of theft or escape, or move into locations normally inaccessible—fall within the movement expertise category. These foci usually have methods of granting either offense or defense through movement, though they may provide some means of doing both.

The classic movement expertise focus is one that relies on speed to make more attacks and avoid being hit, though general agility might also provide the same benefit. Other foci in this category might fall within the theme by granting a character the ability to become immaterial, to change their form into something like water or air, or to instantly move via teleportation.

Connection: Choose four relevant connections from the Focus Connections list.

Additional Equipment: Any object necessary to achieve great speeds, change state, or otherwise gain the benefit of the focus should be granted as additional equipment. Some foci in this category don't require anything to gain or retain their benefits.

Minor Effect Suggestions: The target is dazed, and their next action is hindered.

Major Effect Suggestions: The target is stunned and loses their next action.

ABILITY SELECTION GUIDELINES

Tier 1: Choose a low-tier ability that grants the basic benefit of the specific movement style, whether that's enhanced speed, agility, immateriality, and so on.

Sometimes an additional low-power ability is appropriate, depending on the focus. If the basic benefit of the movement demands some kind of additional understanding or training, this ability could be that. Alternatively, if the movement provided seems like it should also unlock a basic offensive or defensive benefit (relying on the use of the initial basic ability), append it as well.

Tier 2: Choose a low-tier ability that provides a new offensive or defensive capability related to the focus's theme.

Alternatively, this ability might provide some additional capability related to the form of movement that grants useful information to the character that would normally be inaccessible to someone without the focus.

Tier 3: Choose two mid-tier abilities. Give both of them as options for the focus; a PC will choose one or the other.

One option should provide an additional movement capacity or further improve the basic movement capacity, related to the focus's theme. This isn't directly offensive or defensive, but provides the character with a new level of ability or an all-new ability related to their basic movement ability.

The other option should provide either an offensive or a defensive capability related to the specific form of movement the focus provides.

Tier 4: Choose a mid-tier ability that further enhances the advantages provided by focus's movement-enhancing paradigm. This could provide a new or better form of defense (directly, or indirectly if moving to a location or time where danger doesn't threaten), or a new or better form of offense.

Tier 5: Choose a high-tier penultimate use of the movement-related ability. For instance, if the focus-provided movement is temporal, this ability might allow actual (if brief) jaunts of time travel. If the focus enhances speed, this ability might allow the character to move up to a very long distance with one action. And so on.

Alternatively, unlock an as-yet-unexplored related ability that could derive from the basic movement power provided by the focus.

Tier 6: Choose two high-tier abilities. Give both of them as options for the focus; a PC will choose one or the other.

One of the options should provide either an offensive or a defensive ability, opposite the ability provided at tier 4 (though high tier rather than mid tier).

The other option should be something that further explores the use of the basic movement ability. If the tier 5 choice was the penultimate ability, this might be an even better ultimate ability related to the movement.

> ### MOVEMENT EXPERTISE FOCI
> The following are examples and not meant to provide a complete list of all possible foci in this category.
> - Exists Partially Out of Phase
> - Moves Like a Cat
> - Moves Like the Wind
> - Runs Away
> - Shreds the Walls of the World
> - Travels Through Time
> - Works the Back Alleys

STRIKER COMBAT FOCI

The following are examples and not meant to provide a complete list of all possible foci in this category.

- Battles Robots
- Fights Dirty
- Fights With Panache
- Hunts
- Is Licensed to Carry
- Looks for Trouble
- Masters Weaponry
- Murders
- Needs No Weapon
- Performs Feats of Strength
- Rages
- Slays Monsters
- Throws With Deadly Accuracy
- Wields Two Weapons at Once

Focus connections, page 61

STRIKER COMBAT

Striker combat foci prioritize dealing damage in battle over other concerns. Foci in this category offer defensive abilities as well, but they emphasize abilities that provide ways to spike damage to heights that other foci normally don't reach.

To achieve this end, a striker combat focus might offer mastery of a particular style of martial combat, which could be training with a particular weapon or martial art, or the use of a unique tool (or even a kind of energy). A style might be something as singular as being the best at fighting a particular kind of enemy, or something much broader, such as adopting a particularly vicious or unsporting style. A striker combatant might use fire, force, or magnetism as their preferred method of spiking damage.

Connection: Choose four relevant connections from the Focus Connections list.

Additional Equipment: The weapon, tool, or other special item or substance (if any) required to engage in the particular style of combat. For instance, a dose of level 5 poison for Fights Dirty or Murders, a trophy from a previously defeated foe for Battles Robots, or stylish clothes for Fights With Panache.

Minor Effect Suggestions: The target is so dazzled by your expertise that it is dazed for one round, hindering all of its tasks.

Major Effect Suggestions: Make an immediate additional attack using an attack provided by the focus as part of your turn.

ABILITY SELECTION GUIDELINES

Tier 1: Choose a low-tier ability that inflicts additional damage when a character attacks using the focus's particular fighting style, energy, or attitude, or when used against a chosen enemy.

Sometimes an additional low-power ability is appropriate, depending on the focus. For instance, a focus that grants proficiency in a special weapon might offer training in crafting tasks associated with that weapon. A focus that grants increased damage against a particular kind of foe might offer training in skills to recognize, locate, or just have general knowledge about that foe. A fighting style that involves fighting in a vicious or dirty manner might provide training in intimidation. And so on.

If the focus is about fighting a particular enemy, additional secondary powers (more than might otherwise be offered) may be appropriate. Those either further enhance effectiveness against the chosen enemy, or offer broader but related abilities that give the character who takes the focus some functionality even when not fighting that enemy.

Tier 2: Choose a low-tier ability that provides some form of defense using the weapon, weapon style, or chosen energy. If the weapon style is being especially good at fighting a certain kind of foe, the ability should be a defense against that kind of foe. Alternatively, the focus might offer another method for increasing damage within the chosen paradigm.

Sometimes an additional low-power ability is appropriate at tier 2. If so, choose whichever low-power ability wasn't gained at tier 1.

Tier 3: Choose two mid-tier abilities. Give both of them as options for the focus; a PC will choose one or the other.

One option should inflict additional damage when using the focus's fighting style, energy, or attitude, or when used against a chosen enemy. That could be as simple as an ability that offers an additional attack of that kind.

The other option should provide a method to temporarily neutralize a foe by disarming them, dazing or stunning them, slowing or holding them, or otherwise discombobulating them by using the focus's fighting style, energy, or attitude, or when used against a chosen enemy.

Tier 4: Choose a mid-tier ability that further enhances the advantages provided by the focus's paradigm. Often, this includes training in a particular kind of attack. Alternatively, the ability might increase the advantages provided by achieving a certain combat status, such as gaining surprise.

Tier 5: Choose a high-tier ability that inflicts damage. Alternatively, if focused on fighting a particular kind of foe, this ability might give the character a chance to completely neutralize, destroy, blind, or kill a singular target of up to level 3 (or higher, if the focus is on a singular foe).

Tier 6: Choose two high-tier abilities. Give both of them as options for the focus; a PC will choose one or the other.

One of the options should use the focus paradigm to inflict an exceptional amount of damage.

The other option could be a different way of inflicting damage, either using the focus paradigm or just dealing lots of damage in general (and relying on previous focus tier abilities to improve targeting). This could be against multiple targets if the first option was for a single target, to outright kill or neutralize a target (starting with level 4, but with guidance for using Effort to increase the level of the target), or to select yet another foe, make another attack, or get away in order to fight another day.

CYPHER SYSTEM

> **SUPPORT FOCI**
> The following are examples and not meant to provide a complete list of all possible foci in this category.
> - Defends the Weak
> - Entertains
> - Helps Their Friends
> - Metes Out Justice
> - Shepherds the Community
> - Siphons Power
> - Works Miracles

Metes Out Justice straddles the line between a support focus and a striker combat focus, depending on the ability options a PC chooses at tiers 3 and 6.

Focus connections, page 61

Draw an attack, page 227

SUPPORT

Foci that allow a character to help others succeed, defend others, heal others who are hurt, and so on are support foci. Of course, most foci abilities are often used in aid of others, but support foci (such as Siphons Power) prioritize aiding, healing, and improving the character who takes the focus.

Support foci rely on a variety of methods to provide their help, including martial training used in defense, supernatural or sci-fi means of providing healing, or simply easing the cares of others through entertainment.

Connection: Choose four relevant connections from the Focus Connections list.

Additional Equipment: Any object necessary to provide support. For instance, someone with a focus that uses entertainment to help others would require an instrument or similar object in aid of their craft. Some foci in this category don't require anything to gain or retain their benefits.

Minor Effect Suggestions: You can draw an attack without having to use an action at any point before the end of the next round.

Major Effect Suggestions: You can take an extra action in aid of an ally.

ABILITY SELECTION GUIDELINES

Tier 1: Choose a low-tier ability that provides some form of defense, aid or entertainment, benefit to recovery or healing, or protection. That defense or protection could be to the PC and not to an ally, as one cannot protect another without first being able to protect themselves (and sometimes protecting themselves is the entire point).

Sometimes an additional low-power ability is appropriate, depending on the focus. Often, this is an ability that grants skill training in a related area of knowledge or a related skill, but it might be something that works with the initial ability that, by itself, wouldn't do much.

Tier 2: Choose a low-tier ability that follows up on the support style opened in the previous tier. If the previous tier's ability provided a means of protection only for the focus taker, this tier 2 ability should specifically provide aid to another. If the previous tier specifically provided aid to another, this tier 2 ability could defend the focus taker or provide an offensive capability grounded, if possible, in the focus's theme.

Tier 3: Choose two mid-tier abilities. Give both of them as options for the focus; a PC will choose one or the other.

One option should work within the focus's theme to aid, heal, protect, or otherwise help another.

The other option should be something that benefits the character, either an offensive or defensive ability, or something that broadens their expertise in some fashion. Alternatively, it could be another, different method of helping someone else.

Tier 4: Choose a mid-tier ability that gives an ally a direct boon or provides the character with a way to help another. It could also be an ability that harms or nullifies a foe, as removing foes certainly helps allies.

Tier 5: Choose a high-tier ability that provides an offensive or defensive option for the character, if none have been provided yet. If this need has been previously addressed or is deemed unnecessary, choose a high-tier ability that provides some form of defense, aid or entertainment, benefit to recovery or healing, or protection to another. For example, a tier 5 ability might grant an ally an additional free action or allow them to repeat a failed action.

Tier 6: Choose two high-tier abilities. Give both of them as options for the focus; a PC will choose one or the other.

One of the options should provide an ultimate method of helping another in the theme of the focus.

The other option could provide an alternative ultimate method of helping another; many foci in this category do. However, an option that provides high-tier offense or defense is also completely reasonable.

TANK COMBAT

Foci that prioritize being able to take a lot of punishment and soak up excess damage from foes fall within the tank combat category. These foci provide offensive abilities too, as well as additional abilities related to the particular method by which improved protection is achieved, but defensive abilities are most pronounced.

Some tank combat foci involve a physical transformation that grants additional protection, and others rely on specialized training, use tools like shields or heavy armor, or provide the ability to heal incredibly fast. The kinds of physical transformation that a tank focus provides, if any, vary widely. A focus might turn a character's skin to stone, reinforce their body with metal, turn them into a monstrous being, make them so big it becomes harder to hurt them, and so on.

Connection: Choose four relevant connections from the Focus Connections list.

Additional Equipment: Any object necessary to maintain a physical transformation (such as a tool for repair if partly robotic, a shield or other defensive tool used if skilled, or possibly some kind of amulet or serum). Some tank combat foci don't require anything to gain or retain their benefits.

Minor Effect Suggestions: +2 to Armor for a few rounds.

Major Effect Suggestions: Regain 2 points to Might Pool.

ABILITY SELECTION GUIDELINES

Tier 1: Choose a low-tier ability that provides defense within the focus's theme. If the theme is simply intense training or the use of a defensive tool, the ability might be as simple as a bonus to Armor. If protection comes from physical transformation, this ability provides the base form effects, benefits, and in some cases drawbacks for making the transformation. A low-tier enhanced healing ability would also be appropriate at first tier.

Sometimes an additional low-power ability is appropriate, depending on the focus. If the character transforms, this ability may provide a knock-on effect, though in the case of some transformations, it might be a description of how someone with an abnormal physiognomy can fully heal. Other times, the secondary power may simply be training in a related skill, or it may unlock the ability to use a particular armor or shield without penalty.

Tier 2: If the theme of the focus isn't physical transformation, choose a low-tier ability that provides an additional method of defending, healing damage, or avoiding attacks.

If the theme of the focus is physical transformation, choose a low-tier ability that unlocks a new capability related to the form the character takes. That might mean gaining better control of the transformation, unlocking a robotic interface, or otherwise more fully unlocking that form. This ability is not necessarily defensive, though it could be.

Tier 3: Choose two mid-tier abilities. Give both of them as options for the focus; a PC will choose one or the other.

One option should provide an additional form of protection in keeping with the focus's theme, such as more defensive capabilities unlocked from a transformation (which might also come with additional offensive capabilities) or a simple physical enhancement if defense is gained by skills or enhanced healing.

The other option should provide an offensive capability, especially if creating a non-transformation focus that doesn't already have offensive benefits. That capability could be an enhanced attack or provide some other benefit useful in combat, such as quickly evading or (on the other end of the continuum) becoming immovable.

Tier 4: Choose a mid-tier ability that further enhances the advantages provided by the focus's damage-soaking paradigm. Often, this includes training in a particular kind of defense. Alternatively, it might increase the advantages provided by previously unlocked defensive abilities, whether that means gaining greater control over a transformation, gaining additional chances to avoid damage or retry tasks related to enhanced determination, and so on. If the focus is lacking in offensive options, this is a good place to include one.

Tier 5: Choose a high-tier ability that provides protection, possibly in the form of shrugging off a debilitating condition (including death). If the focus offers a physical transformation, this ability might further unlock an additional related ability, whether offensive, defensive, or something related to exploration or interaction (such as flight if the form is winged, intimidation if the form is fearsome, and so on).

TANK COMBAT FOCI
The following are examples and not meant to provide a complete list of all possible foci in this category.
- Abides in Stone
- Brandishes an Exotic Shield
- Defends the Gate
- Fuses Flesh and Steel
- Grows to Towering Heights
- Howls at the Moon
- Lives in the Wilderness
- Masters Defense
- Never Says Die
- Stands Like a Bastion

Tier 6: Choose two high-tier abilities. Give both of them as options for the focus; a PC will choose one or the other.

One option should use the focus paradigm to increase the defense, protection, or ability to shrug off damage.

The other option could be a different way of being defensive. In some cases, the best defense is a good offense, so this option could provide a high-tier offensive ability in keeping with the focus's theme, whether that's a straight-up damage boost on attacks or better control of an unstable physical transformation.

CUSTOMIZING FOCI

Sometimes not everything about a focus is right for a character's concept, or perhaps the GM needs additional guidelines for creating a new focus. Either way, the solution lies in looking at foci abilities at their most basic default levels.

At any tier, a player can select one of the following abilities in place of the ability granted by the tier. Many of these replacement abilities, particularly at the higher tiers, might involve body modification, integration with high-tech devices, learning powerful magic spells, uncovering forbidden secrets, or something similar appropriate to the genre.

TIER 1
- Combat Prowess (120)
- Enhanced Potential (135)

TIER 2
- Lower-tier ability: choose any tier 1 replacement ability, above.
- Skill With Defense (183)
- Practiced With All Weapons (171)
- Skill With Attacks (183)

TIER 3
- Lower-tier ability: choose any tier 1 or 2 replacement ability, above.
- Incredible Health (153)
- Fusion Armor (144)

TIER 4
- Lower-tier ability: choose any tier 1, 2, or 3 replacement ability, above.
- Poison Resistance (170)
- Built-in Weaponry (116)

TIER 5
- Lower-tier ability: choose any tier 1, 2, 3, or 4 replacement ability, above.
- Adaptation (108)
- Defensive Field (127)

TIER 6
- Lower-tier ability: choose any tier 1, 2, 3, 4, or 5 replacement ability, above.
- Reactive Field (174)

Chapter 9
ABILITIES

This chapter presents a vast catalog of more than a thousand abilities a character can gain from their type, flavor (if any), and focus. They are sorted alphabetically by the ability's name.

A character's type, flavor, and focus assign an appropriate tier to each ability. However, if you're creating a brand-new focus or type, we provide a couple of additional tools.

The first is a power grade for each ability, which tells you about how potent it is in relation to other abilities. Abilities appropriate for tiers 1 and 2 characters are called "low-tier" abilities. Abilities appropriate for tiers 3 and 4 are called "mid-tier" abilities. Abilities appropriate for tiers 5 and 6 are called "high-tier" abilities.

These abilities are further sorted into ability categories based on the kinds of things they do—abilities that improve physical attacks are in the attack skill category, abilities that assist allies are in the support category, and so on.

ABILITY CATEGORIES AND RELATIVE POWER

Abilities can be divided into several categories based on the kinds of things they do—improve your physical attacks, assist allies, provide defense, give you a special attack form, and so on. Under each of the following category descriptions is a list of abilities that fit that category, sorted into low-, medium-, and high-tier abilities.

The categories are mainly used by GMs when designing new foci for a campaign, allowing them to search a short list of abilities instead of trying to find something appropriate among the thousand or so abilities in this chapter. For example, the GM might have a custom focus in their campaign called "Is Born of the Swamp" and want a defensive ability for tier 5, so they can look at the high-tier abilities in the protection category and quickly narrow down what options are available.

It may be possible that a character gains the same ability from more than one source (such as from their type and their descriptor). Unless the two abilities are obviously additive (such as two abilities that each add 3 points to your Might Pool, which together would give the character +6 Might points), the duplicated ability might be improved in some way, such as having a longer duration or greater effect, or automatically providing an asset. Some abilities give suggestions on how to do this; otherwise, the player and the GM should work out whether and how the ability is improved.

Players may find it useful to note on their character sheets the page numbers where their ability descriptions are found.

The ability categories are not intended to be rigid or comprehensive. Some abilities fall into more than one category, and it could be argued that some abilities could be included in more categories than are listed here.

These categories have some overlap with the focus categories in chapter 8. For example, there is a support category here and a support category in the Focus chapter. They aren't intended to be exact parallels and they don't mean exactly the same thing. That said, if you're creating a support-centric focus, many of the abilities in the support ability category would be appropriate choices.

Focus categories, page 82

Follower, page 233

ATTACK SKILL

Gives you training or specialization in a specific physical attack (like swords or unarmed combat), a category of physical attacks (light bladed, heavy bashing, and so on), or another physical skill primarily used to inflict harm (such as breaking objects).

LOW TIER:
- Heads-Up Display (148)
- Practiced With Guns (171)
- Practiced With Medium Weapons (171)
- Practiced With Swords (171)
- Quarry (173)
- Unarmed Fighting Style (194)

MID TIER:
- Blood Fever (115)
- Cognizant Offense (119)
- Greater Skill With Defense (147)
- Practiced With All Weapons (171)
- Robot Fighter (178)
- Serv-0 Aim (181)
- Serv-0 Brawler (181)
- Skill With Attacks (183)
- Sniper's Aim (184)
- Specialized Throwing (185)

HIGH TIER:
- As Foretold in Prophecy (110)
- Duel to the Death (132)
- Greater Skill With Attacks (147)
- Hunter's Drive (149)
- Master of Unarmed Fighting Style (160)
- Mastery With Attacks (161)
- Specialized Basher (185)

COMPANION

Gives you a follower, modifies a follower, or gives you an additional benefit when interacting with or near your follower. This category includes humanoid followers, beast companions, and temporary companions like summoned swarms, conjured spirits, and so on.

LOW TIER:
- Basic Follower (112)
- Beast Companion (112)
- Bound Magic Creature (115)
- Control Swarm (122)
- Critter Companion (123)
- Duplicate (132)
- Entourage (136)
- Influence Swarm (153)
- Necromancy (165)
- Resilient Duplicate (176)
- Robot Assistant (178)
- Serv-0 (181)
- Spirit Accomplice (185)

MID TIER:
- Beast Eyes (112)
- Call Swarm (118)
- Expert Follower (137)
- Fellow Explorer (139)
- Fiery Hand of Doom (139)
- Gain Unusual Companion (144)
- Greater Necromancy (147)
- Improved Object Bond (152)
- Living Armor (158)
- Machine Companion (159)
- Mount (164)
- Retinue (177)
- Shipspeak (183)
- Stronger Together (187)
- Summon Giant Spider (188)
- Superior Duplicate (188)
- Time Doppelganger (191)
- Time Loop (192)

HIGH TIER:
- As If One Creature (110)
- Band of Desperados (112)
- Band of Followers (112)
- Beast Call (112)
- Call Dead Spirit (117)
- Call in Favor (117)
- Call Otherworldly Spirit (117)
- Call Through Time (118)
- Conjuration (121)
- Deadly Swarm (125)
- Dragon's Maw (131)
- Fire Servant (140)
- Improved Apportation (151)
- Improved Companion (151)
- Improved Machine Companion (152)
- Insect Eruption (154)
- Legal Intern (157)
- Masterful Armor Modification (160)
- Multiplicity (165)
- Object Bond Mastery (167)
- Recruit Deputy (175)
- Robot Fleet (179)
- Summon Demon (188)
- Time Doppelganger (191)
- True Necromancy (194)

ABILITIES

CONTROL

Controls or influences minds in ways outside of what could be done with conventional intimidation and persuasion, such as using psychic mind control, fear gas, and so on.

LOW TIER:
- Calm Stranger (118)
- Charm Machine (119)
- Cloud Personal Memories (119)
- Community Activist (121)
- Fast Talk (138)
- Goad (145)
- Hack the Impossible (147)
- Robot Control (178)
- Soothe the Savage (184)
- Terrifying Presence (190)

MID TIER:
- Calm (118)
- Captivate or Inspire (118)
- Captivate With Starshine (118)
- Command (120)
- Command Machine (120)
- Command Spirit (121)
- Crowd Control (123)
- Daydream (124)
- Grand Deception (146)
- Interruption (155)
- Mind Control (162)
- Psychic Suggestion (172)

HIGH TIER:
- Advanced Command (108)
- Assume Control (111)
- Brainwashing (116)
- Change the Paradigm (119)
- Control Machine (121)
- Control the Savage (122)
- Defuse Situation (127)
- Flee (141)
- Psychic Passenger (172)
- Show Them the Way (183)
- Suggestion (188)
- Word of Command (199)

The small numbers you see after abilities throughout this book are page numbers for easy reference.

CRAFT

Creates useful physical things, such as mundane tools (hammers, crowbars), limited-use devices (manifest cyphers, artifacts), or independent beings (robots, elementals, zombies). Includes blueprints, plans, and effects that aid or speed crafting.

LOW TIER:
- Create Deadly Poison (123)
- Fortification Builder (143)
- Junkmonger (156)
- Machine Efficiency (159)
- Modify Device (164)
- Natural Crafter (165)
- Quick Work (174)
- Robot Builder (178)
- Trapster (193)
- Weapon Crafter (197)

MID TIER:
- Dream Becomes Reality (132)
- Expert Crafter (137)
- Ice Creation (150)
- Poison Crafter (170)
- Robot Upgrade (179)
- Sculpt Light (180)

HIGH TIER:
- Create (122)
- Dark Matter Structure (124)
- Improved Sculpt Light (152)
- Innovator (154)
- Jury-Rig (156)
- Modify Artifact Power (163)
- Reshape (176)

CURE

Cures damage, adds or improves recovery rolls, or negates, cures, suspends, or otherwise gives immunity to a harmful effect or condition, such as poison, disease, mental attacks, moving down on the damage track, or dying.

LOW TIER:

- Alleviate (109)
- Crystalline Body (123)
- Destined for Greatness (127)
- Diver (130)
- Drain Creature (131)
- Drain Machine (131)
- Endurance (134)
- Escape (136)
- Extra Recovery (138)
- Foil Danger (142)
- Healing Touch (149)
- Ignore the Pain (150)
- Improved Recovery (152)
- Living Off the Land (158)
- Push on Through (173)
- Quick Recovery (173)
- Repair Flesh (176)
- Restful Presence (177)
- Speedy Recovery (185)
- Surging Confidence (188)
- Totally Chill (192)
- Water Adaptation (196)
- Will of Legend (199)

MID TIER:

- Aquatic Combatant (110)
- Biomorphic Healing (113)
- Damage Transference (124)
- Drain Charge (131)
- Fight On (139)
- Font of Healing (142)
- Healing Pulse (148)
- Ignore Affliction (150)
- Immovable (150)
- Incredible Health (153)
- Miraculous Health (163)
- Noble's Courage (166)
- One With the Wild (167)
- Poison Resistance (170)
- Preternatural Senses (171)
- Regeneration (175)
- Store Energy (186)
- Thinking Ahead (191)
- Tough As Nails (192)
- Unmovable (195)
- Unraveling Consumption (195)
- Wilderness Encouragement (198)
- Willing Sacrifice (199)

HIGH TIER:

- Deep Reserves (126)
- Final Defiance (139)
- Free to Move (143)
- Gamer's Fortitude (144)
- Gaming God (144)
- Greater Healing Touch (147)
- Incredible Recovery (153)
- Infuse Spirit (153)
- Inspiration (154)
- Inspire the Innocent (154)
- Mind Surge (162)
- Negate Danger (165)
- Not Dead Yet (166)
- Rapid Recovery (174)
- Regenerate (175)
- Restore Life (177)
- Resuscitate (177)
- Share the Power (182)
- Stay the Course (186)
- Trick Driver (194)
- Vigilant (196)

The small numbers you see after abilities throughout this book are page numbers for easy reference.

ABILITIES

ENVIRONMENT

Manipulates the environment or things in the environment, such as with telekinesis, weather control, gravity control, illusions, and so on.

LOW TIER:
- Create Water (123)
- Dreamcraft (132)
- Fetch (139)
- Grasping Foliage (146)
- Hedge Magic (149)
- Hidden Closet (149)
- Illuminating Touch (150)
- Illusory Duplicate (150)
- Impetus (151)
- Legerdemain (157)
- Lock (159)
- Minor Illusion (162)
- Move Metal (164)
- Slip Into Shadow (183)
- Telekinesis (189)
- Wilderness Explorer (199)

MID TIER:
- Daydream (124)
- Define Down (127)
- Field of Gravity (139)
- Force Field Barrier (143)
- Force to Reckon With (143)
- Illusory Selves (150)
- Living Wall (158)
- Major Illusion (160)
- Nullify Sound (166)
- Projection (172)
- Storm Seed (187)
- Sunlight (188)

HIGH TIER:
- Adaptation (108)
- Control Weather (122)
- Diamagnetism (128)
- Force Wall (143)
- Generate Force Field (145)
- Grandiose Illusion (146)
- Granite Wall (146)
- Inferno Trail (153)
- Move Mountains (164)
- Permanent Illusion (169)
- Relocate (176)
- Terrifying Image (190)
- Wall of Lightning (196)
- The Wild Is on Your Side (198)

INFORMATION

Gives the ability to learn information about something, whether chosen by the GM like Scan, by asking a question and the GM giving the answer, or by learning a language.

LOW TIER:
- Babel (112)
- Communication (121)
- Community Knowledge (121)
- Decipher (126)
- Dream Thief (132)
- Eye for Detail (138)
- Gather Intelligence (144)
- Lab Analysis (157)
- Mind Reading (162)
- Monster Lore (164)
- Network Tap (165)
- Predictive Model (171)
- Premonition (171)
- Question the Spirits (173)
- Retrieve Memories (177)
- Salvage and Comfort (179)
- Scan (179)
- See History (180)
- Speaker for the Dead (184)
- Telepathic (189)

MID TIER:
- Creature Insight (123)
- Device Insight (128)
- Draw Conclusion (131)
- Find the Hidden (140)
- Got a Feeling (145)
- Know Their Faults (156)
- Machine Telepathy (159)
- Mechanical Telepathy (161)
- Reading the Room (175)
- Sensor Array (181)
- Serv-0 Scanner (181)
- Soul Interrogation (184)
- Spot Weakness (185)
- Wilderness Awareness (198)

HIGH TIER:
- Deep Consideration (126)
- Drawing on Life's Experiences (131)
- Information Gathering (153)
- Knowing the Unknown (156)
- Mind of a Leader (162)
- Read the Signs (174)
- Telepathic Network (190)

META

Modifies an existing ability or character trait's effects or parameters, such as increasing range or, damage, easing the difficulty, giving you additional noncombat actions each turn, rerolling a failed attempt, or treating a number on the die as something different than normal.

LOW TIER:

- A Smile and a Word (108)
- Arcane Flare (110)
- Artifact Tinkerer (110)
- Augment Cypher (111)
- Careful Shot (118)
- Charge (119)
- Coaxing Power (119)
- Combat Prowess (120)
- Crushing Blow (123)
- Crystalline Body (123)
- Curious (123)
- Distant Interface (130)
- Double Strike (131)
- Drain Creature (131)
- Driving on the Edge (132)
- Elusive (133)
- Energize Object (134)
- Enhanced Body (134)
- Extra Use (138)
- Find the Way (140)
- Fists of Fury (140)
- Fleet of Foot (141)
- Frenzy (143)
- Golem Body (145)
- Gunner (147)
- Hacker (147)
- Hold Breath (149)
- Improved Designation (151)
- Investigator (155)
- Lead From the Front (157)
- Machine Efficiency (159)
- Mind for Might (162)
- Modify Device (164)
- Monster Bane (164)
- Natural Crafter (165)
- No Need for Weapons (166)
- Object Bond (167)
- Overload Machine (168)
- Precision (171)
- Quick Death (173)
- Quick Work (174)
- Range Increase (174)
- Reload (176)
- Something in the Road (184)
- Tinker (192)
- Weapon Master (197)
- Wreck (200)

MID TIER:

- Amazing Effort (109)
- Betrayal (113)
- Better Living Through Chemistry (113)
- Capable Warrior (118)
- Cast Illusion (118)
- Cyphersmith (124)
- Deadly Aim (125)
- Deep Resources (126)
- Disarming Strike (129)
- Dodge and Resist (131)
- Drain at a Distance (131)
- Energized Shield (134)
- Enhanced Intellect (135)
- Enhanced Intellect Edge (135)
- Enhanced Might (135)
- Enhanced Might Edge (135)
- Enhanced Physique (135)
- Enhanced Potential (135)
- Enhanced Speed (135)
- Enhanced Speed Edge (135)
- Experienced in Armor (136)
- Expert Cypher Use (137)
- Expert Skill (137)
- Fast Kill (138)
- Flameblade (140)
- From the Shadows (144)
- Fury (144)
- Fusion (144)
- Greater Beast Form (146)
- Greater Designation (146)
- Greater Enhanced Intellect (146)
- Greater Enhanced Might (146)
- Greater Enhanced Physique (146)
- Greater Enhanced Potential (146)
- Greater Enhanced Speed (146)
- Greater Frenzy (146)
- Guide Bolt (147)
- Guild Training (147)
- Heroic Monster Bane (149)
- Hidden Reserves (149)
- Huge (149)
- Immovable (150)
- Improved Absorb Kinetic Energy (151)
- Improved Edge (151)
- Improved Monster Bane (152)
- Improved Sensor (152)
- Incomparable Pilot (152)
- Increased Effects (153)
- Iron Fist (155)
- Know Where to Look (156)
- Lunge (159)
- Machine Bond (159)
- Machine Vulnerabilities (159)
- Minor Wish (162)
- Never Fumble (165)
- One With the Wild (167)
- Outlast the Foe (167)
- Outwit (168)
- Overcharge Energy (168)
- Perfect Stranger (169)
- Precise Cut (171)
- Punish the Guilty (173)
- Push Off and Throw (173)
- Quick Wits (174)
- Rapid Processing (174)
- Resilient Ice Armor (176)
- Roaming Third Eye (178)
- Robot Improvement (179)
- Seize the Moment (181)
- Shepherd's Fury (182)
- Slippery Customer (183)
- Space Fighting (184)
- Speed Burst (185)
- Stone Breaker (186)
- Store Energy (186)
- Strategize (187)
- Think Your Way Out (191)
- Tower of Will (193)
- Trust to Luck (194)
- Uncanny Luck (194)
- Wall With Teeth (196)
- Weaponization (197)
- Willing Sacrifice (199)
- Wrest From Chance (200)

ABILITIES

HIGH TIER:
- Adroit Cypher Use (108)
- Again and Again (109)
- Agile Wit (109)
- All-Out Con (109)
- Artifact Scavenger (110)
- Blurring Speed (115)
- Burst of Escape (116)
- Charging Horde (119)
- Coordinated Effort (122)
- Damage Dealer (124)
- Damn the Guilty (124)
- Deep Reserves (126)
- Disarming Attack (129)
- Discipline of Watchfulness (129)
- Divide Your Mind (130)
- Dual Distraction (132)
- Duel to the Death (132)
- Effective Skill (133)
- Enhanced Beast Form (134)
- Enhanced Phased Attack (135)
- Escape Plan (136)
- Extreme Mastery (138)
- Force and Accuracy (142)
- Gambler (144)
- Go to Ground (145)
- Hard to Kill (148)
- Horde Tactics (149)
- Impart Understanding (151)
- Improved Command Spirit (151)
- Improved Gravity Cleave (151)
- Improved Machine Companion (152)
- Improved Success (152)
- Inventor (155)
- Lethal Damage (158)
- Machine Enhancement (159)
- Maneuvering Adept (160)
- Master Cypher Use (160)
- Master Machine (160)
- Masterful Armor Modification (160)
- Moderate Wish (163)
- Modify Artifact Power (163)
- Multiple Quarry (164)
- Multiplicity (165)
- Overcharge Device (168)
- Perfect Control (169)
- Perfect Speed Burst (169)
- Physically Gifted (170)
- Recycled Cyphers (175)
- Reinforcing Field (175)
- Resonant Frequency (177)
- Robot Evolution (178)
- Seize the Initiative (181)
- Shield Burst (182)
- Shred Existence (183)
- Subtle Tricks (187)
- Thief's Luck (191)
- Trick Driver (194)
- Twist of Fate (194)
- Two Things at Once (194)
- Ultra Enhancement (194)
- Using What's Available (195)
- Usurp Cypher (195)
- Weightless Shot (197)
- Weird Science Breakthrough (197)
- Wild Vitality (198)
- Winter Gauntlets (199)

The small numbers you see after abilities throughout this book are page numbers for easy reference.

MOVEMENT

Increases your movement (such as increasing your basic movement speed from short to long) or adds a new type of movement (such as flight, wallcrawling, phasing, or teleporting).

LOW TIER:
- Bolt Rider (115)
- Contortionist (121)
- Danger Instinct (124)
- Far Step (138)
- Get Away (145)
- Hover (149)
- Phase Sprint (170)
- Void Wings (196)
- Walk Through Walls (196)

MID TIER:
- Apportation (110)
- Blink of an Eye (115)
- Bypass Barrier (116)
- Controlled Fall (122)
- Ghost (145)
- Mobile Fighter (163)
- Obstacle Running (167)
- Phase Door (170)
- Runner (179)
- Swim (188)
- Temporal Dislocation (190)
- Up to Speed (195)
- Windrider (199)
- Wings of Fire (199)
- Wormhole (200)

HIGH TIER:
- Alley Rat (109)
- Blurring Speed (115)
- Chamber of Dreams (119)
- Electrical Flight (133)
- Embraced by Darkness (133)
- Fast Travel (139)
- Flash Across the Miles (141)
- Flight (141)
- Impossible Walk (151)
- Incredible Running Speed (153)
- Jaunt (155)
- Juggernaut (156)
- Living Light (158)
- Masterful Armor Modification (160)
- Mental Projection (161)
- Return to the Obelisk (177)
- Teleportation (190)
- Time Travel (192)
- Traverse the Worlds (194)
- Very Long Sprinting (196)
- Wind Chariot (199)
- Windwracked Traveler (199)

PROTECTION

Gives training or specialization in one or more types of combat defenses (Might, Speed, or Intellect), provides or increases Armor, or otherwise helps prevent damage.

LOW TIER:

- Absorb Kinetic Energy (108)
- Block (115)
- Closed Mind (119)
- Courageous (122)
- Crystalline Body (123)
- Defense Against Robots (126)
- Defensive Phasing (127)
- Deflect Attacks (127)
- Distortion (130)
- Enhanced Body (134)
- Enveloping Shield (136)
- Fearsome Reputation (139)
- Field of Destruction (139)
- Flesh of Stone (141)
- Flight Not Fight (141)
- Force Field Shield (143)
- Fortified Position (143)
- Go Defensive (145)
- Golem Body (145)
- Hard to Distract (148)
- Hard to Hit (148)
- Hardiness (148)
- Have Spacesuit, Will Travel (148)
- Ice Armor (150)
- Just a Bit Mad (156)
- Magic Shield (159)
- Mentally Tough (162)
- Out of Harm's Way (167)
- Phase Sprint (170)
- Powered Armor (171)
- Practiced in Armor (171)
- Quick Block (173)
- Repel Metal (176)
- Resist the Elements (176)
- Resist Underwater Hazards (176)
- Resonance Field (176)
- Safe Fall (179)
- Serv-0 Defender (181)
- Shield Master (182)
- Shroud of Flame (183)
- Skill With Defense (183)
- Sound Conversion Barrier (184)
- Stare Them Down (186)
- Sturdy (187)
- Trained Without Armor (193)
- Unarmored Fighter (194)
- Ward (196)
- Warding Shield (196)
- Weapon Defense (197)
- Weather the Vicissitudes (197)
- Wind Armor (199)

MID TIER:

- Absorb Pure Energy (108)
- Anticipate Attack (110)
- Blood Fever (115)
- Cloak of Opportunity (119)
- Confounding Banter (121)
- Confuse Enemy (121)
- Counter Danger (122)
- Countermeasures (122)
- Dark Matter Shell (124)
- Dark Matter Shroud (124)
- Discerning Mind (129)
- Divert Attacks (130)
- Dodge and Respond (131)
- Dual Defense (132)
- Electric Armor (133)
- Elemental Protection (133)
- Energy Protection (134)
- Energy Resistance (134)
- Experienced in Armor (136)
- Experienced Defender (136)
- Force Field Barrier (143)
- Fusion Armor (144)
- Hard-Won Resilience (148)
- Horde Fighting (149)
- Huge (149)
- Illusory Evasion (150)
- Magnetic Field (159)
- Matter Cloud (161)
- Minor Wish (162)
- Moving Like Water (164)
- Nimble Swimmer (166)
- Outlaw Reputation (168)
- Poison Crafter (170)
- Rapid Processing (174)
- Resilience (176)
- Resilient Ice Armor (176)
- Robot Fighter (178)
- Shield Training (182)
- Subconscious Defense (187)
- Temporal Acceleration (190)
- Tough It Out (193)
- Tower of Intellect (193)
- Tower of Will (193)
- Tumbling Moves (194)
- Versatile Mind (196)
- Vigilance (196)
- Wraith Cloak (200)

HIGH TIER:

- Defense Master (127)
- Defensive Augmentation (127)
- Defensive Field (127)
- Energize Creature (134)
- Energize Crowd (134)
- Evasion (136)
- Field-Reinforced Armor (139)
- Hard Target (148)
- Hard to Kill (148)
- Lost in the Chaos (159)
- Masterful Armor Modification (160)
- Mastery in Armor (161)
- Mastery With Defense (161)
- Microgravity Avoidance (162)
- Moderate Wish (163)
- Nothing but Defend (166)
- Parry (168)
- Precognition (171)
- Reactive Field (174)
- See the Future (180)
- Still As a Statue (186)
- Ultra Enhancement (194)
- Untouchable (195)
- Untouchable While Moving (195)
- Wear It Well (197)

SENSES

Enhances your senses (seeing in the dark, seeing underwater or through mist, sensing danger, finding optimal places to stand in combat, and so on), but doesn't provide direct answers to questions like an information ability does.

LOW TIER:
- Eyes Adjusted (138)
- Familiarize (138)
- Find an Opening (139)
- Heads-Up Display (148)
- Link Senses (158)
- Mental Link (161)
- Reveal (178)
- See the Unseen (180)
- See Through Matter (180)
- Sense Ambush (181)
- Share Senses (182)
- Third Eye (191)

MID TIER:
- Animal Senses and Sensibilities (109)
- Awareness (111)
- Beast Eyes (112)
- Break the Line (116)
- Detect Life (128)
- Distance Viewing (130)
- Echolocation (133)
- Experienced Finder (136)
- Inhabit Crystal (154)
- Remote Viewing (176)
- Sensing Package (181)
- Sensor (181)
- Serv-0 Spy (181)
- Trapfinder (193)
- Use Senses of Others (195)

HIGH TIER:
- Amplify Sounds (109)
- Battlefield Tactician (112)
- Dark Explorer (124)
- Infer Thoughts (153)
- Master Machine (160)
- See Through Time (181)
- True Senses (194)

SOCIAL

Gives you an indirect social benefit, such as providing a useful contact in a city or letting you take advantage of your social status.

LOW TIER:
- Connected (121)
- Debate (126)
- Demeanor of Command (127)
- Impart Ideal (151)
- Misdirect Blame (163)
- Negotiate (165)
- Perks of Stardom (169)
- Powerful Rhetoric (171)
- Privileged Nobility (172)
- Underworld Contacts (195)
- Unexpected Betrayal (195)

MID TIER:
- Betrayal (113)
- Flamboyant Boast (140)
- Informer (153)
- Oratory (167)
- Perfect Stranger (169)

HIGH TIER:
- Group Friendship (147)

SPECIAL ATTACK

Gives the ability to make a special melee or ranged attack (weapon, energy blast, psychic, and so on). The attack might do damage, have a special effect (disarm, hinder, move the target, and so on), or both. This also includes abilities like Spray that let you attack multiple targets as your action.

LOW TIER:

- Advantage to Disadvantage (109)
- Aggression (109)
- Arcane Flare (110)
- Bash (112)
- Bloodlust (115)
- Concussive Blast (121)
- Control the Field (121)
- Cutting Light (123)
- Dazzling Sunburst (125)
- Disincentivize (129)
- Disrupting Touch (129)
- Drain Machine (131)
- Dream Thief (132)
- Dual Light Wield (132)
- Entangling Force (136)
- Enthrall (136)
- Erase Memories (136)
- Eye Gouge (138)
- Flash (140)
- Force Bash (142)
- Frost Touch (144)
- Golem Grip (145)
- Grasping Foliage (146)
- Hemorrhage (149)
- Hurl Flame (149)
- Misdirect (163)
- Onslaught (167)
- Opportunist (167)
- Overwatch (168)
- Pierce (170)
- Push (173)
- Quick Throw (174)
- Ray of Confusion (174)
- Release Energy (175)
- Resonance Field (176)
- Ribbons of Dark Matter (178)
- Scramble Machine (179)
- Scratch Existence (180)
- Seeds of Fury (181)
- Shatter (182)
- Shock (183)
- Stasis (186)
- Successive Attack (187)
- Surprise Attack (188)
- Swipe (188)
- Thrust (191)
- Thunder Beam (191)
- Weighty (197)

The small numbers you see after abilities throughout this book are page numbers for easy reference.

MID TIER:

- Acrobatic Attack (108)
- Ambusher (109)
- Answering Attack (110)
- Better Surprise Attack (113)
- Bolts of Power (115)
- Built-in Weaponry (116)
- Burning Light (116)
- Castigate (118)
- Center of Attention (119)
- Crystal Lens (123)
- Dark Matter Strike (124)
- Dazing Attack (125)
- Debilitating Strike (126)
- Destroy Metal (127)
- Disable Mechanisms (128)
- Disarming Strike (129)
- Divine Radiance (130)
- Dodge and Respond (131)
- Drain Charge (131)
- Dual Medium Wield (132)
- Everything Is a Weapon (136)
- Exile (136)
- Feint (139)
- Fire and Ice (140)
- Fire Bloom (140)
- Fling (141)
- Force at Distance (142)
- Force Blast (142)
- Freezing Touch (143)
- Golem Stomp (145)
- Grab (146)
- Gravity Cleave (146)
- Ignition (150)
- Improved Object Bond (152)
- Knock Out (156)
- Matter Cloud (161)
- Mind Games (162)
- Momentum (164)
- Overawe (168)
- Overcome All Obstacles (168)
- Phase Detonation (169)
- Phased Attack (170)
- Power Strike (171)
- Pry Open (172)
- Psychic Burst (172)
- Psychosis (172)
- Push Off and Throw (173)
- Quick Strike (174)
- Rapid Attack (174)
- Reaction (174)
- Remote Control (176)
- Run and Fight (179)
- Shattering Shout (182)
- Slice (183)
- Snap Shot (183)
- Snipe (183)
- Spray (185)
- Sprint and Grab (186)
- Taking Advantage (188)
- Tall Tale (189)
- Throw (191)
- Throw Force Shield (191)
- Trick Shot (194)

ABILITIES

HIGH TIER:
- Absorb Energy (108)
- Arc Spray (110)
- Assassin Strike (110)
- Asserting Your Privilege (110)
- Attack and Attack Again (111)
- Biomorphic Detonation (113)
- Blind Machine (114)
- Blinding Attack (115)
- Bouncing Shield (115)
- Break the Ranks (116)
- Break Their Mind (116)
- Call the Storm (117)
- Cold Burst (119)
- Concussion (121)
- Deactivate Mechanisms (125)
- Deadly Strike (125)
- Death Touch (125)
- Defense Master (127)
- Destroyer (127)
- Dirty Fighter (128)
- Disarming Attack (129)
- Divine Intervention (130)
- Divine Symbol (131)
- Do You Know Who I Am? (131)
- Drain Power (131)
- Dust to Dust (133)
- Earthquake (133)
- Embrace the Night (133)
- Explosive Release (138)
- Finishing Blow (140)
- Fire Tendrils (140)
- Foul Aura (143)
- Ice Storm (150)
- Iron Punch (155)
- Jump Attack (156)
- Lethal Ploy (158)
- Lethal Vibration (158)
- Murderer (165)
- Nightmare (165)
- Phase Foe (170)
- Protective Wall (172)
- Psychokinetic Attack (172)
- Punish All the Guilty (173)
- Resonant Quake (177)
- Return to Sender (177)
- Shatter Mind (182)
- Special Shot (184)
- Spin Attack (185)
- Spring Away (186)
- Stun Attack (187)
- Sun Siphon (188)
- Taunt Foe (189)
- Terrifying Gaze (190)
- Twisting the Knife (194)
- Undo (195)
- Vindictive Performance (196)
- Weapon and Body (196)
- Weight of the World (197)
- Weightless Shot (197)
- Whirlwind of Throws (198)
- Winter Gauntlets (199)
- Word of Death (200)

SUPPORT

Gives some sort of benefit to an ally rather than yourself, such as an extra action or an asset on their roll.

LOW TIER:
- Advice From a Friend (109)
- Anecdote (109)
- Attack Flourish (111)
- Defend the Innocent (126)
- Enable Others (133)
- Encouragement (134)
- Encouraging Presence (134)
- Force Field (143)
- Friendly Help (143)
- Good Advice (145)
- Inspire Action (154)
- Inspire Aggression (154)
- Inspiring Ease (154)
- Protector (172)
- Rally to Me (174)
- Reveal (178)
- Sculpt Flesh (180)
- Teamwork (189)

MID TIER:
- Accelerate (108)
- Applying Your Knowledge (110)
- Buddy System (116)
- Combat Challenge (120)
- Defend All the Innocent (126)
- Dual Wards (132)
- Elemental Protection (133)
- In Harm's Way (152)
- Lead by Inquiry (157)
- Pay It Forward (168)
- Play to the Crowd (170)
- Spur Effort (186)
- Take Command (188)
- True Guardian (194)

HIGH TIER:
- Able Assistance (108)
- Battle Management (112)
- Block for Another (115)
- Energize Creature (134)
- Energize Crowd (134)
- Impart Understanding (151)
- Inspiration (154)
- Inspire Coordinated Actions (154)
- Inspiring Success (154)
- Regenerate Other (175)
- Share Defense (181)
- Stimulate (186)
- Teach Trick (189)
- Transcend the Script (193)
- True Defender (194)
- Undo (195)
- Will of a Leader (199)
- Work the Friendship (200)

TASK

Gives training, specialization, or an asset in one or more noncombat skills (climbing, healing, computers, initiative, and so on).

LOW TIER:

- Advantages of Being Big (109)
- Anticipation (110)
- Assassin Skills (110)
- Athlete (111)
- Autodoctor (111)
- Balance (112)
- Bestiary Knowledge (113)
- Blameless (113)
- Breaker (116)
- Car Surfer (118)
- Careful Aim (118)
- Celebrity Talent (119)
- Computer Programming (121)
- Contortionist (121)
- Courageous (122)
- Crafter (122)
- Danger Sense (124)
- Datajack (124)
- Debate (126)
- Deep Water Guide (126)
- Designation (127)
- Devoted Defender (128)
- Disguise (129)
- Divine Knowledge (130)
- Driver (132)
- Enlightened (136)
- Exploratory Experience (137)
- Extra Skill (138)
- Feat of Strength (139)
- Flex Lore (141)
- Freakishly Large (143)
- Game Lessons (144)
- Gamer (144)
- Good Advice (145)
- Hand to Eye (148)
- Handy (148)
- Hard Choices (148)
- Heads-Up Display (148)
- Higher Mathematics (149)
- How Others Think (149)
- Impersonate (151)
- Impressive Display (151)
- Infiltrator (153)
- Inner Defense (154)
- Insight (154)
- Inspire Aggression (154)
- Interaction Skills (155)
- Interface (155)
- Investigate (155)
- Investigative Skills (155)
- Knowing (156)
- Knowledge of the Law (156)
- Knowledge Skills (157)
- Late Inspiration (157)
- Learning the Path (157)
- Levity (158)
- Life Lessons (158)
- Machine Affinity (159)
- Machine Hunting (159)
- Machine Interface (159)
- Magic Training (159)
- Make Judgment (160)
- Master Identifier (160)
- Master Thief (160)
- Microgravity Adept (162)
- Monster Lore (164)
- Movement Skills (164)
- Muscles of Iron (165)
- Natural Charisma (165)
- Oneirochemy (167)
- Open Mind (167)
- Opening Statement (167)
- Physical Skills (170)
- Pilot (170)
- Poetic License (170)
- Post-Apocalyptic Survivor (170)
- Powerful Rhetoric (171)
- Predictive Equation (171)
- Privileged Nobility (172)
- Quarry (173)
- Quick Study (174)
- Quick to Flee (174)
- Quicker Than Most (174)
- Resist Tricks (176)
- Ruin Lore (179)
- Sailor (179)
- Salvage and Comfort (179)
- Sense Attitudes (181)
- Serv-0 Repair (181)
- Sharp Senses (182)
- Sleuth (183)
- Slippery (183)
- Sneak (183)
- Stalker (186)
- Stand Watch (186)
- Stealth Skills (186)
- Straightforward (187)
- Superb Explorer (188)
- Superb Infiltrator (188)
- Taking Advantage (188)
- Task Training (189)
- Tech Skills (189)
- There's Your Problem (190)
- Tool Mastery (192)
- Tracker (193)
- Trained Excavator (193)
- Trained Interlocutor (193)
- Trained Swimmer (193)
- Travel Skills (193)
- Understanding (194)
- Vacuum Skilled (196)
- Wilderness Life (199)
- Wilderness Lore (199)
- Wound Tender (200)
- Zero Dark Eyes (200)

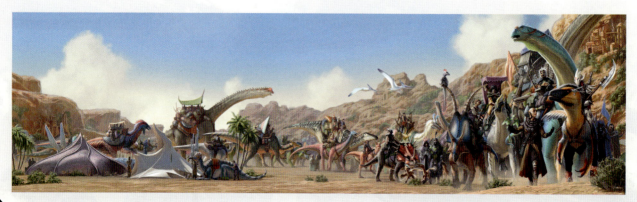

ABILITIES

MID TIER:
- Action Processor (108)
- Agent Provocateur (109)
- Animal Senses and Sensibilities (109)
- Confidence Artist (121)
- Dark Matter Shell (124)
- Enhance Strength (134)
- Expert Driver (137)
- Expert Pilot (137)
- Find the Guilty (139)
- Flex Skill (141)
- Ghost (145)
- Hard to See (148)
- Heightened Skills (149)
- Improvise (152)
- Increasing Determination (153)
- Intelligent Interface (155)
- Intense Interaction (155)
- Knowledge Is Power (156)
- Master Crafter (160)
- Meticulous Planner (162)
- Minor Wish (162)
- Nightstrike (166)
- Outlast the Foe (167)
- Passing Mechanic (168)
- Preternatural Senses (171)
- Pull a Fast One (173)
- Rapid Processing (174)
- Rider (178)
- Sea Legs (180)
- Sensing Package (181)
- Serv-0 Aim (181)
- Serv-0 Brawler (181)
- Sharp-Eyed (182)
- Ship Footing (182)
- Silent As Space (183)
- Skill With Attacks (183)
- Soothe Mind and Body (184)
- Subtle Steps (187)
- Targeting Eye (189)
- Task Specialization (189)
- Telling (190)
- Temporal Acceleration (190)
- Trained Basher (193)
- Trained Gunner (193)
- Trained Slayer (193)
- Verbal Misdirection (196)
- You Studied (200)

HIGH TIER:
- Amplify Sounds (109)
- As Foretold in Prophecy (110)
- Coordinated Effort (122)
- Dark Explorer (124)
- Explains the Ineffable (137)
- Exploit Advantage (137)
- Further Mathematics (144)
- Learned a Few Things (157)
- Like the Back of Your Hand (158)
- Magnificent Moment (159)
- Master Entertainer (160)
- Multiple Skills (165)
- No One Knows Better (166)
- Precognition (171)
- See the Future (180)
- Subsonic Rumble (187)
- Total Awareness (192)
- Trick Driver (194)
- Using the Environment (195)

The small numbers you see after abilities throughout this book are page numbers for easy reference.

TRANSFORM

A significant change that temporarily enhances you, such as growing bigger, turning into a werewolf, and so on. Also includes apparent transformations like disguises and invisibility.

LOW TIER:
- Beast Form (112)
- Bigger (113)
- Controlled Change (122)
- Enlarge (135)
- Face Morph (138)
- Golem Healing (145)
- Illusory Disguise (150)
- Phased Pocket (170)
- Spin Identity (185)
- Vanish (196)

MID TIER:
- Bigger Beast Form (113)
- Blend In (113)
- Evanesce (136)
- Greater Controlled Change (146)
- Hard to See (148)
- Huge (149)
- Invisible Phasing (155)
- Moon Shape (164)

HIGH TIER:
- Colossal (120)
- Command Metal (120)
- Disappear (128)
- Gargantuan (144)
- Invisibility (155)
- Mask (160)
- Moderate Wish (163)
- Outside Reality (168)
- Perfect Control (169)
- Wild Camouflage (198)

If you select an ability for your new focus or type that refers to or modifies a lower-tier ability, also include that lower-tier ability in your type or focus as a selection a PC can make at a lower tier.

Free level of Effort, page 209

Minor effect, page 211

ABILITIES—A

○ **A Smile and a Word:** When you use Effort on any action involving interactions—even those having to do with calming animals or communicating with someone or something whose language you do not speak—you gain a free level of Effort on the task. Action.

○ **Able Assistance:** When you help someone with a task and they apply a level of Effort, they get a free level of Effort on that task. Enabler.

○ **Absorb Energy (7 Intellect points):** You touch an object and absorb its energy. If you touch a manifest cypher, you render it useless. If you touch an artifact, roll for its depletion. If you touch another kind of powered machine or device, the GM determines whether its power is fully drained. In any case, you absorb energy from the object touched and regain 1d10 Intellect points. If this would give you more Intellect than your Pool's maximum, the extra points are lost, and you must make a Might defense roll. The difficulty of the roll is equal to the number of points over your maximum you absorbed. If you fail the roll, you take 5 points of damage and are unable to act for one round. You can use this ability as a defense action when you're the target of an incoming ability. Doing so cancels the incoming ability, and you absorb the energy as if it were a device. Action.

○ **Absorb Kinetic Energy:** You absorb a portion of the energy of a physical attack or impact. You negate 1 point of damage you would have suffered and store that point as energy. Once you have absorbed 1 point of energy, you continue to negate 1 point of damage from any incoming blow or impact, but the residual energy bleeds off with a flare of harmless light (you cannot store more than 1 point at a time). Enabler.

○ **Absorb Pure Energy:** When you use Absorb Kinetic Energy, you can also absorb and store energy from attacks made with pure energy (focused light, radiation, transdimensional, psychic, etc.) or from conduits that direct energy, if you can make direct contact. This ability does not change how many points of energy you can store. If you also have Improved Absorb Kinetic Energy, you can absorb 2 points of damage from other energy sources as well. Enabler.

○ **Accelerate (4+ Intellect points):** Your words imbue the spirit of a character within immediate range who is able to understand you, accelerating them so they gain an asset on initiative tasks and Speed defense rolls for ten minutes. In addition to the normal options for using Effort, you can choose to use Effort to affect more targets; each level of Effort affects one additional target. You must speak to additional targets to accelerate them, one target per round. Action per target to initiate.

○ **Acrobatic Attack (1+ Speed points):** You leap into the attack, twisting or flipping through the air. If you roll a natural 17 or 18, you can choose to have a minor effect rather than deal extra damage. If you apply Effort to the attack, you get a free level of Effort on the task. You can't use this ability if your Speed Effort costs are reduced from wearing armor. Enabler.

○ **Action Processor (4 Intellect points):** Drawing upon stored information and the ability to process incoming data at amazing speeds, you are trained in one physical task of your choice for ten minutes. For example, you can choose running, climbing, swimming, Speed defense, or attacks with a specific weapon. Action to initiate.

○ **Adaptation:** Thanks to a latent mutation, a device implanted in your spine, a ritual performed with dragon's blood, or some other gift, you now remain at a comfortable temperature; never need to worry about dangerous radiation, diseases, or gases; and can always breathe in any environment (even the vacuum of space). Enabler.

○ **Adroit Cypher Use:** You can bear four cyphers at a time. Enabler.

○ **Advanced Command (7 Intellect points):** A target within short range obeys any command you give as long as they can hear and understand you. Further, as long as you continue to do nothing but issue commands (taking no other action), you can give that same target a new command. This effect ends when you stop issuing commands or they are out of short range. Action to initiate.

Abilities—A

○ **Advantage to Disadvantage (3 Speed points):** With a number of quick moves, you make an attack against an armed foe, inflicting damage and disarming them so that their weapon is now in your hands or 10 feet (3 m) away on the ground—your choice. This disarming attack is hindered. Action.

○ **Advantages of Being Big:** When you use Enlarge, you're so big that you can move massive objects more easily, climb buildings by using hand- and footholds unavailable to regular-sized people, and jump much farther. While you enjoy the effects of Enlarge, all climbing, lifting, and jumping tasks are eased. Enabler.

○ **Advice From a Friend (1 Intellect point):** You know your friend's strengths and weaknesses, and how to motivate them to succeed. When you give an ally a suggestion involving their next action, the character is trained in that action for one round. Action.

○ **Again and Again (8 Speed points):** You can take an additional action in a round in which you have already acted. Enabler.

○ **Agent Provocateur:** Choose one of the following to be trained in: attacking with a weapon of your choice, demolitions, or sneaking and lockpicking (if you choose this last option, you are trained in both). Enabler.

○ **Aggression (2 Might points):** You focus on making attacks to such an extent that you leave yourself vulnerable to your opponents. While this ability is active, you gain an asset on your melee attacks, and your Speed defense rolls against melee and ranged attacks are hindered. This effect lasts for as long as you wish, but it ends if no combat is taking place within range of your senses. Enabler.

○ **Agile Wit:** When attempting a Speed task, you instead can roll (and spend points) as if it were an Intellect action. If you apply Effort to this task, you can spend points from your Intellect Pool instead of your Speed Pool (in which case you also use your Intellect Edge instead of your Speed Edge). Enabler.

○ **All-Out Con (7 Intellect points):** You put everything into it. You add three free levels of Effort to the next task you attempt. You can't use this ability again until after you've taken a ten-hour recovery action. Action.

○ **Alleviate (3 Intellect points):** You attempt to cancel or cure one malady (such as disease or poison) in one creature. Action.

○ **Alley Rat (6 Intellect points):** While in a city, you find or create a significant shortcut, secret entrance, or emergency escape route where it looked like none existed. Doing so requires that you succeed on an Intellect action whose difficulty is set by the GM based on the situation. You and the GM should work out the details. Action.

○ **Amazing Effort:** When you apply at least one level of Effort to a noncombat task, you get a free level of Effort on that task. When you choose this ability, decide if it applies to Might Effort or Speed Effort. Enabler.

○ **Ambusher:** When you attack a creature that has not yet acted during the first round of combat, your attack is eased. Enabler.

○ **Amplify Sounds (2 Might points):** For one minute, you can amplify distant or small sounds so that you can hear them clearly, even if it's a conversation or the sound of a small animal moving through an underground burrow up to a very long distance away. You can attempt to perceive the sound even if interceding barriers block it or the sound is very slight, though this requires a few additional rounds of concentration. To discriminate the sound you wish in a noisy environment might also require a few additional rounds of concentration as you audibly explore the surrounding soundscape. Given enough time, you could pinpoint every conversation, every breathing creature, and every device creating noise within range. Action to initiate, up to several rounds to complete, depending on the difficulty of the task.

○ **Anecdote (2 Intellect points):** You can lift the spirits of a group of creatures and help them bond together by entertaining them with an uplifting or pointed anecdote. For the next hour, those who pay attention to your story are trained in a task you choose that's related to the anecdote, as long as it's not an attack or defense task. Action to initiate, one minute to complete.

○ **Animal Senses and Sensibilities:** You are trained in listening and spotting things. In addition, most of the time, the GM should alert you if you're about to walk into an ambush or a trap that is lower than level 5. Enabler.

Enlarge, page 135

109

○ **Answering Attack (3 Speed points):** If you are struck in melee, you can make an immediate melee attack against that attacker once per round. The attack is hindered, and you can still take your normal action during the round. Enabler.

○ **Anticipate Attack (4 Intellect points):** You can sense when and how creatures attacking you will make their attacks. Speed defense rolls are eased for one minute. Action.

○ **Anticipation (1 Intellect point):** You look ahead to see how your actions might unfold. The first task you perform before the end of the next round gains an asset. Action.

○ **Applying Your Knowledge:** When you help another character undertake any action that you're untrained in, you are treated as if you are trained in it. Action.

○ **Apportation (4 Intellect points):** You call a physical object to you. You can choose any piece of normal equipment on the standard equipment list, or (no more than once per day) you can allow the GM to determine the object randomly. If you call a random object, it has a 10 percent chance of being a manifest cypher or artifact, a 50 percent chance of being a piece of standard equipment, and a 40 percent chance of being a bit of worthless junk. You can't use this ability to take an item held by another creature. Action.

○ **Aquatic Combatant:** You ignore penalties for any action (including fighting) in underwater environments. Enabler.

○ **Arc Spray (3 Speed points):** If a weapon has the ability to fire rapid shots without reloading (usually called a rapid-fire weapon, such as a crank crossbow), you can fire your weapon at up to three targets (all next to one another) at once. Make a separate attack roll against each target. Each attack is hindered. Action.

○ **Arcane Flare (1 Intellect point):** You enhance the damage of another attack spell with an extra charge of energy so that it deals 1 additional point of damage. Alternatively, you attack a target within long range by projecting a flare of raw magic that inflicts 4 points of damage. Enabler for enhancement; action for long-range attack.

○ **Artifact Scavenger (6 Intellect points + 2 XP):** You've developed a sixth sense for searching for the most valuable items in the wasteland. If you spend the time required to succeed on two scavenging tasks, you can exchange all the results you would otherwise obtain for a chance to gain an artifact of the GM's choosing if you succeed on a difficulty 6 Intellect task. You can use this ability at most once per day, and never within the same general area. Action to initiate, several hours to complete.

○ **Artifact Tinkerer:** If you spend at least one day tinkering with an artifact in your possession, it functions at one level higher than normal. This applies to all artifacts in your possession, but they retain this bonus only for you. Enabler.

○ **As Foretold in Prophecy:** You accomplish something that proves you are truly the chosen one. The next task you attempt is eased by three steps. You can't use this ability again until after you've taken a one-hour or a ten-hour recovery action. Action.

○ **As If One Creature:** When you and your beast (from your Beast Companion ability) are within immediate distance of each other, you can share damage inflicted on either of you. For instance, if one of you is struck by a weapon for 4 points of damage, divide the damage between the two of you as you see fit. Only the Armor and resistances of the target initially damaged come into play. So if you have 2 Armor and are struck by a force blast for 4 points of damage, your beast can take the 2 points of damage you would suffer, but their Armor does not come into play, nor does their immunity to force blasts, if any. Enabler.

○ **Assassin Skills:** You are trained in stealth and disguise tasks. Enabler.

○ **Assassin Strike (5 Intellect points):** If you successfully attack a creature that was previously unaware of your presence, you deal 9 additional points of damage. Enabler.

○ **Asserting Your Privilege (3 Intellect points):** Acting as only a privileged person can, you verbally harangue a foe who can hear and understand you so forcefully that they are unable to take any action, including attacks, for one round. Whether you succeed or fail, the next action the target takes is hindered. Action.

Scavenging, page 296

Equipment, page 201

Beast Companion, page 112

Water, page 221

Abilities—A

○ **Assume Control (6+ Intellect points):** You control the actions of another creature you have interacted with or studied for at least a round. This effect lasts for ten minutes. The target must be level 2 or lower. Once you have assumed control, the target acts as if it wants to accomplish your desire to the best of its ability, freely using its own best judgment unless you use an action to give it a specific instruction on an issue-by-issue basis. In addition to the normal options for using Effort, you can choose to use Effort to increase the maximum level of the target. Thus, to attempt to command a level 5 target (three levels above the normal limit), you must apply three levels of Effort. When the effect ends, the target remembers everything that happened and reacts according to its nature and your relationship to it; assuming control might have soured that relationship if it was previously a positive one. Action to initiate.

○ **Athlete:** You are trained in carrying, climbing, jumping, and smashing. Enabler.

○ **Attack and Attack Again:** Rather than granting additional damage or a minor or major effect, a natural 17 or higher on your attack roll allows you the option of immediately making another attack. Enabler.

○ **Attack Flourish:** With your attack, you add stylish moves, entertaining quips, or a certain something that entertains or impresses others. One creature you choose within short range who can see you gains an asset to its next task if taken within a round or two. Enabler.

○ **Augment Cypher (2+ Intellect points):** When you activate a cypher, add +1 to its level. In addition to the normal options for using Effort, you can choose to use Effort to increase the level of the cypher by an additional +1 (per level of Effort applied). You can't increase the cypher's level above 10. Enabler.

○ **Autodoctor:** You are trained in healing, performing surgical procedures, and withstanding pain. You can perform surgeries on yourself, remaining conscious while you do so. Enabler.

○ **Awareness (3 Intellect points):** You become hyperaware of your surroundings in order to better locate your target. For ten minutes, you are aware of all living things within long range (including their general position), and by concentrating (another action), you can attempt to learn the general health and power level of any one of them. Action.

Minor and major effects, page 211

ABILITIES—B

○ **Babel:** After hearing a language spoken for a few minutes, you can speak it and make yourself understood. If you continue to use the language to interact with native speakers, your skills improve rapidly, to the point where you might be mistaken for a native speaker after just a few hours of speaking the new language. Enabler.

○ **Balance:** You are trained in balancing. Enabler.

○ **Band of Desperados:** Your reputation draws a band of six level 2 desperado NPC followers who are completely devoted to you. You and the GM must work out the details of these followers. If a follower dies, you gain a new one after at least two weeks and proper recruitment. Enabler.

○ **Band of Followers:** You gain four level 3 followers. They are not restricted on their modifications. Enabler.

○ **Bash (1 Might point):** This is a pummeling melee attack. Your attack inflicts 1 less point of damage than normal, but dazes your target for one round, during which time all tasks it performs are hindered. Action.

○ **Basic Follower:** You gain a level 2 follower. One of their modifications must be persuasion. You can take this ability multiple times, each time gaining another level 2 follower. Enabler.

○ **Battle Management (4 Intellect points):** As long as you use your action each round giving orders or advice, attack and defense actions taken by your allies within short range are eased. Action.

○ **Battlefield Tactician (2+ Intellect points):** You scrutinize your surroundings, learning whatever facts the GM feels are pertinent about attacking, defending, maneuvering, and dealing with environmental hazards within a short distance. For example, you might notice a pile of rubble you can stand on for an advantage in melee, a sheltered corner to help protect against enemy attacks, a less-slippery part of a frozen lake, or a place where the poison gas is thinner than elsewhere. If you (or someone you tell) move to that location, you (or they) gain an asset on tasks related to that optimal position (such as attack rolls from the high ground, Speed defense rolls from the sheltered corner, balance rolls on the frozen lake, or Might defense rolls against the poisonous cloud). Instead of gaining an advantageous location, you might learn of a disadvantageous location that you could use against your enemies, such as maneuvering them into an awkward corner that hinders their melee attacks or a weak spot on the frozen lake that will break if they stand on it. You can apply Effort to learn one additional good or bad location within range (one location per level of Effort), increase the range of this ability (another short distance per level of Effort), or both. Enabler.

○ **Beast Call (5 Intellect points):** You summon a horde of small animals or a single level 4 beast to help you temporarily. These creatures do your bidding for as long as you focus your attention, but you must use your action each turn to direct them. Creatures are native to the area and arrive under their own power, so if you're in an unreachable place, this ability won't work. Action.

○ **Beast Companion:** A level 2 creature of your size or smaller accompanies you and follows your instructions. You and the GM must work out the details of your creature, and you'll probably make rolls for it in combat or when it takes actions. The beast companion acts on your turn. As a level 2 creature, it has a target number of 6 and 6 health and it inflicts 2 points of damage. Its movement is based on its creature type (avian, swimmer, and so on). If your beast companion dies, you can hunt in the wild for 1d6 days to find a new one. Enabler.

○ **Beast Eyes (3 Intellect points):** By linking to the creature from your Beast Companion ability, you can perceive through its senses if it is within 1 mile (1.5 km) of you. This effect lasts up to ten minutes. Action to establish.

○ **Beast Form:** On five consecutive nights each month, you change into a monstrous beast for up to one hour each night. In this new form, you gain +8 to your Might Pool, +1 to your Might Edge, +2 to your Speed Pool, and +1 to your Speed Edge. While in beast form, you can't spend Intellect points for any reason other than to try to change to your normal form before the one-hour duration is over (a difficulty 2 task). In addition, you attack any and every living creature within short range. After you revert to your normal form, you take a –1 penalty to all rolls for one hour. If you did not kill and eat at least one substantial creature while in beast form, the penalty increases to –2 and affects all your rolls for the next 24 hours. Action to change back.

Followers, page 233

A creature's level determines its target number, health, and damage, unless otherwise stated. So a level 2 beast companion has a target number of 6 and a health of 6, and it inflicts 2 points of damage. A level 4 beast companion has a target number of 12 and a health of 12, and it inflicts 4 points of damage. And so on.

Creatures, page 312

When you use Basic Follower, the GM may require that you actually look for a suitable follower.

Abilities—B

○ **Bestiary Knowledge:** You are trained in the lore of flesh-eating, nonhumanoid creatures—recognizing them, knowing their weaknesses, and knowing their habits and behaviors. Enabler.

○ **Betrayal:** Any time you convince a foe that you are not a threat and then suddenly attack it (without provocation), the attack deals 4 additional points of damage. Enabler.

○ **Better Living Through Chemistry (4 Intellect points):** You've developed drug cocktails specifically designed to work with your own biochemistry. Depending on which one you inject, it makes you smarter, faster, or tougher, but when it wears off, the crash is a doozy, so you use it only in desperate situations. You gain 2 to your Might Edge, Speed Edge, or Intellect Edge for one minute, after which you can't gain the benefit again for one hour. During this follow-up hour, every time you spend points from a Pool, increase the cost by 1. Action.

○ **Better Surprise Attack:** If attacking from a hidden vantage, with surprise, or before an opponent has acted, you get an asset on the attack (if you have Surprise Attack, this is in addition to the asset from that ability). On a successful hit with this surprise attack, you inflict 2 additional points of damage (for a total of 4 additional points of damage if you have Surprise Attack). Enabler.

○ **Bigger:** When you use Enlarge, you can choose to grow up to 12 feet (4 m) in height, and you add 3 more temporary points to your Might Pool. Enabler.

○ **Bigger Beast Form:** When you use Beast Form, your beast form grows bigger than before, during which time you achieve a height of 12 feet (4 m). Being so large, your beast form gains the following additional bonuses: +1 to Armor, +5 to your Might Pool, and you are trained in using your fists as heavy weapons (if you weren't already). However, your Speed defense tasks are hindered. While bigger, you also gain an asset to tasks that are easier for a larger creature to perform, like climbing, intimidating, wading rivers, and so on. Enabler.

○ **Biomorphic Detonation (7+ Might points):** You radiate a pulse of biomorphic energy up to a short distance away, but you tune it to disrupt life in an area an immediate distance across. All within the detonation take 5 points of damage that ignores Armor (unless it is Armor provided by a force field effect). If you apply additional Effort to increase the damage, you deal 2 additional points of damage per level of Effort (instead of 3 points); targets in the area take 1 point of damage even if you fail the attack roll. Action.

○ **Biomorphic Healing (4+ Might points):** You consciously send out a pulse of your biomorphic field (a strange energy your body generates) and focus it on a living creature within short range. The target gains a free and immediate one-action recovery roll. You can't use this ability again on that creature until after its next ten-hour rest. Action.

○ **Blameless:** You are trained in one of the following: deception, stealth, or disguise. Enabler.

○ **Blend In (4 Intellect points):** When you blend in, creatures still see you, but they attach no importance to your presence for about a minute. While blending in, you are specialized in stealth and Speed defense tasks. This effect ends if you do something to reveal your presence or position—attacking, using an ability, moving a large object, and so on. If this occurs, you can regain the remaining period of effect by taking an action to focus on seeming innocuous and as if you belong. Action to initiate or reinitiate.

Surprise Attack, page 188

Enlarge, page 135

Although people probably look upon a creature transforming into another creature as mystical lycanthropy, if the genre allows, the process might instead be accessing other dimensions of reality. A character either draws mass from an extradimensional space (perhaps somehow warping higher-dimensional mass into our lower dimensions) or switches places with a larger, more savage ultraterrestrial creature for a time. In this latter case, the character and the creature have a bond that allows them to share general intentions. The character, while shunted to another dimension, likely remains in stasis, unaware of anything until returning to the normal world.

113

Blessing of the Gods is an ability most commonly associated with the Channels Divine Blessings focus on page 65.

○ **Blessing of the Gods:** As a servant of the gods, you can call up blessings in their name. This blessing depends on the god's general demeanor and area of influence. Choose two of the abilities described below.

Authority/Law/Peace (3 Intellect points). You prevent a foe that can hear and understand you from attacking anyone or anything for one round. Action.

Benevolence/Righteousness/Spirit (2+ Intellect points). One level 1 demon, spirit, or similar creature within short range is destroyed or banished. In addition to the normal options for using Effort, you can choose to use Effort to increase the maximum level of the target. Thus, to destroy or banish a level 5 target (four levels above the normal limit), you must apply four levels of Effort. Action.

Death/Darkness (2 Intellect points). A target you choose within short range withers, suffering 3 points of damage. Action.

Desire/Love/Health (3 Intellect points). With a touch, you restore 1d6 points to one stat Pool of any creature, including yourself. This ability is a difficulty 2 Intellect task. Each time you attempt to heal the same creature, the task is hindered by an additional step. The difficulty returns to 2 after that creature rests for ten hours. Action.

Earth/Stone. You are trained in climbing, stonecraft, and spelunking. Enabler.

Knowledge/Wisdom (3 Intellect points). Choose up to three creatures (potentially including yourself). For one minute, a particular type of task (but not an attack roll or defense roll) is eased for those creatures, but only while they remain within immediate range of you. Action.

Nature/Animals/Plants. You are trained in botany and handling natural animals. Enabler.

Protection/Silence (3 Intellect points). You create a quiet bubble of protection around you to an immediate radius for one minute. The bubble moves with you. All defense rolls for you and all creatures you designate within the bubble are eased, and no noise, regardless of its origin, sounds louder than a normal speaking voice. Action to initiate.

Sky/Air (2 Intellect points). A creature you touch is immune to airborne toxins or contaminants for ten minutes. Action.

Sun/Light/Fire (2 Intellect points). You cause one creature or object within short range to catch fire, inflicting 1 point of ambient damage each round until the fire is extinguished (requiring an action). Action.

Trickery/Greed/Commerce. You are trained in detecting the deceptions of other creatures. Enabler.

War (1 Intellect point). A target you choose within short range (potentially yourself) deals 2 additional points of damage with its next successful weapon attack. Action.

Water/Sea (2 Intellect points). A target you touch can breathe water for ten minutes. Action.

○ **Blind Machine (6 Speed points):** You deactivate the sensory apparatus of a machine, making it effectively blind until it can be repaired. You must either touch the target or strike it with a ranged attack (inflicting no damage). Action.

Abilities—B

○ **Blinding Attack (3 Speed points):** If you have a source of light, you can use it to make a melee attack against a target. If successful, the attack deals no damage, but the target is blinded for one minute. Action.

○ **Blink of an Eye (4 Speed points):** You move up to 1,000 feet (300 m) in one round. Action.

○ **Block (3 Speed points):** You automatically block the next melee attack made against you within the next minute. Action to initiate.

○ **Block for Another:** If you use a light or medium weapon, you can block attacks made against an ally near you. Choose one creature within immediate range. You provide an asset to that creature's Speed defense tasks. You can't use Quick Block while using Block for Another. Enabler.

○ **Blood Fever:** When you have no points in one or two Pools, you gain an asset to attacks or defense rolls (your choice). Enabler.

○ **Bloodlust (3 Might points):** If you take down a foe, you can move a short distance, but only if you move toward another foe. You don't need to spend the points until you know that the first foe is down. Enabler.

○ **Blurring Speed (7 Speed points):** You move so quickly that until your next turn, you look like a blur. While you are blurred, if you apply Effort to a melee attack task or Speed defense task, you get a free level of Effort on that task; you can move a short distance as part of another action or a long distance as your entire action. Enabler.

○ **Bolt Rider (4 Intellect points):** You can move a long distance from one location to another almost instantaneously, carried by a bolt of lightning. You must be able to see the new location, and there must be no intervening barriers. Action.

○ **Bolts of Power (5+ Intellect points):** You blast a fan of lightning out to short range in an arc that is approximately 50 feet (15 m) wide at the end. This discharge inflicts 4 points of damage. If you apply Effort to increase the damage rather than to ease the task, you deal 2 additional points of damage per level of Effort (instead of 3 points); targets in the area take 1 point of damage even if you fail the attack roll. Action.

○ **Bouncing Shield:** When you use Throw Force Shield, instead of dissipating after one attack (whether it hits or misses), it will attack up to two additional targets within short range. Effort or other modifiers applied to the first attack affect all other targets as well. Whether you hit all, some, or none of your targets, the shield dissipates and then reforms in your grasp. (If you choose Bouncing Shield and have previously taken the Throw Force Shield ability, you have the option to exchange that ability for Healing Pulse.) Enabler.

○ **Bound Magic Creature:** You have a magic ally bound to a physical object (perhaps a minor djinn bound to a lamp, a lesser demon bound to a coin, or a spirit bound to a mirror). The magic ally doesn't yet have the full power that one of its kind could possess when mature. Normally, the ally remains quiescent in its bound object. When you use an action to manifest it, it appears next to you as a creature that can converse with you. The creature has its own personality determined by the GM and is a level higher than its base level for one area of knowledge (such as local history). The GM determines whether the magic ally has a long-term goal of its own.

Each time the magic ally becomes physically manifest, it remains so for up to one hour. During that period, it accompanies you and follows your instructions. The magic ally must remain an immediate distance from you; if it moves farther away, it is yanked back into its object at the end of your following turn and cannot return until after your next ten-hour recovery roll. It doesn't attack creatures, but it can use its action to serve as an asset for any one attack you make on your turn. Otherwise, it can take actions on its own (though you'll likely roll for it).

If the creature is reduced to 0 health, it dissipates. It reforms in its object in 1d6 + 2 days.

If you lose the bound object, you retain a sense of the direction in which it lies. Action to manifest the magic creature.

Force Field Shield, page 143

Throw Force Shield, page 191

Healing Pulse, page 148

Bound magic creature: *level 3*

Quick Block, page 173

Free level of Effort, page 209

OBJECT DAMAGE TRACK

Intact: The default state for an object.

Minor damage: A slightly damaged state. An object with minor damage reduces its level by 1.

Major damage: A critically damaged state. An object with major damage is broken and no longer functions.

Destroyed: The object is ruined. It no longer functions and cannot be repaired.

○ **Brainwashing (6+ Intellect points):** You use trickery, well-spoken lies, and mind-affecting chemicals (or other means, like magic or high technology) to make others temporarily do what you want them to do. You control the actions of another creature you touch. This effect lasts for one minute. The target must be level 3 or lower. You can allow it to act freely or override its control on a case-by-case basis as long as you can see it. In addition to the normal options for using Effort, you can choose to use Effort to increase the maximum level of the target or increase the duration by one minute. Thus, to control the mind of a level 6 target (three levels above the normal limit) or control a target for four minutes (three minutes above the normal duration), you must apply three levels of Effort. When the duration ends, the creature doesn't remember being controlled or anything it did while under your influence. Action to initiate.

○ **Break the Line (4 Intellect points):** You have an eye for group discipline and hierarchy, even among your foes. If a group of foes is gaining any kind of benefit from working together, you can attempt to disrupt that benefit by pointing out the weak spot in the enemy's line, formation, or swarm attack. This effect lasts for up to a minute or until all the affected foes spend a round assessing and resetting themselves to regain their normal advantage. Action to initiate.

○ **Break the Ranks (6 Speed points):** You move up to a short distance and attack up to four different foes as a single action as long as they are all along your path. Any modifiers that apply to one attack apply to all the attacks you make. If you have another special ability that allows you to move and take an action, when you use Break the Ranks, you gain an asset to attacking these foes. Action.

○ **Break Their Mind (7+ Intellect points):** Using your clever words and knowledge of others, and given a couple of rounds of conversation to gain a few specific pieces of context regarding your target, you can utter a sentence designed to cause your target immediate psychological distress. If the target can hear and understand you, it suffers 6 points of Intellect damage (ignores Armor) and forgets the last day of its life, which might mean it forgets you and how it came to be where it currently is. In addition to the normal options for using Effort, you can choose to use Effort to attempt to break the mind of one additional target who can hear and understand you. Action to initiate, action to complete.

○ **Breaker:** You are trained in tasks related to damaging objects with the goal of breaking, piercing, or demolishing them. It is a Might action to damage an object, and on a success, the object moves one step down the object damage track. If the Might roll exceeds the difficulty by two steps, the object instead moves two steps down the object damage track. If the Might roll exceeds the difficulty by four steps, the object moves three steps down the object damage track and is immediately destroyed. Brittle material reduces the effective level of the object, while hard material like wood or stone adds 1 to the effective level or 2 for very hard objects like those made of metal. Enabler.

○ **Brute Strike (4 Might points):** You deal 4 additional points of damage with all melee attacks until the end of the next round. Enabler.

○ **Buddy System (3 Intellect points):** Choose one character standing next to you. That character becomes your buddy for ten minutes. You are trained in all tasks involving finding, healing, interacting with, and protecting your buddy. Also, while you stand next to your buddy, both of you have an asset on Speed defense tasks. You can have only one buddy at a time. Action to initiate.

○ **Built-in Weaponry:** Biomechanical implants, a magical jewel fused to your forehead, or something just as wild now provides you with inherent weaponry. This allows you to fire a blast of energy up to long range that inflicts 5 points of damage. There is no cost for you to use this ability. Action.

○ **Burning Light (3 Intellect points):** You send a beam of light at a creature within long range and then tighten the beam until it burns, inflicting 5 points of damage. Action.

○ **Burst of Escape (5 Speed points):** You can take two separate actions this round, as long as one of them is to hide or to move in a direction that is not toward a foe. Enabler.

○ **Bypass Barrier (6+ Intellect points):** You get past a door, force field, or other barrier up to 3 feet (1 m) thick that is blocking your way. Depending on the barrier, this might involve finding a weak spot you can push through, pressing the right button by luck, just breaking through, or even weirder explanations like touching a thin place between dimensions or an unexpected interaction with your equipment. The difficulty of the task is the level of the barrier. This ability allows you alone to pass through, not anyone else, and the way through closes at the end of your turn (which might mean you're trapped on the far side). You have an asset in any attempts to get through it again. In addition to the normal options for using Effort, you can choose to use Effort to increase the maximum thickness of the barrier, each level adding 3 feet (1 m). Action.

ABILITIES—C

◯ **Call Dead Spirit (6 Intellect points):** At your touch, the remains of a creature dead no longer than seven days appears as a manifest (and apparently physical) spirit, whose level is the same as it had in life. The raised spirit persists for up to a day (or less, if it accomplishes something important to it before then), after which it fades away and cannot return again.

The raised spirit remembers everything it knew in life and possesses most of its previous abilities (though not necessarily its equipment). In addition, it gains the ability to become insubstantial as an action for up to a minute at a time. The raised spirit is not beholden to you, and it does not need to stay near you to remain manifest. Action to initiate.

◯ **Call in Favor (4 Intellect points):** A guard, doctor, technician, or hired thug in the employ of or allied with a foe is secretly your ally or owes you a favor. When you call in the favor, the target does what they can to help you out of a specific fix (unties you, slips you a knife, leaves a cell door unlocked) in a way that minimizes their risk of revealing their divided loyalties to their employer or other allies. This ability is a difficulty 3 Intellect task. Each additional time you use this ability, the task is hindered by an additional step. The difficulty returns to 3 after you rest for ten hours. Action.

◯ **Call Otherworldly Spirit (6 Intellect points):** You summon a spirit creature that manifests for up to a day (or less, if it accomplishes something important to it before then), after which it fades away and cannot be summoned again. The spirit is a creature of level 6 or lower, and it can be substantial or insubstantial as it wishes (using an action to change). The spirit is not beholden to you, and it does not need to stay near you to remain manifest. Action to initiate.

◯ **Call the Storm (7+ Intellect points):** If you are outside or in a location that has a ceiling at least 300 feet (90 m) above the floor, you summon a boiling layer of lightning-lit, rumbling clouds up to 1,500 feet (460 m) in diameter for ten minutes. During daylight hours, natural illumination beneath the storm is reduced to dim light. While the storm rages, you can use an action to send a lightning bolt from the cloud to attack a target you can see directly, inflicting 4 points of damage (you can spend Effort normally on each individual lightning bolt attack). Three actions to initiate; action to call down a lightning strike.

When a dead spirit is called, it is likely to have a unique personality, a name, and perhaps even unfinished business that it might relate to the character.

Influence Swarm, page 153

Enthrall, page 136

Calming a stranger with words might rely on pure training, a way with people, or, if the setting utilizes magic or psionics, a more fantastic manipulation of reality.

Minor Illusion, page 162

○ **Call Swarm (4 Intellect points):** If you're in a location where it's possible for the creatures from your Influence Swarm ability to come, you call a swarm of them for one hour. During this hour, they do as you telepathically command as long as they are within long range. They can swarm about and hinder any or all opponents' tasks. While the creatures are in long range, you can speak to them telepathically and perceive through their senses. Action to initiate.

○ **Call Through Time (6+ Intellect points):** You call a creature or person of up to level 3 from the recent past, and it appears next to you. You can choose a creature that you've previously encountered (even if it is now dead), or (no more than once per day) you can allow the GM to determine the creature randomly. If you call a random creature, it has a 10 percent chance of being a creature of up to level 5. The creature has no memory of anything before being called by you, though it can speak and has the general knowledge a creature of its type should possess. The time-shifted creature does your bidding for as long as you concentrate on it, but you must use your action each turn to direct it; otherwise it returns to the past.

In addition to the normal options for using Effort, you can choose to use Effort to call a more powerful creature; each level of Effort used in this way increases the creature's level by 1. For example, applying one level of Effort calls a specific creature of up to level 4 or a random creature with a 10 percent chance of being up to level 6. Action.

○ **Calm (3 Intellect points):** Through jokes, song, or other art, you prevent a living foe from attacking anyone or anything for one round. Action.

○ **Calm Stranger (2+ Intellect points):** You can cause one intelligent creature to remain calm as you speak. The creature doesn't need to speak your language, but it must be able to see you. It remains calm as long as you focus all your attention on it and it is not attacked or otherwise threatened. In addition to the normal options for using Effort, you can choose to use Effort to calm additional creatures allied with your initial target, one additional creature per level of Effort applied. Action.

○ **Capable Warrior:** Your attacks deal 1 additional point of damage. Enabler.

○ **Captivate or Inspire:** You can use this ability in one of two ways. Either your words keep the attention of all NPCs that hear them for as long as you speak, or your words inspire all NPCs that hear them to function as if they were one level higher for the next hour. In either case, you choose which NPCs are affected. If anyone in the crowd is attacked while you're trying to speak to them, you lose the crowd's attention. Action to initiate.

○ **Captivate With Starshine:** For as long as you speak, you keep the attention of all level 2 or lower NPCs who can hear you. If you also have the Enthrall ability, you can similarly captivate all level 3 NPCs. Action to initiate.

○ **Car Surfer:** You can stand or move about on a moving vehicle (such as on the hood, on the roof, in the open door well, etc.) with a reasonable expectation of not falling off. Unless the vehicle veers sharply, stops suddenly, or otherwise engages in extreme maneuvers, standing or moving about on a moving vehicle is a routine task for you. If the vehicle engages in extreme maneuvers like those described, any tasks to remain on the vehicle's surface are eased. Enabler.

○ **Careful Aim:** You are trained in attacks with all weapons that you throw. Enabler.

○ **Careful Shot:** You can spend points from either your Speed Pool or your Intellect Pool to apply levels of Effort to increase your gun damage. Each level of Effort adds 3 points of damage to a successful attack, and if you spend a turn lining up your shot, each level of Effort instead adds 5 points of damage to a successful attack. Enabler.

○ **Cast Illusion:** You can increase the range at which you create and maintain your immediate-range illusions (such as from Minor Illusion) to anywhere within short range that you can perceive. Enabler.

○ **Castigate (4 Intellect points):** You intimidate any opponent within long range who understands speech (even if it is not your language) so much that they lose their next action and all the rest of their actions are hindered for one minute. Each additional time you attempt this ability against the same target, you must apply one more level of Effort than you applied on the previous attempt. Action.

ABILITIES—C

○ **Celebrity Talent:** You are trained in two of the following areas: writing, journalism, a particular style of art, a particular sport, chess, science communication, acting, news presentation, or some related noncombat skill that led to your celebrity. Enabler.

○ **Center of Attention (5 Intellect points):** A literal (or metaphorical, depending on the genre) beam of pure radiance descends from on high and spotlights you. All creatures you choose within immediate range fall to their knees and lose their next action. Affected targets cannot defend themselves and are treated as helpless. Action.

○ **Chamber of Dreams (8 Intellect points):** You and your allies can step into a chamber of dreams, decorated as you wish, that contains a number of doors. The doors correspond with other locations that you have visited or know reasonably well. Stepping through one of the doors delivers you to the desired location. This is a difficulty 2 Intellect-based task (which could be modified upward by the GM if the location is warded). Action to step into chamber of dreams; action to move through a door in the chamber.

○ **Change the Paradigm (6+ Intellect points):** You sway the worldview of a creature you spend at least one round speaking to, as long as it can understand you. The creature changes its mind on a significant belief, which could include something as straightforward as helping you instead of trying to kill you, or it could be something more esoteric. This effect lasts for at least ten minutes, but it can last longer if the creature wasn't previously your foe. During this time, the creature takes actions in accordance with the wisdom you have imparted to it. The target must be level 2 or lower. In addition to the normal options for using Effort, you can choose to use Effort to increase the maximum level of the target by one for each level of Effort applied. Action to initiate.

○ **Charge (1+ Intellect points):** You can charge an artifact or other device (except a cypher) so that it can be used once. The cost is 1 Intellect point plus 1 point per level of the device. Action.

○ **Charging Horde (7 Might points):** You and two or more of your followers next to you can act like a single creature to make a charge attack. When you do, all of you move up to a short distance, during which time you can attack anything that comes within immediate range along your path with an asset to the attack. Targets that take damage take an additional 3 points and are knocked prone. Action.

○ **Charm Machine (2 Intellect points):** You convince an unintelligent machine to "like" you. A machine that likes you is 50 percent less likely to function if said function would cause you harm. Thus, if a foe attempts to detonate a bomb near you controlled by a detonator that likes you, there is a 50 percent chance that it won't explode. Action to initiate.

○ **Cloak of Opportunity (5 Intellect points):** You set small objects from the environment (rocks, broken items, clumps of dirt, and so on) swirling about you for up to ten minutes, which grants you +2 Armor. Action to initiate.

○ **Closed Mind:** You are trained in Intellect defense tasks and have +2 Armor against damage that selectively targets your Intellect Pool (which normally ignores Armor). Enabler.

○ **Cloud Personal Memories (3 Intellect points):** If you interact with or study a target for at least a round, you gain a sense of how its mind works, which you can use against it in the most blunt fashion possible. You can attempt to confuse it and make it forget what's just happened. On a success, you erase up to the last five minutes of its memory. Action to prepare; action to initiate.

○ **Coaxing Power (2 Intellect points):** You boost the power or function of a machine so that it operates at one level higher than normal for one hour. Action to initiate.

○ **Cognizant Offense:** During combat, your brain shifts into a sort of battle mode where all potential attacks you could make are plotted on vector graphs in your mind's eye, which always provides the best option. Your attacks are eased. Enabler.

○ **Cold Burst (5+ Intellect points):** You emit a burst of cold in all directions, up to short range. All within the burst (except you) take 5 points of damage. If you apply Effort to increase the damage rather than to ease the task, you deal 2 additional points of damage per level of Effort (instead of 3 points); targets in the area take 1 point of damage even if you fail the attack roll. Action.

Cloak of Opportunity can be quite flashy and intimidating to others, especially before they know its purpose.

Artifact, page 204
Cypher, page 377

Follower, page 233

Enlarge, page 135

Gargantuan, page 144
Bigger, page 113
Huge, page 149

Destroy Metal, page 127

○ **Colossal:** When you use Enlarge, you can choose to grow up to a base height of 60 feet (18 m). When you do, you add 5 more temporary points to your Might Pool (plus any from Gargantuan and Bigger), and you deal an additional 2 points of damage with melee attacks (plus any from your Huge ability). For each level of Effort you apply to increase your height further, your total height increases by 10 feet (3 m), and you add 1 more point to your Might Pool. Thus, the first time you use Enlarge after a ten-hour recovery roll, if you apply two levels of Effort, your base height is 80 feet (24 m), and you add a total of 17 temporary points to your Might Pool. Enabler.

○ **Combat Challenge:** All attempted tasks that draw an attack to yourself (and away from someone else) are eased by two steps. Enabler.

○ **Combat Prowess:** You add +1 damage to one type of weapon attack of your choice: melee weapon attacks or ranged weapon attacks. Enabler.

○ **Command (3 Intellect points):** Through sheer force of will, you can issue a simple imperative command to a single living creature, who then attempts to carry out your command as its next action. The creature must be within short range and able to understand you. The command can't inflict direct harm on the creature or its allies, so "Commit suicide" won't work, but "Flee" might. In addition, the command can require the creature to take only one action, so "Unlock the door" might work, but "Unlock the door and run through it" won't. A commanded creature can still defend itself normally and return an attack if one is made on it. If you possess another ability that allows you to command a creature, you can target two creatures at once as your base effect if you use either ability. Action.

○ **Command Machine (4 Intellect points):** If you've charmed an unintelligent machine or have spoken telepathically with an intelligent machine, you can attempt to command it to take one action within its capabilities on its next turn. (If you use this ability to command an intelligent machine, it likely becomes hostile to you afterward.) Action.

○ **Command Metal (5 Intellect points):** You reshape a metallic item as you desire. The item must be within sight and within short range, and its mass can be no greater than your own. You can affect multiple items at once as long as their combined mass falls within these limits. You can fuse multiple items together. You can use this power to destroy a metal object (as the Destroy Metal ability), or you can craft it into another desired shape (crudely, unless you have the proper crafting skills). You can then move the new object anywhere within range. For example, you could take a few metal shields, fuse them together, and use the resulting shape to block a doorway. You can use this ability to make an attack—causing a foe's armor to constrict, rendering a metal item into shards that you fling across the battlefield, and so on—against one target within short range. Regardless of the form of the attack, it is an Intellect action that deals 7 points of damage. Action.

Abilities—C

Command Spirit (3 Intellect points): You can command a spirit or animated dead creature of up to level 5 within short range. If you are successful, the target cannot attack you for one minute, during which time it follows your verbal commands if it can hear and understand you. Action to initiate.

Communication (2 Intellect points): You can convey a basic concept to a creature that normally can't speak or understand speech. The creature can also give you a very basic answer to a simple question. Action.

Community Activist: When speaking to others in a community you have a strong connection to, you are trained in persuasion and intimidation tasks about topics that directly relate to the community. Enabler.

Community Knowledge (2 Intellect points): If you've invested yourself in a community and have spent at least a few months living there, you can learn things about it through a variety of methods. Sometimes contacts slip the information to you. Other times, you're able to draw conclusions simply by what you can see and hear. When you use this ability, you can ask the GM one question about the community and get a very short answer. Action.

Computer Programming: You are trained in using (and exploiting) computer software, you know one or more computer languages well enough to write basic programs, and you are fluent in internet protocol. Enabler.

Concussion (7 Intellect points): You cause a pulse of concussive force to explode out from a point you choose within long range. The pulse extends up to short range in all directions, dealing 5 points of damage to everything in the area. Even if you fail the attack roll, targets in the area take 1 point of damage. Action.

Concussive Blast (2 Intellect points): You release a beam of pure force that smashes into a creature within short range, inflicting 5 points of damage and moving it back an immediate distance. Action.

Confidence Artist: When you're hacking into a computer system, running a con, picking a pocket, fooling or tricking a dupe, sneaking something by a guard, and so on, you gain an asset on the task. Enabler.

Confounding Banter (4 Intellect points): You spew a stream of nonsense to distract a foe within immediate range. On a successful Intellect roll, your defense roll against the creature's next attack before the end of the next round is eased. Action.

Confuse Enemy (4 Intellect points): Through a clever bit of misdirection involving a flourish of your coat, ducking at just the right moment, or a similar stratagem, you can attempt to redirect a physical melee attack that would otherwise hit you. When you do, the misdirected attack hits another creature you choose within immediate range of both you and the attacking foe. This ability is a difficulty 2 Intellect task. Enabler.

Conjuration (7 Intellect points): You produce, as if from thin air, a level 5 creature of a kind you have previously encountered. The creature remains for one minute and then returns home. While present, the creature acts as you direct, but this requires no action on your part. Action.

Connected: You know people who get things done—not just respected people in positions of authority, but also a variety of online hackers and regular street criminals. These people are not necessarily your friends and might not be trustworthy, but they owe you a favor. You and the GM should work out the details of your contacts. Enabler.

Contortionist (2 Speed points): You can wriggle free from bindings or squeeze through a tight spot. You are trained in escaping. When you use an action to escape or move through a tight area, you can immediately use another action. You may use this action only to move. Enabler.

Control the Field (1 Might point): This melee attack inflicts 1 less point of damage than normal, and regardless of whether you hit the target, you maneuver it into a position you desire within immediate range. Action.

Control Machine (6 Intellect points): You can attempt to control the functions of any machine, intelligent or otherwise, within short range for ten minutes. Action.

Abilities that rely on the character being a part of the community give the GM additional material for scenarios. For instance, even as the character gains benefits from those in the community, other NPCs in the community might call on the character to help them solve some of their issues, too.

Duplicate, page 132

Influence Swarm, page 153

Using Counter Danger is usually a matter of the character applying quick thinking in the face of immediate danger. The ability doesn't rely on supernatural means, but rather a practical act.

Foil Danger, page 142

Storm Seed, page 187

Beast Form, page 112
Crafting, page 227

Control the Savage (6 Intellect points): You can control a calm nonhuman beast within 30 feet (9 m). You control it for as long as you focus all your attention on it, using your turn each round. The GM has final say over what counts as a nonhuman beast, but unless some kind of deception is at work, you should know whether you can affect a creature before you attempt to use this ability on it. Aliens, extradimensional entities, very intelligent creatures, and robots never count. Action.

Control Swarm (2 Intellect points): Your swarm creatures from your Influence Swarm ability within short range do as you telepathically command for ten minutes. Even common insects (level 0) in large enough numbers can swarm about a single creature and hinder its tasks. Action to initiate.

Control Weather (10 Intellect points): You change the weather in your general region. If performed indoors, this creates minor effects, such as mist, mild temperature changes, and so on. If performed outside, you can create rain, fog, snow, wind, or any other kind of normal (not overly severe) weather. The change lasts for a natural length of time so that a storm might last for an hour, fog for two or three hours, and snow for a few hours (or for ten minutes if it's out of season). For the first ten minutes after activating this ability, you can create more dramatic and specific effects, such as lightning strikes, giant hailstones, twisters, hurricane-force winds, and so on. These effects must occur within 1,000 feet (300 m) of your location. You must spend your turn concentrating to create an effect or maintain it in a new round. These effects inflict 6 points of damage each round. If you have this ability from another source, the cost for the ability is 7 Intellect points instead of 10. If you already have the Storm Seed ability, you can immediately replace it with a new ability of the same tier. Action to initiate.

Controlled Change: You can try to use your Beast Form ability to change into your beast form on any night you wish (a difficulty 3 Intellect task). Any transformations you make using this power are in addition to the five nights per month that you change involuntarily. Action to change.

Controlled Fall: When you fall while you are able to use actions and within reach of a vertical surface, you can attempt to slow your fall. Make a Speed roll with a difficulty of 1 for every 20 feet (6 m) you fall. On a success, you take half damage from the fall. If you reduce the difficulty to 0, you take no damage. Enabler.

Coordinated Effort (3 Intellect points): When you and the duplicate from your Duplicate ability would attack the same creature, you can choose to make one attack roll with an asset. If you hit, you inflict damage with both attacks and treat the attacks as if they were one attack for the purpose of subtracting Armor from the damage. Action.

Counter Danger (4 Intellect points): You negate a source of potential danger related to one creature or object within immediate distance for one minute (instead of one round, as with Foil Danger). This could be a weapon or device held by someone, a creature's natural ability, or a trap triggered by a pressure plate. You can also try to counter an action (like moving or making a conventional mundane attack with a weapon, a claw, etc.). Action.

Countermeasures (4 Intellect points): You immediately end one ongoing effect (such as an effect created by a character ability) within immediate range. Alternatively, you can use this as a defense action to cancel any incoming ability targeted at you, or you can cancel any device or the effect of any device for 1d6 rounds. You must touch the effect or device to cancel it. Action.

Courageous: You are trained in Intellect defense tasks and initiative tasks. Enabler.

Crafter: You are trained in the crafting of two kinds of items. Enabler.

Create (7 Intellect points): You create something from nothing. You can create any item you choose that would ordinarily have a difficulty of 5 or lower (using the crafting rules). Once created, the item lasts for a number of hours equal to 6 minus the difficulty to create it. Thus, if you create a set of sturdy manacles (difficulty 5), it would last for one hour. Action.

○ **Create Deadly Poison (3+ Intellect points):** You create one dose of a level 2 poison that either inflicts 5 points of damage or hinders the poisoned creature's actions for ten minutes (your choice each time you create the poison). You can apply this poison to a weapon, food, or drink as part of the action of creating it. In addition to the normal options for using Effort, you can choose to use Effort to increase the level of the poison; each level of Effort used in this way increases the poison level by 1. If unused, the poison loses its potency after one hour. Action.

○ **Create Water (2 Intellect points):** You cause water to bubble up from a spot on the ground you can see. The water flows from that spot for one minute, creating about 1 gallon (4 liters) by the time it stops. Action to initiate.

○ **Creature Insight (3 Intellect points):** When examining any nonhuman creature, you can ask the GM one question to gain an idea of its level, its capabilities, what it eats, what motivates it, what its weaknesses are (if any), how it can be repaired, or any other similar query. This is for difficult or strange creatures beyond those readily identified by using skills. Action.

○ **Critter Companion:** A level 1 creature accompanies you and follows your instructions. This creature is no larger than a large cat (about 20 pounds, or 9 kg) and is normally some sort of domesticated species. You and the GM must work out the details of your creature, and you'll probably make rolls for it in combat or when it takes actions. The critter companion acts on your turn. As a level 1 creature, it has a target number of 3 and 3 health, and it inflicts 1 point of damage. Its movement is based on its creature type (avian, swimmer, and so on). If your critter companion dies, you can search an urban or wild environment for 1d6 days to find a new one. Enabler.

○ **Crowd Control (6+ Intellect points):** You control the actions of up to five creatures in short range. This effect lasts for one minute. All targets must be level 2 or lower. Your control is limited to simple verbal commands like "Stop," "Run away," "Follow that guard," "Look over there," or "Get out of my way." All affected creatures respond to the command unless you specifically command them otherwise. In addition to the normal options for using Effort, you can choose to use Effort to increase the maximum level of the targets or affect an additional five people. Thus, to control a group that has a level 4 target (two levels above the normal limit) or a group of fifteen people, you must apply two levels of Effort. When the Crowd Control ability ends, the creatures remember your commands but don't remember being controlled—your commands seemed reasonable at the time. Action to initiate.

○ **Crushing Blow (2 Might points):** When you use a bashing or bladed weapon in both hands and apply Effort on the attack, you get a free level of Effort on the damage. (If fighting unarmed, this attack is made with both fists or both feet together.) Action.

○ **Crystal Lens:** You can focus the inherent energy surging through you from your Crystalline Body ability. This allows you to fire a blast of energy that inflicts 5 points of damage on a target within very long range. Action.

○ **Crystalline Body:** You are composed of animate, translucent crystal the color of amber. Work with your GM to decide your exact form, though it is likely about the shape and size of a humanoid. Your crystal body grants you +2 to Armor and +4 to your Might Pool. However, you're not quick and your Speed defense tasks are hindered. Certain conditions, like mundane diseases and poisons, do not affect you. Your crystalline body repairs itself more slowly than a body of living flesh would. You have only the one-round, one-hour, and ten-hour recovery rolls available each day; you do not have a ten-minute recovery roll available. Any ability you have that requires a ten-minute recovery roll instead requires a one-hour recovery roll. Enabler.

○ **Curious:** You're always curious about your surroundings, even on a subconscious level. Whenever you use Effort to attempt navigation, perception, or initiative tasks in an area that you've only rarely or never visited before, you can apply an additional free level of Effort. Enabler.

○ **Cutting Light (2 Intellect points):** You emit a thin beam of energized light from your hand. This inflicts 5 points of damage to a single foe in immediate range. The beam is even more effective against immobile, nonliving targets, slicing up to 1 foot (30 cm) of any material that is level 6 or lower. The material can be up to 1 foot thick. Action.

Free level of Effort, page 209

A Critter Companion might have an interesting quirk, such as having a thing for chasing bugs, always wanting to be petted by another NPC, getting lost, and so on.

○ **Cyphersmith:** All manifest cyphers you use function at one level higher than normal. If given a week and the right tools, chemicals, and parts, you can tinker with one of your manifest cyphers, transforming it into another cypher of the same type that you had in the past. The GM and player should collaborate to ensure that the transformation is logical—for example, you probably can't transform a pill into a helmet. Enabler.

ABILITIES—D

○ **Damage Dealer:** You inflict an additional 3 points of damage with your chosen weapon. Enabler.

○ **Damage Transference:** When you or your duplicate (from the Duplicate ability) would take damage, you can transfer 1 point of damage from one to the other provided that you and your duplicate are within 1 mile (1.5 km) of each other. Enabler.

○ **Damn the Guilty (3 Intellect points):** You speak words of revelation and judgment to everyone within close range. Those whom you have designated as guilty with your Designation ability take an additional 3 points of damage from any attack they receive from anyone who heard your judgment. This judgment lasts for up to one minute or until they move at least a long distance away from you. Action.

○ **Danger Instinct (3 Speed points):** If you are attacked by surprise, whether by a creature, a device, or simply an environmental hazard (a tree falling on you), you can move an immediate distance before the attack occurs. If moving prevents the attack, you are safe. If the attack can still potentially affect you—if the attacking creature can move to keep pace, if the attack fills an area too big to escape, etc.—the ability offers no benefit. Enabler.

○ **Danger Sense (1 Speed point):** Your initiative task is eased. You pay the cost each time the ability is used. Enabler.

○ **Dark Explorer:** You ignore penalties for any action (including fighting) in extremely dim light or in cramped spaces. If you also have the Eyes Adjusted ability, you can act without penalty even in total darkness. You are trained in sneaking tasks while in dim or no light. Enabler.

○ **Dark Matter Shell (5 Intellect points):** For the next minute, you cover yourself with a shell of dark matter. Your appearance becomes a dark silhouette, and you gain an asset to sneaking tasks and gain +1 to your Armor. The dark matter shell works seamlessly with your desires, and if you apply a level of Effort to any physical task while the shell persists, you can apply an additional free level of Effort to that same task. Action to initiate.

○ **Dark Matter Shroud (4 Intellect points):** Ribbons of dark matter condense and swirl about you for up to one minute. This shroud eases your Speed defense tasks, inflicts 2 points of damage to anyone who tries to touch you or strike you with a melee attack, and gives you +1 Armor. Action to initiate.

○ **Dark Matter Strike (4 Intellect points):** When you attack a foe within long range, dark matter condenses around your target and entangles its limbs, holding it in place and easing your attack by two steps. The ability works for whatever kind of attack you use (melee, ranged, energy, and so on). Enabler.

○ **Dark Matter Structure (5 Intellect points):** You can form dark matter into a large structure consisting of up to ten 10-foot (3 m) cubes. The structure can be somewhat complex, though everything has the same matte black color from which no light shines. Otherwise, the structure can possess different densities, textures, and capacities. This means it can include windows, doors with locks, furnishings, and even decor, as long as it is all black as pitch. For example, you could shape the dark matter into a large, defensible structure; a sturdy 100-foot (30 m) bridge; or anything similar. The structure is a level 6 creation and lasts for 24 hours. You can't keep more than one such structure solid at any one time. Action.

○ **Datajack (1 Intellect point):** With computer access, you jack in instantly and learn a bit more about something you can see. You get an asset on a task involving that person or object. Action.

○ **Daydream (4 Intellect points):** You pull someone into a daydream, substituting a dream of your own creation for the target's reality for up to one minute. You can affect a target within long range that you can see, or a target within 10 miles (16 km) that you have hair or skin clippings from. To all outward appearances, an affected

Free level of Effort, page 209

Duplicate, page 132

Designation, page 127

Surprise, page 220

Initiative, page 214

Eyes Adjusted, page 138

target stands (or lies) unmoving. But inside, the substituted reality (or dream within a dream, if the target was sleeping) is what the target experiences. If the target is under duress, it can attempt another Intellect defense roll each round to break free, though the target may not realize its state. Either the dream unfolds according to a script you prepared when you used this ability, or if you use your own actions (forcing you into a similar state as the target), you can direct the unfolding dream from round to round. Using this ability on a sleeping target eases the initial attack. Action to initiate; if you direct the dream, action to direct per round.

◐ **Dazing Attack (3 Might points):** You hit your foe in just the right spot, dazing them so that tasks they attempt on their next turn are hindered. This attack inflicts normal damage. Action.

◐ **Dazzling Sunburst (2 Intellect points):** You send a barrage of dazzling colors at a creature within short range and, if successful, inflict 2 points of damage on the target. In addition, the creature's attacks are hindered on its next turn, unless the target relies primarily on senses other than sight. Action.

◐ **Deactivate Mechanisms (5+ Speed points):** You make a melee attack that inflicts no damage against a machine. Instead, if the attack hits, make a second Speed-based roll. If successful, a machine of level 3 or lower is deactivated for one minute. For each additional level of Effort applied, you can affect one higher level of machine or you can extend the duration for an additional minute. If you have the Scramble Machine or Disable Mechanisms ability (or an ability that works similarly), when you apply a level of Effort to any of them, you gain an additional free level of Effort. Action.

◐ **Deadly Aim (3 Speed points):** For the next minute, all ranged attacks you make inflict 2 additional points of damage. Action to initiate.

◐ **Deadly Strike (5 Might points):** If you strike a foe of level 3 or lower with a weapon you're practiced with, you kill the target instantly. Action.

◐ **Deadly Swarm (6 Intellect points):** If you're in a location where it's possible for your swarm of creatures from your Influence Swarm ability to come, you call a swarm of them for ten minutes. During this time, they do as you telepathically command as long as they are within long range. They can swarm about and hinder any or all opponents' tasks, or they can focus the swarm and attack all opponents within immediate range of each other (all within long range of you). The attacking swarm inflicts 4 points of damage. While the creatures are in long range, you can speak to them telepathically and perceive through their senses. Action to initiate.

◐ **Death Touch (6 Intellect points):** You gather disrupting energy in your fingertip and touch a creature. If the target is an NPC or a creature of level 3 or lower, it dies. If the target is a PC of any tier, they move down one step on the damage track. Action.

Swarms don't usually have game stats, but if needed, a typical swarm is level 2. Only attacks that affect a large area affect the swarm.

Damage track, page 218
Scramble Machine, page 179
Disable Mechanisms, page 128
Influence Swarm, page 153

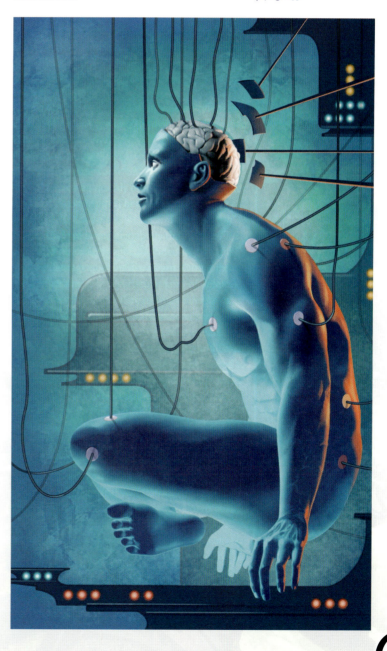

○ **Debate (3 Intellect points):** In any gathering of two or more people trying to establish the truth or come to a decision, you can sway the verdict with masterful rhetoric. If you are given one minute or more to argue your point, either the decision goes your way or, if someone else effectively argues a competing point, any associated persuasion or deception task is eased by two steps. Action to initiate; one minute to complete.

○ **Debilitating Strike (4 Speed points):** You make an attack to deliver a painful or debilitating strike. The attack is hindered. If it hits, the creature takes 2 additional points of damage at the end of the next round, and its attacks are hindered until the end of the next round. Action.

○ **Decipher (1 Intellect point):** If you spend one minute examining a piece of writing or code in a language you do not understand, you can make an Intellect roll of difficulty 3 (or higher, based on the complexity of the language or code) to get the gist of the message. Action to initiate.

○ **Deep Consideration (6 Intellect points):** When you develop a plan that involves you and your friends working together to accomplish a goal, you can ask the GM one very general question about what is likely to happen if you carry out the plan, and you will get a simple, brief answer. In addition, all of you gain an asset to one roll related to enacting the plan you developed together, as long as you put the plan into action within a few days of the plan's creation. Action.

○ **Deep Reserves:** When others are exhausted, you can push through. Once each day, you can transfer up to 5 points among your Pools in any combination, at a rate of 1 point per round. For example, you could transfer 3 points of Might to Speed and 2 points of Intellect to Speed, which would take a total of five rounds. Action.

○ **Deep Resources:** You gain an additional 6 points to your Speed Pool. Enabler.

○ **Deep Water Guide:** While underwater, any creature you choose that can see you has an asset on swimming tasks. Enabler.

○ **Defend All the Innocent:** You protect everyone within immediate range whom you have designated as innocent with your Designation ability. Speed defense rolls made by such creatures gain an asset. Enabler.

○ **Defend the Innocent (2 Speed points):** For the next ten minutes, if someone you have designated as innocent with the Designation ability stands next to you, that creature shares any defensive advantages that you might have, other than mundane armor. These advantages include the Speed defense from your shield, the Armor offered from a force field, and so on. In addition, Speed defense rolls made by the innocent creature gain an asset. You can protect only one innocent creature at a time. Action to initiate.

○ **Defense Against Robots:** You have studied your enemy and are trained in anticipating the actions that a robot or machine is likely to take in a fight. Defense tasks you attempt against these foes are eased. Enabler.

Designation, page 127

Abilities—D

○ **Defense Master:** Every time you succeed at a Speed defense task, you can make an immediate attack against your foe. (If you have Dodge and Respond, you can exchange that ability for Dodge and Resist.) Your attack must be the same type (melee weapon, ranged weapon, or unarmed) as the attack you defend against. If you don't have an appropriate type of weapon ready, you can't use this ability. Enabler.

○ **Defensive Augmentation:** By upgrading your nervous and immune systems, you are trained in Might defense and Speed defense tasks. Enabler.

○ **Defensive Field:** Thanks to subdermal implants, a permanent spell, alien modifications, or something similar, you now have a force field that radiates 1 inch (2.5 cm) from your body and provides you with +2 Armor. Enabler.

○ **Defensive Phasing (2 Intellect points):** You can change your phase so that some attacks pass through you harmlessly. For the next ten minutes, you gain an asset to your Speed defense tasks, but during this time you lose any benefit from armor you wear. Action to initiate.

○ **Define Down (4 Intellect points):** The natural gravity within an area a short distance across that you are within immediate range of changes directions so that it flows in the direction you determine (up, up and to the south, west, and so on) for a few seconds, then snaps back. Affected targets could be tossed up to 20 feet (6 m) and take a few points of damage. Action.

○ **Deflect Attacks (1 Intellect point):** Using your mind, you protect yourself from incoming attacks. For the next ten minutes, you are trained in Speed defense tasks. Action to initiate.

○ **Defuse Situation:** During the course of an investigation, your questions sometimes elicit an angry or even violent response. Through dissembling, verbal distraction, or similar evasion, you prevent a living foe from attacking anyone or anything for one round. Action.

○ **Demeanor of Command (2 Intellect points):** You project confidence, knowledge, and charisma to all who see you for the next hour. Your demeanor is such that those who see you automatically understand that you are someone important, accomplished, and with authority. When you speak, strangers who are not already attacking give you at least a round to have your say. If speaking to a group that can understand you, you can attempt to have them produce their leader or ask that they take you to their leader. You gain a free level of Effort that can be applied to one persuasion task you attempt during this period. Action to initiate.

○ **Designation:** You assign an innocent or guilty label to one creature within immediate range, based on your assessment of a given situation or a predominant feeling. In other words, someone who is labeled innocent can be innocent in a certain circumstance, or they can be generally innocent of terrible crimes (such as murder, major theft, and so on). Likewise, you can declare that a creature is guilty of a particular crime or of terrible deeds in general. The accuracy of your assessment isn't important as long as you believe it to be the truth; the GM may require you to give a rationale. Henceforth, your tasks to socially interact with someone you designate as innocent gain an asset, and your attacks against those you designate as guilty gain an asset. You can change your assessment, but it requires another designation action. The benefits of the designation last until you change it or until you are shown proof that it is wrong. Action.

○ **Destined for Greatness:** You enjoy uncanny luck as if something was watching over you and keeping you from harm. When you would otherwise descend a step on the damage track, make an Intellect defense roll versus the difficulty set by the level of the foe or effect. If you succeed, you do not descend that step. If the step was because you fell to 0 points in a Pool, you are still at 0 points; you just don't suffer the negative effects of being impaired or debilitated. If you would otherwise descend the final step on the damage track to death, a successful defense roll keeps you at 1 point in one Pool, and you remain debilitated. Enabler.

○ **Destroy Metal (3 Intellect points):** You instantly tear, rip, or burst a metal object that is within sight, within short range, and no bigger than half your size. Attempt an Intellect task to destroy the object; the task is eased by three steps compared to breaking it with brute strength. Action.

○ **Destroyer (6 Might points):** If you succeed on a Might task to damage an object, instead of descending one step on the object damage track, the object descends all three steps and is destroyed. Action.

Dodge and Respond, page 131

Dodge and Resist, page 131

Free level of Effort, page 209

The benefits provided by Designation apply to the character using the ability, their allies, and anyone who hears or is told of their judgment and believes their assessment.

A character could use Define Down to help propel allies to a location they can't otherwise climb to.

Damage track, page 218

Object damage track, page 116

○ **Detect Life (3+ Might points):** You consciously send out a pulse of your your life energy. You detect all living creatures within short range, even if they are behind cover, though not if they're behind a force field. When you detect a creature, you detect its general location (to within an immediate range). If you apply two additional levels of Effort, you can increase the range of detection to long. Action.

○ **Device Insight (3 Intellect points):** When examining any unknown, alien, or high-technology device, you can ask the GM one question to gain an idea of its capabilities, how it functions, how it can be activated or deactivated, what its weaknesses are (if any), how it can be repaired, or any other similar query. This is for difficult or strange things beyond those readily identified by using the appropriate knowledge or technical skill. Action.

○ **Devoted Defender (2 Might or Intellect points):** Choose one character you can see. That character becomes your ward. You are trained in all tasks involving finding, healing, interacting with, and protecting that character. You can have only one ward at a time. Action to initiate.

○ **Diamagnetism:** You magnetize any nonmetallic object within short range so that it can be affected by your other magnetic powers. Thus, with Move Metal, you can move any object. With Repel Metal, you are trained in all Speed defense tasks, regardless of whether the incoming attack uses metal. And so on. Enabler.

○ **Dirty Fighter (2 Speed points):** You distract, blind, annoy, hamper, or otherwise interfere with a foe, hindering their attacks and defenses for one minute. Action.

○ **Disable Mechanisms (3 Speed points):** With a keen eye and quick moves, you disrupt some functions of a robot or machine and inflict upon it one of the following maladies:
- All its tasks are hindered for one minute.
- Its speed is halved.
- It can take no action for one round.
- It deals 2 fewer points of damage (minimum 1 point) for one minute.

You must touch the robot or machine to disrupt it (if you are making an attack, it inflicts no damage). Action.

○ **Disappear (4 Intellect points):** You bend light that falls on you so you seem to disappear. You are invisible to other creatures for ten minutes. While invisible, you are specialized in stealth and Speed defense tasks. This effect ends if you do something to reveal your presence or position—attacking, using an ability, moving a large object, and so on. If this occurs, you can regain the remaining invisibility effect by taking an action to focus on hiding your position. Action to initiate or reinitiate.

Even though light bends around a character with the Disappear ability, they can still sense their surroundings. If the GM wants to throw a bone to realism, the invisible character's perception tasks are hindered.

Move Metal, page 164
Repel Metal, page 176

○ **Disarming Attack (5 Speed points):** You attempt a Speed task to disarm a foe as part of your melee attack. If you succeed, your attack inflicts 3 additional points of damage and the target's weapon is knocked from their grip, landing up to 20 feet (6 m) away. If you fail, you still attempt your normal attack, but you don't inflict the extra damage or disarm the opponent if you hit. Action.

○ **Disarming Strike (3 Speed points):** Your attack inflicts 1 point less damage and disarms your foe so that their weapon is now 10 feet (3 m) away on the ground. (If your chosen weapon is a whip, you can instead deposit the disarmed weapon into your hands; if your chosen weapon is a bow or other ranged weapon that fires physical rounds, you can instead "nail" the disarmed weapon to a nearby object or structure. Choosing to do either of these hinders your attack.) Action.

○ **Discerning Mind:** You have +3 Armor against damaging attacks and damaging effects that target your mind and Intellect. Defense rolls you make against attacks that attempt to confuse, persuade, frighten, or otherwise influence you are eased. Enabler.

○ **Discipline of Watchfulness (7 Intellect points):** You keep your allies on their toes with occasional questions, jokes, and even mock drills for those who care to join in. After spending 24 hours with you, your allies can apply a free level of Effort to any initiative tasks they attempt. This benefit is ongoing while you remain in the allies' company. It ends if you leave, but it resumes if you return to the allies' company within 24 hours. If you leave the allies' company for more than 24 hours, you must spend another 24 hours together to reactivate the benefit. You must spend the Intellect point cost each 24 hours you wish to keep the benefit active. Enabler.

○ **Disguise:** You are trained in disguise. You can alter your posture, voice, mannerisms, and hair to look like someone else for as long as you keep up the disguise. However, it is extremely difficult to adopt the appearance of a specific individual without a disguise kit at your disposal. Enabler.

○ **Disincentivize (1 Intellect point):** You hinder all actions attempted by any number of targets within short range who can understand you. You choose which targets are affected. Affected targets' actions are hindered for one round. Enabler.

○ **Disrupting Touch (1+ Might points):** You can turn your Phase Sprint into a melee attack by purposefully grazing another creature as you run. When you do, the touch releases a violent blast of energy that inflicts 2 points of damage to the target (ignores Armor). Whether you hit or miss, your movement (and turn) ends immediately, which puts you within immediate distance of your target. If you apply Effort to increase damage rather than to ease the task, you deal 2 additional points of damage per level of Effort (instead of 3 points); the target takes 1 point of damage even if you fail the attack roll. Enabler.

Phase Sprint, page 170

Free level of Effort, page 209

The Distortion ability grants a creature an asset to their Speed defense. Defense actions are described on page 225.

○ **Distance Viewing (5 Intellect points):** You know that space and distance are illusions. You concentrate to create an invisible, immobile sensor at a location you have previously visited or viewed (at the GM's discretion, you may have to succeed at an Intellect task if the location is warded). The sensor lasts for one hour. Once it is created, you can concentrate to see, hear, and smell through the sensor. It doesn't grant you sensory capabilities beyond the norm. Action to create; action to check.

○ **Distant Interface (2 Intellect points):** You can activate, deactivate, or control a machine at long range as if you were next to it, even if normally you would have to touch or manually operate it. If you have never interacted with the particular machine before, the task is hindered by two steps. To use this ability, you must understand the function of the machine, it must be your size or smaller, and it can't be connected to another intelligence (or be intelligent itself). Action.

Major Effect, page 212

○ **Distortion (2 Intellect points):** You modify how a willing creature within short range reflects light for one minute. The target rapidly shifts between its normal appearance and a blot of darkness. The target has an asset on Speed defense rolls until the effect wears off. Action to initiate.

○ **Diver:** You can safely dive into water from heights of up to 100 feet (30 m), and you can withstand pressure when in water as deep as 100 feet. Enabler.

○ **Divert Attacks (4 Speed points):** For one minute, you automatically deflect or dodge any ranged projectile attacks. However, on your next turn after you're attacked with ranged projectiles, all your other actions are hindered. Action to initiate.

○ **Divide Your Mind (7 Intellect points):** You split your consciousness into two parts. For one minute, you can take two actions on each of your turns, but only one of them can be to use a special ability. Action.

○ **Divine Intervention (2 Intellect points, or 2 Intellect points + 4 XP):** You ask the divine to intervene on your behalf, usually against a creature within long range, changing the course of its life in a small way by introducing a major special effect upon it. The major special effect is akin to what occurs when you roll a natural 20 on an attack. If you want to try for a larger effect, and if the GM allows it, you can attempt a divine intervention with a more far-reaching effect, which is more like the kind of GM intrusion initiated by the GM on their players. In this case, Divine Intervention also costs 4 XP, the effect may not work out exactly like you hope, and you may not make another plea for divine intervention for a week. Action.

○ **Divine Knowledge:** You are trained in all tasks related to knowledge of godly beings. Enabler.

○ **Divine Radiance (2 Intellect points):** Your prayer calls divine radiance from the heavens to punish an unworthy target within long range, inflicting 4 points of damage. If the target is a demon, spirit, or something similar, it also stands in unwilling awe of the divine energy coursing through it and is unable to act on its next turn. Once exposed to this blessing, the target can't be awed by this attack again for several hours. Action.

ABILITIES—D

○ **Divine Symbol (5+ Intellect points):** You invoke divine power by scribing a glowing symbol in the air with your fingers. Writhing pillars of divine radiance spear up to five targets within long range. A successful attack on a target inflicts 5 points of damage. If you apply Effort to increase the damage, you deal 2 additional points of damage per level of Effort (instead of 3 points); targets take 1 point of damage even if you fail the attack roll. Action.

○ **Do You Know Who I Am? (3 Intellect points):** Acting only as someone who is famous and used to privilege can, you verbally harangue a living foe who can hear and understand you so forcefully that it is unable to take any action, including making attacks, for one round. Whether you succeed or fail, the next action the target takes after your attempt is hindered. Action.

○ **Dodge and Resist (3 Speed points):** You can reroll any of your Might, Speed, or Intellect defense rolls and take the better of the two results. Enabler.

○ **Dodge and Respond (3 Might points):** If a melee attack misses you, you can immediately make a melee attack in return, but no more than once per turn. Enabler.

○ **Double Strike (3 Might points):** When you wield two weapons, you can choose to make one attack roll against a foe. If you hit, you inflict damage with both weapons plus 2 additional points of damage, and because you made a single attack, the target's Armor is subtracted only once. Action.

○ **Dragon's Maw (6 Intellect points):** You fashion and control a "hovering" phantasmal construct of magic within long range that resembles a dragon's head. The construct lasts for up to an hour, until it is destroyed, or until you cast another spell. It is a level 4 construct that inflicts 6 points of damage with its bite when directed. While the construct persists, you can use it to manipulate large objects, carry heavy items in its mouth, or attack foes. If you use it to attack foes, you must use your action to directly control the phantom maw for each attack. Action to initiate.

○ **Drain at a Distance:** Your Drain Machine and Drain Creature abilities work on a target within short range. Enabler.

○ **Drain Charge:** You can drain the power from an artifact or device, allowing you to regain 1 Intellect point per level drained. You regain points at the rate of 1 point per round and must give your full concentration to the process each round. The GM determines whether the device is fully drained (likely true of most handheld or smaller devices) or retains some power (likely true of large machines). Action to initiate; action each round to drain.

○ **Drain Creature (3+ Intellect points):** You can drain energy from a living creature you touch, inflicting 3 points of damage and restoring 3 points to your Might or Speed Pool. Action.

○ **Drain Machine (3+ Intellect points):** You can drain the power from an artifact or powered device you touch. If the target is a robot, you inflict 3 points of damage and restore 3 points to your Might or Speed Pool. If the target is an object, you restore points to your Might or Speed Pool equal to the level of the target. If the target is a manifest cypher, it is fully drained and useless. Artifacts and similar devices must immediately check for depletion (items with a depletion of "—" are either immune to this ability or have a depletion of 1 in 1d10 when attacked with this ability). Action.

○ **Drain Power (5 Speed points):** You affect the main power source of a robot or machine, inflicting upon it all four conditions in Disable Mechanisms at once. You must touch the robot to do this (if you are making an attack, it inflicts no damage). Action.

○ **Draw Conclusion (3 Intellect points):** After careful observation and investigation (questioning one or more NPCs on a topic, searching an area or a file, and so on) lasting a few minutes, you can learn a pertinent fact. This ability is a difficulty 3 Intellect task. Each additional time you use this ability, the task is hindered by an additional step. The difficulty returns to 3 after you rest for ten hours. Action.

○ **Drawing on Life's Experiences (6 Intellect points):** You've seen a lot and done a lot, and that experience comes in handy. Ask the GM one question, and you'll receive a general answer. The GM assigns a level to the question, so the more obscure the answer, the more difficult the task. Generally, knowledge that you could find by looking somewhere other than your current location is level 1, and obscure knowledge of the past is level 7. Action.

The GM decides if a target you want to drain is protected in some way, which hinders your attack, or doesn't have any power you can tap.

Disable Mechanisms, page 128

When using Drawing on Life's Experiences, the player is encouraged to make up an anecdote, even if only in overview, that serves as a basis for gaining the ability's benefit.

○ **Dream Becomes Reality (4 Intellect points):** You create a dream object of any shape you can imagine that is your size or smaller, which takes on apparent substance and heft. The object is crude and can have no moving parts, so you can make a sword, a shield, a short ladder, and so on. The dream object has the approximate mass of the real object, if you choose. Your dream objects are as strong as iron, but if you do not remain within long range of them, they function for only one minute before fading away. Action.

○ **Dream Thief (2 Intellect points):** You steal a previous dream from a living creature within short range. The creature loses 2 points of Intellect (ignores Armor), and you learn something the GM chooses to reveal about the creature—its nature, a portion of its plans, a memory, and so on. Action.

○ **Dreamcraft (1 Intellect point):** You pull an image from a dream into the waking world and place it somewhere within long range. The dream lasts for up to one minute, and it can be tiny or fill an area an immediate distance in diameter. Though it appears solid, the dream is intangible. The dream (a scene, a creature, or an object) is static unless you use your action each round to animate it. As part of that animation, you could move the dream up to a short distance each round, as long as it remains within long range. If you animate the dream, it can make sound but does not produce odor. Direct physical interaction or sustained interaction with the dream shatters it into dispersing mist. For example, attacking the dream shatters it, as does the strain of keeping up appearances when an NPC moves through a dream scene or engages a dream creature in conversation for more than a couple of rounds. Action to initiate; action to animate.

○ **Driver:** You are trained in all tasks related to driving a car, truck, or motorcycle, including mechanical repair tasks. Enabler.

○ **Driving on the Edge:** You can make an attack with a light or medium ranged weapon and attempt a driving task as a single action. Enabler.

○ **Dual Defense:** When you wield two weapons, you are trained in Speed defense tasks. Enabler.

○ **Dual Distraction (1+ Speed points):** When you wield two weapons, your opponent's next attack is hindered, and if you apply Effort on your next attack against that same foe, you get a free level of Effort on the task. Enabler.

○ **Dual Light Wield:** You can use two light weapons at the same time, making two separate attacks on your turn as a single action. You remain limited by the amount of Effort you can apply on one action, but because you make separate attacks, your opponent's Armor applies to both. Anything that modifies your attack or damage applies to both attacks, unless it's specifically tied to one of the weapons. Enabler.

○ **Dual Medium Wield:** You can use two light weapons or medium weapons at the same time (or one light weapon and one medium weapon), making two separate attacks on your turn as a single action. This ability otherwise works like the Dual Light Wield ability. Enabler.

○ **Dual Wards:** You can have two wards from Devoted Defender at a time. Choosing a second ward can be its own action, or you can choose two wards with one action (and only pay the cost once for doing so). The wards must remain within an immediate distance of each other. Benefits provided by Devoted Defender apply to both your wards. If your wards separate, you choose which retains the benefit. If they come back together, both regain the benefit immediately. Enabler.

○ **Duel to the Death (5 Speed points):** Choose a target (a single individual creature that you can see). You are trained in all tasks involving fighting that creature. When you successfully attack that target, you inflict +5 damage, or +7 damage if the creature is engaging someone else instead of you. You can duel only one creature at a time. A duel lasts up to one minute, or until you break it off. Action to initiate.

○ **Duplicate (2 Might points):** You cause a duplicate of yourself to appear at any point you can see within short range. The duplicate has no clothing or possessions when it appears. The duplicate is a level 2 NPC with 6 health. The duplicate obeys your commands and does as you direct it. The duplicate remains until you dismiss it using an action or until it is killed. When the duplicate disappears, it leaves behind anything it was wearing or carrying. If the duplicate disappears because it was killed, you take 4 points of damage that ignore Armor, and you lose your next action. Action to initiate.

Free level of Effort, page 209

Devoted Defender, page 128

Training in driving makes the character practiced in using a vehicle as a weapon. If the vehicle is used to run over a victim or ram an enemy vehicle, treat a motorcycle as a medium weapon and treat a car or truck as a heavy weapon.

ABILITIES—D–E

○ **Dust to Dust (7 Intellect points):** You disintegrate one object that is smaller than you and whose level is less than or equal to your tier. You must touch the object to affect it. If the GM feels it appropriate to the circumstances, you can disintegrate a portion of an object (the total volume of which is smaller than you) rather than the entire thing. Action.

ABILITIES—E

○ **Earthquake (7 Might points):** You direct your destructive resonance into the ground and trigger an earthquake centered on a spot you can see within very long range. The ground within short range of that spot heaves and shakes for five minutes, causing damage to structures and terrain in the area. Buildings and terrain features shed debris and rubble. Each round, creatures in the area take either 3 points of damage due to the general shaking, or 6 points of damage if in or adjacent to a structure or terrain feature shedding debris. Action to initiate.

○ **Echolocation:** You are especially sensitive to sound and vibration, so much so that you can sense your environment within a short distance regardless of your ability to see. Enabler.

○ **Effective Skill:** Choose one noncombat skill when you gain this ability. You get a minor effect with that skill when you roll a natural 14 or higher (the d20 shows "14" or more). You get a major effect with that skill when you roll a natural 19 or higher (the d20 shows "19" or higher). You can select this ability more than once. Each time you select it, you must choose a different noncombat skill. Enabler.

○ **Electric Armor (4 Intellect points):** When you wish it, electricity crackles across your body for ten minutes, granting you +1 Armor. While electrified, you have an additional +2 Armor versus electrical damage specifically, and you inflict 2 points of damage on any creature that touches you or attacks you with a melee weapon that conducts electricity. Enabler.

○ **Electrical Flight (5 Intellect points):** You exude an aura of crackling electricity that lets you fly a long distance each round for ten minutes. You can't carry other creatures with you. Action to activate.

○ **Elemental Protection (4+ Intellect points):** You and every target you designate within immediate range gains +5 Armor against one type of direct elemental damage (such as fire, lightning, shadow, or thorn) for one hour, or until you cast this spell again. Each level of Effort applied increases the elemental protection by +2. Action to initiate.

○ **Elusive (2 Speed points):** When you succeed on a Speed defense action, you immediately gain an action. You can use this action only to move. Enabler.

○ **Embrace the Night (7+ Intellect points):** You fashion a truly horrifying facade of a creature from swirling ribbons of dark matter and launch it at your foes within long range. Each round, you can attack a target within long range using the creation as your weapon. When you attack, the creature inserts hair-fine tendrils of shadow into the target's eyes and brain. The target takes 3 points of Intellect damage (ignores Armor) and is stunned for one round so that it loses its next turn. Alternatively, you can cause the creature to take other actions, as long as you are able to see it and mentally control it as your action. The creature disperses after about a minute. Action to initiate.

○ **Embraced by Darkness (6 Intellect points):** For the next hour, you take on some characteristics of a shadow thanks to a fundamental adaptation of your flesh or a device you've kept secret. Your appearance is a dark silhouette. When you apply a level of Effort to sneaking tasks, you get a free level of Effort on the task. During this time, you can move through the air at a rate of a short distance per round, and you can move through solid barriers (even those that are sealed to prevent the passage of light or shadow), but not energy barriers, at a rate of 1 foot (30 cm) per round. You can perceive while passing through a barrier or object, which allows you to peek through walls. As a shadow, you can't affect or be affected by normal matter. Likewise, you can't attack, touch, or otherwise affect anything. However, attacks and effects that rely on light can affect you, and sudden bursts of light can potentially make you lose your next turn. Action to initiate.

○ **Enable Others:** You can use the helping rules to provide a benefit to another character attempting a physical task. Unlike the normal helping rules, this doesn't require you to use your action helping the other character with the task. This requires no action on your part. Enabler.

Minor effect, page 211

Major effect, page 212

Helping, page 226

Force Field Shield, page 143

○ **Encouragement (1 Intellect point):** While you maintain this ability through ongoing inspiring oration, your allies within short range ease one of the following task types (your choice): defense tasks, attack tasks, or tasks related to any skill that you are trained or specialized in. Action.

○ **Encouraging Presence (2 Intellect points):** For one minute, allies within short range gain an asset on defense rolls. Action.

○ **Endurance:** Any duration dealing with physical actions is either doubled or halved, whichever is better for you. For example, if the typical person can hold their breath for thirty seconds, you can hold it for one minute. If the typical person can march for four hours without stopping, you can do so for eight hours. In terms of harmful effects, if a poison paralyzes its victims for one minute, you are paralyzed for thirty seconds. The minimum duration is always one round. Enabler.

Absorb Kinetic Energy, page 108

○ **Energize Creature (6+ Might points):** You extend your Absorb Kinetic Energy ability to one creature within immediate range so that they also can absorb energy from physical attacks and impacts for one hour. That creature, however, cannot release excess energy as a blast. For each level of Effort you apply, you can increase the number of targets you affect by one. If you have Absorb Pure Energy or Improved Absorb Kinetic Energy, those abilities are also duplicated in your target when you use Energize Creature. Action to initiate.

Absorb Pure Energy, page 108

Improved Absorb Kinetic Energy, page 151

○ **Energize Crowd (9 Might points):** You extend your Absorb Kinetic Energy ability to up to thirty creatures within short range so that they also can absorb energy from physical attacks and impacts for one hour. If you have Absorb Pure Energy or Improved Absorb Kinetic Energy, these creatures can use those abilities as well. The creatures, however, cannot release excess energy as a blast. Action to initiate.

Beast Form, page 112

"Steel can't feel, but when it gets cold out, the places where it joins to my flesh sting and ache worse than anything."
~Grandpa Iron

○ **Energize Object:** By focusing your Absorb Kinetic Energy ability on an object (like a weapon), you infuse it with your power. The object holds the energy until it is touched by anyone but you, so putting it into your melee weapon or the ammo of a ranged weapon allows the weapon to trigger the energy in combat. The energy inflicts 3 points of damage on the creature touched in addition to any damage the weapon itself might do. You cannot have more than one energized object on your person at a time. Action to initiate.

○ **Energized Shield:** Your force shield from your Force Field Shield ability now pulses with dangerous energy whenever you manifest it. Each time you use your shield as a melee or ranged weapon, it inflicts an additional 3 points of damage. Enabler.

○ **Energy Protection (3+ Intellect points):** Choose a discrete type of energy that you have experience with (such as heat, sonic, electricity, and so on). You gain +10 to Armor against damage from that type of energy for ten minutes. Alternatively, you gain +1 to Armor against damage from that energy for 24 hours. You must be familiar with the type of energy; for example, if you have no experience with a certain kind of extradimensional energy, you can't protect against it. In addition to the normal options for using Effort, you can choose to use Effort to protect more targets; each level of Effort used in this way affects up to two additional targets. You must touch additional targets to protect them. Action to initiate.

○ **Energy Resistance:** Choose a discrete type of energy that you have experience with (such as heat, sonic, electricity, and so on). You gain +5 to Armor against damage from that type of energy. You must be familiar with the type of energy; for example, if you have no experience with a certain kind of extradimensional energy, you can't protect against it. You can select this ability more than once. Each time you select it, you must choose a different kind of energy. Enabler.

○ **Enhance Strength (3 Intellect points):** For the next ten minutes, you gain an asset on tasks that depend on brute force, such as moving a heavy object, smashing down a door, or hitting someone with a melee weapon. Action to initiate.

○ **Enhanced Beast Form:** When you use Beast Form, your beast form gains the following additional bonuses: +3 to your Might Pool, +2 to your Speed Pool, and +2 to Armor. Enabler.

○ **Enhanced Body:** Your machine parts grant you +1 to Armor, +3 to your Might Pool, and +3 to your Speed Pool. Traditional healing skills, medicines, and techniques work only half as well for you. Each time you start at full health, the first 5 points of damage you take can never be healed in these ways or recovered normally. Instead, you must use repairing skills and abilities to restore those points. For example, if you start with a full Might Pool of 10 and take 8 points of damage, you can use recovery rolls to restore 3 points, but the remaining 5 points must be restored with repair tasks. Enabler.

- **Enhanced Intellect:** You gain 3 points to your Intellect Pool. Enabler.

- **Enhanced Intellect Edge:** You gain +1 to your Intellect Edge. Enabler.

- **Enhanced Might:** You gain 3 points to your Might Pool. Enabler.

- **Enhanced Might Edge:** You gain +1 to your Might Edge. Enabler.

- **Enhanced Phased Attack (5 Intellect points):** This ability works like the Phased Attack ability except that your attack also disrupts the foe's vitals, dealing an additional 5 points of damage. Enabler.

- **Enhanced Physique:** You gain 3 points to divide among your Might and Speed Pools however you wish. Enabler.

- **Enhanced Potential:** You gain 3 points to divide among your stat Pools however you wish. Enabler.

- **Enhanced Speed:** You gain 3 points to your Speed Pool. Enabler.

- **Enhanced Speed Edge:** You gain +1 to your Speed Edge. Enabler.

- **Enlarge (1+ Might point):** You trigger an enzymatic reaction that draws additional mass from another dimension, and you (and your clothing or suit) grow larger. You achieve a height of 9 feet (3 m) and stay that way for about a minute. During that time, you add 4 points to your Might Pool, add +1 to Armor, and add +2 to your Might Edge. While you are larger than normal, your Speed defense rolls are hindered, and you are practiced in using your fists as heavy weapons.

    When the effects of Enlarge end, your Armor and Might Edge return to normal, and you subtract a number of points from your Might Pool equal to the number you gained (if this brings the Pool to 0, subtract the overflow first from your Speed Pool and then, if necessary, from your Intellect Pool). Each additional time you use Enlarge before your next ten-hour recovery roll, you must apply an additional level of Effort. Thus, the second time you use Enlarge, you must apply one level of Effort; the third time you use Enlarge, two levels of Effort; and so on.
    Action to initiate.

Phased Attack, page 170

A character with an Enhanced Physique is likely to be either a bit bulkier or somewhat leaner as a result.

○ **Enlightened:** You are trained in any perception task that involves sight. Enabler.

○ **Entangling Force (1+ Intellect point):** A target within short range is subject to a snare constructed of semi-tangible lines of force for one minute. The force snare is a level 2 construct. A target caught in the force snare cannot move from its position, but it can attack and defend normally. The target can also use its action attempting to break free. You can increase the level of the force snare by 1 per level of Effort applied. Action to initiate.

○ **Enthrall (1 Intellect point):** While talking, you grab and keep another creature's attention, even if the creature can't understand you. For as long as you do nothing but speak (you can't even move), the other creature takes no actions other than to defend itself, even over multiple rounds. If the creature is attacked, the effect ends. Action.

○ **Entourage:** You gain an entourage of five level 1 twenty-somethings that accompanies you wherever you go unless you purposefully disband it for a particular outing. You can ask them to deliver things for you, run messages, pick up your dry cleaning—pretty much whatever you want, within reason. They can also run interference if you're trying to avoid someone, help hide you from media attention, help you muscle through a crowd, and so on. On the other hand, if a situation becomes physically violent, they retreat to safety. Enabler.

○ **Enveloping Shield:** Your Force Field Shield ability produces an envelope of force that enfolds you while you are holding the shield, granting you +1 to Armor. Enabler.

○ **Erase Memories (3 Intellect points):** You reach into the mind of a creature within immediate range and make an Intellect roll. On a success, you erase up to the last five minutes of its memory. Action.

○ **Escape (2 Speed points):** You slip your restraints, squeeze through the bars, break the grip of a creature holding you, pull free from sucking quicksand, or otherwise get loose from whatever is holding you in place. Action.

○ **Escape Plan:** When you kill a foe, you can attempt a stealth task to immediately hide from anyone around, assuming that a suitable hiding place is nearby. Enabler.

○ **Evanesce (3 Speed points):** You step into shadows or behind cover, and everyone who was observing you completely loses track of you. Although you're not invisible, you can't be seen until you reveal yourself again by moving out of the shadows or from behind cover (or by making an attack). Action.

○ **Evasion:** You're hard to affect when you don't want to be affected. You are trained in all defense tasks. Enabler.

○ **Everything Is a Weapon:** You can take any small object—a coin, a pen, a bottle, a stone, and so on—and throw it with such force and precision that it inflicts damage as a light weapon. Enabler.

○ **Exile (5 Intellect points):** You send a target that you touch hurtling into another random dimension or universe, where it remains for ten minutes. You have no idea what happens to the target while it's gone, but at the end of ten minutes, it returns to the precise spot it left. Action.

○ **Experienced Defender:** When wearing armor, you gain +1 to Armor. Enabler.

○ **Experienced Finder (6+ Intellect points):** When you are looking for something specific, such as a particular rare component, a chemical needed to complete a vaccine for a disease, a spare part required to repair a damaged device, the tracks of a specific beast, or the sword that a thief stole from you, this ability is of great use. For the next 24 hours, if you come within short range of the thing and circumstances are such that it is possible for you to perceive the thing (for example, it's not in a locked chamber for which you do not have the key), you find it. This ability assumes that you are constantly on the lookout, always looking everywhere possible, peering behind obstacles, and so on—if you're running for your life, sleeping, or otherwise occupied, this ability does not help you. You use this ability in lieu of making a roll to find the thing, but only if the difficulty for finding the object is level 6 or below. You can apply Effort to increase the maximum level of the thing you're trying to find (each level of Effort used this way increases the maximum level by 1). Action to initiate.

○ **Experienced in Armor:** The cost reduction from your Practiced in Armor ability improves. You now reduce the Speed cost by 2. Enabler.

Defense tasks, page 225

Force Field Shield, page 143

Erasing memories can be a tricky business. On a failed attempt to erase a creature's memories, an interesting GM intrusion might have the effect target an ally or the character.

Practiced in Armor, page 171

ABILITIES—E

○ **Expert Crafter:** Instead of rolling, you can choose to automatically succeed on a crafting task you're trained in. The task must be difficulty 4 or lower. If you are able to reduce the assessed difficulty of a crafting task to 4 or lower, this ability also applies to each subtask, assuming something doesn't interrupt you during the ensuing time to build. Enabler.

○ **Expert Cypher Use:** You can bear three cyphers at a time. Enabler.

○ **Expert Driver:** You are specialized in all tasks related to driving a car, truck, or motorcycle, including mechanical repair tasks. Enabler.

○ **Expert Follower:** You gain a level 3 follower. They are not restricted on their modifications. You can take this ability multiple times, each time gaining another level 3 follower. Alternatively, you could choose to advance a level 2 follower you already have to level 3 and then gain a new level 2 follower. Enabler.

○ **Expert Pilot:** You are specialized in all tasks related to piloting a starcraft. Enabler.

○ **Expert Skill:** Instead of rolling a d20, you can choose to automatically succeed on a task you're trained in. The task must be difficulty 4 or lower, and it can't be an attack roll or a defense roll. Enabler.

○ **Explains the Ineffable:** Through anecdotes, historical retellings, and citing knowledge that few but you have previously understood, you enlighten your friends. After spending 24 hours with you, once per day, each of your friends can ease a particular task by two steps. This benefit is ongoing while you remain in your friends' company. It ends if you leave, but it resumes if you return to your friends' company within 24 hours. If you leave your friends' company for longer than that, you must spend another 24 hours together to reactivate the benefit. Enabler.

○ **Exploit Advantage:** Even if you can do something well, you've learned that you can always do it even better. Whenever you have an asset for a roll, you ease the task by one additional step. Enabler.

○ **Exploratory Experience:** You are trained in two additional skills in which you are not already trained. Choose from the following: navigation, perception, sensing danger, initiative, peacefully opening communications with strangers, and tracking. Enabler.

Crafting, page 227

Follower, page 233
Modifications, page 233

Store Energy, page 186

○ **Explosive Release (6 Intellect points):** You can amplify the energy stored in your Siphon Pool (from your Store Energy ability) and release it in a massive blast that affects either one target within short range or everything within immediate range. If you choose a single target, it takes 2 points of damage for every point in your Siphon Pool. If you choose an area, everything in the area (except you) takes 1 point of damage per point in your Siphon Pool (or half that if your attack fails against them). This drains your Siphon Pool to 0 points. Action.

○ **Extra Recovery:** You gain an additional one-action recovery each day. Enabler.

If building a focus, Extra Skill can often be granted as a secondary ability in addition to another more potent ability at the same tier.

○ **Extra Skill:** You are trained in one skill of your choice (other than attacks or defense) in which you are not already trained. You can select this ability multiple times. Each time you select it, you must choose a different skill. Enabler.

○ **Extra Use (3 Intellect points):** You attempt to gain an extra use from an artifact without triggering a depletion roll. The difficulty of the task is equal to the level of the artifact. If you crafted the artifact, you gain an asset to the task. On a failure, the depletion roll occurs normally. You could also try to use a manifest cypher without burning it out, but the task is hindered. A failed attempt to gain an additional use from a manifest cypher destroys it before it can produce the desired effect. Action.

○ **Extreme Mastery (6 Might or 6 Speed points):** When using your chosen weapon, you can reroll any attack roll you wish and take the better of the two results. Enabler.

○ **Eye for Detail (2 Intellect points):** When you spend five minutes or so thoroughly exploring an area no larger than a short distance in diameter, you can ask the GM one question about the area. The GM must answer you truthfully. You cannot use this more than one time per area per 24 hours. Action to initiate, five minutes to complete.

When a PC uses Fast Talk, encourage them to provide the broad gist of how they're trying to persuade their target.

○ **Eye Gouge (2 Speed points):** You make an attack against a creature with an eye. The attack is hindered, but if you hit, the creature has trouble seeing for the next hour. During this time, the creature's tasks that rely on sight (which is most tasks) are hindered. Action.

○ **Eyes Adjusted:** You can see in extremely dim light as though it were bright light. You can see in total darkness as if it were extremely dim light. Enabler.

ABILITIES—F

○ **Face Morph (2+ Intellect points):** You alter your features and coloration for one hour, hiding your identity or impersonating someone. This affects only your face, not the rest of your body. You can't perfectly duplicate someone else's face, but you can be accurate enough to fool someone who knows that person casually. You have an asset in all tasks involving disguise. You must apply a level of Effort to be able to impersonate a different species (such as a human morphing into a humanoid alien). Action.

○ **Familiarize:** You can familiarize yourself with a new area if you spend at least one hour studying a region up to a long distance across that you are able to directly access and move about in. Once you've familiarized yourself with an area, all your tasks related to perception, navigation, salvaging and scavenging, defense, and moving about the area gain an asset. Each time you familiarize yourself with a new area, you lose focus on a previous area unless you spend 1 XP to retain the familiarity permanently. Action to initiate, one hour to complete.

○ **Far Step (2 Intellect points):** You leap through the air and land some distance away. You can jump up, down, or across to anywhere you choose within long range if you have a clear and unobstructed path to that location. You land safely. Action.

○ **Fast Kill (2 Speed points):** You know how to kill quickly. When you hit with a melee or ranged attack, you deal 4 additional points of damage. You can't make this attack in two consecutive rounds. Action.

○ **Fast Talk (1 Intellect point):** When speaking with an intelligent creature who can understand you and isn't hostile, you convince that creature to take one reasonable action in the next round. A reasonable action must be agreed upon by the GM; it should not put the creature or its allies in obvious danger or be wildly out of character. Action.

Abilities—E–F

○ **Fast Travel (7 Intellect points):** You warp time and space so that you and up to ten other creatures within immediate distance travel overland at ten times the normal rate for up to eight hours. At this speed, most dangerous encounters or regions of rough terrain are ignored, though the GM may declare exceptions. Outright barriers still present a problem. Action to initiate.

○ **Fearsome Reputation (3 Intellect points):** You and those you travel with have earned a fearsome reputation in some parts. If your foes have heard of you, affected targets within earshot become afraid, and all attacks they make against you are hindered until one or more of them successfully inflicts damage on you or one of your allies, at which time their fear abates. Action.

○ **Feat of Strength (1 Might point):** Any task that depends on brute force is eased. Examples include smashing down a barred door, tearing open a locked container, lifting or moving a heavy object, or striking someone with a melee weapon. Enabler.

○ **Feint (2 Speed points):** If you use one action creating a misdirection or diversion, in the next round you can take advantage of your opponent's lowered defenses. Make a melee attack roll against that opponent. You gain an asset on this attack. If your attack is successful, it inflicts 4 additional points of damage. Action.

○ **Fellow Explorer:** You gain a level 2 follower. One of their modifications must be for tasks related to perception. Enabler.

○ **Fetch (3 Intellect points):** You cause an object to disappear and reappear in your hands or somewhere else nearby. Choose one object that can fit inside a 5-foot (2 m) cube and that you can see within long range. The object vanishes and appears in your hands or in an open space anywhere you choose within immediate range. Action.

○ **Field of Destruction (4 Might points):** When you cause an object to descend one or more steps on the object damage track, you gain 1 additional point of Armor for one minute. Enabler.

○ **Field of Gravity (4 Intellect points):** When you wish it, a field of manipulated gravity around you pulls incoming ranged projectile attacks to the ground. You are immune to such attacks until your turn in the next round. You must be aware of an attack to foil it. This ability does not work on energy attacks. Enabler.

○ **Field-Reinforced Armor:** You gain +1 to Armor while wearing the power armor from your Powered Armor ability. Enabler.

○ **Fiery Hand of Doom (3 Intellect points):** While your Shroud of Flame is active, you can reach into your halo and produce a hand made of animate flame that is twice the size of a human's hand. The hand acts as you direct, floating in the air. Directing the hand is an action. Without a command, the hand does nothing. It can move a long distance in a round, but it never moves farther away from you than long range. The hand can grab, move, and carry things, but anything it touches takes 1 point of damage per round from the heat. The hand can also attack. It's a level 3 creature and deals 1 extra point of damage from fire when it attacks. Once created, the hand lasts for ten minutes. Action to create; action to direct.

○ **Fight On:** You do not suffer the normal penalties for being impaired on the damage track. If debilitated, instead of suffering the normal penalty of being unable to take most actions, you can continue to act; however, all tasks are hindered. Enabler.

○ **Final Defiance:** When you would normally be dead, you instead remain conscious and active for one more round plus one additional round each time you succeed on a difficulty 5 Might task. During these rounds, you are debilitated. If you do not receive healing or otherwise gain points in a Pool during your final round(s) of activity, you are subject to the effects of Not Dead Yet. Enabler.

○ **Find an Opening (1 Intellect point):** You use trickery to find an opening in your foe's defenses. If you succeed on a Speed roll against one creature within immediate range, your next attack against that creature before the end of the next round is eased. Action.

○ **Find the Guilty:** If you have used Designation on a target, you are trained in tracking them, spotting them when they are hidden or disguised, or otherwise finding them. Enabler.

Powered Armor, page 171

Shroud of Flame, page 183

Damage track, page 218

Followers, page 233

Not Dead Yet, page 166

Object damage track, page 116

Designation, page 127

Shroud of Flame, page 183

Free level of Effort, page 209

A Flash user sometimes has a signature shape and color for their explosion of energy, such as an orange roaring lion silhouette, a neon violet stinging wasp, and so on.

○ **Find the Hidden (4+ Intellect points):** You see the traceries of objects as they move through space and time. You can sense the distance and direction of any specific inanimate object that you once touched. This takes anywhere from one action to hours of concentration, depending on what the GM feels is appropriate due to time, distance, or other mitigating circumstances. However, you don't know in advance how long it will take. If you use at least two levels of Effort, once you have established the distance and direction, you remain in contact with the object for one hour per level of Effort used. Thus, if it moves, you are aware of its new position. Action to initiate; action each round to concentrate.

○ **Find the Way:** When you apply Effort to a navigation task because you don't know the way, are lost, are attempting to blaze a new route, need to choose between two or more otherwise similar paths to take, or something very similar, you can apply a free level of Effort. Enabler.

○ **Finishing Blow (5 Might points):** If your foe is prone, stunned, or somehow helpless or incapacitated when you strike, you inflict 7 additional points of damage on a successful hit. Enabler.

○ **Fire and Ice (4 Intellect points):** You cause a target within short range to become either very hot or very cold (your choice). The target suffers 3 points of ambient damage (ignores Armor) each round for up to three rounds, although a new roll is required each round to continue to affect the target. Action to initiate.

○ **Fire Bloom (4+ Intellect points):** Fire blooms within long range, filling an area 10 feet (3 m) in radius and inflicting 3 points of damage on all affected targets. Effort applied to one attack counts for all attacks against targets in the area of the bloom. Even on an unsuccessful attack, a target in the area still takes 1 point of damage. Flammable objects in the area may catch fire. Action.

○ **Fire Servant (6 Intellect points):** While your Shroud of Flame is active, you reach into your halo and produce an automaton of fire that is your general shape and size. It acts as you direct each round. Directing the servant is an action, and you can command it only when you are within long range of it. Without a command, the servant continues to follow your previous command. You can also give it a simple programmed action, such as "Wait here, and attack anyone who comes within short range until they're dead." The servant lasts for ten minutes, is a level 5 creature, and deals 1 extra point of damage from fire when it attacks. Action to create; action to direct.

○ **Fire Tendrils (5 Intellect points):** When you wish it, your halo (from your Shroud of Flame ability) sprouts three tendrils of flame that last for up to ten minutes. As an action, you can use the tendrils to attack, making a separate attack roll for each. Each tendril inflicts 4 points of damage. Otherwise, the attacks function as standard attacks. If you don't use the tendrils to attack, they remain but do nothing. Enabler.

○ **Fists of Fury:** You inflict 2 additional points of damage with unarmed attacks. Enabler.

○ **Flamboyant Boast (1 Intellect point):** You boastfully describe an act that you will accomplish, and then as part of the same action, you attempt it. If an average person would find the action difficult (or impossible) and you succeed on it, creatures who witnessed it who are not your allies are potentially dazed on their next turn, and all tasks they attempt are hindered. The GM will help you determine whether your boast is something that would impress onlookers so significantly. If you attempt the task you boast about but fail to accomplish it, all your attempts to affect or attack onlookers who saw you are hindered for about ten minutes. Enabler.

○ **Flameblade (4 Intellect points):** When you wish it, you extend your Shroud of Flame to cover a weapon you wield in flame for one hour. The flame ends if you stop holding or carrying the weapon. While the flame lasts, the weapon inflicts 2 additional points of damage. Enabler.

○ **Flash (4 Intellect points):** You create an explosion of energy at a point within close range, affecting an area up to immediate range from that point. You must be able to see the location where you intend to center the explosion. The blast inflicts 2 points of damage to all creatures or objects within the area. If you apply Effort to increase the damage, you deal 2 additional points of damage per level of Effort (instead of 3 points); targets in the area take 1 point of damage even if you fail the attack roll. Action.

Abilities—F

◯ **Flash Across the Miles (6+ Intellect points):** You can move to an open location on the planet that you're familiar with almost instantaneously, transformed into a bolt of lightning. If you apply a level of Effort, you can attempt to penetrate covered locations that you're aware of as long as a route exists from the open air to the area you want to reach that electricity can easily follow. Action.

◯ **Flee (6 Intellect points):** All non-allies within short distance who can hear your dreadful, intimidating words flee from you at top speed for one minute. Action.

◯ **Fleet of Foot (1+ Speed points):** You can move a short distance as part of another action. You can move a long distance as your entire action for a turn. If you apply a level of Effort to this ability, you can move a long distance and make an attack as your entire action for a turn, but the attack is hindered. Enabler.

◯ **Flesh of Stone:** You have +1 to Armor if you do not wear physical armor. Enabler.

◯ **Flex Lore:** After each ten-hour recovery roll when you have access to a high-technology digital reference library (such as one that might be found in a starship or in a learning center), choose one field of knowledge related to a specific planet or some other location. The field might be habitations, customs, governments, characteristics of the main species, important figures, and so on. You're trained in that field until you use this ability again. You could use this ability with an area of knowledge you're already trained in to become specialized. Enabler.

◯ **Flex Skill:** At the beginning of each day, choose one task (other than attacks or defense) on which you will concentrate. For the rest of that day, you're trained in that task. You can't use this ability with a skill in which you're already trained to become specialized. Enabler.

◯ **Flight (4+ Intellect points):** You can float and fly through the air for one hour. For each level of Effort applied, you can affect one additional creature of your size or smaller. You must touch the creature to bestow the power of flight. You direct the other creature's movement, and while flying, it must remain within sight of you or fall. In terms of overland movement, a flying creature moves about 20 miles (32 km) per hour and is not affected by terrain. Action to initiate.

◯ **Flight Not Fight:** If you use your action only to move, all Speed defense tasks are eased. Enabler.

◯ **Fling (4 Intellect points):** You violently launch a creature or object about your size or smaller within short range and send it flying a short distance in any direction. This is an Intellect attack that inflicts 4 points of damage to the object being flung when it lands or strikes a barrier. If you aim the primary target at another creature or object (and succeed on a second attack), the secondary target also takes 4 points of damage. Action.

○ **Foil Danger (2 Intellect points):** You negate one source of potential danger related to one creature or object that you are aware of within immediate distance for one round. This could be a weapon or device held by someone, a trap triggered by a pressure plate, or a creature's natural ability (something special, innate, and dangerous, like a dragon's fiery breath or a giant cobra's venom). You can also try to foil a foe's mundane action (such as an attack with a weapon or claw), so that the action isn't made this round. Make your roll against the level of the attack, danger, or creature. Action.

○ **Font of Healing:** With your approval, other creatures can touch you and regain 1d6 points to either their Might Pool or their Speed Pool. This healing costs them 2 Intellect points. A single creature can benefit from this ability only once each day. Enabler.

○ **Force and Accuracy:** You inflict 3 additional points of damage with attacks using weapons that you throw. Enabler.

○ **Force at Distance (4+ Intellect points):** You temporarily bend the fundamental law of gravity around a creature or object (up to twice your mass) within short range. The target is caught in your telekinetic grip, and you can move it up to a short distance in any direction each round that you retain your hold. A creature in your grip can take actions, but it can't move under its own power. Each round after the initial attack, you can attempt to keep your grip on the target by spending 2 additional Intellect points and succeeding at a difficulty 2 Intellect task. If your concentration lapses, the target drops back to the ground. In addition to the normal options for using Effort, you can choose to use Effort to increase the amount of mass you can affect. Each level allows you to affect a creature or object twice as massive as before. For example, applying one level of Effort would affect a creature four times as massive as you, two levels would affect a creature eight times as massive, three levels would affect a creature sixteen times as massive, and so on. Action to initiate.

○ **Force Bash (1 Might point):** This is a pummeling melee attack you make with your Force Field Shield. Your attack inflicts 1 less point of damage than normal but dazes your target for one round, during which time all tasks it performs are hindered. Enabler.

○ **Force Blast:** You figure out how to project blasts of pure force from the gauntlets of the power armor from your Powered Armor ability. This allows you to fire a blast of force that inflicts 5 points of damage with a range of 200 feet (60 m). Action.

When Font of Healing is used, describe the sensation and visual effects you think are appropriate, if any.

Force Field Shield, page 143

Powered Armor, page 171

- **Force Field (3 Intellect points):** You create an invisible energy barrier around a creature or object you choose within short range. The force field moves with the creature or object and lasts for ten minutes. The target has +1 to Armor until the effect ends. Action.

- **Force Field Barrier (3+ Intellect points):** You create an opaque, stationary barrier of solid energy (a force field) within immediate range. The barrier is 10 feet by 10 feet (3 m by 3 m) and of negligible thickness. It is a level 2 barrier and lasts for ten minutes. It can be placed anywhere it fits, whether against a solid object (including the ground) or floating in the air. Each level of Effort you apply strengthens the barrier by one level. For example, applying two levels of Effort creates a level 4 barrier. Action.

- **Force Field Shield:** You manifest a small plane of pure force, which takes on a shield-like shape with the barest flicker of a thought. You can dismiss it just as easily. To use the force shield, you must hold it in one of your hands. You are practiced in using your exotic shield in one hand as a light melee weapon; however, if you attack with both your shield and a weapon held in the other hand, both attacks are hindered. When you are unconscious or sleeping, the force field dissipates. Enabler.

- **Force to Reckon With:** You can break through force fields and energy barriers as if they were physical walls. Enabler.

- **Force Wall (5 Intellect points):** You can trigger the energy in your Force Field Shield to expand outward in all directions to create an immobile plane of solid force up to 20 feet by 20 feet (6 m by 6 m) for up to one hour or until you take your shield back. (The force shield becomes the force wall.) The plane of the force wall conforms to the space available. While the force wall remains in place, you cannot use any of your other abilities that require Force Field Shield. Action to initiate.

- **Fortification Builder:** Whenever you attempt a crafting task—or help in the crafting task—to build a wall or other fortification, you ease the crafting difficulty by two steps, to a minimum of difficulty 1. Enabler.

- **Fortified Position (2 Might points):** For the next minute, you gain +1 Armor and an asset to your Might defense tasks, as long as you haven't moved more than an immediate distance since your last turn. Action to initiate.

- **Foul Aura (5+ Intellect points):** Your words, gestures, and touch invest an object no larger than yourself with an aura of doom, fear, and doubt for one day. Creatures that can hear and understand you feel an urge to move at least a short distance away from the object. If a creature does not move away, all tasks, attacks, and defenses it attempts while within the aura are hindered. The duration of the aura is extended by one day per level of Effort applied. The aura is temporarily blocked while the object is covered or contained. Action to initiate.

- **Freakishly Large:** Your increased size intimidates most people. While you enjoy the effects of Enlarge, all intimidation tasks you attempt are eased. Enabler.

- **Free to Move:** You ignore all movement penalties and adjustments due to terrain or other obstacles. You can fit through any space large enough to fit your head. Tasks involving breaking free of bonds, a creature's grip, or any similar impediment gain three free levels of Effort. Enabler.

- **Freezing Touch (4 Intellect points):** Your hands become so cold that your touch freezes solid a living target of your size or smaller, rendering it immobile for one round. If you have another cold ability activated by touch (such as Frost Touch), you can use it as part of the Freezing Touch attack. Action.

- **Frenzy (1 Intellect point):** When you wish, while in combat, you can enter a state of frenzy. While in this state, you can't use Intellect points, but you gain +1 to your Might Edge and your Speed Edge. This effect lasts as long as you wish, but it ends if no combat is taking place within range of your senses. Enabler.

- **Friendly Help:** If your friend tries a task and fails, they can try again without spending Effort if you help. You provide this advantage to your friend even if you are not trained in the task that they are retrying. Enabler.

A shield, including one produced by a force field, provides an asset to a character's Speed defense task while it is held in one hand.

Enlarge, page 135

Free level of Effort, page 209

Frost Touch, page 144

Crafting difficulty, page 228

○ **From the Shadows:** If you successfully attack a creature that was previously unaware of your presence, you deal 3 additional points of damage. Enabler.

○ **Frost Touch (1 Intellect point):** Your hands become so cold that the next time you touch a creature, you inflict 3 points of damage. Alternatively, you can use this ability on a weapon, and for ten minutes, it inflicts 1 additional point of damage from the cold. Action for touch; enabler for weapon.

○ **Further Mathematics:** You are specialized in higher mathematics. If you are already specialized, choose some other sphere of knowledge to become trained in. Enabler.

○ **Fury (3 Might points):** For the next minute, all melee attacks you make inflict 2 additional points of damage. Action to initiate.

○ **Fusion:** You can fuse your manifest cyphers and artifacts with your body. These fused devices function as if they were one level higher. Enabler.

○ **Fusion Armor:** A procedure gives you biometal implants in major portions of your body, you grow metal-hard skin, the blessings of an angel protect you, or something similar happens. These changes give you +1 to Armor even when you're not wearing physical armor. Enabler.

ABILITIES—G

○ **Gain Unusual Companion:** You gain a special specimen as a constant companion. It is level 4, probably the size of a small dog, and follows your telepathic commands. You and the GM must work out the details of your creature, and you'll probably make rolls for it in combat or when it takes actions. The companion acts on your turn. If your companion dies, you can hunt in the wild for 1d6 days to find a new one. Enabler.

○ **Gambler:** Each day, choose two different numbers from 2 to 16. One number is your lucky number, and the other is your unlucky number. Whenever you make a roll that day and get a number matching your lucky number, your next task is eased. Whenever you make a roll that day and get a number matching your unlucky number, your next task is hindered. Enabler.

○ **Game Lessons:** You've played so many games that you've picked up some real knowledge. Choose any two noncombat skills. You are trained in those skills. Enabler.

○ **Gamer:** Pick any one style of game such as real-time strategy games, games of chance in the style of poker, roleplaying games, and so on. You can apply an asset to a task related to playing that style of game once between each recovery roll. Enabler.

○ **Gamer's Fortitude:** Sitting and playing a game for twelve hours straight is not something most people can do, but you've figured it out. Once after each ten-hour recovery roll, you can transfer up to 5 points between your Pools in any combination, at a rate of 1 point per round. For example, you could transfer 3 points of Might to Speed and 2 points of Intellect to Speed, which would take a total of five rounds. Action.

○ **Gaming God:** Any time you use Effort on an Intellect action, add one of the following enhancements to the action (your choice):
• Free level of Effort
• Automatic minor effect
Enabler.

○ **Gargantuan:** When you use Enlarge, you can choose to grow up to 30 feet (9 m) in height, and you add 3 more temporary points to your Might Pool (if you also have the Bigger ability, the temporary points from Gargantuan are in addition to the points from Bigger). Enabler.

○ **Gather Intelligence (2 Intellect points):** When in a group of people (a caravan, a palace, a village, a city, etc.) you can ask around about any topic you choose and come away with useful information. You can ask a specific question, or you can simply obtain general facts. You also get a good idea of the general layout of the location involved, note the presence of all major sites, and perhaps even notice obscure details. For example, not only do you find out if anyone in the palace has seen the missing boy, but you also get a working knowledge of the layout of the palace itself, note all the entrances and which are used more often than others, and take notice that everyone seems to avoid the well in the eastern courtyard for some reason. Action to initiate, about an hour to complete.

Cypher, page 377
Artifact, page 204

Free level of Effort, page 209
Minor effect, page 211

Enlarge, page 135

Bigger, page 113

Abilities—F-G

○ **Generate Force Field (9+ Intellect points):** You create six planes of solid force (level 8), each 30 feet (9 m) to a side, which persist for one hour. The planes must be contiguous, and they retain the position that you choose when initiating this ability. For instance, you could arrange the planes linearly, creating a wall 180 feet (55 m) long, or you could create a closed cube. The planes conform to the space available. Each additional level of Effort you apply increases the level of the barrier by one (to a maximum of level 10) or increases the number of hours it remains by one. Action to initiate.

○ **Get Away (2 Speed points):** After your action on your turn, you move up to a short distance or get behind or beneath cover within immediate range. Enabler.

○ **Ghost (4 Intellect points):** For the next ten minutes, you gain an asset to sneaking tasks. During this time, you can move through solid barriers (but not energy barriers) at a rate of 1 foot (30 cm) per round, and you can perceive while phased within a barrier or object, which allows you to peek through walls. Action to initiate.

○ **Go Defensive (1 Intellect point):** When you wish, while in combat, you can enter a state of heightened awareness of threat. While in this state, you can't use points from your Intellect Pool, but you gain +1 to your Speed Edge and gain two assets to Speed defense tasks. This effect lasts as long as you wish or until you attack a foe or no combat is taking place within range of your senses. Once the effect of this ability ends, you can't enter it again for one minute. Enabler.

○ **Go to Ground (4 Speed points):** You move up to a long distance and attempt to hide. When you do, you gain an asset on the stealth task to blend in, disappear, or otherwise escape the senses of everyone previously aware of your presence. Action.

○ **Goad (1 Intellect point):** You can attempt to goad a target into a belligerent—and probably foolish—reaction that requires the target to try to close the distance between you and attempt to physically strike you on its next turn. They attempt this action even if this would cause them to break formation or to give up cover or a tactically superior position. Whether the target strikes you or fails to do so, they come to their senses immediately afterward, after which further tasks attempting to goad the target again are hindered. Action to initiate.

○ **Golem Body:** You gain +1 to Armor, +1 to your Might Edge, and 5 additional points to your Might Pool. You do not need to eat, drink, or breathe (though you do need rest and sleep). You move more stiffly than a creature of flesh, which means you can never be trained or specialized in Speed defense rolls. Furthermore, you are practiced in using your stone fists as a medium weapon. Enabler.

○ **Golem Grip (3 Might points):** Your attack with the stone fists from your Golem Body ability is eased. If you hit, you can grab the target, preventing it from moving on its next turn. While you hold the target, its attacks or attempts to break free are hindered. If the target attempts to break free instead of attacking, you must make a Might-based roll to maintain your grip. If the target fails to break free, you can continue to hold it each round as your subsequent actions, automatically inflicting 4 points of damage each round by squeezing. Enabler.

○ **Golem Healing:** Your stone form from the Golem Body ability is more difficult to repair than flesh, which means you are unable to use the first, single-action recovery roll of the day that other PCs have access to. Thus, your first recovery roll on any given day requires ten minutes of rest, the second requires an hour of rest, and the third requires ten hours. Enabler.

○ **Golem Stomp (4 Might points):** You stomp on the ground with all of your strength, creating a shock wave that attacks all creatures in immediate range. Affected creatures take 3 points of damage and are either pushed out of immediate range or fall down (your choice). Action.

○ **Good Advice:** Anyone can help an ally, easing whatever task they're attempting. However, you have the benefit of clarity and wisdom. When you help another character, they gain an additional asset. Enabler.

○ **Got a Feeling (4 Intellect points):** You have an uncanny intuition when it comes to finding things. While exploring, you can extend your senses up to 1 mile (1.5 km) in any direction and ask the GM a very simple, general question—usually a yes-or-no question—about that area, such as "Is there an orc encampment nearby?" or "Is there dark matter to be found in that rusted hulk?" If the answer you seek is not in the area, you receive no information. Action.

The skin of people with Golem Body and Golem Grip is like stone, either smooth stone like a statue with strange resilience, or cracked and craggy stone constantly breaking and reforming as the character moves.

Helping, page 226

○ **Grab:** While you are using the Enlarge ability, you can attack by attempting to wrap your massive hands around a target the size of a normal human or smaller. While you maintain your hold as your action, you keep the target from moving or taking physical actions (other than attempts to escape). The target's escape attempt is hindered by two steps due to your size. If you wish, you can automatically inflict 3 points of damage each round on the target while you hold it, but you can also keep it protected (by taking all attacks otherwise meant for the target). Action.

○ **Grand Deception (3 Intellect points):** You convince an intelligent creature that can understand you and isn't hostile of something that is wildly and obviously untrue. Action.

○ **Grandiose Illusion (8 Intellect points):** You create a fantastically complex scene of images that fit within a 1-mile (1.5 km) cube that you are also within. You must be able to see the images when you create them. The images can move in the cube and act in accordance with your desires. They can also act logically (such as reacting appropriately to fire or attacks) when you aren't directly observing them. The illusion includes sound and smell. For example, armies can clash in battle, with air support from machines or flying creatures, on and above terrain of your creation. The illusion lasts for one hour (or longer, if you concentrate on it after that time). Action.

○ **Granite Wall (7+ Intellect points):** You create a level 6 granite wall within short range. The wall is 1 foot (30 cm) thick and up to 20 feet by 20 feet (6 m by 6 m) in size. It appears resting on a solid foundation and lasts for about ten hours. If you apply three levels of Effort, the wall is permanent until destroyed naturally. Action to initiate.

○ **Grasping Foliage (3+ Intellect points):** Roots, branches, grass, or other natural foliage in the area snags and holds a foe you designate within short range for up to one minute. A foe caught in the grasping foliage can't move from its position, and all physical tasks, attacks, and defenses are hindered, including attempts to free itself. In addition to the normal options for using Effort, you can choose to use Effort to deal damage with the initial attack. Each level applied inflicts 2 additional points of damage when Grasping Foliage first snags and holds your foe.

Enlarge, page 135

Effects of Gravity, page 276

Beast Form, page 112

Designation, page 127

Frenzy, page 143

You can also use this ability to clear an area of entangling growth in the immediate radius, such as an area of tall grass, thick brush, impenetrable vines, and so on. Action.

○ **Gravity Cleave (3 Intellect points):** You can harm a target within short range by rapidly increasing gravity's pull on one portion of the target and decreasing it on another, inflicting 6 points of damage. Action.

○ **Greater Beast Form:** When using Beast Form, your beast form gains the following additional bonuses: +1 to your Might Edge, +2 to your Speed Pool, and +1 to your Speed Edge. Enabler.

○ **Greater Controlled Change:** It's easier to change into and out of the shape granted by your Beast Form ability. Transforming either way is now a difficulty 2 Intellect task. Enabler.

○ **Greater Designation:** You can assign an innocent or guilty label to all creatures within immediate range when you use Designation. The one label applies to all affected creatures. This lasts until you use Greater Designation again. Action.

○ **Greater Enhanced Intellect:** You gain 6 points to your Intellect Pool. Enabler.

○ **Greater Enhanced Might:** You gain 6 points to your Might Pool. Enabler.

○ **Greater Enhanced Physique:** You gain 6 points to divide among your Might and Speed Pools however you wish. Enabler.

○ **Greater Enhanced Potential:** You gain 6 points to divide among your stat Pools however you wish. Enabler.

○ **Greater Enhanced Speed:** You gain 6 points to your Speed Pool. Enabler.

○ **Greater Frenzy (4 Intellect points):** When you wish, while in combat, you can enter a state of frenzy. While in this state, you can't use Intellect points, but you gain +2 to your Might Edge and your Speed Edge. This effect lasts as long as you wish, but it ends if no combat is taking place within range of your senses. If you have the Frenzy ability, you can use it or this ability, but you can't use both at the same time. Enabler.

○ **Greater Healing Touch (4 Intellect points):** You touch a creature and restore its Might Pool, Speed Pool, and Intellect Pool to their maximum values, as if it were fully rested. A single creature can benefit from this ability only once each day. Action.

○ **Greater Necromancy (5+ Intellect points):** This ability works like the Necromancy ability except that it creates a level 3 creature. Action to animate.

○ **Greater Skill With Attacks:** Choose one type of attack, even one in which you are already trained: light bashing, light bladed, light ranged, medium bashing, medium bladed, medium ranged, heavy bashing, heavy bladed, or heavy ranged. You are trained in attacks using that type of weapon. If you're already trained in that type of attack, you instead are specialized in that type of attack. Enabler.

○ **Greater Skill With Defense:** Choose one type of defense task, even one in which you are already trained: Might, Speed, or Intellect. You are trained in defense tasks of that type, or specialized if you are already trained. You can select this ability up to three times. Each time you select it, you must choose a different type of defense task. Enabler.

○ **Group Friendship (4 Intellect points):** You convince a sentient creature to regard you (and up to ten creatures that you designate within immediate distance of you) positively, as they would a potential friend. Action.

○ **Guide Bolt (4+ Intellect points):** When you make an attack with a metallic bolt or metal-tipped arrow on a target within short range, you can improve the attack's aim and velocity, which grants an asset to the attack and inflicts an additional 2 points of damage. If you apply a level of Effort, you grant the same benefits to a ranged attack made by an ally within immediate range. In any case, you can use this ability only once per round. Enabler.

○ **Guild Training:** Your type abilities that have durations last twice as long. Your type abilities that have short ranges reach to long range instead. Your type abilities that inflict damage deal 1 additional point of damage. Enabler.

○ **Gunner:** You inflict 1 additional point of damage with guns. Enabler.

ABILITIES—H

○ **Hack the Impossible (3 Intellect points):** You can persuade robots, machines, and computers to do your bidding. You can discover an encrypted password, break through security on a website, briefly turn off a machine such as a surveillance camera, or disable a robot with a moment's worth of fiddling. Action.

○ **Hacker (2 Intellect points):** You gain quick access to a desired bit of information in a computer or similar device, or you access one of its primary functions. Action.

Necromancy, page 165

When you're hacking the impossible, the GM will decide if your hack is reasonable and determine its level of difficulty. For comparison, discovering a normal password when you have direct access to the system is a difficulty 2 task for you.

○ **Hand to Eye (2 Speed points):** This ability provides an asset to any tasks involving manual dexterity, such as pickpocketing, lockpicking, games involving agility, and so on. Each use lasts up to a minute; a new use (to switch tasks) replaces the previous use. Action to initiate.

○ **Handy:** You work for a living and are trained in tasks related to carpentry, plumbing, and electrical repair. Your knowledge in these realms also gives you an asset to craft entirely new items within your spheres of knowledge and the limits of possibility within the setting. Enabler.

○ **Hard Choices:** Sometimes, you believe that you've got to lie to those who trust you for their own good. You are specialized in deception tasks. Enabler.

○ **Hard Target:** If you move a short distance or farther on your turn, all Speed defense rolls are eased. Enabler.

○ **Hard to Distract:** You are trained in Intellect defense tasks. Enabler.

○ **Hard to Hit:** You are trained in Speed defense tasks. Enabler.

○ **Hard to Kill:** You can choose to reroll any defense task you make but never more than once per round. Enabler.

○ **Hard to See:** When you move, you are a blur. It is impossible to make out your identity as you run past, and in a round where you do nothing but move, stealth tasks and Speed defense tasks are eased. Enabler.

Have Spacesuit, Will Travel is associated with the Loves the Void focus on page 71.

Powered Armor, page 171

○ **Hard-Won Resilience:** In your explorations of dark places, you've been exposed to all sorts of terrible things and are developing a general resistance. You gain +1 to Armor and are trained in Might defense tasks. Enabler.

○ **Hardiness:** You are trained in Might defense tasks. Enabler.

○ **Have Spacesuit, Will Travel:** Somehow or another, you became the legal owner of a fully functional and advanced spacesuit. The spacesuit provides +1 Armor and, more important, allows you to survive in the vacuum of space using suit reserves for up to twelve hours at a time with enough reaction mass to get around in zero gravity on jets of ionized gas for that same period. After each use, the suit must be recharged, either with already-charged cartridges of air and reaction mass or by allowing the suit to sit idle in an area with breathable atmosphere for at least two hours, during which time it will recharge both air and reaction mass using integrated solid state mechanisms. The suit's power supply is a radioisotope thermoelectric generator, which means it'll function for a few decades before needing to be changed out. Enabler.

○ **Heads-Up Display (2+ Intellect points):** Your Powered Armor ability comes with systems that help you make sense of, analyze, and use your weapons in your environment. When you trigger this ability, you gain an asset on one attack roll as the suit perfectly outlines foes and steadies your aim, regardless of whether you're making a melee or ranged attack.

Alternatively, you can use the heads-up display to magnify your vision, increasing your vision range to 5 miles (8 km) for two rounds. If you apply one level of Effort, you can also see through mundane materials (such as wood, concrete, plastic, and stone) to a short distance in false color images. If you apply two levels of Effort, you can see through special materials (such as solid lead or other substances) to an immediate distance in false color images; however, the GM might require you to succeed at an Intellect-based task first, depending on the material blocking your armor's sensors. Enabler.

○ **Healing Pulse (3 Intellect points):** You and all targets you choose within immediate range gain the immediate benefits of using one of their recovery rolls (as long as it is not their ten-hour recovery roll) without having to spend an action,

ten minutes, or one hour. Targets regain points to their Pools immediately but mark off that recovery use. PCs who have already used up their one-action, ten-minute, and one-hour recovery rolls for the day gain no benefit from this ability. NPCs targeted by this ability regain a number of health points equal to their level. Action.

Healing Touch (1 Intellect point): With a touch, you restore 1d6 points to one stat Pool of any creature. This ability is a difficulty 2 Intellect task. Each time you attempt to heal the same creature, the task is hindered by an additional step. The difficulty returns to 2 after that creature rests for ten hours. Action.

Hedge Magic (1 Intellect point): You can perform small tricks: temporarily change the color or basic appearance of a small object, cause small objects to float through the air, clean a small area, mend a broken object, prepare (but not create) food, and so on. You can't use Hedge Magic to harm another creature or object. Action.

Heightened Skills: You are trained in two tasks of your choosing (other than attacks or defense). If you choose a task you're already trained in, you instead become specialized in that task. You can't choose a task you're already specialized in. Enabler.

Hemorrhage (2+ Might points): You make a powerful and precise strike that inflicts additional damage later. On your next turn, the target of this attack takes an additional 3 points of damage (ignores Armor). The target can prevent this additional damage by making a recovery roll, using any ability that heals it, or using its action to attend to the injury. In addition to the normal options for using Effort, you can choose to use Effort to increase this duration by one round. Action.

Heroic Monster Bane: When you inflict damage to creatures more than twice as large or massive as you, you inflict 3 additional points of damage. Enabler.

Hidden Closet: The magic ally from your Bound Magic Creature ability can store items for you within its bound object, including extra sets of clothing, tools, food, and so on. The interior of the object is, in effect, a 10-foot (3 m) square pocket dimension that normally only the magic ally can access. Enabler.

Hidden Reserves: When you use an action to make a recovery roll, you also gain +1 to both your Might Edge and your Speed Edge for ten minutes thereafter. Enabler.

Higher Mathematics: You are trained in standard and higher mathematics. Enabler.

Hold Breath: You can hold your breath for up to five minutes. Enabler.

Horde Fighting: When two or more foes attack you at once in melee, you can use them against each other. You gain an asset to Speed defense rolls or attack rolls (your choice each round) against them. Enabler.

Horde Tactics (7 Might points): For up to one hour a day, you and at least three other allies can act like a single creature. Use your stats, but add +8 to your Might Pool, +1 to your Might Edge, +2 to your Speed Pool, +1 to your Speed Edge, and +1 to your Armor. Enabler.

Hover (2 Intellect points): You float slowly into the air. If you concentrate, you can control your movement to remain motionless in the air or float up to a short distance as your action; otherwise, you drift with the wind or with any momentum you have gained. This effect lasts for up to ten minutes. Action to initiate.

How Others Think: You have a sense of how people think. You're trained in one of the following tasks: persuasion, deception, or detecting falsehoods. Enabler.

Huge: When you use Enlarge, you can choose to grow up to 16 feet (5 m) in height. When you do, you add +1 to Armor (a total of +2 to Armor) and deal 2 additional points of damage with melee attacks. Enabler.

Hunter's Drive (5 Intellect points): Through force of will, when you wish it, you grant yourself greater prowess in the hunt for ten minutes. During this time, you gain an asset to all tasks involving your quarry, including attacks. Your quarry is the creature you selected with your Quarry ability. Enabler.

Hurl Flame (2 Intellect points): While your Shroud of Flame is active, you can reach into your halo and hurl a handful of fire at a target. This is a ranged attack with short range that deals 4 points of fire damage. Action.

Enlarge, page 135

Bound Magic Creature, page 115

Quarry, page 173

Shroud of Flame, page 183

ABILITIES—I

Ice Armor (1 Intellect point): When you wish it, your body is covered in a sheen of ice for ten minutes that gives you +1 to Armor. While the sheen is active, you feel no discomfort from normal cold temperatures and have an additional +2 to Armor versus cold damage specifically. Enabler.

Ice Creation (4+ Intellect points): You create a solid object of ice that is your size or smaller. The object is crude and can have no moving parts, so you can make a sword, a shield, a short ladder, and so on. Your ice objects are as strong as iron, but if you're not in constant contact with them, they function for only 1d6 + 6 rounds before breaking or melting. For example, you can make and wield an ice sword, but if you give it to another PC, the sword won't last as long for that character. In addition to the normal options for using Effort, you can choose to use Effort to create objects larger than you. For each level of Effort used in this way, you can create an object up to twice again as large as you. Action.

Ice is usually frosty and opaque, unless the character specifies transparent ice.

Ice Storm: You attempt an additional Intellect task as part of your Cold Burst attack, and if successful, you blind foes for up to one minute with a layer of freezing ice. All tasks of blinded creatures are hindered by two steps. Enabler.

Cold Burst, page 119

Ignition (4 Intellect points): You designate a creature or flammable object you can see within short range to catch fire. This is an Intellect attack. The target takes 6 points of ambient damage per round until the flames are extinguished, which a creature can do by dousing itself in water, rolling on the ground, or smothering the flames. Usually, putting out the flames takes an action. Action to initiate.

Ignore Affliction (5 Might points): If you are affected by an unwanted condition or affliction (such as disease, paralysis, mind control, broken limb, and so on, but not damage), you can ignore it and act as if it does not affect you for one hour. If the condition would normally last less than an hour, it is entirely negated. Action.

Impaired, debilitated: see damage track, page 218

Ignore the Pain: You ignore the impaired condition and treat the debilitated condition as impaired. Enabler.

Free level of Effort, page 209

Illuminating Touch (1 Intellect point): You touch an object, and that object sheds light to illuminate everything in short range. The light remains until you use an action to touch the object again, or until you've illuminated more objects than you have tiers, in which case the oldest objects you illuminated go dark first. Action.

Illusory Disguise (2+ Intellect points): You appear to be someone or something else, roughly of your size and shape, for up to one hour. Once created, the disguise requires no concentration. For each additional Intellect point you spend, you can disguise one other creature. All disguised creatures must stay within sight of you or lose their disguise. Action to create.

Illusory Duplicate (2 Intellect points): You create a single image of yourself within immediate range. The image looks like you as you are now (including how you are dressed). The image can move (for example, you could make it walk or attack), but it can't move more than an immediate distance from where you created it. The illusion includes sound and smell. It lasts for ten minutes and changes as you direct (no concentration is needed). If you move beyond short range of the illusion, it vanishes. Action to create.

Illusory Evasion (5 Intellect points): When you would be hit by an attack, you teleport an immediate distance away, leaving behind an illusory copy of yourself to be struck by that attack instead of you. This destroys the illusion but leaves you unharmed by the attack. If the attack affects an area and the teleportation can't get you out of that area, the attack still affects you normally. Enabler.

Illusory Selves (4 Intellect points): You create four holographic duplicates of yourself within short range. The duplicates last for one minute. You mentally direct their actions, and the duplicates aren't mirror images—each one can do different things. If struck violently, they either disappear permanently or freeze motionless (your choice). Action to create.

Immovable: You gain +3 to your Might Pool. You can attempt a Might task to avoid being knocked down, pushed back, or moved against your will even if the effect attempting to move you doesn't allow it. If you apply Effort to this task, you can apply two free levels of Effort. Enabler.

150

Abilities—1

○ **Impart Ideal (3 Intellect points):** After interacting for at least one minute with a creature who can hear and understand you, you can attempt to temporarily impart an ideal to it that you could not otherwise convince it to adopt. An ideal is different than a specific suggestion or command; an ideal is an overarching value such as "All life is sacred," "My political party is the best," "Children should be seen, not heard," and so on. An ideal influences a creature's behavior but doesn't control it. The imparted ideal lasts as long as befits the situation, but usually at least a few hours. The ideal is jeopardized if someone friendly to the creature spends a minute or more bringing it back to its senses. Action.

○ **Impart Understanding:** Your Learning the Path ability works more effectively, allowing you to ease a task by two steps or to provide two assets to a friend's task, instead of easing normally. Enabler.

○ **Impersonate (2 Intellect points):** For one hour, you alter your voice, posture, and mannerisms, whip together a disguise, and gain an asset on an attempt to impersonate someone else, whether it is a specific individual (Bob the cop) or a general role (a police officer). Action to initiate.

○ **Impetus (2 Intellect points):** A loose object within short range that you could carry in one hand is drawn to your free hand. If the object is stuck or held by another creature, you must succeed on a Might roll to rip it free, or the object remains where it is. Action.

○ **Impossible Walk (5+ Speed points):** You can walk (or crawl or run) on steep inclines and horizontal surfaces (such as walls and cliffs) for the next minute as if they were flat ground. When using this ability, "down" for you is either the surface you are walking on or the normal orientation of gravity (your choice). If you apply one level of Effort, you can also walk on the ceiling or on a liquid or semi-liquid surface such as water, mud, quicksand, or even lava (although touching a dangerous surface like lava still harms you). If you apply two levels of Effort, you can also walk on air as if it were solid ground. Enabler.

○ **Impressive Display (2 Might points):** You perform a feat of strength, speed, or combat, impressing those nearby. For the next minute you gain an asset on all interaction tasks with people who saw you use this ability. Action.

○ **Improved Absorb Kinetic Energy:** When you use Absorb Kinetic Energy, instead of being able to absorb 1 point of damage from a physical attack or impact, you can absorb 2 points. You can also store up to 2 points of energy from any source. However, you can still release energy only 1 point at a time. Enabler.

Absorb Kinetic Energy, page 108

○ **Improved Apportation (6 Intellect points):** You call a creature of up to level 3, which appears next to you. You can choose a creature that you've previously encountered, or (no more than once per day) you can allow the GM to determine the creature randomly. If you call a random creature, it has a 10 percent chance of being a creature of up to level 5. The creature has no memory of anything before being called by you, though it can speak and has the general knowledge a creature of its type should possess. The creature is receptive to communication and helping you (unless shown that it should do otherwise). Action.

Learning the Path, page 157

○ **Improved Command Spirit:** When you use your Command Spirit ability, you can command a spirit or animate undead creature of up to level 7. Enabler.

Command Spirit, page 121

○ **Improved Companion:** Your companion (such as a controlled beast) or follower increases to level 4. As a level 4 creature, it has a target number of 12 and 12 health, and it inflicts 4 points of damage (though in most cases, instead of attacking, it provides an asset to your attacks). You can gain this ability once per tier. Each additional time you select it, it increases your companion or follower's level by 1. Enabler.

Controls Beasts, page 65
Follower, page 233

○ **Improved Designation:** When you use Designation, you can designate one additional creature to be innocent or guilty, which means up to two creatures at a time may be innocent, or two guilty, or one innocent and one guilty. Enabler.

Designation, page 127

○ **Improved Edge:** Choose one of your Edge stats that is 0. It increases to 1. Enabler.

○ **Improved Gravity Cleave (9 Intellect points):** You can harm a group of targets within long range by rapidly increasing gravity's pull on one portion of each target and decreasing it on another, inflicting 6 points of damage. The targets must be within immediate range of each other. Action.

Recovery rolls, page 218
Machine Companion, page 159

Bound Magic Creature, page 115
Bound magic creature: *level 4*

Improvise can be used on a task a character has an inability in, but instead of gaining an asset, the character just loses the inability penalty.

Sensor, page 181

○ **Improved Machine Companion:** The machine from your Machine Companion ability improves, becoming a level 5 creature with the ability either to fly a long distance each round (and carry you) for up to ten minutes at a time, or to carry an extra cypher for you that doesn't count against your cypher limit. Enabler.

○ **Improved Monster Bane:** When you inflict damage to creatures more than twice as large or massive as you, you inflict 3 additional points of damage. Enabler.

○ **Improved Object Bond (5 Intellect points):** When you manifest the ally from your Bound Magic Creature ability, it is now a level 4 creature. Also, the creature gains a pulse attack that renders all artifacts, machines, manifest cyphers, and lesser magic devices within short range inoperable for one minute. After the creature uses this ability, it must retreat to its object to rest for three hours. Enabler.

○ **Improved Recovery:** Your ten-minute recovery roll takes only one action instead, so that your first two recovery rolls are one action, the third is one hour, and the fourth is ten hours. Enabler.

○ **Improved Sculpt Light (7+ Intellect points):** You create an object of solid light in any shape you can imagine whose base size can fit within a 10-foot (3 m) cube. The object appears in an area adjacent to you or floating freely in space up to a long distance away, and the object lasts for a few days. The object is crude and can have no moving parts, so you can make a wall segment, a block, a box, stairs, and so on. The sculpted object has the approximate mass of the real object and is level 6. If you apply Effort to increase the size of the object, each level applied increases the size by an additional 10-foot (3 m) cube. Action.

○ **Improved Sensor (2 Intellect points):** When you use Sensor, you can place the sensor anywhere you choose within long range. Enabler.

○ **Improved Success:** When you roll a 17 or higher on an attack roll that deals damage, you deal 1 additional point of damage. For instance, if you roll a natural 18, which normally deals 2 extra points of damage, you instead deal 3 extra points. If you roll a natural 20 and choose to deal damage instead of achieve a special major effect, you deal 5 extra points of damage. Enabler.

○ **Improvise (3 Intellect points):** When you perform a task in which you are not trained, you can improvise to gain an asset on the task. The asset might be a tool you cobble together, a sudden insight into overcoming a problem, or a rush of dumb luck. Enabler.

○ **In Harm's Way (3 Intellect points):** When you put your friends before yourself as your action, you ease all defense tasks for all characters you choose that are adjacent to you. This lasts until the end of your next turn. If one of your friends would be damaged, you can choose to take up to half the number of points of damage they would otherwise take, but only if you're not already impaired or debilitated. Enabler.

○ **Incomparable Pilot:** While on a starcraft you own or have a direct connection with, your Might Edge, Speed Edge, and Intellect Edge increase by 1. When you make a recovery roll on a starcraft you're familiar with, you recover 5 additional points. Enabler.

Abilities—1

○ **Increased Effects:** You treat rolls of natural 19 as rolls of natural 20 for either Might actions or Speed actions (your choice when you gain this ability). This allows you to gain a major effect on a natural 19 or 20. Enabler.

○ **Increasing Determination:** If you fail at a noncombat physical task (pushing open a door or climbing a cliff, for example) and then retry the task, the task is eased. If you fail again, you gain no special benefits. Enabler.

○ **Incredible Feat of Science (12 Intellect points):** You do something amazing in the lab. This takes parts and materials equivalent to three expensive items. Possible incredible feats include:
- Reanimate and command a dead body for one hour.
- Create an engine that runs on perpetual motion.
- Create a teleportation gate that remains open for one minute.
- Transmute one substance into another substance.
- Cure one person with an incurable disease or condition.
- Create a weapon designed to hurt something that can't otherwise be hurt.
- Create a defense designed to protect against something that can't otherwise be stopped.

Action to initiate; a full day of work to complete.

○ **Incredible Health:** Thanks to a dip in a magical pool, an injection of artificial antibodies and immune defense nanobots into your bloodstream, exposure to strange radiation, or something else, you are now immune to diseases, viruses, and mutations of any kind. Enabler.

○ **Incredible Recovery (6 Might points):** You move up one step on the damage track or shake off any unwanted ongoing condition. Action.

○ **Incredible Running Speed:** You move much farther than normal in a round. This means as a part of another action, you can move up to a long distance. As an action, you can move up to 200 feet (60 m), or up to 500 feet (150 m) as a Speed-based task with a difficulty of 4. Enabler.

○ **Infer Thoughts (4 Intellect points):** If you interact with or study a target for at least a round, you can attempt to read its surface thoughts, even if the subject doesn't want you to. You must be able to see the target. Once you have gained a sense of what it's thinking—through its body language, its speech, and what it does and doesn't say—you can continue to infer the target's surface thoughts for up to one minute as long as you can still see and hear the target. Action to prepare; action to initiate.

○ **Inferno Trail (6 Intellect points):** For the next minute, you leave a trail of flame in your wake. The trail matches your path and lasts for up to a minute, creating a wall of flame about 6 feet (2 m) high that inflicts 5 points of damage to any creature that passes through it, potentially catching them on fire for an additional 1 point of damage each round (if they are flammable) until they spend a round putting out the fire. Action.

○ **Infiltrator:** You are trained in interactions involving lies or trickery. Enabler.

○ **Influence Swarm (1 Intellect point):** You master one type of small creature (such as insects, rats, bats, or even birds) and they respond to you in number. Your creatures within short range will not harm you or those you designate as allies for one hour. Action to initiate.

○ **Information Gathering (5 Intellect points):** You speak telepathically with any or all machines within 1 mile (1.5 km). You can ask one basic question about themselves or anything happening near them and receive a simple answer. For example, while in an area with many machines, you could ask about the location of a specific creature or individual, and if they are within a mile of you, one or more machines will probably provide the answer. Action.

○ **Informer:** You gain an informer within an allied community. They act as your secret (or known) informer. If something of note happens in your informer's location, they will use whatever means they have available to tell you about it. Enabler.

○ **Infuse Spirit:** When you kill a creature or destroy a spirit with an attack, if you choose, its spirit (if unprotected) immediately infuses you, and you regain 1d6 points to one of your Pools (your choice). The spirit is stored within you, which means it cannot be questioned, raised, or restored to life by any means unless you allow it. Enabler.

Major effect, page 212

Incredible Feat of Science is an ability often associated with the Conducts Weird Science focus on page 65.

Damage track, page 218

A character should specify where they place the crystal for the Inhabit Crystal ability before using it, even if it's just on the ground at their feet.

Designation, page 127

Recovery roll, page 218

○ **Inhabit Crystal (4 Intellect points):** You transfer your body and whatever you are carrying into a crystal at least the size of your index finger. While in the crystal, you are aware of what is going on around it, seeing and hearing through the crystal. You can even speak through the crystal and carry on conversations. You cannot take actions other than to exit the crystal. You remain within as long as you wish, but you are not in stasis and should exit to eat, drink, sleep, and so on as normal (breathing is not an issue). If the crystal is destroyed or takes major damage while you are within it, you immediately exit, cannot act for three rounds, and move two steps down the damage track. Action to enter and exit.

○ **Inner Defense:** Life's trials have toughened you and made you hard to read. You are trained in any task to resist another creature's attempt to discern your true feelings, beliefs, or plans. You are likewise trained in resisting torture, telepathic intrusion, and mind control. Enabler.

○ **Innovator:** You can modify any artifact to give it different or better abilities as if that artifact were one level lower than normal, and the modification takes half the normal time. Enabler.

○ **Insect Eruption (6 Intellect points):** You call a swarm of insects in a place where it is possible for insects to appear. They remain for one minute, and during this time, they do as you command while they are within long range. They can swarm about and hinder any or all creatures' tasks, or you can focus the swarm and attack all targets within immediate range of each other (all within long range of you). The attacking swarm inflicts 2 points of damage per round. You can also command the swarm to move heavy objects through collective effort, eat through wooden walls, and perform other actions suitable for a supernatural swarm. Action to initiate.

○ **Insight:** You are trained in tasks to discern others' motives and to ascertain their general nature. You have a knack for sensing whether or not someone is truly innocent. Enabler.

○ **Inspiration (6 Intellect points):** You speak words of encouragement and inspiration. All allies within short range who can hear you immediately gain a recovery roll, gain an immediate free action, and have an asset for that free action. The recovery roll does not count as one of their normal recovery rolls. Action.

○ **Inspire Action (4 Intellect points):** If one ally can see and easily understand you, you can instruct that ally to take an action. If the ally chooses to take that exact action, they can do so as an additional action immediately. Doing so doesn't interfere with the ally taking a normal action on their turn. Action.

○ **Inspire Aggression (2 Intellect points):** Your words twist the mind of a character within short range who is able to understand you, unlocking their more primitive instincts. As a result, they gain an asset on their Might-based attack rolls for one minute. Action to initiate.

○ **Inspire Coordinated Actions (9 Intellect points):** If your allies can see and easily understand you, you can instruct each of them to take one specific action (the same action for all of them). If any of them choose to take that exact action, they can do so as an additional action immediately. This doesn't interfere with them taking their normal actions on their turns. Action.

○ **Inspire the Innocent (3 Intellect points):** You speak words of encouragement and inspiration to everyone within immediate range whom you have designated as innocent with your Designation ability. They immediately gain a free recovery roll. One person you choose can gain an immediate free action instead of a free recovery roll. If you also have the Inspiration ability, the target who gains a free action also gains an asset on it. Action.

○ **Inspiring Ease:** Through stories, songs, art, or other forms of entertainment, you inspire your friends. After spending 24 hours with you, once per day each of your friends can ease a task. This benefit is ongoing while you remain in the friend's company. It ends if you leave, but it resumes if you return to the friend's company within 24 hours. If you leave the friend's company for more than 24 hours, you must spend another 24 hours together to reactivate the benefit. Enabler.

○ **Inspiring Success (6 Intellect points):** When you succeed on a roll to perform a task related to the stat that you choose upon selecting this ability, and you applied at least one level of Effort, you may choose another character within short range. That character has an asset on the next task they attempt using that stat on their next turn. Enabler.

Abilities—I

○ **Intelligent Interface (3 Intellect points):** You can speak telepathically with any intelligent machine within long range. Further, you are trained in all interactions with intelligent machines. Such machines and robots that normally would never communicate with a human might talk to you. Enabler.

○ **Intense Interaction (3 Intellect points):** You gain an asset on intimidating, persuading, and influencing people for ten minutes. Action.

○ **Interaction Skills:** You are trained in two skills in which you are not already trained. Choose two of the following: deceiving, persuading, public speaking, seeing through deception, or intimidation. You can select this ability multiple times. Each time you select it, you must choose two different skills. Enabler.

○ **Interface:** By directly plugging into a device, you can identify and learn to operate it as though the task were one level lower. Enabler.

○ **Interruption (4 Intellect points):** Your vociferous, booming command prevents a creature within short range from taking any action for one round. It can defend itself if attacked, but when it does so, its defense is hindered by two steps. Each additional time you attempt this ability against the same target, you must apply one more level of Effort than you applied on the previous attempt. Action.

○ **Inventor:** You can create new artifacts in half the time, as if they were two levels lower, by spending half the normal XP. Enabler.

○ **Investigate:** You are trained in perception, cryptography, deceiving, and breaking into computers. Enabler.

○ **Investigative Skills:** You are trained in two skills in which you are not already trained. Choose two of the following: perception, identifying, lockpicking, assessing danger, or tinkering with devices. You can select this ability multiple times. Each time you select it, you must choose two different skills. Enabler.

○ **Investigator:** To really shine as an investigator, you must engage your mind and body in your deductions. You can spend points from your Might Pool, Speed Pool, or Intellect Pool to apply levels of Effort to any Intellect-based task. Enabler.

○ **Invisibility (4 Intellect points):** You become invisible for ten minutes. While invisible, you are specialized in stealth and Speed defense tasks. This effect ends if you do something to reveal your presence or position—attacking, using an ability, moving a large object, and so on. If this occurs, you can regain the remaining invisibility effect by taking an action to hide your position. If you have another ability that also confers invisibility, using either one allows you to remain invisible for twice as long as the duration specified. Action to initiate or reinitiate.

○ **Invisible Phasing (4 Might points):** You become invisible while using Phase Sprint and during the following round. While invisible, stealth is eased by two steps and Speed defense is eased by two steps (this replaces the asset to Speed defense tasks provided by Phase Sprint). The first attack you make using any Shreds the Walls of the World attack abilities is also eased by two steps; however, if you attack a creature, Invisible Phasing ends immediately instead of lasting for one additional round. If you have the Invisibility ability, you can remain invisible during the entire round, which means that if you use Scratch Existence or Shred Existence, attacking each target along your path is eased by two steps. Enabler.

○ **Iron Fist:** Your unarmed attacks deal 4 points of damage. Enabler.

○ **Iron Punch (5+ Intellect points):** You magnetically pick up a metallic heavy object within short range and hurl it at someone within short range, an Intellect action that deals 6 points of damage to the target and to the hurled object. For each additional level of Effort applied, you can pick up a slightly larger object, allowing you to affect one additional target within short range as long as it is next to the prior target. Action.

Abilities—J

○ **Jaunt (5+ Intellect points):** You instantaneously teleport yourself to any location within long distance that you can see. In addition to the normal options for using Effort, you can choose to use Effort to increase the distance you can travel; each level of Effort used in this way increases the range by another 100 feet (30 m). Action.

Phase Sprint, page 170

Shreds the Walls of the World, page 76

Scratch Existence, page 180

Shred Existence, page 183

○ **Juggernaut (5 Might points):** Until the end of the next round, you can move through solid objects such as doors and walls. Only 2 feet (60 cm) of wood, 1 foot (30 cm) of stone, or 6 inches (15 cm) of metal can stop your movement. Enabler.

○ **Jump Attack (5+ Might points):** You attempt a difficulty 4 Might roll to jump high into the air as part of your melee attack action. If you succeed at the jump and your attack hits, you inflict 3 additional points of damage and knock the foe prone. If you fail at the jump, you still make your normal attack roll, but you don't inflict the extra damage or knock down the opponent if you hit. In addition to the normal options for using Effort, you can choose to use Effort to enhance your jump; each level of Effort used in this way adds +2 feet to the height and +1 damage to the attack. Action.

○ **Junkmonger (2 Intellect points):** You are trained in crafting two kinds of items using scavenged junk. If you have scavenged (or otherwise obtained) at least two pieces of junk in different categories (electronic, plastic, dangerous, metallic, glass, or textile), you have the materials you need to craft a new item in one of your areas of training (unless the GM deems otherwise). Enabler.

○ **Jury-Rig (5 Intellect points):** You quickly create an object using what would seem to be entirely inappropriate materials. You can make a bomb out of a tin can and household cleaners, a lockpick out of aluminum foil, or a sword out of broken furniture. The level of the item determines the difficulty of the task, but the appropriateness of the materials eases or hinders it as well. Generally, the object can be no larger than something you can hold in one hand, and it functions once (or, in the case of a weapon or similar item, is essentially useful for one encounter). If you spend at least ten minutes on the task, you can create an item of level 5 or lower. You can't change the nature of the materials involved. For example, you can't take iron rods and make a pile of gold coins or a wicker basket. Action.

○ **Just a Bit Mad:** You are trained in Intellect defense tasks. Enabler.

Useful Stuff table, page 298

Junk table, page 298

Crafting, Building, and Repairing, page 227

If you're creating a focus, Knowing is the kind of ability that can be given in addition to some other ability at the same tier.

ABILITIES—K

○ **Knock Out (5+ Might points):** You make a melee attack that inflicts no damage. Instead, if the attack hits, make a second Might-based roll. If successful, a foe of level 3 or lower is knocked unconscious for one minute. For each level of Effort used, you can affect one higher level of foe, or you can extend the duration for an additional minute. Action.

○ **Know Their Faults:** If a creature that you can see has a special weakness, such as a vulnerability to loud noises, a negative modification to perception, and so on, you know what it is. Ask and the GM will tell you; usually, this is not associated with a roll, but in certain cases the GM may decide that there is a chance for you not to know. In these cases, you are specialized in knowing creature weaknesses. Enabler.

○ **Know Where to Look:** Whenever the GM obtains a result for you on the Useful Stuff table, you get two results instead of one. If the GM is using some other method to generate rewards for finding valuables, you should gain double the result you would otherwise obtain. Enabler.

○ **Knowing:** You are trained in one area of knowledge of your choice. Enabler.

○ **Knowing the Unknown (6 Intellect points):** By accessing the resources appropriate to your character, you can ask the GM one question and get a general answer. The GM assigns a level to the question, so the more obscure the answer, the more difficult the task. Generally, knowledge that you could find by looking somewhere other than your current location is level 1, and obscure knowledge of the past is level 7. Gaining knowledge of the future is impossible. Action.

○ **Knowledge of the Law:** You're trained in the law of the land. If you don't know the answer to a question of law, you know where and how to research it (a university's law library is a good place to start, but you've also got online sources). Enabler.

○ **Knowledge Is Power:** Choose two noncombat skills in which you are not trained. You are trained in those skills. Enabler.

ABILITIES—J-L

○ **Knowledge Skills:** You are trained in two skills in which you are not already trained. Choose two areas of knowledge such as history, geography, archeology, and so on. You can select this ability multiple times. Each time you select it, you must choose two different skills. Enabler.

ABILITIES—L

○ **Lab Analysis (3 Intellect points):** You analyze the scene of a crime, the site of a mysterious incident, or a series of unexplained phenomena, and maybe learn a surprising amount of information about the perpetrators, the participants, or the force(s) responsible. To do so, you must collect samples from the scene. Samples are paint or wood scrapings, dirt, photographs of the area, hair, an entire corpse, and so on. With samples in hand, you can discover up to three pertinent pieces of information about the scene, possibly clearing up a lesser mystery and pointing the way to solving a greater one. The GM will decide what you learn and what level of difficulty is needed to learn it. (For comparison, discovering that a victim was killed not by a fall, as seems immediately obvious, but rather by electrocution, is a difficulty 3 task for you.) The task is eased if you take the time to transport the samples to a permanent lab (if you have access to one), as opposed to conducting the analysis with your field science kit. Action to initiate, 2d20 minutes to complete.

○ **Late Inspiration (3 Intellect points):** You retry a task you failed within the past one minute, using the same difficulty and modifiers, except this time you have an asset on the task. If this retry fails, you can't use this ability to retry it again. Enabler.

○ **Lead by Inquiry:** You keep your allies on their toes with occasional questions, jokes, and even mock drills for those who care to join in. After spending 24 hours with you, your allies are treated as if trained in tasks related to perception. This benefit is ongoing while you remain in your allies' company. It ends if you leave, but it resumes if you return to the allies' company within 24 hours. If you leave the allies' company for more than 24 hours, you must spend another 24 hours together to reactivate the benefit. Enabler.

○ **Lead From the Front:** You gain 3 new points to divide among your stat Pools however you wish. Enabler.

○ **Learned a Few Things:** You are trained in two areas of knowledge of your choice, or specialized in one area of knowledge of your choice. Enabler.

○ **Learning the Path (2 Intellect points):** You observe or study a creature, object, or location for at least one round. The next time you interact with it (possibly in the following round), a related task (such as persuading the creature, attacking it, or defending from its attack) is eased. Action.

○ **Legal Intern:** You gain a level 4 follower who is mostly interested in helping with your law-related tasks, but who might also help you in other areas. Enabler.

○ **Legerdemain (1 Speed point):** You can perform small but seemingly impossible tricks. For example, you can make a small object in your hands disappear and move into a desired spot within reach (like your pocket). You can make someone believe that they have something in their possession that they do not have (or vice versa). You can switch similar objects right in front of someone's eyes. Action.

Follower, page 233

○ **Lethal Damage:** Choose one of your existing attacks that inflicts points of damage (depending on your type and focus, this might be a specific weapon, a special ability such as a blast of fire, or your unarmed attacks). When you hit with that attack, you inflict an additional 5 points of damage. Enabler.

○ **Lethal Ploy (5+ Intellect points):** Long experience has revealed to you that subterfuge is your friend in desperate situations. You push, attack, or distract the target in some seemingly inconsequential way that leads to the target's death. The target must be level 2 or lower. In addition to the normal options for using Effort, you can choose to use Effort to increase the maximum level of the target by 1. Thus, to kill a level 5 target (three levels above the normal limit), you must apply three levels of Effort. Action.

○ **Lethal Vibration (7 Might points):** You set up a lethal vibration in your own body and pass it to a creature you touch with a successful attack. If the target is level 2 or lower, it dies, exploding in a peal of thunder. If the target is level 3 or higher, it sustains 6 points of damage and is stunned on its next action. If the target is a PC of any tier, they move down one step on the damage track. In addition to the normal options for using Effort, you can choose to use Effort to affect a more powerful target (one level of Effort means a target of up to level 3 explodes and a target of level 4 or higher takes damage and is stunned, and so on). Action.

○ **Levity:** Through wit, charm, humor, and grace, you are trained in all social interactions other than those involving coercion or intimidation. During rests, you put friends and comrades at ease so much that they gain +1 to their recovery rolls. Enabler.

○ **Life Lessons:** Choose any two noncombat skills. You are trained in those skills. Enabler.

○ **Like the Back of Your Hand:** All tasks directly related to a starcraft that you own or have a direct connection with are eased. Tasks include repair, refueling, finding a breach in the hull, finding a stowaway, and so on. The same goes for any attack or defense rolls you make within the starcraft against enemy boarders, as well as any attack or defense rolls you make with the ship against enemy ships. Enabler.

○ **Link Senses (2 Intellect points):** You touch a willing creature and link its senses to yours for one minute. At any time during that duration, you can concentrate to see, hear, and smell what that creature is experiencing, instead of using your own senses. If you or the creature move out of long range, the connection is broken. Action to initiate.

○ **Living Armor (4 Intellect points):** If you're in a location where it's possible for your creatures from Influence Swarm to come, you call a swarm around you for one hour. They crawl over your body or fly around you in a cloud. During this time, your Speed defense tasks are eased, and you gain +1 to Armor. Action to initiate.

○ **Living Light (6+ Intellect points):** Your body dissolves into a cloud of photons that instantly travel to a location you choose and then reform. You can choose any open space big enough to contain you that you can see within very long range, or any place you have lit by Illuminating Touch that is still shining. You disappear and almost instantly reappear in the space you chose. It takes until the end of the round for your body to become fully solid, so until the start of the next round, you take a maximum of 1 point of damage from any given attack or source of damage. Each level of Effort you apply allows you to bring along one additional person besides yourself, as long as they are within immediate range when you depart. Action.

○ **Living Off the Land:** Given an hour or so, you can always find edible food and potable water in the wilderness. You can even find enough for a small group of people, if need be. Further, since you're so hardy and have gained resistance over time, you are trained in resisting the effects of natural poisons (such as those from plants or living creatures). You're also immune to natural diseases. Enabler.

○ **Living Wall (3 Might points):** You specify a confined area—such as an open doorway, a hallway, or a space between two trees—where you stand. For the next ten minutes, if anyone attempts to enter or pass through that area and you don't wish it, you make an automatic attack against them. If you hit, not only do you inflict damage, but they must also stop their movement. Enabler.

Influence Swarm, page 153

Illuminating Touch, page 150

Damage track, page 218

ABILITIES—L–M

○ **Lock (2+ Intellect points):** A door, gate, chest, drawer, locket, or other object that can be closed within long range snaps shut and is magically locked (level 3 effect) for one hour. If an object or creature is physically holding the target object open, you must also succeed on an Intellect-based attack. For each level of Effort you apply, the quality of the magical lock increases by one level. Action to initiate.

○ **Lost in the Chaos:** When faced with several foes at once, you have developed tactics for using their numbers against them. When two or more foes attack you at once in melee, you play one off the other. Speed defense rolls or attack rolls (your choice) against them are eased. Enabler.

○ **Lunge (2 Might points):** This ability requires you to extend yourself for a powerful stab or smash. The awkward lunge hinders the attack roll. If your attack is successful, it inflicts 4 additional points of damage. Action.

ABILITIES—M

○ **Machine Affinity:** You are trained in tasks involving electrical machines. Enabler.

○ **Machine Bond:** From very long range, you can activate and control a device (including a robot or vehicle) that you have bonded with. For example, you can detonate a manifest cypher even when it is held by someone else, or cause an automated turret to fire where you direct. Bonding is a process that requires 24 hours of meditation in the presence of the machine. Action.

○ **Machine Companion:** You create a level 3 animate, intelligent machine that accompanies you and acts as you direct. As a level 3 machine companion, it has a target number of 9 and 9 health, and it inflicts 3 points of damage. If it's destroyed, it takes you one month to create a new one. Enabler.

○ **Machine Efficiency (3 Intellect points):** You can make a blaster shoot farther, coax more speed from a skycycle, improve the clarity of a camera, jury-rig a light to be brighter, speed up a network connection, and so on. You increase an object's level by 2 for one minute, or you treat the object as an asset that eases an associated task by two steps for one minute (your choice). Action to initiate.

○ **Machine Enhancement:** Any time you use Effort on an Intellect action, add one of the following enhancements to the action (your choice):
- Free level of Effort
- Automatic minor effect

Enabler.

○ **Machine Hunting:** You are trained in tasks associated with tracking, spotting, or otherwise finding robots and animate machines. You are also trained in all stealth tasks. Enabler.

○ **Machine Interface (2 Intellect points):** For one minute you gain an asset on tasks to discern the level, function, and activation of technological devices that you touch. Enabler.

○ **Machine Telepathy (3 Intellect points):** You can read the surface thoughts of a machine within short range, even if the machine doesn't want you to. You must be able to see the machine. Once you have established contact, you can read the target's thoughts for up to one minute. If you or the target move out of range, the connection is broken. If you have the Mind Reading ability, when you apply Effort to Machine Telepathy, you gain a free level of Effort. Action to initiate.

○ **Machine Vulnerabilities:** You inflict 3 additional points of damage against robots and animate machines of all kinds. Enabler.

○ **Magic Shield (1 Intellect point):** You gain +1 to Armor for an hour. Action to initiate.

○ **Magic Training:** You are trained in the basics of magic (including the operation of magic artifacts and cyphers) and can attempt to understand and identify its properties. Enabler.

○ **Magnetic Field (4 Intellect points):** When you wish it, a field of magnetism around you pulls incoming, ranged, metallic projectile attacks (such as arrows, bullets, a thrown metal knife, and so on) to the ground. You are immune to such attacks for one round. You must be aware of an attack to foil it. Enabler.

○ **Magnificent Moment:** If you make an attack or attempt a task with the immediate action you gain by using Seize the Moment, the attack or task is eased. Enabler.

Free level of Effort, page 209

Minor effect, page 211

Mind Reading, page 162

Seize the Moment, page 181

Inspiration, page 154

Machine Bond, page 159

Trained, page 207

Powered Armor, page 171

Free level of Effort, page 209

○ **Major Illusion (3 Intellect points):** You create a complex scene of images within immediate range. The entire scene must fit within a 100-foot (30 m) cube. The images can move, but they can't leave the area defined by the cube. The illusion includes sound and smell. It lasts for ten minutes and changes as you direct (no concentration is needed). If you move beyond immediate range of the cube, the illusion vanishes. Action to create.

○ **Make Judgment:** You are trained in discerning the truth of a situation, seeing through lies, or otherwise overcoming deception. Enabler.

○ **Maneuvering Adept:** If you apply at least one level of Effort to a task involving climbing, jumping, balancing, or some other kind of maneuvering, you get a free level of Effort. Enabler.

○ **Mask (5 Intellect points):** You transform your body to become someone else. You can change any physical characteristic you wish, including coloration, height, weight, gender, and distinguishing markings. You can also change the appearance of whatever you are wearing or carrying. Your stats, as well as the stats of your items, do not change. You remain in this form for up to a day or until you use an action to resume your normal appearance. Action to initiate.

○ **Master Crafter:** You are trained in the crafting of two kinds of items, or you are specialized in two kinds of items that you are already trained in. Enabler.

○ **Master Cypher Use:** You can bear five cyphers at a time. Enabler.

○ **Master Entertainer:** Your Inspiration ability works more effectively, easing your friends' tasks by two steps rather than one step. Enabler.

○ **Master Identifier:** You are trained in identifying the function of any kind of device. Enabler.

○ **Master Machine (8 Intellect points):** You can control the functions of a machine you have bonded with using Machine Bond, intelligent or otherwise. In addition, if you use an action to concentrate on a machine, you are aware of what is going on around it (you see and hear as if you were standing next to it, no matter how far away you are). You must touch the machine to create the bond, but afterward, there is no range limitation. This bond lasts for one week. You can bond with only one machine at a time. Action to initiate.

○ **Master of Unarmed Fighting Style:** You are specialized in unarmed attacks. If you are already specialized in unarmed attacks, you instead deal 2 additional points of damage with unarmed attacks. Enabler.

○ **Master Thief:** You are trained in climbing, escaping from bonds, slipping through narrow places, and other contortionist moves. Enabler.

○ **Masterful Armor Modification:** Choose one of the following modifications to make to the Powered Armor from your Powered Armor ability. If you choose to make a different modification later, you can do so, but you must spend 2 XP each time and substitute the updated modification for the previous modification.

Cypher Pod. The power armor provides an insulated pod in which you can carry one additional manifest cypher beyond what your cypher limit normally allows. Enabler.

Drone (3 Intellect points). A level 4 drone no larger than 1 foot (30 cm) on a side launches from your armor for one hour, flying up to a long distance each round. The drone accompanies you and follows your instructions. It has manipulators, allowing it to attempt to accomplish physical tasks. You'll probably make rolls for your drone when it takes actions. A drone in combat usually doesn't make separate attacks but helps with yours. On your action, if the drone is next to you, it serves as an asset for one attack you make on your turn. If the drone is destroyed, you must spend another 2 XP to rebuild it or choose another Masterful Armor Modification. Action to initiate.

ABILITIES—M

Improved Field Reinforcement. You gain +1 to Armor while wearing your power armor. Enabler.

Jet-Assisted Flight (3+ Might points). You modify your power armor to allow you to blast off the ground and fly for one minute at a time. For each level of Effort applied, you can increase the duration by an additional minute. Action.

◖ **Mastery in Armor:** The cost reduction from your Practiced in Armor ability improves. You now reduce the Speed Effort cost for wearing armor to 0. Enabler.

◖ **Mastery With Attacks:** Choose one type of attack in which you are trained: light bashing, light bladed, light ranged, medium bashing, medium bladed, medium ranged, heavy bashing, heavy bladed, or heavy ranged. You are specialized in attacks using that type of weapon. Enabler. (If you aren't trained in an attack, select Skill With Attacks to become trained in that attack.)

◖ **Mastery With Defense:** Choose one type of defense task in which you are trained: Might, Speed, or Intellect. You are specialized in defense tasks of that type. You can select this ability up to three times. Each time you select it, you must choose a different type of defense task. Enabler.

◖ **Matter Cloud (5 Intellect points):** Pebbles, dirt, sand, and debris rise into the air around you to form a swirling cloud. The cloud extends out to immediate range, moves with you, and lasts for one minute. When it ends, all the materials fall to the ground around you. The cloud makes it harder for other creatures to attack you, giving you an asset on Speed defense rolls. In addition, while the cloud is around you, you can use an action to whip the material so that it abrades everything within immediate range, dealing 1 point of damage to each creature and object in the area. Action to initiate.

◖ **Mechanical Telepathy (3 Intellect points):** By touching a thinking machine, you gain access to its surface "thoughts." Action.

◖ **Memory Becomes Action (4+ Intellect points):** You can duplicate a one-action character ability, performing it as if it were natural for you. You must have seen the ability used within the past week, it must be third tier or lower, and it must be an ability with a point cost. In addition to the point cost of Memory Becomes Action, you must pay the Might, Speed, or Intellect cost of the ability you are copying. For example, if you want to copy a friend's Lunge attack (which normally costs 2 Might points), you'd pay 4 Intellect points to activate Memory Becomes Action and 2 Might points to use Lunge. In addition to the normal options for using Effort, you can choose to use Effort to copy an ability you saw longer than one week ago; each level of Effort used in this way extends the time period by one week. Enabler.

◖ **Mental Link (1+ Intellect point):** You open a pathway to another creature's mind via a light touch, which allows you to transmit thoughts and images to each other. The mental link remains regardless of distance and lasts for one hour. In addition to the normal options for using Effort, you can choose to use Effort to extend the duration by one hour for each level of Effort applied. Action to initiate.

◖ **Mental Projection (6+ Intellect points):** Your mind fully leaves your body and manifests anywhere you choose within immediate range. Your projected mind can remain apart from your body for up to 24 hours. This effect ends early if your Intellect Pool is reduced to 0 or if your projection touches your resting body.

Your disembodied mind is a psychic construct that looks like you, though its frayed edges trail off into nothingness. You control this body as if it were your normal body and can act and move as you normally would with a few exceptions. You can move through solid objects as if you were phased, and you ignore any terrain feature that would impede your movement.

Your attacks inflict 3 fewer points of damage (to a minimum of 1) and you take 3 fewer points of damage (to a minimum of 1) from physical attacks, unless they can affect transdimensional or phased beings, in which case you take full damage. Regardless of the source, you take all damage as Intellect damage first.

Your mind can travel up to 1 mile (1.5 km) from your body. Each level of additional Effort applied extends the range that you can travel by 1 mile (1.5 km).

Your physical body is helpless until this effect ends. You cannot use your physical senses to perceive anything. For example, your body could sustain a significant injury, and you wouldn't know it. Your body cannot take Intellect damage, so if your body takes enough damage to reduce both your Might Pool and your Speed Pool to 0, your mind snaps back to your body, and you are stunned until the end of the next round as you try to reorient yourself to your predicament. Action to initiate.

Lunge, page 159

Practiced in Armor, page 171

Skill With Attacks, page 183

Mentally projecting characters may attract psychic entities and predators that PCs normally don't have to deal with, run into weather psychic phenomena that risks severing their connection, and possibly even become lost on a different metaphysical plane.

○ **Mentally Tough:** Staring into the naked weave of hyperspace, warped space, or a similar effect related to faster-than-light travel is hard on the mind, but you've developed resistance. You're trained in Intellect defense tasks. Enabler.

○ **Meticulous Planner:** If you spend a long time planning an action, you gain an asset on performing it. The time to study and plan for the action is ten times as long as it takes to perform the action. For example, if you want to jump across a hole in the floor (one action), you can study the area for ten rounds (about a minute), and when you attempt to jump over the hole, you have an asset on the jump. This benefit applies to only one roll—if you want to perform the task again with the benefit of an asset, you need to study and plan again. Enabler.

○ **Microgravity Adept:** You ignore all the ill effects of low gravity and no gravity on movement; you are trained in low-gravity maneuvers and zero-gravity maneuvers. (You might still be subject to negative biological effects of long-term exposure, if any.) Enabler.

Effect of Gravity, page 276

○ **Microgravity Avoidance:** By taking advantage of microgravity conditions, you gain an asset to Speed defense tasks while in zero-gravity or low-gravity conditions. Enabler.

Recovery roll, page 218

○ **Mind Control (6+ Intellect points):** You control the actions of another creature you touch. This effect lasts for one minute. The target must be level 2 or lower. Once you have established control, you maintain mental contact with the target and sense what it senses. You can allow it to act freely or override its control on a case-by-case basis. In addition to the normal options for using Effort, you can choose to use Effort to increase the maximum level of the target or increase the duration by one minute. Thus, to control the mind of a level 5 target (three levels above the normal limit) or control a target for four minutes (three minutes above the normal duration), you must apply three levels of Effort. When the duration ends, the creature doesn't remember being controlled or anything it did while under your command. Action to initiate.

Bound Magic Creature, page 115

○ **Mind for Might:** When performing a task that would normally require spending points from your Intellect Pool, you can spend points from your Might Pool instead, and vice versa. Enabler.

○ **Mind Games (3 Intellect points):** You use lies and trickery, mockery, and perhaps even hateful, obscene language against a foe that can understand you. If successful, the foe is stunned for one round and cannot act, and it is dazed in the following round, during which time its tasks are hindered. Action.

○ **Mind of a Leader (6 Intellect points):** When you develop a course of action to deal with a future situation, you can ask the GM one very general question about what is likely to happen if you carry out the plan, and you will get a simple, brief answer. Action.

○ **Mind Reading (2 Intellect points):** You can read the surface thoughts of a creature within short range, even if the target doesn't want you to. You must be able to see your target. Once you have established contact, you can read the target's thoughts for up to one minute. If you also have the Mind Reading special ability from another source, you can use this ability at long range, and you don't need to be able to see the target (but you do have to know that the target is within range). Action to initiate.

○ **Mind Surge:** In addition to your normal recovery rolls each day, you can—at any time between ten-hour rests—recover 1d6 + 6 points to your Intellect Pool. Action.

○ **Minor Illusion (1 Intellect point):** You create a single image of a creature or object within immediate range. The image must fit within a 10-foot (3 m) cube. The image can move (for example, you could make the illusion of a person walk or attack), but it can't leave the area defined by the cube. The illusion includes sound but not smell. It lasts for ten minutes, but if you want to change the original illusion significantly—such as making a creature appear to be wounded—you must concentrate on it again (though doing so doesn't cost additional Intellect points). If you move beyond immediate range of the cube, the illusion vanishes. Action to create; action to modify.

○ **Minor Wish:** At your request, the magic ally from your Bound Magic Creature ability can use its action to cast a minor spell on you. Afterward, it must retreat to its bound object to rest for one hour. The effects it can produce include the following. Action to initiate.

Golden Anger. A golden light touches your eyes. For the next several minutes, if you attack a target, you inflict 2 additional points of damage.

ABILITIES—M

Golden Ward. You gain +1 to Armor for one hour from a translucent sheen of golden light.

Light of Truth. Whenever you attempt to discern falsehood during the next hour, the task is eased by two steps.

Touch of Grace. With the magic ally's touch, you add 3 points to any stat Pool. If you are not damaged, you add the points to your chosen Pool's maximum. They remain until you spend them, you lose them to damage, or an hour passes.

◉ **Miraculous Health:** When you would descend a step on the damage track, you can attempt a Might task to resist, with a difficulty equal to the level of the foe or effect that harmed you. If successful, you don't descend the step and you regain 1 point in any Pool that is bereft of points. You can't use this ability again until after your next ten-hour rest. Enabler.

◉ **Misdirect (3 Speed points):** When an opponent misses you, you can redirect their attack to another target (a creature or object) of your choosing that's within immediate range of you. Make an unmodified attack roll against the new target (do not use any of your or the opponent's modifiers to the attack roll, but you can apply Effort for accuracy). If the attack hits, the target takes damage from your opponent's attack. Enabler.

◉ **Misdirect Blame (2+ Intellect points):** Using your clever words and knowledge of others, you can attempt to alter the narrative so that a target of up to level 3 within short range becomes uncertain of its conviction in one simple area, such as their conviction that you just stole a fruit from their stand or their belief that they've never met you before. This effect usually lasts only for the period of time you spend speaking, and perhaps up to a minute longer, before the target realizes its error. In addition to the normal options for using Effort, you can choose to use Effort to increase the target level that can be affected. Afterward, all your tasks to persuade or otherwise socially interact with the target are hindered. Action.

◉ **Mobile Fighter (3 Speed points):** As part of your attack, you can leap on or over obstacles, swing from ropes, run along narrow surfaces, or otherwise move around the battlefield at your normal speed as if such tasks were routine (difficulty 0). You can't use this ability if your Speed Effort costs are reduced from wearing armor. Enabler.

> **MAKING A WISH**
>
> If a character asks the magic ally from their Bound Magic Creature ability for a real wish instead of a minor or moderate spell, the creature may grant it, especially if the PC is tier 3 or higher. If so, the magic ally is then free of its compulsion to serve the character, who should work with the GM to adopt a new focus. Even if the wish is granted, the character may not get exactly what they want, especially if a wish is poorly worded or has multiple interpretations. The level of the effect granted is no greater than level 7, as determined by the GM, who can modify the effect of the wish accordingly. (The larger the wish, the more likely the GM will limit its effect.)

◉ **Moderate Wish:** At your request, the magic ally from your Bound Magic Creature ability can spend its action casting a moderate spell on you. Afterward, it must retreat to its bound object to rest for at least one hour. The effects it can produce include the following. Action to initiate.

Golden Armor. You gain +3 to Armor for one hour from a translucent sheen of golden light.

Golden Fury. A golden light blazes in your eyes. For the next three minutes, if you attack a target, you inflict 5 additional points of damage.

Improved Touch of Grace. With the magic ally's touch, you add 6 points to any stat Pool. If you are not damaged, you add the points to your chosen Pool's maximum. They remain until you spend them, you lose them to damage, or an hour passes.

Invisible. With a touch, the magic ally bends light that falls on you, so you seem to disappear. You are invisible to other creatures for ten minutes. While invisible, you are specialized in stealth and Speed defense tasks. This effect ends if you do something to reveal your presence or position—attacking, using an ability, moving a large object, and so on. If this occurs, you can regain the remaining invisibility effect by taking an action to focus on hiding your position. Action to initiate.

◉ **Modify Artifact Power (6 Intellect points):** You permanently add +1 to the level of an artifact of up to level 5. The difficulty of this task is equal to the modified higher level of the artifact. If the task is failed, the artifact makes a depletion roll and is not advanced in level. Once modified, the artifact can't be similarly boosted again. Action.

Damage track, page 218

○ **Modify Device (4 Intellect points):** You jury-rig a piece of mechanical or electrical equipment to make it function above its rated specs for a very limited time. To do so, you must use spare parts equal to an expensive item, have a field science kit (or a permanent lab, if you have access to one), and succeed at a difficulty 3 Intellect-based task. When complete, using the device eases all tasks performed in conjunction with the device, until the device inevitably breaks. For example, you could overclock a computer so research tasks using it are easier, modify an espresso maker so that each cup of coffee made with it is better, modify a car's engine so that it goes faster (or modify its steering so it handles better), and so on. Each use of the modified device requires a depletion roll of 1–5 on a d20. Action to initiate, one hour to complete.

○ **Momentum:** If you use an action to move, your next attack made using a melee weapon before the end of the next round inflicts 2 additional points of damage. Enabler.

○ **Monster Bane:** You inflict 1 additional point of damage with weapons. When you inflict damage to creatures more than twice as large or massive as you, you inflict 3 additional points of damage. Enabler.

○ **Monster Lore:** You are trained in the names, habits, suspected lairs, and related topics regarding the monsters of your world. You can make yourself understood in their languages (if they have one). Enabler.

○ **Moon Shape (4+ Intellect points):** You change into a monstrous natural beast, such as a wolf, bear, or other terrestrial creature, for up to one hour. If you try to change during daylight hours when you are not deep underground (or otherwise away from the daylight), you must apply a level of Effort. In your new form, you add 8 points to your Might Pool, gain +2 to your Might Edge, add 2 points to your Speed Pool, and gain +2 to your Speed Edge. Reverting to your normal form is a difficulty 2 task. While in beast form, you are prone to fits of rage (triggered by GM intrusion), during which you attack every living creature within short range, and the only way to end the rage is to revert to your normal form. Either way, after you revert to your normal form, you take a –1 penalty to all rolls for one hour. If you did not kill and eat at least one substantial creature while in beast form, the penalty increases to –2 and affects all your rolls for the next day. Action to change; action to revert.

○ **Mount:** A level 3 creature serves you as a mount and follows your instructions. While you're mounted on it, the creature can move and you can attack on your turn, which provides an asset to your attack. You and the GM must work out the details of the creature, and you'll probably make rolls for it when it takes noncombat actions. The mount acts on your turn. If your mount dies, you can hunt in the wild for 3d6 days to find a new one. Enabler.

○ **Move Metal (1 Intellect point):** You can exert force on metal objects within short range for one round. Once activated, your power has an effective Might Pool of 10, a Might Edge of 1, and an Effort of 2 (approximately equal to the strength of a fit, capable, adult human), and you can use it to move metal objects, push against metal objects, and so on. For example, in your round, you could lift and pull a light metal object anywhere within range to yourself or move a heavy object (like a piece of furniture) about 10 feet (3 m). This power lacks the fine control to wield a weapon or move objects with much speed, so in most situations, it's not a means of attack. You can't use this ability on your own body. The power lasts for one hour or until its Might Pool is depleted, whichever comes first. Action.

○ **Move Mountains (9 Intellect points):** You exert a tremendous amount of physical force within 250 feet (75 m) of you. You can push up to 10 tons (9 t) of material up to 50 feet (15 m). This force can collapse buildings, redirect small rivers, or perform other dramatic effects. Action.

○ **Movement Skills:** You are trained in climbing and jumping. Enabler.

○ **Moving Like Water (3 Speed points):** You spin and move so that your defense and attacks are aided by your fluid motion. For one minute, all your attacks and Speed defense tasks gain an asset. Enabler.

○ **Multiple Quarry (6 Intellect points):** This ability functions like the Quarry ability except that you can select up to three creatures as quarry. You must be able to see all three creatures when you initiate this ability. If you have Hunter's Drive, it applies to all three creatures. Action to initiate.

Expensive item, page 202

Depletion, page 204

Quarry, page 173

Hunter's Drive, page 149

ABILITIES—M-N

○ **Multiple Skills:** You are trained in three skills of your choice in which you are not already trained. You can select this ability multiple times. Each time you select it, you must choose three different skills. Enabler.

○ **Multiplicity (6 Might points):** This ability functions as Duplicate, except you can create two duplicates. Action to initiate.

○ **Murderer (8+ Speed points):** With a swift and sudden attack, you strike a foe in a vital spot. If the target is level 4 or lower, it is killed outright. For each additional level of Effort you apply, you can increase the level of the target by 1. Action.

○ **Muscles of Iron (2 Might points):** For the next ten minutes, all Might-based actions other than attack rolls that you attempt are eased. If you already have this ability from another source, the effect of this ability lasts for one hour instead of ten minutes. Enabler.

ABILITIES—N

○ **Natural Charisma:** You are trained in all social interactions, whether they involve charm, learning a person's secrets, or intimidating others. Enabler.

○ **Natural Crafter:** All commonplace objects or structures you craft are effectively one level higher than an average example of that object or structure. For instance, if you craft a defensive wall that would normally be level 4, its effective level is 5. Enabler.

○ **Necromancy (3+ Intellect points):** You animate the body of a dead creature of approximately your size or smaller, creating a level 1 creature. It has none of the intelligence, memories, or special abilities that it had in life. The creature follows your verbal commands for one hour, after which it becomes an inert corpse. Unless the creature is killed by damage, you can reanimate it again when its time expires, but any damage it had when it became inert applies to its newly reanimated state. If you have access to multiple bodies, you can create an additional undead creature for each additional Intellect point you spend when you activate the ability. Action to animate.

○ **Negate Danger (7 Intellect points):** You permanently negate a source of potential danger related to one creature or object within immediate distance. This could be a weapon or device held by someone, a creature's natural ability, or a trap triggered by a pressure plate. Action.

○ **Negotiate (3 Intellect points):** In any gathering where two or more people are trying to establish the truth or come to a decision, you can sway the verdict with masterful rhetoric. If you are given a few rounds or more to argue your point, either the decision goes your way or, if someone else effectively argues a competing point, any associated persuasion or deception task is eased by two steps. Action to initiate, one or more rounds to complete.

○ **Network Tap (4 Intellect points):** You can ask the GM one question and get a very short answer if you succeed on an Intellect roll against a difficulty assigned by the GM. The more obscure the answer, the more difficult the task. On a failed roll, feedback or perhaps some defense from the network you're accessing inflicts 4 points of Intellect damage on you (ignores Armor). Action.

○ **Never Fumble:** If you roll a natural 1 when attacking with your chosen weapon, you can ignore or countermand the GM intrusion for that roll. You can never be disarmed of your chosen weapon, nor will you ever drop it accidentally. Enabler.

○ **Nightmare (5 Intellect points):** You pull a horrifying creature from your worst nightmare into the waking world and sic it on your foes. The nightmare persists each round while you use your action concentrating on it (or until you disperse it or it is destroyed). It has one of the following abilities, which you choose when you call it.
   Confusion. Instead of making a normal attack, the nightmare's attack confuses the target for one round. On its next action, the target attacks an ally.
   Horrify. Instead of making a normal attack, the nightmare's attack horrifies the target, which drops to its knees (or similar appendages). The target takes 3 points of damage that ignore Armor and is dazed for one round, during which time all its tasks are hindered.
   Pustule Eruption. Instead of making a normal attack, the nightmare's attack causes rancid,

Duplicate, page 132

Generally, knowledge that you could find by looking somewhere other than your current location is level 1, while obscure knowledge of the past is level 7. Gaining knowledge of the future is impossible.

Nightmare: level 5; health 15; inflicts 5 points of damage

painful pustules to rise all over the target's skin for one minute. If the target takes a forceful action (such as attacking another creature or moving farther than an immediate distance), the pustules burst, dealing 5 points of damage that ignore Armor. Action to initiate, action each round to concentrate.

◉ **Nightstrike:** When you attack a foe in dim light or darkness, you get a free level of Effort on the attack. Enabler.

◉ **Nimble Swimmer:** You are trained in all defense actions while underwater. Enabler.

◉ **No Need for Weapons:** When you make an unarmed attack (such as a punch or kick), it counts as a medium weapon instead of a light weapon. Enabler.

◉ **No One Knows Better:** You are trained in two of the following skills: persuasion, deception, intimidation, research, knowledge in one area, or seeing through deception. If you choose a skill in which you're already trained, you become specialized in that skill instead. Enabler.

◉ **Noble's Courage (3+ Intellect points):** Your noble lineage teaches that courage is necessary to do things that are difficult, tedious, or dangerous. When your mind would be negatively affected by an effect of up to level 4, whether something as overt as a psychic command or illness or something as subtle as fear or even boredom, your courage neutralizes the effect for up to a minute or, if you're actively being attacked, until the next attack. For each level of Effort applied, you can increase the level of the effect you can neutralize by 1. Enabler.

◉ **Not Dead Yet:** When you would normally be dead, you instead fall unconscious for one round and then awaken. You immediately gain 1d6 + 6 points to restore your stat Pools, and you are treated as if debilitated until you rest for ten hours. If you die again before you make your ten-hour recovery roll, you are truly dead. If you also have this ability from another source, your healing from this ability increases to 1d6 + 12. Enabler.

◉ **Nothing but Defend:** If you do nothing on your turn but defend, you are specialized in all defense tasks for one round. Action.

◉ **Nullify Sound (3 Might points):** You pulse perfectly misaligned sounds within short range to create a zone of absolute quiet up to an immediate distance across for one minute. All sound is canceled in the zone. Action to initiate.

Free level of Effort, page 209

Debilitated: see damage track, page 218

Recovery roll, page 218

ABILITIES—O

Object Bond (3 Intellect points): When you manifest the magic ally from your Bound Magic Creature ability, it can move up to 300 feet (90 m) from you before being returned to its bound object. Also, it can remain manifest for an extended period, lasting until the end of your next ten-hour recovery roll. Finally, if you give permission, the magic ally can emerge from and enter the bound object on its own initiative. Enabler.

Object Bond Mastery (7 Intellect points): When you manifest the magic ally from your Bound Magic Creature ability, it is now a level 7 creature. It can remain manifest for only three minutes, after which it must return to its object and rest for three days before you can manifest it again.

The magic ally can make its own magic touch attacks (when it does, you roll for it). If it uses its pulse attack from Improved Object Bond, instead of deactivating items, it can take control of one item within short range for one minute, if applicable.

Finally, the magic ally can transform into smoke and flame as its action, giving it +10 to Armor but rendering it incapable of attacking foes. In this form, it can fly a long distance each round, and the first time each day it returns to flesh (as an action), it regains 25 points of health. Enabler.

Obstacle Running (3 Speed points): For the next minute, you can ignore obstacles that slow your movement, allowing you to travel at normal speed through areas with rubble, fences, tables, and similar objects that you would have to climb over or move around. This movement might include sliding on a railing, briefly running along a wall, or even stepping on a creature to boost yourself over something. If an obstacle would normally require a Might or Speed task to overcome, such as swinging on a rope, balancing on a rope, or jumping over a hole, you are trained in that task. Enabler.

One With the Wild (6 Intellect points): For the next hour, natural animals and plants within long range will not knowingly harm you or those you designate. In addition, your Might Edge, Speed Edge, and Intellect Edge increase by 1, and if you make any recovery rolls during this period, you recover twice as many points. Action to initiate.

Oneirochemy: You are trained in tasks related to sleep and mixing natural elixirs to help creatures fall asleep. Enabler.

Onslaught (1 Intellect point): You attack a foe using energies that assail either their physical form or their mind. In either case, you must be able to see your target. If the attack is physical, you emit a short-range ray of force that inflicts 4 points of damage. If the attack is mental, you focus your mental energy to blast the thought processes of another creature within short range. This mindslice inflicts 2 points of Intellect damage (ignores Armor). Some creatures without minds (such as robots) might be immune to your mindslice. Action.

Open Mind (3 Intellect points): You open your mind to increase your awareness. You gain an asset to any task involving perception. While you have this asset and you are conscious and able to take actions, other characters gain no benefit from surprising you. The effect lasts for one hour. Action.

Opening Statement: You're trained in tasks related to persuasion, deception, and detecting the falsehoods of others. Enabler.

Opportunist: You have an asset on any attack roll you make against a creature that has already been attacked at some point during the round and is within immediate range. Enabler.

Oratory (4 Intellect points): When speaking with a group of intelligent creatures that can understand you and aren't hostile, you convince them to take one reasonable action in the next round. A reasonable action should not put the creatures or their allies in obvious danger or be wildly out of character. Action.

Out of Harm's Way: No matter how careful, an investigator sometimes ends up in a scrap. Knowing how to survive is more than half the battle. You are trained in Speed defense tasks. Enabler.

Outlast the Foe: If you have been in combat for five full rounds, you have an asset for all tasks in the remainder of the combat, and you deal 1 additional point of damage per attack. Enabler.

Bound Magic Creature, page 115

Onslaught is a particularly useful ability in that it can be used to either inflict physical damage or inflict damage directly to someone's mind. Even though the latter usage inflicts only 2 points of damage, it's a great ability to use against a heavily armored foe. Especially if a level of Effort is applied to inflict 3 additional points of damage.

Improved Object Bond, page 152

○ **Outlaw Reputation (3 Intellect points):** People know of your notorious exploits, which have been told and retold so many times that they bear little resemblance to reality. But people fear your name when they recognize you (or you declare yourself). They become so afraid that all attacks made against you by affected targets within earshot are hindered until one or more of them successfully inflicts damage on you or one of your allies, at which time their fear abates. Enabler.

○ **Outside Reality (6+ Intellect points):** You exist outside of everything until the start of your next turn. To you, a few seconds pass while you are alone in a cool void. To everyone else, you seem to vanish for a few seconds and reappear in the same place. While in this unreal state, you can use abilities or objects on yourself, but you can't perceive, interact with, or affect the rest of the world, and vice versa. Time-based effects already on you (like a poison that inflicts damage every round) are paused while you exist outside reality, but when this ability ends they resume as if no time had passed. In addition to the normal options for using Effort, you can choose to use Effort to increase the duration; each level of Effort used in this way adds one round to how long you spend outside reality. Enabler.

○ **Outwit:** When you make a Speed defense roll, you can use your Intellect in place of your Speed. Enabler.

○ **Overawe (5 Intellect points):** A blast of divine radiance from the heavens spotlights a target you select within long range, pushing the target to its knees (or similar appendages, if any) and rendering it helpless in the light for up to ten minutes, or until it breaks free. The overawed target cannot defend itself, make attacks, or attempt anything other than to shake free of the divine awe each round. If the target is a demon, spirit, or something similar, it also takes 1 point of damage that ignores Armor each round it remains affected. Action to initiate.

○ **Overcharge Device:** You infuse 1 point of energy gained from using Absorb Energy or related ability into a device, such as an artifact, raising its effective level on its next use by three (to a maximum of 10). Action.

○ **Overcharge Energy:** When you use Release Energy, it inflicts an additional 2 points of damage. Enabler.

○ **Overcome All Obstacles (3+ Intellect points):** Those who stand against you do so at their peril and eventually shrink away in your presence. When you focus on a particular foe within long range, the target suffers 2 points of Intellect damage (ignores Armor) each round for one minute or until the target can throw off the effect. This ability can only be active on one target at a time. You can apply Effort to increase damage during the first round, and for any one round in which you apply Effort and use another action. Action to initiate.

○ **Overload Machine (3+ Intellect points):** Through the robot assistant from your Serv-0 ability, you infuse a powered device of level 3 or lower with more energy than it can handle. If affected, the device is destroyed or disabled for at least one minute, depending on its size and complexity. The GM may rule that the disabling effect lasts until the device is repaired. In addition to the normal options for using Effort, you can choose to use Effort to increase the maximum level of the target. Thus, to overload a level 5 device (two levels above the normal limit), you must apply two levels of Effort. Action.

○ **Overwatch (1 Intellect point):** You use a ranged weapon to target a limited area (such as a doorway, a hallway, or the eastern side of the clearing) and make an attack against the next viable target to enter that area. This works like a wait action, but you also negate any benefit the target would have from cover, position, surprise, range, illumination, or visibility. Further, you inflict 1 additional point of damage with the attack. You can remain on overwatch as long as you wish, within reason. Action.

ABILITIES—P

○ **Parry (5 Speed points):** You can deflect incoming attacks quickly. When you activate this ability, for the next ten rounds you ease all Speed defense rolls. Enabler.

○ **Passing Mechanic:** You are trained in tasks related to the repair and maintenance of a starcraft. Enabler.

○ **Pay It Forward (3 Intellect points):** You can pass on what you've learned. When you give another character a suggestion involving their next action that is not an attack, their action is eased for one minute. Action.

○ **Perfect Control:** You no longer need to make a roll to use Beast Form or change into your normal form. You can change back and forth as your action. When you return to your normal form, you no longer take a penalty to your rolls. Enabler.

○ **Perfect Speed Burst (6 Speed points):** You can take two separate actions this round. Enabler.

○ **Perfect Stranger (3 Intellect points):** You alter your posture and way of speaking and make a small but real alteration to an outfit (such as putting on or taking off a hat, reversing a cloak, and so on). For the next hour (or as long as you keep up the alteration), even creatures that know you well don't recognize you. All tasks related to hiding your true identity during this period gain one free level of Effort. Action to initiate.

○ **Perks of Stardom:** You are adept at claiming the rewards that fame can generate. When you are recognized, you can be seated at any restaurant, be let into any government building, be invited to any show or sports event (even if they're sold out), get a seat at a private function of any sort, or get into any club, no matter how exclusive. When dealing with someone who can't or won't immediately give in to your desire, you gain an asset on all tasks related to persuasion if that person recognizes you or is convinced that you're a celebrity even if they don't recognize you. Enabler.

○ **Permanent Illusion (9 Intellect points):** An illusion (or portion of an illusion) that you create using Minor Illusion or related ability that fits within a 10-foot (3 m) cube becomes permanent. You can permanently end the illusion as an action, but others must expend exceptional ingenuity to prevent the illusion from regenerating even if it has apparently been dispersed. Enabler.

○ **Phase Detonation (2+ Might points):** When you use Phase Sprint or Walk Through Walls, you can choose to significantly damage normal matter around you with a blast of transdimensional energy when you first go into or come out of phase (your choice). This detonation inflicts 4 points of damage that ignores Armor to all creatures and objects within immediate range. If you apply Effort to increase the damage rather than ease the task, you deal 2 additional points of damage per level of Effort (instead of 3 points); targets in the area take 1 point of damage even if you fail the attack roll. Enabler.

Beast Form, page 112

Minor Illusion, page 162

Phase Sprint, page 170

Walk Through Walls, page 196

Free level of Effort, page 209

○ **Phase Door (4 Intellect points):** You can phase into a solid object's surface and then phase out of any other solid object within long range of the first, even if the two objects are not connected. There must be no intervening barriers between the two objects, and you must be aware of or able to see the destination object. Action.

○ **Phase Foe (6+ Intellect points):** You gather disrupting energy in your fingertip and touch a creature. If the target is an NPC or a creature of level 3 or lower, it becomes phased as if it had used the Ghost ability. However, unless it can figure out how to control its movement while being phased, which most creatures have no experience with, it begins to sink through solid matter. If it can't control itself or end the effect, it might be gone for good because when it becomes solid again after ten minutes, it's probably deep in the earth. For each additional level of Effort you apply, you can attempt to affect a target of one level higher. Action.

○ **Phase Sprint (1+ Speed points):** You can run up to a long distance as long as you take no other actions. During your action and until the beginning of your next turn, you are partially phased, and some attacks pass through you harmlessly. While phased, you gain an asset to your Speed defense tasks, but you lose any benefit from armor you wear.
   Note that some of your other special abilities may enable specific actions that you can take while using Phase Sprint. For instance, when using Disrupting Touch, you can make one touch attack while moving (though this ends your movement). Action.

○ **Phased Attack (3 Intellect points):** The attack you make on this turn ignores your foe's armor. The ability works for whatever kind of attack you use (melee, ranged, energy, and so on). Enabler.

○ **Phased Pocket (2+ Intellect points):** You connect yourself for one hour to a small space that is out of phase and moves with you. You can access this space as if it were a convenient pocket or bag, but nobody else can perceive or access the space unless they have the ability to interact with transdimensional areas. The space can hold up to 1 cubic foot. The space is a part of you, so you can't use it to carry more cyphers than your limit, a detonation cypher activated inside the space harms you, and so on. When the connection ends, anything in the space falls out. For each 2 additional Intellect points you spend, the pocket lasts an additional hour. Enabler.

○ **Physical Skills:** You are trained in two skills in which you are not already trained. Choose two of the following: balancing, climbing, jumping, running, or swimming. You can select this ability multiple times. Each time you select it, you must choose two different skills. Enabler.

○ **Physically Gifted:** Any time you spend points from your Might Pool or Speed Pool on an action for any reason, if you roll a 1 on the associated die, you reroll, always taking the second result (even if it's another 1). Enabler.

○ **Pierce (1 Speed point):** This is a well-aimed, penetrating ranged attack. You make an attack and inflict 1 additional point of damage if your weapon has a sharp point. Action.

○ **Pilot:** You are trained in all tasks related to piloting a starcraft. Generally speaking, piloting tasks are Speed-based tasks, though using sensors and communication instruments are Intellect-based tasks. Enabler.

○ **Play to the Crowd (3 Intellect points):** You give a speech that is both rousing and terrifying. Those within short range who can hear and understand you have their next action either eased (an asset) or hindered—you choose, and it can be different for each individual. Action; a few rounds to complete.

○ **Poetic License:** You are trained in all social interactions, including persuasion, deception, and intimidation. You also know two additional languages. Enabler.

○ **Poison Crafter:** You are trained in crafting, sensing, identifying, and resisting poisons. Your poison crafting has given you some immunity to poisons; you have +5 Armor that applies specifically to poison damage. Enabler.

○ **Poison Resistance:** Thanks to an injection of biological agents, a quaff of a magical elixir, a ring from a dying alien, or something just as extreme, you are now immune to poisons, toxins, or any kind of particulate threat. You are not immune to viruses, bacteria, or radiation. Enabler.

○ **Post-Apocalyptic Survivor:** You are trained in stealth and Might defense tasks. Enabler.

Ghost, page 145

You don't have to run in one long, straight line when using Phase Sprint, but can instead zig and zag, curve, or even return to where you started.

Other abilities can be used with Phase Sprint to unlock additional effects, including Disrupting Touch, Scratch Existence, Invisible Phasing, and Phase Detonation. These abilities are additive enablers, requiring the user to spend points for both abilities, and sometimes from two different Pools.

Disrupting Touch, page 129
Scratch Existence, page 180
Invisible Phasing, page 155
Phase Detonation, page 169

Poison, page 219

There are other ways for characters to learn how to make poisons, such as the Create Deadly Poison ability, page 123.

Detonation cypher, page 386

Abilities—P

- **Power Strike (3+ Might points):** If you successfully attack a target, you knock it prone in addition to inflicting damage. The target must be your size or smaller. You can knock down a target larger than you if you apply a level of Effort to do so (rather than to ease the attack). Enabler.

- **Powered Armor:** You have a suit of powered armor. It is effectively medium armor (+2 to Armor); however, you suffer no Speed penalties for wearing it. Also, your suit grants other benefits: it provides breathable air for up to eight hours and a comfortable environment even in bitter heat, cold, vacuum, or underwater to a depth of 4 miles (6 km); and it allows you to see in the dark up to a short distance. Getting into the suit requires an action (and, of course, access to your suit). Enabler.

- **Powerful Rhetoric (1 Intellect point):** After engaging a creature in conversation for at least a minute, you can attempt to influence how that creature is perceived, promoting it as a friend, dismissing it as a fool, or denouncing it as an enemy. Your words are so well chosen that even you and it are affected, because your conviction and its doubt are paramount. The accuracy of your assessment isn't important as long as you keep up the rhetoric. From then on (or until you change your rhetoric or the creature offers a convincing defense to those who've heard your label), the friend's social interactions gain an asset, the fool's social interactions are hindered, or the enemy's defenses are hindered. Action to initiate, one minute to complete.

- **Practiced in Armor:** You can wear armor for long periods of time without tiring and can compensate for slowed reactions from wearing armor. You reduce the Speed cost for wearing armor by 1. You start the game with a type of armor of your choice. Enabler.

- **Practiced With All Weapons:** You become practiced with light, medium, and heavy weapons and suffer no penalty when using any kind of weapon. Enabler.

- **Practiced With Guns:** You are practiced with guns and suffer no penalty when using one. Enabler.

- **Practiced With Medium Weapons:** You can use light and medium weapons without penalty. If you wield a heavy weapon, attacks with it are hindered. Enabler.

- **Practiced With Swords:** You are practiced with swords and can use them without penalty. Enabler.

- **Precise Cut:** You inflict 1 additional point of damage with light weapons. Enabler.

- **Precision:** You deal 2 additional points of damage with attacks using weapons that you throw. Enabler.

- **Precognition (6 Intellect points):** You dimly sense the future for the next ten minutes. This has the following effects until the duration expires:
  - Your defense tasks gain an asset.
  - You can predict the actions of those around you. You gain an asset to seeing through deceptions and attempts to betray you as well as avoiding traps and ambushes.
  - You know what people are probably thinking and what they will say before they say it, which gives you an edge. You gain an asset to all interaction skills.

  Enabler.

- **Predictive Equation (2 Intellect points):** You observe or study a creature, object, or location for at least one round. The next time you interact with it (possibly in the following round), a related task (such as persuading the creature, attacking it, or defending from its attack) is eased. Action.

- **Predictive Model (2+ Intellect points):** If you've used Predictive Equation on a creature, object, or location within the last few days, you can learn one random fact about the subject that is pertinent to a topic you designate. If you also have the magic flavor ability Premonition, one use of either ability grants you two random but related facts about the subject. In addition, you can use Predictive Model on the same subject multiple times (even if you've learned a creature's level), but each time you do, you must apply one additional level of Effort than on your previous use. Action.

- **Premonition (2 Intellect points):** You learn one random fact about a creature or location that is pertinent to a topic you designate. Alternatively, you can choose to learn a creature's level; however, if you do so, you cannot learn anything else about it later with this ability. Action.

- **Preternatural Senses:** While you are conscious and able to use an action, you cannot be surprised. In addition, you are trained in initiative actions. Enabler.

Powered Armor is an ability commonly associated with Wears Power Armor, on page 78.

Practiced, page 207

A character should using Psychic Passenger should consider secreting their actual body someplace away from prying eyes and wild beasts, or they may return to an unfortunate situation.

○ **Privileged Nobility:** You are adept at claiming the rewards that a noble background can generate. When recognized, you can be seated at any eating establishment no matter how full, get a room in an inn even if that means others are turned out, be let into any court or other structure where laws are decided or nobility rules, be invited to any gala, and get a seat at a private function of any sort. In addition, you are trained in persuasion. Enabler.

○ **Projection (4 Intellect points):** You project an image of yourself to any location you have seen or previously visited. Distance does not matter as long as the location is on the same world as you. The projection copies your appearance, movements, and any sounds you make for the next ten minutes. Anyone present at the location can see and hear you as if you were there. However, you do not perceive through your projection. Action to initiate.

○ **Protective Wall (6+ Might points):** When engaging in combat that directly relates to defending a community you are associated with, you can attack up to five different foes as a single action as long as they are all within immediate range. If you hit an attacker, they are pushed back an immediate distance. All of the attacks have to be the same sort of attack (melee or ranged). Make a separate attack roll for each foe. You remain limited by the amount of Effort you can apply on one action. Anything that modifies your attack or damage applies to all of these attacks. In addition to the normal options for using Effort, you can choose to use Effort to increase the number of foes you can attack with this ability, one additional foe per level of Effort. Enabler.

○ **Protector:** You designate a single character to be your charge. You can change this freely every round, but you can have only one charge at a time. As long as that charge is within immediate range, they gain an asset for Speed defense tasks because you have their back. Enabler.

○ **Pry Open (4 Intellect points):** You tear apart the defenses of a creature within long range. Any energy-based defenses it has (such as a force field or a Ward ability) are negated for 1d6 + 1 rounds. If the creature has no energy defenses, its Armor is reduced by 2 for one minute. If it has no energy-based defenses or Armor, attacks against it are eased for one minute. Action.

Ward, page 196

○ **Psychic Burst (3+ Intellect points):** You blast waves of mental force into the minds of up to three targets within short range (make an Intellect roll against each target). This burst inflicts 3 points of Intellect damage (ignores Armor). For each 2 additional Intellect points you spend, you can make an Intellect attack roll against an additional target. Action.

○ **Psychic Passenger (6 Intellect points):** You place your mind into the body of a willing creature you choose within short range and remain in that body for up to one hour. Your own body falls down and becomes insensate until this ability ends.

You see, hear, smell, touch, and taste using the senses of the creature whose body you inhabit. When you speak, the words come from your defenseless body, and the creature you inhabit hears those words in their mind.

The creature you inhabit can use your Intellect Edge in place of their own. In addition, you and the creature have an asset on any task that involves perception.

When you take an action, you use the creature's body to perform that action if they allow it. Action to initiate.

○ **Psychic Suggestion (4 Intellect points):** You attempt to make the target take the action you indicate on its next turn. If the action you wish the target to take would cause direct harm to itself or its allies, your mental attack is hindered. Action.

○ **Psychokinetic Attack (5 Intellect points):** You can use this attack in one of two ways. The first is to pick up a heavy object and hurl it at someone within short range. This attack is an Intellect action, and if successful, it deals 6 points of damage to the target and to the hurled object (which could be another foe, although that would require two rolls—one roll to grab the first foe and another roll to hit the second foe with the first). The second way is to unleash a shattering burst of power that works only against an inanimate object no larger than half your size. Make an Intellect roll to instantly destroy the object; the task is eased by three steps compared to breaking it with brute strength. Action.

○ **Psychosis (4 Intellect points):** Your words inflict a destructive psychosis in the mind of a target within long range that can understand you, dealing 6 points of Intellect damage (ignores Armor) per round. The psychosis can be dispersed if a target uses an action doing nothing but calming and centering itself. Action to initiate.

○ **Pull a Fast One (3 Intellect points):** When you're running a con, picking a pocket, fooling or tricking a dupe, sneaking something by a guard, and so on, you gain an asset on the task. Enabler.

○ **Punish All the Guilty (3 Speed points):** You can attack up to five foes within immediate range that you have designated as guilty with your Designation ability, all as part of the same action in one round. Make separate attack rolls for each foe, but all attacks count as a single action in a single round. You remain limited by the amount of Effort you can apply on one action. Anything that modifies your attack or damage applies to all attacks. If you also have the Spin Attack ability, you inflict 1 additional point of damage when you use Punish All the Guilty. Action.

○ **Punish the Guilty (2 Might points):** For the next ten minutes, if you attack someone you have designated as guilty with your Designation ability, you inflict 2 additional points of damage. Action to initiate.

○ **Push (2 Intellect points):** You telekinetically push a creature or object an immediate distance in any direction you wish. You must be able to see the target, which must be your size or smaller, must not be affixed to anything, and must be within short range. The push is quick, and the force is too crude to be manipulated. For example, you can't use this ability to pull a lever or close a door. Action.

○ **Push Off and Throw (3 Speed points):** You can make precise, point-to-point jumps in microgravity, which means you can move up to a long distance and make a melee attack or attempt to grab a foe of your size or smaller. If you successfully grab your foe, you move your foe up to a short distance from its original position.

Alternatively, while you come to a standstill (or move off in an immediate distance per round in any direction you choose) you can launch your foe in a chosen direction through space at a rate of a short distance per round. Action.

○ **Push on Through (2 Might points):** You ignore the effects of terrain while moving for one hour. Enabler.

ABILITIES—Q

○ **Quarry (2 Intellect points):** Choose a quarry (a single individual creature that you can see). You are trained in all tasks involving following, understanding, interacting with, or fighting that creature. You can have only one quarry at a time. Action to initiate.

○ **Question the Spirits (2 Intellect points):** You can call a spirit to you and petition it to answer a few questions (usually no more than three before the spirit fades).

First, you must summon a spirit. If it is a spirit of the dead, you must have personally known the creature, have an object that was owned by the creature, or touch the physical remains of the creature. For other spirits, you must know the spirit's full name or have a great deal of an element (such as fire or earth) that the spirit is associated with.

If the spirit responds, it can manifest as an insubstantial shade that answers for itself, it can inhabit an object or any remains you provide, or it can manifest as an invisible presence that you speak for.

The spirit may not wish to answer your questions, in which case you must persuade it to help. You can attempt to psychically wrestle the spirit into submission (an Intellect task), or you can try diplomacy, deception, or blackmail ("Answer me, or I'll tell your children that you were a philanderer" or "I'll destroy this relic that belonged to you").

The GM determines what the spirit might know, based on the knowledge it possessed in life. Action to initiate.

○ **Quick Block:** If you use a light or medium weapon, you are trained in Speed defense tasks. Enabler.

○ **Quick Death (2 Speed points):** You know how to kill quickly. When you hit with a melee or ranged attack, you deal 4 additional points of damage. You can't make this attack in two consecutive rounds. Action.

○ **Quick Recovery:** Your second recovery roll (usually requiring ten minutes) is only a single action. Enabler.

"The alleyways are the true streets. The main thoroughfares are just for prey."

~a Clever Speaker who Works the Back Alleys

Designation, page 127

Spin Attack, page 185

○ **Quick Strike (4 Speed points):** You make a melee attack with such speed that it is hard for your foe to defend against, and it knocks them off balance. Your attack is eased by two steps, and the foe, if struck, takes normal damage but is dazed so that their tasks are hindered for the next round. Action.

○ **Quick Study:** You learn from repetitive actions. You gain a +1 bonus to rolls for similar tasks after the first time (such as operating the same device or making attacks against the same foe). Once you move on to a new task, the familiarity with the old task fades—unless you start doing it again. Enabler.

○ **Quick Throw (2 Speed points):** After using a thrown light weapon, you draw another light weapon and make another thrown attack against the same target or a different one. Action.

○ **Quick to Flee:** You are trained in stealth and movement tasks. Enabler.

○ **Quick Wits:** When performing a task that would normally require spending points from your Intellect Pool, you can spend points from your Speed Pool instead. Enabler.

○ **Quick Work (3+ Intellect points):** One use of any artifact (or one minute of its continuous function) is increased by one level if you use it within the next minute. If you spend 4 additional Intellect points, the use is increased by two levels if you use it within the next minute. Action.

○ **Quicker Than Most:** Experience has honed your reaction times, because those who act first gain the advantage in most situations. You're trained in tasks related to initiative, seeing underlying patterns, and solving puzzles. Enabler.

ABILITIES—R

○ **Rally to Me (2 Intellect points):** You cry out, blow a battle horn, or otherwise signal to everyone within very long range that you require aid. All allied creatures who respond by moving to within an immediate distance of you within the next few rounds gain one asset on any one attack or defense task within the next hour that you suggest, such as "Hold the gate," "Charge that group of orcs," or something similar. Action to initiate.

○ **Range Increase:** Ranges for you increase by one step. Immediate becomes short, short becomes long, long becomes very long, and very long becomes 1,000 feet (300 m). Enabler.

○ **Rapid Attack (3 Speed points):** Once per round, you can make an additional attack with your chosen weapon. Enabler.

○ **Rapid Processing (6 Intellect points):** You or a target you touch experiences a higher level of mental and physical reaction time for about a minute. During that period, all Speed tasks (including Speed defense rolls) are eased. In addition, the target can take one extra action at any time before the ability's duration expires. Action.

○ **Rapid Recovery:** You can make most recovery rolls faster than normal. You can make your one-action recovery roll as part of another action or when it isn't your turn, your ten-minute recovery roll takes you only one action, and your one-hour recovery roll takes you only ten minutes (your ten-hour rest is unchanged). If you make a recovery roll when it isn't your turn, until the end of your next turn all of your tasks are hindered. Enabler.

○ **Ray of Confusion (2 Intellect points):** You project a grey beam of confusion at a creature within short range, inflicting 1 point of damage that ignores Armor. In addition, until the end of the next round, all tasks, attacks, and defenses the target attempts are hindered. Action.

○ **Reaction:** If a creature you attacked on your last turn with a melee attack uses its action to move out of immediate range, you gain an action to attack the creature as a parting blow, even if you have already taken a turn in the round. Enabler.

○ **Reactive Field:** Thanks to a remarkable enhancement of science, magic, psionics, or something even stranger, you now have a force field that radiates 1 inch (2.5 cm) from your body and provides you with +2 to Armor. In addition, if struck by a melee attack, the field creates a backlash that inflicts 4 points of electricity damage to the attacker. Enabler.

○ **Read the Signs (4 Intellect points):** You examine an area and learn precise, useful details about the past (if any exist). You can ask the GM up to four questions about the immediate area; each requires its own roll. Action.

Recovery roll, page 218

O **Reading the Room (3 Intellect points):** You gain knowledge about an area by speaking with dead spirits or reading residual energies from the past. You can ask the GM a single, matter-of-fact question about the location and get an answer if you succeed on the Intellect roll. "What killed the cattle in this barn?" is a good example of a simple question. "Why were these cattle killed?" is not an appropriate question because it has more to do with the mindset of the killer than the barn. Simple questions usually have a difficulty of 2, but extremely technical questions or those that involve facts meant to be kept secret can have a much higher difficulty. Action.

O **Recruit Deputy:** You gain a level 4 follower. They are not restricted on their modifications. Alternatively, you can choose to advance a level 3 follower you already have to level 4 and then gain a new level 3 follower. Enabler.

O **Recycled Cyphers:** All manifest cyphers you use function at one level higher than normal. In addition, if given a week and at least ten items of junk from the Junk table, you can tinker with one of your manifest cyphers, transforming it into another cypher of the same type that you had in the past. The GM and player should collaborate to ensure that the transformation is logical— for example, you probably can't transform a pill into a helmet. Enabler.

O **Regenerate:** Your ability to heal (whether from a potent spell, unique mutation, or cybernetic graft) continues to function even if you die from violence, as long as your body is mostly intact. One minute after your death, this ability activates and brings you back to life; however, you come back with a permanent 2-point deduction from your Intellect Pool. Enabler.

O **Regenerate Other (9 Might points):** You can confer your Regenerate ability on another creature that you touch and attempt to return it to life, as long as its body is mostly intact. (If you don't have the Regenerate ability, you gain it, but can use it only on yourself.) The difficulty of the task is equal to 3 plus the number of days the target has been dead. (If the body has been perfectly preserved in stasis or through some other non-damaging preservation mechanism, no time limit applies.) Enabler.

O **Regeneration (6 Intellect points):** You restore points to a target's Might or Speed Pool in one of two ways: either the chosen Pool regains up to 6 points, or it is restored to a total value of 12. You make this decision when you initiate this ability. Points are regenerated at a rate of 1 point each round. You must remain within immediate range of the target the whole time, either touching them or conversing with them. In no case can this raise a Pool higher than its maximum. Action.

O **Reinforcing Field (6+ Intellect points):** You can reinforce any object or structure by infusing it with a force field for one hour. The force field increases the level of the object or structure by 2 for tasks related to durability and withstanding damage and destruction. Action to initiate.

O **Release Energy:** You release 1 point of energy you've absorbed with your Absorb Kinetic Energy ability, magnifying and focusing it into a blast of energy that strikes a single foe within long range for 4 points of damage. (If you don't have any kinetic energy absorbed, you can still use this ability, but it requires that you transform a fraction of yourself into the blast, which costs 1 point of Might.) Action.

Follower, page 233

Absorb Kinetic Energy, page 108

Junk table, page 298

A character might discover that Regenerate is both a blessing and a curse, because relying on it too much leads to a kind of malaise that vitality alone can't fix.

Crafting, page 227

Remote Control is a masterful attempt to jam or hack an enemy spacecraft, a task normally requiring multiple rolls, and you only succeed if you roll a total of three successes before rolling a total of two failures. However, all such tasks are hindered by at least two steps due to hardened spacecraft electronic security.

Duplicate, page 132

Sensor, page 181
Ice Armor, page 150

Damage track, page 218

Minor effect, page 211

Major effect, page 212

○ **Reload (1 Speed point):** When using a weapon that normally requires an action to reload, such as a heavy crossbow, you can reload and fire (or fire and reload) in the same action. Enabler.

○ **Relocate (7 Intellect points):** Choose one creature or object within immediate range. You instantly transport it to a new position within long range that you can see. The new position can be any direction from you, but it cannot be inside a solid object. Action.

○ **Remote Control (5 Intellect points):** You can use a starcraft's communication and sensor arrays to launch an attack that briefly renders an enemy starcraft within 20 miles (32 km) inoperative for up to a minute. Action.

○ **Remote Viewing (6 Intellect points):** Distance is an illusion, as all space is one space. With great concentration, you can see another place. This ability can be used in one of two ways:
- Distance and direction. Pick a spot a specific distance away and in a specific direction. You can see from that vantage point as if you had used the Sensor ability there, but only for one minute.
- Think of a place you have seen before, either conventionally or using the other application of this power. You can see from that vantage point as if you had used the Sensor ability there, but only for one or two rounds.

Either application takes anywhere from one action to hours of concentration, depending on what the GM feels is appropriate due to time, distance, or other mitigating circumstances. However, you don't know in advance how long it will take. Action to initiate; action each round to concentrate.

○ **Repair Flesh (3 Intellect points):** When you touch an impaired or debilitated character, you can move them up one step on the damage track (for example, a debilitated PC becomes impaired, and an impaired one becomes hale). Alternatively, if you use this ability on a PC during a rest, you grant them a +2 bonus to their recovery roll. Action.

○ **Repel Metal:** By manipulating magnetism, you are trained in Speed defense tasks against any incoming attack that uses metal. Enabler.

○ **Reshape (5 Intellect points):** You reshape matter within short range in an area no larger than a 5-foot (1.5 m) cube. If you use only one action on this ability, the changes you make are crude at best. If you spend at least ten minutes and succeed at a hindered appropriate crafting task, you can make complex changes to the material. You can't change the nature of the material, only its shape. Thus, you can make a hole in a wall or floor, or you can seal one up. You can fashion a rudimentary sword from a large piece of iron. You can break or repair a chain. With multiple uses of this ability, you could bring about large changes, making a bridge, a wall, or a similar structure. Action.

○ **Resilience:** You have 1 point of Armor against any kind of physical damage, even physical damage that normally ignores Armor. Enabler.

○ **Resilient Duplicate:** Increase the health of any duplicate you create (such as with Duplicate) by 5. Enabler.

○ **Resilient Ice Armor:** The sheen of ice you generate using your Ice Armor ability gives you an additional +1 to Armor. Enabler.

○ **Resist the Elements:** You resist heat, cold, and similar extremes. You have a special +2 to Armor against ambient damage or other damage that would normally ignore Armor. Enabler.

○ **Resist Tricks:** You're trained in solving puzzles and recognizing tricks from years of game playing. Enabler.

○ **Resist Underwater Hazards:** Whether you're resisting crushing waters while exploring the depths or a sting from a poisonous fish, all defense tasks while submerged in water are eased. Enabler.

○ **Resonance Field (1 Intellect point):** Faint lines in a color you choose form a tracery over your entire body and emit faint light. The effect lasts for one minute. Whenever a creature within immediate range makes an attack against you, the pattern energizes to block the attack. You can make an Intellect defense roll in place of the defense roll you would normally make. If you do so and you get a minor effect, the creature attacking you takes 1 point of damage. If you get a major effect, the creature attacking you takes 4 points of damage. Action to initiate.

Abilities—R

○ **Resonant Frequency:** You can infuse an item of up to level 7 that you can hold in one hand with a special vibration generated from your core. The object then functions as if two levels higher for one minute. At the end of that minute, the resonant frequency ramps up exponentially until the object finally shatters from the energy buildup. Anything within immediate range of the detonation suffers 5 points of damage. Action to initiate.

○ **Resonant Quake (7 Intellect points):** You can infuse the ground beneath you with a special vibration generated from your core. This creates a small quake whose epicenter you can select within a very long distance. Everyone within short range of the epicenter is subject to 8 points of damage (from shaking and being struck by toppling objects, crumbling walls, and so on). However, you are dazed for a round afterward yourself, during which time all your tasks are hindered. If you have the Move Mountains ability, both abilities cost 3 fewer Intellect points to use. Action.

○ **Restful Presence:** Creatures who make a recovery roll within short range of you add +1 to their roll. Enabler.

○ **Restore Life (9+ Intellect points):** You can attempt to restore life to a dead creature of up to level 3, as long as the corpse is no more than a day old and is mostly intact. You can also attempt to restore life to a corpse that is much older but is especially well preserved. The difficulty of the Intellect task is equal to the level of the creature you're attempting to restore to life. For each additional level of Effort applied, you can attempt to restore the life of a creature whose level is 1 higher. When first restored to life, a creature is dazed for at least a day, and all tasks they attempt are hindered. Action; one minute to initiate.

○ **Resuscitate (6 Intellect points):** You can resuscitate a character who is up to two steps down on the damage track as your action. The target ascends one step on the damage track. If a character has dropped all three steps on the damage track (dead) but is otherwise in one piece and less than a minute has passed since they descended to the third step, you can resuscitate them if you succeed at a level 6 healing task. If you use this ability on an NPC who has no health but has been dead for less than a minute and is otherwise in one piece, the NPC is resuscitated with 1 health. Action.

○ **Retinue:** Four level 2 followers join you (and your first follower, if you have one). One of their modifications must be for tasks related to serving as your personal assistants. In addition to other tasks they might individually take on your behalf, they can also work together to run interference if you're trying to avoid someone, help hide you from the attention of others, help you muscle through a crowd, and so on. If a situation becomes physically violent, they provide an asset to your Speed defense tasks and, if you command it, try to hold a foe's attention while you escape. Enabler.

○ **Retrieve Memories (3 Intellect points):** You touch the remains of a recently killed creature and make an Intellect-based roll to restore its mind to life long enough to learn information from it. The GM sets the difficulty based on the amount of time that has passed since the creature died. A creature that has been dead for only a few minutes is a difficulty 2 task, one that has been dead for an hour is a difficulty 4 task, and one that has been dead for a few days is a difficulty 9 task. If you succeed, you awaken the corpse, causing its head to animate and perceive things as if it were alive. This enables communication for about one minute, which is how long it takes for the creature to realize that it's dead. The creature is limited to what it knew in life, though it cannot recall minor memories, only big events of importance to it. When the effect ends, or if you fail the roll, the creature's brain dissolves to mush and cannot be awakened again. Action.

○ **Return to Sender (3 Speed points):** If you succeed at a Speed defense task against a melee attack, you can make an immediate melee attack against your foe. You can use this ability only once per round. Enabler.

○ **Return to the Obelisk (7+ Intellect points):** You transfer your body and personal possessions into a crystal of any size that you can touch, and you exit from another crystal of any size, including any crystal obelisks that you are aware of. You must know of the crystal you are going to use as an exit before you enter the first crystal. You can take one additional creature with you for each level of Effort applied. Action.

Followers, page 233

Move Mountains, page 164

177

Third Eye, page 191

○ **Reveal (2+ Intellect points):** You adjust a creature's eyesight so that it can see normally in areas of dim light and darkness. You can affect one willing creature within immediate range for one hour. In addition to the normal options for using Effort, you can choose to use Effort to affect more targets; each level of Effort applied affects two additional targets. You must touch additional targets to affect them. Action to initiate.

○ **Ribbons of Dark Matter (2 Intellect points):** For the next minute, dark matter condenses within an area within long range that is no bigger than an immediate distance in diameter, manifesting as swirling ribbons. All tasks attempted by creatures in the area are hindered, and leaving the area requires a creature's entire action to move. You can dismiss the dark matter early as an action. Action to initiate.

Healing, page 228

Evolved robot assistant: level 5; health 15; inflicts 5 points of damage

○ **Rider:** You are trained in riding any kind of creature that serves as a mount, such as a noble warhorse. Enabler.

○ **Roaming Third Eye (3 Intellect points):** When you use your Third Eye ability, you can place the sensor anywhere within long range. In addition, until that ability ends, you can use an action to move the sensor anywhere within short range of its starting position. Enabler.

○ **Robot Assistant:** A level 2 robot of your size or smaller (built by you) accompanies you and follows your instructions. You and the GM must work out the details of your robot. You'll probably make rolls for it when it takes actions. A robot assistant in combat usually doesn't make separate attacks but helps with yours. On your action, if the artificial assistant is next to you, it serves as an asset for one attack you make on your turn. If the robot is destroyed, you can repair the original with a few days' worth of tinkering, or build a new one with a week's worth of half-time labor. Enabler.

○ **Robot Builder:** You are trained in tasks related to building and repairing robots. For the purposes of repair, you can use this skill to heal robots that use similar technology. Enabler.

○ **Robot Control (2+ Intellect points):** You use your knowledge of robot command and control (and possibly devices that transmit on the proper frequency) to affect any mechanized system or robot of level 2 or lower within short range. You can render several targets inactive for as long as you focus all your attention on them. If you focus on just one target, you can attempt to take active control of it for one minute, commanding it to do simple tasks on your behalf while you concentrate. In addition to the normal options for using Effort, you can choose to use Effort to increase the maximum level of the mechanized system or robot. Thus, to affect a level 4 target (two levels above the normal limit), you must apply two levels of Effort. Action to initiate.

○ **Robot Evolution:** Your first artificial assistant from the Robot Assistant ability increases to level 5, and each of your level 2 robots from Robot Fleet increases to level 3. Instead of choosing this option, you may instead choose one upgrade from the Robot Upgrade ability. Enabler.

○ **Robot Fighter:** When fighting a robot or intelligent machine, you are trained in attacks and defense. Enabler.

○ **Robot Fleet:** You build up to four level 2 robot assistants, each no larger than yourself. (They are in addition to the assistant you built at first tier with Robot Assistant, which may have seen a few upgrades since then.) You and the GM must work out the details of these additional robots. If a robot is destroyed, you can build a new one (or repair the old one from its parts) after a week of half-time labor. Instead of this ability, you can select one of the following abilities: Expert Follower, Robot Control, or Robot Upgrade. Enabler.

○ **Robot Improvement:** Your artificial assistant from the Robot Assistant ability increases to level 4. Enabler.

○ **Robot Upgrade:** You modify your artificial assistant from the Robot Assistant ability with one new capability. Standard options include the following. Work with your GM if you prefer a different capability.
  Cypher Pod. The robot can carry one extra manifest cypher for you. Enabler.
  Flight. The robot can fly a long distance each round. It can carry you, but only for up to an hour between each of your ten-hour recovery rolls. Enabler.
  Force Shield. The robot can erect an opaque level 5 force field around itself and anyone within 10 feet (3 m) of it for one minute (or until it is destroyed). It cannot do so again until after your next recovery roll. Action.
  Mounted Laser Configuration. The robot can reconfigure itself and become an immobile laser weapon on a gimbal mount. In this configuration, the robot is a heavy weapon that deals 7 points of damage. If the robot acts as an autonomous turret, treat it as one level lower than its normal level. However, if the laser is fired by you or someone else who has your permission, the laser attacks are eased. Action to reconfigure; action to return to normal robot configuration.

○ **Ruin Lore:** You are trained in scavenging, which means you're more likely to find useful things, and junk that can potentially be turned into useful things in the ruins of what came before. Enabler.

○ **Run and Fight (4 Might points):** You can move a short distance and make a melee attack that inflicts 2 additional points of damage. Action.

○ **Runner:** Your standard movement increases from short to long. Enabler.

ABILITIES—S

○ **Safe Fall:** You reduce the damage from a fall by 5 points. Enabler.

○ **Sailor:** You are trained in tasks related to sailing and trained in the geography of islands and coastlines. Enabler.

○ **Salvage and Comfort (2 Intellect points):** You're familiar with open space. If you spend an hour using your spacecraft's sensors and make a difficulty 3 Intellect roll, you can find salvage in the form of abandoned spacecraft, drifting motes of matter that were once inhabited, or a place to hide from pursuit in what most people would otherwise assume to be empty space (such as in a nebula, an asteroid field, or the shadow of a moon). Salvage you turn up includes enough food and water for you and several others, as well as the possibility of weapons, clothing, technological artifacts, survivors, or other usable items. In other contexts, this ability counts as training in tasks related to perception. Action to initiate, one hour to complete.

○ **Scan (2 Intellect points):** You scan an area equal in size to a 10-foot (3 m) cube, including all objects or creatures within that area. The area must be within short range. Scanning a creature or object always reveals its level. You also learn whatever facts the GM feels are pertinent about the matter and energy in that area. For example, you might learn that the wooden box contains a device of metal and plastic. You might learn that the glass cylinder is full of poisonous gas, and that its metal stand has an electrical field running through it that connects to a metal mesh in the floor. You might learn that the creature standing before you is a mammal with a small brain. However, this ability doesn't tell you what the information means. Thus, in the first example, you don't know what the metal and plastic device does. In the second, you don't know if stepping on the floor causes the cylinder to release the gas. In the third, you might suspect that the creature is not very intelligent, but scans, like looks, can be deceiving. Many materials and energy fields prevent or resist scanning. Action.

○ **Scramble Machine (2 Intellect points):** You render one machine within short range unable to function for one round. Alternatively, you can hinder any action by the machine (or by someone attempting to use the machine) for one minute. Action.

Expert Follower, page 137

Improved robot assistant: *level 4; health 12; inflicts 4 points of damage*

Scavenging, page 296

Phase Sprint, page 170

Disrupting Touch, page 129

○ **Scratch Existence (1+ Might points):** You can choose to phase in a way that "scratches" normal matter in a long streak as you run using Phase Sprint. This tears a bit at you, too, reflected by the Might cost. When you use Phase Sprint, you inflict 2 points of damage (ignores Armor) to one target you select as you pass within immediate range, without triggering Disrupting Touch. In addition to the normal options for using Effort, you can choose to use Effort to increase the number of targets along your path that you can attack as part of the same action. Make a separate attack roll for each foe. You remain limited by the amount of Effort you can apply on one action. Anything that modifies your attack or damage applies to all of these attacks.

Alternatively, if you apply Effort to increase the damage rather than ease the task, you deal 2 additional points of damage per level of Effort (instead of 3 points); the target takes 1 point of damage even if you fail the attack roll. Enabler.

○ **Sculpt Flesh (2 Intellect points):** You cause a willing creature's fingers to lengthen into claws and their teeth to grow into fangs. The effect lasts for ten minutes. The damage dealt by the target's unarmed strikes increases to 4 points. Action.

○ **Sculpt Light (4 Intellect points):** You create an object of solid light in any shape you can imagine that is your size or smaller, and it persists for about an hour. The object appears in an area adjacent to you. It is crude and can have no moving parts, so you can make a sword, a shield, a short ladder, and so on. The object has the approximate mass of the real object and is level 4. Action.

○ **Sea Legs:** You have gotten used to rough seas and unexpected surges. You are trained in balance. Any movement task that would be hindered by a pitching deck, moving through rigging, and so on is a routine task for you. Enabler.

○ **See History (4 Intellect points):** You touch an object, read the subtle echoes of its existence through time, ask the GM a question about the object's past, and get a general answer. The answers are often in the form of brief images or sensations rather than specific answers in a language you know. The GM assigns a level to the question, so the more obscure the answer, the more difficult the task. Generally, knowledge that you could find by looking somewhere other than your current location is level 1, and obscure knowledge of the past is level 7. After you use this ability, you have an asset on identifying the object. Action.

○ **See the Future (6 Intellect points):** Based on all the variables you perceive, you can predict the next few minutes. This has the following effects:
- For the next ten minutes, your defense rolls gain an asset.
- You have a sort of danger sense. For the next ten minutes, you gain an asset in seeing through deceptions and attempts to betray you, as well as avoiding traps and ambushes.
- You know what people are probably thinking and what they will say before they say it. For the next ten minutes, you gain an asset to tasks involving interaction and deception. Enabler.

○ **See the Unseen:** You can automatically perceive creatures and objects that are normally invisible, out of phase, or only partially in this universe. When looking for things more conventionally hidden, the task is eased. Enabler.

○ **See Through Matter (3+ Intellect points):** You can see through matter as if it were transparent. You can see through up to 6 inches (15 cm) of material for one round. Doing so is a task whose difficulty is equal to the material or object's level. In addition to the normal options for using Effort, you can choose to use Effort to see through another 6 inches of material for each additional level of Effort you apply toward that goal. Action.

"Obscure" is a relative term—a sage might not know how a vampire acquired a specific artifact, but someone using See History on that artifact would have an easy time sensing that event.

ABILITIES—S

○ **See Through Time (7 Intellect points):** Time is an illusion, as all time is one time. With great concentration, you can see into another time. You specify a time period regarding the place where you now stand. Interestingly, the easiest time to view is about one hundred years in the past or future. Viewing farther back or ahead is a nearly impossible task.

This takes anywhere from one action to hours of concentration, depending on what the GM feels is appropriate due to time, distance, or other mitigating circumstances. However, you don't know in advance how long it will take. Action to initiate; action each round to concentrate.

○ **Seeds of Fury (1 Intellect point):** You throw a handful of seeds in the air that ignite and speed toward a target within long range, scratching the air with twisting smoke trails. The attack deals 3 points of damage and catches the target on fire, which inflicts 1 additional point of damage per round for up to a minute or until the target uses an action to douse the flames. Action.

○ **Seize the Initiative (5 Intellect points):** Within one minute of successfully using your Draw Conclusion ability, you can take one additional, immediate action, which you can take out of turn. After using this ability, you can't use it again until after your next ten-hour recovery roll. Enabler.

○ **Seize the Moment (4+ Speed points):** If you succeed on a Speed defense roll to resist an attack, you gain an action. You can use the action immediately even if you have already taken a turn in the round. You don't take an action during the next round, unless you apply a level of Effort when you use Seize the Moment. Enabler.

○ **Sense Ambush:** You are never surprised by an attack. Enabler.

○ **Sense Attitudes:** You are trained in sensing lies and whether a person is likely to (or already does) believe your lies. Enabler.

○ **Sensing Package:** You can see in dim light and darkness as if it were bright light, and you can see up to a short distance through fog, smoke, and other obscuring phenomena. In addition, if you apply a level of Effort to perception or searching tasks, you get a free level of Effort on that task. Enabler.

○ **Sensor (4 Intellect points):** You create an immobile, invisible sensor within immediate range that lasts for 24 hours. At any time during that duration, you can concentrate to see, hear, and smell through the sensor, no matter how far you move from it. The sensor doesn't grant you sensory capabilities beyond the norm. If you also have this ability from another source, it lasts twice as long. Action to create; action to check.

○ **Sensor Array (3 Intellect points):** You are trained in using starcraft sensory instruments. These instruments allow users to answer general questions about a location, such as "How many people are in the mining colony?" or "Where did the other spacecraft crash?" Action.

○ **Serv-0:** You build a tiny robot assistant. It is level 1 and cannot take independent actions or leave your immediate area. In truth, it's more an extension of you than a separate being. It gains a modification in using machines and other technological devices. Enabler.

○ **Serv-0 Aim:** Your Serv-0 aids you in ranged combat. It gains a modification in ranged attacks. Enabler.

○ **Serv-0 Brawler:** Your Serv-0 aids you in melee combat. It gains a modification in melee attacks. Enabler.

○ **Serv-0 Defender:** Your Serv-0 aids you in combat by blocking attacks. It gains a modification in Speed defense. Enabler.

○ **Serv-0 Repair:** Your Serv-0 aids you in repairing other devices. It gains a modification in repair. Enabler.

○ **Serv-0 Scanner (2 Intellect points):** Your Serv-0 gains the Scan ability. Enabler.

○ **Serv-0 Spy (3 Intellect points):** You can send your Serv-0 up to a long distance away for up to ten minutes and see and hear through it as though its senses were your own. You direct its movement. Action to initiate.

○ **Share Defense:** If your training in a defense task is greater than that of an ally within short range, your advice and insight allow them to substitute your training for that defense task. Enabler.

An impossible task has a difficulty of 10.

Follower modifications, page 233

To use Serv-0 Defender, Serv-0 Repair, Serv-0 Scanner, and similar abilities, you must have a Serv-0 assistant.

Draw Conclusion, page 131

Surprise, page 220

Scan, page 179

Free level of Effort, page 209

181

Drain Creature, page 131
Drain Machine, page 131

Store Energy, page 186

Drain at a Distance, page 131

Duplicate, page 132

Force Field Shield, page 143

The vegetative state created by Shatter Mind can be healed by advanced magic or science, or by a condition remover cypher that cures psychosis.

Condition remover cypher, page 385

○ **Share the Power:** When you use Drain Creature or Drain Machine to drain energy, you can transfer it to another creature, restoring points to their Might or Speed Pools (or health for an NPC) instead of yourself. You can spend points from your Siphon Pool (from the Store Energy ability) in the same way. You must touch the creature you want to heal, unless you have the Drain at a Distance ability, in which case they can be up to a short distance away. Enabler.

○ **Share Senses:** While your duplicate created by the Duplicate ability is in existence and within 1 mile (1.5 km), you know everything it experiences and can communicate with it telepathically. Enabler.

○ **Sharp Senses:** You are trained in all tasks involving perception. Enabler.

○ **Sharp-Eyed:** Because you must always keep an eye out when you're traveling, you are trained in all tasks related to perception and navigation. Enabler.

○ **Shatter (2+ Intellect points):** You interrupt the fundamental force holding normal matter together for a moment, causing the detonation of an object you choose within long range. The object must be a small, mundane item composed of homogeneous matter (such as a clay cup, an iron ingot, a stone, and so on). The object explodes in an immediate radius, dealing 1 point of damage to all creatures and objects in the area. If you apply Effort to increase the damage, you deal 2 additional points of damage per level of Effort (instead of 3 points); targets in the area take 1 point of damage even if you fail the attack roll. Action.

○ **Shatter Mind (7+ Intellect points):** Your words reverberate destructively in the brain of an intelligent level 1 target within short range that can hear and understand you. They destroy tissue, memories, and personality, triggering a vegetative state. In addition to the normal options for using Effort, you can choose to use Effort to increase the maximum level of the target. Thus, to shatter the mind of a level 5 target (four levels above the normal limit), you must apply four levels of Effort. Action.

○ **Shattering Shout (5+ Might points):** Your focused shout sets up a destructive resonance in a creature or object within long range. Nothing happens on the round you strike your target other than an ominous humming or buzzing sound emitted by the target. But on your next turn, the resonance shatters discrete inanimate objects, inflicts major damage to structures, or inflicts 4 points of damage on a creature (ignores Armor).

If you shatter a discrete object, it shatters explosively, inflicting 1 point of damage on all creatures and objects within immediate range of it. If you apply Effort to increase the damage rather than ease the task, you deal 2 additional points of damage per level of Effort (instead of 3 points); targets in the area take 1 point of damage even if you fail the attack roll. Action to initiate.

○ **Shepherd's Fury:** You inflict 3 additional points of damage when engaging in combat that directly relates to advancing the needs of a community you are associated with. (You and the GM can decide whether a particular situation warrants the additional damage.) Enabler.

○ **Shield Burst:** When you make a melee or ranged attack and hit with your Force Field Shield, it releases an explosion of energy, inflicting an additional 2 points of damage on the target and everything within immediate range of the target. If you applied Effort to inflict additional damage as part of the attack, each level of Effort inflicts only 2 additional points to all targets instead of 3 points. If you use Shield Burst with a melee attack, you and creatures behind you are not affected by this explosion. If you use Shield Burst with a ranged attack, the shield dissipates after the attack and then reforms in your grasp. Enabler.

○ **Shield Master:** When you use a shield, in addition to the asset it gives you (easing Speed defense tasks), you can act as if you are trained in Speed defense tasks. However, in any round in which you use this benefit, your attacks are hindered. Enabler.

○ **Shield Training:** If you use a shield, Speed defense tasks are eased by two steps instead of one. Enabler.

○ **Ship Footing (3 Speed points):** For ten minutes, all tasks you attempt while on a spaceship are eased. Action to initiate.

Abilities—S

○ **Shipspeak:** You can make basic maneuvers from a planetary distance with a starship that you have bonded with using Machine Bond. You can send it to a designated place, call it to you, have it land, allow or deny entrance, and so on, even if you are not on board. Bonding is a process that requires a day of meditation while jacked into the ship. Action.

○ **Shock (1 Intellect point):** Your hands crackle with electricity, and the next time you touch a creature, you inflict 3 points of damage. Alternatively, if you wield a weapon, for ten minutes it crackles with electricity and inflicts 1 additional point of damage per attack. Action for touch; enabler for weapon.

○ **Show Them the Way (6+ Intellect points):** Your presence overwhelms a creature that you touch and ask to aid you. Essentially, if the creature fails to defend against your presence, you control its actions for up to ten minutes. The target must be level 3 or lower. Once you have established control, you maintain control through verbal instruction. You can allow the target to act freely or override control on a case-by case basis. In addition to the normal options for using Effort, you can choose to use Effort to increase the maximum level of the target. Thus, to affect a level 5 target (two levels above the normal limit), you must apply two levels of Effort. When the effect ends, the creature vaguely remembers doing your will, but it's as blurry as a dream. Action to initiate.

○ **Shred Existence:** When you use Disrupting Touch, Scratch Existence, or Phase Detonation, you inflict an additional 5 points of damage that ignores Armor. Enabler.

○ **Shroud of Flame (1 Intellect point):** At your command, your entire body becomes shrouded in flames that last up to ten minutes. The fire doesn't burn you, but it automatically inflicts 2 points of damage to anyone who tries to touch you or strike you with a melee attack. Flames from another source can still hurt you. While the shroud is active, you gain +2 Armor against damage from fire from another source. Enabler.

○ **Silent As Space:** By taking advantage of microgravity conditions, you gain an asset to stealth and initiative tasks while in zero-gravity or low-gravity conditions. Enabler.

○ **Skill With Attacks:** Choose one type of attack in which you are not already trained: light bashing, light bladed, light ranged, medium bashing, medium bladed, medium ranged, heavy bashing, heavy bladed, or heavy ranged. You are trained in attacks using that type of weapon. You can select this ability multiple times. Each time you select it, you must choose a different type of attack. Enabler.

○ **Skill With Defense:** Choose one type of defense task in which you are not already trained: Might, Speed, or Intellect. You are trained in defense tasks of that type. Enabler.

○ **Sleuth:** Finding the clues is the first step in solving a mystery. You are trained in perception. Enabler.

○ **Slice (2 Speed points):** This is a quick attack with a bladed or pointed weapon that is hard to defend against. You are trained in this task. If the attack is successful, it deals 1 less point of damage than normal. Action.

○ **Slip Into Shadow (2+ Intellect points):** You attempt to slip away from a selected target and hide from view in a nearby shadow, behind a tree or a furnishing, or in the next room, even if in full view of the target. For each level of Effort applied, you can attempt to affect one additional target, as long as all your targets are next to each other. Action to initiate.

○ **Slippery:** You are trained in escaping any kind of bond or grasp. Enabler.

○ **Slippery Customer:** When you apply Effort to tasks involving escaping from bonds, fitting in tight spaces, and other contortionist tasks, you get a free level of Effort on the task. Thanks to your experience, you are also trained in Speed defense tasks while wearing light armor or no armor. Enabler.

○ **Snap Shot:** You can make two gun attacks as a single action, but the second attack is hindered by two steps. Enabler.

○ **Sneak:** You are trained in stealth and initiative tasks. Enabler.

○ **Snipe (2 Speed points):** If you spend one action aiming, in the next round you can make a precise ranged attack. You have an asset on this attack. If your attack is successful, it inflicts 4 additional points of damage. Action.

If you become trained with a weapon that you have an inability in, the inability and training cancel each other out.

Machine Bond, page 159

Disrupting Touch, page 129
Scratch Existence, page 180
Phase Detonation, page 169

Free level of Effort, page 209

Initiative, page 214

○ **Sniper's Aim:** By dint of almost constant practice playing games that simulate making ranged attacks, your hand-eye coordination is off the chart. You have an asset on all ranged attacks. Enabler.

○ **Something in the Road:** When you use a vehicle as a weapon, you inflict 5 additional points of damage. Enabler.

Healing, page 228

○ **Soothe Mind and Body:** The body and the mind are connected. All healing tasks you attempt are eased by two steps. Enabler.

○ **Soothe the Savage (2 Intellect points):** You calm a nonhuman beast within 30 feet (9 m). You must speak to it (although it doesn't need to understand your words), and it must see you. It remains calm for one minute or for as long as you focus all your attention on it. The GM has final say over what counts as a nonhuman beast, but unless some kind of deception is at work, you should know whether you can affect a creature before you attempt to use this ability on it. Aliens, extradimensional entities, very intelligent creatures, and robots never count. Action.

○ **Soul Interrogation (5 Intellect points):** You determine the weaknesses, vulnerabilities, qualities, and mannerisms of a single creature within long range. The GM should reveal the creature's level, basic abilities, and obvious weaknesses (if any). All actions you attempt that affect that creature—attack, defense, interaction, and so on—are eased for a few months afterward. Action.

○ **Sound Conversion Barrier:** Attacks that hit you—especially energy attacks like focused light, heat, radiation, and transdimensional energy—are partially converted to surges of harmless noise similar to the sound of a wave crashing to shore. This ability grants you +1 Armor against all attacks and an additional +2 Armor against energy attacks. Enabler.

○ **Space Fighting:** By taking advantage of microgravity conditions, you can use inertia and mass to your advantage. If you spend a round setting up a melee attack (or an attack from a thrown or launched object) while in zero-gravity or low-gravity conditions, the attack inflicts 6 additional points of damage. Enabler.

○ **Speaker for the Dead (2+ Intellect points):** You can ask a question of a dead being whose corpse you are touching. Because the answer comes through the filter of the being's understanding and personality, it can't answer questions that it wouldn't have understood in life, and it can't provide answers that it wouldn't have known in life. In fact, the being is not compelled to answer at all, so you might need to interact with it in a way that would have convinced it to answer while it was alive. For each additional Intellect point you spend when you activate the ability, you can ask the being an additional question. Action.

○ **Special Shot:** When you hit a target with a gun attack, you can choose to reduce the damage by 1 point but hit the target in a precise spot. Some of the possible effects include (but are not limited to) the following:
- You can shoot an object out of someone's hand.
- You can shoot the leg, wing, or other limb it uses to move, reducing its maximum movement speed to immediate for a few days or until it receives expert medical care.
- You can shoot a strap holding a backpack, armor, or a similarly strapped-on item so that it falls off.

Enabler.

ABILITIES—S

○ **Specialized Basher:** You are specialized in using the stone fists from your Golem Body ability as a medium weapon. Enabler.

○ **Specialized Throwing:** You are specialized in attacks with all weapons that you throw. Enabler.

○ **Speed Burst (4 Speed points):** You can take two separate actions in this round. In the following round, all actions are hindered. You cannot use this ability two rounds in a row. Enabler.

○ **Speedy Recovery (3 Intellect points):** Your words enhance the normal regenerative ability of a character within short range who is able to understand you. When they make a recovery roll, they must spend only half the normal amount of time required to do so (minimum one action). Action.

○ **Spin Attack (5+ Speed points):** You stand still and make attacks against up to five foes, all as part of the same action in one round. All of the attacks have to be the same sort of attack (melee or ranged). Make a separate attack roll for each foe. You remain limited by the amount of Effort you can apply on one action. Anything that modifies your attack or damage applies to all of these attacks. In addition to the normal options for using Effort, you can choose to use Effort to increase the number of foes you can attack with this ability (one additional foe per level of Effort used in this way). Action.

○ **Spin Identity (2+ Intellect points):** You convince all intelligent creatures who can see, hear, and understand you that you are someone or something other than who you actually are. You don't impersonate a specific individual known to the victim. Instead, you convince the victim that you are someone they do not know belonging to a certain category of people. "We're from the government." "I'm just a simple farmer from the next town over." "Your commander sent me." A disguise isn't necessary, but a good disguise will almost certainly be an asset to the roll involved. If you attempt to convince more than one creature, the Intellect cost increases by 1 point per additional victim. Fooled creatures remain so for up to an hour, unless your actions or other circumstances reveal your true identity earlier. Action.

○ **Spirit Accomplice:** A level 3 spirit accompanies you and follows your instructions. The spirit must remain within immediate range—if it moves farther away, it fades at the end of your following turn and cannot return for a day. You and the GM must work out the details of your spirit accomplice, and you'll probably make rolls for it when it takes actions. The spirit accomplice acts on your turn, can move a short distance each round, and exists partially out of phase (allowing it to move through walls, though it makes a poor porter). The spirit takes up residence in an object you designate, and it manifests as either an invisible presence or a ghostly shade. Your spirit accomplice is specialized in one knowledge skill the GM determines.

The spirit is normally insubstantial, but if you use an action and spend 3 Intellect points, it accretes enough substance to affect the world around it. As a level 3 creature with substance, it has a target number of 9 and a health of 9. It doesn't attack creatures, but while substantial, it can use its action to serve as an asset for any one attack you make on your turn.

While corporeal, the spirit can't move through objects or fly. A spirit remains corporeal for up to ten minutes at a time, but fades back to being insubstantial if not actively engaged. If your spirit accomplice is destroyed, it reforms in 1d6 days, or you can attract a new spirit in 2d6 days. Enabler.

○ **Spot Weakness:** If a creature that you can see has a special weakness, such as a vulnerability to fire, a negative modification to perception, or so on, you know what it is. (Ask and the GM will tell you.) Enabler.

○ **Spray (2 Speed points):** If a weapon has the ability to fire rapid shots without reloading (usually called a rapid-fire weapon, such as a crank crossbow or submachine gun), you can spray multiple shots around your target to increase the chance of hitting. This ability uses 1d6 + 1 rounds of ammo (or all the ammo in the weapon, if it has less than the number rolled). You are trained in making this attack. If the attack is successful, it deals 1 less point of damage than normal. You can also use this ability on multiple thrown weapons (stones, shuriken, daggers, and so on) if you're carrying them on your person or they are all within reach. Action.

Golem Body, page 145

An insubstantial creature can't affect or be affected by anything unless indicated otherwise, such as when an attack is made with a special weapon. An insubstantial creature can pass through solid matter without hindrance, but solid energy barriers, such as magical fields of force, keep it at bay.

O **Spring Away (5 Speed points):** Whenever you succeed on a Speed defense roll, you can immediately move up to a short distance. You cannot use this ability more than once in a given round. Enabler.

O **Sprint and Grab (2 Speed points):** You can run a short distance and make a melee attack to grab a foe of your size or smaller. A successful attack means you grab the foe and bring it to a halt if it was moving (this can be treated as a tackle, if appropriate). Action.

O **Spur Effort (5 Intellect points):** You select an ally within immediate range. If that character applies Effort to a task on their next turn, they can apply a free level of Effort on that task. Enabler.

Free level of Effort, page 209

O **Stalker:** You gain an asset to all types of movement tasks (including climbing, swimming, jumping, and balancing). Enabler.

O **Stand Watch (2 Intellect points):** While standing watch (mostly remaining in place for an extended period of time), you unfailingly remain awake and alert for up to eight hours. During this time, you are trained in perception tasks as well as stealth tasks to conceal yourself from those who might approach. Action to initiate.

Golem Body, page 145

O **Stare Them Down:** One doesn't play games of chicken with other maniac drivers without gaining mental strength. You're trained in Intellect defense tasks. Enabler.

O **Stasis (3 Intellect points):** You surround a foe of your size or smaller with scintillating energy, keeping it from moving or acting for one minute, as if frozen solid. You must be able to see the target, and it must be within short range. While in stasis, the target is impervious to harm, cannot be moved, and is immune to all effects. Action.

O **Stay the Course (5 Intellect points):** When your companions are flagging, you can help inspire them with a well-timed word or two. Any ally (except you) within immediate range can make a recovery roll that is not an action and does not count toward their daily limit. Action.

O **Stealth Skills:** You are trained in your choice of two of the following skills: disguise, deception, lockpicking, pickpocketing, seeing through deception, sleight of hand, or stealth. You can choose this ability multiple times, but you must select different skills each time. Enabler.

O **Still As a Statue (5 Might points):** Drawing upon the power of your Golem Body, you freeze in place, burying your essence deep in your stone core. During this time, you lose all mobility as well as the ability to take physical actions. You cannot sense what's happening around you, and no time seems to pass for you. While Still As a Statue, you gain +10 to Armor against damage of all sorts. Under normal circumstances, you automatically rouse to normal wakefulness and mobility a day later. If an ally you trust shakes you hard enough (with a minimum cost of 2 Might points), you rouse earlier. Action to initiate.

O **Stimulate (6 Intellect points):** Your words encourage a target you touch who can understand you. The next action it takes is eased by three steps. Action.

O **Stone Breaker:** Your attacks against objects inflict 4 additional points of damage when you use a melee weapon that you wield in two hands. Enabler.

O **Store Energy:** When you drain energy with your focus abilities, you can store some of it for later in a Siphon Pool. You can spend points from your Siphon Pool as if they were from your Might or Speed Pool, or use an action to spend them to restore an equal number of points to your Might or Speed Pool. Your Siphon Pool can safely store up to 3 points; each point beyond that hinders all of your tasks. Enabler.

Abilities–S

○ **Storm Seed (3 Intellect points):** If outside or in a large-enough enclosed space, you can seed a natural storm of a kind common to the area. Doing so requires at least an hour's concentration as you use your connection to the air (whether this is due to nanobots, elemental spirits, magic, or some other source) to initiate proper conditions, though it could take longer if the GM feels there are additional obstacles at play. Once the storm begins, it lasts for about ten minutes. Once during that period, you can create a more dramatic and specific effect appropriate to that kind of storm, such as a lightning strike, a squall of giant hailstones, the brief touchdown of a twister, a single gust of hurricane-force winds, and so on. These effects must occur within long range of your location. You must spend your turn concentrating to create the effect, which occurs a round later. The effect inflicts 6 points of damage, after which the storm begins to disperse. Action to initiate, an hour or more to complete.

○ **Straightforward:** You are trained in one of the following tasks (choose one): breaking things, climbing, jumping, or running. Enabler.

○ **Strategize (6 Intellect points):** Having an action plan in place before facing a challenge improves the odds of success, even if that plan is eventually changed or discarded once it's put into play. If you and your allies spend at least ten minutes going over a plan of action, all of you gain one free level of Effort that can be applied to one task you attempt during the execution of that plan within the next 24 hours. The plan of action must be something concrete and executable in order to gain this benefit. Action to initiate, ten minutes to complete.

○ **Stronger Together:** When you and your companion from the Beast Companion ability are within immediate distance of each other, you inflict 2 additional points of damage when you attack and both of you gain an asset to defense actions. Enabler.

○ **Stun Attack (6 Speed points):** You attempt a difficulty 5 Speed task to stun a creature as part of your melee or ranged attack. If you succeed, your attack inflicts its normal damage and stuns the creature for one round, causing it to lose its next turn. If you fail, you still make your normal attack roll, but you don't stun the opponent if you hit. If you also have this ability from another source (such as having it as a type ability and a focus ability), using this costs you only 3 points instead of 6 points. Action.

○ **Sturdy:** You are trained in Might defense tasks. Enabler.

○ **Subconscious Defense:** Your subconscious constantly runs predictive models for avoiding danger. You gain an asset on your Speed defense tasks. Enabler.

○ **Subsonic Rumble (2 Intellect points):** For one minute or until you use some other sound manipulation ability, you emit a subsonic rumble that most living creatures can't hear but which has an effect on them all the same. The effect lasts for one minute and affects all creatures you select within short range. All tasks related to resisting persuasion, intimidation, and fear are hindered by two steps for affected targets. Action to initiate.

○ **Subtle Steps:** When you move no more than a short distance, you can move without making a sound, regardless of the surface you move across. Enabler.

○ **Subtle Tricks:** You can use your skills and special abilities in ways that don't look like you're doing anything. If the skill or ability would normally require an obvious movement, phrase, or other action by you, it instead seems to happen on its own. Instead of using your tools to pick a lock, the lock clicks open as you stand near it. Instead of manipulating a computer screen, the information you want appears on the screen when you look at it. Instead of bluffing your way past some guards, they step aside as you approach and let you through. This ability usually only works up to an immediate distance. You still must spend points and make rolls to use your skills and abilities with Subtle Tricks. Using a skill or ability in a subtle way hinders the task. This ability can't be used to conceal your attack or defense rolls. Enabler.

○ **Successive Attack (2 Speed points):** If you take down a foe, you can immediately make another attack on that same turn against a new foe within your reach. The second attack is part of the same action. You can use this ability with melee attacks and ranged attacks. Enabler.

Storm Seed usually calls thunderstorms, but in an area where stranger weather is common, a Storm Seed could call that instead. For instance, some settings have particular kinds of magical weather.

Beast Companion, page 112

Stun, page 219

Duplicate, page 132

- **Suggestion (5+ Intellect points):** You suggest an action to a creature within immediate range. If the action is something that the target might normally do anyway, it follows your suggestion. If the suggestion is something that is outside of the target's nature or express duty (such as asking a guard to let an intruder pass), the suggestion fails. The creature must be level 2 or lower. The effect of your suggestion lasts for up to a minute.

  In addition to the normal options for using Effort, you can choose to use Effort to increase the maximum level of the target you can affect by 1. Thus, to affect a level 5 target (three levels above the normal limit), you must apply three levels of Effort.

  When the effects of the ability end, the creature remembers following the suggestion but can be persuaded to believe that it chose to do so willingly. Action to initiate.

Demon, page 322

- **Summon Demon (7+ Intellect points):** A demon appears within immediate range. If you applied a level of Effort as part of the summoning, the demon is amenable to your instructions; otherwise, it acts according to its nature. Regardless, the demon persists for up to one minute before it fades away—you hope. Action to initiate.

Giant spider, page 335

- **Summon Giant Spider (4+ Intellect points):** A giant spider appears within immediate range. If you applied a level of Effort as part of the summoning, the spider is amenable to your instructions; otherwise, it acts according to its nature. Regardless, the creature persists for up to one minute before it fades away. Action to initiate.

Store Energy, page 186

- **Sun Siphon:** The safe limit of your Siphon Pool from the Store Energy ability increases by 3 points. If you spend an hour in sunlight (or an hour in contact with a suitable powerful energy source), you automatically fill your Siphon Pool to its safe limit. You can't refill your Siphon Pool this way again until after your next ten-hour recovery roll. Enabler.

Free level of Effort, page 209

Damage track, page 218

- **Sunlight (3 Intellect points):** A mote of light travels from you to a spot you choose within long range. When the mote reaches that spot, it flares and casts bright light in a 200-foot (60 m) radius, and darkness within 1,000 feet (300 m) of the mote becomes dim light. The light lasts for one hour or until you use an action to dismiss it. Action.

- **Superb Explorer:** You are trained in searching, listening, climbing, balancing, and jumping tasks. Enabler.

- **Superb Infiltrator:** You are trained in lockpicking and tinkering with devices in an effort to make them work, or at least work for you. Enabler.

- **Superior Duplicate (2 Might points):** When you use your Duplicate ability, you can create a superior duplicate instead of a normal duplicate. A superior duplicate is a level 3 NPC with 15 health. Enabler.

- **Surging Confidence (1 Might point):** When you use an action to make your first recovery roll of the day, you immediately gain another action. Enabler.

- **Surprise Attack:** If attacking from a hidden vantage, with surprise, or before your opponent has acted, you get an asset on the attack. On a successful hit, you inflict 2 additional points of damage. Enabler.

- **Swim (1+ Intellect points):** You can swim like a fish through water and similar liquid for one hour. For each level of Effort applied, you can extend the duration by one hour. You swim about 10 miles (16 km) per hour, and you are not affected by currents in the water. Action to initiate.

- **Swipe (1 Speed point):** This is a quick, agile melee attack. Your attack inflicts 1 less point of damage than normal but dazes your target for one round, during which time all tasks it performs are hindered. Action.

ABILITIES—T

- **Take Command (3 Intellect points):** You issue a specific command to another character. If that character chooses to listen, any attack they attempt on their next turn is eased, and a hit deals 3 additional points of damage. If your command is to perform a task other than an attack, the task is eased as if it benefited from a free level of Effort. Action.

- **Taking Advantage:** When your foe is weakened, dazed, stunned, moved down the damage track, or disadvantaged in some other way, your attacks against that foe are eased beyond any other modifications due to the disadvantage. Enabler.

Abilities—S-T

○ **Tall Tale (3 Intellect points):** You tell a short anecdote to a foe that can understand you about something you've witnessed in your life that's so over the top yet so convincing that, if you are successful, the foe is dazed for one minute, during which time its tasks are hindered. Action.

○ **Targeting Eye:** You are trained in any physical ranged attack that is a character ability or comes from a device. For example, you are trained when using an Onslaught force blast because it's a physical attack, but not when using an Onslaught mindslice because it's a mental attack. Enabler.

○ **Task Specialization:** Choose one task (other than attacks or defense) that you are trained in. You become specialized in that task. (You can instead use this ability as Task Training to become trained in a task you aren't trained in.) Enabler.

○ **Task Training:** Choose one task (other than attacks or defense) that you are not trained or specialized in. You become trained in that task. Enabler.

○ **Taunt Foe (4 Might or Intellect points):** You can make an attack on a foe as part of drawing an attack (which is not something you can do normally when attempting to draw an attack). In cases where an intelligent or determined foe isn't drawn to you, you can attempt an Intellect action as part of the attack. If that Intellect action is successful, the foe attacks you. Your defenses against that attack are hindered by one step, instead of being hindered by two steps as normal when drawing an attack. Enabler.

○ **Teach Trick (5+ Intellect points):** You spend an hour instructing someone on how to perform a type ability that you know. The ability must be no higher than fourth tier. For one hour after you teach them, the student can perform that ability as if it were natural for them. They must pay the Might, Speed, or Intellect cost (if any) to use that ability. The student must be able to understand your instructions. In addition to the normal options for using Effort, you can choose to use Effort to increase how long the student can use the ability or to teach additional students at the same time; each level of Effort used in this way increases the duration by one hour or the number of students by one. One hour to initiate. Action; hour to complete.

○ **Teamwork:** Through example, acts of camaraderie, stories of martial prowess, or other forms of instruction, you and your allies work better together as a cohesive unit. During any round in which you rally your team (by spending 2 Intellect points as part of another action), you and your allies inflict 1 additional point of damage in combat. This benefit applies only to allies with whom you have spent the last 24 hours. It ends if you leave, but it resumes if you return to your allies' company within 24 hours. If you leave for more than 24 hours, you must spend another 24 hours together to reactivate the benefit. Enabler.

○ **Tech Skills:** You are trained in two skills in which you are not already trained. Choose two of the following: crafting, computers, identifying, machines, piloting, repairing, or vehicle driving. You can select this ability multiple times. Each time you select it, you must choose two different skills. Enabler.

○ **Telekinesis (2 Intellect points):** You can exert force on objects within short range. Once activated, your power has an effective Might Pool of 10, a Might Edge of 1, and an Effort of 2 (approximately equal to the strength of a fit, capable adult human), and you can use it to move objects, push against objects, and so on. For example, you could lift and pull a light object anywhere within range to yourself or move a heavy object (like a piece of furniture) about 10 feet (3 m). This power lacks the fine control to wield a weapon or move objects with much speed, so in most situations, it's not a means of attack. You can't use this ability on your own body. The power lasts for one hour or until its Might Pool is depleted, whichever comes first. Action.

○ **Telepathic (1+ Intellect points):** You can speak telepathically with others who are within short range. Communication is two-way, but the other party must be willing and able to communicate. You don't have to see the target, but you must know that it's within range. You can have more than one active contact at once, but you must establish contact with each target individually. Each contact lasts up to ten minutes. If you apply a level of Effort to increase the duration rather than ease the task, the contact lasts for 24 hours. Action to establish contact.

Onslaught, page 167

If you're using Telekinesis to move an object across the room, and an average fit human could do it with their arms, you can do it with your psychokinesis. You have to use the power's Might Pool, Might Edge, and Effort only if a PC would have to do so, such as if a character tried to push open a barred door.

Draw the Attack, page 227

○ **Telepathic Network (0+ Intellect points):** When you wish it, you can contact up to ten creatures known to you, no matter where they are. All targets must be willing and able to communicate. You automatically succeed at establishing a telepathic network; no roll is required. All creatures in the network are linked and can communicate telepathically with one another. They can also "overhear" anything said in the network, if they wish. Activating this ability doesn't require an action and doesn't cost Intellect points; to you, it's as easy as speaking out loud. The network lasts until you choose to end it. If you spend 5 Intellect points, you can contact twenty creatures at once, and for every 1 Intellect point you spend above that, you can add ten more creatures to the network. These larger networks last for ten minutes. Creating a network of twenty or more creatures does require an action to establish contact. Enabler.

○ **Teleportation (6+ Intellect points):** You instantaneously transmit yourself to any location that you have seen or been to, no matter the distance, as long as it is on Earth (or whatever world you're currently on). In addition to the normal options for using Effort, you can choose to use Effort to bring other people with you; each level of Effort used in this way affects up to three additional targets. You must touch any additional targets. Action.

○ **Telling (2 Intellect points):** This ability provides an asset to any tasks for attempting to deceive, persuade, or intimidate. Each use lasts up to a minute; a new use (to switch tasks) replaces the previous use. Action to initiate.

○ **Temporal Acceleration (5 Intellect points):** You or one willing creature you touch moves more quickly through time. The effect lasts for one minute. Everything moves more slowly for the affected character, while to all others, the character seems to move at preternatural speed. The character has an asset on all tasks until the effect ends. After the effect ends, the target is exhausted and disoriented by the experience, hindering all tasks for one hour. Action.

○ **Temporal Dislocation (7 Intellect points):** You disappear and travel up to one hour into the future or the past. While dislocated in time, you perceive events as they transpire from your position using your normal senses, but you can't interact with or change anything. If you project yourself into the past, you remain there for one hour, at which point you've caught up to the present (to anyone with you in the present, you only seem to flicker out of existence for a moment). If you project yourself into the future, you remain there until the present catches up to you (to anyone with you in the present, you vanish for one hour and reappear in the place you left). Action.

○ **Terrifying Gaze (6 Intellect points):** You project a chilling gaze at all living creatures within short range who can see you. Make a separate Intellect attack roll for each target. Success means that the creature is frozen in fear, not moving or taking actions for one minute or until it is attacked. Some creatures without minds (such as robots) might be immune to Terrifying Gaze. Action.

○ **Terrifying Image (6 Intellect points):** You use a bit of subtle telepathy to learn which images would appear terrifying to creatures that you choose within long range. Those images appear within that area and menace the appropriate creatures. Make an Intellect attack roll against each creature you want to affect. Success means the creature flees in terror for one minute, pursued by its nightmares. Failure means the creature ignores the images, which do not hamper it in any way. Action.

○ **Terrifying Presence (2+ Intellect points):** You convince one intelligent target of level 3 or lower that you are its worst nightmare. The target must be within short range and be able to understand you. For as long as you do nothing but speak (you can't even move), the target is paralyzed with fear, runs away, or takes some other action appropriate to the circumstances. In addition to the normal options for using Effort, you can choose to use Effort to increase the maximum level of the target. Thus, to terrorize a level 5 target (two levels above the normal limit), you must apply two levels of Effort. Action.

○ **There's Your Problem:** You are trained in tasks related to figuring out how to solve problems with multiple solutions (like the best way to pack a truck, calm an enraged customer, give a cat a shot of insulin, or find a route through the city for maximum speed). Enabler.

> *The PC and GM should work together to determine what kind of effect, if any, accompanies a use of Teleportation. Does the character step in and out of an exploding blast of vapor? Into a brief wormhole portal? Or is there simply no effect other than simply being gone and somewhere else?*

ABILITIES—T

○ **Thief's Luck:** Luck is not the chaotic ocean of random chance most people believe it to be. If you fail on a task (including an attack roll or a defense roll), you can change the die result to a natural 20. That still might not be enough to succeed if the difficulty is higher than 6. Once you use this ability, it is not available again until after you make a ten-hour recovery roll. (Thief's Luck doesn't work if you roll a natural 1 for an attempted task, unless you also have and use the ability Wrest From Chance.) Enabler.

○ **Think Your Way Out:** When you wish it, you can use points from your Intellect Pool rather than your Might Pool or Speed Pool on any noncombat action. Enabler.

○ **Thinking Ahead (variable Intellect points):** You produce a remedy that removes a negative condition because you've previously spent considerable time thinking ahead and preparing for your current situation. For instance, if another character is poisoned, you produce an antidote, or if they're blinded, you produce a salve that returns sight (assuming they weren't blinded because their eyes were destroyed). The Intellect cost for using this ability is equal to the level of effect or creature that caused the negative condition. Action.

○ **Third Eye (1 Intellect point):** You visualize a place within short range and cast your mind to that place, creating an immobile, invisible sensor for one minute or until you choose to end this ability. While using your third eye, you see through your sensor instead of your eyes using your normal visual abilities. You may perceive the area around your body using your other senses as normal. Action.

○ **Throw (2 Might points):** When you are using Enlarge and deal damage to a creature of your size or smaller with an unarmed attack, you can choose to throw that creature up to 1d20 feet away from you. The creature lands prone. Enabler.

○ **Throw Force Shield:** You can throw your Force Field Shield up to short range as a light ranged weapon. Whether the shield hits or misses, it immediately dissipates and then reforms in your grasp. Enabler.

○ **Thrust (1 Might point):** This is a powerful melee stab. You make an attack and inflict 1 additional point of damage if your weapon has a sharp edge or point. Action.

○ **Thunder Beam (2 Might points):** You direct a beam of focused sound at a target within long range, inflicting 2 points of damage and inducing a resonant destructive wave in their body. Each round after this initial attack, you can make another roll for the destructive wave to inflict an additional 1 point of damage to the target. If you fail this roll, the destructive wave ends. Unlike the initial attack, the destructive wave ignores Armor.

Alternatively, you can set up a destructive resonance in a physical melee weapon for one minute or until you let go of it. All attacks made with the target weapon inflict 1 additional point of damage. Action to initiate.

○ **Time Doppelganger (6+ Intellect points):** A perfect copy of you appears within an immediate distance. This doppelganger is probably a version of you from another timeline or the past. The doppelganger is a level 5 NPC with 15 health. It has your mind and memories, and you control it as if it were you in another body. In effect, while this ability is active, you have two bodies.

If the doppelganger uses any of your abilities that cost points, those points come from your Pools (including spending Effort). Controlling two bodies at once is difficult and distracting; while this ability is active, all tasks performed by you or the doppelganger are hindered. The doppelganger has no equipment other than simple clothing.

It remains for up to one minute, but disappears if killed or if you use an action to dismiss it. If the doppelganger is killed, you take 5 points of damage that ignore Armor, and you lose your next action. If you are killed while the doppelganger is present, you live on as the doppelganger (it becomes your character instead of being an NPC that disappears). In addition to the normal options for using Effort, you can choose to use Effort to increase the duration of this ability; each level of Effort used in this way adds one minute to the doppelganger's existence.

If you also have this ability from another source, you may use either ability, the doppelganger is 1 level higher, and it has 3 additional health. Action.

Wrest from Chance, page 200

Enlarge, page 135

Force Field Shield, page 143

191

> ### FOR THE GM: MANAGING TIME TRAVEL
> Although time travel offers plenty of grist for the storytelling mill, it also brings plenty of complications. If a player chooses the Travels Through Time focus and you allow it, you need to decide whether the character can change history by traveling through time (at least, once they advance to a high-enough tier).
>
> The easiest way to manage time travel is to say that the PC jumps to a different timeline when they move forward or backward through time. Anything they do while displaced in time only affects events on that timeline.
>
> The point the PC left becomes a nexus of many timelines. A character returning to that point might find themselves in their original timeline, in which case nothing they altered in the past affects their present or future, or they might be in a different timeline, where their past actions have had a great effect on the current world.
>
> The biggest benefit of the multiple timelines approach is that it sidesteps the problems of paradoxes. Whenever a paradox would occur, the characters create another timeline instead. So if a PC goes back in time to a point before they were born and kills their young grandparent, they erase themselves from that timeline but not from their own timeline. Thus, the character would continue to exist in the (main) campaign timeline.
>
> You can also use other methods for managing time travel, allowing characters to change past events to create a new future, paradoxes be damned. Or you might have the PCs merely observe, unable to interact with anything outside of the point you decide is the present.
>
> If a time-traveling PC's choice at sixth tier is restricted to the Call Through Time ability instead of Time Travel, many of the issues discussed here never come into play.

Travels Through Time, page 77

Call Through Time, page 118

Time Loop (4 Intellect points): You call yourself from a few moments in the future to help you in the present. On the round you use this ability, your future self appears anywhere you choose within immediate range and takes an action. On the second round, you and your future self both take actions, and your future self's action is eased. On the third round, you and your future self both disappear. On the fourth round, you catch up to your future self, reappear wherever your future self initially appeared in the first round, and can take your actions normally.

Your future self shares your stats, so any damage that either of you takes applies to the same stat Pools. If your future self is killed, you and your future self disappear in the third round (as normal) and you reappear, dead, in the fourth round. Neither you nor your future self can use Time Loop again until you reappear as your future self in the fourth round. Action.

Time Travel (10+ Intellect points): You and up to three willing characters you choose within immediate range travel to a point in time that you specify when you use this ability. The point in time must be within ten years of the present. For each level of Effort applied, you can travel ten more years or bring three more creatures with you. When you appear in the new moment in time, you do so in the same position you were in when you used this ability. Upon arriving at your temporal destination, you and the other time travelers are stunned for one minute. In order to return to your original time, you must use this ability again. Action.

Tinker (1 Intellect point): You make a device do something different from its original purpose. For example, a blaster becomes a bomb. A scanner becomes a signal booster for a radio transmitter. A music player becomes a battery for another device. The effective level of the modified device is 1 lower than normal, and the device is rendered unusable (for its original purpose) until repaired. Action to initiate.

Tool Mastery: When you have an asset from using a tool, the time required to perform the task is cut in half (minimum one round). Enabler.

Total Awareness: You possess such a high level of awareness that it's very difficult to surprise, hide from, or sneak up on you. When you apply a level of Effort to initiative and perception tasks, you gain two free levels of Effort. Enabler.

Totally Chill: Your ten-minute recovery roll takes you only one round. Enabler.

Tough As Nails: When you are impaired or debilitated on the damage track, Might-based tasks and defense rolls you attempt are eased. If you also have Ignore the Pain, make a difficulty 1 Might defense roll when you reach 0 points

In effect, Time Loop lets "you" take an action on the round you use it, two actions on the second round, and zero actions on the third round, and then you're back to normal after that.

Free level of Effort, page 209

Damage track, page 218

Ignore the Pain, page 150

A character can't apply Effort or other abilities to any task accomplished using Tough As Nails.

in all three of your Pools to immediately regain 1 Might point and avoid dying. Each time you attempt to save yourself with this ability before your next ten-hour recovery roll, the task is hindered. Enabler.

O **Tough It Out:** Working for a living has toughened you over time. You have +1 to Armor against any kind of physical damage, even damage that normally ignores Armor. Enabler.

O **Tower of Intellect:** You are trained in Intellect defense tasks. If you are already trained, you are specialized in those tasks instead. Enabler.

O **Tower of Will:** You are trained in Intellect defense tasks and gain +3 points to your Intellect Pool. Enabler.

O **Tracker:** You are trained in following and identifying tracks. Enabler.

O **Trained Basher:** You are trained in using the stone fists from your Golem Body as a medium weapon. Enabler.

O **Trained Excavator:** You are trained in perception, climbing, and salvaging tasks. Enabler.

O **Trained Gunner:** You can choose from one of two benefits. Either you are trained in using guns, or you have the Spray ability (which costs 2 Speed points): If a weapon has the ability to fire rapid shots without reloading (usually called a rapid-fire weapon, such as an automatic pistol), you can spray multiple shots around your target to increase the chance of hitting. This move uses 1d6 + 1 rounds of ammo (or all the ammo in the weapon, if it has less than the number rolled). The attack roll is eased. If the attack is successful, it deals 1 less point of damage than normal. Enabler (being trained in using guns) or action (Spray).

O **Trained Interlocutor:** Through wit, charm, humor, and grace (or sometimes rudeness, threatening posture, and obscenity), you're better able to talk others into what you want. You are trained in all interactions. Enabler.

O **Trained Slayer:** You are trained in using swords. Enabler.

O **Trained Swimmer:** While underwater, you are trained in escaping, perception, sneaking, and swimming tasks, as well as in tasks to identify aquatic creatures and geography. Enabler.

O **Trained Without Armor:** You are trained in Speed defense tasks when not wearing armor. Enabler.

O **Transcend the Script (5 Intellect points):** Whether they are lines you wrote, acted, reported on, or otherwise incorporated into your talent, you compose an oratory on the fly that is so wonderful that even you believe it. For each ally who hears it (and you too), a task attempted within the next hour is eased by two steps. Action.

O **Trapfinder (3+ Intellect points):** You find any traps (like a floor that would give way beneath you) or mechanical triggers to a trap or defense system that might pose a threat. You can do this without setting them off and in lieu of making a roll to find them. This ability can find traps of level 4 or below. In addition to the normal options for using Effort, you can choose to use Effort to increase the level of traps that can be found by 2, so using two levels of Effort can find all traps of level 8 or below. Action.

O **Trapster:** You are trained in creating simple traps for human-sized or smaller targets, especially many varieties of deadfalls and snares using natural objects from the surrounding environment. When you lay a trap, decide whether you want to hold the victim in place (a snare) or inflict damage (a deadfall). Creating a snare is a difficulty 3 task, while the difficulty of creating a deadfall is equal to the number of points of damage you want it to inflict. For example, if you want to inflict 4 points of damage, that's a difficulty 4 task (the training that comes with this ability eases the task).

On a success, you create your one-use trap in about one minute, and it is considered level 3 for the purposes of avoiding detection before it is sprung and for a victim trying to struggle free (if a snare). Action to initiate, one minute or one hour to complete.

O **Travel Skills:** You are trained in two skills in which you are not already trained. Choose two of the following: navigation, riding, running, piloting, or vehicle driving. You can select this ability multiple times. Each time you select it, you must choose two different skills. Enabler.

When a character uses Transcend the Script, ask the player to provide a broad overview of what their character is doing that is so amazing that others are inspired.

Golem Body, page 145

Spray, page 185

○ **Traverse the Worlds (8+ Intellect points):** You instantaneously transmit yourself to another planet, dimension, plane, or level of reality. You must know that the destination exists; the GM will decide if you have enough information to confirm its existence and the level of difficulty to reach the destination. In addition to the normal options for using Effort, you can choose to use Effort to bring other people with you; each level of Effort used in this way affects up to three additional targets. You must touch any additional targets. Action.

○ **Trick Driver:** While driving a car, truck, or motorcycle, your Might Edge, Speed Edge, and Intellect Edge increase by 1. When you make a recovery roll while driving, you recover 5 additional points. When you attempt a driving task or an extreme trick—such as jumping a ravine or other vehicle, spinning in the air, landing safely on another vehicle, and so on—the task is eased. Enabler.

○ **Trick Shot (2 Speed points):** As part of the same action, you make a ranged attack against two targets that are within immediate range of each other. Make a separate attack roll against each target. The attack rolls are hindered. Action.

○ **True Defender (6 Might or Intellect points):** This ability functions as the Devoted Defender ability, except the benefit applies to up to three characters you choose. If you choose just one character, you become specialized in the tasks described under the Devoted Defender ability. Action to initiate.

Devoted Defender, page 128

○ **True Guardian (2 Might or Intellect points):** When you stand guard as your action, allies within immediate range of you gain an asset to their defense tasks. This lasts until the end of your next turn. Enabler.

Guarding, page 228

○ **True Necromancy (8+ Intellect points):** This ability works like the Necromancy ability except that it creates a level 5 creature. Action to animate.

Minor effect, page 211
Major effect, page 212
Necromancy, page 165

○ **True Senses:** You can see in complete darkness up to 50 feet (15 m) as if it were dim light. You recognize holograms, disguises, optical illusions, sound mimicry, and other such tricks (for all senses) for what they are. Enabler.

○ **Trust to Luck (3 Intellect points):** Sometimes, you've just got to roll the dice and hope things add up in your favor. When you use Trust to Luck, roll a d6. On any even result, the task you're attempting is eased by two steps. On a roll of 1, the task is hindered. Enabler.

○ **Tumbling Moves (5 Speed points):** When you use an action to move, Speed defense rolls are eased until the end of your next turn. Enabler.

○ **Twist of Fate:** Experience has taught you a lot, including that sometimes luck is something that you have to make for yourself. When you roll a 1, you can reroll. You must use the new result, even if it's another 1. Enabler.

○ **Twisting the Knife (4 Speed points):** In a round after successfully striking a foe with a melee weapon, you can opt to automatically deal standard damage to the foe with that same weapon without any modifiers (2 points for a light weapon, 4 points for a medium weapon, or 6 points for a heavy weapon). Action.

○ **Two Things at Once (6 Intellect points):** The ultimate test: you divide your attention and take two separate actions this round. Enabler.

ABILITIES—U

○ **Ultra Enhancement:** You gain +1 to Armor and +5 to each of your three stat Pools. Enabler.

○ **Unarmed Fighting Style:** You are trained in unarmed attacks. Enabler.

○ **Unarmored Fighter:** While unarmored, you are trained in Speed defense tasks. Enabler.

○ **Uncanny Luck (4 Speed points):** When you roll for a task and succeed, roll again. If the second number rolled is higher than the first, you get a minor effect. If you roll the same number again, you get a major effect. If you have Uncanny Luck from another source or a similar ability, it's your choice (no roll required) whether you get a minor effect, a major effect, or a free activation of one of your tier 1–3 focus abilities. Enabler.

○ **Understanding (1 Intellect point):** You observe or study a creature or object. Your next interaction with that creature or object gains one asset. Action.

Abilities—T–U

○ **Underworld Contacts:** You know many people in a variety of communities who engage in illegal activities. These people are not necessarily your friends and might not be trustworthy, but they recognize you as a peer. You and the GM should work out the details of your underworld contacts. Enabler.

○ **Undo (5 Intellect points):** You turn back time a few seconds, effectively undoing a single creature's most recent action. That creature can then immediately repeat the same action or try something different. Action.

○ **Unexpected Betrayal:** Within a round or two of successfully using Enthrall, Fast Talk, or a similar ability on a target within short range, the first attack you make on that target is eased by two steps. Once you use Unexpected Betrayal on a target, using your abilities or attempting simple persuasion on that target is permanently hindered by two steps. Enabler.

○ **Unmovable (3 Might points):** You avoid being knocked down, pushed back, or moved against your will as long as you are upright and able to take actions. Enabler.

○ **Unraveling Consumption:** You can drain energy from a living creature by touching it and concentrating for a minute or more. Each minute you spend in contact with and concentrating on the creature deals it 1 point of damage (ignores Armor) and restores 1 point to your Might or Speed Pool. Because of the extended contact required for this ability, normally you can use it only on a willing or helpless creature. If the creature takes enough damage to knock it unconscious or kill it, it crumbles into ash, dust, or some other inert material. Action to initiate.

○ **Untouchable (6 Intellect points):** You change your phase state for the next minute so that you can't affect or be affected by normal matter or energy. Only mental attacks and special transdimensional energies, devices, or abilities can affect you, but likewise you can't attack, touch, or otherwise affect anything. Action to initiate.

○ **Untouchable While Moving (4 Intellect points):** You change your phase state for the next minute so that you can't affect or be affected by normal matter or energy, as long as you move at least an immediate distance each round while phased. If you don't move on your turn, the effect ends. While you are phased, only mental attacks and special transdimensional energies, devices, or abilities can affect you, but likewise you can't attack, touch, or otherwise affect anything. Action to initiate.

○ **Up to Speed:** If you do nothing but move for three actions in a row, you accelerate greatly and can move up to 200 mph (about 2,000 feet each round) for up to ten minutes (about 35 miles), after which you must stop and make a recovery roll. (Move up to 322 kph [about 600 m each round] for up to ten minutes [about 56 km].) Enabler.

○ **Use Senses of Others (4 Intellect points):** You can see, hear, smell, touch, and taste through the senses of anyone with whom you have telepathic contact by using Telepathic or similar abilities. You can attempt to use this ability on a willing or unwilling target within long range; an unwilling target can try to resist. You don't need to see the target, but you must know that it's within range. Your shared senses last ten minutes. Action to establish.

○ **Using the Environment (4 Intellect points):** You find some way to use the environment to your advantage in a fight. For the next ten minutes, attack rolls and Speed defense rolls are eased. Action to initiate.

○ **Using What's Available (4 Intellect points):** If you have the time and the freedom to scrounge for everyday materials in your environment, you can fashion a temporary asset that will aid you once to accomplish a specific task. For example, if you need to climb a wall, you could create some sort of climbing assistance device; if you need to break out of a cell, you can find something to use as a lockpick; if you need to create a small distraction, you could put together something to make a loud bang and flash; and so on. The asset lasts for a maximum of one minute, or until used for the intended purpose. One minute to assemble materials; action to create asset.

○ **Usurp Cypher:** Choose one cypher that you carry. The cypher must have an effect that is not instantaneous. You destroy the cypher and gain its power, which functions for you continuously. You can choose a cypher when you gain this ability, or you can wait and make the choice later. However, once you usurp a cypher's power, you cannot later switch to a different cypher—the usurping ability works only once. Action to initiate.

Enthrall, page 136
Fast Talk, page 138
Telepathic, page 189

ABILITIES—V

Vacuum Skilled: You are trained in two of the following skills: vacuum welding, algae farming, ecosystem design, circuit design, spacecraft maintenance and repair, or some similar skill related to traveling and colonizing planets, moons, and stations located in the solar system. Enabler.

Vanish (2 Intellect points): You become invisible for a short amount of time. While invisible, you have an asset on stealth and Speed defense tasks. The invisibility ends at the end of your next turn, or if you do something to reveal your presence or position—attacking, using an ability, moving a large object, and so on. Action.

Verbal Misdirection (2+ Intellect points): With fast talk and bewildering words, you can confuse and distract anyone that you're speaking with, giving you an asset on social interactions with that person for ten minutes. In addition to the normal options for using Effort, you can choose to use Effort to affect additional creatures (one per level of Effort). Enabler.

Versatile Mind: When you make a Speed defense roll, you can use your Intellect in place of your Speed. Enabler.

Very Long Sprinting: When you use Phase Sprint, you can travel up to a very long distance as your action instead of a long distance. Enabler.

Vigilance (2 Intellect points): You take a cautious approach to combat, focusing more on protecting yourself than on hurting your opponents. While this ability is active, you gain an asset on Speed defense rolls against melee and ranged attacks, and your melee and ranged attacks are hindered. This effect lasts for as long as you wish, but it ends if no combat is taking place within range of your senses. Action to initiate.

Vigilant (5 Might points): When affected by an attack or effect that would daze or stun you, you are not dazed or stunned. Enabler.

Vindictive Performance (5 Intellect points): When you tell a joke, perform a song or poem, draw a picture, relate an anecdote, or otherwise provide entertainment, you can select one individual from the audience who is able to understand you. During your performance, you heap indirect but biting derision on this target.

If you succeed, the target doesn't realize that they've become the victim of your performance until you wrap up the entertainment at a moment you choose in a way that strikes home. The target suffers 6 points of Intellect damage (ignores Armor) and loses their next turn. One or more actions to initiate.

Void Wings (3 Intellect points): Swirling ribbons of weird matter grasp you and lift you up, allowing you to fly for one round as quickly as you can move. Enabler.

ABILITIES—W

Walk Through Walls (2 Intellect points): You can slowly pass through physical barriers at a rate of 1 inch (2.5 cm) per round (minimum of one round to pass through any barrier). You can't act (other than moving) or perceive anything until you pass entirely through the barrier. You can't pass through energy barriers. Action.

Wall of Lightning (6 Intellect points): You create a barrier of crackling electricity up to 2,500 square feet (230 sq. m) in size, shaped as you wish. The wall is a level 7 barrier. Anyone within immediate distance of the wall automatically takes 10 points of damage. The wall lasts for one hour. Action to create.

Wall With Teeth: You inflict 2 additional points of damage with all attacks when using your Living Wall ability. Enabler.

Ward: You have a shield of energy around you at all times that helps deflect attacks. You gain +1 to Armor. Enabler.

Warding Shield: You have +1 to Armor while you are using a shield. Enabler.

Water Adaptation: You can breathe water as easily as you breathe air. Enabler.

Weapon and Body (5 Speed points): After making a melee weapon or ranged weapon attack, you follow up with a punch or kick as an additional attack, all as part of the same action in one round. The two attacks can be directed at different foes. Make a separate attack roll for each attack. You remain limited by the amount of Effort you can apply on one action. Anything that modifies your attack or damage applies to both attacks, unless it is tied specifically to your weapon. Action.

Phase Sprint, page 170

Living Wall, page 158

Cautious Adepts rely on Ward. Depending on what you work out with your GM, the energy shield might be completely invisible, visible only when you are attacked, always visible as a faint glimmer surrounding you, or something else.

○ **Weapon Crafter:** You are trained in crafting tasks associated with your chosen weapon. For instance, if your weapon is a bow, you are trained in tasks related to crafting bows and fletching arrows; if your weapon is a sword, you are trained in tasks for forging swords and sharpening blades; and so on. Enabler.

○ **Weapon Defense:** While your chosen weapon is in your hand(s), you are trained in Speed defense rolls. Enabler.

○ **Weapon Master:** You inflict an additional 1 point of damage with your chosen weapon. Enabler.

○ **Weaponization:** One light or medium melee weapon of your choice is built into your body, and you are trained in using it. The weapon is concealed until you wish to use it. Enabler.

○ **Wear It Well:** When you wear armor of any kind, you gain an additional +1 to Armor. Enabler.

○ **Weather the Vicissitudes:** Helping your friends means being able to stand up to everything the world throws at you. You have +1 to Armor. Also, you resist heat, cold, and similar extremes and have an additional +1 to Armor against ambient damage or other damage that would normally ignore Armor. Enabler.

○ **Weight of the World (6+ Intellect points):** You can increase a target's weight dramatically. The target is pulled to the ground and can't move physically under its own power for one minute. The target must be within short range. In addition to the normal options for using Effort, you can choose to use Effort to affect additional creatures (one per level of Effort). Action.

○ **Weightless Shot:** You have a sixth sense when it comes to lining up trajectories and moving in low-gravity and zero-gravity environments, which also translates to making ranged attacks. When you hit a target with a ranged attack in microgravity conditions, you can choose to reduce the damage by 2 points but hit the target in a precise spot. Some of the possible effects include (but are not limited to) the following:

- You punch a hole in the target's suit, so it begins to leak air into the vacuum slowly, or all at once (your choice).
- You hit the reaction mass of the target's maneuvering pack, which means the target can no longer change their trajectory, or they go spinning off in a random direction (your choice).
- You can shoot a spacecraft, and degrade one ship system by one step (systems include engines, weapons, and atmosphere).

Enabler.

○ **Weighty (1 Intellect point):** You briefly increase the weight of a target within short range enough to stop them in their tracks, preventing the target from moving and hindering any attempted tasks on their next turn. Action.

○ **Weird Science Breakthrough (5+ Intellect points):** Your research leads to a breakthrough, and you imbue an object with a truly amazing property, though you can use the item only once. To do so, you must buy spare parts equivalent to an expensive item, have a field science kit (or a permanent lab, if you have access to one), and succeed at a difficulty 4 Intellect-based roll to create a random manifest cypher of up to level 2. The GM decides the nature of the cypher you create. Attempting to create a specified cypher hinders the task by two steps. Creating a cypher does not allow you to surpass your normal cypher limit. In addition to the normal options for using Effort, you can choose to use Effort to increase the level of the cypher you create; each level of Effort increases the level of the cypher and the difficulty of the Intellect task to create it. Action to initiate, one hour to complete.

Some foci, such as Masters Weaponry, have you pick a specific weapon and develop your unusual abilities with that weapon. Masters Weaponry, page 72.

- **Whirlwind of Throws (5 Speed points):** With a large handful of small objects—tiny knives, shuriken, stones, jagged bits of metal, coins, or whatever is on hand—you attack every creature in an immediate area within short range. You must make attack rolls against each target. Each attack is hindered. You inflict 3 points of damage on targets you hit. Action.

- **Wild Camouflage (4 Intellect points):** By drawing your clothing about you just so and using various tricks and your deep knowledge of your surroundings, you become invisible in the wilderness for ten minutes. While you are invisible, this asset eases your stealth and Speed defense tasks by two steps. This effect ends if you do something to reveal your presence or position—attacking, using an ability, moving a large object, and so on. If this occurs, you can regain the remaining invisibility effect by taking an action to focus on hiding your position. Action to initiate or reinitiate.

Orc, page 347

- **The Wild Is on Your Side (5 Intellect points):** While you're in the wilderness, foes within short range are tripped by rocks, tangled in vines, bitten by insects, and distracted or confused by small animals, which hinders all their tasks for ten minutes. Action to initiate.

Recovery roll, page 218

- **Wild Vitality (4 Intellect points):** You attune with the life force of a natural creature (your size or bigger) within long range that you can see. This is a level 2 Intellect task. If you succeed, the creature is not harmed, but through resonance with its wild vitality, you gain several benefits for up to one minute: an asset to all your Might-based tasks (including attacks and defenses), +2 to your Might Edge and Speed Edge, and 2 additional points of damage on all successful melee attacks. Action to initiate.

- **Wilderness Awareness (4 Intellect points):** Your connection to the natural world extends to a degree that some would call supernatural. While in the wilderness, you can extend your senses up to a mile in any direction and ask the GM a very simple, general question about that area, such as "Where is the orc camp?" or "Is my friend Deithan still alive?" If the answer you seek is not in the area, you receive no information. Action.

- **Wilderness Encouragement (3 Intellect points):** While in the wilderness, or when talking about your time in the wilderness, your stirring words of encouragement grant a target within short range that can understand you 1d6 points to one Pool. You can't use this ability on the same creature again until they've made a recovery roll. Action.

○ **Wilderness Explorer:** While taking any action (including fighting) in the wild, you ignore any penalties due to natural causes such as tall grass, thick brush, rugged terrain, weather, and so on. Enabler.

○ **Wilderness Life:** You are trained in two of the following: climbing, swimming, navigation, or identifying plants and creatures. Enabler.

○ **Wilderness Lore:** You are trained in wilderness navigation and in identifying plants and creatures. Enabler.

○ **Will of a Leader (9 Intellect points):** You harden your allies' dedication and capabilities. Each ally within immediate range gains +1 Edge to one stat of their choice for one hour. You also gain this benefit to one stat of your choice. Action.

○ **Will of Legend:** You are immune to attacks that would captivate, mesmerize, charm, or otherwise influence your mind. Enabler.

○ **Willing Sacrifice:** When you take an attack meant for another character, you know how to take the attack in a way that minimizes its effect. The attack automatically strikes you, but instead of taking 1 additional point of damage, you take 1 less point of damage (to a minimum of 1 point). Additionally, you can take more than one attack in a given round provided that all the attacks were originally meant for one target. Enabler.

○ **Wind Armor (1 Intellect point):** When you wish it, a cyclone of wind surrounds your body for ten minutes, giving you +1 to Armor and an additional +2 to Armor against physical projectile weapons specifically. While the cyclone is active, you feel no discomfort from the wind, and you can interact with other creatures and objects normally because the wind flow automatically diverts to enable such interaction. Enabler.

○ **Wind Chariot (7+ Intellect points):** You summon winds that pick you up and allow you to fly for up to a long distance each round in combat or with an overland speed of up to 200 miles per hour (320 kph) for up to ten hours. For each level of Effort you apply, you can bring one ally of about your size with you through the air or increase the duration of the effect by one hour. Action to initiate.

○ **Windrider (4+ Intellect points):** You summon winds that pick you up and allow you to fly for one minute at a rate of up to a long distance each round. For each level of Effort you apply, you can carry one ally of about your size with you through the air or increase the duration of the effect by one minute. Action to initiate.

○ **Windwracked Traveler (4+ Intellect points):** You condense a wide wing of dark matter that can carry you through the air for a period of up to one hour. For each level of Effort applied, you can add one hour to the duration or carry one additional creature of your size or smaller. You must touch the additional creatures for them to be tucked under your wing. They must remain relatively still while the wing lasts or they will fall. In terms of overland movement, you fly at about 20 miles (32 km) per hour and are not affected by terrain. Action to initiate.

○ **Wings of Fire (4 Intellect points):** While your Shroud of Flame is active, you can spread wings of fire and can levitate, moving at a rate of up to 20 feet (6 m) per round in any direction for one minute. You can also take one other non-movement action on your turn. Action.

○ **Winter Gauntlets:** When you use Frost Touch, you inflict an additional 3 points of damage if you touch a creature, or an additional 2 points of damage if you infuse a weapon. In addition, damaged targets are frozen in place (if standing on a solid surface) and can't move from their location until they use an action to break free. The target can still attack and defend. Action for touch; enabler for weapon.

○ **Word of Command (6 Intellect points + level 6 cypher):** You utter a word so powerful that to fully invest it, you sacrifice a cypher in your possession that is level 6 or higher. You issue the word to one creature within long range that you can see. The affected target must obey the command for several hours before it is free to act as it wishes. Targets that are attacked while under the effect of the command can defend themselves. Typical commands include "retreat," "calm," "come," and "stay." The GM decides how the target acts once a command is given. Action.

Shroud of Flame, page 183

Two characters attempting to draw an attack at the same time cancel each other out.

Frost Touch, page 144

In some settings, using Word of Death may gradually stain a character's soul, making them vulnerable to future temptations or evil creatures they might otherwise be able to ignore.

- **Word of Death (5+ Intellect points):** Your attack is the utterance of a magic word so terrible that it snuffs the life from a living target within short range. The target must be level 1. In addition to the normal options for using Effort, you can choose to use Effort to increase the maximum level of the target. Thus, to kill a level 5 target (four levels above the normal limit), you must apply four levels of Effort. Action.

- **Work the Friendship (4 Intellect points):** You know just what to say to draw a little extra effort from an ally. This grants one creature you choose within short range an additional, immediate action, which it can take out of turn. The creature uses the additional action however it wishes. Action.

- **Wormhole (6 Intellect points):** You create a doorway through time and space. The shortcut manifests as a hole in reality large enough to accommodate you and creatures of your size or smaller. One side of the doorway appears anywhere within immediate range, and the other side opens at a spot you choose anywhere within long range. Any character or object moving into one side exits from the other. The door remains open for one minute or until you use an action to close it. Action to initiate.

Healing, page 228

- **Wound Tender:** You are trained in healing. Enabler.

Spirit Accomplice, page 185

- **Wraith Cloak:** At your command, the spirit from your Spirit Accomplice ability wraps itself around you for up to ten minutes. The spirit automatically inflicts 4 points of damage to anyone who tries to touch you or strike you with a melee attack. While the wraith cloak is active, all tasks to evade the perceptions of others are eased. Enabler.

- **Wreck:** Using two hands, you wield a weapon or a tool with a powerful swing. (If fighting unarmed, this attack is made with both fists or both feet together.) When using this as an attack, you take a −1 penalty to the attack roll, and you inflict 3 additional points of damage. When attempting to damage an object or barrier, you are trained in the task. Action.

- **Wrest From Chance:** If you roll a natural 1 on a d20, you can reroll the die. If you reroll, you avoid a GM intrusion—unless you roll a second 1—and might succeed on your task. Once you use this ability, it is not available again until after you make a ten-hour recovery roll. Enabler.

ABILITIES—Y

- **You Studied:** To be able to put two and two together to reach a deduction, you have to know a few things. You are trained in two areas of knowledge of your choosing (as long as they are not physical actions or combat related) or specialized in one area. Enabler.

ABILITIES—Z

- **Zero Dark Eyes:** Some people's eyes are degraded by constantly playing games. And maybe that'll happen to you, but not yet. You're still young and instead of degrading, your vision is actually better thanks to all your practice. You can see in very dim light as though it were bright light. You can see in total darkness as if it were very dim light. Enabler.

Chapter 10
EQUIPMENT

Equipment in the Cypher System plays only a small role. It's far more important to focus on what you can do than on what you have. Still, sometimes it's important to know if you've got enough rope, or what kind of gun your space pilot has at their hip.

CURRENCY AND PRICES

Dollars, pounds, euros, credits, gold pieces, Martian solval beads, Corso moons and stars, bottle caps—a lot of different currencies might be used in your game, depending on the setting and the genre. You should use whatever you like. In the Cypher System rules, we talk in generalities rather than specifics. Not unlike saying immediate or short distance rather than giving precise numbers, we talk about goods and services in terms of inexpensive, moderately priced, expensive, very expensive, or exorbitant.

The GM can figure out what those things mean in their setting. In a fantasy setting, an inexpensive item might be 1 or 2 copper pennies, while an expensive item might require gold on the table. The exact amount can vary, and in many campaigns, the exact amount will matter. The GM will develop a detailed price list for their setting, and players will track their money on their character sheets to determine what they can afford, often ignoring the terms inexpensive, moderately priced, and so on.

But some GMs might want to keep things simple and use only the general terms, indicating currency just as flavor now and then. In a space opera game, where the PCs are the crew of a starship blazing about the galaxy in search of adventure and profit, fuel and upkeep for the ship might be expensive. Hauling a few passengers from Epsilon Eridani back to Earth might earn enough to purchase six expensive items but cost the equivalent of two expensive items, leaving the crew with the means to refuel and maintain the ship for two further voyages. In such a game, where money only means keeping the ship flying, no one has to talk in specific amounts. Characters might refer to "galactic credits" or something similar, but amounts might not be tracked on the character sheets.

For any game set in the present day, catalogs or shopping websites can provide prices for any kind of item that you might need.

PRICE CATEGORIES

There are five price categories for goods and services.

An **inexpensive item** is something that common people buy. A simple meal or a drink in the bar. A pen and some paper. A book or magazine.

A **moderately priced item** is something that common people buy, but not too often and not in great quantities. A small piece of furniture. A major entertainment. An expensive meal. A new outfit.

An **expensive item** is something that would strain a common person's finances. Rent on a simple apartment. A major piece of furniture. A very nice outfit. The cost to travel a long distance (if appropriate to the setting).

A **very expensive item** is probably out of the reach of most people except in very special circumstances. Jewelry. Luxury furnishings.

An **exorbitant item** is something only the very rich can afford. A very nice house. A ship. Extremely expensive jewelry or art.

Think of the categories as powers of 10. That is to say, a moderately priced item is ten times more costly than an inexpensive item. An expensive item is ten times more costly than a moderately priced item, and thus 100 times the cost of something inexpensive. A very expensive item is ten times the cost of an expensive one, 100 times the cost of a moderate one, and 1,000 times the cost of an inexpensive one. An exorbitant item is priced ten times beyond that.

USING THE PRICE CATEGORIES

Regardless of how precise you want to be with prices and currency, you can use the price categories in a variety of ways.

It's easy for a GM to say to a player "You can afford two extra moderately priced things at the start of the game." The player can look on the list and pick two moderately priced items without worrying about their cost. Plus, this approach makes it clear that they get two items, not twenty inexpensive items or one more expensive item that perhaps would not be appropriate for a starting character. The categories make it easy to lump similar items together.

The GM can also say "You can have whatever inexpensive items you want, and don't worry about the cost." At higher tiers, when the PCs have more wealth, followers, and so on, the GM can do this with moderate or even expensive items. This allows the group to skip over playing through a shopping trip to get supplies, and players don't have to track prices down to the last coin.

Finally, the categories can be shorthand when evaluating loot, dividing up the spoils among the PCs, and resolving other story-based occurrences that crop up in the game without dealing in the minutiae of exact prices. This is of particular use in high-powered games where the PCs are rich and powerful.

ARMOR

Characters expecting danger frequently wear armor. Even the simplest protective covering helps against stabs and cuts, and more sophisticated or heavier armor protects against graver threats.

You can wear only one type of armor at a time—you cannot wear chainmail hauberk and scale armor together, for example. However, Armor bonuses from multiple sources combine to provide a total Armor rating. For example, if you have subdermal implants that give you +1 to Armor, a force field that offers another +1 to Armor, and beastskin that grants +2 to Armor, you have a total of +4 to Armor.

In general, light armor is a moderately priced item, medium armor is expensive, and heavy armor is very expensive. The genre chapters offer more specific details on the kinds of armor available in a given setting. Keep in mind that in many genres, it's quite odd, at best, to run around in armor tougher than a leather jacket.

USING ARMOR

Anyone can wear any armor, but it can be taxing. Wearing armor increases the cost of using a level of Effort when attempting a Speed-based action. So if you're wearing light armor and want to use two levels of Effort on a Speed-based roll to run across difficult terrain, it costs 7 points from your Speed Pool rather than 5 (3 for the first level of Effort, plus 2 for the second level of Effort, plus 1 per level for wearing light armor). Edge reduces the overall cost as normal. If you are not experienced with a certain type of armor but wear it anyway, this cost is further increased by 1. Having experience with a type of armor is called being practiced with the armor.

Armor	Speed Effort Additional Cost Per Level
Light	+1
Medium	+2
Heavy	+3

In some settings, even the generalization offered by the pricing categories might be too specific or cumbersome. In many superhero games, for example, prices are relatively moot. After saving the city, typical superheroes don't worry about paying rent or how much dinner will cost. (On the other hand, in a grittier superhero game, maybe that's exactly what they worry about.)

Some characters have abilities that reduce or even negate the costs of wearing armor.

EQUIPMENT

WEAPONS

Not all characters are familiar with all weapons. Warriors know their way around most types, but Explorers prefer light or medium weapons, and Adepts and Speakers usually stick to light weapons. If you wield a weapon that you have no experience with, an attack with that weapon is hindered. Having experience with a weapon is called being practiced with the weapon.

Light weapons inflict only 2 points of damage, but attacks with them are eased because they are fast and easy to use. Light weapons are punches, kicks, knives, handaxes, darts, very small pistols, and so on. Weapons that are particularly small are light weapons.

Medium weapons inflict 4 points of damage. Medium weapons include broadswords, battleaxes, maces, crossbows, spears, typical handguns, light rifles, sawed-off shotguns, and so on. Most weapons are medium. Anything that could be used in one hand (even if it's often used in two hands, such as a quarterstaff or spear) is a medium weapon.

Heavy weapons inflict 6 points of damage, and you must use two hands to attack with them. Heavy weapons are huge swords, great hammers, massive axes, halberds, heavy crossbows, rifles, regular shotguns, assault rifles, and so on. Anything that must be used in two hands is a heavy weapon.

Weapon	Damage
Light	2 points (attack eased)
Medium	4 points
Heavy	6 points

In general, light weapons are moderately priced items, medium weapons are expensive, and heavy weapons are very expensive. Ammunition for a ranged weapon is inexpensive. The genre chapters offer more specific details on weapons available in a given setting. Keep in mind that in many genres, it's not acceptable to run around carrying dangerous weapons.

EXPLOSIVE WEAPONS

Bombs, grenades, missiles, and other explosives operate differently than other weapons. They affect all targets within an area (usually an immediate area) and inflict damage to all of them. A separate attack roll is required for each (or a Speed defense roll if the PCs are the targets of such an attack), although to simplify, the player can make one attack roll and compare it to the difficulty to attack each target. Usually, even if the attack roll fails (or the Speed defense roll succeeds), the targets still suffer a smaller amount of damage, often 1 point.

Explosives like grenades can be thrown a short distance. Otherwise, another launcher weapon is needed to project them a long distance (or farther).

MISCELLANEOUS ITEMS AND SERVICES

Although the types of items for sale vary greatly based on the setting, a few things are always present, like food, lodging, and clothing. However, these goods and services can span the price categories. For example, you can get an inexpensive meal, a moderately priced meal, an expensive meal, and so on. An inexpensive meal is light and probably not very nutritious. An expensive meal is available only in nice restaurants in certain locations. An exorbitant meal is probably a feast for a crowd, with the finest foods and drink available.

Nightly lodging is similar, although the bottom end starts out worse. An inexpensive night's lodging is probably a flea-ridden mat on the floor of a room filled with other lodgers. Typical lodging (a private room with a decent bed) is probably in the moderately priced range. Very expensive lodging might be a suite of rooms with delicious meals and personal services (such as massages and grooming) included.

Inexpensive clothing is just a step up from rags, but moderately priced clothing is decent enough. For a formal party, you'd want expensive clothing. The very rich likely wear very expensive clothing most of the time, and exorbitant clothing (and jewelry) when they go to their elite galas.

Other sorts of miscellaneous items can be found in the genre chapters.

Some explosives create smoke, poison gas, flame, or other effects.

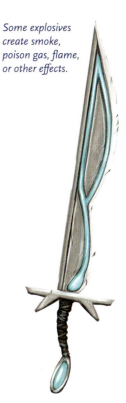

Level of Equipment
Mundane equipment is about level 4—less if of inferior quality or materials, more if of superior quality or materials. This means that in a setting based on the distant past, the default level might be 3, while in the future it might be 5 or 6. So an average serf's tool in the Dark Ages is level 3, easily broken, while an average tool on a space station is level 6, made of advanced polymers.

For GM information on artifacts, see page 421.

Repair, page 227

> ## CONTEXT
> Context in pricing is important. A match is almost worthless in a modern setting (many establishments give away books of them), but consider how valuable it would be in 1000 BC. Likewise, a sword might be expensive in a fantasy setting, but mostly worthless in the far future other than as a collector's item (although it hurts just the same if you're hit with it), making it either inexpensive or very expensive. A motorcycle would be expensive in a modern setting, moderate at best in a future setting—again, unless it's a collector's item—and utterly priceless if it somehow found its way to 1000 BC (where it would be an artifact). Maybe in a fantasy setting, assuming a fair bit of magic, the same motorcycle would merely be exorbitant compared to the flying carpets and whatnot that are available.
>
> This is why you can't have a standardized price list that applies to every setting, genre, and time period. It's all about context.

CYPHERS

Cyphers can sometimes be physical items like equipment, but they work very differently. To be entirely accurate, cyphers might have the veneer of equipment, but don't fall into the trap of confusing the two. Cyphers are far more akin to PC special abilities than to gear. In a fantasy game, they might be potions, scrolls, or charms. In a science fiction game, cyphers might be interesting throwaway devices or alien crystals of unknown providence. In other games, they might just represent good fortune or sudden inspiration. See chapter 24 for more details.

ARTIFACTS

Artifacts are more powerful than equipment and can't simply be purchased. The genre chapters offer a few sample artifacts appropriate for various settings.

Each artifact has a level and a rate of power depletion. When an artifact is used or activated, the player rolls the designated die (1d6, 1d10, 1d20, or 1d100). If the die shows the depletion number(s), the item works, but that is its last use. A depletion entry of "—" means that the artifact never depletes, and an entry of "automatic" means that it can be used only once.

Depowered artifacts can sometimes be recharged using the repair rules, depending on the item's nature. Other special abilities can also repower an expended item, but probably for only one use.

FINDING, IDENTIFYING, AND USING ARTIFACTS

Characters can sometimes find artifacts while on adventures. They might be in ancient ruins, either intact or in need of manipulation to get them working. They could have been stolen from well-guarded military installations. They might be granted as rewards or taken from fallen foes. Sometimes they can even be purchased from a specialized source, but this occurs more rarely than most PCs would probably like.

After the characters find an artifact, identifying it is a separate Intellect task. The GM sets the difficulty of the task, but it is usually equal to the artifact's level. Identifying it takes fifteen minutes to three hours. If the PCs can't identify an artifact, they can bring it to an expert to be identified or, if desired, traded or sold.

Characters can attempt to use an artifact that has not been identified, which is usually an Intellect task equal to the artifact's level + 2. Failure might mean that the PCs can't figure out how to use the artifact or they use it incorrectly (GM's discretion). Of course, even if characters use an unidentified artifact correctly the first time, they have no idea what the effect might be.

Once characters identify an artifact, using it for the first time requires an additional Intellect action; this process is far more complex than pushing a button. It can involve manipulating touchscreens, reciting the proper arcane words, or anything else that fits the setting. The GM sets the difficulty, but it is usually equal to the artifact's level.

Part 2
RULES

Chapter 11: RULES OF THE GAME   206
Chapter 12: EXPERIENCE POINTS   237

Chapter 11
RULES OF THE GAME

Cypher System games are played in the joint imagination of all the players, including the GM. The GM sets the scene, the players state what their characters attempt to do, and the GM determines what happens next. The rules and the dice help make the game run smoothly, but it's the people, not the rules or the dice, that direct the action and determine the story—and the fun. If a rule gets in the way or detracts from the game, the players and the GM should work together to change it.

Task Difficulty table, page 8, 208

This is how you play the Cypher System:

1. The player tells the GM what they want to do. This is a character action.

2. The GM determines if that action is routine (and therefore works without needing a roll) or if there's a chance of failure.

Demigod, page 321

3. If there is a chance of failure, the GM determines which stat the task uses (Might, Speed, or Intellect) and the task's difficulty—how hard it will be on a scale from 1 (really easy) to 10 (basically impossible).

Might, page 14
Speed, page 14
Intellect, page 14

4. The player and the GM determine if anything about the character—such as training, equipment, special abilities, or various actions—can modify the difficulty up or down by one or more steps. If these modifications reduce the difficulty to less than 1, the action is routine (and therefore works with no roll needed).

Training, page 207
Equipment, page 201
Special abilities, page 18

5. If the action still isn't routine, the GM uses its difficulty to determine the target number—how high the player must roll to succeed at the action (see the Task Difficulty table). The GM doesn't have to tell the player what the target number is, but they can give the player a hint, especially if the character would reasonably know if the action was easy, average, difficult, or impossible.

6. The player rolls a d20. If they roll equal to or higher than the target number, the character succeeds.

That's it. That's how to do anything, whether it's identifying an unknown device, calming a raging drunk, climbing a treacherous cliff, or battling a demigod. Even if you ignored all the other rules, you could still play the Cypher System with just this information. The key features here are: character actions, determining task difficulty, and determining modifications.

TAKING ACTION

Each character gets one turn each round. On a character's turn, they can do one thing—an action. All actions fall into one of three categories: Might, Speed, or Intellect (just like the three stats). Many actions require die rolls—rolling a d20.

KEY CONCEPTS

ACTION: Anything a character does that is significant—punch a foe, leap a chasm, activate a device, use a special power, and so on. Each character can take one action in a round.

CHARACTER: Any creature in the game capable of acting, whether it is a player character (PC) run by a player or a nonplayer character (NPC) run by the game master (GM). In the Cypher System, even bizarre creatures, sentient machines, and living energy beings can be "characters."

DIFFICULTY: A measure of how easy it is to accomplish a task. Difficulty is rated on a scale from 1 (lowest) to 10 (highest). Altering the difficulty to make a task harder is called "hindering." Altering it to make a task easier is called "easing." All changes in difficulty are measured in steps. Difficulty often equates directly with level, so opening a level 3 locked door probably has a difficulty of 3.

EASE: A decrease in a task's difficulty, usually by one step. If something doesn't say how many steps it eases a task, then it reduces the difficulty by one step.

EFFORT: Spending points from a stat Pool to reduce the difficulty of a task. A PC decides whether or not to apply Effort on their turn before the roll is made. NPCs never apply Effort.

HINDER: An increase in a task's difficulty, usually by one step. If something doesn't say how many steps it hinders a task, then it increases the difficulty by one step.

INABILITY: The opposite of trained—you're hindered whenever you attempt a task that you have an inability in. If you also become trained in the task, the training and the inability cancel each other out and you become practiced.

LEVEL: A way to measure the strength, difficulty, power, or challenge of something in the game. Everything in the game has a level. NPCs and objects have levels that determine the difficulty of any task related to them. For example, an opponent's level determines how hard they are to hit or avoid in combat. A door's level indicates how hard it is to break down. A lock's level determines how hard it is to pick. Levels are rated on a scale from 1 (lowest) to 10 (highest). PC tiers are a little like levels, but they go only from 1 to 6 and mechanically work very differently than levels—for example, a PC's tier does not determine a task's difficulty.

PRACTICED: The normal, unmodified ability to use a skill—not trained, specialized, or an inability. Your type determines what weapon skills you're practiced in; if you aren't practiced with a type of weapon, you have an inability in it.

ROLL: A d20 roll made by a PC to determine whether an action is successful. Although the game occasionally uses other dice, when the text simply refers to "a roll," it always means a d20 roll.

ROUND: A length of time about five to ten seconds long. There are about ten rounds in a minute. When it's really important to track precise time, use rounds. Basically, it's the length of time to take an action in the game, but since everyone more or less acts simultaneously, all characters get to take an action each round.

SPECIALIZED: Having an exceptional amount of skill in a task. Being specialized eases the task by two steps. So, if you are specialized in climbing, all your climbing tasks are eased by two steps.

STAT: One of the three defining characteristics for PCs: Might, Speed, or Intellect. Each stat has two values: Pool and Edge. Your Pool represents your raw, innate ability, and your Edge represents knowing how to use what you have. Each stat Pool can increase or decrease over the course of play—for example, you can lose points from your Might Pool when struck by an opponent, spend points from your Intellect Pool to activate a special ability, or rest to recover points in your Speed Pool after a long day of marching. Anything that damages a stat, restores a stat, or boosts or penalizes a stat affects the stat's Pool.

TASK: Any action that a PC attempts. The GM determines the difficulty of the task. In general, a task is something that you do and an action is you performing that task, but in most cases they mean the same thing.

TRAINED: Having a reasonable amount of skill in a task. Being trained eases the task. For example, if you are trained in climbing, all climbing tasks for you are eased. If you become very skilled at that task, you become specialized instead of trained. You do not need to be trained to attempt a task.

TURN: The part of the round when a character or creature takes its actions. For example, if a Warrior and an Adept are fighting an orc, each round the Warrior takes an action on their turn, the Adept takes an action on their turn, and the orc takes an action on its turn. Some abilities or effects last only one turn, or end when the next turn is started.

Every action performs a task, and every task has a difficulty that determines what number a character must reach or surpass with a die roll to succeed.

Most tasks have a difficulty of 0, which means the character succeeds automatically. For example, walking across a room, opening a door, and throwing a stone into a nearby bucket are all actions, but none of them requires a roll. Actions that are usually difficult or that become difficult due to the situation (such as shooting at a target in a blizzard) have a higher difficulty. These actions usually require a roll.

Some actions require a minimum expenditure of Might, Speed, or Intellect points. If a character cannot spend the minimum number of points needed to complete the action, they automatically fail at the task.

DETERMINING TASK STAT

Every task relates to one of a character's three stats: Might, Speed, or Intellect. Physical activities that require strength, power, or endurance relate to Might. Physical activities that require agility, flexibility, or fast reflexes relate to Speed. Mental activities that require force of will, memory, or mental power relate to Intellect. This means you can generalize tasks into three categories: Might tasks, Speed tasks, and Intellect tasks. You can also generalize rolls into three categories: Might rolls, Speed rolls, and Intellect rolls.

The category of the task or roll determines what kind of Effort you can apply to the roll and may determine how a character's other abilities affect the roll. For example, an Adept may have an ability that makes them better at Intellect rolls, and a Warrior may have an ability that makes them better at Speed rolls.

DETERMINING TASK DIFFICULTY

The most frequent thing a GM does during the game—and probably the most important thing—is set a task's difficulty. To make the job easier, use the Task Difficulty table, which associates a difficulty rating with a descriptive name, a target number, and general guidance about the difficulty.

Every difficulty from 1 to 10 has a target number associated with it. The target number is easy to remember: it's always three times the difficulty. The target number is the minimum number a player needs to roll on a d20 to succeed at the task. Moving up or down on the table is called hindering or easing, which is measured in steps.

For example, reducing a difficulty 5 task to a difficulty 4 task is "easing the difficulty by one step" or just "easing the difficulty" or "easing the task." Most modifiers affect the difficulty rather than the player's roll. This has two consequences:

- Low target numbers such as 3 or 6, which would be boring in most games that use a d20, are not boring in the Cypher System. For example, if you need to roll a 6 or higher, you still have a 25% chance to fail.
- The upper levels of difficulty (7, 8, 9, and 10) are all but impossible because the target numbers are 21 or higher, which you can't roll on a d20. However, it's common for PCs to have abilities or equipment that ease a task and thus lower the target number to something they *can* roll on a d20.

A character's tier does not determine a task's level. Things don't get more difficult just because a character's tier increases—the world doesn't instantly become a more difficult place.

Unless for some reason you tell the players directly, they'll never know if you change an NPC's stats or a task's difficulty on the fly. If you do it to make a better story, that's your purview.

TASK DIFFICULTY

Task Difficulty	Description	Target No.	Guidance
0	Routine	0	Anyone can do this basically every time.
1	Simple	3	Most people can do this most of the time.
2	Standard	6	Typical task requiring focus, but most people can usually do this.
3	Demanding	9	Requires full attention; most people have a 50/50 chance to succeed.
4	Difficult	12	Trained people have a 50/50 chance to succeed.
5	Challenging	15	Even trained people often fail.
6	Intimidating	18	Normal people almost never succeed.
7	Formidable	21	Impossible without skills or great effort.
8	Heroic	24	A task worthy of tales told for years afterward.
9	Immortal	27	A task worthy of legends that last lifetimes.
10	Impossible	30	A task that normal humans couldn't consider (but one that doesn't break the laws of physics).

RULES OF THE GAME

Fourth-tier characters don't deal only with level 4 creatures or difficulty 4 tasks (although a fourth-tier character probably has a better shot at success than a first-tier character does). Just because something is level 4 doesn't necessarily mean it's meant only for fourth-tier characters. Similarly, depending on the situation, a fifth-tier character could find a difficulty 2 task just as challenging as a second-tier character does.

Therefore, when setting the difficulty of a task, the GM should rate the task on its own merits, not on the power of the characters.

MODIFYING THE DIFFICULTY

After the GM sets the difficulty for a task, the player can try to modify it for their character. Any such modification applies only to this particular attempt at the task. In other words, rewiring an electronic door lock normally might be difficulty 6, but since the character doing the work is skilled in such tasks, has the right tools, and has another character assisting them, the difficulty in this instance might be much lower. That's why it's important for the GM to set a task's difficulty without taking the character into account. The character comes in at this step.

By using skills and assets, working together, and—perhaps most important—applying Effort, a character can ease a task by multiple steps to make it easier. Rather than adding bonuses to the player's roll, reducing the difficulty lowers the target number. If they can reduce the difficulty of a task to 0, no roll is needed; success is automatic. (An exception is if the GM decides to use a GM intrusion on the task, in which case the player would have to make a roll at the original difficulty.)

There are three basic ways in which a character can ease a task: skills, assets, and Effort. Each method eases the task by at least one step—never in smaller increments.

SKILLS

Characters may be skilled at performing a specific task. A skill can vary from character to character. For example, one character might be skilled at lying, another might be skilled at trickery, and a third might be skilled in all interpersonal interactions. The first level of being skilled is called being trained, and it eases that task by one step. More rarely, a character can be incredibly skilled at performing a task. This is called being specialized, and it eases the task by two steps instead of one. Skills can never decrease a task by more than two steps—any more than two steps from being trained and specialized don't count.

ASSETS

An asset is anything that helps a character with a task, such as having a really good crowbar when trying to force open a door or being in a rainstorm when trying to put out a fire. Appropriate assets vary from task to task. The perfect awl might help when woodworking, but it won't make a dance performance much better. An asset usually eases a task by one step. Assets can never ease a task by more than two steps—any more than two steps from assets don't count.

EFFORT

A player can apply Effort to ease a task. To do this, the player spends points from the stat Pool that's most appropriate to the task. For example, applying Effort to push a heavy rock off a cliff requires a player to spend points from the character's Might Pool; applying Effort to activate an unusual machine interface requires them to spend points from the character's Intellect Pool. For every level of Effort spent on a task, the task is eased. It costs 3 points from a stat Pool to apply one level of Effort, and it costs 2 additional points for every level thereafter (so it costs 5 points for two levels of Effort, 7 points for three levels of Effort, and so on). A character must spend points from the same stat Pool as the type of task or roll—Might points for a Might roll, Speed points for a Speed roll, or Intellect points for an Intellect roll.

Every character has a maximum level of Effort they can apply to a single task. Effort can never ease a task by more than six steps—any more than six steps from applying Effort doesn't count.

Free Level of Effort: A few abilities give you a free level of Effort (these usually require you to apply at least one level of Effort to a task). In effect, you're getting one more level of Effort than what you paid for. This free level of Effort can exceed the Effort limit for your character, but not the six-step limit for easing a task.

ROLLING THE DIE

To determine success or failure, a player rolls a die (always a d20). If they roll the target number or higher, they succeed. Most of the time, that's the end of it—nothing else needs to be done. Rarely, a character might apply a small modifier to the roll. If they have a +2 bonus when attempting specific actions, they add 2 to the number rolled. However, the original roll matters if it's a special roll.

GM intrusion, page 408

By using skills, assets, and Effort, you can ease a task by a maximum of ten steps.

The important thing to remember is that a skill can reduce the difficulty by no more than two steps, and assets can reduce the difficulty by no more than two steps, regardless of the situation. Thus, no task's difficulty will ever be reduced by more than four steps without using Effort.

Special roll, page 210

If a character applies a modifier to the die roll, it's possible to get a result of 21 or higher, in which case they can attempt a task with a target number above 20. But if there is no possibility for success—if not even rolling a natural 20 (meaning the d20 shows that number) is sufficient to accomplish the task—then no roll is made. Otherwise, characters would have a chance to succeed at everything, even impossible or ridiculous tasks such as climbing moonbeams, throwing elephants, or hitting a target on the opposite side of a mountain with an arrow.

If a character's modifiers add up to +3, treat them as an asset instead. In other words, instead of adding a +3 bonus to the roll, reduce the difficulty by one step. For example, if a Warrior has a +1 bonus to attack rolls from a minor effect, a +1 bonus to attack rolls from a special weapon quality, and a +1 bonus to attack rolls from a special ability, they do not add 3 to their attack roll—instead, they reduce the difficulty of the attack by one step. So if they attack a level 3 foe, they would normally roll against difficulty 3 and try to reach a target number of 9, but thanks to their asset, they roll against difficulty 2 and try to reach a target number of 6.

This distinction is important when stacking skills and assets to decrease the difficulty of an action, especially since reducing the difficulty to 0 or lower means no roll is needed.

THE PLAYER ALWAYS ROLLS

In the Cypher System, players always drive the action. That means they make all the die rolls. If a PC leaps out of a moving vehicle, the player rolls to see if they succeed. If a PC searches for a hidden panel, the player rolls to determine whether they find it. If a rockslide falls on a PC, the player rolls to try to get out of the way. If a PC and an NPC arm wrestle, the player rolls, and the NPC's level determines the target number. If a PC attacks a foe, the player rolls to see if they hit. If a foe attacks the PC, the player rolls to see if they dodge the blow.

As shown by the last two examples, the PC rolls whether they are attacking or defending. Thus, something that improves defenses might ease or hinder their rolls. For example, if a PC uses a low wall to gain cover from attacks, the wall eases the player's defense rolls. If a foe uses the wall to gain cover from the PC's attacks, it hinders the player's attack rolls.

SPECIAL ROLLS

If a character rolls a natural 1, 17, 18, 19, or 20 (meaning the d20 shows that number), special rules come into play. These are explained in more detail in the following sections.

1: GM Intrusion. The GM makes a free intrusion (see below) and doesn't award experience points (XP) for it.

17: Damage Bonus. If the roll was a damage-dealing attack, it deals 1 additional point of damage.

18: Damage Bonus. If the roll was a damage-dealing attack, it deals 2 additional points of damage.

19: Minor Effect. If the roll was a damage-dealing attack, it deals 3 additional points of damage or the PC gets a minor effect in addition to the normal results of the task. If the roll was something other than an attack, the PC gets a minor effect in addition to the normal results of the task.

20: Major Effect. If the roll was a damage-dealing attack, it deals 4 additional points of damage or the PC gets a major or minor effect in addition to the normal results of the task. If the roll was something other than an attack, the PC gets a major effect in addition to the normal results of the task. If the PC spent points from a stat Pool on the action, the point cost for the action decreases to 0, meaning the character regains those points as if they had not spent them at all.

GM INTRUSION

GM intrusion is explained in more detail in chapter 25, but essentially it means that something occurs to complicate the character's life. The character hasn't necessarily fumbled or done anything wrong (although perhaps they did). It could just be that the task presents an unexpected difficulty or something unrelated affects the current situation.

For GM intrusion on a defense roll, a roll of 1 might mean that the PC takes 2 additional points of damage from the attack, indicating that the opponent got in a lucky blow.

MINOR EFFECT

A minor effect happens when a player rolls a natural 19. Most of the time, a minor effect is slightly beneficial to the PC, but not overwhelming.

A climber gets up the steep slope a bit faster. A repaired machine works a bit better. A character jumping down into a pit lands on their feet. Either the GM or the player can come up with a possible minor effect that fits the situation, but both must agree on what it should be.

Don't waste a lot of time thinking of a minor effect if nothing appropriate suggests itself. Sometimes, in cases where only success or failure matters, it's okay to have no minor effect. Keep the game moving at an exciting pace.

In combat, the easiest and most straightforward minor effect is dealing 3 additional points of damage with an attack. The following are other common minor effects for combat:

Damage object: Instead of striking the foe, the attack strikes what the foe is holding. If the attack hits, the character makes a Might roll with a difficulty equal to the object's level. On a success, the object moves one or more steps down the object damage track.

Distract: For one round, all of the foe's tasks are hindered.

Knock back: The foe is knocked or forced back a few feet. Most of the time, this doesn't matter much, but if the fight takes place on a ledge or next to a pit of lava, the effect can be significant.

Move past: The character can move a short distance at the end of the attack. This effect is useful to get past a foe guarding a door, for example.

Strike a specific body part: The attacker strikes a specific spot on the defender's body. The GM rules what special effect, if any, results. For example, hitting a creature's tentacle that is wrapped around an ally might make it easier for the ally to escape. Hitting a foe in the eye might blind it for one round. Hitting a creature in its one vulnerable spot might ignore Armor.

Usually, the GM just has the desired minor effect occur. For example, rolling a 19 against a relatively weak foe means it is knocked off the cliff. The effect makes the round more exciting, but the defeat of a minor creature has no significant impact on the story. Other times, the GM might rule that an additional roll is needed

For complete details about GM intrusion and how to use it to best effect in the game, see page 408.

Object damage track, page 116

to achieve the effect—the special roll only gives the PC the *opportunity* for a minor effect. This mostly happens when the desired effect is very unlikely, such as pushing a 50-ton battle automaton off a cliff. If the player just wants to deal 3 additional points of damage as the minor effect, no extra roll is needed.

MAJOR EFFECT

A major effect happens when a player rolls a natural 20. Most of the time, a major effect is quite beneficial to the character. A climber gets up the steep slope in half the time. A jumper lands with such panache that those nearby are impressed and possibly intimidated. A defender makes a free attack on a foe.

Either the GM or the player can come up with a possible major effect that fits the situation, but both must agree on what it should be. As with minor effects, don't spend a lot of time agonizing over the details of a major effect. In cases where only success or failure matters, a major effect might offer the character a one-time asset (a modification of one step) to use the next time they attempt a similar action. When nothing else seems appropriate, the GM can simply grant the PC an additional action on their turn that same round.

In combat, the easiest and most straightforward major effect is dealing 4 additional points of damage with an attack. The following are other common major effects for combat.

Disarm: The foe drops one object that it is holding.

Impair: For the rest of the combat, all tasks the foe attempts are hindered.

Knock down: The foe is knocked prone. It can get up on its turn.

Stun: The foe loses its next action.

As with minor effects, usually the GM just has the desired major effect occur, but sometimes the GM might require an extra roll if the major effect is unusual or unlikely.

RETRYING A TASK AFTER FAILURE

If a character fails a task (whether it's climbing a wall, picking a lock, trying to figure out a mysterious device, or something else) they can attempt it again, but they must apply at least one level of Effort when retrying that task. A retry is a new action, not part of the same action that failed, and it takes the same amount of time as the first attempt did.

Sometimes the GM might rule that retries are impossible. Perhaps a character has one chance to convince the leader of a group of thugs not to attack, and after that, no amount of talking will stop them.

This rule doesn't apply to something like attacking a foe in combat because combat is always changing and fluid. Each round's situation is new, not a repeat of a previous situation, so a missed attack can't be retried.

INITIAL COST

The GM can assign a point cost to a task just for trying it. Called an initial cost, it's simply an indication that the task is particularly taxing. For example, let's say a character wants to try a Might action to open a heavy cellar door that is partially rusted shut. The GM says that forcing the door open is a difficulty 5 task, and there's an initial cost of 3 Might points simply to try. This initial cost is in addition to any points the character chooses to spend on the roll (such as when applying Effort), and the initial cost points do not affect the difficulty of the task. In other words, the character must spend 3 Might points to attempt the task at all, but that doesn't help them open the door. If they want to apply Effort to ease the task, they have to spend more points from their Might Pool.

> ### OPTIONAL RULE: CHOOSING A COMBAT EFFECT AHEAD OF TIME
>
> While normally you get a minor or major effect based on your die roll, sometimes a character in combat tries to achieve a minor or major effect as a part of a deliberate strategy, such as disarming a foe they don't want to harm or shooting a huge beast in the eye to blind it so they can run away. A character can choose a minor or major combat effect ahead of time so they can achieve it without rolling a natural 19 or 20 on the die, but the attack is modified in these ways:
>
> - For a minor effect, you subtract 4 from your damage, and the attack is hindered.
> - For a major effect, you subtract 8 from your damage, and the attack is hindered by two steps.
>
> In either case, if your attack would deal 0 points of damage or less, there is no damage or effect at all.

Edge helps with the initial cost of a task, just as it does with any expenditure from a character's Pool. In the previous example, if the character had a Might Edge of 2, they would have to spend only 1 point (3 points minus 2 from their Might Edge) for the initial cost to attempt the task. If they also applied a level of Effort to open the door, they couldn't use their Edge again—Edge applies only once per action—so using the Effort would cost the full 3 points. Thus, they'd spend a total of 4 points (1 for the initial cost plus 3 for the Effort) from their Might Pool.

The rationale of the initial cost rule is that even in the Cypher System, where things like Effort can help a character succeed on an action, logic still suggests that some actions are very difficult and taxing, particularly for some PCs more than others.

DISTANCE

Distance is simplified into four basic categories: immediate, short, long, and very long.

Immediate distance from a character is within reach or within a few steps; if a character stands in a small room, everything in the room is within immediate distance. At most, immediate distance is 10 feet (3 m). Immediate distance is sometimes referred to as close, or even point-blank, particularly when referring to ranges.

Short distance is anything greater than immediate distance but less than 50 feet (15 m) or so.

Long distance is anything greater than short distance but less than 100 feet (30 m) or so.

Very long distance is anything greater than long distance but less than 500 feet (150 m) or so.

Beyond that range, distances are always specified—1,000 feet (300 m), 1 mile (1.5 km), and so on.

All weapons and special abilities use these terms for ranges. For example, all melee weapons have immediate range—they are close-combat weapons, and you can use them to attack anyone within immediate distance. A thrown knife (and most other thrown weapons) has short range. A small handgun also has short range. A rifle has long range.

A character can move an immediate distance as a part of another action. In other words, they can take a few steps to the light switch and flip it on. They can lunge across a small room to attack a foe. They can open a door and step through.

A character can move a short distance as their entire action for a turn. They can also try to move a long distance as their entire action, but the player might have to roll to see if the character slips, trips, or stumbles for moving so far so quickly.

GMs and players don't need to determine exact distances. For example, if the PCs are fighting a group of star troopers, any character can likely attack any foe in the general melee—they're all within immediate range. However, if one trooper stays back to fire a blaster, a character might have to use their entire action to move the short distance required to attack that foe. It doesn't matter if the trooper is 20 feet (6 m) or 40 feet (12 m) away—it's simply considered short distance. It does matter if the trooper is more than 50 feet (15 m) away because that distance would require a long move.

OTHER DISTANCES

In rare cases where distances beyond very long are needed, real-world distances are best (1 mile, 100 kilometers, and so on). However, the following shorthand distances can be useful in some settings:

Planetary: On the same planet.
Interplanetary: Within the same solar system.
Interstellar: Within the same galaxy.
Intergalactic: Anywhere in the same universe.
Interdimensional: Anywhere.

TIMEKEEPING

Generally, keep time the same way that you normally would, using minutes, hours, days, and weeks. Thus, if the characters walk overland for 15 miles (24 km), about eight hours pass, even though the journey can be described in only a few seconds at the game table. Precision timekeeping is rarely important. Most of the time, saying things like "That takes about an hour" works fine.

This is true even when a special ability has a specific duration. In an encounter, a duration of "one minute" is mostly the same as saying "the rest of the encounter." You don't have to track each round that ticks by if you don't want to. Likewise, an ability that lasts for ten minutes can safely be considered the length of an in-depth conversation, the time it takes to quickly explore a small area, or the time it takes to rest after a strenuous activity.

Star troopers are guards; see page 374.

The words "immediate" and "close" can be used interchangeably to talk about distance. If a creature or object is within arm's reach of the character, it can be considered both immediate and close.

TIMEKEEPING

Action	Time Usually Required
Walking a mile over easy terrain	About fifteen minutes
Walking a mile over rough terrain (forest, snow, hills)	About half an hour
Walking a mile over difficult terrain (mountains, thick jungle)	About forty-five minutes
Moving from one significant location in a city to another	About fifteen minutes
Sneaking into a guarded location	About fifteen minutes
Observing a new location to get salient details	About fifteen minutes
Having an in-depth discussion	About ten minutes
Resting after a fight or other strenuous activity	About ten minutes
Resting and having a quick meal	About half an hour
Making or breaking camp	About half an hour
Shopping for supplies in a market or store	About an hour
Meeting with an important contact	About half an hour
Referencing a book or website	About half an hour
Searching a room for hidden things	At least half an hour, perhaps one hour
Searching for cyphers or other valuables amid a lot of stuff	About an hour
Identifying and understanding a cypher	Fifteen minutes to half an hour
Identifying and understanding an artifact	At least fifteen minutes, perhaps three hours
Repairing a device (assuming parts and tools available)	At least an hour, perhaps a day
Building a device (assuming parts and tools available)	At least a day, perhaps a week

ENCOUNTERS, ROUNDS, AND INITIATIVE

Sometimes in the course of the game, the GM or players will refer to an "encounter." Encounters are not so much measurements of time as they are events or instances in which something happens, like a scene of a movie or a chapter in a book. An encounter might be a fight with a foe, a dramatic crossing of a raging river, or a stressful negotiation with an important official. It's useful to use the word when referring to a specific scene, as in "My Might Pool is low after that encounter with the soul sorcerer yesterday."

A round is about five to ten seconds. The length of time is variable because sometimes one round might be a bit longer than another. You don't need to measure time more precisely than that. You can estimate that on average there are about ten rounds in a minute. In a round, everyone—each character and NPC—gets to take one action.

To determine who goes first, second, and so on in a round, each player makes a Speed roll called an initiative roll. Most of the time, it's only important to know which characters act before the NPCs and which act after the NPCs. On an initiative roll, a character who rolls higher than an NPC's target number takes their action before the NPC does. As with all target numbers, an NPC's target number for an initiative roll is three times the NPC's level. Many times, the GM will have all NPCs take their actions at the same time, using the highest target number from among all the NPCs. Using this method, any characters who rolled higher than the target number act first, then all the NPCs act, and finally any characters who rolled lower than the target number act.

The order in which the characters act usually isn't important. If the players want to go in a precise order, they can act in initiative order (highest to lowest), by going around the table, by going oldest to youngest, and so on.

For example, Charles, Tammie, and Shanna's characters are in combat with two level 2 security guards. The GM has the players make Speed rolls to determine initiative. Charles rolls an 8, Shanna rolls a 15, and Tammie rolls a 4. The target number for a level 2 creature is 6, so each round Charles and Shanna act before the guards, then the guards act, and finally Tammie acts. It doesn't matter whether Charles acts before or after Shanna, as long as they think it's fair.

After everyone—all PCs and NPCs—in the combat has had a turn, the round ends and a new round begins. In all rounds after the first, everyone acts in the same order as they did in the first round. The characters cycle through this

An initiative roll is a d20 roll. Since your initiative depends on how fast you are, if you spend Effort on the roll, the points come from your Speed Pool.

RULES OF THE GAME

order until the logical end of the encounter (the end of the fight or the completion of the event) or until the GM asks them to make new initiative rolls. The GM can call for new initiative rolls at the beginning of any new round when conditions drastically change. For example, if the NPCs gain reinforcements, the environment changes (perhaps the lights go out), the terrain changes (maybe part of the balcony collapses under the PCs), or something similar occurs, the GM can call for new initiative rolls.

Since the action moves as a cycle, anything that lasts for a round ends where it started in the cycle. If Umberto uses an ability on an opponent that hinders its defenses for one round, the effect lasts until Umberto acts on his next turn.

Faster Initiative (Optional Rule): To make an encounter move faster, if at least one character rolls high enough to beat the target number of the NPC(s), all the characters act before the NPC(s). If nobody rolls high enough to beat that target number, all the characters act after the NPC(s). On the characters' turn, go clockwise around the table. If you're playing using an online video chat or virtual table, start with the leftmost player and move right; repeat.

ACTIONS

Anything that your character does in a round is an action. It's easiest to think of an action as a single thing that you can do in five to ten seconds. For example, if you use your dart thrower to shoot a strange floating orb, that's one action. So is running for cover behind a stack of barrels, prying open a stuck door, using a rope to pull your friend up from a pit, or activating a cypher (even if it's stored in your pack).

Opening a door and attacking a security guard on the other side are two actions. It's more a matter of focus than time. Drawing your sword and attacking a foe is all one action. Putting away your bow and pushing a heavy bookcase to block a door are two actions because each requires a different train of thought.

If the action you want to accomplish is not within reach, you can move a little bit. Essentially, you can move up to an immediate distance to perform your action. For example, you can move an immediate distance and attack a foe, open a door and move an immediate distance into the hallway beyond, or grab your hurt friend lying on the ground and pull them back a few steps. This movement can occur before or after your action, so you can move to a door and open it, or you can open a door and move through it.

The most common actions are:
- Attack
- Activate a special ability (one that isn't an attack)
- Move
- Wait
- Defend
- Do something else

> ### A CLOSER LOOK AT SITUATIONS THAT DON'T INVOLVE PCs
> Ultimately, the GM is the arbiter of conflicts that do not involve the PCs. They should be adjudicated in the most interesting, logical, and story-based way possible. When in doubt, match the level of the NPCs (characters or creatures) or their respective effects to determine the results. Thus, if a level 4 NPC fights a level 3 NPC, the level 4 NPC will win, but if they face a level 7 NPC, they'll lose. Likewise, a level 4 creature resists poisons or devices of level 3 or lower but not those of level 5 and above.
>
> The essence is this: in the Cypher System, it doesn't matter if something is a creature, a poison, or a gravity-dispelling ray. If it's a higher level, it wins; if it's a lower level, it loses. If two things of equal level oppose each other, there might be a long, drawn-out battle that could go either way.

ACTION: ATTACK

An attack is anything that you do to someone that they don't want you to do. Slashing a foe with a curved dagger is an attack, blasting a foe with a lightning artifact is an attack, wrapping a foe in magnetically controlled metal cables is an attack, and controlling someone's mind is an attack. An attack almost always requires a roll to see if you hit or otherwise affect your target.

In the simplest kind of attack, such as a PC trying to stab a thug with a knife, the player rolls and compares their result to the opponent's target number. If their roll is equal to or greater than the target number, the attack hits. Just as with any kind of task, the GM might modify the difficulty based on the situation, and the player might have a bonus to the roll or might try to ease the task using skills, assets, or Effort.

215

A less straightforward attack might be a special ability that stuns a foe with a mental blast. However, it's handled the same way: the player makes a roll against the opponent's target number. Similarly, an attempt to tackle a foe and wrestle it to the ground is still just a roll against the foe's target number.

Attacks are sometimes categorized as "melee" attacks, meaning that you hurt or affect something within immediate reach, or "ranged" attacks, meaning that you hurt or affect something at a distance.

Melee attacks can be Might or Speed actions—player choice. Physical ranged attacks (such as bows, thrown weapons, and blasts of fire from a mutation) are almost always Speed actions, but those that come from special abilities tend to be Intellect actions.

Special abilities that require touching the target require a melee attack. If the attack misses, the power is not wasted, and you can try again each round as your action until you hit the target, use another ability, or take a different action that requires you to use your hands. These attempts in later rounds count as different actions, so you don't have to keep track of how much Effort you used when you activated the ability or how you used Edge. For example, let's say that in the first round of combat, you activate a special ability that requires you to touch your foe and you use Effort to ease the attack, but you roll poorly and miss your foe. In the second round of combat, you can try attacking again and use Effort to ease the attack roll.

The GM and players are encouraged to describe every attack with flavor and flair. One attack roll might be a stab to the foe's arm. A miss might be the PC's sword slamming into the wall. Combatants lunge, block, duck, spin, leap, and make all kinds of movements that should keep combat visually interesting and compelling. Chapter 25 has much more guidance in this regard.

Common elements that affect the difficulty of a combat task are cover, range, and darkness. The rules for these and other modifiers are explained in the Attack Modifiers and Special Situations section of this chapter.

Object damage track, page 116

Attack Modifiers and Special Situations, page 220

Attacking objects, page 223

Onslaught, page 167

DAMAGE

When an attack strikes a character, it usually means the character takes damage.

An attack against a PC subtracts points from one of the character's stat Pools—usually the Might Pool. Whenever an attack simply says it deals "damage" without specifying the type, it means Might damage, which is by far the most common type. Intellect damage, which is usually the result of a mental attack, is always labeled as Intellect damage. Speed damage is often a physical attack, but attacks that deal Speed damage are fairly rare.

NPCs don't have stat Pools. Instead, they have a characteristic called health. When an NPC takes damage of any kind, the amount is subtracted from its health. Unless described otherwise, an NPC's health is always equal to its target number. Some NPCs might have special reactions to or defenses against attacks that would normally deal Speed damage or Intellect damage, but unless the NPC's description specifically explains this, assume that all damage is subtracted from the NPC's health.

Objects don't have stat Pools or health. They have an object damage track, just like how PCs have a damage track. Attacking objects might move them down their damage track.

Damage is always a specific amount determined by the attack. For example, a slash with a broadsword or a blast with a spike thrower deals 4 points of damage. An Adept's Onslaught deals 4 points of damage. Often,

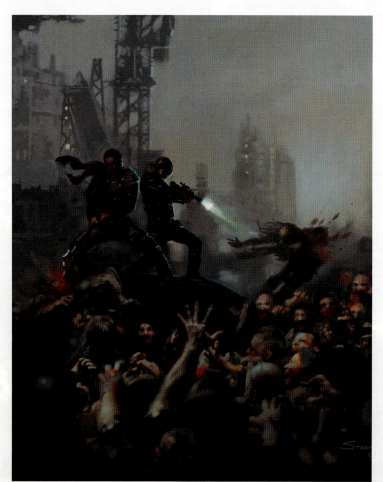

there are ways for the attacker to increase the damage. For example, a PC can apply Effort to deal 3 additional points of damage, and rolling a natural 17 on the attack roll deals 1 additional point of damage.

ARMOR

Pieces of equipment and special abilities protect a character from damage by giving them Armor. Each time a character takes damage, subtract their Armor value from the damage before reducing their stat Pool or health. For example, if a Warrior with 2 Armor is hit by a gunshot that deals 4 points of damage, they take only 2 points of damage (4 minus 2 from their Armor). If Armor reduces the incoming damage to 0 or lower, the character takes no damage from the attack. For example, the Warrior's 2 Armor protects them from all physical attacks that deal 1 or 2 points of damage.

The most common way to get Armor is to wear physical armor, such as a leather jacket, a bulletproof vest, a chainmail hauberk, bioengineered carapace grafts, or something else, depending on the setting. All physical armor comes in one of three categories: light, medium, or heavy. Light armor gives the wearer 1 point of Armor, medium gives 2 points of Armor, and heavy gives 3 points of Armor.

When you see the word "Armor" capitalized in the game rules (other than in the name of a special ability), it refers to your Armor characteristic—the number you subtract from incoming damage. When you see the word "armor" in lowercase, it refers to any physical armor you might wear.

Other effects can add to a character's Armor. If a character is wearing chainmail (+2 to Armor) and has an ability that covers them in a protective force field that grants +1 to Armor, their total is 3 Armor. If they also use a cypher that hardens their flesh temporarily for +1 to Armor, their total is 4 Armor.

Some types of damage ignore physical armor. Attacks that specifically deal Speed damage or Intellect damage ignore Armor; the creature takes the listed amount of damage without any reduction from Armor. Ambient damage (see below) usually ignores Armor as well.

A creature may have a special bonus to Armor against certain kinds of attacks. For example, a protective suit made of a sturdy, fire-resistant material might normally give its wearer +1 to Armor but count as +3 to Armor against fire attacks. An artifact worn as a helmet might grant +2 to Armor only against mental attacks.

AMBIENT DAMAGE

Some kinds of damage aren't direct attacks against a creature, but they indirectly affect everything in the area. Most of these are environmental effects such as winter cold, high temperatures, or background radiation. Damage from these kinds of sources is called ambient damage. Physical armor usually doesn't protect against ambient damage, though a well-insulated suit of armor can protect against cold weather.

DAMAGE FROM HAZARDS

Attacks aren't the only way to inflict damage on a character. Experiences such as falling from a great height, being burned in a fire, and spending time in severe weather also deal damage. Although no list of potential hazards could be comprehensive, the Damage From Hazards table includes common examples.

DAMAGE FROM HAZARDS

Source	Damage	Notes
Falling	1 point per 10 feet (3 m) fallen (ambient damage)	—
Minor fire	3 points per round (ambient damage)	Torch
Major fire	6 points per round (ambient damage)	Engulfed in flames; lava
Acid splash	2 points per round (ambient damage)	—
Acid bath	6 points per round (ambient damage)	Immersed in acid
Cold	1 point per round (ambient damage)	Below freezing temperatures
Severe cold	3 points per round (ambient damage)	Liquid nitrogen
Shock	1 point per round (ambient damage)	Often involves losing next action
Electrocution	6 points per round (ambient damage)	Often involves losing next action
Crush	3 points	Object or creature falls on character
Huge crush	6 points	Roof collapse; cave-in
Collision	6 points	Large, fast object strikes character

The damage track allows you to know how far from death you are. If you're hale, you're three steps from death. If you're impaired, you're two steps from death. If you're debilitated, you are only one small step from death's door.

When NPCs (who have only health) suffer Speed or Intellect damage, normally this is treated the same as Might damage. However, the GM or the player has the option to suggest an appropriate alternate effect—the NPC suffers a penalty, moves more slowly, is stunned, and so on.

Enthrall, page 136

THE EFFECTS OF TAKING DAMAGE

When an NPC reaches 0 health, it is either dead or (if the attacker wishes) incapacitated, meaning unconscious or beaten into submission.

As previously mentioned, damage from most sources is applied to a character's Might Pool. Otherwise, stat damage always reduces the Pool of the stat it affects.

If damage reduces a character's stat Pool to 0, any further damage to that stat (including excess damage from the attack that reduced the stat to 0) is applied to another stat Pool. Damage is applied to Pools in this order:

1. Might (unless the Pool is 0)
2. Speed (unless the Pool is 0)
3. Intellect

Even if the damage is applied to another stat Pool, it still counts as its original type for the purpose of Armor and special abilities that affect damage. For example, if a character with 2 Armor is reduced to 0 Might and then is hit by a creature's claw for 3 points of damage, it still counts as Might damage, so their Armor reduces the damage to 1 point, which then is applied to their Speed Pool. In other words, even though they take the damage from their Speed Pool, it doesn't ignore Armor like Speed damage normally would.

In addition to taking damage from their Might Pool, Speed Pool, or Intellect Pool, PCs also have a damage track. The damage track has four states (from best to worst): hale, impaired, debilitated, and dead. When one of a PC's stat Pools reaches 0, they move one step down the damage track. Thus, if they are hale, they become impaired. If they are already impaired, they become debilitated. If they are already debilitated, they become dead.

Some effects can immediately shift a PC one or more steps on the damage track. These include rare poisons, cellular disruption attacks, and massive traumas (such as falls from very great heights, being run over by a speeding vehicle, and so on, as determined by the GM).

Some attacks, like a serpent's poisonous bite or a Speaker's Enthrall, have effects other than damage to a stat Pool or shifting the PC on the damage track. These attacks can cause unconsciousness, paralysis, and so on.

THE DAMAGE TRACK

As noted above, the damage track has four states: hale, impaired, debilitated, and dead.

Hale is the normal state for a character: all three stat Pools are at 1 or higher, and the PC has no penalties from harmful conditions. When a hale PC takes enough damage to reduce one of their stat Pools to 0, they become impaired. Note that a character whose stat Pools are much lower than normal can still be hale.

Impaired is a wounded or injured state. When an impaired character applies Effort, it costs 1 extra point per level applied. For example, applying one level of Effort costs 4 points instead of 3, and applying two levels of Effort costs 7 points instead of 5.

An impaired character ignores minor and major effect results on their rolls, and they don't deal as much extra damage in combat with a special roll. In combat, a roll of 17 or higher deals only 1 additional point of damage. When an impaired PC takes enough damage to reduce one of their stat Pools to 0, they become debilitated.

Debilitated is a critically injured state. A debilitated character may not take any actions other than to move (probably crawl) no more than an immediate distance. If a debilitated character's Speed Pool is 0, they can't move at all. When a debilitated PC takes enough damage to reduce a stat Pool to 0, they are dead.

Dead is dead.

RECOVERING POINTS IN A POOL

After losing or spending points in a Pool, you recover those points by resting. You can't increase a Pool past its maximum by resting—just back to its normal level. Any extra points gained go away with no effect. The amount of points you recover from a rest, and how long each rest takes, depends on how many times you have rested so far that day.

When you rest, make a recovery roll. To do this, roll a d6 and add your tier. You recover that many points, and you can divide them among your stat Pools however you wish. For example, if your recovery roll is 4 and you've lost 4 points of Might and 2 points of Speed, you can recover 4 points of Might, or 2 points of Might and 2 points of Speed, or any other combination adding up to 4 points.

The first time you rest each day, it takes only a few seconds to catch your breath. If you rest this way in the middle of an encounter, it takes one action on your turn.

The second time you rest each day, you must rest for ten minutes to make a recovery roll. The third time you rest each day, you must rest for one hour to make a recovery roll. The fourth time you rest each day, you must rest for ten hours to make a recovery roll (usually, this occurs when you stop for the day to eat and sleep).

After that much rest, it's assumed to be a new day, so the next time you rest, it takes only a few seconds. The next rest takes ten minutes, then one hour, and so on, in a cycle.

If you haven't rested yet that day and you take a lot of damage in a fight, you could rest a few seconds (regaining 1d6 points + 1 point per tier) and then immediately rest for ten minutes (regaining another 1d6 points + 1 point per tier). Thus, in one full day of doing nothing but resting, you could recover 4d6 points + 4 points per tier.

Each character chooses when to make recovery rolls. If a party of five PCs rests for ten minutes because two of them want to make recovery rolls, the others don't have to make rolls at that time. Later in the day, those three can decide to rest for ten minutes and make recovery rolls.

Recovery Roll	Rest Time Needed
First recovery roll	One action
Second recovery roll	Ten minutes
Third recovery roll	One hour
Fourth recovery roll	Ten hours

RESTORING THE DAMAGE TRACK

Using points from a recovery roll to raise a stat Pool from 0 to 1 or higher also automatically moves the character up one step on the damage track.

If all of a PC's stat Pools are above 0 and the character has taken special damage that moved them down the damage track, they can use a recovery roll to move up one step on the damage track instead of recovering points. For example, a character who is debilitated from a hit with a cell-disrupting biotech device can rest and move up to impaired rather than recover points in a Pool.

SPECIAL DAMAGE

In the course of playing the game, characters face all manner of threats and dangers that can harm them in a variety of ways, only some of which are easily represented by points of damage.

Dazed and Stunned: Characters can be dazed when struck hard on the head, exposed to extremely loud sounds, or affected by a mental attack. When this happens, for the duration of the daze effect (usually one round), all of the character's tasks are hindered. Similar but more severe attacks can stun characters. Stunned characters lose their turn (but can still defend against attacks normally).

Poison and Disease: When characters encounter poison—whether the venom of a serpent, rat poison slipped into a burrito, cyanide dissolved in wine, or an overdose of acetaminophen—they make a Might defense roll to resist it. Failure to resist can result in points of damage, moving down the damage track, or a specific effect such as paralysis, unconsciousness, disability, or something stranger. For example, some poisons affect the brain, making it impossible to say certain words, take certain actions, resist certain effects, or recover points to a stat Pool.

Diseases work like poisons, but their effect occurs every day, so the victim must make a Might defense roll each day or suffer the effects. Disease effects are as varied as poisons: points of damage, moving down the damage track, disability, and so on. Many diseases inflict damage that cannot be restored through conventional means.

Paralysis: Paralytic effects cause a character to drop to the ground, unable to move. Unless otherwise specified, the character can still take actions that require no physical movement.

Other Effects: Other special effects can render a character blind or deaf, unable to stand without falling over, or unable to breathe. Stranger effects might negate gravity for the character (or increase it a hundredfold), transport them to another place, render them out of phase, mutate their physical form, implant false memories or senses, alter the way their brain processes information, or inflame their nerves so they are in constant, excruciating pain. Each special effect must be handled on a case-by-case basis. The GM adjudicates how the character is affected and how the condition can be alleviated (if possible).

NPCs AND SPECIAL DAMAGE

The GM always has final say over what special damage will affect an NPC. Human NPCs usually react like characters, but nonhuman creatures might react very differently. For example, a tiny bit of venom is unlikely to hurt a gigantic dragon, and it won't affect an android or a demon at all.

If an NPC is susceptible to an attack that would shift a character down the damage track, using that attack on the NPC usually renders it unconscious or dead. Alternatively, the GM could apply the debilitated condition to the NPC, with the same effect as it would have on a PC.

GMs should always remember that above all else, describing the action and how it fits into the situation at hand is more important than the mechanics of it.

Precise ranges are not important in the Cypher System. The broadly defined "immediate," "short," "long," and "very long" ranges let the GM quickly make a judgment call and keep things moving. Basically, the idea is: your target is right there, your target is close, your target is pretty far away, or your target is extremely far away.

The GM might allow a character with a ranged weapon to attack beyond extreme range, but the attack would be hindered by two steps for each range category beyond the normal limit. Attacks with hard limits, such as the blast radius of a bomb, can't be modified.

Movement, page 223

In certain situations, such as a PC on top of a building looking across an open field, the GM should allow ranged attacks to exceed their maximum range. For example, in perfect conditions, a good archer can hit a large target with a bow and arrow at 500 feet (150 m), much farther than a bow's typical long range.

ATTACK MODIFIERS AND SPECIAL SITUATIONS

In combat situations, many modifiers might come into play. Although the GM is at liberty to assess whatever modifiers they think are appropriate to the situation (that's their role in the game), the following suggestions and guidelines might make that easier. Often the modifier is applied as a step in difficulty. So if a situation hinders attacks, that means if a PC attacks an NPC, the difficulty of the attack roll is increased by one step, and if an NPC attacks a PC, the difficulty of the defense roll is decreased by one step. This is because players make all rolls, whether they are attacking or defending—NPCs never make attack or defense rolls.

When in doubt, if it seems like it should be harder to attack in a situation, hinder the attack rolls. If it seems like attacks should gain an advantage or be easier in some way, hinder the defense rolls.

COVER

If a character is behind cover so that a significant portion of their body is behind something sturdy, attacks against the character are hindered.

If a character is entirely behind cover (their entire body is behind something sturdy), they can't be attacked unless the attack can go through the cover. For example, if a character hides behind a thin wooden screen and their opponent shoots the screen with a rifle that can penetrate the wood, the character can be attacked. However, because the attacker can't see the character clearly, this still counts as cover (attacks against the character are hindered).

POSITION

Sometimes where a character stands gives them an advantage or a disadvantage.

Prone Target: In melee, a prone target is easier to hit (attacks against them are eased). In ranged combat, a prone target is harder to hit (attacks against them are hindered).

Higher Ground: In either ranged or melee combat, attacks by an opponent on higher ground are eased.

SURPRISE

When a target isn't aware of an incoming attack, the attacker has an advantage. A ranged sniper in a hidden position, an invisible assailant, or the first salvo in a successful ambush are all eased by two steps. For the attacker to gain this advantage, however, the defender truly must have no idea that the attack is coming.

If the defender isn't sure of the attacker's location but is still on guard, the attacks are eased by only one step.

RANGE

In melee, you can attack a foe who is adjacent to you (next to you) or within reach (immediate range). If you enter into melee with one or more foes, usually you can attack most or all of the combatants, meaning they are next to you, within reach, or within reach if you move slightly or have a long weapon that extends your reach.

The majority of ranged attacks have only two ranges: short range and long range (a few have very long range). Short range is generally less than 50 feet (15 m) or so. Long range is generally from 50 feet (15 m) to about 100 feet (30 m). Very long range is generally 100 feet (30 m) to 500 feet (150 m). Greater precision than that isn't important in the Cypher System. If anything is longer than very long range, the exact range is usually spelled out, such as with an item that can fire a beam 1,000 feet (300 m) or teleport you up to 1 mile (1.5 km) away.

Thus, the game has four measurements of distance: immediate, short, long, and very long. These apply to movement as well. A few special cases—point-blank range and extreme range—modify an attack's chance to successfully hit.

Point-Blank Range: If a character uses a ranged weapon against a target within immediate range, the attack is eased.

Extreme Range: Targets just at the limit of a weapon's range are at extreme range. Attacks against such targets are hindered.

ILLUMINATION

What characters can see (and how well they can see) plays a huge factor in combat.

Dim Light: Dim light is approximately the amount of light on a night with a bright full moon or the illumination provided by a torch, flashlight, or desk lamp. Dim light allows you to see out to short range. Targets in dim light are harder to hit. Attacks against such targets are hindered. Attackers trained in low-light spotting negate this modifier.

Very Dim Light: Very dim light is approximately the amount of light on a starry night with no visible moon, or the glow provided by a candle or an illuminated control panel. Very dim light allows you to see clearly only within immediate range and perceive vague shapes to short range. Targets in very dim light are harder to hit. Attacks against targets within immediate range are hindered, and attacks against those in

RULES OF THE GAME

short range are hindered by two steps. Attackers trained in low-light spotting modify these difficulties by one step in their favor. Attackers specialized in low-light spotting modify these difficulties by two steps in their favor.

Darkness: Darkness is an area with no illumination at all, such as a moonless night with cloud cover or a room with no lights. Targets in complete darkness are nearly impossible to hit. If an attacker can use other senses (such as hearing) to get an idea of where the opponent might be, attacks against such targets are hindered by four steps. Otherwise, attacks in complete darkness fail without the need for a roll unless the player spends 1 XP to "make a lucky shot" or the GM uses GM intrusion. Attackers trained in low-light spotting ease the task. Attackers specialized in low-light spotting ease the task by two steps.

VISIBILITY

Similar to illumination, factors that obscure vision affect combat.

Mist: A target in mist is similar to one in dim light. Ranged attacks against such targets are hindered. Particularly dense mist makes ranged attacks nearly impossible (treat as darkness), and even melee attacks are hindered.

Hiding Target: A target in dense foliage, behind a screen, or crawling amid the rubble in a ruin is hard to hit because they're hard to see. Ranged attacks against such targets are hindered.

Invisible Target: If an attacker can use other senses (such as hearing) to get an idea of where the opponent might be, attacks against such targets are hindered by four steps. Otherwise, attacks against an invisible creature fail without the need for a roll unless the player spends 1 XP to "make a lucky shot" or the GM uses GM intrusion.

WATER

Being in shallow water can make it hard to move, but it doesn't affect combat. Being in deep water can make things difficult, and being underwater entirely can seem as different as being on another world.

Deep Water: Being in water up to your chest (or the equivalent thereof) hinders your attacks. Aquatic creatures ignore this modifier.

Underwater Melee Combat: For nonaquatic creatures, being completely underwater makes attacking very difficult. Attacks with stabbing weapons are hindered, and melee attacks with slashing or bashing weapons are hindered by two steps. Aquatic creatures ignore these penalties.

GM intrusion, page 408

Cooperative actions, page 226

Underwater Ranged Combat: As with melee combat, nonaquatic creatures have problems fighting underwater. Some ranged attacks are impossible underwater—you can't throw things, fire a bow or crossbow, or use a blowgun. Many firearms also do not work underwater. Attacks with weapons that do work underwater are hindered. Ranges underwater are reduced by one category; very-long-range weapons work only to long range, long-range weapons work only to short range, and short-range weapons work only to immediate range.

MOVING TARGETS

Moving targets are harder to hit, and moving attackers have a difficult time as well.

Target Is Moving: Attackers trying to hit a foe who is moving very fast are hindered. (A foe moving very fast is one who is doing nothing but running, mounted on a moving creature, riding on a vehicle or moving conveyance, and so on.)

Attacker Is Moving: An attacker trying to make an attack while moving under their own power (walking, running, swimming, and so on) takes no penalties. Attacks from a moving mount or moving vehicle are hindered; an attacker trained in riding or driving ignores this penalty.

Attacker Is Jostled: Being jostled, such as while standing on a listing ship or a vibrating platform, makes attacking difficult. Such attacks are hindered. Characters trained in balancing or sailing would ignore penalties for being on a ship.

GRAVITY

In a spacefaring campaign, characters may travel to worlds with stronger or weaker gravity than Earth's. Likewise, strange technology or magic can cause gravity to fluctuate even in an Earth-based campaign. Characters who have a large amount of metal (wearing metal armor, using metal weapons, and so on) can be affected by fluctuating magnetism just as a character is affected by gravity.

Low Gravity: Weapons that rely on weight, such as all heavy weapons, deal 2 fewer points of damage (dealing a minimum of 1 point of damage). Weapons with short range can reach to long range, and long-range weapons can reach to very long range. Characters trained in low-gravity maneuvering ignore the damage penalty.

High Gravity: It's hard to make effective attacks when the pull of gravity is very strong. Attacks (and all physical actions) made in high gravity are hindered. Ranges in high gravity are reduced by one category (very-long-range weapons reach only to long range, long-range weapons reach only to short range, and short-range weapons reach only to immediate range). Characters trained in high-gravity maneuvering ignore the change in difficulty but not the range decreases.

Zero Gravity: It's hard to maneuver in an environment without gravity. All physical actions (including attacks) made in zero gravity are hindered. Weapons with short range can reach to long range, long-range weapons can reach to very long range, and very-long-range weapons can reach to about 1,000 feet (300 m) instead of 500 feet (150 m). Characters trained in zero-gravity maneuvering ignore the change in difficulty.

SPECIAL SITUATION: COMBAT BETWEEN NPCs

When an NPC ally of the PCs attacks another NPC, the GM can designate a player to roll and handle it like a PC attacking. Often, the choice is obvious. For example, a character who has a trained attack animal should roll when their pet attacks enemies. If an NPC ally accompanying the party leaps into the fray, that ally's favorite PC rolls for them. NPCs cannot apply Effort. Of course, it's perfectly fitting (and easier) to have the NPC ally use the cooperative action rules to aid a PC instead of making direct attacks, or to compare the levels of the two NPCs (higher wins).

SPECIAL SITUATION: COMBAT BETWEEN PCs

When one PC attacks another PC, the attacking character makes an attack roll, and the other character makes a defense roll, adding any appropriate modifiers. If the attacking PC has a skill, ability, asset, or other effect that would ease the attack if it were made against an NPC, the character adds 3 to the roll for each step reduction (+3 for one step, +6 for two steps, and so on). If the attacker's final result is higher, the attack hits. If the defender's result is higher, the attack misses. Damage is resolved normally. The GM mediates all special effects.

SPECIAL SITUATION: AREA ATTACKS

Sometimes, an attack or effect affects an area rather than a single target. For example, a grenade or a landslide can potentially harm or affect everyone in the area.

In an area attack, all PCs in the area make appropriate defense rolls against the attack to determine its effect on them. If there are any

NPCs in the area, the attacker makes a single attack roll against all of them (one roll, not one roll per NPC) and compares it to the target number of each NPC. If the roll is equal to or greater than the target number of a particular NPC, the attack hits that NPC.

Some area attacks always deal at least a minimum amount of damage, even if the attacks miss or if a PC makes a successful defense roll.

For example, consider a character who uses Shatter to attack six cultists (level 2; target number 6) and their leader (level 4; target number 12). The PC applies Effort to increase the damage and rolls an 11 for the attack roll. This hits the six cultists, but not the leader, so the ability deals 3 points of damage to each of the cultists. The description of Shatter says that applying Effort to increase the damage also means that targets take 1 point of damage if the PC fails the attack roll, so the leader takes 1 point of damage. In terms of what happens in the story, the cultists are caught flat-footed by the sudden detonation of one of their knives, but the leader ducks and is shielded from the blast. Despite the leader's quick moves, the blast is so intense that a few bits of metal slice them.

SPECIAL SITUATION: ATTACKING OBJECTS

Attacking an object is rarely a matter of hitting it. Sure, you can hit the broad side of a barn, but can you damage it? Attacking inanimate objects with a melee weapon is a Might action. Objects have levels and thus target numbers. Objects have a damage track that works like the damage track for PCs.

Intact is the default state for an object.

Minor damage is a slightly damaged state. An object with minor damage reduces its level by 1.

Major damage is a critically damaged state. An object with major damage is broken and no longer functions.

Destroyed is destroyed. The object is ruined, no longer functions, and cannot be repaired.

If the Might action to damage an object is a success, the object moves one step down the object damage track. If the Might roll exceeded the difficulty by 2 levels, the object instead moves two steps down the object damage track. If the Might roll exceeded the difficulty by 4 levels, the object instead moves three steps down the object damage track. Objects with minor or major damage can be repaired, moving them one or more steps up the object damage track.

Brittle or fragile objects, like paper or glass, decrease the effective level of the object for the purposes of determining if it is damaged. Hard objects, like those made of wood or stone, add 1 to the effective level. Very hard objects, like those made of metal, add 2. (The GM may rule that some exotic materials add 3.)

The tool or weapon used to attack the object must be at least as hard as the object itself. Further, if the amount of damage the attack could inflict—not modified by a special die roll—does not equal or exceed the effective level of the object, the attack cannot damage the object no matter what the roll.

ACTION: ACTIVATE A SPECIAL ABILITY

Special abilities are granted by foci, types, and flavors, or provided by cyphers or other devices. If a special ability affects another character in any kind of unwanted manner, it's handled as an attack. This is true even if the ability is normally not considered an attack. For example, if a character has a healing touch, and their friend doesn't want to be healed for some reason, an attempt to heal their unwilling friend is handled as an attack.

Plenty of special abilities do not affect another character in an unwanted manner. For example, a PC might use Hover on themselves to float into the air. A character with a matter-reorganizing device might change a stone wall into glass. A character who activates a phase changer cypher might walk through a wall. None of these requires an attack roll (although when turning a stone wall to glass, the character must still make a roll to successfully affect the wall).

If the character spends points to apply Effort on the attempt, they might want to roll anyway to see if they get a major effect, which would reduce the cost for their action.

ACTION: MOVE

As a part of another action, a character can adjust their position—stepping back a few feet while using an ability, sliding over in combat to take on a different opponent to help a friend, pushing through a door they just opened, and so on. This is considered an immediate distance, and a character can move this far as part of another action.

In a combat situation, if a character is in a large melee, they're usually considered to be next to most other combatants, unless the GM rules that they're farther away because the melee is especially large or the situation dictates it.

Shatter, page 182

Hover, page 149

Phase changer, page 394

Damage track, page 218

Repair, page 227

If they're not in melee but still nearby, they are considered to be a short distance away—usually less than 50 feet (15 m). If they're farther away than that but still involved in the combat, they are considered to be a long distance away, usually 50 to 100 feet (15 to 30 m), or possibly even a very long distance away, usually more than 100 feet to 500 feet (30 to 150 m).

In a round, as an action, a character can make a short move. In this case, they are doing nothing but moving up to about 50 feet (15 m). Some terrain or situations will change the distance a character can move, but generally, making a short move is considered to be a difficulty 0 action. No roll is needed; they just get where they're going as their action.

A character can try to make a long move—up to 100 feet (30 m) or so—in one round. This is a Speed task with a difficulty of 4. As with any action, they can use skills, assets, or Effort to ease the task. Terrain, obstacles, or other circumstances can hinder the task. A successful roll means the character moved the distance safely. Failure means that at some point during the move, they stop or stumble (the GM determines where this happens).

A character can also try to make a short move and take another (relatively simple) physical action, like make an attack. As with the attempt to make a long move, this is a Speed task with a difficulty of 4, and failure means that the character stops at some point, slipping or stumbling or otherwise getting held up.

LONG-TERM MOVEMENT

When talking about movement in terms of traveling rather than round-by-round action, typical characters can travel on a road about 20 miles (32 km) per day, averaging about 3 miles (5 km) per hour, including a few stops. When traveling overland, they can move about 12 miles (19 km) per day, averaging 2 miles (3 km) per hour, again with some stops. Mounted characters, such as those on horseback, can go twice as far. Other modes of travel (cars, airplanes, hovercraft, sailing ships, and so on) have their own rates of movement.

MOVEMENT MODIFIERS

Different environments affect movement in different ways.

Rough Terrain: A surface that's considered rough terrain is covered in loose stones or other material, uneven or with unsure footing, unsteady, or a surface that requires movement across a narrow space, such as a cramped corridor or a slender ledge. Stairs are also considered rough terrain. Rough terrain does not slow normal movement on a round-by-round basis, but hinders move rolls. Rough terrain cuts long-term movement rates in half.

Difficult Terrain: Difficult terrain is an area filled with challenging obstacles—water up to waist height, a very steep slope, an especially narrow ledge, slippery ice, a foot or more of snow, a space so small that one must crawl through it, and so on. Difficult terrain hinders move rolls and halves movement on a round-by-round basis. This means that a short move is about 25 feet (8 m), and a long move is about 50 feet (15 m). Difficult terrain reduces long-term movement to a third of its normal rate.

Water: Deep water, in which a character is mostly or entirely submerged, hinders move rolls and reduces round-by-round and long-term movement to one quarter its normal rate. This means that a short move is about 12 feet (4 m), and a long move is about 25 feet (7.5 m). Characters trained in swimming halve their movement only while in deep water.

Low Gravity: Movement in low gravity is easier but not much faster. All move rolls are eased.

High Gravity: In an environment of high gravity, treat all moving characters as if they were in difficult terrain. Characters trained in high-gravity maneuvering negate this penalty. High gravity reduces long-term movement to a third of its normal rate.

Zero Gravity: In an environment without gravity, characters cannot move normally. Instead, they must push off from a surface and succeed at a Might roll to move (the difficulty is equal to one-quarter the distance traveled in feet). Without a surface to push off from, a character cannot move. Unless the character's movement takes them to a stable object that they can grab or land against, they continue to drift in that direction each round, traveling half the distance of the initial push.

SPECIAL SITUATION: A CHASE

When a PC is chasing an NPC or vice versa, the player should attempt a Speed action, with the difficulty based on the NPC's level. If the PC succeeds at the roll, they catch the NPC (if chasing), or they get away (if chased). In terms of the story, this one-roll mechanic can be the result of a long chase over many rounds.

Alternatively, if the GM wants to play out a long chase, the character can make many rolls (perhaps one per level of the NPC) to finish the pursuit successfully. For every failure, the PC

RULES OF THE GAME

must make another success, and if they ever have more failures than successes, the PC fails to catch the NPC (if chasing) or is caught (if chased). As with combat, the GM is encouraged to describe the results of these rolls with flavor. A success might mean the PC has rounded a corner and gained some distance. A failure might mean that a basket of fruit topples over in front of them, slowing them down. Vehicle chases are handled similarly.

ACTION: WAIT

You can wait to react to another character's action.

You decide what action will trigger your action, and if the triggering action happens, you get to take your action first (unless going first wouldn't make sense, like attacking a foe before they come into view). For example, if an orc threatens you with a halberd, on your turn you can decide to wait, stating "If it stabs at me, I'm going to slash it with my sword." On the orc's turn, it stabs, so you make your sword attack before that happens.

Waiting is also a good way to deal with a ranged attacker who rises from behind cover, fires an attack, and ducks back down. You could say "I wait to see them pop up from behind cover and then I shoot them."

ACTION: DEFEND

Defending is a special action that only PCs can do, and only in response to being attacked. In other words, an NPC uses its action to attack, which forces a PC to make a defense roll. This is handled like any other kind of action, with circumstances, skill, assets, and Effort all potentially coming into play. Defending is a special kind of action in that it does not happen on the PC's turn. It's never an action that a player decides to take; it's always a reaction to an attack. A PC can take a defense action when attacked (on the attacking NPC's turn) and still take another action on their own turn.

The type of defense roll depends on the type of attack. If a foe attacks a character with an axe, they can use Speed to duck or block it with what they're holding. If they're struck by a poisoned dart, they can use a Might action to resist its effects. If a psi-worm attempts to control their mind, they can use Intellect to fend off the intrusion.

Sometimes an attack provokes two defense actions. For example, a poisonous reptile tries to bite a PC. They try to dodge the bite with a Speed action. If they fail, they take damage from the bite, and they must also attempt a Might action to resist the poison's effects.

If a character does not know an attack is coming, usually they can still make a defense roll, but they can't add modifiers (including the modifier from a shield), and they can't use any skill or Effort to ease the task. If circumstances warrant—such as if the attacker is right next to the character—the GM might rule that the surprise attack simply hits.

A character can always choose to forgo a defense action, in which case the attack automatically hits.

Some abilities (such as the Countermeasures special ability) may allow you to do something special as a defense action.

Vehicle chases, page 230

Countermeasures, page 122

Waiting is also a useful tool for cooperative actions (page 226).

Orc, page 347

225

ACTION: DO SOMETHING ELSE

Players can try anything they can think of, although that doesn't mean anything is possible. The GM sets the difficulty—that's their primary role in the game. Still, guided by the bounds of logic, players and GMs will find all manner of actions and options that aren't covered by a rule. That's a good thing.

Players should not feel constrained by the game mechanics when taking actions. Skills are not required to attempt an action. Someone who's never picked a lock can still try. The GM might hinder the task, but the character can still attempt the action.

Thus, players and GMs can return to the beginning of this chapter and look at the most basic expression of the rules. A player wants to take an action. The GM decides, on a scale of 1 to 10, how difficult that task is and what stat it uses. The player determines whether they have anything that might modify the difficulty and considers whether to apply Effort. Once the final determination is made, they roll to see if their character succeeds. It's as easy as that.

As further guidance, the following are some of the more common actions a player might take.

Difficult terrain, page 224
Inability, page 207

CLIMBING

When a character climbs, the GM sets a difficulty based on the surface being climbed. Climbing is like moving through difficult terrain: the move roll is hindered and the movement is half speed. Unusual circumstances, such as climbing while under fire, pose additional step penalties.

CLIMBING DIFFICULTY

Difficulty	Surface
2	Surface with lots of handholds
3	Stone wall or similar surface (a few handholds)
4	Crumbling or slippery surface
5	Smooth stone wall or similar surface
6	Metal wall or similar surface
8	Smooth, horizontal surface (climber is upside down)
10	Glass wall or similar surface

COOPERATIVE ACTIONS

There are many ways multiple characters can work together. None of these options, however, can be used at the same time by the same characters.

Helping: If you use your action to help someone with a task, you ease the task. If you have an inability in a task, your help has no effect. If you use your action to help someone with a task that you are trained or specialized in, the task is eased by two steps. Help is considered an asset, and someone receiving help usually can't gain more than two assets on a single task if that help is provided by another character.

For example, if Scott is trying to climb a steep incline and Sarah (who is trained in climbing) spends her turn helping him, Scott's task is eased by two steps.

Sometimes you can help by performing a task that complements what another person

RULES OF THE GAME

is attempting. If your complementary action succeeds, you ease the other person's task. For example, if Scott tries to persuade a ship captain to let him on board, Sarah could try to supplement Scott's words with a flattering lie about the captain (a deception action), a display of knowledge about the region where the ship is headed (a geography action), or a direct threat to the captain (an intimidation action). If Sarah's roll is a success, Scott's persuasion task is eased.

Distraction: When a character uses their turn to distract a foe, that foe's attacks are hindered for one round. Multiple characters distracting a foe have no greater effect than a single character doing so—a foe is either distracted or not. A distraction might be yelling a challenge, firing a warning shot, or a similar activity that doesn't harm the foe.

Draw the Attack: When an NPC attacks a character, another PC can prominently present themselves, shout taunts, and move to try to get the foe to attack them instead. In most cases, this action succeeds without a roll—the opponent attacks the prominent PC instead of their companions. In other cases, such as with intelligent or determined foes, the prominent character must succeed at an Intellect action to draw the attack. If that Intellect action is successful, the foe attacks the prominent character, whose defenses are hindered by two steps. Two characters attempting to draw an attack at the same time cancel each other out.

Take the Attack: A character can use their action to throw themselves in front of a foe's successful attack to save a nearby comrade. The attack automatically succeeds against the sacrificial character, and it deals 1 additional point of damage. A character cannot willingly take more than one attack each round in this way.

CRAFTING, BUILDING, AND REPAIRING

Crafting is a tricky topic in the Cypher System because the same rules that govern building a spear also cover repairing a machine that can take you into hyperspace. Normally, the level of the item determines the difficulty of creating or repairing it as well as the time required. For cyphers, artifacts, other items that require specialized knowledge, or items unique to a world or species other than your own (such as a Martian tripod walker), add 5 to the item's level to determine the difficulty of building or repairing it.

Sometimes, if the item is artistic in nature, the GM will add to the difficulty and time required. For example, a crude wooden stool might be hammered together in an hour. A beautiful finished piece might take a week or longer and would require more skill on the part of the crafter.

The GM is free to overrule some attempts at creation, building, or repair, requiring that the character have a certain level of skill, proper tools and materials, and so forth.

A level 0 object requires no skill to make and is easily found in most locations. Sling stones and firewood are level 0 items—producing them is routine. Making a torch from spare wood and oil-soaked cloth is simple, so it's a level 1 object. Making an arrow or a spear is fairly standard but not simple, so it's a level 2 object.

Generally speaking, a device to be crafted requires materials equal to its level and all the levels below it. So a level 5 device requires level 5 material, level 4 material, level 3 material, level 2 material, and level 1 material (and, technically, level 0 material).

The GM and players can gloss over much of the crafting details, if desired. Gathering all the materials to make a mundane item might not be worth playing out—but then again, it might be. For example, making a wooden spear in a forest isn't very interesting, but what if the characters have to make a spear in a treeless desert? Finding the wreckage of something made of wood or forcing a PC to fashion a spear out of the bones of a large beast could be interesting situations.

The time required to create an item is up to the GM, but the guidelines in the crafting table are a good starting point. Generally, repairing an item takes somewhere between half the creation time and the full creation time, depending on the item, the aspect that needs repairing, and the circumstances. For example, if creating an item takes one hour, repairing it takes thirty minutes to one hour.

Sometimes a GM will allow a rush job if the circumstances warrant it. This is different than using skill to reduce the time required. In this case, the quality of the item is affected. Let's say that a character needs to create a tool that will cut through solid steel with a laser (a level 7 item), but they have to do it in one day. The GM might allow it, but the device might be extremely volatile, inflicting damage on the user, or it might work only once. The device is still considered a level 7 item to create in all other respects. Sometimes the GM will rule that reducing the

In some fights, it might be to your advantage to help another PC who is more effective in combat than you are, either by helping them attack or by distracting their opponent. Just because you're not making an attack roll doesn't mean you're not contributing to your side's success.

In the Cypher System, players are not rewarded for killing foes in combat, so using a smart idea to avoid combat and still succeed is just good play. Likewise, coming up with an idea to defeat a foe without hammering on it with weapons is encouraged—creativity is not cheating!

Players are encouraged to come up with their own ideas for what their characters do rather than looking at a list of possible actions. That's why there is a "do something else" action. PCs are not pieces on a game board—they are people in a story. And like real people, they can try anything they can think of. (Succeeding is another matter entirely.) The task difficulty system provides GMs with the tools they need to adjudicate anything the players come up with.

227

CRAFTING DIFFICULTY AND TIME

Difficulty	Craft	General Time to Build
0	Something extremely simple like tying a rope or finding an appropriately sized rock	A few minutes at most
1	Torch	Five minutes
2	Spear, simple shelter, piece of furniture	One hour
3	Bow, door, basic article of clothing	One day
4	Sword, chainmail vest	One to two days
5	Common technological item (electric light), nice piece of jewelry or art object	One week
6	Technological item (watch, transmitter), really nice piece of jewelry or art object, elegant craftwork	One month
7	Technological item (computer), major work of art	One year
8	Technological item (something from beyond Earth)	Many years
9	Technological item (something from beyond Earth)	Many years
10	Technological item (something from beyond Earth)	Many years

Circumstances really matter. For example, sewing a dress by hand might take five times as long (or more) as using a sewing machine.

The GM is free to overrule some attempts at creation, building, or repair, requiring that the character have a certain level of skill, proper tools and materials, and so forth.

Obviously, what is considered "weird stuff" will vary from setting to setting, and sometimes the concept might not apply at all. But many times, there will be something in the setting that is too strange, too alien, too powerful, or too dangerous for PCs to mess around with (or at least mess around with easily). Einstein may have been extraordinary, but that doesn't mean he could reverse-engineer a teleporter made in another dimension.

time is not possible. For example, a single human can't make a chainmail vest in one hour without some kind of machine to help.

Possible crafting skills include:

Armoring	Glassblowing
Bowyering/fletching	Gunsmithing
Chemistry	Leatherworking
Computer science	Metalworking
Electronics	Neural engineering
Engines	Weaponsmithing
Genetic engineering	Woodcrafting

Characters might try to make a cypher, an artifact, or an alien psionic starship do something other than its intended function. Sometimes, the GM will simply declare the task impossible. You can't turn a vial of healing elixir into a two-way communicator. But most of the time, there is a chance of success.

That said, tinkering with weird stuff is not easy. Obviously, the difficulty varies from situation to situation, but difficulties starting at 7 are not unreasonable. The time, tools, and training required would be similar to the time, tools, and training needed to repair a device. If the tinkering results in a long-term benefit for the character—such as creating an artifact that they can use—the GM should require them to spend XP to make it.

GUARDING

In a combat situation, a character can stand guard as their action. They do not make attacks, but all their defense tasks are eased. Further, if an NPC tries to get by them or take an action that they are guarding against, the character can attempt an eased Speed action based on the level of the NPC. Success means the NPC is prevented from taking the action; the NPC's action that turn is wasted. This is useful for blocking a doorway, guarding a friend, and so forth.

If an NPC is standing guard, use the same procedure, but to get past the guard, the PC attempts a hindered Speed action against the NPC. For example, Diana is an NPC human with a level 3 bodyguard. The bodyguard uses their action to guard Diana. If a PC wants to attack Diana, the PC first must succeed at a difficulty 4 Speed task to get past the guard. If the PC succeeds, they can make their attack normally.

HEALING

You can administer aid through bandaging and other succor, attempting to heal each patient once per day. This healing restores points to a stat Pool of your choice. Decide how many points you want to heal, and then make an Intellect action with a difficulty equal to that number. For example, if you want to heal someone for 3 points, that's a difficulty 3 task with a target number of 9.

INTERACTING WITH CREATURES

The level of the creature determines the target number, just as with combat. Thus, bribing a guard works much like punching them or affecting them with an ability. This is true of persuading someone, intimidating someone, calming a wild beast, or anything of the kind. Interaction is an Intellect task. Interacting usually requires a common language or some other way to communicate. Learning new languages is the same as learning a new skill.

JUMPING

Decide how far you want to jump, and that sets the difficulty of your Might roll. For a standing jump, subtract 4 from the distance in feet to determine the difficulty of the jump. For example, jumping 10 feet (3 m) has a difficulty of 6.

If you run an immediate distance before jumping, it counts as an asset, easing the jump.

If you run a short distance before jumping, divide the jump distance (in feet) by 2 and then subtract 4 to determine the difficulty of the jump. Because you're running an immediate distance (and then some), you also count your running as an asset. For example, jumping a distance of 20 feet (6 m) with a short running start has a difficulty of 5 (20 feet divided by 2 is 10, minus 4 is 6, minus 1 for running an immediate distance).

For a vertical jump, the distance you clear (in feet) is equal to the difficulty of the jumping task. If you run an immediate distance, it counts as an asset, easing the jump.

LOOKING OR LISTENING

Generally, the GM will describe any sight or sound that's not purposefully difficult to detect. But if you want to look for a hidden enemy, search for a secret panel, or listen for someone sneaking up on you, make an Intellect roll. If it's a creature, its level determines the difficulty of your roll. If it's something else, the GM determines the difficulty of your roll.

MOVING A HEAVY OBJECT

You can push or pull something very heavy and move it an immediate distance as your action.

The weight of the object determines the difficulty of the Might roll to move it; every 50 pounds (23 kg) hinders the task by one step. So moving something that weighs 150 pounds (68 kg) is difficulty 3, and moving something that weighs 400 pounds (180 kg) is difficulty 8. If you can ease the task to 0, you can move a heavy object up to a short distance as your action.

OPERATING OR DISABLING A DEVICE, OR PICKING A LOCK

As with figuring out a device, the level of the device usually determines the difficulty of the Intellect roll. Unless a device is very complex, the GM will often rule that once you figure it out, no roll is needed to operate it except under special circumstances. So if the PCs figure out how to use a hovercraft, they can operate it. If they are attacked, they might need to roll to ensure that they don't crash the vehicle into a wall while trying to avoid being hit.

Unlike operating a device, disabling a device or picking a lock usually require rolls. These actions often involve special tools and assume that the character is not trying to destroy the device or lock. (A PC who *is* attempting to destroy it probably should make a Might roll to smash it rather than a Speed or Intellect roll requiring patience and know-how.)

RIDING OR PILOTING

If you're riding an animal that's trained to be a mount, or driving or piloting a vehicle, you don't need to make a roll to do something routine such as going from point A to point B (just as you wouldn't need to make a roll to walk there). However, staying mounted during a fight or doing something tricky with a vehicle requires a Speed roll to succeed. A saddle or other appropriate gear is an asset and eases the task.

RIDING OR PILOTING DIFFICULTY

Difficulty	Maneuver
0	Riding
1	Staying on the mount (including a motorcycle or similar vehicle) in a battle or other difficult situation
3	Staying on a mount (including a motorcycle or similar vehicle) when you take damage
4	Mounting a moving steed
4	Making an abrupt turn with a vehicle while moving fast
4	Getting a vehicle to move twice as fast as normal for one round
5	Coaxing a mount to move or jump twice as fast or far as normal for one round
5	Making a long jump with a vehicle not intended to go airborne (like a car) and remaining in control

SNEAKING

The difficulty of sneaking by a creature is determined by its level. Sneaking is a Speed roll. Moving at half speed eases the sneaking task. Appropriate camouflage or other gear may count as an asset and ease the task, as will dim lighting conditions and having plenty of things to hide behind.

SWIMMING

If you're simply swimming from one place to another, such as across a calm river or lake, use the standard movement rules, noting the fact that your character is in deep water. However, sometimes, special circumstances require a Might roll to make progress while swimming, such as when trying to avoid a current or being dragged into a whirlpool.

There's nothing wrong with the GM simply assigning a difficulty level to a jump without worrying about the precise distance. The rules here are just so everyone has some guidelines.

UNDERSTANDING, IDENTIFYING, OR REMEMBERING

When characters try to identify or figure out how to use a device, the level of the device determines the difficulty. For a bit of knowledge, the GM determines the difficulty.

Difficulty	Knowledge
0	Common knowledge
1	Simple knowledge
3	Something a scholar probably knows
5	Something even a scholar might not know
7	Knowledge very few people possess
10	Completely lost knowledge

VEHICULAR MOVEMENT

Vehicles move just like creatures. Each has a movement rate, which indicates how far it can move in a round. Most vehicles require a driver, and when moving, they usually require that the driver spends every action controlling the movement. This is a routine task that rarely requires a roll. Any round not spent driving the vehicle hinders the task in the next round and precludes any change in speed or direction. In other words, driving down the road normally is difficulty 0. Spending an action to retrieve a backpack from the back seat means that in the following round, the driver must attempt a difficulty 1 task. If they instead use their action to pull a handgun from the backpack, in the next round the difficulty to drive will be 2, and so on. Failure results are based on the situation but might involve a collision or something similar.

During a vehicular battle, particularly a space battle, there's a lot of chatter about shields failing, hull integrity, being outmaneuvered, coming in too fast, and whatnot. These sorts of details are great, but they're all flavor, so they're represented in the rules generally, rather than specifically.

For more details about vehicles, refer to the appropriate genre chapter.

In a vehicular chase, drivers attempt Speed actions just like in a regular chase, but the task may be based either on the level of the driver (modified by the level and movement rate of the vehicle) or on the level of the vehicle (modified by the level of the driver). So if a PC driving a typical car is chasing a level 3 NPC driving a level 5 sports car, the PC would make three chase rolls with a difficulty of 5. If the PC's car is a souped-up custom vehicle, it might grant the PC an asset in the chase. If the PC is not in a car at all, but riding a bicycle, it might hinder the chase rolls by two or three steps, or the GM might simply rule that it's impossible.

VEHICULAR COMBAT

Much of the time, a fight between foes in cars, boats, or other vehicles is just like any other combat situation. The combatants probably have cover and are moving fast. Attacks to disable a vehicle or a portion of it are based on the level of the vehicle. If the vehicle is an armored car or a tank, all attacks are likely aimed at the vehicle, which has a level and probably an appropriate Armor rating, not unlike a creature.

The only time this isn't true is with battles where only vehicles and not characters are involved. Thus, if the PCs are in a shootout with bank robbers and both groups are in cars, use the standard rules. However, battles between starships of various kinds—from gigantic capital ships to single-pilot fighters—are a frequent occurrence in far-future science fiction settings. A submarine battle between two deep sea craft could be quite exciting. Characters in a modern-day game might find themselves in a tank fight. If PCs are involved in combat in which they are entirely enclosed in vehicles (so that it's not really the characters fighting, but the vehicles), use the following quick and easy guidelines.

On this scale, combat between vehicles isn't like traditional combat. Don't worry about health, Armor, or anything like that. Instead, just compare the levels of the vehicles involved. If the PCs' vehicle has the higher level, the difference in levels is how many steps the PCs' attack and defense rolls are eased. If the PCs' vehicle has the lower level, their rolls are hindered. If the levels are the same, there is no modification.

These attack and defense rolls are modified by skill and Effort, as usual. Some vehicles also have superior weapons, which ease the attack (since there is no "damage" amount to worry about), but this circumstance is probably uncommon in this abstract system and should not affect the difficulty by more than one or maybe two steps.

Further, if two vehicles coordinate their attack against one vehicle, the attack is eased. If three or more vehicles coordinate, the attack is eased by two steps.

The attacker must try to target a specific system on or portion of an enemy vehicle. This hinders the attack based on the system or portion targeted.

That's a lot of modifications. But it's not really that hard. Let's look at an example of a space battle. A PC in a small level 2 fighter attacks a level 4 frigate. Since the frigate is level 4, the difficulty of the attack starts at 4. But the attacking craft is weaker than the defender, so the attack is hindered equal to the difference in their levels (2). The fighter pilot must make a difficulty 6 attack on the frigate. However, the fighter is trying to swoop in and damage the frigate's drive, which hinders the attack by another three steps, for a total difficulty of 9. If the fighter pilot is trained in space combat, they reduce the difficulty to 8, but it's still impossible without help. So let's say that two other PCs—also in level 2 fighters—join in and coordinate their attack. Three ships coordinating an attack on one target eases the task by two steps, resulting in a final difficulty of 6. Still, the attacking PC would be wise to use Effort.

Then the frigate retaliates, and the PC needs to make a defense roll. The level difference between the ships (2) means the PC's defense is hindered by two steps, so the difficulty of the PC's defense roll starts out at 6. But the frigate tries to take out the fighter's weapons, hindering their attack (easing the PC's defense) by two steps. Thus, the PC needs to succeed at a difficulty 4 task or lose their main weapons systems.

It's important to remember that a failed attack doesn't always mean a miss. The target ship might rock and reel from the hit, but the bulk of the damage was absorbed by the shields, so there's no significant damage.

This bare-bones system should allow the GM and players to flesh out exciting encounters involving the whole group. For example, perhaps while one PC pilots a ship, another mans the guns, and another frantically attempts to repair damage to the maneuvering thrusters before they crash into the space station they're trying to defend.

Targeting Task	Attack Hindered	Effect
Disable weapons	Two steps	One or more of the vehicle's weapons no longer function
Disable defenses (if applicable)	Two steps	Attacks against the vehicle are eased
Disable engine/drive	Three steps	Vehicle cannot move, or movement is hampered
Disable maneuverability	Two steps	Vehicle cannot alter its present course
Strike power core or vital spot	Five steps	Vehicle is completely destroyed

OPTIONAL RULE: GAINING INSIGHT

Sometimes GMs like to keep lots of mystery in their games and present the players with many unknowns. This can be fun, and it's realistic—there's always some unknown factor in any situation that can creep up and cause trouble. And trouble is good because it makes things more interesting. These unknown factors are usually best portrayed as GM intrusions.

However, when a master thief plans to break into a vault and steal the jewels, they don't go in unless they are sure. They might know exactly what sorts of alarms are rigged to the door, or what schedule the security guards follow when patrolling. This isn't guesswork. The thief knows these things for certain. That's how they came up with their break-in plan in the first place. It's what separates the master thief from bumbling criminals.

Similarly, the PCs are competent individuals—sometimes even experts—and such people can make decisions and devise plans with confidence. Yet players often find this difficult for two reasons. First, while their characters might be world-class con artists, infiltration specialists, or demolition experts, the players are not. And second, they're hindered by all the previously mentioned unknowns.

This is why PCs can gain Insights to help them. If a character is thinking about a plan, doing research, gathering information, casing a job, or scouting ahead, they can spend 3 Intellect points and one action to gain a single bit of special knowledge from the GM that they can count on with certainty. Insights are always presented as absolutes, and once established, they should never be changed, unless it is through the direct and deliberate intervention of the PCs. For example, if the PCs gain an Insight

If there are no Insights to be gained in a particular situation (or no more Insights to be gained), the PC looking for one still loses the Intellect points.

The cost of gaining Insight is not reduced by any Edge you may have.

that giving the guard at the gate a bottle of booze by 10 p.m. ensures that the guard is drunk by midnight, and they kill that guard and a new one is stationed there, the Insight is invalidated and all bets are off. (Likewise if they use a psychic power to make the guard hate alcohol.) Either way, it changes only because the PCs changed it deliberately. Thus, they know for certain, ahead of time, that the Insight has become invalid.

Insights are never an end in themselves—they are a means to an end. If the whole point of an adventure is to identify a murderer, the characters can't get an Insight to learn the killer's identity. They could, however, use Insights to help them along. For example, they might learn that the murderer is left-handed, or that the accountant is definitely *not* the murderer.

Ultimately, the GM decides each Insight's revelation, so there's no chance that the PCs will gain too much information (if such a thing is even possible). But GMs are highly, highly encouraged to give a valuable Insight if the characters look for one (by spending Intellect points and an action), even if it must be made up on the spot. Doing so allows the players to make intelligent plans and feel confident and—more important—competent.

Short-term benefit, page 239

GM-INSTIGATED INSIGHTS

Sometimes, the GM can flag a potential Insight to a player in a given area. Usually, this is something the GM has specifically designed ahead of time for this purpose. After the PCs have explored an area and are ready to leave, the GM might say "There's an Insight to be had here." This kind of Insight can't be gained by spending Intellect points. Instead, if the character wants to follow up on the GM's comment, they spend 2 XP as if they were buying a short-term benefit. No player is required to make this expenditure—they can always choose to not spend the XP and not learn that Insight.

OPTIONAL RULE: GETTING AN XP ADVANCE

By introducing a story complication based on their character's background, a player can start the game with a significant amount of XP (and can spend them immediately if desired, even to purchase enough benefits to advance to the next tier). The GM has final approval over this option, and it should be used only in groups that don't insist on all characters having precisely the same power levels. This story-based concept allows a player to create exactly the character they want at the outset at the cost of building a narrative complication into the PC.

SAMPLE INSIGHTS
- The mob boss's bodyguard always falls asleep after a big lunch.
- The mayor won't press charges if they think their child is involved.
- There must be a secret room at the center of the level because the walls don't match up.
- The guard at the gate can't be bribed.
- The starship captain won't believe anything a Narvelian says.
- The shopkeeper knows they must sell the stolen goods by the end of the day and will do anything to do so.
- The queen is having an affair with the noblewoman.
- The magic amulet sank to the bottom of the Garvanas Trench in the Talvar Sea when the ship went down.
- The kidnappers are holding the boy as far away from the cathedral as possible.
- Orcs hate the taste of anise.
- The castle's defenses include counterspells that negate invisibility effects.
- The bridge will collapse if more than one person walks across it.
- The judge knows who the murderer is.
- The two magic rings will cancel each other out.
- The alarm system is wired to every door, but not to the windows on the second floor.
- The fugitives couldn't be more than one hour's drive away.
- The ambassador shows the telltale signs of being a shapeshifter.
- The dwarves of the ancient fortress always put exactly three traps on their doors.
- The general's assistant is fiercely loyal and will never betray them.

FOLLOWERS

Player characters have the option to gain followers as they advance in tier, as provided by type or focus special abilities. Followers do not need to be paid, fed, or housed, though a character who gains followers can certainly make such arrangements if they wish. A follower is someone whom a character has inspired (or asked) to come work with the character for a time, aiding them in a variety of endeavors. A follower puts the PC's interests ahead of, or at least on par with, their own.

The PC generally makes rolls for their follower when the follower takes actions, though usually a follower's modifications provide an asset to a specific action taken by the PC they follow.

Modifications: A follower can help a PC in one or more tasks, granting the PC an asset to that task. The level of the follower indicates the number of different tasks they can help with. The tasks that the follower is able to help with are predetermined, usually chosen by the PC when they gain the follower. A level 2 follower who the player determines is a spy could grant a PC an asset on two different tasks, such as stealth and deception. Followers cannot help with tasks that they don't have modifications for; for the purpose of helping, treat the follower as if they had inabilities in all nonmodified tasks.

When the follower acts autonomously rather than helping the PC, they act like a normal NPC that has modifications. Thus, the modification increases their effective level for the associated task by one step. For example, the level 2 spy follower with modifications for stealth and deception attempts stealth and deception tasks as if they were level 3 and all other tasks as level 2.

Follower Assets to Combat and Defense: A follower cannot grant an asset to a character's attacks or defense until the follower is level 3 or higher. Even then, the follower can help with attacks and defense only if they have a modification for that kind of task.

Some abilities may grant a special exception to this rule. For instance, the Serv-0 Defender ability gives your level 1 Serv-0 follower (a machine companion) a modification for Speed defense.

Follower Level Progression: A follower increases in level by 1 each time a PC advances two tiers after gaining that follower. When the follower gains a level, the PC also chooses the task that the follower gains a modification for.

Exceptional Follower: When a character gains a follower, there's a small chance that the follower will be exceptional in some way, a cut above other followers of their kind. The GM determines when an exceptional follower is found, possibly as an additional reward for smart or engaging roleplaying where the PCs impress or otherwise positively interact with one or more NPCs, some of whom may later go on to become one of their followers. An exceptional follower has the same qualities as a regular follower but is 1 level higher.

Pet: Any PC can potentially gain a pet, though a pet typically doesn't provide modifications. If a character wants a pet that can do this, they must gain the pet through an an ability or focus that grants followers. On the other hand, a well-cared-for pet grants an asset to a PC's tasks related to achieving peace of mind, finding comfort, and resisting loneliness.

BREATHING LIFE INTO FOLLOWERS

The modifications provided by followers could come across as fairly dry and mechanical. To avoid that, you could present each follower in a way that makes them more compelling and interesting. Here are a few examples of how to describe a follower, depending on their mix of modifications.

- A firebrand diplomat able to convince an enemy horde to back down.
- A veteran commander whose presence bolsters the entire community's military might.
- A genius medic who invigorates everyone with their healing techniques.
- An imaginative architect whose works both beautify and defend the city.
- A tricky spy whose intelligence on enemy movements is invaluable.

Helping, page 226

Controls Beasts, page 65

Modifications, page 313

If a follower dies, the character gains a new one after at least two weeks and proper recruitment.

Serv-0 Defender, page 181

Followers cannot help with tasks that they don't have modifications for; treat the follower as if they had inabilities in all nonmodified tasks for the purpose of helping.

For example, a player might want to start the game with a robotic companion or a beam weapon. Under the normal rules, these options aren't available to a beginning player (unless such a thing is their explanation for a type or focus ability), but they could find or build a companion or weapon given time (and perhaps after spending XP). With the optional rule, the character gets an advance XP amount that can be used to "buy" the automaton or weapon, and in exchange, the GM decides they have an inability with all NPC interactions.

Inability, page 207

As another example, let's say a player doesn't want to start by playing a new, young character—they want to play someone who is older and more experienced. Although the Cypher System does not assume that all starting characters are fresh young recruits, the player's vision doesn't quite sound like a first-tier character. So the player comes up with a significant drawback, such as a severe addiction to a costly drug, in exchange for an advance of XP that allows them to start at the second tier, with all the benefits of a second-tier character.

The following story complications are worth an advance of 4 to 6 XP:

- People find the character extremely unlikable. No matter what they say or do, intelligent creatures and animals find them unpleasant. All interaction tasks are hindered. Further, the GM should make a default assumption that all people treat the PC with distaste and contempt as a baseline.
- The character has a bum leg. It acts up every now and then (at least once per adventure, and usually once per session), and when it does, all Speed tasks are hindered.
- The character has an inability with a significant task, such as attacks, defense, movement, or something of that nature. As a result, all such tasks are hindered.
- The character has an occasionally debilitating condition, such as a bad back, alcoholism, eating issues, and so on. This problem results in a significant penalty once per session.
- The character is wanted by the law and must keep a low profile. This can cause story-based complications rather than mechanical ones, but it can make life difficult for them at times.
- The character has a defenseless relative or friend who is often at risk. Again, this is not a mechanical issue, but one that will affect how the character is played. At times, they will have to stop what they are doing to help the person out of a jam. At other times, the person's life might be truly in jeopardy, compelling the PC to action.
- The character must perform a regular action to retain their abilities. For example, each morning, they must "commune" with an ultrapowerful, artificially intelligent "god" who grants them their powers. If this communion is disturbed or prevented, or if the transmission is broken or blocked, the PC does not have access to their abilities that day.
- The character must have a particular item to be able to use their abilities. For example, they need a power cell, a focusing crystal, or another object that can be lost, stolen, or destroyed. Perhaps, like a power cell, it needs to be replaced or recharged from time to time.

The following story complications are worth an advance of 12 to 20 XP:

- The character is wanted by the law and is actively pursued by multiple NPCs. This isn't just a matter of lying low when they are in town. Instead, NPCs will show up at the worst possible times and attempt to abduct or kill them.
- The character has a condition such that all tasks involving combat and NPC interaction are hindered.
- The character has a truly debilitating condition, such as blindness, deafness, being crippled, severe drug addiction, and so on.
- The character has a defenseless relative or friend who (for some vital reason) must accompany them at least 75 percent of the time. The character will spend many actions protecting this person instead of doing what they'd rather be doing.
- The character's abilities rely on a rare drug that is difficult to obtain. Without a regular dose of this substance, they are virtually powerless.
- The character was experimented on as a young child, which gave them powers and abilities. Now, to gain any new abilities, they must find the original experimenter and replicate the process. This is a major mission and could result in a long delay in character advancement (effectively giving them a boost in power at the beginning of the game but no boosts for a long time afterward).

OPTIONAL RULE: SKILLS FROM BACKGROUNDS

A Warrior's background says that they worked in a smithy as a child. But there's no way a Warrior can begin with weaponsmithing as a skill (they can get this skill as they progress). Should they start with that skill? This question has four potential answers.

1. *No.* They might know the basics of the task. However, a skill doesn't represent a simple familiarity, but extensive training, experience, or talent. Not everyone who works in a restaurant is a chef.

2. *Sure.* In the scope of things, will weaponsmithing wreck the game or make the character unplayable? Is it unfair to the other players? Probably not. For that matter, the GM could give all the characters a background skill. Require that it ties into the character's background and doesn't have a lot of direct adventuring applications. For example, a PC can have cooking, animal care, philosophy, or woodworking, but not climbing, sneaking, or anything similar, and certainly not a skill with attack or defense.

3. *Yes.* Use the optional rules for giving experience point advances, where the character takes on a story complication in exchange for receiving 4 XP to buy the new skill (4 XP is the normal cost to buy a new skill as a Character Advancement).

4. *Yes.* Allow the player to have an XP deficit. The character starts with the desired skill, but before they can gain any of the four benefits required to advance to the next tier, they must pay off this deficit. It's probably unwise to allow a character to start with a deficit of greater than 4 XP.

OPTIONAL RULE: USING MINIATURES

Some players like to use miniatures, counters, or other tokens to represent their characters, particularly in a battlefield situation. Miniatures showing the location of the PCs, NPCs, and terrain features can be useful visual aids. They help people see who is closest to the door, which foe stands where, and who will be crushed if the dangerously weak part of the ceiling caves in.

DISTANCE

Often, players who use miniatures also use a grid to represent distance. If you do this, it's probably best to say that each 1-inch (2.5 cm) square represents about 5 feet (1.5 m). Simply move your figure the right number of squares; for example, a short distance would be ten squares.

Character Advancement, page 240

XP advances, page 232

However, a grid isn't necessary in the Cypher System. Since most things have one of four possible distances—immediate, short, long, and very long—that's all you need to worry about. Thus, you could cut four lengths of string: one 2 inches (5 cm) long, one 10 inches (25 cm) long, one 20 inches (51 cm) long, and one 50 inches (127 cm) long. If something has immediate range, stretch the 2-inch string from the origin point to see how far it goes. Any character whose figure is within 2 inches of another figure can make a melee attack against that figure. (The attacker is assumed to move closer to the target, so slide the figures together.) If a character wants to move a short distance, use the 10-inch string to measure from their starting point to their intended destination. If the string can reach that far, so can they. For long range, anything you can reach with the 20-inch string is in range. For very long range, anything you can reach with the 50-inch string is in range (of course, that's longer than the map space on most home gaming tables, so anything on the table is probably within very long range). Soon, you'll find that you can eyeball the distances—precision isn't that important.

SIZE

In some games that use miniatures, the size of the miniature's base is important. In the Cypher System, such precision isn't necessary. However, it certainly helps if larger creatures have larger bases, representing that they take up more room.

Speaking of which, GMs are free to consider any appropriate creature "big." An appropriate creature would likely be one that is more than 10 feet (3 m) tall or 10 feet (3 m) long. Big creatures don't have to move their miniature when making a melee attack within immediate distance. They can just reach that far.

GMs can also designate some creatures "huge." Huge creatures are 20 feet (6 m) tall or 20 feet (6 m) long. For them, immediate distance is a string 4 inches (10 cm) long—or four squares on a grid—and they don't have to move to make melee attacks.

Line of sight is a gaming term meaning that an attacker can directly see their target and make an attack. If you can draw a straight line from the attacker to the target without hitting obstacles, you have line of sight. You could have line of sight in an open field, or through an open doorway or window, but probably not around a corner or through a wall.

As a rule of thumb, the maximum number of attackers that can attack a single creature is the same as the number of figures whose bases can fit around the creature. In general, this means that larger creatures can be attacked by more foes.

TACTICAL PLAY

When you use miniatures, some aspects of the game become more important, including range, movement, and special effects that move characters. If a character is knocked back, move their miniature back 1 or 2 inches (or squares), as appropriate.

That means terrain is more important, too. If a deep chasm is nearby, the players need to know exactly where it is in relation to their figures in case they have the opportunity to knock a foe into that chasm (or face that same risk themselves). Likewise, things to hide behind, the layout of interior chambers, and so on become important and must be depicted along with the miniatures. Many people enjoy playing this kind of game on a dry-erase or wet-erase surface so they can draw the features and place the figures right in the action. Sketching them on paper works fine, too, as does using books, pencils, or other things to represent ledges, walls, and so forth. And, of course, terrain pieces can be used for extra flavor. Some pieces are made of paper to keep them inexpensive.

Line of sight also becomes more important, and if you already cut a string to measure distance, it works for this purpose as well. Place the string anywhere on the base of the character taking the action, and stretch the string toward the target. If the string can be stretched to any part of the base of the target, without having to bend around or over an obstacle, the attacker has line of sight.

POSSIBLE DRAWBACKS

The downside to using miniatures is that the exacting detail they offer sometimes gets in the way of the GM's narrative control. For example, without miniatures, a GM can introduce an intrusion and say "You are standing on the trapdoor when it opens." With miniatures, a player usually knows exactly where they are standing at any given moment.

Also, psychologically, miniatures seem to encourage combat. If you place a miniature on the game table representing a new creature that the PCs encounter, some players assume that they need to engage with it in tactical combat rather than talk to it, sneak past it, or try some other course of action.

Chapter 12
EXPERIENCE POINTS

Experience points (XP) are the currency by which players gain benefits for their characters. The most common ways to earn XP are through GM intrusions and by accomplishing things the PCs set out to do. Sometimes experience points are earned during a game session, and sometimes they're earned between sessions. In a typical session, a player might earn 2 to 4 XP, and between sessions, perhaps another 2 XP (on average). The exact amounts depend on the events of the session.

GM INTRUSION

At any time, the GM can introduce an unexpected complication for a character. When they intrude in this way, they must give that character 2 XP. That player, in turn, must immediately give one of those XP to another player and justify the gift (perhaps the other player had a good idea, told a joke, or performed an action that saved a life).

Often, the GM intrudes when a player attempts an action that should be an automatic success. However, the GM is free to intrude at other times. As a general rule, the GM should intrude at least once each session, but no more than once or twice each session per character.

Anytime the GM intrudes, the player can spend 1 XP to refuse the intrusion, though that also means they don't get the 2 XP. If the player has no XP to spend, they can't refuse.

If a player rolls a 1 on a die, the GM can intrude without giving the player any XP.

Example 1: Through skill and the aid of another character, a fourth-tier PC eases a wall-climbing task from difficulty 2 to difficulty 0. Normally, they would succeed at the task automatically, but the GM intrudes and says "No, a bit of the crumbling wall gives way, so you still have to make a roll." As with any difficulty 2 task, the target number is 6. The PC attempts the roll as normal and gains 2 XP because the GM intruded. They immediately give one of those XP to another player.

Example 2: During a fight, a PC swings their axe and damages a foe with a slice across the shoulder. The GM intrudes by saying that the foe turned just as the axe struck, wrenching the weapon from the character's grip and sending it clattering across the floor. The axe comes to a stop 10 feet (3 m) away. Because the GM intruded, the PC gains 2 XP, and the player immediately gives one of those XP to another player. Now the character must deal with the dropped weapon, perhaps drawing a different weapon or using their next turn to scramble after the axe.

For much more on GM intrusion, see page 408.

CHARACTER ARCS

Character arcs are the means by which players can invest themselves more in great stories and character depth and development.

Just like in a book or a television show, characters progress through their own personal story and change over time. A PC with a character arc decides for themselves what they do and why. Character arcs are like stated goals for a character, and by progressing toward that goal, the character advances. The key word there is *progressing*. A PC doesn't have to succeed at achieving the goal to earn advancement—it's not an all-or-nothing prospect. Each arc is keyed to a single character, but just like in a book or show, characters can take part in the larger story arc that the whole group participates in, while also progressing in their own personal arc.

Character arcs have different steps that mark the character's progress through the arc. Each arc eventually reaches a climax, and then finishes with a step that is a final resolution. Each step reached earns the character 2 XP. Character arcs are the most straightforward way that a character earns XP.

At character creation, a player can choose one character arc for their PC at no cost. Players have the option to not choose one, but it's probably a good idea to do so. First and foremost, it is a character-defining factor. If they begin the campaign with a desire to find the woman who killed their brother, that says a lot about the character: they had a brother, he was likely close to them, he had been in at least one dangerous situation, and the character is probably motivated by anger and hate, at least somewhat. Even after the character finishes this first arc, they'll undoubtedly have (at least one) more because they can gain new arcs as the campaign progresses.

Once play begins, players can take on a new arc whenever they wish, as fits the character's ongoing story. Taking a new arc has a cost of 1 XP. While there's no hard limit on how many arcs a character can have at one time, realistically most PCs couldn't reasonably have more than three or four.

However, as mentioned above, arcs have a beginning cost that must be paid, reflecting the character's devotion to the goal. The character will earn this investment back (probably many times over) if the arc is completed.

Character arcs are always player-driven. A GM cannot force one on a character. That said, the events in the narrative often present story arc opportunities and inspire character arcs for the PCs. It's certainly in the GM's purview to suggest possible arcs related to the events going on. For example, if the GM presents an encounter in which an NPC wishes to learn from the PC, it might make sense to suggest taking the Instruction arc. Whether or not the PC takes on the student, the player doesn't have to adopt the Instruction arc unless they want to.

At the end of a session, review the actions you took and describe how they might equate to the completion of a step (or possibly more than one step) in their character arc. If the GM agrees, the character gets their reward.

This chapter presents many sample character arcs, starting on page 241.

GM AWARDS

Sometimes, a group will have an adventure that doesn't deal primarily with a PC's character arc. In this case, it's a good idea for the GM to award XP to that character for accomplishing other tasks. First and foremost, awards should be based on discovery. Discovery can include finding a significant new location, such as a hidden chamber, a secret fortress, a lost land, a new planet, or an unexplored dimension. In this fashion, PCs are explorers. Discovery can also include a new significant aspect of a setting, such as a secret organization, a new religion, and so on.

It can also mean finding a new procedure or device (something too big to be considered a piece of equipment) or even previously unknown information. This could include a source of magical power, a unique teleportation device, or the cure for a plague. These are all discoveries. The common thread is that the PCs discover something that they can understand and put to use.

Last, depending on the GM's outlook and the kind of campaign the group wants to play, a discovery could be a secret, an ethical idea, an adage, or even a truth.

Artifacts: When the group gains an artifact, award XP equal to the artifact's level and divide it among the PCs (minimum 1 XP for each character). Round down if necessary. For example, if four PCs discover a level 5 artifact, they each get 1 XP. Money, standard equipment, and cyphers are not worth XP.

Miscellaneous Discoveries: Various other discoveries might grant 1 XP to each PC involved.

Other Awards: If a character is focused on activities that don't relate to a character arc or a discovery, as a general rule, a mission should be

---

Typically, PCs will earn about half their total experience points from arcs or other GM awards.

When in doubt, if one character accomplishes a step in their arc but another character does not, the first character should get the 2 XP reward, but the other character should probably still get, at minimum, 1 XP for the session.

It's a fine line, but ultimately the GM decides what constitutes a discovery as opposed to just something weird in the course of an adventure. Usually, the difference is, did the PCs successfully interact with it and learn something about it? If so, it's probably a discovery.

Experience point awards for artifacts should usually apply even if the artifact was given to the PCs rather than found, because often such gifts are the rewards for success.

worth at least 1 XP per game session involved in accomplishing it. For example, saving a family on an isolated farm beset by raiding cultists might be worth 1 XP for each character. Of course, saving the family doesn't always mean killing the bad guys; it might mean relocating them, parlaying with the cultists, or chasing off the raiders.

SPENDING EXPERIENCE POINTS

Experience points are meant to be used. Hoarding them is not a good idea; if a player accumulates more than 10 XP, the GM can require them to spend some.

Generally, experience points can be spent in four ways: immediate benefits, short- and medium-term benefits, long-term benefits, and character advancement.

IMMEDIATE BENEFITS

The most straightforward way for a player to use XP is to reroll any roll in the game—even one that they didn't make. This costs 1 XP per reroll, and the player chooses the best result. They can continue to spend XP on rerolls, but this can quickly become an expensive proposition. It's a fine way to try to prevent disaster, but it's not a good idea to use a lot of XP to reroll a single action over and over.

A player can also spend 1 XP to refuse a GM intrusion.

SHORT- AND MEDIUM-TERM BENEFITS

By spending 2 XP, a character can gain a skill—or, more rarely, an ability—that provides a short-term benefit. Let's say a character notices that the computer terminals in the facility they're infiltrating are similar to those used by the company they once worked for. They spend 2 XP and say that they have a great deal of experience in using these. As a result, they are trained in operating (and breaking into) these computers. This is just like being trained in computer use or hacking, but it applies only to computers found in that particular location. The skill is extremely useful in the facility, but nowhere else.

Medium-term benefits are usually story based. For example, a character can spend 2 XP while climbing through mountains and say that they have experience with climbing in regions like these, or perhaps they spend the XP after they've been in the mountains for a while and say that they've picked up the feel for climbing there. Either way, from now on, they're trained in climbing in those mountains. This helps them now and any time they return to the area, but they're not trained in climbing everywhere.

This method allows a character to get immediate training in a skill for half the normal cost. (Normally, it costs 4 XP to become trained in a skill.) It's also a way to gain a new skill even if the PC has already gained a new skill as a step toward attaining the next tier.

In rare cases, a GM might allow a character to spend 2 XP to gain an entirely new ability—such as a device, a special ability, or a special mental power—for a short time, usually no longer than the course of one scenario. The player and the GM should agree on a story-based explanation for the benefit. Perhaps the ability has a specific rare requirement, such as a tool, a battery, a drug, or some kind of treatment. For example, a character who wants to explore a submerged location has several biotech enhancements, and they spend 2 XP to cobble together a device that lets them breathe underwater. This gives them the ability for a considerable length of time, but not permanently—the device might work for only eight hours. Again, the story and the logic of the situation dictate the parameters.

LONG-TERM BENEFITS

In many ways, the long-term benefits a PC can gain by spending XP are a means of integrating the mechanics of the game with the story. Players can codify things that happen to their characters by talking to the GM and spending 3 XP.

Things that a PC can acquire as a long-term benefit can be thought of as being story based, and they allow the player to have some narrative control over the story. In the course of play, a player might decide that their character gains a friend (a contact) or builds a log cabin (a home). Because a player spent XP, however, they should have some agency over what they've gained, and it shouldn't be easily taken away. The player should help come up with the details of the contact or the design of their home.

It's also possible to gain these benefits through events in the story, without spending XP. The new contact comes to the PC and starts the relationship. The new home is granted to them as a reward for service to a powerful or wealthy patron, or maybe the character inherits the home from a relative. However, because these came from the GM and not the player (and no XP were spent), the player has no narrative control over them and the GM makes up the details.

Long-term benefits can include the following.

Contact: The character gains a long-term NPC contact of importance—someone who will help

Experience points should not be a goal unto themselves. Instead, they are a game mechanic to simulate how—through experience, time, toil, travail, and so on—characters become more skilled, more able, and more powerful. Spending XP to explain a change in a character's capabilities that occurred in the course of the story, such as if the PC made a new device or learned a new skill, isn't a waste of XP—it's what XP are for.

GMs and players should work together to make XP awards and expenditures fit the ongoing story. If a PC stays in a location for two months to learn the inhabitants' unique language, the GM might award the character a few XP, which are then immediately spent to grant them the ability to understand and speak that language.

Inability, page 207

them with information, equipment, or physical tasks. The player and GM should work out the details of the relationship.

Home: The PC acquires a full-time residence. This can be an apartment in a city, a cabin in the wilderness, a base in an ancient complex, or whatever fits the situation. It should be a secure place where the PC can leave their belongings and sleep soundly. Several characters could combine their XP and buy a home together.

Title or job: The PC is granted a position of importance or authority. It might come with responsibilities, prestige, and rewards, or it might be an honorary title.

Wealth: The PC comes into a considerable amount of wealth, whether it's a windfall, an inheritance, or a gift. It might be enough to buy a home or a title, but that's not really the point. The main benefit is that the PC no longer needs to worry about the cost of simple equipment, lodging, food, and so on. This wealth could mean a set amount—perhaps 50,000 dollars (or whatever is appropriate in the setting)—or it could bestow the ability to ignore minor costs, as decided by the player and GM.

CHARACTER ADVANCEMENT

Progressing to the next tier involves four steps. When a PC has spent 4 XP on each of the steps, they advance to the next tier and gain all the type and focus benefits of that tier. The four steps can be purchased in any order, but each can be purchased only once per tier. In other words, a PC must buy all four steps and advance to the next tier before they can buy the same steps again.

Increasing Capabilities: You gain 4 new points to add to your stat Pools. You can allocate the points among your Pools however you wish.

Moving Toward Perfection: You add 1 to your Might Edge, your Speed Edge, or your Intellect Edge (your choice).

Extra Effort: Your Effort score increases by 1.

Skills: Choose one skill other than attacks or defense, such as climbing, jumping, persuading, sneaking, or history. You become trained in that skill. You can also choose to be knowledgeable in a certain area of study, such as history or geology. You can even choose a skill based on your character's special abilities. For example, if your character can make an Intellect roll to blast an enemy with mental force, you can become trained in that ability, easing the task of using it.

If you choose a skill that you are already trained in, you become specialized in that skill, easing the task by two steps instead of one.

If you choose a skill that you have an inability in, the training and the inability cancel each other out (you aren't eased or hindered in that task). For example, if you have an inability in perception, becoming trained in that cancels out the inability.

Other Options: Players can also spend 4 XP to purchase other special options. Selecting one of these options counts as purchasing one of the four stages necessary to advance to the next tier. The other three need to be from the other categories. The special options are as follows:

- Reduce the cost for wearing armor. This option lowers the Speed penalty for wearing armor by 1.
- Add 2 to your recovery rolls.
- Select another focus ability available to you at tier 3. (You must be tier 3 or higher to do this. Characters advancing beyond tier 6 can use this option to select their other tier 6 focus ability.)
- Select another character ability from your type, such as a tier 2 Warrior selecting Reload or Crushing Blow.

EQUAL ADVANCEMENT

It's worthwhile if all characters advance through the six tiers at about the same rate—an important issue for some players. A good GM can achieve this result by carefully handing out XP rewards, some during play (which will tend to get used immediately) and some after play concludes, especially after completing a major story arc or quest so the GM can hand out 4 XP in one go (which will tend to get used for advancement). Many groups will discover while playing that equal advancement isn't an important issue in the Cypher System, but people should get to play the game the way they want to play it.

TIER ADVANCEMENT IN THE CYPHER SYSTEM

Tiers in the Cypher System aren't entirely like levels in other roleplaying games. In the Cypher System, gaining tiers is not the players' only goal or the only measure of achievement. Starting (first-tier) characters are already competent, and there are only six tiers. Character advancement has a power curve, but it's only steep enough to keep things interesting. In other words, gaining a new tier is cool and fun, but it's not the only path to success or power. If you spend all your XP on immediate, short-term, and medium-term benefits, you will be different from someone who spends their points on long-term benefits, but you will not be "behind" that character.

This chapter has a selection of sample character arcs, but you can create your own too. The arcs are intentionally broad to encompass many different characters and stories. For example, Revenge is a very simple and straightforward character arc. The player who chooses this arc for their character decides who they want revenge on, and why. It's up to the players and the GM to make the details fit.

Once you're specialized in a skill, you can't improve your training in that skill further (you can ease a task by up to two steps with training). You can still make that task easier with assets and a few rare abilities that don't count as an asset or training.

The general idea is that most characters will spend half their XP on tier advancement and long-term benefits, and the rest on immediate benefits and short- and medium-term benefits (which are used during gameplay). Some groups might decide that XP earned during a game is to be spent on immediate and short- and medium-term benefits (gameplay uses), and XP awarded between sessions for discoveries is to be spent on character advancement (long-term uses).

Ultimately, the idea is to make experience points into tools that the players and the GM can use to shape the story and the characters, not just a bookkeeping hassle.

SAMPLE CHARACTER ARCS

The rest of this chapter presents sample character arcs for PCs. The writeup of each arc describes the parts involved in progressing through the arc:

Opening: This sets the stage for the rest of the arc. It involves some action, although that might just be the PC agreeing to do the task or undertake the mission. It usually has no reward.

Step(s): This is the action required to move toward the climax. In story terms, this is the movement through the bulk of the arc. It's the journey. The rising tension. Although there might be just one step, there might also be many, depending on the story told. Each results in a reward of 2 XP.

Climax: This is the finale—the point at which the PC likely succeeds or fails at what they've set out to do. Not every arc ends with victory. If the character is successful, they earn a reward of 4 XP. If they fail, they still earn a reward of 2 XP. If a character fails the climax, they very likely ignore the resolution.

Resolution: This is the wrap-up or denouement. It's a time for the character to reflect on what happened, tie up any loose ends, and figure out what happens next. When things are more or less resolved, the character earns a 1 XP reward.

Within the arc, most of the time a part is probably optional, depending on the situation—although it's hard to envision most arcs without some kind of opening, climax, or resolution. Steps other than the opening, the climax, and the resolution can be done in any order.

Character arcs should always take at least weeks in game time, and no more than two parts in an arc should be accomplished in a game session (and most of the time, it should be one part, if any). If neither of these two things is true, then it's not really a character arc. You can't, for example, use the Creation arc to guide you through something you can make in an hour or two.

The following are common character arcs that you can choose for your character. If you and the GM want to make a new one, it should be fairly easy after looking through these models.

Often the best scenarios are the ones in which the players take the initiative and are proactive about attaining a goal that they set for themselves. Whether they want to case and rob a noble's estate, start their own business, clear out an area of the wilderness to make their home, or anything else, sometimes players should make their own adventures.

AID A FRIEND

Someone needs your help.

When a PC friend takes a character arc, you can select this arc to help them with whatever their arc is (if appropriate). The steps and climax depend entirely on their chosen arc. If the friend is an NPC, the steps and climax are lifted from another arc appropriate to whatever they seek to do.

It's difficult, but possible, to aid a friend with an arc even if that friend is unwilling to accept (or is ignorant of) your help.

The cost and rewards for a character with this arc are the same as those described in the original character arc.

Opening: Answering the Call. Offering to help (or responding to a request for help).

Step(s) and Climax: Depends on the friend's arc. Rewards are the same for you as for the friend.

Resolution: You speak with your friend and learn if they are satisfied. Together, you share what you've learned (if anything) and where you will go from here.

ASSIST AN ORGANIZATION

You set out to accomplish something that will further an organization. You're probably allied with them or they are rewarding you for your help in some fashion.

Opening: Responding to the Call. You work out all the details of what's expected of you, and what rewards (if any) you might get. You also get the specifics of what's required to join and advance.

Step: Sizing up the Task. This requires some action. A reconnaissance mission. An investigation.

Step(s): Undertaking the Task. Because this arc can vary so widely based on the task involved, there might be multiple steps like this one.

Climax: Completing the Task.

Resolution: Collecting your reward (if any) and conferring with the people in the organization that you spoke to. Perhaps getting access to higher-ranking people in the organization. You can choose to have your connection to the organization increase rather than take the standard reward.

AVENGE

Someone close to you or important to you in some way has been wronged. The most overt version of this arc would be to avenge someone's death. Avenging is different than revenge, as revenge is personal—you are the wronged party. But in the Avenge character arc, you are avenging a wrong done to someone else.

Opening: Declaration. You publicly declare that you are going to avenge the victim(s). This is optional.

Step(s): Tracking the Guilty. You track down the guilty party. This might not be physically finding them if you already know where they are. Instead, it might be discovering a way to get at them if they are distant, difficult to reach, or well protected. This step might be repeated multiple times, if applicable.

Step: Finding the Guilty. You finally find the guilty party, or find a path or make a plan to reach them. Now all that's left is to confront them.

Climax: Confrontation. You confront the guilty party. This might be a public accusation and demonstration of guilt, a trial, or an attack to kill, wound, or apprehend them—whatever you choose to be appropriate.

Resolution: You resolve the outcome and the ramifications of the confrontation and decide what to do next.

BIRTH

You are becoming a parent.

The Birth character arc assumes you already have a partner or a surrogate. If you want your character to find a romantic partner or spouse, you can use the Romance arc. And of course, nonhuman characters might reproduce in other ways.

This arc is usually followed by the Raise a Child arc.

Opening: Impregnation.

Step: Finding a Caretaker. This might be a physician, midwife, doula, or similar person. This is optional.

Step: Complication. A complication arises that threatens the pregnancy, the birth parent, or both.

Step: Preparation. You prepare a place for the delivery as well as a safe place for the infant to live once born.

Climax: Delivery. The baby is born. Success means the child survives.

Resolution: You get the baby to the place you have prepared and settle in, deciding what to do next.

Some players might not want to use character arcs. The GM, however, can still use them as a benchmark for awarding XP. If the PCs are going off to explore a strange planet, the GM can essentially give them the Explore arc.

BUILD

You are going to build a physical structure—a house, a fortress, a workshop, a defensive wall, and so on. This arc would also cover renovating an existing structure or substantially adding to one. Of course, this doesn't have to be physical construction. You might build something with spells or other supernatural abilities.

Opening: Make a Plan. This almost certainly involves literally drawing up blueprints or plans.

Step(s): Find a Site. This might be extremely straightforward—a simple examination of the site—or it might be an entire exploratory adventure. (If the latter, it might involve multiple such steps.)

Step(s): Gather Materials. Depending on what you are building and what it is made out of, this could involve multiple steps. There probably are substantial costs involved as well.

Step(s): Construction. Depending on what you are building, this could involve multiple steps. It might also take a considerable amount of time and work.

Climax: Completion. The structure is finished.

Resolution: You put the structure to its desired use and see if it holds up.

CLEANSE

Someone or something has been contaminated, probably by evil spirits, radiation, a deadly virus, foul magic, or the like, and you want to rid them of such influences or contaminants. This could also be a curse, a possession, an infestation, or something else.

Opening: Analyzing the Threat. You determine the nature of the contamination.

Step: Find the Solution. Almost every contamination has its own particular solution, and this likely involves research and consultation.

Step: Getting Ready. The solution probably involves materials, spells, or other things that you must gather and prepare.

Climax: The Cleansing. You confront the contamination.

Resolution: You reflect on the events that have transpired and what effects they might have on the future. How can you keep this from happening again?

CREATION

You want to make something. This might be a magic item, a painting, a novel, or a machine.

Opening: Make a Plan. You figure out what you need, what you're going to do, and how you're going to do it.

Step(s): Gather Materials. Depending on what you are creating and what it is made out of, this could involve multiple steps. There probably are substantial costs involved as well.

Step(s): Progress. Depending on what you are creating, this could involve multiple steps. It might also take a considerable amount of time and work.

Climax: Completion. It's finished! Is it what you wanted? Does it work?

Resolution: You think about what you have learned from the process and use or enjoy the fruits of your labor.

DEFEAT A FOE

Someone stands in your way or is threatening you. You must overcome the challenge they represent. Defeat doesn't always mean kill or even fight. Defeating a foe could mean beating them in a chess match or in competition for a desired mentor.

Opening: Sizing up the Competition. This requires some action. A reconnaissance mission. An investigation.

Step: Investigation. This requires some action. A reconnaissance mission. An investigation.

Step(s): Diving In. You travel toward your opponent, overcome their lackeys, or take steps to reach them so you can confront them. This step can take many forms, and there might be more than one such step. This step is always active.

Climax: Confrontation. The contest, challenge, fight, or confrontation occurs.

Resolution: You reflect on what you've learned and what the consequences of your actions might be.

DEFENSE

A person, place, or thing is threatened, and you want to protect it.

Opening: Analyze the Situation. What are you defending, and what threats are involved?

Step: Account for Your Resources. How are you going to defend?

Step(s): Fend Off Danger. The forces threatening what you are protecting probably make an initial threat that you'll have to defeat. It's not the main threat, though. There might be multiple such initial threats.

Climax: Protect. The true threat reveals itself and you confront it.

Resolution: A time for reflection on everything that occurred, and an assessment of the person, place, or thing's safety going forward.

DEVELOP A BOND

You want to get closer to another character. This might be to make a friend, find a mentor, or establish a contact in a position of power. It might be to turn a friend into a much closer friend. The character might be an NPC or a PC.

Opening: Getting to Know You. You learn what you can about the other character.

Step: Initial Attempt. You attempt to make contact. This might involve sending messages or gifts through a courier, using an intermediary, or just going up and saying hello, depending on the situation.

Step(s): Building a Relationship. There might be many such steps as you develop the relationship.

Climax: Bond. You succeed or fail at forging the bond.

Resolution: You enjoy the fruits of your new relationship.

ENTERPRISE

You want to create and run a business or start an organization. Maybe you're a craftsperson who wants to sell your creations. Maybe you like baking and you want to start a catering service. Or maybe you want to start a secret society or found a school to teach young mutants how to use their powers. You'll almost certainly have to make new connections, find (and somehow pay for) a location, and deal with all manner of administrative duties.

Opening: Drawing up a Plan. What's your goal, and how are you going to achieve it?

Step: Account for Your Resources. How much financing does the enterprise need compared to what you've got? If you need more, how will you get it? How many people other than yourself are needed to begin, and how many will you need to sustain things once they are up and running?

Step: Finding a Location. You probably need a place to run your enterprise—a store, a workshop, a base of operations, and so on. You find a location and look into what it will take to buy or rent it.

Step(s): Building the Enterprise. You procure the needed equipment or personnel. You make the connections and deals to get things started. You obtain important permits or other legal documents. You test new products. You actually start the business. Each of these developments (and likely others) can be counted as a separate step, so there will be many steps.

Climax: Profit and Loss. You determine whether your enterprise will take off and carry on into the future, or fall apart before it gets a chance to blossom. This occurs in a single dramatic moment—your first major client, your organization's first big meeting or mission, or whatever else is appropriate.

Resolution: A time for reflection on everything that occurred, and how you're going to move forward.

ESTABLISHMENT

You want to prove yourself as someone of importance. This can take many forms—socially, within your order, financially, or even romantically.

Opening: Assessment. You assess yourself as well as who you need to prove yourself to.

Step(s): Appearances Matter. You improve your look. Enhance your wardrobe. Spruce up your house. Whatever it takes to get attention from the right people. There might be many such steps.

Step(s): Self-Aggrandizement. You need to get the word out to get people talking about you. There might be many such steps.

Climax: Grabbing Attention. You do something big, like host a party for influential people or produce a play that you wrote. You make a big splash or a big crash.

Resolution: You reflect on what you did and where you go from here.

EXPLORE

Something out there is unknown and you want to explore its secrets. This is most likely an area of wilderness, a new planet, an otherworldly dimension, or something similar.

Opening: Make a Plan. Not only do you draw up a plan for your exploration, but if appropriate, you also make a formal declaration to relevant parties of what you're going to do.

Step(s): Gather Resources. You get the supplies, vehicles, and help you need. Depending on where you are going and what is required, this could involve multiple steps. There probably are substantial costs involved as well.

Step(s): Travel. You go where you wish to explore. There might be many such steps, depending on how long it takes to get there.

Step(s): Exploration. This is the meat of the arc, but it's probably a series of small moves and minor victories. There might be many such steps.

Climax: Conquest. You make the big discovery or truly master the area. You might not have explored every inch of the place, but if you are successful, you can claim to be done.

Resolution: You return home and possibly share your findings.

FALL FROM GRACE

This is an odd character arc in that it's (presumably) not something that a character would want. It is something that a player selects on a meta level for the character because it makes for an interesting story. It also sets up the potential for future arcs, such as Redemption. It's important that this involve actions you take. For example, you fall into substance abuse. You treat people badly. You make mistakes that endanger others. In other words, the fall isn't orchestrated by someone else—it's all your own doing.

Opening: The Descent. Things go bad.

Step(s): Further Descent. Things get worse. Depending on the situation, this might involve many steps.

Step: Lashing Out. You treat others poorly as you descend.

Climax: Rock Bottom. There is no chance for success here. Only failure.

Resolution: You wallow in your own misery.

FINISH A GREAT WORK

Something that was begun in the past must now be completed. This might involve destroying an evil artifact, finishing the construction of a monument, developing the final steps of a cure for a disease, or uncovering a lost temple forgotten to the ages.

Opening: Assessing the Past. You look at what has come before and where it still needs to go. This almost certainly involves some real research.

Step: Conceive a Plan. You make a plan on how to move forward.

Step(s): Progress. You make significant progress or overcome a barrier to completion. This may involve multiple such steps.

Climax: Completion. This involves the big finish to the past work.

Resolution: You reflect on what you did and where you go from here.

GROWTH

Willingly or unwillingly, you are going to change. This is another meta arc. It's less about a goal and more about character development. While it's possible that the growth involved is intentional, in most people's lives and stories, it is emergent. A character might become less selfish, braver, a better leader, or experience some other form of growth.

Opening: The Beginning. Change usually begins slowly, in a small, almost imperceptible way.

Step(s): Change. Growth involves many small steps.

Step: Overcoming an Obstacle. The temptation to resort to your old ways is always present.

Climax: Self-Evident Change. This is a dramatic about-face. This is the moment where you do something the "old you" would never have done, and it has a profound effect on you and those around you. With either success or failure, growth is possible.

Resolution: You recognize the change in yourself and move forward.

INSTRUCTION

You teach a pupil. You have knowledge on a topic and are willing to share. This can be a skill, an area of lore, a combat style, or the use of a special ability. This is usually a fairly long-term arc. Sometimes teaching a pupil is a side matter, and sometimes the pupil takes on more of an apprentice role and spends a great deal of time with you, traveling with you and perhaps even living in your house (or you living in theirs).

Opening: Taking on the Student.

Step: Getting to Know Them. You assess your pupil's strengths and weaknesses and try to get an idea of what they need to learn and how you can teach it to them.

Step(s): The Lessons. Teaching is often a slow, gradual process.

Step: Breakdown. Many times, a student needs to have a moment of crisis to really learn something. Maybe they get dejected, or maybe they rebel against your teaching techniques.

Climax: Graduation. This is when you recognize that the pupil has learned what they need. It usually comes at a dramatic moment.

Resolution: You and the pupil say your goodbyes, and you look toward the future.

JOIN AN ORGANIZATION

You want to join an organization. This might be a military organization, a corporation, a secret society, a religion, or something else.

Opening: Getting the Details. You learn all you can about the organization and how one becomes a member.

Step(s): Making a Contact. Friends on the inside are always important.

Step(s): Performing a Deed. The organization might want to test your worth, or this might be a ceremony you must take part in. It might include paying some sort of dues or fee. Or all of these things.

Climax: Proving Your Worth. This is the point at which you attempt to show the organization that they would be better off with you as a member.

Resolution: You consider your efforts and assess what your membership gets you.

JUSTICE

You try to right a wrong or bring a wrongdoer to justice.

Opening: Declaration. You publicly declare that you are going to bring justice in this situation. This is optional.

Step(s): Tracking the Guilty. You track down the guilty party, assuming there is one. This might not be physically finding them if you already know where they are. Instead, it might be discovering a way to get at them if they are distant, difficult to reach, or well protected. This step might be repeated multiple times, if applicable.

Step: Helping the Victim. Righting a wrong does not always involve confronting a wrongdoer. Part of it might be about helping those who were wronged.

Climax: Confrontation. You confront the guilty party. This might be a public accusation and demonstration of guilt, a trial, or an attack to kill, wound, or apprehend them—whatever you choose to be appropriate.

Resolution: You resolve the outcome and ramifications of the confrontation and decide what to do next.

LEARN

You want to learn something. This isn't the same as the Uncover a Secret arc, in which you're looking for a bit of information. This is a skill or whole area of knowledge you want to gain proficiency with. This is learning a new language, how to play an instrument, or how to be a good cook. Thus, it's not about gaining a level or rank in climbing, but learning to be an experienced mountaineer.

Opening: Focusing on the Problem.

Step: Finding a Teacher or a Way to Teach Yourself. Now you can truly begin.

Step(s): Learn. Depending on what you're learning, this could involve one step or quite a few.

Climax: The Test. You put your new knowledge to the test in a real situation.

Resolution: You relax a bit and decide what to do next.

MASTER A SKILL

You're skilled, but you want to become the best. This arc might logically follow the Learn arc. As with the Learn arc, this can involve any kind of training at all, not just a skill.

Opening: Finding the Path. You've learned the basics. Now it's time for the advanced material.

Step: Discovering a Master. You find a master to help you become a master.

Step(s): Learn. Depending on what you're mastering, this could involve one step or quite a few.

Step: The Last Step. Eventually, you realize that even a master cannot teach you the last step. You must learn it on your own.

Climax: The Test. You put your mastery to the test in a real situation—and considering your goal, it's probably a very important situation.

Resolution: You relax a bit and decide what to do next.

MYSTERIOUS BACKGROUND

You don't know who your parents were, but you want to find out. The mystery might be something other than your parentage, but that's a common theme in this kind of arc. You want to know where you come from—there's some kind of mystery in your past.

Opening: Beginning the Search.

Step: Research. You look into your own family background, if possible.

Step(s): Investigation. You talk to people who might know. You follow clues.

Climax: Discovery. You discover the secret of your own background. You determine if what you learn is good or bad, but either way discovery means success.

Resolution: You contemplate how this new knowledge sits with you.

NEW DISCOVERY

You want to invent a new device, process, spell, or something similar. A cure for a heretofore unknown disease? An invocation with a result you've never heard of before? A method for getting into an impregnable vault? Any of these and more could be your discovery. While similar to the Creation arc and the Learn arc, the New Discovery arc involves blazing a new trail. No one can teach you what you want to know. You've got to do it on your own.

Opening: The Idea. You draw up plans for the thing you want to invent or discover.

Step: Research. You learn what people have done before and recognize where they fell short.

Step(s): Trial and Error. You test your hypothesis. This often ends in many failures before you get a success.

Climax: Eureka! It's time to put the discovery to the true test.

Resolution: You reflect on your discovery and probably compile your notes and write it all down, for posterity's sake if nothing else.

RAISE A CHILD

You raise a child to adulthood. It can be your biological child or one you adopt. It can even be a child taken under your wing, more a young protégé than a son or daughter. This is obviously a very long-term arc.

Opening: Sharing Your Home. The child now lives with you.

Step: Care and Feeding. You learn to meet the child's basic needs.

Step(s): Basic Instruction. You teach them to walk, talk, and read. You teach them to care for themselves.

Step(s): The Rewards Are Many. The child loves you. Relies on you. Trusts you. Eventually, helps you.

Step(s): Ethical Instruction. You instill your basic ethics in the child, hoping that they will mature into an adult you can be proud of.

Climax: Adulthood. At some point the child leaves the proverbial nest. You determine, at this point, your own success or failure.

Resolution: You reflect on the memories you have made.

RECOVER FROM A WOUND (OR TRAUMA)

You need to heal. This isn't just for healing simple damage. This involves recovering from a major debilitating injury, illness, or shock. Severe damage, the loss of a body part, and emotional trauma all fall into this category.

Opening: Rest. The first thing you need to do is rest.

Step: Self Care. You take care of your own needs.

Step: Getting Aid. Someone helps.

Step: Medicine. Some kind of drug, cure, poultice, potion, or remedy aids your recovery.

Step: Therapy. With the help of someone else, you exercise your injury or cope with your trauma.

Climax: Acceptance or Recovery. You try to move on and use what has been damaged (or learn how to function without it).

Resolution: You get on with your life.

REDEMPTION

You've done something very wrong, but you want to atone and make it right again. This is like the Justice arc or the Undo a Wrong arc, except you are the wrongdoer. This could be a follow-up to the Fall From Grace arc.

Opening: Regret. You are determined to rebuild, recover, and restore.

Step: Forgiveness. You apologize and ask for forgiveness.

Step: Identifying the Needs. You determine what needs to be done to atone for your transgression.

Climax: Making Good. You perform an act that you hope will redeem your past misdeed.

Resolution: You reflect on what has happened but now look to the future.

REPAY A DEBT

You owe someone something, and it's time to make good.

Opening: Debts Come Due. You determine to do what is needed to make good on the debt. It might involve repaying money, but more appropriately it's performing a deed or a series of deeds.

Step: Talking It Over. You discuss the matter with the person you owe, if possible. You ensure that what you're doing is what they want.

Climax: Repayment. Either you do something to earn the money or goods you owe, or you undertake a major task that will compensate the other person.

Resolution: You relax knowing that your debt is repaid, and you look to the future.

RESCUE

Someone or something of great importance has been taken, and you want to get them or it back.

Opening: Heeding the Call. You determine what has happened, and who or what is missing.

Step: Tracking. You discover who has taken them, and where.

Step: Travel. You go to where they are being held and get information on the location and who is involved. Maybe make a plan.

Climax: Rescue Operation. You go in and get them.

Resolution: You return them home.

RESTORATION

You're down but not out. You want to restore your good name. Recover what you've lost. Rebuild what has been destroyed. You've fallen down or have been knocked down, but either way you want to pick yourself up. This is a possible follow-up to the Fall From Grace arc.

Opening: Vow to Yourself. You are determined to rebuild, recover, and restore.

Step(s): Work. You rebuild, recover, and restore. If all your money was stolen, you make more. If your house was destroyed, you rebuild it. If your reputation was tarnished, you perform deeds that restore your good name.

Climax: The Final Act. You undertake one last major task that will bring things back to where they were (or close to it). A lot is riding on this moment.

Resolution: You enjoy a return to things the way they were before.

REVENGE

Someone did something that harmed you. Unlike the Avenge arc, this arc probably isn't about tracking down a murderer, but it might involve pursuing someone who stole from you, hurt you, or otherwise brought you grief. The key is that it's personal. Otherwise, use the Justice arc.

Opening: Vow. You swear revenge.

Step(s): Finding a Clue. You find a clue to tracking down the culprit.

Climax: Confrontation. You confront the culprit.

Resolution: You deal with the aftermath of the confrontation and move on. You think about whether you are satisfied by gaining your revenge.

ROMANCE

You want to strike up a relationship with a romantic partner. Perhaps you have a specific person in mind, or maybe you're just interested in a relationship in general.

Opening(s): Caught Someone's Eye. You meet someone you are interested in. (Since this can be short-lived, it's possible to have this opening occur more than once.)

Step(s): Courtship. You begin seeing the person regularly. Although not every "date" is a step in the arc, significant moments are, and there may be a few of them.

Climax: Commitment. You may or may not be interested in a monogamous relationship. Regardless, you and your love have made some kind of commitment to each other.

Resolution: You think about the future. Marriage? Children? These are only some of the possibilities.

SOLVE A MYSTERY

Different from the Learn arc and the Uncover a Secret arc, this arc is about solving a crime or a similar action committed in the fairly recent past. It's not about practice or study, but about questions and answers. In theory, the mystery doesn't have to be a crime. It might be "Why is this strange caustic substance leaking into my basement?"

Opening: Pledging to Solve the Mystery.

Step: Research. You get some background.

Step(s): Investigation. You ask questions. You look for clues. You cast divinations. This likely encompasses many such steps.

Climax: Discovery. You come upon what you believe to be the solution to the mystery.

Resolution: In this step, which is far more active than most resolutions, you confront the people involved in the mystery with what you've discovered, or you use the information in some way (such as taking it to the proper authorities).

THEFT

Someone else has something you want.

Opening: Setting Your Sights. You make a plan.

Step: Casing the Joint. You scout out the location of the thing (or learn its location).

Step(s): Getting to the Object. Sometimes, many steps are involved before you reach the object you wish to take. For example, if, in order to steal something from a vault, you need to approach one of the guards while they are off duty and bribe them to look the other way when you break in, that is covered in this step.

Climax: The Attempt. You make your heist.

Resolution: You decide what to do with the thing you've stolen and contemplate the repercussions you might face for stealing it.

TRAIN A CREATURE

You want to domesticate and train an animal or other creature. While the beast doesn't need to be wild, it must not already be domesticated and trained.

Opening: Getting Acquainted. You get to know the creature a bit, and it gets to know you.

Step: Research. You get information on the type of creature or advice from others who have trained one.

Step: Domestication. After some work, the creature is no longer a threat to you or anyone else, and it can live peacefully in your home or wherever you wish.

Step(s): Training. Each time you use this step, you teach the creature a new, significant command that it will obey regularly and immediately.

Climax: Completion. Believing the creature's training to be complete, you put it in a situation where that is put to the test.

Resolution: You reflect on the experience.

TRANSFORMATION

You want to be different in a specific way. Because the Growth arc covers internal change, this one focuses primarily on external change. This could take many forms, and probably varies greatly by genre. In some settings, it could even be death, which might turn you into a ghost. For the change to be an arc, it should be difficult and perhaps risky.

Opening: Deciding on the Transformation.

Step: Research. You look into how the change can be made and what it entails.

Step(s): Investigation. This is an active step toward making the change. It might involve getting more information, materials or ingredients, or something else.

Climax: Change. You make the change, with some risk of failure or disaster.

Resolution: You contemplate how this change affects you going forward.

UNCOVER A SECRET

There is knowledge out there that you want. It could be an attempt to find and learn a specific special ability. This could also be a hunt for a lost password or a key that will open a sealed door, the true name of a devil, the secret background of an important person, or how the ancients constructed that strange monolith.

Opening: Naming the Secret. You give your goal a name. "I am seeking the lost martial art of the Khendrix, who could slice steel with their bare hands."

Step(s): Research. You scour libraries and old tomes for clues and information.

Step(s): Investigation. You talk to people to gain clues and information.

Step(s): Tracking. You track down the source of the secret information and travel to it.

Climax: Revelation. You find and attempt to use the secret, whatever that entails.

Resolution: You contemplate how this secret affects you and the world.

UNDO A WRONG

Someone did something horrible, and its ramifications are still felt, even if it happened long ago. You seek to undo the damage, or at least stop it from continuing.

This is different from the Justice arc because this isn't about justice (or even revenge)—it's about literally undoing something bad that happened in the past, such as a great library being burned to the ground, a sovereign people being driven from their land, and so on.

Opening: Vowing to Put Right What Once Went Wrong.

Step: Make a Plan. You learn all you can about the situation and then make a plan to put things right.

Step(s): Progress. This is an active step toward undoing the wrong. It might involve finding something, defeating someone, destroying something, building something, or almost anything else, depending on the circumstances.

Climax: Change. You face the challenge of the former wrong, and either overcome it or fail.

Resolution: You reflect on what you've accomplished and think about the future.

PART 3
GENRES

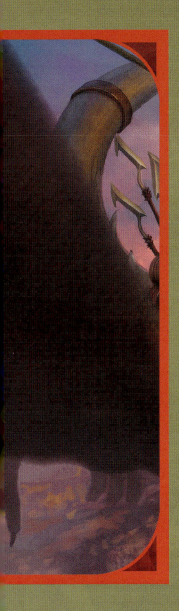
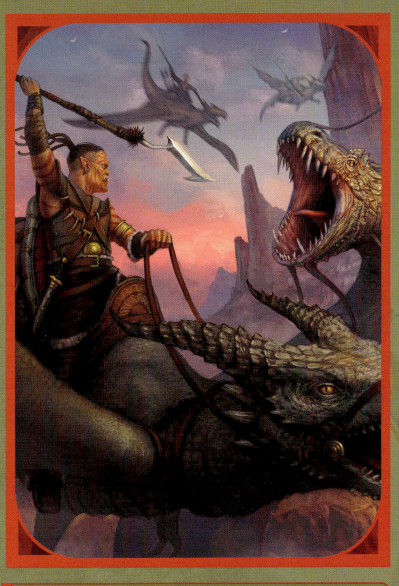

Chapter 13: FANTASY	252
Chapter 14: MODERN	261
Chapter 15: SCIENCE FICTION	270
Chapter 16: HORROR	280
Chapter 17: ROMANCE	286
Chapter 18: SUPERHEROES	289
Chapter 19: POST-APOCALYPTIC	295
Chapter 20: FAIRY TALE	302
Chapter 21: HISTORICAL	307

Chapter 13
FANTASY

Elf, page 258
Dwarf, page 258
Helborn, page 259
Half-giant, page 259

For our purposes, fantasy is any genre that has magic, or something so inexplicable it might as well be magic. The sort of core default of this type is Tolkienesque fantasy, also known as second-world fantasy because it includes a completely new world not our own. Big fantasy epics like those penned by J. R. R. Tolkien (hence the name), C. S. Lewis, George R. R. Martin, Stephen R. Donaldson, David Eddings, Ursula K. Le Guin, and others are indicative of this genre. It usually involves swords, sorcery, nonhuman species (such as elves, dwarves, helborn, and half-giants), and epic struggles.

Of course, fantasy might also involve the modern world, with creatures of myth and sorcerers dwelling among us. It might involve mythic traditions of any number of cultures (elves, dwarves, and the like, usually being decidedly European) or bear little resemblance to anything on Earth, past or present. It might even involve some of the trappings of science fiction, with spaceships and laser guns amid the wizardry and swords (this is often called science fantasy).

Fantasy can also be defined by the amount of fantasy elements within it. A second-world fantasy filled with wizards, ghosts, dragons, curses, and gods is referred to as high fantasy. Fantasy with a firmer grounding in reality as we know it in our world is low fantasy. (In fact, low fantasy often takes place in our world, or in our world's distant past, like the stories of Conan.) No single element indicates concretely that a given fantasy is high or low. It's the prevalence of those elements.

The point is, there are many, many types of fantasy.

CREATING A FANTASY SETTING

There are so many fantasy settings—so many fantasy roleplaying game settings—out there that we don't need to dwell on this topic much. If you're reading this, you've probably played a fantasy RPG. That said, here are a few things to keep in mind.

Default high fantasy needs bad guys in great numbers. That doesn't mean the stories always need to be about fighting, but rather that there is always a threat to cope with, and the threat is always of some dire evil.

Players need to understand the rules of the setting, at least a bit—not the Cypher System rules, but the rules of magic and the fantastical elements of the setting. Are faeries real or superstition? Can dead people be brought back to life? Are the gods real? Is there any limit to what a powerful wizard can do? These are the kinds of questions players need answers to so they can understand the world in which their characters live.

Spend at least a bit of time outlining the parameters of the fantasy elements of the world. Who's the most powerful wizard? Where does one go to find the mightiest artifact? Where does the most fearsome dragon dwell? How do the normal people fit in? Who lives in the little villages the PCs will come upon, and how do they look at their world?

RUNNING A FANTASY GAME

Running a fantasy game means managing a lot of magic, including magic items and mystical creatures. In a default high fantasy, you might want the PCs to discover magic artifacts, like swords (which usually give an increase in damage or an asset to attacks), wands (which usually contain a dramatic power with a small number of uses), or rings (which usually have an always-on power that works like a free skill or asset). Also, keep the following in mind:

The default high fantasy setting is heroic. That is to say, brave heroes face overwhelming odds and win in the end. Good and evil are usually clearly defined. Orcs and demons are evil, and heroes are good.

Low fantasy tends to deal with protagonists struggling against a dark world. Rather than fighting to defeat the evil lord on an epic quest, low-fantasy characters might simply be trying to earn enough coins to pay for their supper. Low fantasy is often about survival. People frequently use words like "grim" and "gritty" to describe such stories.

Default high fantasy, probably more than any other genre, embraces the concept of lowly nobodies rising to great stature and power. "Zero to hero" is the phrase sometimes used. In the Cypher System, that likely means either slightly decreasing the power of the PCs at the lower tiers, or increasing them at higher tiers. The former is tricky, but the latter could come from an increase in opportunities to learn new skills (including attack and defense skills) starting at tier 4.

The other way to increase a fantasy character's power over time is for them to learn a bit of spellcasting, whatever their type.

An interesting player intrusion in a fantasy setting would be to have the fluctuations of magic change the way a spell works, or bring some minor calamity upon an NPC. See player intrusions, page 21.

Spellcasting, page 259

SUGGESTED TYPES FOR A FANTASY GAME

Role	Character Type
Warrior	Warrior
Knight	Warrior
Ranger	Explorer
Barbarian	Explorer flavored with combat
Thief	Explorer flavored with stealth
Wizard	Adept
Cleric	Speaker flavored with magic
Druid	Explorer flavored with magic
Warrior mage	Warrior flavored with magic
Bard	Speaker

Type, page 20

Flavor, page 34

Character focus, page 60

SUGGESTED FOCI FOR A FANTASY GAME

Abides in Stone	Fights With Panache	Rides the Lightning
Awakens Dreams	Focuses Mind Over Matter	Sees Beyond
Bears a Halo of Fire	Howls at the Moon	Separates Mind From Body
Blazes With Radiance	Hunts	Shepherds Spirits
Builds Robots	Infiltrates	Shepherds the Community
Channels Divine Blessings	Keeps a Magic Ally	Siphons Power
Commands Mental Powers	Leads	Slays Monsters
Consorts With the Dead	Lives in the Wilderness	Speaks for the Land
Controls Beasts	Looks for Trouble	Stands Like a Bastion
Crafts Illusions	Masters Defense	Throws With Deadly Accuracy
Crafts Unique Objects	Masters Spells	Thunders
Defends the Gate	Masters the Swarm	Travels Through Time
Defends the Weak	Masters Weaponry	Was Foretold
Descends From Nobility	Metes Out Justice	Wears a Sheen of Ice
Entertains	Moves Like a Cat	Wields Two Weapons at Once
Exists in Two Places at Once	Murders	Works Miracles
Exists Partially Out of Phase	Needs No Weapon	Works the Back Alleys
Explores Dark Places	Never Says Die	
Fights Dirty	Performs Feats of Strength	

Creatures, page 312
NPCs, page 372

SUGGESTED CREATURES AND NPCs FOR A FANTASY GAME

Assassin	Giant	Prince(ss) of summer
Chimera	Giant rat	Shadow elf
Demigod	Giant snake	Skeleton
Demon	Giant spider	Statue, animate
Devil	Goblin	Thug/bandit
Djinni	Golem	Vampire
Dragon	Guard	Wendigo
Elemental	Mechanical soldier	Werewolf
Fallen angel	Occultist	Witch
Ghost	Ogre	Wizard, mighty
Ghoul	Orc	Zombie

OTHER CREATURES AND NPCs FOR A FANTASY GAME

Bat: level 1
Dog: level 2, perception as level 3
Dog, guard: level 3, attacks and perception as level 4
Hawk: level 2; flies a long distance each round
Horse: level 3; moves a long distance each round
Rat: level 1
Viper: level 2; bite inflicts 3 points of Speed damage (ignores Armor)
Warhorse: level 4; moves a long distance each round

Wolf: level 3, perception as level 4
Blacksmith: level 2, metalworking as level 4; health 8
Farmer: level 2, animal handling as level 3; health 8
Merchant: level 2, haggling and assessment tasks as level 3
Villager: level 1

ADDITIONAL FANTASY EQUIPMENT

In the default Medieval Europe-style fantasy setting, the following items (and anything else appropriate to that time period) are usually available.

INEXPENSIVE ITEMS

Weapons	Notes
Arrows (12)	
Crossbow bolts (12)	
Knife (rusty and worn)	Light weapon (won't last long)
Wooden club	Light weapon

Other Items	Notes
Burlap sack	
Candle	
Iron rations (1 day)	
Torch (3)	

MODERATELY PRICED ITEMS

Weapons	Notes
Blowgun	Light weapon, immediate range
Dagger	Light weapon
Handaxe	Light weapon
Sword (substandard)	Medium weapon (won't last long)
Throwing knife	Light weapon, short range

Armor	Notes
Hides and furs	Light armor
Leather jerkin	Light armor

Other Items	Notes
Backpack	
Bedroll	
Crowbar	
Hourglass	
Lantern	
Rope	Hemp, 50 feet
Signal horn	
Spikes and hammer	10 spikes
Tent	

EXPENSIVE ITEMS

Weapons	Notes
Battleaxe	Medium weapon
Bow	Medium weapon, long range
Cutlass	Medium weapon
Light crossbow	Medium weapon, long range
Quarterstaff	Medium weapon (requires 2 hands)
Sword	Medium weapon

Armor	Notes
Breastplate	Medium armor
Brigandine	Medium armor
Chainmail	Medium armor

Other Items	Notes
Bag of heavy tools	
Bag of light tools	

VERY EXPENSIVE ITEMS

Weapons	Notes
Greatsword	Heavy weapon
Heavy crossbow	Heavy weapon, long range
Sword (jeweled)	Medium weapon

Armor	Notes
Dwarven breastplate	Medium armor, encumbers as light armor
Full plate armor	Heavy armor

Other Items	Notes
Disguise kit	Asset for disguise tasks
Healing kit	Asset for healing tasks
Spyglass	Asset for perception tasks at range

EXORBITANT ITEMS

Armor	Notes
Elven chainmail	Medium armor, encumbers as no armor

Other Items	Notes
Sailing ship (small)	

FANTASY ARTIFACTS

In many ways, fantasy is the genre for artifacts. All magic items—wands that shoot lightning, magic carpets, singing swords, rings that make the wearer invisible, and so on—are artifacts. Below are a few sample artifacts to give a template for GMs to follow. Those running a fantasy campaign will likely want to create many magic artifacts.

ANGELIC WARD

Level: 1d6 + 2
Form: Tiny figurine of a winged angel
Effect: Once activated, the figurine's spirit emerges and becomes semisolid as a glowing, human-sized winged angel. It follows within 3 feet (1 m) of the figurine owner. Anything within long range that attacks the owner is attacked by the angelic ward, which sends out a bolt of flesh-rotting energy, doing damage equal to the artifact's level. Once activated, it functions for a day.
Depletion: 1 in 1d10

RING OF DRAGON'S FLIGHT

Level: 1d6 + 2
Form: Green iron ring that appears like a dragon wound around the finger
Effect: When the wearer activates the ring, dragon wings unfurl from their back, and for one minute the wearer can fly up to long range. The ring does not confer the ability to hover or make fine adjustments while in flight.
Depletion: 1 in 1d10

SOULFLAYING WEAPON

Level: 1d6 + 1
Form: Weapon of any type, with engraved glowing runes denoting soulflaying
Effect: This weapon functions as a normal weapon of its kind. The wielder can use an action to activate its soulflaying magic for one minute. During that time, if the weapon scores a hit, it inflicts normal damage, plus 3 additional points of Intellect damage on all creatures that have souls (not automatons, mindless undead, or the like).
Depletion: 1 in 1d100

SPELLBOOK OF THE AMBER MAGE

Level: 1d6
Form: Weighty tome bound in amber filled with pages of spell runes
Effect: When the user incants from the spellbook and succeeds at a level 3 Intellect-based task, the user can attempt to trap a creature within long range inside a block of amber. Only creatures whose level is equal to or lower than the artifact's level can be targeted. A creature successfully caught is preserved in perfect stasis until the encasing amber is broken away (the amber has 10 points of health per level of the artifact).
Depletion: 1 in 1d20

WAND OF FIREBOLTS

Level: 1d6 + 2
Form: Wand of red wood 8 inches (20 cm) long, carved with intricate flamelike images
Effect: When activated, the wand looses a blast of fire at a chosen target within short range, inflicting damage equal to the artifact's level.
Depletion: 1 in 1d20

MIXING IT UP: FANTASY AND SCIENCE FICTION

Sword and planet. Science fantasy. There are many ways to mix fantasy and science fiction. If the base is fantasy, the science fiction elements usually are exceptions, with out-of-place high technology seeming almost like another kind of magic. Maybe a starship from another planet crashed in the fantasy world, or perhaps the occasional relic surfaces from a highly advanced civilization that flourished in ancient history. Perhaps a wizard opened a gate to the future or to a technological world and brought back wonders of science. The sudden appearance of a robot as the defender of a fantasy castle, or an evil knight producing a blaster rifle after being unhorsed in a joust, can be a fun and surprising twist on the genre.

Artifacts, page 204

SPECIES DESCRIPTORS

In a high fantasy setting, some GMs may want dwarves and elves to be mechanically different from humans. Below are some possibilities for how this might work.

DWARF

You're a stocky, broad-shouldered, bearded native of the mountains and hills. You're also as stubborn as the stone in which the dwarves carve their homes under the mountains. Tradition, honor, pride in smithcraft and warcraft, and a keen appreciation of the wealth buried under the roots of the world are all part of your heritage. Those who wish you ill should be wary of your temper. When dwarves are wronged, they never forget.

You gain the following characteristics:

Stalwart: +2 to your Might Pool.

Skill: You are trained in Might defense rolls.

Skill: You are trained in tasks related to stone, including sensing stonework traps, knowing the history of a particular piece of stonecraft, and knowing your distance beneath the surface.

Skill: You are practiced in using axes.

Skill: You are trained in using the tools required to shape and mine stone.

Vulnerability: When you fail an Intellect defense roll to avoid damage, you take 1 extra point of damage.

Additional Equipment: You have an axe.

Initial Link to the Starting Adventure: From the following list of options, choose how you became involved in the first adventure.

1. You found the PCs wandering a maze of tunnels and led them to safety.

2. The PCs hired you to dig out the entrance to a buried ruin.

3. You tracked down the thieves of your ancestor's tomb and found they were the PCs. Instead of killing them, you joined them.

4. Before dwarves settle down, they need to see the world.

ELF

You haunt the woodlands and deep, natural realms, as your people have for millennia. You are the arrow in the night, the shadow in the glade, and the laughter on the wind. As an elf, you are slender, quick, graceful, and long lived. You manage the sorrows of living well past many mortal lifetimes with song, wine, and an appreciation for the deep beauties of growing things, especially trees, which can live even longer than you do.

You gain the following characteristics:

Agile: +2 to your Speed Pool.

Long-Lived: Your natural lifespan (unless tragically cut short) is thousands of years.

Skill: You are specialized in tasks related to perception.

Skill: You are practiced in using one bow variety of your choice.

Skill: You are trained in stealth tasks. In areas of natural woodland, you are specialized in stealth tasks.

Fragile: When you fail a Might defense roll to avoid damage, you take 1 extra point of damage.

Additional Equipment: You have a bow and a quiver of arrows to go with it.

Initial Link to the Starting Adventure: From the following list of options, choose how you became involved in the first adventure.

1. Before putting an arrow in the forest intruders, you confronted them and met the PCs, who were on an important quest.

2. Your heart yearned for farther shores, and the PCs offered to take you along to new places.

3. Your home was burned by strangers from another place, and you gathered the PCs along the way as you tracked down the villains.

4. An adventure was in the offing, and you didn't want to be left behind.

HALF-GIANT

You stand at least 12 feet (4 m) tall and tower over everyone around you. Whether you are a full-blooded giant or merely have giant heritage from large ancestors, you're massive. Always large for your age, it became an issue only once you reached puberty and topped 7 feet (2 m) in height, and kept growing from there.

You gain the following characteristics:

Tough: +4 to your Might Pool.

Mass and Strength: You inflict +1 point of damage with your melee attacks and attacks with thrown weapons.

Breaker: Tasks related to breaking things by smashing them are eased.

Inability: You're too large to accomplish normal things. Tasks related to initiative, stealth, and fine manipulation of any sort (such as lockpicking or repair tasks) are hindered.

Additional Equipment: You have a heavy weapon of your choice.

Initial Link to the Starting Adventure: From the following list of options, choose how you became involved in the first adventure.

1. You fished the PCs out of a deep hole they'd fallen into while exploring.

2. You were the PCs' guide in the land of giants and stayed with them afterward.

3. The PCs helped you escape a nether realm where other giants were imprisoned by the gods.

4. You kept the PCs from being discovered by hiding them behind your bulk when they were on the run.

HELBORN

Demons of the underworld sometimes escape. When they do, they can taint human bloodlines. Things like you are the result of such unnatural unions. Part human and part something else, you are an orphan of a supernatural dalliance. Thanks to your unsettling appearance, you've probably been forced to make your own way in a world that often fears and resents you. Some of your kin have large horns, tails, and pointed teeth. Others are more subtle or more obvious in their differences—a shadow of a knife-edge in their face and a touch that withers normal plants, a little too much fire in their eyes and a scent of ash in the air, a forked tongue, goatlike legs, or the inability to cast a shadow. Work with the GM on your particular helborn appearance.

You gain the following characteristics.

Devious: +2 to your Intellect Pool.

Skill: You are trained in tasks related to magic lore and lore of the underworld.

Fire Adapted: +2 to Armor against damage from fire only.

Helborn Magic: You are inherently magical. Choose one low-tier ability from chapter 9. If the GM agrees it is appropriate, you gain that ability as part of your helborn heritage, and can use it like any other type or focus ability.

Inner Evil: You sometimes lose control and risk hurting your allies. When you roll a 1, the GM has the option to intrude by indicating that you lose control. Once you've lost control, you attack any and every living creature within short range. You can't spend Intellect points for any reason other than to try to regain control (a difficulty 2 task). After you regain control, you suffer a –1 penalty to all rolls for one hour.

Inability: People distrust you. Tasks to persuade or deceive are hindered.

Initial Link to the Starting Adventure: From the following list of options, choose how you became involved in the first adventure.

1. You were nearly beaten to death by people who didn't like your look, but the PCs found and revived you.

2. The PCs hired you for your knowledge of magic.

3. Every so often you get visions of people trapped in the underworld. You tracked those people down and found the PCs, who'd never visited the underworld. Yet.

4. Your situation at home became untenable because of how people reacted to your looks. You joined the PCs to get away.

OPTIONAL RULE: SPELLCASTING

Fantasy settings prioritize magic as an essential ingredient. But why restrict that magic to just wizards and similar characters? It's not uncommon in fantasy literature for a thief or warrior to learn a few spells as they steal or brawl through their adventures. Leiber's Gray Mouser knew some spells, Moorcock's Elric knew a lot, pretty much everyone in Anthony's Xanth books knew at least one, and so on. Of course, wizards and sorcerers specialize in spellcasting, which gives them clear superiority in magic use. But whether a character is a fireball-flinging wizard or a belligerent barbarian, anyone can learn some spellcasting under this optional rule.

Under the spellcasting rule, any character, no matter their role or type, can choose to learn a spell as a long-term benefit. After they learn one spell, they may learn more later if they wish, or just stick with the one.

Chapter 9: Abilities, page 95

Helborn are sometimes called cambions.

Potentially, learning spells could be a character arc for a PC who isn't some kind of magic user already.

Character arcs, page 238

Long-term benefits, page 239

Chapter 9: Abilities, page 95

Recovery rolls, page 218

Ward, page 196
Telekinesis, page 189

FIRST SPELL

Any character can gain a spell by spending 3 XP and working with the GM to come up with an in-game story of how the PC learned it. Maybe they learned it as a child from their parent and practiced it enough to actually do it; perhaps they spent a month hiding in a wizard's library reading; it could be that they found a weird magical amulet that imbues them with the spell; and so on.

Next, choose one low-tier ability from chapter 9. If the GM agrees it is appropriate, the character gains that ability as their spell, with a few caveats. The spell can't be used like a normal ability gained through a PC's type or focus. Instead, a character must either use a recovery roll or spend many minutes or longer evoking their spell, in addition to paying its Pool cost (if any).

Using a Recovery Roll to Cast a Spell: If the character uses a one-action, ten-minute, or one-hour recovery roll as part of the same action to cast the spell (including paying any Pool costs), they can use the ability as an action. This represents a significant mental and physical drain on the character, because the normal benefit of recovering points in a Pool is not gained.

Spending Time to Cast a Spell: If the character takes at least ten minutes chanting, mumbling occult phonemes, concentrating deeply, or otherwise using all their actions, they can cast a low-tier spell (if they also pay any Pool costs). An hour is required to cast mid-tier spells. Ten hours are required to cast a high-tier spell.

MORE SPELLS

Once a character has learned at least one spell, they can opt to learn additional spells later. Each time, they must spend an additional 3 XP and work with the GM to come up with an in-game story of how the character's magical learning has progressed.

Two additional rules for learning additional spells apply:
- First, a character must be at least tier 3 and have previously gained one low-tier spell before they can learn a mid-tier spell.
- Second, a character must be at least tier 5 and have previously gained one mid-tier spell before they can learn a high-tier spell.

Otherwise, gaining and casting additional spells are as described for the character's first spell.

WIZARDS AND THE OPTIONAL SPELLCASTING RULE

Wizards (usually Adepts) and characters with explicit spellcasting foci like Masters Spells, Channels Divine Blessings, Speaks for the Land, and possibly others are also considered to be spellcasters, and moreover, specialized ones. Their spells—abilities provided by their type or focus—are used simply by paying their Pool costs. Extra time or physical effort isn't required to cast them. That's because, in the parlance of the fantasy genre, these spells are considered to be "prepared."

But specialized casters can also use the optional spellcasting rule to expand their magic further. They can learn additional spells via the optional spellcasting rule just like other characters, with the same limitations.

Optionally, specialized casters who record their arcane knowledge in a spellbook (or something similar) gain one additional benefit. The spellbook is a compilation of spells, formulas, and notes that grants the specialized caster more flexibility than those who've simply learned a spell or two. With a spellbook, a PC can replace up to three prepared spells with three other spells they've learned of the same tier. To do so, they must spend at least one uninterrupted hour studying their spellbook. Usually, this is something that requires a fresh mind, and must be done soon after a ten-hour recovery.

For instance, if a wizard exchanges Ward (an ability gained from their type) with Telekinesis (an ability gained from the optional spellcasting rule), from now on the character can cast Ward only by spending time or using a recovery roll (as well as spending Pool points). On the other hand, they can use Telekinesis normally, because now it's prepared. Later, the wizard could spend the time studying to change out their prepared spells with others they've learned using the optional spellcasting rule.

> A PC might choose the 4 XP character advancement option to select a new type-based ability from their tier or a lower tier. If so, the ability gained doesn't count as a spell, and the spellcasting rule limitations do not apply to the ability so gained. If the PC is a wizard and uses the 4 XP character advancement option, treat the ability as one more prepared spell.

CHAPTER 14

MODERN

The modern setting is easy because it's just the real world, right? Well, yes and no. It's easy for players to understand the context of a modern setting. They know the default assumptions—cities, cars, cell phones, the internet, and so on. It's also easier for some players to get into character, because their character could be someone they might very well pass on the street. It can be easier to wrap your mind around a history professor than a thousand-year-old elf wizard. These things make it easier on the GM as well.

But for the same reason, it's not easy. The setting is the real world we all know, so it's easy to get facts wrong or let them bog you down. What happens when you pull the fire alarm on the thirty-fifth floor of a major hotel in a large city? How fast do the authorities arrive? In truth, the facts aren't as important as the story you're creating, but some verisimilitude is nice.

CREATING A MODERN SETTING

You don't have to create a setting if the whole game takes place in London, Dallas, or the Outback, because those places really exist. The only time you need to do any worldbuilding is if you're creating original places (an amusement park that you made up) or organizations (a secret spy group that the PCs belong to). Still, that doesn't mean you have no work to do. The modern world has implications to consider.

In a world with GPS, mobile phones, and the internet, it's very difficult to imagine getting seriously lost, not being in communication, or not knowing the answer to a question. Rather than constantly thwart these truths (no cell phone reception here!), think of ways to use them.

You need to figure out what happens if the PCs just call the police rather than deal with a situation themselves.

You need to go the extra mile to make NPCs realistic and believable, because the players have real people to compare them to.

You need to decide if your campaign setting will remain in the real world or deviate from it. In other words, can campaign events break from the believable world we see around us? If aliens land in Nebraska in your game, and everyone knows it, the setting is no longer the world we see outside our window. (There is no wrong choice, but you still need to decide.)

RUNNING A MODERN GAME

Preparation is important in a modern game, and most of that entails being ready with realistic ramifications of potential PC actions. How quickly will the authorities arrive if the characters start a shootout with gangsters? What happens if the PCs are arrested? In a fantasy game, you can make things up as you go along—who's to say that the queen's guards wouldn't show up that quickly, or that faeries can't see in the dark? When the world is fictional, you have freedom. But when it's real, you need to know what you're talking about. Consider the following tips.

Use an online directory or a phone book to generate names for your NPCs.

Use real-world resources to get maps, photo references, forms, and similar items to enhance the game. You'll be surprised what you can find online for free.

Incorporate the PCs' real-world lives into the game. If the characters have jobs, work with the players to generate some details about those occupations. Real-world people have families, homes, friends, hobbies, and so on. Not only is that great for character development, but you can also work it into the story. If a PC always goes to the gym on Tuesday, have a significant plot encounter happen there.

Commands Mental Powers, page 65

Focuses Mind Over Matter, page 68

Flavor, page 34

Calm, page 40

Doesn't Do Much, page 67

Would Rather Be Reading, page 79

MOLDING CHARACTERS FOR A MODERN GAME

If you're trying to portray a psychic with a few basic powers, you might not want to use the Adept character type. Instead, choose a different type (perhaps a Speaker) and encourage foci such as Commands Mental Powers or Focuses Mind Over Matter. Some of the Adept's powers might be too over the top for the genre.

Similarly, the technology flavor is probably too high-tech for a modern game. For someone with technical skills, use the skills and knowledge flavor instead.

Sometimes, the types might be more physical than is always desirable for a modern game, but that's because the least physical type, the Adept, is often inappropriate for other reasons. The Calm descriptor is very good for such characters, not only granting them a great deal of skill and knowledge, but also reducing their physical capabilities.

Last, don't forget foci such as Doesn't Do Much or Would Rather Be Reading for "normal" characters who have useful skills but not much in the way of flashy abilities.

SUGGESTED TYPES FOR A MODERN GAME

Role	Type
Police officer	Explorer with combat flavor
Detective	Explorer with stealth flavor
Soldier	Warrior
Criminal	Explorer with stealth flavor
Teacher	Speaker
Professional (accountant, writer, etc.)	Speaker with skills and knowledge flavor
Technical profession	Explorer with skills and knowledge flavor
Dilettante	Speaker with skills and knowledge flavor
Doctor/Nurse	Explorer with skills and knowledge flavor
Politician	Speaker
Lawyer	Speaker
Scholar	Explorer with skills and knowledge flavor
Spy	Speaker with stealth flavor
Occultist	Adept
Mystic/Psychic	Adept

SUGGESTED FOCI FOR A MODERN GAME

Calculates the Incalculable
Commands Mental Powers*
Conducts Weird Science
Consorts With the Dead*
Crafts Unique Objects
Doesn't Do Much
Drives Like a Maniac
Entertains
Explores Dark Places
Fights Dirty
Focuses Mind Over Matter
Helps Their Friends
Howls at the Moon*
Hunts
Infiltrates
Interprets the Law
Is Idolized by Millions
Is Licensed to Carry
Leads
Learns Quickly
Lives in the Wilderness
Looks for Trouble
Masters the Swarm*
Masters Weaponry
Moves Like a Cat
Murders
Needs No Weapon
Never Says Die
Operates Undercover
Plays Too Many Games
Runs Away
Sees Beyond*
Separates Mind From Body*
Slays Monsters*
Solves Mysteries
Throws With Deadly Accuracy
Wields Two Weapons at Once
Works for a Living
Works the Back Alleys
Works the System
Would Rather Be Reading

* Only if the setting has a supernatural element

Character focus, page 60

SUGGESTED CREATURES AND NPCs FOR A MODERN GAME

Assassin
Cannibal
Crime boss
Detective
Ghost
Giant rat
Giant snake
Giant spider
Guard (works for police officers and soldiers as well)
Hacker
Killer clown
Occultist
Politician
Priest
Secret agent
Soldier
Thug/bandit

OTHER CREATURES AND NPCs FOR A MODERN GAME

Businessperson: level 1, business tasks as level 3
Cat: level 1, Speed defense as level 3
Clerk: level 1
Dog: level 2, perception as level 3
Dog, guard: level 3, attacks and perception as level 4
Horse: level 3; moves a long distance each round
Rat: level 1
Worker: level 2; health 8

ADDITIONAL MODERN EQUIPMENT

In a modern setting, the following items (and anything else appropriate to the real world) are usually available.

INEXPENSIVE ITEMS

Weapons	Notes
Ammo (box of 50 rounds)	
Knife (simple)	Light weapon (won't last long)

Other Items	Notes
Duct tape roll	Useful and ubiquitous
Flashlight	
Padlock with keys	
Trail rations (1 day)	

MODERATELY PRICED ITEMS

Weapons	Notes
Hand grenade	Explosive weapon, inflicts 4 points of damage in immediate radius
Hunting knife	Light weapon
Machete	Medium weapon
Nightstick	Light weapon

Armor	Notes
Leather jacket	Light armor

Other Items	Notes
Backpack	
Bag of heavy tools	
Bag of light tools	
Binoculars	Asset for perception tasks at range
Bolt cutters	
Cell phone	
Climbing gear	
Crowbar	
Electric lantern	
First aid kit	Asset for healing tasks
Handcuffs	
Rope	Nylon, 50 feet
Sleeping bag	
Tent	

EXPENSIVE ITEMS

Weapons	Notes
Light handgun	Light weapon, short range
Medium handgun	Medium weapon, long range
Bow	Medium weapon, long range
Rifle	Medium weapon, long range
Shotgun	Heavy weapon, immediate range

Armor	Notes
Kevlar vest	Medium armor

Other Items	Notes
Camera designed to be concealed	Transmits at long range
Microphone designed to be concealed	Transmits at long range
Cold weather camping gear	
Nightvision goggles	
Scuba gear	
Smartphone	
Straightjacket	

VERY EXPENSIVE ITEMS

Weapons	Notes
Heavy handgun	Heavy weapon, long range
Assault rifle	Heavy weapon, rapid-fire weapon, long range
Heavy rifle	Heavy weapon, 300-foot (90 m) range
Submachine gun	Medium weapon, rapid-fire weapon, short range

Armor	Notes
Lightweight body armor	Medium armor, encumbers as light armor
Military body armor	Heavy armor

Other Items	Notes
Disguise kit	Asset for disguise tasks
Used car	Level 3
Small boat	Level 3

EXORBITANT ITEMS

Other Items	Notes
Large boat	Level 5
Luxury car	Level 5
Sports car	Level 6

MODERN ARTIFACTS

The concept of artifacts is probably inappropriate for a modern setting without some kind of supernatural, fantastical, or science fiction element. The exception to this would be in an espionage-focused game, where characters are given special high-tech items that have limited uses, such as a jacket with buttons that can be used as grenades, or a watch that conceals a laser. If your modern setting has supernatural elements, look to one of the other appropriate genre chapters for artifact ideas.

MIXING IT UP: MODERN AND FANTASY

Often labeled "urban fantasy," stories of wizards and fantastic creatures living among us in the modern world (usually covertly, but not always) can make for a fun campaign. It mixes the crazy weirdness of fantasy with the comfortable familiarity of the real world. The PCs could be lurkers in the shadows, combating evil spellcasters, vampires, werewolves, and other creatures to safeguard the world we know. Alternatively, the characters could be young wizards just discovering their powers, perhaps gathering at a school to master their abilities.

CHILDHOOD ADVENTURE

Childhood adventure books, television shows, and movies are often set in a modern genre with elements of horror or science fiction. But the focus of the genre is on the kids, usually in the range of eleven to seventeen years of age, who encounter strange and unexplained happenings and must do something about it. Childhood adventure distinguishes its young characters as active heroes, not victims. Normally, protecting children is a common motivating influence for adult characters in all kinds of stories and games. By focusing on the child as the protagonist instead, a reader, a viewer, or a roleplaying game player gains a real sense that the stakes are somehow higher.

Popular childhood adventure scenarios include children finding and aiding a misunderstood alien, children dealing with the aftermath of a disaster in the absence of all the adults who are dead or missing, or children fending off the attacks of a horrific monster that adults believe to be imaginary. Many other childhood adventures are possible, and fiction is littered with them. One of the most popular follows the exploits of Harry Potter and his friends as he learns of his wizarding background and begins instruction in the magical arts, courtesy of J. K. Rowling. Another recent example

---

A player intrusion in a modern setting could be the appearance of a police car on patrol just when it's needed, or, conversely, the police car passing by gets a more important call and leaves before noticing the character is up to something illegal. See player intrusions, page 21.

"Modern" games set in the past are "historical." See Chapter 21: Historical on page 307.

is the TV series *Stranger Things* by the Duffer Brothers, but many more examples exist. In fact, childhood adventure stories are so popular that literature has a term for the genre: Young Adult fiction (usually abbreviated to YA fiction), though of course there is a lot of YA fiction that doesn't actually feature children. So some might say that childhood adventure, as described here, is a subset of YA fiction.

RUNNING A CHILDHOOD ADVENTURE

A major theme of childhood adventure is simple: kids helping kids. Sure, kid PCs might also help their parents, their mentors, and so on. But helping your friend who is lost, missing, different, or being haunted is a great place to start.

Another theme is how kid PCs deal with issues either without the notice of the adult world or in the face of outright disbelief and claims of "imaginary friends" and similar from adults. Some parents simply don't have time to listen to their child describe what is immediately assumed to be just a story. Others will listen and pretend to go along with a tall tale of monsters in the garden shed, but they don't actually believe it. Pretty soon, kid PCs must realize they've got to take care of the problem on their own.

That said, kid protagonists might require a patron or mentor to help them accomplish goals that can only be accomplished in the adult realm. For instance, in the Danny Dunn series (*Danny Dunn and the Homework Machine*; *Danny Dunn, Time Traveler*; *Danny Dunn, Invisible Boy*; and so on), the protagonists rely to a greater or lesser extent on Professor Euclid Bullfinch as their patron. A professor makes a great patron, but other NPCs could accomplish similar tasks. An uncle who's a soldier. An older sibling who's a priest. Maybe even an aunt who's secretly a witch.

OPTIONAL RULE: HANDLING PCs AS CHILDREN

The regular character creation process makes fully competent, adult characters. To account for playing children, the GM could adopt this optional rule. First, the players make their characters normally, and then they apply the following adjustments to their PCs, as appropriate to their age category. You might also consider applying a tier cap of 3 to childhood adventure games with kids of up to thirteen years old, and a tier cap of 4 for childhood adventure games featuring PCs who are aged fourteen to seventeen.

AGE 9 TO 13

Slight: –4 to your Might Pool.
Vulnerable: Adults look out for you. You are trained in all pleasant social interactions with adults.
Inability: Might-based tasks are hindered.
Inability: Tasks involving knowledge are hindered.

AGE 14 TO 17

Youthful: –2 to your Might Pool.
Inability: Tasks involving knowledge are hindered.

CHILDHOOD ADVENTURE THREATS

The Childhood Adventure Threats table provides more dangers to throw at kid PCs. These dangers can be incidental to the larger plot or help you generate a larger plot. They're not meant to be the major story arc, though you could probably spin some of them out to serve that purpose. Most of these threats should be presented as GM intrusions. If you are rolling for results instead of choosing, ignore or change results that don't fit your game. For instance, if the PCs are dealing with a science fiction-inspired alien, ignore the results that suggest that ghosts or killer clowns come after the characters.

MODERN

CHILDHOOD ADVENTURE THREATS

d20	Threat
1	**Bullies in the alley:** Three bullies (level 2) ambush one or more of the PCs at an unexpected location or time.
2	**Freak storm (level 1):** Inflicts 1 point of ambient damage each minute the PC fails a difficulty 3 Might defense task; reduces vision and chills characters, threatening worse with prolonged exposure.
3	**Rotten board (level 3):** While exploring the haunted house, old farm, or similar structure, a rotten board plunges the PC into the basement, inflicting 3 points of damage on a failed difficulty 4 Speed defense roll.
4	**Bicycle breakdown:** A character's bike throws a chain, requiring a difficulty 3 Intellect task to repair it.
5	**Detention:** A character is set up by an NPC child, who threatens to embroil the PC in an altercation where a teacher or other authority figure will be forced to step in and punish the offenders with detention, a truancy violation, or an unexpected trip home.
6	**Sinister authority figure:** A principal, a police officer, a mysterious man in a suit with a government badge, or some other authority figure takes an interest in the character(s) and begins to work against them.
7	**Bad dreams:** One PC suffers from a series of debilitating nightmares and must succeed on a difficulty 3 Intellect defense task or be treated as dazed for several hours, hindering all tasks.
8	**Unexpected roadblock:** Before the PCs can proceed, they are stopped by a parade blocking their path through town, a parent who demands that they finish their homework before leaving the house, a stolen bike, or some similar delay.
9	**Dilapidated house (level 4):** The old house, underpass tunnel, or cellar under the crazy old man's house collapses. Characters suffer 4 points of damage, and on a failed difficulty 4 Speed task are buried under suffocating rubble until they can escape or are rescued.
10	**Spiders:** Spiders of abnormal size infest this locked room, sub-basement, or subway tunnel.
11	**Ghost:** While the PCs investigate, a potentially friendly ghost appears before them. It doesn't realize it's dead, and the PCs might not realize until later that the strange NPC who told them important information has been dead for thirty years.
12	**Dire circus:** Is the circus in town just a regular troupe of entertainers, or is one of the clowns secretly a killer?
13	**Missing parent:** One of the PCs' parents mysteriously goes missing. Is it related to the adventure they're already on, or unrelated? Did something bad happen, or did the parent's car just break down?
14	**Missing younger sibling:** As with a missing parent, a younger sibling doesn't show up when called. Are they at a friend's house, or does the disappearance have something to do with the adventure the PCs are on? Either way, the PC is likely to be blamed ("You were supposed to be watching your sister!").
15	**Suspicious stranger:** The PCs realize that someone in a white van is following them around but trying to appear inconspicuous. Are they a random creeper, an agent of the organization the PCs have discovered as being involved in their adventure, or a detective hired by an estranged parent to keep tabs on one of the kid PCs?
16	**Accident:** A car threatens to barrel into a PC on a bike, or a car the PCs are getting a ride in suddenly blows a tire.
17	**Childhood illness:** One or more of the characters is struck down with a childhood illness like chicken pox, strep throat, or a similar sickness for a couple of days, hindering all their tasks by two steps.
18	**Bees or wasps:** The PCs accidentally disturb a hive or nest of stinging insects, which boil out of their home and attack as a swarm like a level 1 creature.
19	**Bear:** A black bear (escaped from the zoo or its natural environment) is disturbed while dumpster diving or investigating the garbage dump. The bear could be scared off but might be dangerous.
20	**Eggs:** The PCs find large eggs that were laid in a hidden spot. They could be glowing alien eggs, dinosaur eggs, or something less dramatic, like ostrich or turtle eggs. If the eggs are disturbed, whatever laid them comes looking for the PCs.

Giant spider, page 335
Ghost, page 331

Killer clown, page 339

Black bear, page 314

267

CRIME AND ESPIONAGE

A crime and espionage setting is often an extension of the modern genre. A crime and espionage game enjoys many of the same benefits and has some of the same challenges that other modern games face. On the plus side, players can easily understand the context. They know what the internet is, the utility of a smartphone, what they can expect from law enforcement, and much more. This familiarity allows players to get into character more easily, in some ways. For the same reason, the GM has it easier—unless players and GMs let themselves get bogged down in checking facts because everyone knows that information about how long it takes authorities to arrive after a 911 call is out there, just an internet search away. Verisimilitude is key.

The particular subgenre of crime and espionage is one where most if not all of the PCs are involved in some capacity with law enforcement, crime forensics, espionage, and/or international spying. This means that for most players, personal familiarity fails to bridge this gap—unless you're talking entertainment, which is replete with examples.

Characters in this case might be agents of a special department of a national government intelligence agency such as the FBI, CIA, NSA, or a black agency you create for your game. Of course, remember that not all spying is sponsored by nation-states. A lot of it is corporate spying, and many semi-secret organizations exist that sell their services to said corporations.

In an espionage game, PCs might get a mission briefing from their handler or patron to get things rolling. Mission briefings tend to be slightly more useful than visiting a fresh crime scene, because forensic specialists and related investigators have presumably already compiled a list of clues and put it in the briefing. The job of a PC spy is to follow up on the information provided, take out the enemy intelligence agents, and do so while retaining their cover and avoiding getting bogged down with red herrings.

TRADECRAFT

"Tradecraft" came to be a term associated with working as a spy during World War II. However, the word association was cemented during the Cold War. Tradecraft includes several skills such as deception, infiltration, maintaining a false cover identity, ferreting information out of files or computer networks, and hiding one's intrusion after the fact. Sometimes detectives (whether working for the police or as private investigators) must also employ tradecraft when trying to solve cases.

Of course, it wouldn't be necessary to go to such lengths if criminals and enemy operatives weren't constantly working against characters trying to accomplish their goals. During the investigation, PCs face many challenges, such as those described in the Tradecraft Challenge table. Use it when you need inspiration. Most of the elements noted on the table should be presented as GM intrusions.

TRADECRAFT CHALLENGE

d20	Challenge
1	**Poisoned (level 4):** Inflicts 3 points of Speed damage for four rounds on a failed Might defense task.
2	**Polonium poisoning (level 6):** Inflicts 5 points of Speed damage for six rounds on a failed Might defense task.
3	**Double agent:** An NPC ally has been turned by an enemy criminal or foreign organization.
4	**Interoffice politics:** Someone who seems unfit for the position replaces the PC's handler.
5	**Falsely accused:** The characters are brought in for questioning; a serious offense was leveled against them.
6	**Equipment failure:** The radio, vehicle, microphone, GPS tracker, or other piece of equipment important to the mission fails and requires repair or replacement.
7	**Cover questioned:** The character's cover identity comes into doubt, and hard questions must be answered to assure those asking that the PCs are who they pretend to be.
8	**Media exposure:** The character is photographed or shown in a video that gets wide distribution, risking their investigation should anyone recognize them.
9	**Hit squad:** An elite team of former military soldiers turned mercenaries is hired to eliminate the characters.
10	**Unexploded ordnance (level 5):** Explosive inflicts 5 points of damage to everyone within short range.
11	**Secret agent:** An enemy secret agent tracks down the PCs and tries to subvert their goals.
12	**Random police stop:** The local police force doing sobriety checks randomly selects the PCs (if they're driving) for questions. If characters are not driving, the police patrol encounters them accidentally.
13	**Network compromised (level 6):** An enemy hacker has broken into a PC's encrypted network and is in the process of learning their secrets. Do the characters even realize it?
14	**Forged papers:** A forged arrest warrant threatens to put the PCs on ice unless they can prove they did no wrong (at least, not in this case).
15	**Witness attacked:** A witness, informant, or other NPC with valuable information is brutally attacked, and winds up either dead or severely hurt and in a coma.
16	**Serial killer:** An NPC who the characters interact with in some capacity is secretly a psychotic killer, but is also a master at keeping their homicidal activities secret, even as they begin to taunt the PCs via anonymous texts, emails, and social media posts.
17	**Cover blown:** The PC's cover story is blown, and there's nothing for it but to deal with the aftermath.
18	**In the wind:** A suspect the PCs were investigating becomes aware of the surveillance and goes to ground.
19	**Body part found:** Either the PCs find the body part of an NPC they were hoping to question, or authorities find a body part the PCs attempted to dispose of.
20	**Captured:** The criminal gang or enemy operatives ambush the PCs at their base using sleep gas (level 6) and other tricks, hoping to knock them out and bring them to the enemy headquarters for questioning.

Chapter 15
SCIENCE FICTION

Science fiction is an incredibly broad category. It covers UFOs, space opera, near-future dystopias, otherworldly epics, hard science fiction, and everything in between. Even when compared to fantasy, science fiction is so wide that it almost isn't a single genre at all. Truthfully, there's not all that much to tie, say, *The Time Machine* by H. G. Wells with a dark cyberpunk story except for the technology involved, which is at a higher level than we possess or understand today. But even that part of science fiction is contentious. Should the science be purely that which obeys the laws of physics as we understand them today (often called hard science fiction), or is it more of an "anything goes" proposition? Is science we can't explain really just magic?

For our purposes, we'll treat fantastic science fiction as the default: aliens, spaceships that allow travel to other stars, energy weapons and shields, and so on. It's a familiar setting to almost everyone interested in science fiction. That said, we've also got some additional guidance for hard science fiction, where what's possible is more grounded in what we currently scientifically extrapolate. But your science fiction setting can be anything you can imagine.

A careful definition of each genre isn't important here. Whether your setting is fantasy or science fiction is up to you. The difference is just nomenclature.

Hard science fiction, page 276

CREATING A SCIENCE FICTION SETTING

Crafting a futuristic science fiction setting is a lot of work. You've got to think about technology levels, the history that led up to the setting, future society, future government, communications, alien species, and more. Consider the following suggestions.

Don't reinvent the wheel. If there's a science fiction setting that does a lot of what you like, steal liberally from it. If it's useful to your players, be upfront about the setting you're borrowing from to give them context.

Don't explain more than you need to. Your setting has faster-than-light travel? Great. Unless it's integral to the story (or fun for you), don't worry about explaining it.

Don't create more than you need to. Be ready to tell the PCs what they see and who they encounter when they set down on a new planet, but don't design a lot of alien species, cultures, and worlds that they will probably never see.

Use broad strokes. Give each alien species and planet one or maybe two unique aspects. Don't worry about creating a fully conceived culture or environment. More than likely, your PCs will hang around for only a session at most before they rocket off to someplace new.

RUNNING A SCIENCE FICTION GAME

The main reason that science fiction roleplaying games become problematic is that the players don't fully understand their options. If the PCs are the crew of a starship, the players don't know all the things the ship can and can't do. To make matters worse, they don't know where they can and can't travel in the ship, and what the ramifications of their travel will be. Modern settings and even fantasy settings have an inherent context that players grab hold of almost instinctively.

Similarly, GMs of science fiction settings sometimes flounder wondering what PCs should do. Fantasy is easier because there are very manageable genre tropes (go into the dungeon and fight the dark lord) and explanations for whatever the GM wants to have happen (it's magic). But science fiction involves, well, science, and we don't all have a mastery of advanced biology or quantum mechanics. The trick is not to worry about it too much. As Arthur C. Clarke said, "Any sufficiently advanced technology is indistinguishable from magic," so you can often toss off very high-tech explanations for almost anything without having an advanced degree. On the other hand, it's okay to have people in a science fiction setting act like people in the modern world (commute to work, go to restaurants, live in apartments, enjoy a variety of entertainment, and so on). Just change the trappings a bit to seem more futuristic. You're not trying to predict the future of culture and society as it is shaped by technology and events. You're trying to run an entertaining game session.

Here are a few other tips to consider.

Be generous with players who want to extrapolate the science elements of the game. If someone wants to reconfigure the ship's sensor array to do something odd but useful, let them try.

Don't be afraid of a little exposition. Explain the normal procedures for docking with another spaceship, and then let the PCs decide if they should do that or something else. Don't forget that the characters have a lot of knowledge that the players do not.

When trying to figure out what the PCs should do, steal plots from science fiction stories you like, whether it's *Star Trek* or *The Expanse*. Science fiction rarely has dungeons to explore or evil wizards to defeat (although versions of both are possible), so coming up with the story can be more challenging.

Science fiction has room for small stories as well as those in which the heroes save the whole galaxy. In such a large setting, in fact, small, character-driven stories are probably best.

Want a science fiction dungeon? How about a derelict alien spacecraft drifting in space? "Dungeon" exploration in environment suits gives the experience a whole new wrinkle.

Type, page 20

Flavor, page 34

SUGGESTED TYPES FOR A SCIENCE FICTION GAME

Role	Type
Soldier	Warrior
Technician	Explorer with technology flavor
Pilot	Explorer with technology flavor
Diplomat	Speaker
Doctor	Speaker with skills and knowledge flavor
Spy	Explorer with stealth flavor
Scientist	Explorer with skills and knowledge flavor
Psion	Adept
Psychic knight	Warrior with magic flavor

Character focus, page 60

SUGGESTED FOCI FOR A SCIENCE FICTION GAME

Absorbs Energy
Battles Robots
Builds Robots
Calculates the Incalculable
Commands Mental Powers
Conducts Weird Science
Dances With Dark Matter
Doesn't Do Much
Entertains
Fights Dirty
Fights With Panache
Focuses Mind Over Matter
Fuses Flesh and Steel

Fuses Mind and Machine
Hunts
Infiltrates
Interprets the Law
Is Idolized by Millions
Learns Quickly
Looks for Trouble
Loves The Void
Masters Defense
Masters Weaponry
Moves Like a Cat
Murders
Needs No Weapon

Never Says Die
Operates Undercover
Pilots Starcraft
Siphons Power
Solves Mysteries
Talks to Machines
Travels Through Time
Wears Power Armor
Works for a Living
Works the Back Alleys
Works the System
Would Rather Be Reading

Creatures, page 312
NPCs, page 372

A player intrusion in a science fiction game could be that the player knows how to reconfigure a piece of technology to do something other than what it's supposed to do—reconfigure the sensor array, so to speak. See player intrusions, page 21.

SUGGESTED CREATURES AND NPCs FOR A SCIENCE FICTION GAME

Assassin
Chronophage
CRAZR
Deinonychus
Enthraller
Fusion hound
Ghoul
Giant spider
Grey

Guard
Kaiju
Mechanical soldier
Mi-go
Mokuren
Neveri
Puppet tree
Ravage bear
Replicant

Secret agent
Thug/bandit
Tyrannosaurus rex
Vat reject
Wardroid
Xenoparasite
Zhev
Zombie

OTHER CREATURES AND NPCs FOR A SCIENCE FICTION GAME

Innocuous rodent: level 1
Guard beast: level 3, perception as level 4

Corporate drone: level 1
Physical laborer: level 2; health 8

ADDITIONAL SCIENCE FICTION EQUIPMENT

In a science fiction setting, the following items (and anything else appropriate to the setting) are usually available.

INEXPENSIVE ITEMS

Weapons	Notes
Energy pack (50 shots)	
Knife (simple)	Light weapon

Other Items	Notes
Flashlight	
Survival rations (1 day)	

MODERATELY PRICED ITEMS

Weapons	Notes
Hunting knife	Light weapon

SCIENCE FICTION

Machete	Medium weapon
Grenade (sonic)	Explosive weapon, inflicts 2 points of damage in immediate radius, plus Might defense roll or lose next turn
Grenade (thermite)	Explosive weapon, inflicts 5 points of damage in immediate radius

Armor	Notes
Leather jacket	Light armor

Other Items	Notes
Backpack	
Bag of heavy tools	
Bag of light tools	
Binoculars	Asset for perception tasks at range
Breather	8 hours of breathable air
Climbing gear	Asset for climbing tasks
Communicator	Planetary range
Crowbar	
Environment tent	
First aid kit	Asset for healing tasks
Handcuffs	
Nightvision goggles	
Portable lamp	
Rope	Nylon, 50 feet
Sleeping bag	

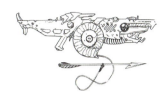

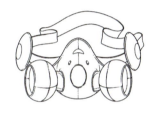

EXPENSIVE ITEMS

Weapons	Notes
Light blaster	Light weapon, short range
Medium blaster	Medium weapon, long range
Needler	Light weapon, long range
Shotgun	Heavy weapon, immediate range
Stunstick	Medium weapon, inflicts no damage but human-sized or smaller target loses next action

Armor	Notes
Armored bodysuit	Medium armor
Lightweight body armor	Medium armor

Other Items	Notes
Camera designed to be concealed	Transmits at long range
Microphone designed to be concealed	Transmits at long range
Environment suit	Provides 24 hours of atmosphere and +10 to Armor against extreme temperatures
Wrist computer	Asset for most knowledge-based tasks

Remember, armor (lowercase a) is something you wear. Armor (capital A) is the bonus you get. You can have only one type of armor at a time, but you can have many sources of Armor, theoretically.

VERY EXPENSIVE ITEMS

Weapons	Notes
Heavy blaster	Heavy weapon, long range
Heavy blaster rifle	Heavy weapon, 300-foot (90 m) range
Pulse laser gun	Medium weapon, rapid-fire weapon, long range

Armor	Notes
Battlesuit	Heavy armor, also works as environment suit

Other Items	Notes
Disguise kit	Asset for disguise tasks
Gravity regulator	Belt-mounted device that regulates gravity to 1G for wearer if within 0 G to 3 G conditions
Handheld scanner	Asset for identifying tasks
Hovercraft	Level 4
Infiltrator	Asset for lockpicking tasks when used with electronic locks
Jetpack	Level 4
Stealthsuit	Asset for stealth tasks

EXORBITANT ITEMS

Weapons	Notes
Blast cannon	10 points of damage, 500-foot (150 m) range, requires a tripod and two people to operate

Armor	Notes
Force field	Not armor, offers +1 to Armor

Other Items	Notes
Luxury hovercar	Level 5
Robot servant	Level 3
Small spaceship	Level 4

SCIENCE FICTION ARTIFACTS

Artifacts in a science fiction game can be strange relics from an unknown alien source or tech items that aren't yet widely available. In a galactic setting, for example, it's easy to imagine that innovations or specialized items might not have spread everywhere.

AMBER CASEMENT
Level: 1d6 + 4
Form: Series of short, rounded tubes and hoses about 12 inches (30 cm) long
Effect: The device solidifies the air in a 10-foot (3 m) cube of space, the center of which must be within short range. The air is turned into an amberlike substance, and those trapped in it will likely suffocate or starve.
Depletion: 1–4 in 1d6

METABOLISM BUD
Level: 1d6
Form: Organic pod, almost like a small, hemispherical bit of brain; once grafted to a host, the host's flesh grows over the pod until it is only a lump
Effect: The pod grafts onto any living host (usually near the brain or spine) and injects chemicals that boost the creature's metabolism. This permanently raises the host's Speed Pool maximum by 5 points.
Depletion: —

MIND IMAGER
Level: 1d6 + 2
Form: Handheld device with a plastic panel screen and wires that must be affixed to the head of a creature
Effect: This device shows a visual image of what a creature is thinking. The affected creature need not be conscious.
Depletion: 1 in 1d20

PSYCHIC CRYSTAL
Level: 1d6 + 4
Form: Violet crystal the size of a fist
Effect: The crystal allows the user to transmit their thoughts telepathically at an interstellar distance. Even at that range, communication is instantaneous. Each use allows about a minute's worth of communication, and the communication is entirely one way (so having two crystals would be handy).
Depletion: 1 in 1d10

REPAIR SPHERE
Level: 1d6 + 2
Form: Small spherical automaton about 8 inches (20 cm) in diameter
Effect: This device comes with a small module that can be affixed to a machine. Floating along, the sphere attempts to follow within immediate range of the module (though it can be directed to remain where it is). It moves a short distance each round. It can come to the module from a range of up to 10 miles (16 km) away. If the module is attached to a machine and that machine takes damage, the sphere moves to repair the damage with sophisticated tools that restore 1d6 − 2 points per round (meaning that if a 1 or 2 is rolled, no damage is repaired that round). This requires no action on the part of the machine being repaired. The sphere can attempt to repair a machine a number of times per day equal to its level. The sphere must be newly activated each day.
Depletion: 1 in 1d100

Since it's frighteningly easy to die in a space battle if your ship is destroyed, most ships have escape pods. Even fighter craft have ejection systems that put the pilot out into space in an environment suit. In other words, GMs should try to give PCs a way out of immediately dying if they get on the wrong end of a space battle.

STARSHIPS
Here are a few sample starship types:

Starship	Level	Crew	Weapon Systems
Fighter	1	1	1
Interceptor	2	1	1
Freighter	3 (4 for defense)	4	1
Frigate	4	20	4
Cruiser	4	25	5
Battleship	10	1,000	36

"Crew" indicates the minimum number of people needed to operate the ship. Many ships can carry more passengers. "Weapon Systems" indicates the maximum number of different enemies the ship can target at once (but only one attack per target in any circumstance).

HARD SCIENCE FICTION

Hard science fiction is distinguished from regular science fiction by the perception of scientific accuracy. Which means hard science fiction often precludes technology deemed impossible by mainstream scientific theory, including such mainstays as faster-than-light travel and time travel. Another way of conceptualizing hard science fiction is "near future."

Many examples of hard science fiction are out there, ready for you to mine for concepts and ideas.

Solar System Colonization: The novel and TV series called *The Expanse* by James S. A. Corey is a prime example of human colonization of the solar system, but many other examples exist, including the Mars trilogy by Kim Stanley Robinson, *Cold as Ice* and *Dark as Day* by Charles Sheffield, *Mars* (and other novels) by Ben Bova, and many more.

Rise of AI: A favorite movie and novel trope, examples of artificial intelligence can be found in movies beginning with the classic *2001: A Space Odyssey* by Stanley Kubrick and Arthur C. Clarke. Other movie and TV examples of human AI emergence include *Ex Machina*, *Terminator*, *Battlestar Galactica*, *A. I. Artificial Intelligence*, and more. Novels include *Carnival* by Elizabeth Bear, *Accelerando* by Charles Stross, *Wake* and other books in the WWW trilogy by Robert J. Sawyer, and more.

Advanced Biotech: Like the previous categories, too many stories about advanced biotech exist to list them all, so here are just a few (that don't overtly stray into horror). Movies include *Gattaca*, *Elysium*, and *Blade Runner*. Novels include *The Windup Girl* by Paolo Bacigalupi, *Blood Music* and *Darwin's Radio* by Greg Bear, and the Rifter series by Peter Watts.

EFFECTS OF GRAVITY

In a hard science fiction game, variable effects of gravity can't be waved away by tech that simulates normal gravity on spacecraft, space stations, and other worlds. Instead, it's an issue people must overcome.

Short-Term Microgravity Exposure: People new to low gravity might get space sickness. Newcomers must succeed on a difficulty 3 Might task or suffer mild nausea for about two to four days, during which time all their tasks are hindered. A few unlucky travelers (usually those who roll a 1 or otherwise face a GM intrusion) are almost completely incapacitated, and find all tasks hindered by three steps.

Sometimes hard science fiction asks readers to accept one element of the impossible along with other more scientifically grounded speculative fiction.

Don't worry about the AI that passes the Turing Test. Worry about the ones intentionally failing it.

Science Fiction

INTERPLANETARY TRAVEL

Origin	Destination	Travel Time Using Nuclear Plasma Engine
Earth/Moon	Mars	20 + 1d20 days
Mars	Asteroid belt	30 + 1d20 days
Asteroid belt	Jupiter and its moons	30 + 1d20 days
Jupiter	Saturn and its moons	60 + 1d20 days
Saturn	Uranus	90 + 1d20 days

Long-Term Microgravity Exposure: Long-term exposure to microgravity environments without medical interventions degrades health. How long one spends in such conditions is directly relevant. The GM may assign long-term penalties to PCs if the situation warrants it, though the use of advanced space medicine, proper exercise, and recommended steroids and other hormones can avoid these complications.

Low Gravity: Weapons that rely on weight, such as all heavy weapons, inflict 2 fewer points of damage (dealing a minimum of 1 point). Short-range weapons can reach to long range, and long-range weapons can reach to very long range. Characters trained in low-gravity maneuvering ignore the damage penalty.

High Gravity: It's hard to make effective attacks when the pull of gravity is very strong. Attacks (and all physical actions) made in high gravity are hindered. Ranges in high gravity are reduced by one category (very-long-range weapons reach only to long range, long-range weapons reach only to short range, and short-range weapons reach only to immediate range). Characters trained in high-gravity maneuvering ignore the change in difficulty but not the range decreases.

Zero Gravity: It's hard to maneuver in an environment without gravity. Attacks (and all physical actions) made in zero gravity are hindered. Short-range weapons can reach to long range, and long-range weapons can reach to very-long range.

EFFECTS OF VACUUM

Vacuum is lethal. There's no air to breathe, and the lack of pressure causes havoc on an organic body. An unprotected character moves one step down the damage track each round. However, at the point where they should die, they instead fall unconscious and remain so for about a minute. If they are rescued during that time, they can be revived. If not, they die.

TRAVELING THE SOLAR SYSTEM AND ORBITAL MECHANICS

In a hard science fiction setting, you might be interested in evoking the reality of travel times between colonies on planets and moons in the solar system. Even so, plotting a course between locations in the solar system isn't simple, because everything is always moving with respect to everything else. You could determine exactly how long a trip would take with some internet research. Or you could just evoke the effect of orbital mechanics and varying accelerations on interplanetary travel. Use the Interplanetary Travel Table to do so. For a trip between locations not directly compared, add up the destinations in between. The travel times assume a nuclear plasma engine of a kind already being tested today (but better), a steady thrust toward the destination, and an equally long and steady braking thrust over the last half of the trip before orbit insertion. Such propulsion systems can change velocity and sustain thrust for days at a time, which reduces bone loss, muscle atrophy, and other long-term effects of low gravity.

Regardless, the travel times between distant locations bring home one thing: space is big and lonely.

Damage track, page 218

HARD SCIENCE FICTION THREATS

This table provides more dangers you can throw at PCs playing in a setting where physics trumps fantasy. The results are not meant to be the major story arc, though you could spin some of them out to serve that purpose. Most of these threats should be presented as GM intrusions.

d20	Threat
1	**Solar flare (level 3):** A freak solar flare sends hard radiation sleeting through the character's vessel or location, inflicting 3 points of ambient radiation damage each minute the character fails a difficulty 3 Might defense task; might lead to cancer if not treated later.
2	**Belligerent asteroid miner:** Four space-suited asteroid miners ambush one or more of the PCs at an unexpected location or time.
3	**Spacesuit issue:** One PC's spacesuit has a control malfunction, requiring a series of Intellect tasks (difficulty ranging from 3 to 5) to repair it before the malfunction leads to a lethal outcome.
4	**Unexpected shake (level 5):** The spacecraft, station, vacuum habitat, or similar structure convulses for not immediately obvious reasons, inflicting 5 points of damage on a failed difficulty 5 Speed defense roll and possibly leading to additional repercussions.
5	**Space debris:** A falling satellite, space station, or other craft threatens to impact the moon, planet, or craft of interest. PCs might need to board the failing relic or otherwise try to change its trajectory to avoid impact.
6	**AI malfunction:** The artificial intelligence, so charming and helpful, secretly decides to kill the crew, the habitat population, or something even more dire.
7	**Diplomatic event:** Is the diplomatic event on the station that the PCs have been invited to a reason to celebrate, or an opportunity for an assassin hidden among the delegation to strike?
8	**Tunnel collapse (level 6):** The tunnel connecting two craft, subsurface moon tunnel, or spacecraft corridor collapses. Characters suffer 6 points of damage and on a failed difficulty 6 Speed task are either set adrift in the vacuum of space or buried under sparking rubble until they can find some resolution or die.
9	**Toxic reaction:** One PC suffers from a reaction to a solvent, food additive, or gas leak and must succeed on a difficulty 4 Might defense task or be treated as dazed for several hours, during which time all their tasks are hindered.
10	**Micrometeorite:** A tiny meteorite holes the craft, station, or habitat, with a chance to hit one character who fails a difficulty 7 Speed defense task and inflict 10 points of damage. If in a vacuum, repairing the punctures requires two difficulty 3 Intellect tasks plus something to seal the holes.

Asteroid miner: level 3; Armor 2

Assassin, page 373

Science Fiction

MIXING IT UP: SCIENCE FICTION AND MODERN

The truth is out there. What if there are aliens among us? What if scientists and secret cabals are using fringe science to create weapons and devices that modern society can't even comprehend? The theme here is that science—alien or otherwise—with all its wonders and horrors is intruding upon our normal lives. Lurking in the shadows, PCs in such a campaign would have glimpses of the truth but would always be questing for more. Perhaps they work for a secret society or a covert government agency assigned to deal with the growing alien menace. Conspiracies, intrigue, and secrets are the hallmarks of this kind of campaign, which could easily incorporate elements of horror as well.

SPECIES DESCRIPTORS

In a science fiction setting, some GMs may want to offer alien species or androids, who are mechanically different from humans, as options for player characters. This can be accomplished by using descriptors. Two examples are below.

ARTIFICIALLY INTELLIGENT

You are a machine—not just a sentient machine, but a sapient one. Your awareness might make you an exception, or there may be many like you, depending on the setting.

Artificially intelligent characters have machine minds of one type or another. This can involve an advanced computer brain, but it could also be a liquid computer, a quantum computer, or a network of smart dust particles creating an ambient intelligence. You might even have been an organic creature whose mind was uploaded into a machine.

Your body, of course, is also a machine. Most people refer to you as a robot or an android, although you know neither term describes you very well, as you are as free-willed and free-thinking as they are.

You gain the following characteristics:

Superintelligent: +4 to your Intellect Pool.
Artificial Body: +3 to your Might Pool and your Speed Pool.
Shell: +1 to Armor.
Limited Recovery: Resting restores points only to your Intellect Pool, not to your Might Pool or your Speed Pool.
Mechanics, Not Medicines: Conventional healing methods, including the vast majority of restorative devices and medicines, do not restore points to any of your Pools. You can recover points to your Intellect Pool only by resting, and you can recover points to your Speed and Might Pools only through repair. The difficulty of the repair task is equal to the number of points of damage sustained, to a maximum of 10. Repairing your Might and Speed Pools are always two different tasks.

Machine Vulnerabilities and Invulnerabilities: Damaging effects and other threats that rely on an organic system—poison, disease, cell disruption, and so on—have no effect on you. Neither do beneficial drugs or other effects. Conversely, things that normally affect only inorganic or inanimate objects can affect you, as can effects that disrupt machines.

Uncanny Valley: You have a hard time relating to organic beings, and they don't react well to you. All positive interaction tasks with such beings are hindered by two steps.

QUINTAR

You are a quintar from the planet Quint. You are basically humanoid but taller, thinner, and blue skinned. Your hands end in three very long fingers. Quintar have five genders, but all quintar prefer to be addressed as female when communicating with more binary species. Human emotions and sexuality fascinate them, but not because they don't have such concepts—quintar emotions and sexuality are just very different from those of humans. In general, quintar are more cerebral than other species, valuing knowledge over all else.

Quint is relatively Earthlike, with slightly less gravity but a slightly denser atmosphere.

You gain the following characteristics:

Cerebral: +4 to your Intellect Pool.
Skill: You are trained in one type of knowledge task of your choice.
Skill: Quintar fascination with human behavior eases all interaction rolls (pleasant or not) with humans.
Difficult Rest: Quintar subtract 2 from all recovery rolls (minimum 1).

Chapter 16

HORROR

Although it's very likely a subset of the modern genre, horror as a genre gets special treatment. Unlike the other genres, horror doesn't necessarily suggest a setting. Any setting can be horrific. Horror is more of a style. An approach. A mood.

You could easily have horror in other times and settings, but for our purposes, we'll deal with a default setting in the modern day. The PCs are probably normal people, not secret agents or special investigators (although being a part of a secret agency that deals with monsters in the shadows could make for a fine horror game).

Suggested foci, types, and additional equipment for a horror setting are the same as in a modern setting, so refer to chapter 14 for that information.

Chapter 14: Modern, page 261

CREATING A HORROR SETTING

Whatever the setting, the main thing to remember when preparing to run a horror-themed game is that if everything is terrifying, nothing is. Think about every good horror movie you've seen or story you've read, in which scenes of horror are paced nicely with scenes of normal life. The key is the contrast. People need rising and falling tension, or they will break from the story. So you need a setting that has ordinary scenes, encounters, and events as well as horrific ones. Even a world overcome by hordes of zombies needs to offer moments of respite for the characters.

RUNNING A HORROR GAME

Running a good horror game is difficult. You've got to maintain mood and atmosphere at almost all times. Consider the following tips.

Give the players time to develop their characters before going to the haunted house, spooky cemetery, or mysterious ruin. Let them get attached to the characters, at least a little, so that when those PCs are in jeopardy, the players will be frightened.

Use music, lighting, and the environment to help create a mood. Don't hesitate to use candles or flashlights in a dark room rather than conventional lighting. Shake things up—if you normally play in the dining room when you run sessions in other genres, play in the basement for your horror game.

Unnerve your players as well as the characters. As you describe a scene in the game, occasionally glance out the window or toward the door, particularly if it's behind one or more players, as though you hear something strange. Make it seem like creepy things are going on, but be subtle. Make the players sense it without being fully aware of it.

Startle the players as well as the characters. When the monster finally appears, shout at the top of your lungs! Turn out the lights suddenly. Do something shocking.

Horror games are often one-shot sessions or a short arc of a few sessions. They are very difficult to run as long-term campaigns, but it's possible. If that's what you want, remember that you need rising and falling tension. There must be respites and calm moments between the horror.

Horror needs to be brutal and ruthless, even if—or rather, especially if—other games you run are relatively safe for PCs. Kill characters. Maim characters.

Focus on the startling and unexpected when possible. Blood and gore can be shocking sometimes, but only in a context in which they are unexpected. In other words, they might be expected on a battlefield, but not in the middle of a happy religious ceremony or family gathering.

Fear of the unknown is the greatest, most primal fear. It's the thing the PCs don't see that scares them the most. Take your time and allow them to hear the horrific creature approach before the encounter begins. Let them see its shadow before they see the rest of it. Let them react to the unknown threat before they can identify it.

CONSENT

Horror games allow us to explore some pretty dark topics from the safety of our own game tables. But before you do that, make sure everyone around your table is okay with that. Find out what your players will find "good uncomfortable," which is something that makes us squirm in our seats in a great horror movie, and "bad uncomfortable," which is something that actually makes a player feel nauseated, unsafe, or offended. Being scared can be fun, but being sickened isn't.

Consider the age and maturity of everyone in the game, perhaps in terms of the movie rating system. Tell the players what you think the game you're running would be rated. If everyone's okay with an R rating, then fine. You can have a spooky game that's on the level of a kids' movie rated G—more like *Scooby-Doo* than *Saw*, in other words. A PG rating might be right for a game that's more creepy than horrific, with ghosts and spooky noises but not axe-wielding maniacs.

The different ratings suggest different kinds of content for your game. Finding a dead body is horrible, but watching someone get decapitated is something else entirely. Getting chased around by an alien that wants to eat you is one thing, but having it gestate and burst out of your own intestines is another. You need to know where the line is for everyone participating, and you need to know it right from the beginning.

A player intrusion in a horror game might involve the player having heard an old legend about the monster in the woods and that it's drawn to the smell of strong perfume. Or maybe something even more dramatic, like the floorboards of the old house give way, dropping the PC into the basement, but away from the zombies. Or perhaps there's a handy meat cleaver in the first kitchen drawer they open. See player intrusions, page 21.

SUGGESTED CREATURES AND NPCs FOR A HORROR GAME

Assassin	Hacker	Secret agent
Cannibal	Killer clown	Skeleton
Chronophage	Killing white light	Slidikin
Crime boss	Mad scientist	Soldier
Deep one	Mi-go	Statue, animate
Demigod	Neveri	Thug/bandit
Demon	Nuppeppo	Vampire
Devil	Occultist	Wendigo
Enthraller	Politician	Werewolf
Ghost	Priest	Witch
Ghoul	Professor	Xenoparasite
Giant rat	Puppet tree	Zombie
Giant spider	Ravage bear	
Guard	Replicant	

Creatures, page 312
NPCs, page 372

OTHER CREATURES AND NPCs

Businessperson: level 1
Cat: level 1, Speed defense as level 3
Clerk: level 1
Dog: level 2, perception as level 3
Dog, vicious: level 3, attacks and perception as level 4

Groundskeeper/caretaker: level 2; health 8
Man in Black: level 4; carries weird weapons, including those with long range
Rat: level 1
Tarantula: level 1

HORROR ARTIFACTS

Most of the time, a horror artifact will be something really weird—an ancient tome of forbidden necromancy, an alien device that humans can barely understand, and so forth. They are often unique items rather than one of a type. Horror artifacts should probably come with a risk, such as a built-in cost, a drawback, or something else that makes using them another way to heighten the tension of the game. Several examples are below.

BOOK OF INVERSION

Level: 8

Form: Very large book of ancient providence, the cover bound in iron and wrapped in chains with a level 6 padlock

Effect: When opened, the Book of Inversion shows a pair of pages that detail a magic spell in the reader's language, complete with disturbing diagrams. The spell's effect varies, but it is always some kind of horrible attack—a target is driven mad, a target is turned inside out, a target seeks to murder their best friend, several targets are cursed with a rotting disease, and so forth. The reader can automatically cast the spell as an action, one time only. More insidiously, if successful, the spell confers pleasure to the caster and fully restores all of their Pools. The caster must make an immediate Intellect defense roll or be compelled to use the book (and thus a new spell) again the next day. This compulsion is so strong that the caster will kill their dearest loved one to complete the task. If they are unable to use the book again, they are driven permanently mad. Woe to the caster who uses the book on the last time before it is depleted (at which point it crumbles to dust).

Depletion: 1 in 1d10

SHADOW BOX

Level: 7

Form: Wooden and black metal box, about 12 inches by 7 inches by 3 inches (30 by 18 by 8 cm), with a hinged lid and a clasp

Effect: When the box opens, shadows seethe out. These shadows coalesce into a form that best represents a deep fear in the subconscious of the person who opened the box. The opener must make an Intellect defense roll to master the shadow thing, which then acts as a level 7 creature under their control for five rounds before fading away. If the roll fails, the creature attacks the opener and anyone else around. To make matters worse, the opener spends the first round frozen in terror, doing nothing.

Depletion: 1–2 in 1d6

SPHERE 23

Level: 1d6 + 4

Form: A 7-inch (18 cm) sphere of what appears to be fluid metal, tinted red

Effect: Possibly one of a number of identical alien artifacts recovered in remote locales across the earth, the so-called sphere 23 will grant a wish to anyone who holds it and uses an action to concentrate on it. The wish can be anything, including something that bends reality: raising the dead, altering time, and so forth. However, the wisher must immediately make a Might defense roll or be consumed by the sphere. If the roll succeeds, they must then make an Intellect defense roll or be driven permanently and irrevocably mad.

Depletion: 1–3 in 1d6

OPTIONAL RULE: SHOCK

When the PCs encounter something shocking, many times the most realistic response is to scream, stand in abject horror, or run. That might not be the smartest thing to do in the situation, but it's genuine. What would your accountant do if they saw an axe-wielding maniac coming at them? Let's face it, unless they truly steeled themselves with all their will, they'd probably scream and run.

When a PC encounters something horrific, utterly disgusting, dreadful, impossible, or otherwise shocking, call for an Intellect defense roll based on the level of the creature involved, or simply an appropriate level as decided by the GM (see the Shock Levels table). Failure might mean that for one round, the player loses control of the character, and the GM decides what the PC does next. This usually means that the character runs, screams, gibbers, stares slack-jawed, or just does nothing. However, GMs should welcome player input into this situation. The point is to portray that when we're shocked, we don't always react in the best way, the smartest way, or even the way we want to. Fear is a powerful thing.

Alternatively, failure on the Intellect defense roll might mean that the character suffers Intellect damage equal to the level of the defense task. This indicates an overall toll that numerous shocks and horrors can have on a person. You might have a situation where a character literally dies of fright.

SHOCK LEVELS

Event	Level
Something unexpected darts or jumps out	1
Something suddenly moves just out of the corner of the eye	2
A sudden loud noise (like a scream)	2
Unexpectedly seeing a corpse	2
Watching someone die	3
Seeing something impossible (like an inanimate object sliding across the floor)	4
Watching a friend die	5
Seeing a monstrous creature	Creature level
Witnessing something supernatural (like a spell)	5
Seeing something mind-bending (like an impossible, multidimensional demigod coalescing out of thin air)	8

OPTIONAL RULE: HORROR MODE

For horror games, GMs can implement a rule called Horror Mode. The idea is to create a feeling of escalating dread and menace by changing one die roll mechanic. In the game, things begin as normal. The PCs interact with each other and the NPCs, investigate, research, travel, and so on. But when they enter the haunted house, the serial killer gets close, the elder things beneath the earth awaken, or whatever horrific situation planned by the GM begins, things change. At this time, the GM announces that the game has gone into Horror Mode.

This is a key for the players (not the characters) to recognize that things are getting bad. It's the RPG equivalent of spooky music beginning to play in a horror film. While in Horror Mode, the rules for GM intrusions governed by die rolls change. Normally this happens only on a roll of 1, but when Horror Mode starts, it becomes a roll of 1 or 2. And then it escalates. As time passes, GM intrusions happen on a roll of 1 to 3, then a roll of 1 to 4, and so on. This potentially means that a die roll in Horror Mode can indicate success in a task and still trigger a GM intrusion.

As the intrusion range changes with each escalation, the GM should announce this to the players. The feeling of rising tension should be dramatic and overt.

ESCALATION RATE

Activity	Intrusion Range Increases by 1
Exploring a large area	Every time a new intrusion is indicated by a die roll
Exploring	Every ten minutes or every time a new intrusion is indicated by a die roll
Combat	Each round

For example, while the PCs are exploring a dark swamp (a large area), the game goes into Horror Mode and intrusions are indicated on a 1 or 2. During this exploration, one of the players rolls a 2. Not only is there an intrusion, but now the range escalates to 1, 2, or 3. The character is almost dragged into a spot of quicksand-like muck. Then the PCs find an old abandoned house in the middle of the swamp. They enter, and now the escalation rate goes up if they roll a 1, 2, or 3, or every ten minutes that passes in the game. They explore the house for twenty minutes (escalating intrusions to 1 to 5), and during the investigation of the kitchen, someone rolls a 3, triggering an intrusion. A cabinet opens mysteriously and a strangely carved clay pot falls, striking the character. This also escalates the intrusion rate, so they now occur on a roll of 1 to 6. When the PCs reach the attic, they encounter the dreaded swamp slayer, a half man, half beast that thrives on blood. It attacks, and now the range goes up during each round of combat. After four rounds of fighting, intrusions happen

Horror Mode is a very "meta" rule. It gives players knowledge that their characters don't have. This is similar to how the viewers of a horror movie or readers of a horror story often know more than the characters on the screen or page. It heightens the tension. Players can express the start of Horror Mode by having their characters talk about goosebumps or a feeling of being watched, but this is not necessary.

on a roll of 1 to 10—half the time. Things are getting dicey, and they're only going to get worse.

When the GM announces that Horror Mode has ended, the GM intrusion rate goes back to normal, happening only on a roll of 1 or when the GM awards XP.

USING GM INTRUSIONS IN HORROR MODE

With the GM intrusions coming fast and furious toward the end of Horror Mode, it's easy to run out of ideas. In combat, intrusions might just mean that the monster or villain gets a surprise extra attack or inflicts more damage. Perhaps a PC is thrown to the ground or nearer to the edge of a cliff. If the characters are running away, one might trip and fall. If the PCs are exploring, a bookcase topples, potentially hitting someone. Think of all the similar moments you've seen in horror films.

Sometimes, if the GM prefers, the GM intrusion can simply be something frightening, like a moan or a whisper. These aren't dangerous to the PCs, but they escalate the tension and indicate that something bad is getting closer.

In fact, while in Horror Mode, GMs should mostly refrain from doing anything bad, ominous, or dangerous unless it's an intrusion (either from a die roll or through the awarding of XP). In a horror game, GM intrusions are an indication that things are bad and getting worse, and whenever possible, the GM should allow the Horror Mode escalation to drive the action. This makes the GM more of a slave to the dice than in other Cypher System situations, but that's okay.

Consider this example. The PCs have tracked something that is probably committing a series of horrific murders to an old factory. They enter the building to explore. The GM knows where the creature is hiding in the factory, but decides that it doesn't become aware of the characters until an intrusion is indicated. The only clue the PCs have is a mysterious noise off in the darkness. The creature doesn't move toward them until another GM intrusion occurs. Now they hear something dragging across the factory floor, coming closer. But it's not until a third intrusion occurs that the creature lunges out from behind an old machine at the PC who rolled the die.

In some ways, the status quo doesn't change until an intrusion happens. This could be seen as limiting the GM and the need for pacing, but remember that the GM can still have an intrusion occur anytime they desire, in addition to waiting for the low die rolls.

OPTIONAL RULE: MADNESS

Having characters descend into madness is an interesting facet of some kinds of horror and can make long-term horror campaigns more interesting. The easiest way to portray blows to a character's sanity is through Intellect damage. When PCs encounter something shocking, as described above, they always take Intellect damage. If they would normally move one step down the damage track due to the damage, they instead immediately regain points (equal to 1d6 + their tier) in their Intellect Pools but lose 1 point from their maximums in that Pool. Characters whose Intellect Pools reach 0 go insane. They lose their current descriptor and adopt the Mad descriptor, regain 1d6 + tier points to their Intellect Pools, and gain +1 to their Intellect Edge. If they ever reach a permanent Intellect Pool maximum of 0 again, they go stark raving mad and are no longer playable.

Intellect Edge offers an interesting means to portray a character who is knowledgeable (and perhaps even powerful in terms of mental abilities) yet mentally fragile. A character with a low Intellect Pool but a high Intellect Edge can perform Intellect actions well (since Edge is very helpful) but is still vulnerable to Intellect damage (where Edge is of no help).

Since Cypher System games are meant to be story based, players should recognize that the

GMs may want to limit the number of intrusions to no more than one per round, no matter what the dice indicate, but that should be based on the situation.

Mad, page 51

degrading sanity of their character is part of the story. A player who feels that their character is going mad can talk to the GM, and the two of them can work out the means to portray that—perhaps by using the Mad descriptor, permanently trading up to 4 points from their Intellect Pool to gain +1 to their Intellect Edge, or anything else that seems appropriate. Mental disorders, manias, psychopathy, schizophrenia, or simple phobias can be added to a character's traits, but they don't need to be quantified in game statistics or die rolls. They're simply part of the character.

Inabilities in personal interaction or any area requiring focus might be appropriate, perhaps allowing the PC to gain training in weird lore or forbidden knowledge. Or maybe the opposite is true—as the character's mind slowly slips away, they become oddly compelled or can obsessively focus on a single task for indefinite periods, and thus they gain training in that topic or skill. These kinds of changes could be balanced with inabilities, such as being unable to remember important details.

As another way to represent madness, the GM could hinder Intellect-based tasks that would be considered routine, such as "remembering your friends and family" or "caring what happens to your best friend" or "stopping yourself from injecting a mysterious substance into your veins." These routine tasks normally have a difficulty of 0, but for a PC who has lost their mind, they might have a difficulty of 1, 2, or even higher. Now the character must make rolls to do even those simple things.

MIXING IT UP: HORROR AND SCIENCE FICTION

Sometimes, it's fun to spring horror on a group that's not expecting it. If the players in a science fiction game set in the not-so-far future are prepared to explore a mysteriously abandoned asteroid-mining facility, how wild would it be to have the facility be haunted by ghosts? The PCs probably expect aliens or some other science fiction threat. How will they deal with spectral beings that ignore their high-tech weaponry and show up on their scanners as odd energy fluctuations?

You can also make a horror game out of standard science fiction tropes. A murderous, nigh-unstoppable alien that is stalking the PCs on their own starship can make for a particularly frightening scenario. Using Horror Mode the entire time the alien is on board heightens the tension and forces the PCs to act quickly to get that thing off their ship. (Bonus points if they do it without resorting to the old out-the-airlock trick.)

Inability, page 207

Chapter 17
ROMANCE

Like horror, romance doesn't automatically suggest a setting. It is more of a mood, or more specifically an approach, to how the game is played. It suggests an emphasis, at least somewhat, on relationships, interactions, and connections.

Suggested foci, types, and additional equipment for a romance setting are the same as in a modern setting, so refer to chapter 14 for that information.

Chapter 14: Modern, page 261

CREATING A ROMANCE SETTING

The key to romance is interaction. That doesn't mean there can't be physical danger or all the other aspects we see in games, just that interactions—between the PCs themselves and between PCs and NPCs (and for that matter, between different NPCs)—are the hub upon which the game turns.

The stakes and probably the motivations of PCs and NPCs in a romance-focused story should always be emotional. It's the key relationship that's at risk. Even if a character is struggling to save the lives of everyone in the city, they're really doing it to save their loved one. Every event in the game should reflect back on the PCs' relationships with each other and with important NPCs.

Romance may seem like a simple concept at first, but hinging everything on emotional ties makes things more complex, not less. People are complex, and much of that complexity comes from the tangled web of our emotions. Who we like, who we love, who we lust after, who we used to love . . . there are as many iterations as there are individuals.

Think about the wide canvas this gives you upon which to create your setting and scenarios. An NPC might be trying to woo away the object of a PC's affections, but perhaps they're doing it not just for love, but because the person they're making a play for is wealthy and they want money. Or because the person knows the code to open the safe where the incriminating evidence lies. Or maybe to force the PC into the arms of another, who has ulterior motives.

Even a traditional adventure can have implications for relationships in a romance-focused game. Imagine the simplest fantasy scenario where the PCs are going to explore a dark dungeon. How does a PC's significant other feel about this? Are they worried about the character? Will they cheat on them while they're gone? Do they insist on going with them? And how will the success or failure in this mission impact the relationship afterward? If the PC returns with little to show for their efforts, will their loved one leave them? Will they suffer because they can't afford the ministrations from the local healer?

RUNNING A ROMANCE GAME

There are some things you absolutely must consider before running a romance game. First and foremost, recognize that emotions, romance, love, and lust make some people uncomfortable. They have no problem blasting aliens with a disintegrator, but the idea of talking about feelings or physical intimacy is not something they'll likely enjoy. It's because romance causes us to risk revealing a bit about ourselves more than violence, problem solving, and other game activities. It can make us feel vulnerable. Only horror, when it explores particularly dark ideas, requires players to open up as much.

It can also sometimes be awkward to roleplay a scene of love or affection with your platonic friends. It's challenging to look someone in the eye and talk about falling in love when it's all just fiction. (Although if you've ever been in a play, you might have done it already.)

One thing you should lay out at the beginning is the distinction between PC romance and PC/NPC romance. It might be easier for some people to have a relationship with an NPC than with another PC. The group should decide ahead of time if everyone is comfortable with either or both.

CONSENT AND BOUNDARIES

You must get consent to cover these topics in a game ahead of time, for all the reasons mentioned above. You don't want to make people uncomfortable. Everyone involved also needs to learn everyone else's boundaries. Someone might not want any part of a romance scene, while others are okay talking about emotional connections but not anything sexual.

Obviously, all of this is doubly important if age is a consideration. If there are younger players involved, romance probably shouldn't go beyond a fairly chaste kiss. (You'll find that kids are sometimes more open to romance in their games than adults, but only because their understanding of the topic is understandably pretty shallow. A kid player might declare that a character is their boyfriend, but it doesn't mean much. And for some adults, that may be the way they want to approach the subject as well.)

Lastly, recognize that there needs to be a clear boundary between the story and real life. Two characters having a relationship has no impact on real-life feelings of the players. Two characters in a game might be in a relationship while each player is in a relationship in the real world with someone else. And maybe they're gaming at the same table! If a player can't distinguish between in-game flirtation or words of endearment and real-world feelings, they shouldn't be in a romance-focused game.

THE CHECK-IN

It's vital that the GM and the players all check in with each other to make sure everyone's still comfortable with what's going on in the game. This is particularly important to maintain the boundary between emotions expressed in the story and how people feel in real life.

OPTIONAL RULE: INFATUATION

When a PC is near someone they are infatuated with, particularly in the early stages of that infatuation, they must make an Intellect defense roll with a difficulty determined by the GM based on the situation (not on the level of the subject of the infatuation). Failure might mean that the character does or says something awkward or embarrassing either in an attempt to impress or when trying to hide the infatuation. Or it could mean that for one round, the player loses control of the character, and the GM decides what the PC does next, such as risk their own safety to help an endangered character. However, GMs should welcome player input into this situation. The point is to portray that when we're distracted by the powerful feelings (and hormones) related to infatuation, we don't always react in the best way, the smartest way, or even the way we want to.

Infatuation can happen whether the PC is attracted to an NPC or a PC.

GM intrusion: *The uncontrollable attraction. The character feels a strong attraction toward a character they meet and must act on it. The heart wants what the heart wants.*

A player intrusion in a romance game might suggest that a sudden attraction to an NPC is mutual, that an NPC encountered is a former lover, or that an NPC the PC is in a relationship with makes an appearance to give some kind of aid. See player intrusions, page 21.

SUGGESTED CREATURES AND NPCs FOR A ROMANCE GAME

Distrustful relative: level 2
Jealous ex: level 1, attacks as level 3
Nosy neighbor: level 1, perception as level 3
Rival suitor: level 2, interactions as level 3
The unattainable: level 3, interactions as level 7, resistance to all interactions as level 9

It's possible for relationship levels to be lopsided, such that the relationship from the point of view of one person is a different level than from the point of view of the other. This should be used sparingly, because it makes things far more complicated.

In the case of polyamory, it is possible to have more than two people in a relationship, but even in these situations the connection between any two individuals should have its own level.

OPTIONAL RULE: RELATIONSHIP LEVELS

When a PC first establishes a relationship with a character (PC or NPC), the GM should assign the relationship a level. If there's no connection at all, there is no relationship (level 0). Otherwise, the starting relationship is probably level 1. In certain circumstances, a relationship might start at level 2, indicating a far stronger initial connection than usual.

As play progresses, the PC can attempt to improve the level of the relationship, indicating a strengthening of the bond between the two characters. The requirements to improve the relationship are twofold. First, some story-based action needs to be taken. This can be dates, gifts, a meaningful speech, a pledge of commitment, some amount of self-sacrifice, or whatever the GM and the player feel is appropriate to the story and the level of the relationship. This action might require the PC to succeed at specific tasks (with appropriate rolls). For example, writing a love poem will require an Intellect-based task, while helping to retrieve a loved one's cat from a tree might require a Speed-based task.

Second, the player must make an Intellect-based roll with the desired level of relationship as the difficulty (modified as the GM sees fit).

A relationship can be improved only one level at a time, and the GM and the player should work out an appropriate time interval. For relationships of levels 5 and above, multiple story-based actions and multiple rolls are almost certainly required.

ROMANTIC RELATIONSHIP LEVELS

Level	Relationship
1	First meeting. Interest or curiosity.
2	A sense of connection above the norm. Strong physical attraction.
3	Affection and a bond that will last longer than a single encounter.
4	Serious affection. Almost certainly physical affection.
5	A profession of love.
6	A serious long-term commitment.
7	A lifelong commitment.
8	Soul mates.
9	A love affair for the ages.
10	A bond that transcends time and space.

Relationship levels can go down as well as up. Neglect, carelessness, inappropriate emotional displays, lies, infidelity, and bungled wooing attempts can all potentially lower a relationship level. This is entirely in the judgment of the GM, although a lowered relationship level is very likely an appropriate use of a GM intrusion.

Relationship levels indicate the strength of the bond and thus help dictate an NPC's actions in regard to a PC. An NPC in a level 5 relationship probably will be more generous and forgiving toward the PC than if the relationship was level 3 or 4. An NPC in a level 6 relationship or higher would likely give their partner most anything, even maybe sacrificing their own well-being or their life for them. (And people in a higher-level relationship certainly would.) Likewise, a relationship level can influence a PC's actions. An Intellect defense roll with a difficulty equal to the relationship level might be appropriate if the PC wants to act against the best interests of their loved one, or if they must keep their cool and act normally when their loved one is in danger.

You can use this optional system in any genre, for any type of relationship, even platonic ones. If desired, the relationship level a PC has with an authority figure, a contact, a relative, or anyone else can be measured, improved, and decreased just as it can with a romantic relationship.

PLATONIC RELATIONSHIP LEVELS

Level	Relationship
1	First meeting. Interest or curiosity.
2	A sense of connection above the norm.
3	A memorable connection. Indications of a mutually beneficial relationship possible.
4	Real friendship.
5	Deep friendship.
6	Relationship akin to that of a close sibling.
7	A pledge of complete partnership.
8	Platonic soul mates. Something akin to a life-debt.
9	A friendship for the ages.
10	A bond that transcends time and space.

Chapter 18
SUPERHEROES

Like horror, the superhero genre is really a subset of the modern genre with extensive special considerations. In many ways, it might appear that the Cypher System is a strange fit for superheroes. But if you think about it, with foci like Bears a Halo of Fire and Wears a Sheen of Ice, the Cypher System makes all genres a little bit "superhero-ish." Character sentences might look like the following:

- Firebrand is a Brash energy projector (Adept) who Bears a Halo of Fire.
- King Brick is a Tough Warrior who Performs Feats of Strength.
- Dimensionar is a Mystical warlock (Adept) who Exists Partially Out of Phase.
- Dark Ronin is a Mysterious crimefighter (Explorer) who Solves Mysteries.
- Speedburst is a Fast crimefighter (Explorer) who Moves Like the Wind.

And so on.

CREATING A SUPERHERO SETTING

Even by roleplaying game standards, superhero games are all about the PCs. Think of the PCs as the main characters of their own comic book. They are the stars of the show. Rather than create a world and have the players make superhero PCs to fit into it, have the players create characters first and build the world around them. They are the superhero team that the setting should revolve around, whether they are a new group or the heroes who have been defending the city for years.

Before you dig in, consider the following topics.

How prevalent are superpowered beings in the world? If they're common, how has the world adapted to this idea? Police or military units particularly suited for superpowered threats, special prisons for holding powered criminals, and special laws for superpowers (is it a crime to rob a bank while under the effects of mind control?) are all obvious issues that will come up. If superbeings are not common, how will ordinary people react when they learn of the PCs? With shock and awe? Fear? Respect?

Are aliens, magic, mutants, and impossible technologies at play in the setting? (The answer is almost certainly yes.) If so, does the majority of the world know about these things, understand them, and accept them?

Superhero games are usually confined to one major city, but occasionally the heroes have adventures that take them around the globe or even into space.

Brash, page 39

Adept, page 24

Bears a Halo of Fire, page 64

Tough, page 57

Warrior, page 20

Performs Feats of Strength, page 73

Mystical, page 53

Exists Partially Out of Phase, page 68

Mysterious, page 52

Explorer, page 27

Solves Mysteries, page 77

Fast, page 45

Moves Like the Wind, page 73

Do the PCs already have arch-foes? If so, developing a bit of history of their previous battles and adventures can add a lot of flavor.

RUNNING A SUPERHERO GAME

Superhero stories, unlike others, rarely have a definitive end. Professor Vengeance may have been defeated this time, but he'll be back with a whole new plan of conquest sooner than anyone expects. Think of your superhero game as a comic book series. Each session is an issue, often ending in an exciting cliffhanger. Stories are told in arcs over multiple issues, but sometimes those arcs overlap. In other words, a new story arc starts while the previous arc is still going on. You can play with this concept further and have special "double-sized" issues for epic confrontations with a lot of "splash pages." If you really want to do something different, let each PC have their own series, playing sessions with just one player, and then have crossover issues where all the characters come together to defeat a powerful threat.

Here are some other tips to consider.

There's a danger that superhero PCs become entirely reactive. They wait for the villains to do something and then try to stop them. If you can occasionally find ways for the heroes to take actions that are more proactive, that's a nice change of pace.

Death for PCs and NPCs should probably be a fluid concept unless you want to go against type. Seemingly impossible events save characters at the last minute or bring them back from the brink. Players probably should not have to fear death much in this genre, which encourages heroic actions.

Similarly, heroes in this genre don't kill. That dictates PC actions somewhat, but it also means that the GM should not create a lot of situations that encourage or force killing. Fights with incredible destruction and serious consequences are fine—you can't have superheroes without them—but in the end, the villains should be knocked out, surrender, or make a frustrating last-minute escape.

Want to run a superhero game? Read a superhero comic or two (or a few dozen). That's all the inspiration and instruction you'll really need.

Type, page 20

Flavor, page 34

SUGGESTED TYPES FOR A SUPERHERO GAME

Role	Type
Strong hero	Warrior
Brawler hero	Warrior with stealth flavor
Gadget hero	Explorer with technology flavor
Pilot	Explorer with technology flavor
Charmer	Speaker
Leader	Speaker with combat flavor
Shadowy vigilante	Explorer with stealth flavor
Scientist hero	Explorer with skills and knowledge flavor
Energy-wielding hero	Adept with combat flavor
Wizard	Adept
Mentalist	Adept
Psychic ninja	Warrior with magic flavor

SUGGESTED FOCI FOR A SUPERHERO GAME

Abides in Stone	Fuses Mind and Machine	Operates Undercover
Absorbs Energy	Grows to Towering Heights	Performs Feats of Strength
Bears a Halo of Fire	Howls at the Moon	Rages
Blazes With Radiance	Hunts	Rides the Lightning
Commands Mental Powers	Infiltrates	Siphons Power
Controls Gravity	Keeps a Magic Ally	Solves Mysteries
Crafts Illusions	Leads	Stands Like a Bastion
Dances With Dark Matter	Looks for Trouble	Talks to Machines
Defends the Weak	Masters Defense	Throws With Deadly Accuracy
Employs Magnetism	Masters Spells	Travels Through Time
Exists in Two Places at Once	Masters Weaponry	Was Foretold
Exists Partially Out of Phase	Metes Out Justice	Wears a Sheen of Ice
Fights With Panache	Moves Like a Cat	Wears Power Armor
Flies Faster Than a Bullet	Moves Like the Wind	
Focuses Mind Over Matter	Needs No Weapon	
Fuses Flesh and Steel	Never Says Die	

Character focus, page 60

In a superhero game, a character's focus is almost certainly more important than their type or descriptor. It's probably the primary manifestation of their superpower.

SUGGESTED CREATURES AND NPCs FOR A SUPERHERO GAME

Abomination	Fusion hound	Replicant
Anathema (supervillain)	Grey	Secret agent
Assassin	Guard	Thug/bandit
Chronophage	Kaiju	Vampire
CRAZR	Killer clown	Vat reject
Crime boss	Magnetar (supervillain)	Wardroid
Detective, master	Mechanical soldier	Wendigo
Djinni	Mister Genocide (supervillain)	Wizard, mighty
Doctor Dread (supervillain)	Mokuren	Wrath (supervillain)
Dragon	Occultist	Zhev
Enthraller	Puppet tree	

Creatures, page 312

NPCs, page 372

OTHER CREATURES AND NPCs FOR A SUPERHERO GAME

Dog, guard: level 3, attacks and perception as level 4
Genetically enhanced bruiser: level 3, attacks as level 4; health 15; 5 points of melee damage
Ninja: level 3, stealth as level 6
Robot minion: level 4; Armor 2
Bystander: level 1
Scientist: level 1, science-related tasks as level 4
Worker: level 2; health 8

TAILORING THE CYPHER SYSTEM FOR SUPERHEROES

In a superhero game, the GM should be generous when allowing players to choose powers, even from outside the ones they normally have access to, so they can create the character they want (as discussed in the Further Customization section in chapter 5). For example, no existing combination of type and focus might easily allow a character to fight well, shoot blasts, and fly, but that's not an unreasonable concept for a hero.

Sometimes an ability a character gets from, say, their focus might not be entirely true to the character concept. For example, our hero who can fight, blast, and fly might be a Tough Adept (with combat flavor) who Controls Gravity. This isn't perfect, however, because Controls Gravity gives them the ability to hover and eventually fly, but the tier 3, 4, and 6 abilities aren't quite right. Rather than not giving them what they want, those tiers give them more than they want. Refer to the Customizing Foci and Creating New Foci sections in chapter 8 for suggestions of what the character might want at those tiers instead.

Last, keep in mind that an optional rule for modifying abilities on the fly is particularly useful for the superhero genre since it lets PCs use their existing abilities in new and original ways.

Customizing foci, page 94

Creating new foci, page 80

Further Customization, page 33

Modifying abilities on the fly, page 419

ADDITIONAL SUPERHERO EQUIPMENT

Suggested additional equipment is the same as in a modern setting, so refer to chapter 14 for that information. Keep in mind, however, that for many heroes, "equipment" can be superfluous. Where do you stash the flashlight and rope when all you're wearing is spandex tights?

Chapter 14: Modern, page 261

Superhero games are perfect for using power boost cyphers. See page 401.

> ### SUPERHEROES AND EQUIPMENT
> Most superheroes don't worry about equipment like backpacks and flashlights. If characters have devices that they regularly use as weapons or that are the source of their power—such as an advanced suit of armor or a utility belt filled with gimmicks—these should be represented by abilities as if they were inherent powers. Thus, a gadget-using hero might be an Adept who has various devices that grant them abilities (to give them more options, they might have the Masters Spells focus, with each spell expressed as a gadget). An armored hero might be a Strong Warrior with the magic flavor and the Abides in Stone focus. The boost in Might from their descriptor and focus, as well as the Armor from the focus, come from the suit of armor they wear. At tier 2, they choose Concussive Blast as their ability from the magic flavor to represent blasters in their gauntlets.
>
> In other words, from a story point of view, the PCs are all about equipment, while from a game mechanic point of view, it's not equipment at all—it's part of their character. If an armored hero is ever caught without their suit of armor, they have no special powers other than their skills, but that's entirely true to the genre, so it works.

Masters Spells, page 72

Magic flavor, page 36
Abides in Stone, page 64

Concussive Blast, page 121

OPTIONAL RULE: POWER SHIFTS

Superheroes can do things that other people cannot. They throw cars, blast through brick walls, leap onto speeding trains, and cobble together interdimensional gateways in a few hours. It's tempting to say that such characters are stronger, faster, or smarter, so they should have higher Might, Speed, or Intellect Pools. However, simply bumping up stat Pools or Edge doesn't fully represent this dramatic increase in power. Instead, consider using an optional rule called power shifts.

Under this rule, all superhero characters get five power shifts. Power shifts are like permanent levels of Effort that are always active. They don't count toward a character's maximum Effort use (nor do they count as skills or assets). They simply ease tasks that fall into specific categories, which include (but are not necessarily limited to) the following.

Accuracy: All attack rolls

Dexterity: Movement, acrobatics, initiative, and Speed defense

Healing: One extra recovery roll per shift (each one action, all coming before other normal recovery rolls)

Intelligence: Intellect defense rolls and all knowledge, science, and crafting tasks

Power: Use of a specific power, including damage (3 additional points per shift) but not attack rolls

Resilience: Might defense rolls and Armor (+1 per shift)

Single Attack: Attack rolls and damage (3 additional points per shift)

Strength: All tasks involving strength, including jumping and dealing damage in melee or thrown attacks (3 additional points of damage per shift) but not attack rolls

Each shift eases the task (except for shifts that affect damage or Armor, as specified in the list above). Applying 2 shifts eases the task by two steps, and applying 3 shifts eases the task by three steps.

A character assigns their five power shifts as desired, but most characters should not be allowed to assign more than three to any one category. Once the shifts are assigned, they should not change.

For example, a superstrong character might put three of their shifts into strength and the other two into resilience. Whenever they lift something heavy, smash through a wall, or throw an object, they ease the task by three steps before applying Effort, skill, or assets. Thus, all difficulties from 0 to 3 are routine for them. They smash through level 3 doors as if they don't exist. As another example, a masked vigilante character with a utility belt full of gadgets and great acrobatic skills might put two shifts in dexterity, one in accuracy, one in intelligence, and one in healing. They're not actually superpowered, just tough and well trained.

Some GMs will want to allow PCs to increase their power shifts. Having a character spend 10 XP to do so would probably be appropriate. Other GMs will want to run superhero games with PCs of greater or lesser power (cosmic-level heroes or street-level heroes, perhaps). In such cases, more or fewer power shifts should be granted to the PCs at the game's start.

SUPERPOWERED NPCs AND POWER SHIFTS

NPC superheroes and villains get power shifts, too. Most of the time, this adds to their level. For example, Blast Star is a level 5 fiery villain who has three power shifts. When she blasts through a level 7 iron security door, she does so easily because in this circumstance, she's actually level 8.

Sometimes, NPC power shifts make things harder for the PCs. For example, Fleetfoot the level 4 speedster puts all three of her shifts in dexterity. When she runs past a character who tries to grab her, the difficulty to do so is increased by three steps to 7.

Typical NPC supers get three power shifts. Exceptional ones usually have five.

EVENING THE ODDS

With power shifts and other mechanics at play, situations will arise where it will be impossible for low-level foes like street thugs to hurt a PC hero. That's okay. There are different ways you can handle it. Allow the hero to wade through them easily—it happens in comic books all the time. Perhaps such a battle need not even be played out using mechanics. Alternatively, use a GM intrusion now and again to represent that the thugs topple a huge stack of crates or produce a bomb that can hurt the hero. And of course, the thugs might not be able to hurt the hero, but what about nearby bystanders who quickly become hostages?

Conversely, the PCs might find themselves in a situation where they can't hurt a powerful villain. Again, this is right out of the pages of comic books. However, many villains aren't overcome by punches, but by heroes who come up with a desperate plan to take them out—or at least put the kibosh on their scheme.

REALLY IMPOSSIBLE TASKS

In superhero games, due to conventions of the genre, difficulty caps at 15 instead of 10. Difficulty 10 is labeled "impossible," but that label is for regular folks. For superpowered characters, "impossible" means something different, thanks to power shifts.

Think of each difficulty above 10 as being one more step beyond impossible. Although a GM in another genre would say there's no chance that a character could leap 100 feet (30 m) from one rooftop to another, in a superhero game, that might just be difficulty 11. Picking up a city bus isn't something normal characters could do, but for a strong superhero, it might be difficulty 12.

In theory, NPCs in such a game can go up to level 15 as well. Levels above 10 represent opponents that only a superhero would consider taking on: a robot that's 1,000 feet (300 m) tall (level 11); Galashal, Empress of Twelve Dimensions (level 14); or a space monster the size of the moon (level 15).

A player intrusion for a superhero game could be the sudden interjection of a surprising connection to a supervillain. Discovering that the villain is actually the hero's boss (in their normal life) or their own clone created by an evil scientist would be very true to comic books. See player intrusions, page 21.

Power shifts work very much like modifications to creatures. Modifications, page 313.

GM intrusions in a superhero game should be big and bold. Buildings collapse. Lightning strikes. A villain who should be dead turns up alive.

Doctor Dread, page 357

SUPERHERO ARTIFACTS

Supervillains build doomsday devices. Ancient artifacts present a threat to all humanity if in the wrong hands. Weird machines from alien dimensions offer solutions to unsolvable problems. Artifacts are an important part of superhero stories. A few examples are below.

DOCTOR DREAD'S TIME PORTAL
Level: 9
Form: Arch of metal big enough to walk through
Effect: Anyone who steps through it goes to a predetermined point in the past or future (a minimum of fifty years in either direction), which can be anywhere on the planet.
Depletion: 1 in 1d20

SERUM X
Level: 1d6 + 2
Form: Vial or syringe of red fluid
Effect: Strips someone of all superpowers (including abilities granted by magic, psionics, mutation, or science) for twenty-four hours. The target retains only skills and abilities that are mundane, as agreed by the GM and player.
Depletion: Automatic

STELLAREX CRYSTAL
Level: 1d6 + 4
Form: Multifaceted purple stone the size of a fist
Effect: Created in the dawning of the universe, this artifact grants the wielder the ability to not only fully restore all their stat Pools, but also increase each Pool temporarily by 10 points. These extra points fade after twenty-four hours if not used.
Depletion: 1–3 in 1d10

MIXING IT UP: SUPERHEROES AND SCIENCE FICTION

Sure, superheroes usually safeguard a city on Earth from criminals, but what if they guard the solar system from alien threats instead? Flying around in spaceships, dealing with foes wielding blasters rather than revolvers, and traveling to new planets every session might be the trappings of a space opera game, but they could easily work for a space-focused superhero game as well. In fact, with the characters' powers and abilities, a space opera science fiction setting might fit superhero PCs even better than a modern setting.

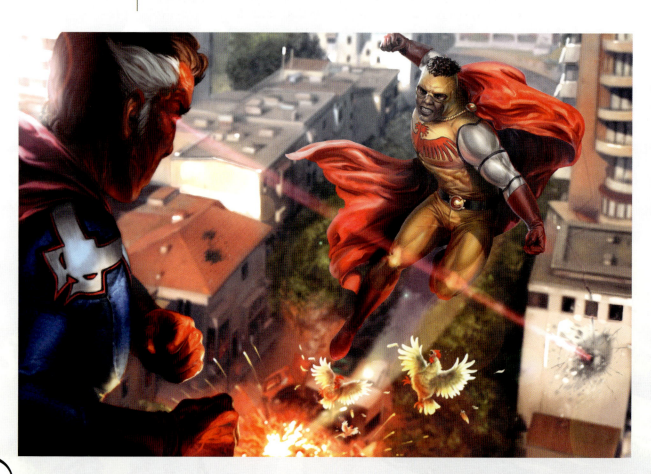

Chapter 19
POST-APOCALYPTIC

Post-apocalyptic literature, movies, and games are a subgenre of science fiction that focuses on the dystopia that follows the fall of civilization. Strictly speaking, post-apocalyptic stories take place after the end of the world. At least, the end of the world for most people. Players take the role of the survivors (or their descendants) trying to persevere in the face of immense hardship. Popular post-apocalyptic scenarios include those set after nuclear war, in the aftermath of a zombie plague, in the months and years following an alien invasion, or after the environment collapses in the face of human overpopulation. Other ways the world could end include a massive meteorite strike, the long-awaited robot uprising, a powerful solar flare that burns out the world's power grids and communications, or even something as prosaic as a global disease pandemic.

CREATING A POST-APOCALYPTIC SETTING

For a post-apocalyptic story to have long-term interest, the world can't be completely dead. Other people are necessary to interact with, help, and compete against for limited resources. A wealth of food, parts, and other supplies should be available so that survivors can live long enough to establish something more long term. Other threats should also manifest—rival survivors, mutant abominations, wild creatures, aliens, disease, poisons, and, yes, possibly even zombies—depending on the post-apocalyptic world you want to create.

Creating a post-apocalyptic setting is almost cheating because you can start with the world as it is now, with its current technology, its history, and all the rest, before ruining it with an apocalypse of your choosing.

Alternatively, you could decide that the apocalypse comes much earlier in the history of the real world, or much later. You might even decide that the apocalypse that defines your setting occurs in another world entirely, perhaps in a fantasy world where the gods all suddenly and inexplicably go extinct.

However, if you stick with the real world as your baseline, consider these additional advantages that you gain. Maps are the biggest benefit. All the maps of the real world are useful as maps of your fictional post-apocalyptic world with a few modifications. Add a crater here, a shanty-town there, and maybe a crashed jet airliner or another oddity, and voila, you've created a high-fidelity map in just minutes.

Another advantage of starting with the real world is that it sets a baseline for designing the

Gods of the Fall, a Cypher System game setting, describes a post-apocalyptic fantasy world where all the gods died out.

A player intrusion in a post-apocalyptic setting could involve noticing something of use amid the ruin in the middle of a crisis, or perhaps the unstable building or even the street an NPC stands within or upon collapses after all this time. See player intrusions, page 21.

post-apocalyptic cultures, wildlife, plant life, architecture, and so on. It's easy to make a major and memorable encounter using something like a bear, even if it's a zombie bear or radioactive bear, or just a huge freaking bear facing off against characters armed with their fists and sticks.

Your players might start a game a little more invested in the setting if they're already familiar with a few of the locations and history, even if those locations are ruined and the history is forgotten by most of the characters. To the players, it's "home." Setting a shootout in a fictional version of a now-ruined nearby supermarket, library, or coffee house will be all the more visceral because the players will be able to imagine it as clearly as if they'd been there themselves. Because they probably have.

Even if your baseline is the real world, you've chosen to run your game after some kind of apocalypse. That means that many encounters and situations faced by the PCs should be colored by that event. Thus, the aforementioned shootout in the grocery store should contain a post-apocalyptic twist. Maybe there's a berserk android in aisle 7, a wounded mutant in the stock room, or a radiation hazard associated with a particular food item.

RUNNING A POST-APOCALYPTIC GAME

It's easy for characters to find motivation in a post-apocalyptic game. Unlike in most other settings, the PCs' basic needs can't be assumed to be met. Even the most basic physiological needs like air, water, and food might be an issue from one day to the next. Thus, scavenging in supermarkets, gas stations, abandoned homes, and warehouses is likely to be an activity that characters must often do, at least as they begin their careers in the world's aftermath. More guidance for this activity is discussed under Scavenging, below.

In addition to meeting their base physiological needs, characters need to locate a place of safety. Finding a location free of radiation, zombies, disease or poison, killer robots, or rival groups of hungry survivors is a must. It's likely that only after these basic needs are met (or a strategy for meeting these needs over the long term is developed) will characters become motivated by goals that apply in other genres, such as saving the innocent, finding the missing heir, defeating the marauders, exploring for monetary gain, and so on.

If you're looking for inspiration, don't be afraid to steal plots from post-apocalyptic stories and games you like. Long-running series and popular games provide a wealth of possible ideas, both in grand campaign arcs and for individual encounters. A single episode that describes a relatively small story can make a great session. If an ally falls down into a ruined structure or needs medicine to recover from sickness, if all the food is stolen, or if a shelter previously thought to be secure is overrun with an external threat, players will react viscerally and become invested.

WASTELAND THREATS

The environment itself is riddled with dangers in many post-apocalyptic scenarios. It's nearly a defining characteristic of the genre. Getting from point A to point B isn't assured because the bridge might be out, the road could be choked with dead vehicles, mutant ants might be living beneath part of the pavement, or a radiation storm could set in. Or the characters could just blunder into a poisoned swamp. These plus a few additional hazards you could throw at the PCs are presented in the Wasteland Threats table. Choose one or roll when you need a threat to throw at your players; if a particular entry on the list doesn't match your conception of the apocalypse, ignore it and use something else. As described under Scavenging, attempts to find a safe place to hole up could also require a roll on the Wasteland Threats table.

CUSTOMIZING YOUR AFTERMATH

One GM's post-apocalyptic game may have mutants and killer robots, maybe even aliens and super-science items. Another GM's game might attempt far more realism because they want to focus on the challenges of simple survival in a ruined world. A wide continuum of scenarios is possible. The threats, useful items, and creatures described and referred to in this chapter attempt to span that continuum. If you're running a "realistic" game, ignore results that you dislike, don't choose them, or modify them so they make sense in your scenario. For instance, a realistic version of psychic lichen might simply be lichen that gives off an invisible spore that results in a similar sleepiness.

SCAVENGING

Characters in a post-apocalyptic setting must usually spend part of each day scavenging for supplies or a place of safety.

Food and Shelter: Generally speaking, characters must spend two to four hours searching through the rubble and ruins before

POST-APOCALYPTIC

WASTELAND THREATS

d10	Threat
1	**Radioactive crater (level 3):** Inflicts 3 points of ambient damage per round and drops character one step on the damage track each day they fail a difficulty 5 Might defense task.
2	**Radioactive storm (level 3):** Treat as a radioactive crater, but one that moves.
3	**Marauder patrol (level 4):** Whether on scavenged trucks or motorcycles, or riding on mutant pigs bred as war mounts (war pigs), a marauder patrol is bad news.
4	**Killer robot depot (level 7):** Designed by robots to kill humans, killer robots may be what caused the apocalypse in the first place.
5	**Dilapidated infrastructure, major (level 5):** The building, underpass tunnel, or cave collapses, or the bridge over which the vehicle is passing crumbles. Characters suffer 5 points of damage, and on a failed difficulty 5 Speed task are buried under suffocating rubble until they can escape or are rescued.
6	**Animate vegetation (level 4):** Kudzu got a lot worse in the aftermath; creatures that fail a Speed defense roll take 4 points of damage each round from strangulation and vine constriction until they can escape.
7	**Toxic spill (level 5):** Sticky orange goo bursts from rusted ancient barrels. Characters who fail a Speed defense task are caught and held in place until they can escape the morass, and suffer 5 points of damage each round they remain stuck.
8	**Quantum singularity (level 6):** Attempts to change the past to avert the apocalypse have consequences, including these points of unstable space-time; characters who fail an Intellect defense task are teleported a short distance in a random direction and possibly several hours forward in time.
9	**Glowing roach infestation:** These glowing roaches the size of dogs have truly come into their own now that they've grown in stature and intelligence. They have little use for survivors, except as food.
10	**Mutant bear:** The house-sized radioactive bear, whose roar can be heard for miles, is something to avoid.

succeeding. Finding enough food for a group of characters to eat for one day is a difficulty 5 Intellect task. Finding a place of relative safety to regroup and rest is also difficulty 5. Characters who succeed on either one of these also get to roll up to once each day on the Useful Stuff table and three times on the Junk table.

Found food often takes the form of canned, processed, dried, or otherwise preserved goods from before the apocalypse, but sometimes it includes fresh fruits and vegetables found growing wild or cultivated by other survivors. Safe places to hole up include homes, RVs, offices, apartments, or any location that can be secured and defended and isn't radioactive, poisoned, or overrun with hostile creatures.

The difficulty of succeeding at finding food, water, and a safe place varies by location and by how many days the characters have already spent in one location. Each week the PCs spend at the same location hinders subsequent scavenging tasks and requires that they succeed on a new task to determine if the place they're staying is still safe. The result of failing to find food and water is obvious. If the PCs fail at the task of finding (or keeping) a safe place, their presence is noticed by hostile forces, or they face a result from the Wasteland Threats table.

Useful Stuff: Food, water, and a safe place to rest are the most important finds, and are the basis of each scavenging task. But other obviously useful stuff is often found along with these basic requirements. When a group of characters successfully finds either food and water or a safe place, consult the Useful Stuff table up to once per day. If it's the first day the PCs have searched in a particular area, each character might find something useful, but in succeeding days, a group normally gets only a single roll to find useful stuff.

Useful stuff also includes a "loot" entry. Loot includes collectible coins from before the apocalypse, such as silver dollars and gold eagles. It also includes jewelry and artwork that survived the disaster and related material that can be used as currency or barter when the characters find other survivors or arrive at a trade town.

Items found on the Useful Stuff table are generally expensive or exorbitant items (except for firearms, which start in the expensive category).

War pig: *level 3; rider has asset on melee attacks, or pig can make a separate tusk attack when rider attacks*

Marauder, page 372

Glowing roach: *level 2; Armor 2; four or more can act as a single level 4 creature whose attack inflicts 4 points of damage; victims must also succeed on a Might defense roll or gain a level 4 disease*

Disease, page 219

Radioactive bear: *level 7; health 30; Armor 3 from carapace; radioactive bite or maul attack inflicts 10 points of damage and on a failed Might defense task, target is stunned and loses its next action*

Useful Stuff table, page 298

Junk table, page 298

Currency and prices, page 201

Scavenges, page 75

Cyphers, page 377

Artifacts, page 204

Junk: Characters who find food and water also find lots of junk. They are free to ignore that junk, but some PCs might have a use for what they find, especially those with the Scavenges focus. All characters gain up to three results on the Junk table each time they successfully scavenge for food or a safe place to stay. Sometimes junk can be fixed, but more often it can be disassembled and used as parts to create something else.

USEFUL STUFF

d100	Item Found
01–10	Tools (provide an asset to tasks related to repair and crafting)
11–20	Medicine (provides an asset to one healing-related task)
21–25	Binoculars
26–35	Chocolate bar or similarly sought-after candy or snack
36–45	Textbook (provides an asset to a knowledge-related task)
46–50	Coffee or tea
51–55	Gun or rifle with ten shells or bullets
56–60	Flashlight
61–65	Loot
66–70	Gasoline (2d6 × 10 gallons)
71–75	Batteries
76–80	Functioning vehicle (sedan, pickup, motorcycle, etc.)
81–85	Generator
86–90	MRE cache (food and water for six people for 1d6 weeks)
91–95	Ammunition cache (100 shells or bullets for 1d6 different weapons)
96–97	Helpful stranger (level 1d6 + 2, stays with the PCs for a week or two)
98–99	Cypher (in addition to any other cyphers the GM awards)
00	Artifact (in addition to any other artifacts the GM awards)

JUNK

d6	Item Found
1	Electronic junk (stereo, DVD/Blu-ray player, smartphone, electric fan, printer, router, etc.)
2	Plastic junk (lawn furniture, baby seat, simple toys, inflatable pool, etc.)
3	Dangerous junk (paint, rat poison, solvents, industrial chemicals, etc.)
4	Metallic junk (car bodies, old playsets, grills, empty barrels, frying pan, etc.)
5	Glass junk (vases, windows, bowls, decorative pieces, etc.)
6	Textile junk (coats, pants, shirts, bathing suits, blankets, rugs, etc.)

SUGGESTED TYPES FOR A POST-APOCALYPTIC GAME

Types, page 20

Flavor, page 34

Role	Type
Survivor	Explorer with stealth flavor
Heavy	Warrior
Dealer	Speaker
Trader	Speaker with skills flavor
Sage	Explorer with knowledge flavor
Evolved	Adept

SUGGESTED FOCI FOR A POST-APOCALYPTIC GAME

Character focus, page 60

Absorbs Energy
Builds Robots
Doesn't Do Much
Drives Like a Maniac
Entertains
Fights Dirty
Helps Their Friends
Hunts

Leads
Learns Quickly
Lives in the Wilderness
Looks for Trouble
Masters Defense
Masters Weaponry
Moves Like a Cat
Murders

Needs No Weapon
Never Says Die
Performs Feats of Strength
Scavenges
Throws With Deadly Accuracy
Wears Power Armor
Wields Two Weapons at Once

POST-APOCALYPTIC

SUGGESTED CREATURES AND NPCs FOR A POST-APOCALYPTIC GAME

Abomination	Giant spider	Slidikin
Assassin	Glowing roach	Soldier
Cannibal	Guard	Thug/bandit
CRAZR	Kaiju	Vat reject
Crime boss	Killing white light	Wardroid
Fusion hound	Marauder	Zhev
Giant rat	Mechanical soldier	Zombie

Creatures, page 312
NPCs, page 372
Glowing roach, page 297

OTHER CREATURES AND NPCs FOR A POST-APOCALYPTIC GAME

Crazy loner: level 3, deception and attacks as level 5
Gamma snake: level 4; bite inflicts 5 points of Speed damage (ignores Armor)
Innocuous rodent: level 1
Mongrel dog: level 4
Survivor, sickened: level 3, interaction and knowledge tasks as level 1; carries level 4 infectious disease
Survivor, typical: level 3

ADDITIONAL POST-APOCALYPTIC EQUIPMENT

In a post-apocalyptic setting, the items on the Additional Modern Equipment table as well as the following items might be available in trade from other survivors, or in the rare trade town.

Additional modern equipment, page 263

INEXPENSIVE ITEMS

Weapons	Notes
Knife	Rusty and worn
Light weapon	Won't last long
Wooden club	

Armor	Notes
Animal hide	
Light armor	Smell hinders stealth tasks

Other Items	Notes
Candle	
Plastic bag	Useful and ubiquitous (won't last long)

MODERATELY PRICED ITEMS

Weapons	Notes
Handaxe	Light weapon
Knife, multipurpose	Light weapon; asset to small repair tasks

Other Items	Notes
Gas mask	Breathable air for four hours
Padlock with keys	
Portable lamp, solar	

EXPENSIVE ITEMS

Other Items	Notes
Radiation detector	
Nightvision goggles	
Radiation tent	Prevents radiation damage for three days
Radiation pill (pack of 5)	Asset for defense tasks against radiation effects for twelve hours

299

POST-APOCALYPTIC ARTIFACTS

Artifacts in a post-apocalyptic game include still-working technology from before the disaster that is not widely available, as well as cobbled-together pieces of tech that can weaponize previously prosaic items. If the apocalypse was related to some kind of alien invasion, artifacts would include even stranger items.

AUTODOC
Level: 1d6
Form: Backpack-sized plastic module from which clamps, forceps, scalpels, and needles can extend
Effect: When strapped to a target (or when someone wearing the autodoc is damaged), the autodoc activates and restores 1 point to a target's Pools each round for ten rounds or until the target is fully healed, whichever happens first.
Depletion: 1 in 1d10

ENVIROSCANNER
Level: 1d6
Form: Forearm-mounted computer tablet
Effect: This multifunction device can receive radio transmissions, automatically map locations the wearer has visited, play various forms of media, keep voice and written records, and provide an asset to any task related to interfacing with other computerized systems or machines. Also, the wearer can scan for specific materials, toxic traces, and life forms within short range.
Depletion: 1 in 1d10 (check per use of scanning function)

MILITARY EXOSKELETON
Level: 1d6 + 1
Form: Articulated metal struts with deformable padding and straps for custom fit to a human frame
Effect: For one hour per use (when the exoskeleton is powered on), the wearer has +1 to their Speed Edge and +1 to their Might Edge.
Depletion: 1 in 1d10

ROCKET FIST
Level: 1d6 + 2
Form: Metal gauntlet with flaring rocket exhaust nozzles
Effect: If the user activates the fist as part of an attack, the punch gains a rocket assist. If the attack is successful, the fist inflicts additional damage equal to the artifact level and throws the target back a short distance.
Depletion: 1 in 1d10

ROCKET-PROPELLED GRENADE
Level: 1d6 + 3
Form: Tube with sight and trigger
Effect: The user can make a long-range attack with a rocket-propelled grenade that inflicts 7 points of damage to the target and every creature and object next to the target.
Depletion: 1 in 1d6

TERAHERTZ SCANNER
Level: 1d6 + 1
Form: Visor fitted with bulky electronics
Effect: By emitting terahertz and long-range infrared light, this device allows a user to see a short distance through most interior walls of standard structures, through normal clothing, and into normal bags and briefcases. Only stone or concrete more than 6 inches (15 cm) thick prevents a scan. Regardless, images are black and white and fuzzy, and lack fine detail.
Depletion: 1 in 1d20

A terahertz scanner uses the same underlying technology as is used in modern airports.

SPECIES DESCRIPTORS

In a post-apocalyptic setting, some GMs may want to offer species affected by the disaster.

MORLOCK

You have lived your life deep underground in artificial bunkers, hidden from the world's destruction and the brutal scavengers that live above. As a morlock, you have a keen mind for the technology salvaged from the before-time. In fact, every morlock comes of age by fitting a piece of morlock technology to its body to provide enhancement and extend its life. This means that you are part flesh and part machine. Your skin is as pale as milk, except where it's been replaced with strips of metal and glowing circuits.

You gain the following characteristics:
Enhanced Intelligence: +2 to your Intellect Pool.
Cyborg Body: +2 to your Might Pool and your Speed Pool.
Partially Metallic: +1 to Armor.
Repair and Maintenance: As an entity of living flesh and humming machinery, you must first succeed on a difficulty 2 repair task before making a recovery roll. On a failure, the recovery roll is not used; however, the normal rules for retrying apply, and you must use Effort on a new roll if you wish to try again. In addition to the normal options for using Effort, you can choose to use Effort to heal additional points to your

Pools (each level of Effort healing an additional 2 points to your Pools if you succeed).

Morlock Prejudice: While among non-morlocks, all positive interaction tasks are hindered.

Initial Link to the Starting Adventure: From the following list of options, choose how you became involved in the first adventure.

1. The PCs found you in a collapsed subterranean tunnel.
2. The other PCs encountered you exploring underground, and you convinced them to allow you to accompany them.
3. You were exiled from the morlock communities and needed help on the surface.
4. The only way to save the morlock community you hail from is to venture to the surface and find a mechanical part needed to repair a failing ancient system.

ROACH

You are born of a species of evolved insects once called "cockroach," but that is far in the past. Radiation and forced evolution have radically increased your size, shape, and ability to think. Your exoskeleton mimics the shape of a human being, though not perfectly. When you move about human society, shadows and cloaks are your ally if you wish to pass unnoticed. When those of your kind are discovered, it usually goes poorly for someone. You, however, have a wandering spirit and seek to explore the fallen world and find a new way forward.

You gain the following characteristics:

Scuttler: Your Speed Edge increases by 1.

Sense by Scent: You can sense your environment even in total darkness.

Cling: You can move an immediate distance each round on walls or clinging to the ceiling.

Carapace: +1 to Armor.

Glide: You can extend small wings from your carapace that grant an asset in jumping tasks and allow you to fall up to a short distance without taking damage.

Skill: You are trained in disguise tasks.

Inability: You are susceptible to disease and poison. Defense rolls against disease or poison are hindered.

Inability: You mimic a human, but you are not as fierce. Tasks involving combat—including attack and defense rolls—are hindered.

Insect Prejudice: While among non-roaches, all positive interaction tasks are hindered.

Initial Link to the Starting Adventure: From the following list of options, choose how you became involved in the first adventure.

1. The PCs didn't realize what you were when they asked for your help.
2. You've managed to hide your roach ancestry so well that everyone thinks you are like them.
3. You are the last of your kind.
4. You have a secret agenda, and the PCs were gullible enough to let you come along.

Chapter 20
FAIRY TALE

*Of an old King in a story
From the grey sea-folk
I have heard
Whose heart was
no more broken
Than the wings of a bird.
[...]
And three tall shadows
were with him
And came at his
command;
And played before
him forever
The fiddles of fairyland.*
—G. K. Chesterton

The genre of fairy tales is a wide one, crossing into almost every culture and encompassing everything from early oral stories passed down from generation to generation to the more modern literary fairy tale. What makes something a fairy tale? While there's a great deal of discussion around that question, most have a number of things in common: a series of far-fetched events; fantastical beings such as talking animals, elves, goblins, mermaids, witches, and dragons; and objects that have magical elements.

One of the powers of a fairy tale—or a game set in a fairy tale-inspired setting—is its ability to create a sense of wonder and to evoke players' imaginations while still allowing them to keep one foot in the known. The very settings themselves are both enchanted and somehow familiar, whether the characters are entering a magical woods, falling down a rabbit hole, or embarking on a voyage to Neverland. Those beasts and beings who stalk such places are equally wondrous, and offer fantastic starting points for any number of adventures.

To heighten the sense of wonder in a fairy tale adventure or campaign, a GM might consider presenting the game in a modern setting. In a modern setting, characters have regular jobs that don't normally involve hunting goblins or helping talking fish solve puzzles. This means that when the moths take shape and become the cloak of a princess of summer come to beg a favor or steal a child, or the house grows legs and runs away one morning, the player characters will be rightfully amazed (and perhaps somewhat terrified).

CREATING A FAIRY TALE SETTING

You could easily have fairy tales in other times and settings, but for our purposes in this chapter, we'll deal with a default setting in the modern day. The player characters are probably normal people, not secret agents or special investigators. Whatever the setting, the main thing to remember when preparing to run a fairy tale-themed game is that it's desirable to invoke a sense of wonder rather than fear. A sense of enticement, of yearning, and the promise of a release from the everyday problems that plague us. What does it matter if your internet provider has jacked up your bill yet another $20 a month when the stray cat on your patio begins to talk about the land of moonbeams, fairy gold, and music that will shiver a soul with everlasting delight?

Of course, every good story—and game—requires a complication, problem, or threat to overcome. Otherwise, what's the point? In a fairy tale, the odd, furry, magical little creatures you've discovered to be responsible for stealing your shoes might turn out to be the nicer cousins of an altogether more vicious version that will also steal the beating heart out of your chest, if given half the chance.

That's when a fairy tale game threatens to become a game of horror. Indeed, horrific elements are certainly a part of fairy tales, particularly those early tales told around the fire. But to retain the style, horror should not predominate. For every erlking, demon, or giant encountered, players should be dazzled and aided by a helpful fairy, a prince of summer, or a talking cat or rabbit that knows secrets of all sorts. And as is noted in the genre chapter on horror, if everything is terrifying, then nothing is. If the thrill of wonder fails to find the PCs more than just on their initial introduction to the game, view it as an opportunity to try again.

If you're looking for inspiration in creating a modern fairy tale adventure or campaign, consider starting with a variety of works by master tale-spinner Neil Gaiman. Of particular note, check out *Coraline*, *Neverwhere*, and *The Ocean at the End of the Lane*. You can also watch an animated version of *Coraline*. Other things to watch for fairy tale inspiration include *The Neverending Story* (story by Michael Ende, directed by Wolfgang Petersen), *Pan's Labyrinth* (written and directed by Guillermo del Toro), *Labyrinth* (screenplay by Terry Jones, directed by Jim Henson), and *Nocturna* (directed by Adrià Garcia & Víctor Maldonado). You could also watch at least the first season of the TV show *Once Upon a Time*, as well as *The Magicians* based on the novels by Lev Grossman.

Other roleplaying games also provide great inspiration. As with stories and movies, there are too many to list them all here, but if you have a chance, take a look at *Mouse Guard* (by Luke Crane, based on the graphic novel series by David Petersen).

RUNNING A FAIRY TALE GAME

Retaining a fairy tale esthetic can be difficult. You've got to maintain mood and atmosphere at all times. Consider these tips.

Lay Non-fantastic Groundwork: Give the players time to develop their characters before they meet the talking cat, the strange little man selling singing chocolate mice, or the raccoon wearing clothing and glasses on the street corner. Let them get attached to their characters, at least a little, so that when those PCs see something wondrous, the players will be thrilled.

Be Evocative: Use descriptive language to paint the picture of what the players see, and use your body language and gestures. For example, if you're describing a faerie forest, don't simply tell them that they see a faerie forest. Instead, as you gesture up and with wide eyes, tell the players something like "The forest canopy stretches high overhead, alight with tumbling motes of firefly light like drifting stars. The air is bracing and smells of the cool night, peppermint, and thunderstorms. From afar, a music like harps and violins gambols, somehow suggesting a great midnight feast taking place someplace deeper within the press of golden trees."

Stay Fresh: Fairy tale games are often one-shot sessions or a short arc of a few sessions. They can be difficult to run as long-term campaigns, but it's possible. If that's what you want to do, remember that you need to keep alive wonder and reward at the same pace as the characters discover the dark side of fairy tales. Gifts of golden armor or magic beans should follow them fighting back forces of the Unseelie Court busy making baby-stealing plans in the modern world.

NATURE OF FAERIE

Faerie (also called by many other names) is a dimension of magic separate from but closely parallel to the mundane world. It doesn't matter whether Faerie is just a collective term for thousands of separate curled-up dimensions hidden in corners, in closets, or at the center of forests, or it's one continuous realm that overlaps the real world where it's thinnest. It's a place those with open hearts can find by following a way between tall trees (or looming library shelves) to a realm where everything is different. Where elves walk, nymphs dance, unicorns gallop, and both natural growths and built structures become vast and enchanting.

Humans don't tend to do well in such a world if they stay too long, as the sensory input is hard on the nervous system. But fey creatures depend on it, like plants to the light. A fey creature too long cut off from its land of origin (or its stream, hill, or burrow) slowly becomes mortal and then dies.

When a fey creature is cut by silvered or cold iron weapons, they temporarily lose the sustaining benefit of their connection to Faerie. This severed connection usually disrupts a fey creature's ability to heal. A silvered weapon is one that contains silver as part of an alloying process, has silver inlay, or has been coated in a dusting of silver powder (which usually lasts only through a single fight). In truth, many items in the modern era are cold-forged, while many others are not. We suggest that any hand-forged item containing iron could be considered a cold-forged weapon for harming fey creatures. Thus, most bullets and other modern items wouldn't be treated as cold iron by this definition, but some would fit the bill.

FAIRY TALE WONDERS

The Fairy Tale Wonders table is a way to quickly generate simple delights and greater wonders appropriate to a fairy tale esthetic. This table is to be used about as often as the one that follows—the Fairy Tale Threats table. If wonders don't beckon to the PCs who step off the path most traveled, why would they leave their jobs as accountants, biologists, journalists, and so on just to be eaten by trolls or imprisoned forever in a fairy tower? Most of these wonders should be presented as GM intrusions.

d20	Wonder
1	**Inheritance:** A letter in a golden envelope arrives in the mail or is found in the attic addressed to a character, letting them know they have inherited a large chest. When found, the chest might contain a faerie artifact and hints as to the character's faerie ancestry.
2	**Musical marvel:** The character finds a musical instrument that allows them to play perfectly while using it, even if they've never studied that instrument before.
3	**Adventure mouse:** An enchanted mouse leads the characters to a clue they need to get on with their adventure.
4	**Friend indeed:** A princess of summer learns of the character's plight, and in the guise of a friendly reporter, lawyer, or police officer, extracts the PCs from a difficult situation with charm so intense it seems supernatural (and probably is).
5	**Faerie path:** The character finds a secret for getting across town using a "shortcut" that turns an hour's drive in traffic to a five-minute walk down a sunny garden path.
6	**Cup of many liquids:** Whatever mundane consumable liquid the character wishes for appears in this small cup: coffee, tea, hot chocolate, brandy, and so on.
7	**Faerie luck:** Tiny human figures with wings flit overhead, wave and smile, and wish the characters a good day. For the rest of the day, the PC has a sense of luck and happiness, and an asset on all noncombat tasks attempted.
8	**Nightmarket:** The character finds a door to a previously unknown market held at night, staffed by all manner of beings—and several talking animals dressed as people—selling the kinds of goods one might find at a flea market, a farmer's market, and in a few cases, a magic shop.
9	**Faithful companion:** A huge shaggy dog shows up, carrying in its mouth something the character lost. (Ask the player to make up something their PC lost.) The dog might continue to follow that character, especially if they care for it.
10	**Hat of perfection:** The character finds a hat that seems to go with everything they wear and provides an asset to all interaction and disguise tasks. A label on the hat brim reads "Property of the King of Good Endings."
11	**Alluring goal:** A floating castle is sometimes glimpsed at sunrise, but only the characters can see it.
12	**Treasure in an egg:** Among the eggs in a bird's nest is found one made of solid gold.
13	**Talking portrait:** A portrait on the wall animates and the person depicted tells a story, which might simply be a story of their life but could also be a warning or directions to someplace else.
14	**Magic bookstore:** A bookshop opens on the corner, offering amazing books whose titles are new to the characters (and are not found anywhere else).
15	**Bonus room:** The character has a dream where they find another room in their house that looks out onto a faerie forest. Upon waking, the room proves to be real.
16	**Mysterious benefactor:** Something amazing happens for the character—they get a book deal, win the lottery, find something thought lost, or similar—after which a silver card smelling of cloves arrives with the message "You're welcome. ~M."
17	**House with legs:** A house across the street stands up on hairy legs, moves a few feet to the left, and settles again, apparently once again as normal as ever.
18	**Flowered jetstream:** A person wearing a long cape flies overhead on what appears to be a broom. Flowers of all varieties drift down in their wake.
19	**Gingerbread winds:** A strong wind blowing in from the east smells of gingerbread, sugar, and wonderful baking things. If followed to its source, a small home is discovered where a fey baker is at work, and willing to share their creations.
20	**Candyfall:** When a storm front rolls in, candy wrapped in golden, copper, and silver foil drops from the clouds.

Prince(ss) of summer, page 348

Shaggy dog: level 3; intelligent but doesn't speak

FAIRY TALE THREATS

The Fairy Tale Threats table provides more dangers you can throw at your PCs in a setting where the unexpected can lead to dire repercussions almost as often as wonders. The results are not meant to be the major story arc, though you could probably spin some of them out to serve that purpose.

Many of the suggestions in the Fairy Tale Threats table work well as GM intrusions.

d20	Threat
1	**Wild Hunt (level 5):** Baying and screeching, a pack of hounds (level 2) carries a sledge through the sky driven by an antlered entity. (Treat as a prince of summer.) The hunt notices characters who fail a difficulty 3 Speed-based task to find cover.
2	**Unexpected eclipse:** A strange moon interposes itself between the characters and the sun. Living shadows ooze out of hard surfaces and attack until the eclipse fades after a minute.
3	**Trolls:** A couple of trolls emerge from the alley, under the overpass, or from the heart of the forest looking to fill their bellies.
4	**Cursed trap (level 4):** A chest, spell, or found object transfers the character bodily to a fairy tower where they are imprisoned unless they succeed on a difficulty 4 Intellect-based task.
5	**Feral trees:** Awakened feral trees attack those who do not know the proper passwords or who are not accompanied by a fey friend.
6	**Razorblade butterflies:** What seems to be a delightful mass of colorful butterflies is revealed as a threat, afflicting victims with hundreds of tiny cuts from fluttering wings.
7	**Item with a mind of its own:** An object gained during the adventure—be it a cypher, a faerie artifact, or a letter to be delivered to the Queen Under the Hill—awakens to limited mind and movement, and decides to play hide and seek.
8	**Gingerbread winds:** A strong wind blowing in from the east smells of gingerbread, sugar, and wonderful baking things. If followed to its source, a small home is discovered where a fey baker is at work, willing to share their creations. But the baker is secretly a cannibal.
9	**Angry noble:** A prince(ss) of summer takes an interest in the characters and begins to work against them.
10	**Greedy wall:** Victims in immediate range of this graffiti-and-art-covered wall must succeed on an Intellect defense task or be drawn into the wall and become one more piece of art. Trapped creatures gain one additional escape attempt. Otherwise, they must be freed, or the wall must be destroyed.
11	**Masquerade:** Fancy invitations on ebony paper with scarlet ink arrive, inviting the PCs to a masquerade ball. However, an evil witch is behind the summons.
12	**Blight:** A faerie wood, path, or other area important to the PCs sickens and begins to die. It might be a curse, or perhaps goblins have taken up residence beneath the ground, poisoning it.
13	**Allergic to magic:** The character reacts unexpectedly to the appearance of a fey being, a spell, a faerie artifact, or similar and must succeed on a difficulty 4 Might defense task or fall into a deep sleep for a day.
14	**Wish upon a star (level 5):** A falling star of green fire streaks down and impacts; PCs who fail a Speed defense task suffer 5 points of damage and must deal with the antagonistic fey creature that steps out of the crater.
15	**Angry ants:** Whispering insults, obscenities, and slurs, angry ants surge up from the ground and attempt to pull the PCs down.
16	**Falling house:** A house on legs stumbles, and the PCs must succeed on a difficulty 4 Speed defense task or suffer 8 points of damage and, on a failed difficulty 6 Might defense task, become buried under the rubble.
17	**Spoken curse:** An entity curses the character(s). Is it a real curse, or just a passing threat? Only time will tell.
18	**Trapped:** When the characters attempt to use the magic door or exit they expect will take them home or to a safe spot, they discover it no longer works, or instead takes them into a dank dungeon where a cruel shadow elf waits.
19	**Three blind mice, see how they run:** A slidikin with a carving knife (medium weapon that ignores Armor) attacks.
20	**Inevitable dragon:** A dragon investigates the PCs in its human shape under false pretenses, before deciding to ambush them and take all their treasures for itself.

Living shadow: level 3; Speed defense level 5 from shadows

Troll, page 306

Feral tree, page 306

Razorblade butterflies, page 306

Greedy wall: level 4; Armor 3

Witch, page 368

Goblin, page 335

Angry ants, page 306

Shadow elf, page 352

Slidikin, page 354

Dragon, page 325

OTHER CREATURES AND NPCs FOR A FAIRY TALE GAME

Most fey creatures of level 2 or higher regain 1 point of health per round while above 0 health, unless wounded by silvered or cold iron weapons.

Angry ants: swarm as a level 1 creature; constantly whisper insults, slurs, and obscenities; those physically attacked must also succeed on a difficulty 3 Might defense task or be stunned and lose their next turn

Erlking: level 6, stealth as level 7; health 27; Armor 4; short-range whisper attack enthralls target for one hour or until attacked; root tendril attacks on up to three separate targets in immediate range; silvered and cold iron weapons ignore the erlking's Armor

Faerie: level 4, deception and Speed defense as level 5; short-range magic dust attack inflicts damage or makes target amenable to faerie suggestions for one minute

An erlking is an animated accumulation of woodland debris—bark, lost teeth, matted weeds, and dirt—that wears a crown of oak leaves and a cloak of mist.

Feral tree: level 3; Armor 3; rooted in place; lashing branches attack up to three characters as a single action and on a failed Might defense task, hold the victim in place until they can escape

Nymph: level 3, stealth and positive social interactions as level 6

Pixie: level 2, stealth and finding lost items as level 6

Razorblade butterflies: level 1; swarm as a level 3 creature able to attack all creatures in an area an immediate distance across

Talking cat: level 1, knowledge tasks as level 7

Troll: level 6; claws inflict 7 points of damage and grab victim until they escape; grabbed creature takes 10 points of damage per round; troll regains 3 points of health per round

SUGGESTED FOCI FOR A FAIRY TALE GAME

The base foci you make available to your players should be the base foci in the genre where your fairy tale is set, with perhaps a few more fantastic foci thrown in (if not already set in the fantasy genre).

SUGGESTED CREATURES AND NPCs FOR A FAIRY TALE GAME

Generally speaking, creatures of the fantasy genre are appropriate for fairy tales when used as the unexpected threat or wonderment in an otherwise normal setting. However, other creatures, including those summarized above, are also useful.

FAIRY TALE ARTIFACTS

Artifacts in a fantasy setting and magic items in other games focused on fantasy would also be suitable for a fairy tale setting. However, every fairy tale artifact should come with a quirk that sets it apart from a simple "wand of fire" or similar item. Come up with your own or roll a quirk on the table below.

d10	Quirk
1	Is sometimes invisible.
2	Cries like a baby if jostled.
3	Becomes cold as ice to the touch and emits cold vapor when danger threatens.
4	Contains a secret compartment that invariably holds a chunk of rock broken from what might be a strange jade sculpture.
5	Also serves as a key to some magically locked doors and chests.
6	Bites owner with tiny teeth if jostled, dealing 1 point of damage.
7	Always muttering and complaining, though useful warnings and other information can sometimes be gained.
8	Jealous of any other manifest cyphers, artifacts, or beautiful objects in the wielder's life.
9	The "painting" of a princess of summer on the object sometimes leaves it, robbing the artifact of power.
10	Causes flowers to grow wherever it is stored or set down.

Chapter 21

HISTORICAL

Setting your campaign in World War 2, the Renaissance, or the 1930s can be fun and interesting. However, setting it in ancient Greece or feudal Japan, for example, probably makes it more like fantasy without all the orcs and magic (although a game set in feudal Japan with orcs and magic could be fascinating).

The big challenge with historical gaming is often the tech (or lack thereof) that the PCs have access to. For example, foci such as Infiltrates and Works the System assume some level of technology or magic. That might mean such foci must be altered (or at least, some of the abilities reimagined) in a game set in the Old West or Napoleonic France.

To prepare for that sort of game, all you need is a good history book on the time period in question. For even more flavorful ideas, look for a book that specifically details what life was like in the time period. This will go beyond battles and dates and give you a good feel for what it was like to live in ancient Egypt or in a Mayan city-state.

Of course, you can mix other genres into a historical game. A horror Old West game, for example, would be fun. Fantasy games set in Medieval Europe or the ancient Middle East are obvious choices. More interesting and innovative might be a fantasy game set in Africa a thousand years ago. And a Victorian science fiction game would simply be steampunk.

A great historical RPG experience is one that balances authenticity with a compelling adventure plot. Given that lots of history fails to record all the people present at any given event, specific dialogue, and other minor details, the GM has a lot of leeway when balancing accurate historical events with elements created to make a particular adventure or campaign memorable.

CREATING A HISTORICAL ADVENTURE

One of the draws of playing in a historical adventure is the thrill of "being there" when something important happens. Thus, in many cases, historical adventures in RPGs shouldn't be designed as campaigns, but instead serve as short-term experiences where players try something new, or at least something they don't normally do: play as figures involved in a momentous historical event.

Historical games should take cues from the closely related areas of historical fiction and historical re-enactment. The lessons of great historical fiction include the following.

The GM should anchor the characters with problems or conflicts that connect them to

HISTORINESS

"Historiness" is the quality of seeming historical or evoking a historical feeling, even if it's not necessarily historical. If you're going for a strictly historical game, replicating events from historical fiction may not be to your liking. That said, there is a gold mine of interesting options in fiction set in historical time. Consider the works of Jane Austen, Charles Dickens, or even William Shakespeare. Imagine a game weaving in and out of *Pride and Prejudice*, *A Tale of Two Cities*, or *Macbeth*.

If you decide that strict historical games aren't for you, you could go a step further by mixing fiction set in historical times with elements of horror or science fiction. Examples of this kind of fiction include *Pride and Prejudice and Zombies* by Seth Grahame-Smith, *Penny Dreadful* (the TV series), *The League of Extraordinary Gentlemen* comic series, and *Shades of Milk and Honey* by Mary Robinette Kowal.

---

the chosen time period; make sure that PC backgrounds contain one relevant detail to the chosen historical setting.

The GM shouldn't fall into the trap of assuming that history was drab just because it is often presented along with old paintings, drawings, or blurred black-and-white photographs. Dramatic events, surprising twists, and unexpected situations are just as likely in a historical adventure as in any other kind.

What's the point of a historical adventure if there is no suspense? Sure, everyone knows what happens at the end of any given historical battle, but the stories of individuals within those fights are not known. Will they live? Will they succeed in their mission? And what are the consequences? Think of all the war movies that rely on that exact latitude to tell great stories.

Make sure you know when the campaign ends. Maybe it's when the PCs successfully accomplish a specific task, but it might be externally timed to when a historical event takes place, whether they are attempting to offer aid, thwart it, or merely be aware of it as they attempt to do something that history hasn't recorded.

Don't create more than you need to. Be ready to tell the PCs what they see and who they encounter when they are introduced to a historical location or person, but don't worry about things that they likely will never see. Yes, figure out what kind of currency is used, but making a super-accurate list of prices just isn't necessary; the players will take your word for the cost of items and many other details. You're evoking a historical setting with your game, not writing a book report.

Be wary about stereotypes and cultural misappropriation. History, as they say, is written by the victors. The ancient Greeks wrote that other cultures were all barbaric, and the European settlers called the natives in North America savages, but that doesn't mean it's true. If all you know about a time period is a movie set in that period, you'll have a skewed version of events and culture. Be willing to go deeper than *Braveheart* or *The Last Samurai*, or maybe choose a different genre.

RUNNING A HISTORICAL GAME

Preparation is important in a historical game, and most of that entails choosing a historical period—or a specific historical event—as the setting. Given that all of history can serve, you won't lack for resources. Below are a few possibilities. Of course, the farther back you

HISTORICAL

set your game, the less information on specific events is available. On the other hand, that frees you up to get creative.

Once you choose the historical period and any special events you want to include in your adventure or campaign, direct your players to an appropriate set of foci. Alternately, you can have your players play as historically significant figures, but if you do this, you may want to create their characters ahead of time. Most GMs will probably want to save historically significant individuals for use as NPCs.

The players will need some kind of grounding in what to expect in the time period you've chosen. Just like they need an idea of what magic can do in a fantasy game, they will need a general idea of what kind of technology is available, the broad strokes of what their characters might know and not know, and so on. Maybe have them read a Wikipedia entry, at the very least.

If you're looking for inspiration for time periods in which to set your historical game, here are some possible ideas: prehistory, classical antiquity, ancient Egypt, the American revolution, ancient China, World War II, Edo Period Japan, Medieval Europe, and the American Old West.

HISTORICAL ARTIFACTS

The concept of artifacts is probably inappropriate for a historical setting without some kind of supernatural, fantastical, or science fiction element. That said, objects of mystery such as the Antikythera mechanism (an ancient analog computer and orrery used to predict eclipses and other astronomical positions) reveal that the ancient world—and by extension more recent historical periods—contained fascinating and useful objects that were anachronistic for their period. Most such artifacts were likely the creations of philosophers, lone geniuses, and similar figures.

TIME TRAVEL GAMING

All material in this chapter is applicable for a campaign revolving around time travel. Bouncing the characters around between World War II, the Renaissance, the 1930s, and ancient Greece can be fun and interesting, especially if the PCs are tracking down some kind of transtemporal problem or criminal (or attempting to loot history, as in the movie *Time Bandits*). Of course, this requires a bit more prep on your part, because rather than researching just one historical setting, the GM must be prepared to allow the PCs to play in several periods, possibly more than one during a given session.

For a time travel game, it's likely that the PCs serve as operatives of some kind of transtemporal agency that's pledged to protect time from saboteurs or perhaps pledged to create a fork in time that wouldn't normally occur so as to improve the chances of the group's existence. Other possibilities exist, of course. A popular time traveling framing device is to serve as companions of a famous time lord whose name is an eternal mystery.

Time-traveling PCs might eventually head into the future, whereupon the contents of the science fiction genre (possibly hard science fiction) described in this book also become useful for preparing for your adventures.

A player intrusion in a historical game could be permission to use metagame knowledge to make a decision based on 21st-century understanding of science, history, and so on. This can manifest as getting a premonition that this young fellow named Adolf Hitler will one day become a monster, or the inspiration that the way to stop infection in the 18th-century hospital is to get doctors to wash their hands. See player intrusions, page 21.

309

Types, page 20
Flavor, page 34

SUGGESTED TYPES FOR A HISTORICAL GAME

Role	Type
Constable (or night watchman)	Explorer with combat flavor
Detective	Explorer with stealth flavor and skills and knowledge flavor
Knight	Warrior
Pirate	Explorer with stealth flavor
Tutor	Speaker
Merchant	Speaker with skills and knowledge flavor
Smith	Speaker with some warrior abilities and skills and knowledge flavor
Playwright	Speaker
Noble	Speaker with skills and knowledge flavor
Explorer	Explorer
Priest	Speaker

Character focus, page 60

SUGGESTED FOCI FOR A HISTORICAL GAME

Calculates the Incalculable	Is Licensed to Carry	Operates Undercover
Crafts Unique Objects	Is Wanted by the Law	Runs Away
Descends From Nobility	Leads	Sailed Beneath the Jolly Roger
Doesn't Do Much	Learns Quickly	Solves Mysteries
Entertains	Lives in the Wilderness	Throws With Deadly Accuracy
Explores Dark Places	Looks for Trouble	Wields Two Weapons at Once
Fights Dirty	Masters Weaponry	Works for a Living
Hunts	Moves Like a Cat	Works the Back Alleys
Infiltrates	Murders	Works the System
Interprets the Law	Needs No Weapon	Would Rather Be Reading
Is Idolized by Millions	Never Says Die	

Creatures, page 312
NPCs, page 372

SUGGESTED CREATURES AND NPCs FOR A HISTORICAL GAME

Assassin	Guard	Professor
Crime boss	Marauder	Secret agent
Detective	Occultist (with no magic)	Soldier
Detective, master	Priest	Thug/bandit

OTHER CREATURES AND NPCs FOR A HISTORICAL GAME

Cat: level 1, Speed defense as level 3
Dodo: level 1
Dog: level 2, perception as level 3
Dog, guard: level 3, attacks and perception as level 4
Horse: level 3; moves a long distance each round
Merchant: level 1, haggling as level 3
Noble: level 2, pleasant social interaction as level 4
Rat: level 1
Serf: level 2, animal handling as level 3
Snake, poisonous: level 1, attacks as level 4
Warhorse: level 4; moves a long distance each round

Part 4
GAME MASTERING

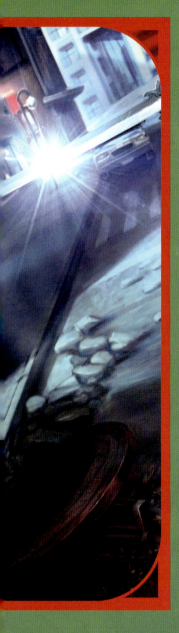

Chapter 22: CREATURES   312
Chapter 23: NPCs   372
Chapter 24: CYPHERS   377
Chapter 25: RUNNING THE CYPHER SYSTEM   402

Chapter 22
CREATURES

The creatures in this chapter are examples to showcase the various kinds of approaches, and not meant to be definitive. Still, it covers some of the obvious bases that you might need, particularly those that can be used in multiple genres, like vampires, zombies, killer robots, dinosaurs, and so on.

This chapter describes many common and uncommon creatures that the characters might meet—and fight—in a Cypher System game and gives their stats. The variety of creatures that populate the possible settings and genres is so great that this chapter only scratches the surface. It does, however, provide examples of kinds of inhabitants—bestial and civilized, living and undead, organic and inorganic—so that you can easily extrapolate and create your own.

UNDERSTANDING THE LISTINGS

Every creature is presented by name, followed by a standard template that includes the following categories.

Level: Like the difficulty of a task, each creature and NPC has a level attached to it. You use the level to determine the target number a PC must reach to attack or defend against the opponent. In each entry, the difficulty number for the creature or NPC is listed in parentheses after its level. As shown on the following table, the target number is three times the level.

Level	Target Number
1	3
2	6
3	9
4	12
5	15
6	18
7	21
8	24
9	27
10	30

Description: Following the name of the creature or NPC is a general description of its appearance, nature, intelligence, or background.

Motive: This entry is a way to help the GM understand what a creature or NPC wants. Every creature or person wants something, even if it's just to be left alone.

Environment: This entry describes whether the creature tends to be solitary or travel in groups and what kind of terrain it inhabits (such as "They travel in packs through dry wastes and temperate lowlands").

CREATURES BY LEVEL

Creature	Level	Creature	Level	Creature	Level
Goblin	1	Ogre	4	Chimera	6
Nuppeppo	2	Mechanical soldier	4	Enthraller	6
Orc	2	Ravage bear	4	Golem	6
Skeleton	2	Shadow elf	4	Puppet tree	6
Deinonychus	3	Werewolf	4	Vampire	6
Fusion hound	3	Abomination	5	Wardroid	6
Giant rat	3	CRAZR	5	Xenoparasite	6
Giant spider	3	Demon	5	Wrath (supervillain)	6
Mokuren	3	Elemental, earth	5	Anathema (supervillain)	7
Vampire, transitional	3	Fallen angel	5	Djinni	7
Vat reject	3	Killer clown	5	Doctor Dread (supervillain)	7
Zombie	3	Killing white light	5	Dragon	7
Chronophage	4	Mi-go	5	Giant	7
Deep one	4	Mister Genocide (supervillain)	5	Neveri	7
Devil	4	Prince(ss) of summer	5	Statue, animate	7
Elemental, fire	4	Replicant	5	Tyrannosaurus rex	7
Ghost	4	Slidikin	5	Magnetar (supervillain)	8
Ghoul	4	Wendigo	5	Demigod	9
Giant snake	4	Witch	5	Kaiju	10
Grey	4	Zhev	5		

Health: A creature's target number is usually also its health, which is the amount of damage it can sustain before it is dead or incapacitated. For easy reference, the entries always list a creature's health, even when it's the normal amount for a creature of its level.

Damage Inflicted: Generally, when creatures hit in combat, they inflict their level in damage regardless of the form of attack. Some inflict more or less or have a special modifier to damage. Intelligent NPCs often use weapons, but this is more a flavor issue than a mechanical one. In other words, it doesn't matter if a level 3 foe uses a sword or claws—it deals the same damage if it hits. The entries always specify the amount of damage inflicted, even if it's the normal amount for a creature of its level.

Armor: This is the creature's Armor value. Sometimes the number represents physical armor, and other times it represents natural protection. This entry doesn't appear in the game stats if a creature has no Armor.

Movement: Movement determines how far the creature can move in a single turn. Creatures have movements of immediate, short, long, or very long, which equate to the ranges of the same name. Most PCs have an effective movement of short, so if they are chasing (or being chased by) a creature with immediate movement, their Speed tasks are eased; if the creature's movement is long or greater, the PCs' Speed tasks are hindered.

Modifications: Use these default numbers when a creature's information says to use a different target number. For example, a level 4 creature might say "defends as level 5," which means PCs attacking it must roll a target number of 15 (for difficulty 5) instead of 12 (for difficulty 4). In special circumstances, some creatures have other modifications, but these are almost always specific to their level.

Combat: This entry gives advice on using the creature in combat, such as "This creature uses ambushes and hit-and-run tactics." At the end of the combat listing, you'll also find any special abilities, such as immunities, poisons, and healing skills. GMs should be logical about a creature's reaction to a particular action or attack by a PC. For example, a mechanical creation is immune to normal diseases, a character can't poison a being of energy (at least, not with a conventional poison), and so on.

Interaction: This entry gives advice on using the creature in interactions, such as "These creatures are willing to talk but respond poorly to threats," or "This creature is an animal and acts like an animal."

Unless noted otherwise, the default assumption is that creatures that automatically regain health each round stop doing so when their health falls to 0.

Use: This entry gives the GM suggestions for how to use the creature in a game session. It might provide general notes or specific adventure ideas.

Loot: This entry indicates what the PCs might gain if they take items from their fallen foes (or trade with or trick them). It doesn't appear in the game stats if the creature has no loot.

GM Intrusion: This optional entry in the stats suggests a way to use GM intrusion in an encounter with the creature. It's just one possible idea of many, and the GM is encouraged to come up with their own uses of the game mechanic.

NORMAL ANIMALS

Unlike many creatures in this chapter, normal animals are simple and understandable enough to be encapsulated by just their level and maybe one or two other stats.

Bear, black: level 3, attacks as level 4
Bear, grizzly: level 5; health 20; Armor 1
Dog: level 2, perception as level 3
Dog, guard: level 3, attacks and perception as level 4
Hawk: level 2; flies a long distance each round
Horse: level 3; moves a long distance each round
Rat: level 1
Rattlesnake: level 2; bite inflicts 3 points of Speed damage (ignores Armor)

ABOMINATION 5 (15)

In a post-apocalyptic setting, abominations were bred in the toxic aftermath of the fall of society. Sometimes they're called mutants. Other times, they're given more colorful monikers, like "ghouls."

An abomination is a hideous bestial humanoid covered with thickened plates of scarlet flesh. Their eyes shine with the stagnant glow of toxic waste dumps. Standing at least 7 feet (2 m) tall, abominations are drawn to movement. Always famished, they consume living prey in great tearing bites.

Motive: Hungers for flesh
Environment: Almost anywhere, hunting alone or in pairs
Health: 22
Damage Inflicted: 6 points
Armor: 2
Movement: Short
Modifications: Might defense as level 6; sees through deception as level 3
Combat: Abominations use scavenged weapons to attack prey at range, but probably switch to biting targets within immediate range. Targets damaged by a bite must also succeed on a Might defense task or descend one step on the damage track as the abomination tears off a big piece of flesh and gulps it down. Those who survive an attack must succeed on a Might defense task a day later when they come down with flu-like symptoms. Those who fail begin the process of transforming into a fresh abomination.

Abominations regain 2 points of health per round and have +5 Armor against damage inflicted by energy (radiation, X-rays, gamma rays, and so on).

Interaction: Most abominations can speak and have vague memories of the people they were before transforming. However, those memories, motivations, and hopes are usually submerged in a hunger that can never be sated.
Use: Abominations hunt ravaged wastelands and bombed-out spacecraft hulks, lurk in basements where mad scientists have conducted illicit experiments, and haunt the dreams of children who've gotten in over their heads.

GM intrusion: *The abomination isn't dead; it stands up on the following round at full health.*

CHIMERA   6 (18)

Chimeras are unsettling hybrids that combine the features of many different animals, often arranged in odd formations. The fusion of animal forms is the only thing that unifies these creatures—otherwise, different chimeras often look very different from each other. They include combinations of goat and lion, lizard and bat, dragon and spider, dinosaur and giant insect. A few even display human features, such as an improbably located face or hands instead of claws. Some chimeras can fly. Others slither across the ground.

A chimera typically has a dominant form to which other animal parts are grafted. The base form must be large enough to support the weight of the extra heads, so lions, bears, and horses are popular as the base form.

Chimeras kill even when not hungry and throw their victims' remains around a wide area in a wild rage. When not feeding or tormenting prey, a chimera that can fly takes to the air, beating its enormous leather wings to scour the landscape for new prey.

Motive: Hungers for human flesh
Environment: Anywhere, usually alone
Health: 21
Damage Inflicted: 4 points
Movement: Short while on the ground; long while flying (if it can fly)
Modifications: Speed defense rolls as level 5 due to size
Combat: All chimeras have a number of ways to kill. The exact methods vary, but most can bite, sting, and gore (three attacks) as a single action, either attacking the same opponent or attacking different foes within immediate range of each other. A chimera's sting carries a powerful toxin, and a stung target must succeed on a Might defense roll or take 4 additional points of damage. Chimeras with spikes can project them at up to three targets within long range as a single action.
Interaction: Chimeras are a lot like wild animals with rabies. They're confused and violent, and they behave erratically. Savage, ferocious beasts, they hate all other creatures and seize any opportunity to kill.
Use: While exploring an island, the PCs find carcasses that have been torn apart, the pieces scattered in all directions. A chimera lairs nearby, and if the characters draw attention to themselves, it hunts them down, too.

GM intrusion: The chimera grabs a character it bites and flies off with the victim.

CHRONOPHAGE 4 (12)

Chronophages are creatures that seem drawn to time paradoxes and disruptions in space-time. They tend to eat those responsible (and those affected), potentially alleviating the disturbance in the fabric of things, though that outcome might just be a side effect. First and foremost, chronophages are parasites that phase into existence near a spatial anomaly and feed to sate their own hunger. However, there are hints that the larvae may represent the first stage of life of a far more powerful and enigmatic entity.

These segmented, 6-foot (2 m) long creatures look partly like larvae that have grown gargantuan and vicious. They appear in places where time moves more slowly or more quickly than normal, where balls and liquids flow upslope, or where a time traveler has visited.

Motive: Hungers for the flesh of those who create, or were created by, time anomalies

Environment: Clutches of four to eight fade into existence within long range of space-time fractures in almost any location.

Health: 18

Damage Inflicted: 5 points

Armor: 1

Movement: Short; can phase into the dimension of time (and disappear) as a move. On its next action, it can phase back into the world up to 300 feet (90 m) from where it disappeared (as an action).

Modifications: Perception as level 5

Combat: A chronophage attacks with its crushing mandibles.

A chronophage can phase back and forth between its home dimension, and it uses this ability to great effect when hunting prey. For instance, it can close on prey otherwise protected by barriers or features of the landscape. It can also use the ability to draw a victim's attention and then launch a surprise attack from behind after it has effectively teleported. However, it is an action for the creature to shift its phase between the dimension of time and normal reality.

Interaction: Chronophages are unswerving in their drive to find prey. Once one marks its target, only killing the creature can sway it from the prey.

Use: When the PCs happen upon a location where the rules of space-time are loose and malleable, or if the PCs trigger a cypher or other device that interferes with time's regular flow, a clutch of chronophages may soon come calling.

Loot: The skin of a chronophage can be salvaged to create a silvery cloak that reflects its surroundings, but the reflection is one hour behind the present.

GM intrusion: *If a chronophage's prey fails its Speed defense roll, the attack ignores Armor, and the prey must make an Intellect defense roll (difficulty 4) or be phased into the chronophage's home dimension of time. Victims automatically phase back into reality on their next turn but are displaced by 100 feet (30 m) straight up or to the closest open space. This usually results in a fall that potentially deals 10 points of damage, knocks victims prone, and dazes them, hindering all actions for a round.*

CRAZR 5 (15)

Machines built for destruction, CRAZRs are designed to run down and destroy targets as quickly and efficiently as possible. CRAZR stands for Canid Robotic Zealous Reapers (the "A" doesn't stand for anything, except to let the acronym evoke the word "crazy," which these machines are). They attack without fear and, despite not being particularly tactical or tough, inflict so much harm in so little time that they can bring down much more powerful targets.

CRAZRs preferentially go after other machines, not creatures of flesh, following programming that assesses a higher chance that another entity like itself is the most dangerous foe, all else being equal. That said, a human with a computer and hacking knowledge is likely able to bring down a CRAZR more quickly than anything else.

Motive: Destroy preprogrammed targets

Environment: Anywhere guards, trackers, or soldiers are deployed

Health: 15

Damage Inflicted: 5 points

Movement: Long

Modifications: Resist hacking attempts as level 7 (see Interaction)

Combat: A CRAZR makes attacks with spinning saw blades designed to chew through the metal hides of other machine creatures. Thus, CRAZR attacks ignore up to 1 point of a target's Armor.

A CRAZR is quick; as a single action, it can move a long distance each round, or move a short distance and attack with all four spinning blades. This quickness comes with a cost: its metallic covering is light, thinner than skin, and just as delicate (which is why CRAZRs have no Armor). It also makes a CRAZR more susceptible to radio-enabled hacking attempts (see Interaction).

A CRAZR can emit a brilliant spotlight to see in the dark, and it's able to track prey by noting small clues in the environment like scratches, footprints, doors left ajar, and so on.

Interaction: CRAZRs constantly operate in berserker mode. Short of destroying one, hacking one is the only way to interact. Someone with a direct connection or a radio-enabled probe can hack a CRAZR and order it to switch off as a level 7 hacking task. Gaining control of a CRAZR or reprogramming it using this method isn't nearly as easy because of built-in failsafes; treat the attempt as a level 8 hacking task.

Use: PCs who enter a sealed area disturb a CRAZR that at first seemed like an inert piece of machinery.

GM intrusion: *A CRAZR's spinning blade risks destroying an important piece of the character's equipment.*

Creatures

DEEP ONE 4 (12)

"Their forms vaguely suggested the anthropoid, while their heads were the heads of fish, with prodigious bulging eyes that never closed. At the sides of their necks were palpitating gills, and their long paws were webbed. They hopped irregularly, sometimes on two legs and sometimes on four. I was somehow glad that they had no more than four limbs. Their croaking, baying voices, clearly used for articulate speech, held all the dark shades of expression which their staring faces lacked ... They were the blasphemous fish-frogs of the nameless design—living and horrible."
—The Shadow Over Innsmouth

Some deep ones dwell in coastal regions on land, usually in isolated villages where they might attempt to pass for human. They are able to breathe both air and water. Most, however, thrive in the ocean depths, in ancient underwater cities like "Cyclopean and many-columned Y'ha-nthlei." Deep ones sometimes breed with insane humans to produce squamous offspring that eventually develop fully into deep ones well after maturity (or even middle age).

Motive: Hungers for flesh
Environment: Anywhere near a large body of salt water
Health: 15
Damage Inflicted: 5 points
Armor: 2
Movement: Short on land; long in the water
Modifications: Swims as level 6; perception as level 3
Combat: Deep ones attack with tooth and claw most often, although occasionally one might use a weapon. They usually give no quarter, nor ask for it. Their skin is subject to drying, and they take 1 extra point of damage (ignores Armor) from any attack that deals fire or heat damage. Because of this weakness, deep ones sometimes retreat from fire and fire attacks.
Interaction: Deep ones are a strange mix of utter alienness and the vestiges of lost humanity. They are foul and degenerate creatures by human standards, however. Many still retain the ability to speak human languages, but all speak their own slurred, unearthly tongue.

Deep ones spend a great deal of time in the sincere adoration of their gods, Mother Hydra, Father Dagon, and Cthulhu. Their religion demands frequent blood sacrifices.

Use: The PCs wander into a small coastal village where everyone seems standoffish and oddly distant. A few people appear to be sickly and malformed, perhaps from mutation or birth defects. Some of the villagers have squamous skin because they are transforming into deep ones. And, of course, true deep ones hide within the community as well.
Loot: A few deep ones will have a cypher.

Two deep ones that have grown colossal and powerful over time are called Mother Hydra and her consort, Father Dagon. Each stands 15 feet (5 m) tall, and they serve as deity-rulers among the deep ones.

Mother Hydra and Father Dagon: level 8; health 38 each; Armor 4; each inflicts 10 points of damage

GM intrusion: *The deep one produces a net and throws it over the character. The only physical action the victim can take is to try to get free, as either a Might-based or a Speed-based action.*

319

DEINONYCHUS 3 (9)

Popularly known as the velociraptor, the dinosaur genus called deinonychus doesn't care if its prey gets the proper terminology sorted. Meat tastes like meat. The "terrible claw" these carnivores are named after refers to their massive, sickle-shaped claws, which are unsheathed from their hind legs when attacking prey.

Deinonychus are pack hunters, which means they work together as a unit, each taking on different roles to scare, flush, and direct even intelligent prey into the claws of an ambush.

Motive: Hungers for flesh

Environment: Wherever they can hunt food, in packs of three to seven

Health: 15

Damage Inflicted: 4 points

Armor: 1

Movement: Short

Modifications: Perception as level 5; attacks and Speed defense as level 4 due to quickness; overcoming obstacles and figuring out tricks as level 4

Combat: When a deinonychus bites its prey, the victim takes damage and must make a Might defense roll. On a failure, the deinonychus holds the victim in place with its jaws while it slices them to ribbons with its terrible claws, automatically inflicting 6 points of damage each round in which they fail a Might-based task to break free (not attempting to break free counts as a failed attempt). For a human-sized or smaller victim held in the jaws, all other tasks are hindered by two steps.

Interaction: Vicious, cunning, and a little too smart to be classified as simple predators, these creatures are unlikely to negotiate, give quarter, or back off from a fight even if contact could be made.

Use: Some fool decided to build a Cretaceous-themed zoo. The only question is: How long before the dinosaurs get loose and take over the local mall?

GM intrusion: *The fleeing deinonychus was actually leading the character over a cliff, into a deadfall trap, or into an ambush with more deinonychus.*

DEMIGOD   9 (27)

> *"With all his speed not yet the sun*
> *Through half his race has run,*
> *Since I, to execute thy dread command,*
> *Have thrice encompass'd sea and land."*
> ~Iris, messenger of the gods, in Handel's *Semele*

Lesser gods, divine children of gods and mortals, and other beings bequeathed with partly divine power are called demigods. Their capacities so radically exceed those of regular people that they have transcended humanity. Demigods are so physically and mentally powerful that it's difficult for them to hide their semi-divine appearance to mortal creatures—not that most would make the effort in the first place.

Motive: Ineffable
Environment: Anywhere other divine entities exist (or once existed)
Health: 99
Damage Inflicted: 12 points
Armor: 5
Movement: Short; long when flying
Combat: Demigods can attack foes up to half a mile (1 km) away with bolts of divine energy (usually in the form of lightning). A demigod can dial up the level of destruction if it wishes, so that instead of affecting only one target, a bolt deals 9 points of damage to all targets within short range of the primary target. Targets caught in the conflagration who succeed on a Speed defense roll still suffer 5 points of damage.

Demigods are just as scary in hand-to-hand combat and can attack all targets within immediate range as an action. They can also call on a variety of other abilities that seem like magic to lesser foes and mimic the effect of any cypher of level 5 or lower.

A demigod doesn't need to alter reality to heal itself, as it automatically regains 2 points of health per round.

Interaction: For all their power, demigods share most human traits and weaknesses. This means it's possible to negotiate with one, though the consequences for angering a demigod in the process are dire.

Use: A demigod was banned from the higher realm of their birth for unknown reasons. Now they seek to show their worth by undertaking a great quest in the mortal world, and they are looking to assemble a group of mortal comrades (sycophants?) to aid them.

Loot: Demigods might carry an artifact related to some aspect of their domain (such as wind, messages, or death), if they have one, and 1d6 cyphers.

GM intrusion: *The divine nature of the demigod allows it to act out of turn, take control of an object (such as an artifact or a cypher) that the PC is about to use against it, and either deactivate the object or turn it against the character.*

DEMON   5 (15)

Demons are formless spirits of the dead tortured in nether realms until all that was good or caring in them was burned away, forging a being of spite and hate.

A demon remembers only fragments of its former life—every good memory is cauterized, and every slight, misfortune, snub, and pain is amplified, motivating the creature to tempt others into the same state.

Having no flesh to call its own, a demon is a shadowed, ephemeral horror able to possess others. A demon can cause great harm in a short time by forcing its host to lie, steal, and harm loved ones.

Motive: Hungers for others' pain and fear
Environment: Anywhere
Health: 25
Damage Inflicted: 6 points
Movement: Short; immediate while flying in immaterial form
Modifications: All stealth tasks as level 7 in immaterial form; deception tasks as level 6
Combat: The immaterial touch of a demon either inflicts 5 points of damage from rot, or allows the demon to attempt to possess the target. The target of an attempted possession must make an Intellect defense roll or become possessed, whereupon the demon's immaterial form disappears into the target.

The first round in which a character is possessed, they can act normally. In the second and all subsequent rounds, the possessing demon can control the actions of the host, but the character can attempt an Intellect defense roll to resist each suggested action. Successful resistance means that the character does nothing for one round. In other rounds, the character can act as they choose. A possessing demon's actions are limited to attempts to control its host and leaving the host.

A possessed target is allowed an Intellect defense roll to eject the demon once per day, barring any exorcism attempts. The defense roll is hindered by one additional step each day of possession after the first seven days. An ejected or cast-out demon is powerless for one or more days.

A demon not possessing another creature is immaterial and can pass through solid objects whose level is lower than its own. While the demon is immaterial, it takes only 1 point of damage from mundane attacks, but it takes full damage from magical, energy, and psychic attacks. While it possesses another creature, the demon is immune to most attacks (though not so the host; killing the host will eject the demon).

Interaction: A demon allows a possessed host to act normally, as long as it doesn't reveal the demon's presence. If its presence is known, the demon might negotiate, but only after a tirade of lies and obscenity, and the demon likely betrays any deal reached.

Use: An ally of the PCs has begun acting differently, and not for the good.

A demon prefers to attempt possession before its potential host is aware of its presence, but it might choose to possess a victim in combat, too.

One way to exorcise a demon is to command it out in the name of an entity that has power over the demon. This can be attempted once per day. It grants the possessed character an additional Intellect defense roll to eject the demon.

GM intrusion: The character who attempts an exorcism of a possessed target is successful, but the demon moves directly from the former victim into the exorcist. The new host can make an Intellect-based roll to eject the demon, but only after the first round of possession.

DEVIL 4 (12)

Devils are manifest evil. As "native fauna" of various tortuous nether realms, devils come in many forms, though most are iterations on a theme that includes a humanoid shape, large batwings, bestial faces, and twisting horns. Most stink of brimstone and sport tails that end in a fork. Devils fill the ranks of hellish armies, guard evil vaults, and appear at the magical summons of warlocks and sorcerers who are not afraid for the sanctity of their own souls.

Motive: Collect souls
Environment: Anywhere in various nether realms; sometimes called by mortal magic
Health: 12
Damage Inflicted: 5 points
Armor: 3
Movement: Short when walking or flying
Modifications: All tasks related to deception as level 7
Combat: When possible, a devil attacks with surprise. If successful, it unfurls two great wings and claws at the ends of its fingers. It leaps into the air, flies up to a short distance toward the nearest foe, and attacks that creature as a single action.

Some devils carry tridents. The weapon inflicts 5 points of damage, and the target must either move to a position within an immediate distance chosen by the devil or take 2 additional points of damage from being impaled (a total of 7 points of damage). Impaled foes automatically take 5 points of damage each round until they use an action to pull themselves free.

Interaction: Evil, cruel, and malevolent, devils are more than happy to talk, especially to those already caught and being readied for torture. Devils serve yet more powerful devils out of fear. If they find someone or something they fear more, they readily betray their master and become obsequious and cringing, though further betrayal is always on the table.

Use: A spate of violent murders grips a city in fear—a devil has escaped into the world of mortals without a leash. It spends nights hunting anyone it spots from its perches atop the city's holy places.

GM intrusion: *A devil anticipates the character's melee attack and brings its wing down "just so" on the attacker's weapon. If the character fails a Speed defense roll, the weapon breaks. Either way, the attack fails to hit the devil.*

DJINNI   7 (21)

Islamic texts describe djinn as inhabiting unseen dimensions beyond the visible universe. Just like normal creatures, djinn are individuals, and they can be good, evil, or unconcerned about the fates and doings of others.

Motive: Unpredictable

Environment: Almost anywhere

Health: 35

Damage Inflicted: 9 points

Movement: Short; long when flying

Modifications: Knowledge of Arabian history as level 8

Combat: With a touch, a djinni can warp a victim's flesh, inflicting damage. Djinn can also use an action to send out a magitech "EMP burst" that renders all artifacts, machines, and lesser magic devices within short range inoperable for one minute. (If the item is part of a character's equipment, they can prevent this outcome by succeeding on a Speed defense roll.) Instead of disabling all devices in range, a djinni can instead take control of one item within range for one minute, if applicable.

A djinni can transform into a being of smoke and flame as its action. While in this form, it has +10 to Armor but can't attack foes. It gains the ability to fly a long distance each round and retains the ability to communicate normally. The first time each day that a djinni returns to physical form after having become smoke, it regains 25 points of health.

Some djinn have the ability to grant wishes, and a few are beholden to do so thanks to an ancient, unexplained agreement with other djinn. Those who grant wishes twist them against the asker, especially if a wish is poorly worded or there are multiple ways to interpret it. The level of the effect granted is no greater than level 7, as determined by the GM, who can modify the effect of the wish accordingly. (The larger the wish, the more likely the GM will limit its effect.)

Interaction: When a djinni interacts with characters, it's narcissistic, certain in its own immense power, and unlikely to let slights pass. That said, low-tier characters could negotiate with one peacefully because even djinn have needs and desires.

Use: Agents of a foreign power retrieved a magic lamp from an ancient Arabian ruin. The PCs' job is to determine whether there is reason for alarm.

Loot: Most djinn carry a couple of cyphers, and some have a magic artifact useful in combat.

Some djinn inhabit pocket dimensions whose entry points are affixed within the mouths of urns, pots, or lamps.

GM intrusion: When the character is touched by a djinni, instead of taking damage, the character is turned to smoke and fire and sent whirling off in a random direction. They lose their next turn and return to normal almost 300 feet (90 m) from where they started.

DRAGON   7 (21)

Dragons are exceptionally territorial, vain, and greedy. Apex predators, dragons must eat large meals on a regular basis. They prefer virgins, though they will settle for whoever, or whatever—such as horses or wild pigs—is available in a pinch. They love games of all sorts, especially when they get to consume the loser. Drawn to wealth and magic, dragons accumulate hoards of golden treasure. A dragon's hoard is not only an end in itself, but part of a never-ending contest between dragons of a certain age to see which one can accumulate the largest trove.

Motive: Self-aggrandizement, hungers for flesh, treasure collection
Environment: Dragons thrive where wilderness meets the civilized frontier.
Health: 45
Damage Inflicted: 10 points
Armor: 3
Movement: Short; long while flying
Modifications: Perception and riddles as level 8; Speed defense as level 6 due to size
Combat: A dragon can bite one target or claw two opponents in immediate range as a single action. When bitten, targets are also immobilized until they succeed on a Might defense roll to break free (or the dragon drops them).

Most dragons have one or more additional magical abilities they can bring to bear in combat, including the following.

Captivate: A dragon with this ability can psychically mesmerize a nondragon target in immediate range who fails an Intellect defense roll. A captivated target does the dragon's verbal bidding for one or more hours. Each time the target is confronted by a third party about its mental condition, the target is allowed another Intellect defense roll to break the effect.

Change Shape: A dragon with this ability can take the form of a human or similar humanoid as its action, or return to its regular shape. When so changed, the dragon's disguise is nearly impenetrable without special knowledge. As a human, the dragon is a level 5 creature.

Fiery Breath: A dragon can breathe a stream of fire up to long range, doing 7 points of damage to all targets within immediate range of each other. Targets who succeed on a Speed defense roll to avoid the full effect of the fire still take 3 points of damage. This ability cannot be used in consecutive rounds.

Interaction: Like the many hues of dragon scales, dragon personalities run the gamut from beastly thug to refined connoisseur. Some dragons lie with every smoky breath, others consider the least bit of dishonesty a personal failing, and most fall somewhere in between. All of them can be flattered and even charmed by someone with courtly manners and grace.

Use: A dragon confronts the PCs, challenging them to a riddle game. If the characters win, they get a cypher. If the dragon wins, the PCs owe it a favor to be specified later . . . unless the dragon is hungry now.

Loot: A dragon's hoard might contain 2d6 cyphers, hard currency equivalent to 1d6 exorbitant items, and possibly a few artifacts (but a hoard is usually well guarded).

GM intrusion: *The dragon breathes fire while the character is caught in its mouth, which automatically inflicts maximum fire damage on them.*

ELEMENTAL

Various elemental beings exist, including those of fire and earth.

ELEMENTAL, FIRE 4 (12)

GM intrusion: A character hit by the fire elemental's attack catches on fire and takes 3 points of damage each round until they use an action patting, rolling, or smothering the flames.

Searing flame in a vaguely humanoid shape, a fire elemental exists only to burn that which is not already ash. They sometimes spin into being where great conflagrations burn.

Motive: Burn
Environment: Anywhere fires can burn
Health: 24
Damage Inflicted: 4 to 7 points; see Combat
Movement: Short

Modifications: See Combat for escalating attack level modification.
Combat: A fire elemental attacks with a flaming limb. The more the elemental burns foes, the more powerful it grows. Its power increases according to the number of successful attacks (that dealt fire damage) it made on another creature during the previous minute.
- *0 successful attacks:* deals 4 points of damage; attacks as level 4
- *1 successful attack:* deals 5 points of damage; attacks as level 5
- *3 successful attacks:* deals 6 points of damage; attacks as level 6
- *4+ successful attacks:* deals 7 points of damage; attacks as level 7

If a fire elemental hasn't burned a foe within the last minute, its combat stats drop back to its level 4 baseline.

A fire elemental is immune to fire attacks but vulnerable to cold; every time it takes 1 point of cold damage, it takes 1 additional point of damage.

Interaction: Fire elementals are barely sapient and usually respond only to those who know spells able to command them. However, there's a chance (about 10%) that a fire elemental commanded to accomplish a particular task breaks free and instead burns whatever's around until it exhausts all possible fuel sources.

Use: A rash of fires leads some people to suspect that an arsonist is on the loose, but the truth is worse.

ELEMENTAL, EARTH 5 (15)

> There are many more kinds of elemental than earth and fire. Most people are familiar with air and water elementals, but elementals of shadow, thorn, and lightning, as well as many others, might also exist in a particular setting.

An excavation, a meteor fall, a still-shuddering earthquake—all these events can summon an earth elemental to take shape and expand the destruction further.

Motive: Crumble and break, reduce things to earth
Environment: Anywhere solid or earthen
Health: 30
Damage Inflicted: 6 points
Armor: 3
Movement: Immediate; short when burrowing
Combat: Earth elementals batter foes with heavy fists. They can also create earthquakes (no more than once every other round) that affect the ground within short range. Creatures standing in the area fall to the ground and take 5 points of damage on a failed Might defense roll.

An earth elemental is vulnerable to water. Any damage it takes while standing in or being doused in water ignores its Armor.

Interaction: Although brooding and slow to respond if encountered as immobile stone, earth elementals are intelligent. The ones that are summoned with a spell have about a 5% chance of breaking the geas and turning on their summoner.

Use: Oddly articulated monoliths were discovered high in the mountains around a shrine containing an ancient treasure. A merchant wants someone to investigate the monoliths in case they represent a trap. In fact, the monoliths are inactive earth elementals.

Structures in the area of a fire elemental's attack might catch on fire; those caught in the area of an earth elemental's earthquake might collapse.

GM intrusion: *A character within range of the earth elemental's earthquake attack must succeed on a Speed defense roll or be covered in an avalanche from a collapsing structure or cliff face.*

ENTHRALLER 6 (18)

Hundreds of thousands of years ago, enthraller ancestors psychically dominated a group of interstellar spacefarers who had the misfortune to land on the enthraller homeworld. Leapfrogging technological prowess by mentally commandeering the know-how of every new species they encountered using their stolen space vessel, the aliens fashioned the Enthraller Dominion, which stretches across vast swaths of space, cemented by the psychic control.

Individual enthrallers are scary, but enthraller overlords are even more powerful thanks to technological aids. These include cranial circlets that give a single enthraller governor the ability to dominate a small city, solar-system-sized ring relays that boost their control across interstellar distances, and more.

Recently, a newly contacted species of aliens developed the technological means to resist the mental influence of the enthrallers. Now war bubbles across the Enthraller Dominion. Sometimes individual enthrallers, stripped of their technological enhancements as a consequence of this war, flee into virgin space, looking for new soldiers to dominate.

Motive: Domination of other creatures
Environment: Almost anywhere, alone or in groups of three
Health: 18
Damage Inflicted: 4 points; see Combat
Armor: 1
Movement: Short
Modifications: Speed defense as level 4; perception and ability to detect falsehoods as level 8
Combat: An enthraller usually relies on dominated minions to make physical attacks on its behalf. An enthraller can make a psychic attack on a creature within short range. On a failed Intellect defense roll, the target acts as the enthraller mentally commands on its next action. If the same target is affected by this dominating attack a second time within a minute, the enthraller's mental control lasts for one minute.

Alternatively, as its action, an enthraller can emit a psychic burst that can target up to three creatures in short range. On a failed Intellect defense roll, a victim suffers 4 points of Intellect damage (ignores Armor) and is unable to take actions on their subsequent turn. If the victim is attacked while so stunned, their defense rolls are hindered by two steps.

The enthraller's attack is a form of mental feeding. If it moves a PC down the damage track, the creature regains 4 points of health.

Interaction: An enthraller can communicate telepathically with characters within short range. It tries to mentally dominate whoever it runs across and will negotiate only with characters who are strong enough to harm it. Even if an enthraller makes a deal, it eventually reneges if it senses any advantage for doing so because it implicitly believes that other creatures are cattle.

Use: A spacecraft (or perhaps an escape pod) crash lands. Inside, a hurt enthraller lies in suspended animation. Investigators are unlikely to realize the enthraller's nature beforehand, but they certainly learn if they wake the alien.

Loot: Enthrallers wear light armor suited for their forms. They might have one or two cyphers and, rarely, an artifact that boosts their already-fearsome mental capabilities.

> **GM intrusion:** The enthraller's intrusion into the character's mind stirs up forgotten memories. The character must deal with the contents of these memories and perhaps why they were repressed.

FALLEN ANGEL   5 (15)

Angels are normally associated with virtue and service to higher moral beings. But just like people, sometimes angels are tempted into impure acts. Those who stray too far over the line may fall from higher realms and be forced to walk the Earth in penance. This experience drives most fallen angels insane.

Fallen angel abilities wax and wane according to the position of the sun. During the day, a fallen angel seems almost sane (and is less dangerous), but at night, it is volatile and threatening to everyone.

Motive: Revenge (but on whom and for what isn't clear, even to the fallen angel)
Environment: Anywhere, sometimes living alone in the wilderness, other times walking the hard streets of large cities
Health: 25
Damage Inflicted: 6 points by day, 8 points at night
Armor: 2
Movement: Short; long when flying
Modifications: At night, perceptions and attacks as level 7
Combat: At night, a fallen angel can attack other creatures by projecting a long-range beam of burning light. Against foes within immediate range, the fallen angel manifests burning wings. A fallen angel can choose to make its attacks ignore Armor, but for each attack so modified, it loses 4 points of health.

On the rare occasion that a fallen angel is within immediate range of another of its kind, both regain 1 point of health per round.

By day, a fallen angel cannot project long-range attacks and has no visible wings with which to make melee attacks, though it may carry a melee weapon.

Interaction: By day, fallen angels are not automatically hostile, and they can be negotiated and reasoned with. They can seem truly angelic, though they are often confused and forgetful of their origin. But when night descends, fallen angels lose control of their faculties as they swell with rage and power. Unless a character directs a fallen angel toward another creature on which it can vent its wrath, the character becomes the object of the fury.

Use: A star slips down from the sky and lands in the country. The next day, travelers come upon a farm in the area and find everyone dead and burned. A trail of scorched earth leads up into the hills.

Loot: Fallen angels collect cyphers and usually have a few.

A fallen angel ultimately seeks revenge against whoever threw it from the higher realms. Since that vengeance is hard to gain, fallen angels take out their frustration on whatever crosses their path.

GM intrusion: *A fallen angel's successful attack causes the character's cypher to detonate (if a grenade) or otherwise activate in a less-than-ideal fashion.*

FUSION HOUND 3 (9)

In radiation-scoured wastelands, either creatures adapt to the deadly energies of their environment, or they die. Fusion hounds are mutant canines able to absorb unbelievable amounts of radiation and thrive on it. They roam in packs, killing and devouring everything they come upon.

A fusion hound's entire head appears to be a blast of flame, and gouts of dangerous radiation flare from its body.

Motive: Hungers for flesh
Environment: Packs of three to eight can be found almost anywhere.
Health: 10
Damage Inflicted: 5 points
Armor: 1
Movement: Long
Modifications: Speed defense as level 4; stealth and climbing as level 2
Combat: Fusion hounds move very fast and use that speed to their advantage in combat. A hound can move a long distance and still attack as a single action. It can also use its action to run about in random patterns, hindering attacks against it by two steps.

A fusion hound's head is completely haloed in a seething mass of radioactive energy, so unlike traditional canines, it has no bite attack. Instead, it pounces on prey with its clawed forelimbs, which causes a burst of radiation to flare from its body, burning whatever it touches.

Anyone within close distance of a fusion hound for more than one round suffers 1 point of damage in each round after the first.

Interaction: Fusion hounds are animals. Creatures immune to radiation sometimes train the hounds to become guardians or hunting dogs, but such creatures are rare.
Use: An NPC delivering something the characters need never made it to the rendezvous. If they backtrack to where the NPC should have come from, the PCs are attacked by a pack of fusion hounds on the road. Clearly, the courier was attacked by the pack as well, and the characters must discover if the NPC is dead or merely injured, and where the package now lies.

> Many people believe that a fusion hound has no head hidden beneath its halo of seething radiation; they think the halo is its head.

> **GM intrusion:** The hound flares with energy and the character must succeed on a Might defense task or go blind for ten minutes.

GHOST   4 (12)

Sounds with no apparent origin, such as the tap of footsteps on the stair, knocking behind the walls, crying from empty rooms, and haunting music, might be signs of a ghost. If the sound is accompanied by a sudden temperature drop and the breath of living creatures begins to steam, it's a certainty.

Ghosts are the spectral remnants of humans, which persist either as fragments of memory or as full-fledged spirits. Though their appearance varies between individuals, many appear somewhat translucent, washed out, or physically warped from their time spent as a phantom.

Motive: Unpredictable (but often seeking to complete unfinished business)
Environment: Almost anywhere
Health: 12
Damage Inflicted: 5 points
Movement: Short
Modifications: Stealth as level 7; tasks related to frightening others as level 6
Combat: A ghost doesn't take damage from mundane physical sources, but it takes half damage from spells and attacks that direct energy, and full damage from weapons designed to affect spirits, psychic attacks, and similar attacks.

A ghost's touch inflicts freezing damage. Some ghosts can kill victims with fear. A ghost with this ability can attack all creatures within short range with a psychic display so horrible that targets who fail an Intellect defense roll take 4 points of Intellect damage (ignores Armor) and become terrified, freezing in place. In each subsequent round, a terrified victim can attempt an Intellect-based task to push away the fright. Each failed attempt moves the victim one step down the damage track. Not attempting to clear one's mind of fear counts as a failed attempt. Those killed by fear are marked by expressions of horror and hair that has turned white.

A ghost can move through solid objects of up to level 7 at will, although it can choose to pick up and manipulate objects if it focuses on them. Ghosts can also go into a state of apparent non-existence for hours or days at a time.

Interaction: Some ghosts are talkative, some don't know they're dead, some want help for a task they failed to accomplish in life, and some only rage against the living and want to bring those who yet breathe into the same colorless existence they endure.

Use: A ghost (that at first appears fully human) wants help in eradicating a guild of ghost hunters that has targeted it and a few others haunting an abandoned structure. The ghost promises to tell secrets of the afterlife to any who accept its strange offer.

Loot: A ghost usually doesn't carry objects, though some might have a keepsake (like an amulet showing the face of a loved one) or an artifact.

The ghost of a high school girl named Emily supposedly haunts a covered bridge in Stowe, Vermont, though the ghost appears only at midnight.

GM intrusion: *The character must succeed on an Intellect defense roll or be possessed by the ghost until they succeed on an Intellect-based task to push it out. While possessed, the character acts just like the ghost did when it was alive.*

GHOUL   4 (12)

Ghouls spend almost as much time beneath the ground as corpses do, but ghouls are very much alive. Their bodies are hairless and so porcelain-smooth that their faces are sometimes mistaken for masks, albeit gore-smeared masks. Ghouls come to the surface at night to gather humanoid remains or steal those recently interred from their graves, though many prefer to eat from still-living victims.

Most ghouls are orgiastic eaters of human flesh, but a rare few ghoul populations are more refined. These wear clothes, have language and sophisticated customs, live in grand subterranean cities of their own design, and fight with milk-white blades of bone. These civilized ghouls claim to hold dominion over the remains of all humans, according to ancient custom, even if they only sometimes assert that privilege. They eat the dead in order to absorb residual memories left in the corpses.

Motive: Hunger for dead flesh; knowledge (in certain rare cases)

Environment: Anywhere above ground at night, usually in groups of three or more, or in subterranean lairs

Health: 12

Damage Inflicted: 5 points

Movement: Short

Modifications: Two areas of knowledge as level 5

Combat: Ghoul saliva contains a paralytic agent. Ghoul bites (and weapons used by ghouls) inflict damage and, on a failed Might defense roll, render the target paralyzed for one minute. A paralyzed target can attempt a Might-based task each round to regain mobility, but for the next minute, attacks, defenses, and movement tasks are hindered.

Ghouls can see in the dark. They're blind in full daylight, but civilized ghouls who travel to the surface carry lenses that cover their eyes, allowing them to see without penalty in full sunlight.

Interaction: Common ghouls can't be negotiated with, though a rare civilized ghoul is an excellent linguist. These latter are willing to deal in return for the body of someone who was knowledgeable or who kept valuable secrets in life.

Use: If a PC needs a piece of information not otherwise obtainable, a trip down into a ghoul city might be worthwhile, for the creatures are rumored to keep lightless libraries below the earth that store knowledge once known by humans.

Loot: If the PCs defeat a group of civilized ghouls, they might find a cypher and a few sets of black goggles that allow the wearer to look directly at the sun and see it as a pale circle.

Civilized ghouls are rare and live in subterranean cities. The primary purpose of each city is to maintain a massive central library filled with winding scrolls printed on vellum pressed from the skin of the dead.

GM intrusion: *The ghoul spits in the character's eye, directly introducing the paralytic into the victim's bloodstream. The victim's Might defense roll to avoid becoming paralyzed is hindered.*

GIANT   7 (21)

Violent storms, earthquakes, typhoons, and other natural disasters draw giants. Standing 20 to 30 feet (6 to 9 m) tall, giants delight in rampaging through the middle of such calamities, creating even more destruction. Some giants grow so powerful that they can trigger natural disasters on their own.

Motive: Destruction
Environment: Underground, deserts, mountaintops, and similar desolate areas
Health: 40
Damage Inflicted: 9 points
Armor: 1
Movement: Short
Modifications: Speed defense as level 5 due to size; breaks and throws objects as level 8; sees through deceptions and tricks as level 3
Combat: Giants smash foes with their fists, possibly catching up to three human-sized targets with the same attack if all the targets are in immediate range of each other.

If a giant attacks a single target, they can choose to do regular damage or to grab hold of the victim, dealing 4 points of damage instead. On their turn, the victim can attempt a Might defense roll to struggle out of the grip, a Speed defense roll to slip out, or an Intellect-based task to distract the giant. If the victim fails, the giant throws the victim as high and as far as they can on their next turn. Damage on impact varies, depending on the environment, but a victim takes an average of 10 points of ambient damage.

A few giants can generate storms, tidal waves, earthquakes, and similar phenomena that can lash an area up to 1,000 feet (300 m) across for up to a minute, inflicting 3 points of damage each round to all creatures and objects not protected by shelter designed to withstand a storm (though few shelters protect against an earthquake).

Interaction: Most giants are not very bright. When a giant is rampaging, someone could attempt to distract them by singing, juggling, or doing some other trick, which some giants will pause to watch for at least one or two rounds.
Use: A giant came down out of the mountains and laid waste to half the nearby village. Survivors will pay someone to venture into the giant's mountain lair and destroy the creature.
Loot: Individual giants carry little, but giant lairs may contain currency equivalent to 1d6 expensive items, 1d6 cyphers, and a couple of artifacts.

Ambient damage, page 217

GM intrusion: *The giant's blow sprains one of the character's limbs, making it useless for ten minutes.*

GIANT RAT 3 (9)

Giant rats are as large as big attack dogs, just as vicious, and more wily. Some giant rats are the lone matriarchs of a pack of ordinary level 1 rats, and others are just one of several making up a colony of oversized rodents. Like their smaller cousins, giant rats are known for harboring virulent disease.

Motive: Defense, reproduction
Environment: Anywhere in ruins or sewers, in groups of one to seven
Health: 18
Damage Inflicted: 4 points
Movement: Short; long when jumping
Modifications: Perception as level 4; tasks related to overcoming obstacles and puzzles as level 5
Combat: Victims damaged by a giant rat's diseased teeth and claws take 4 points of damage and, on a failed Might defense roll, are infected with a level 5 disease. Within twelve hours, the victim's lymph glands swell, creating visible buboes. Every twelve hours thereafter, the victim must succeed on a Might defense roll or take 5 points of ambient damage.
Interaction: Giant rats stubbornly pursue prey, but they flee if that prey proves to be too strong.
Use: A contact of the PCs dies of plague before they can deliver an important message. The PCs will have to backtrack the contact's movements to discover what they wanted to say, which leads to a giant rat colony.

Ambient damage, page 217

GM intrusion: A swarm of twelve ordinary rats—each level 1, but acting like a level 3 swarm—is summoned by the high-pitched squeaking of a giant rat.

GIANT SNAKE 4 (12)

Those about to stumble into the presence of a giant snake at least 50 feet (15 m) long are warned by the skin it shed and discarded and by the cracked, slippery bones of digested victims.

Motive: Hungers for flesh
Environment: Anywhere a giant snake can lurk, including jungles, sewers, caves, and spacecraft access tubes
Health: 18
Damage Inflicted: 5 points or more; see Combat
Armor: 2
Movement: Short
Modifications: Perception and stealth as level 6; Speed defense as level 3 due to size
Combat: A giant snake bites foes, preferably from ambush, hindering the target's Speed defense by two steps. If it succeeds, the snake's bite deals 8 points of damage for that attack. On a failed Might defense roll, a bite also inflicts 3 points of Speed damage (ignores Armor). A giant snake may coil around a sleeping, stunned, or debilitated victim. Caught victims automatically take 5 points of crushing damage each round until they break free.
Giant snakes lose their perception and stealth modifications in cold climates and when attacked with abilities that reduce the temperature. Thus, the creatures retreat from cold.
Interaction: A giant snake is a predator that regards other creatures as food, though it ignores them when it is already busy digesting a meal.
Use: Characters note something amiss as they glimpse lambent eyes peering from the darkness, glaring as if seeking to pin victims in place with cold terror.
Loot: A giant snake's droppings or gullet might hold a few cyphers and possibly an artifact that the creature could not digest.

Once it kills a victim, a giant snake drags off the carcass and swallows it over the course of a minute. It takes the snake several hours to digest a human-sized creature.

GM intrusion: The snake's venom affects the character more strongly. Instead of merely inflicting Speed damage, it also paralyzes the character for one minute, though after a couple of rounds, the victim can make another Might defense roll to throw off the effects of the poison early.

Creatures

GIANT SPIDER 3 (9)

Giant spiders result most commonly from radioactive accidents, magic, or genetic manipulation. Whatever their origin, they're terrifying hunters large enough to predate people. The creatures range from the size of a large dog to the size of a large horse.

Motive: Hungers for blood
Environment: Anywhere webs can be spun in the dark
Health: 12
Damage Inflicted: 3 points
Movement: Short; long when traveling on their webs
Modifications: Perception as level 5; Speed defense as level 4 due to quickness
Combat: A giant spider's envenomed fangs inflict 3 points of damage, plus 3 points of Speed damage (ignores Armor) if a victim fails a Might defense roll. Debilitated victims are not killed but instead cocooned and hung for later dining. Giant spider webs (level 4) can hold victims immobile and unable to take actions until they manage to break free.

Giant spiders lose their perception and Speed defense modifications in bright light and thus often retreat from intense illumination.

Interaction: Most giant spiders are simple predators and react accordingly.
Use: Giant spider webs can infest unlit alleys, dungeon corridors, dark forests, and darkened hallways of decommissioned genetic labs.
Loot: Cocooned corpses of previous victims hanging in a giant spider's web sometimes contain all manner of valuables, including cyphers.

GM intrusion: *Giant spider eggs hatch, and a level 3 swarm of tiny spiders attacks the character.*

GOBLIN 1 (3)

Goblins are wicked, grasping, and perversely resourceful. Usually no larger than children, they can seem like pesky rabble, but that illusion hides something altogether more cunning. Tribe members work together to accomplish their goals of murder, kidnapping, and theft.

Motive: Greed and theft
Environment: Tunnels and caves, usually in groups of ten or more
Health: 3
Damage Inflicted: 2 points
Movement: Short
Modifications: Tasks related to perception, stealth, and setting traps as level 5
Combat: Goblins attack from the shadows with ambushes and hit-and-run tactics. When they have surprise, they attack as level 4 creatures and deal 2 additional points of damage, and they attempt to draw larger prey into level 5 traps they've previously set. They often flee in the face of real danger.
Interaction: Goblins are lying tricksters but can be cowed into cooperating for short periods.
Use: Thieves and murderers, goblins are foes to all, even rival goblin tribes.
Loot: Aside from weapons, each goblin carries a personal stash, including bones, shiny rocks, sticks, and other bits of worthless trash, plus currency equivalent to an inexpensive item.

GM intrusion: *The goblin poisoned its knife. If struck, the character must make a Might defense roll or immediately move one step down the damage track.*

335

GOLEM   6 (18)

Animate creatures of stone created by magic for a specific purpose, golems usually serve as guardians. However, they may also serve as soldiers, couriers, and banner-bearers. Golems that have accomplished their task may spend years without moving, like statuary posed in unexpected places—stained, eroded, and forlorn. But if disturbed, a golem rumbles back to movement and attempts to restart the last task assigned to it by its maker.

Motive: Seeks to fulfill the commands of its creator

Environment: Anywhere that needs a sturdy magical guardian

Health: 30

Damage Inflicted: 8 points

Armor: 5

Movement: Short

Modifications: Intellect defense as level 2; Speed defense as level 4 due to slowness

Combat: Skilled with large two-handed weapons, golems inflict 2 additional points of damage (total of 8 points) when using them. Golems cannot be stunned or dazed. They are immune to most poisons and disease, and 2 of their 5 points of Armor protect against ambient damage (environmental damage, heat, cold, falling, and so on).

On the other hand, golems are activated by light, even light as dim as a candle. In complete darkness, a golem is blind and suffers penalties to attack and defend normally. A golem subject to complete darkness may choose to freeze in place like a statue. When one does so, its Armor increases to 10 (and Armor against ambient damage increases to 5), but it can take no actions, including purely mental actions. Unless something can damage the golem through its Armor, it remains frozen indefinitely or until light returns.

Even if a golem is completely destroyed, the rubble of its form slowly reassembles over the course of three days, unless that rubble is ground to the finest gravel and spread widely.

Interaction: Most golems can't speak. Those that can are mournful, and a few have become cruel in their isolation, but at heart, all are lonely. Many are also tired of their stone existence, in which they can move but not really feel, and they wish for some sort of final end.

Use: Powerful sorcerers sometimes create golems and press them into service with yet more spells. These golems prove to be tough bodyguards, but sometimes the futility of such service overcomes a golem and it turns on the sorcerer, breaking free of the binding spells in its rage over being denied the peace of death.

The preferred pronunciation of golem is GO-lem (as in "go forth"), not GALL-em (as in "my gall bladder aches").

GM intrusion: The character hit by the golem is also grabbed and headbutted for 6 additional points of damage. The victim must break or slip free, or else they remain in the golem's grip.

Creatures

GREY   4 (12)

Greys are enigmatic creatures born of alien stars (or dimensions) who have learned to move across the vast distances that bridge neighboring star systems. The creatures descend through the atmosphere under the cover of night to abduct specimens for study and return the victims later after a thorough examination. Returned abductees are usually befuddled and confused, and they retain little memory of what happened to them. Victims of the greys' examination frequently sport strange marks on their flesh, oddly shaped wounds, gaps where teeth used to be, and strange or unknown metal lodged somewhere under the skin.

A grey stands 3 feet (1 m) tall. It has a narrow body with skinny limbs and a large, bulbous head. Two large black eyes, almond shaped, dominate a face that has only a suggestion of a nose and a narrow mouth. Greys wear skintight uniforms, carry numerous instruments to study their environments, and keep a weapon or two for protection.

Motive: Knowledge
Environment: Greys land their spacecraft in remote areas, where they have minimal risk of discovery.
Health: 12
Damage Inflicted: 6 points
Armor: 1
Movement: Short
Modifications: All tasks related to knowledge as level 6; Speed defense as level 5 due to size and quickness
Combat: A grey carries a powerful ray emitter that can burn holes through solid steel. The grey can use the emitter to attack targets within long range. Against dangerous opponents, a grey can use an action to activate a personal shield that encapsulates it in a bubble of force. The shield gives it +3 to Armor, but while the shield is active, the grey can't fire its ray emitter.

Greys are scientists, but cautious ones. Leaving a trail of corpses as evidence of their existence isn't their preferred mode of operation. For this reason, one grey in every group has a memory eraser. When this grey activates the device, each target other than a grey within short range must succeed on an Intellect defense roll or become stunned for one minute, taking no action (unless attacked, which snaps the victim out of the condition). When the effect wears off naturally, the target has no recollection of encountering little grey creatures.

Interaction: Greys are curious about the places they visit but reluctant to move or act in the open. Secretive and mysterious, they prefer to observe creatures from afar and, on occasion, pick them up for closer inspection. Someone who offers a grey true knowledge might be treated as an equal rather than a lab animal.
Use: The PCs are called to investigate a series of disappearances of animals and people. One by one, the abductees return, usually in odd places, and always bearing physical markings that suggest they were subjected to invasive procedures. To protect others from a similar fate, the PCs must catch the abductors in the act.
Loot: A grey has one or two cyphers and might have a memory eraser that works as described under Combat (depletion roll of 1–2 on a 1d10).

Ray emitter, page 395

GM intrusion: *A grey's ray emitter suffers a terrible mishap and explodes. The device kills the grey and destroys its body completely. For the next day, creatures that come within a short distance of where the grey died take 4 points of ambient damage from the psychic radiation each round they remain there.*

KAIJU   10 (30)

Kaiju come in a variety of shapes, but all share one difficult-to-ignore quality: mind-blowing size. Appearances of these colossal creatures are rare events that usually don't last for more than a few days. In that sense, they're akin to hundred-year storms and at least as destructive. When they emerge, they're attracted by artificial structures, the more densely situated and elaborate the better, which they set to smashing with a vengeance. It's hard to judge the size of things so far outside normal scale, but good estimates put most kaiju at over 300 feet (90 m) in height.

Kaiju rely primarily on their strength and mass, but many have some additional trick or ability that sets them apart from their kin, which usually translates into even more devastation.

The other quality all kaiju share is the talent of hiding after a rampage by diving into a nearby sea or burrowing deep into the earth. Sometimes the same kaiju will appear again days, months, years, or decades later, attacking the same location or someplace entirely new.

Motive: Destruction
Environment: Usually near communities containing many high structures
Health: 140
Damage Inflicted: 18 points
Armor: 5
Movement: Short
Modifications: Speed defense as level 8 due to size
Combat: A kaiju can punch, kick, or deliver a tail or tentacle lash at something within long range. Damage is inflicted on the target and everything within short range of the target, and even those that succeed on a Speed defense roll take 7 points of damage.

Kaiju heal quickly, usually at a rate of 2 points per round.

Kaiju are rare and devastating enough that most are dubbed with a unique identifier by survivors. The entry for each creature below notes only where it varies from the base creature described above.

Rampagion: This kaiju has been estimated to be almost 1,000 feet (300 m) high. Once per day, it can make a charging trample attack, dealing its damage in a line 300 feet (90 m) wide and 2 miles (3 km) long. Rampagion has 10 Armor and deals 20 points of damage with a physical attack (or 8 points if a victim makes a successful Speed defense roll).

Suneko: This kaiju's body, which resembles a cross between a lion and a lizard, is so hot that its skin glows like red coals, its mane like the sun's corona, and its eyes like beaming searchlights. Suneko automatically deals 10 points of damage to everyone within immediate range. The creature can emit twin rays of plasma from its eyes in a focused beam that can reach as far as the horizon, which from Suneko's height above the ground is about 22 miles (35 km). When it makes its eyebeam attack, it stops emitting killing heat in immediate range for about one minute.

Interaction: Most PCs can't directly interact with a kaiju unless they have some special device or association allowing them to get the attention of one of the massive creatures. Doing so could give the characters a chance to trick or lure the beast, or maybe even persuade one kaiju to fight another.

Use: After seeing the devastation caused by a kaiju, the PCs might decide (or be asked) to find a way to stop a projected future appearance by the same creature.

Other named kaiju include Kthama, a many-tentacled creature able to generate a tsunami of black fluid that sweeps away whole neighborhoods, and Tonboju, a massive, insect-like creature whose beating wings can generate windstorms, and whose missile stingers leave dozens of smoke trails in their wake and produce immense explosions when they reach their target.

GM intrusion: The character gains the direct attention of the kaiju. If the kaiju attacks the character, They are awarded 5 XP, only 1 of which they have to give to a friend.

CREATURES

KILLER CLOWN 5 (15)

Clowns are great, but only at the circus.

A clown—whether it's a doll or what seems to be a person wearing clown makeup—could be entirely benign. But if you see one sitting alone in a dark room, lying under your bed, or gazing up at you through the sewer grate in the street, it might be a killer clown. Killer clowns might be evil spirits possessing someone or an insane person living out a homicidal fantasy. Either way, they're as dangerous as anything you'll ever likely meet. If you see a clown, run. Because it might be a killer.

Motive: Homicide
Environment: Almost anywhere
Health: 25
Damage Inflicted: 5 points
Movement: Short
Modifications: Detecting falsehoods, deception, and persuasion as level 7
Combat: A killer clown attempts to deceive its victim into believing that the clown is a friend. In fact, the clown is setting up an ambush where the victim can be strangled to death in private. When a killer clown successfully attacks, it inflicts 5 points of damage and locks its hands around the victim's neck. In each round that the victim does not escape, it suffers 5 points of damage from being strangled.

Some killer clowns know tricks that border on the supernatural. Such a clown may do one of the following as its action during combat.

d6	Clown Trick
1	Reveal a secret that one character is keeping from one or more of their allies.
2	Poke target in the eyes as a level 6 attack, blinding target for one minute.
3	Activate a trapdoor beneath victim that drops them 20 feet (6 m) into a cellar or basement.
4	Disappear into secret door or hatch and reappear somewhere hidden within short range.
5	Jab target in the throat as a level 6 attack; resulting coughing fit causes target to lose next action.
6	Down an elixir or energy drink that heals the killer clown of all damage sustained.

GM intrusion: *The clown snatches a weapon, cypher, or other object from the character's hand as a level 6 attack, and if successful, immediately uses it on the character.*

Interaction: A killer clown is all jokes, magic tricks, and juggling, until it decides it's time to strike.
Use: The creepy circus that just pulled into town is guarded by a killer clown, as late-night investigators soon learn.
Loot: A killer clown might have one or two cyphers in the form of a joy buzzer, cards, and cheap trinkets.

KILLING WHITE LIGHT   5 (15)

"The glow returned last night. It was as bright as a welder's torch! Everyone ran, our shadows leading the way. I escaped the killing white light, but my brother wasn't so lucky."

~Aida Chavez, refugee

Though normally hidden within the nimbus of its brilliant radiation, the core of a killing white light is a solid object about 1 foot (30 cm) in diameter. It looks like a bleached-white chunk of volcanic glass filled with tiny, bubblelike cavities, suggesting that the creature might be some kind of mineral-based life form.

A killing white light isn't a subtle hunter. At a distance, the creature is an eye-watering point of brilliance. When it closes in, it is nothing less than blinding, though its emanation isn't warm. Despite the blazing intensity, a killing white light is as cold as starlight on a December night, sapping heat and life from living things caught in its radiance.

By day, a killing white light is usually inactive. During this period, the creature hibernates in darkened areas, as if unwilling or unable to compete against the sun.

Motive: Eliminate organic life

Environment: Almost anywhere dark

Health: 15

Damage Inflicted: 5 points

Armor: 1

Movement: Short when flying

Combat: An active (glowing) killing white light can attack one target within immediate range each round with a pulse of its brilliant nimbus. A character who fails a Speed defense roll against the attack takes damage and experiences a cooling numbness. A victim killed by the creature is rendered into so much blowing ash, though their clothing and equipment are unharmed.

As it attacks, a killing white light emits a blinding nimbus of illumination that affects all creatures within short range. Targets in the area must succeed on a Might defense roll each round or be blinded for one round. A character in the area can avert their eyes when fighting a killing white light to avoid being blinded, but attacks and defenses are hindered for those who do so.

A killing white light is vulnerable to strong sources of light other than its own. If exposed to daylight or caught in a high-intensity beam of light (such as a spotlight), the killing white light falters and takes no action for one round, after which it can act normally. However, if the competing light persists for more than three or four rounds, the creature usually retreats to a darkened place of safety.

Interaction: A killing white light is too alien for interaction and may not be intelligent in a way humans can understand.

Use: An inactive killing white light (which looks something like an albino lump of volcanic glass) is sometimes mistaken for a cypher whose properties can't quite be identified—until the creature becomes active, at which point its true nature is revealed.

GM intrusion: *Normally resistant to interaction, a killing white light uses its blazing nimbus to burn an alien glyph of uncertain meaning in the character's flesh before the creature fades like a light bulb switched off.*

MECHANICAL SOLDIER 4 (12)

Clockwork automatons powered by steam, these mechanical men patrol about and guard locations of importance to their makers. Lanky and awkward in their movements, these quasi-humanoid automatons stand almost 8 feet (2 m) tall. In their three-fingered hands, they wield a variety of weapons.

A few people have wondered if a gear-driven soldier could ever truly attain sentience. Most scoff at the suggestion, but is that a gleam in the glass lens of its eye?

Motive: Incomprehensible
Environment: Anywhere, usually in groups of three to eight
Health: 15
Damage Inflicted: 4 points
Armor: 3
Movement: Short
Modifications: Perception as level 5; leaps, runs, and balances as level 3
Combat: Mechanical soldiers attack in groups using well-organized tactics. Although they can speak, they transmit information to one another silently and instantly within a 100-mile (160 km) range via wireless radio transmissions.

Soldiers armed with advanced weaponry typically carry rifle-like guns that can fire multiple rapid shots without reloading. The soldiers fire at up to three targets (all next to one another) at once. For each target after the first, defense rolls are eased.

In addition, one in four soldiers carries a back-mounted device that hurls bombs at long range with deadly accuracy. They explode in immediate range for 4 points of damage. Each device holds 1d6 such bombs.

A mechanical soldier that has lost its original weaponry scavenges whatever is available.

Certain frequencies of sound confuse these clockwork soldiers, hindering all their actions by two steps, and other frequencies prevent them from acting at all for 1d6 + 1 rounds.

Interaction: On their own, mechanical soldiers act on prior orders. Otherwise, they listen to and obey their creator—and only their creator.

Use: An enterprising bandit has captured and repurposed a number of mechanical soldiers, probably using sound. These soldiers remember nothing of their former duties and work for their new master as high-tech brigands and pirates. The bandit has no idea how to repair them if they are damaged, much less make new soldiers.

Loot: A determined scientist might scavenge the body of one of these automatons to find a cypher.

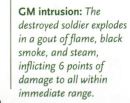

GM intrusion: *The destroyed soldier explodes in a gout of flame, black smoke, and steam, inflicting 6 points of damage to all within immediate range.*

MI-GO   5 (15)

> "The creatures were a sort of huge, light-red crab with many pairs of legs and with two great batlike wings in the middle of the back. They sometimes walked on all their legs, and sometimes on the hindmost pair only, using the others to convey large objects of indeterminate nature. On one occasion they were spied in considerable numbers, a detachment of them wading along a shallow woodland watercourse three abreast in evidently disciplined formation. Once a specimen was seen flying—launching itself from the top of a bald, lonely hill at night and vanishing in the sky after its great flapping wings had been silhouetted an instant against the full moon."
> ~H. P. Lovecraft, "The Whisperer in Darkness"

These extraterrestrial creatures are known as the Fungi from Yuggoth or the Abominable Ones. They are a bizarre amalgam of insect and fungal entity, with many limbs and wings that can carry them aloft. They sometimes enslave humans to work for them in strange factories, mines, or other labor-intensive capacities.

Motive: Knowledge and power

Environment: Usually cold or temperate hills or mountains

Health: 19

Damage Inflicted: 5 points

Armor: 1

Movement: Short; long when flying

Modifications: All knowledge tasks as level 6

Combat: Mi-go defend themselves with pincers and claws but are more likely to use technological devices as weapons. Assume that a mi-go has one of the following abilities from a device:

- Project a blast of electricity at long range that inflicts 6 points of damage
- Emit poison gas in a cloud that fills to short range and inflicts 4 points of Intellect damage if the victim fails a Might defense roll (the mi-go is immune)
- Project a holographic image of itself to one side that hinders attacks aimed at the real mi-go by two steps
- Project a sonic field that provides +2 to Armor

Mi-go have access to other devices as well, including translators, cylinders that can preserve a human's brain without its body, sophisticated tools, collars that control the actions of their wearers, and weird vehicles. Mi-go suffer no damage from cold and do not need to breathe.

Interaction: Although very few mi-go speak human languages, peaceful interaction with these creatures is not impossible. It's just very difficult (level 7), as they see most humans as little more than animals.

Use: The characters are attacked by mi-go intent on capturing and enslaving them. If caught, the PCs are sent to scavenge through primordial ruins for disturbing technological relics.

Loot: Mi-go always have 1d6 cyphers as well as many curious objects that have no obvious human function.

GM intrusion: Fungal spores from the mi-go's body overcome the character, who must succeed at a Might defense roll or lose their next turn. The character faces this risk each round they are within immediate distance of the creature.

MOKUREN   3 (9)

Mokuren are usually no larger than a cat, but they possess the ability to swell until they're the size of a bus (if only briefly). That ability, combined with their flashy pyrokinetic tails, make these creatures a particular favorite with children, at least in stories and picture books. Given that mokuren can "burrow" into paintings and other two-dimensional art, it's possible that some mokuren images are more than simple representations.

Motive: Play
Environment: Almost anywhere, usually as static images on walls or in storybooks
Health: 9
Damage Inflicted: 3 points, unless enlarged; see Combat
Movement: Short; long if flying
Modifications: Defends as level 5 due to size, unless enlarged; see Combat
Combat: A mokuren exists in three states: as an image, as a cat-sized creature, and as a bus-sized behemoth.

As an image, a mokuren can't be harmed. Even if the image is defaced, the mokuren merely "burrows" away and reappears like graffiti on a new flat space within a few miles.

Alternatively, it could emerge from the image and become a physical cat-sized creature as a move. In this form, a mokuren can attack with its claws or bite. It can also direct a stream of fire from its glowing tail at a target within long range. (When a mokuren flies, it's by using its tail to create a jet that rockets it skyward.)

Finally, it can make an enlarged attack, in which it swells to the size of a bus and swipes at, bites, or lands on a target as part of the same action. When enlarged, the mokuren gains +5 to Armor and makes and defends against all attacks as a level 7 creature. On a hit, the enlarged mokuren deals 7 points of damage. However, a mokuren can remain enlarged for a total of only four rounds during any twenty-four-hour period, so it uses this ability sparingly or only when enraged.

Interaction: To see an active mokuren is considered good luck, unless you manage to get on the wrong side of one. Then an offering of sweets must be made to the offended creature. A mokuren can't talk, but it can understand the languages where it lives about as well as a trained courser or hound can.

Use: A mokuren can lead characters into unexplored areas, helping them find places they may have overlooked or skipped. It can also lead PCs into danger, but it usually does so only to bring aid (the characters) to someone else in trouble.

As images, mokuren can exist almost anywhere. They sometimes remain inactive without coming alive off a page for years or decades, until someone new comes along that the mokuren finds interesting.

GM intrusion: *The character hit by the mokuren doesn't take damage. Instead, they must succeed on a Might defense roll or be pulled into the nearest wall, floor, or book with the creature, becoming a two-dimensional image. In this state, the victim is in stasis until the mokuren pulls them free, another creature "pries" them loose, or a day passes and the effect ends naturally.*

NEVERI   7 (21)

In fiction, it's not uncommon to find incredibly powerful Evil Things secured by Ancient Powers in a forgotten prison. But why? Why didn't those Ancient Powers simply destroy the Evil Thing? Many possibilities suggest themselves, but the plainest answer might be right: because the Evil Thing would not die.

A neveri is a floating blob of heaving, writhing flesh, 10 feet (3 m) in diameter, which always oozes pus, dark fluids, and the odor of a thousand graves. A neveri constantly extrudes new sections of skin, mouths, eyes, spines, clawed hands, and whipping tendrils, seemingly force-grown from the mass of dead matter that serves as the nucleus of its body.

Neveri are rare, apparently spending years at a time either inactive or imprisoned from some earlier epoch. When one becomes active (or escapes), it makes a lair in a hard-to-reach location within a day or two of a large population of living things and sets to work feeding its ravenous appetite.

Motive: Hungers for flesh
Environment: Anywhere
Health: 42
Damage Inflicted: 7 points
Armor: 2
Movement: Long when flying; immediate when burrowing
Modifications: Speed defense as level 5 due to size; knowledge tasks as level 8
Combat: A neveri can create specialized organs that spray acid, spit enzymes, or generate bursts of radiation or plasma at long range against up to three targets at one time.

One character in immediate range of a neveri must succeed on a Might defense roll each round or be grasped by a mouth, tendril, or clawed hand. A grabbed character is pulled into contact with the neveri's writhing mass of rotting flesh. Each round, the victim sustains 10 points of damage. A character who dies from this damage is consumed, and their body becomes part of the neveri. A neveri can absorb only one victim at a time.

If a neveri has eaten in the last few days, it regains 3 points of health per round, even if its health drops to 0. If it hasn't eaten recently, a neveri still regains 1 point of health per year (or longer). Even if exploded and dispersed into seeming dust, eventually a neveri begins regaining health again.

Interaction: A neveri has a low-level telepathic ability that allows it to sense when living creatures come near and perhaps to pick up bits of the thinking creature's language. It responds to attempts at communication by forming a mouth that issues horrifying threats. Then it attacks.

Use: An eroded metallic sculpture from an unidentified prehistoric people is discovered. It turns out that the sculpture was a prison, and the intense examination of the prison granted the neveri inside enough impetus to break free.

Loot: If sifted for valuables, the mass of regenerating flesh might contain 1d6 cyphers and an artifact or two.

A neveri is a horror, an entity so malign that its very existence challenges many people's sense of reality. Those who have survived a neveri interaction say that the creature is unkillable, and that the only way to stop one is by confining it or shunting it into an ultimate region of destruction (or inescapable location), such as the sun.

GM intrusion: *A neveri produces a head-sized "childlet" and flings it at a character. If the character fails a Speed defense roll, the childlet adheres and sends mind-controlling rootlets into the victim. Each round the childlet remains attached, the victim must succeed on an Intellect defense roll or willingly come into contact with the neveri if no other victim is currently held in place. Detaching the childlet requires someone in their right mind to rip it free with a Might-based roll.*

NUPPEPPO 2 (6)

Nuppeppos are animated lumps of human flesh that walk on vaguely defined limbs. They smell of decay and death. They're spotted in graveyards, battlefields, coroner's offices, and other places where the dead are kept or interred. When witnessed in other places, nuppeppos seem to wander streets aimlessly, sometimes alone, sometimes in groups, and sometimes following a living person who'd rather be left alone.

Information about these creatures is scarce. They might be the unintended consequence of a reanimation attempt, one that's able to catalyze its animation in similarly dead tissue to form more nuppeppos. On the other hand, they could be particularly gruesome spirits of the dead.

A nuppeppo sometimes follows a living individual around like a silent, smelly pet that shows no affection. No one knows why.

Motive: Wander, graze on dead flesh
Environment: Near places of death at night, alone or in groups of up to eight
Health: 12
Damage Inflicted: 4 points
Armor: 1
Movement: Short
Combat: A nuppeppo can smash a foe with one of its lumpy limbs. If a nuppeppo is touched or struck in melee, the attacker's weapon (or hand) becomes stuck to the nuppeppo and can be pulled free only with a difficulty 5 Might roll.

A victim of a nuppeppo's attack (or someone who touches a nuppeppo) begins to decay at a rate of 1 point of Speed damage (ignores Armor) per round, starting in the round following contact. To stop the spread of the decay, the victim can cut off the layer of affected flesh, which deals 4 points of damage (ignores Armor).

Interaction: If approached, a nuppeppo turns to "face" its interlocutor, but it doesn't respond to questions or orders. However, it may begin to follow its interlocutor from that point forward unless physically prevented—at which point the nuppeppo becomes violent.

Use: The PCs open a grave, a coffin, or a sealed research lab, and several nuppeppos spill out. Unless stopped, the creatures attempt to "adopt" their discoverers.

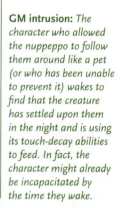

If a nuppeppo begins to follow a character, interaction tasks by that character and their allies are hindered. Most other creatures are put off by a lump of animate human flesh hanging around nearby.

GM intrusion: *The character who allowed the nuppeppo to follow them around like a pet (or who has been unable to prevent it) wakes to find that the creature has settled upon them in the night and is using its touch-decay abilities to feed. In fact, the character might already be incapacitated by the time they wake.*

OGRE 4 (12)

A bestial brute, the ogre is a sadistic, 8-foot (2 m) tall, cannibalistic fiend that preys upon other creatures in the woods, mountains, or other wilderness areas. This often pits them against sylvan beings like elves and fey. Ogres dwelling in more civilized lands are also the enemy of humans, but these ogres usually come no closer to civilization than its very fringes.

Ogres typically dress in ragged, piecemeal clothing or nothing at all.

Motive: Hungers for flesh, sadistic

Environment: Anywhere, usually alone or (rarely) in a band of three or four

Health: 20

Damage Inflicted: 8 points

Armor: 1

Movement: Short

Modifications: Feats of raw strength as level 6; Intellect defense and seeing through deception as level 3; Speed defense as level 3 due to size

Combat: Ogres usually use clubs or large, two-handed weapons with great power. Since they are accustomed to fighting smaller creatures, they are adept at using their size and strength to their advantage. If an ogre strikes a foe smaller than itself, either the victim is knocked back up to 5 feet (1.5 m), or it is dazed, which hinders its next action.

> **GM intrusion:** The ogre's mighty blow (whether it strikes a foe or not) hits the ground or the wall, causing major structural damage and a possible collapse, cave-in, or landslide. It might also expose a hidden underground cave or chamber.

Ogres can also swing their huge weapons in wide arcs, attacking all foes within close range. Defending against this attack is hindered and the attack inflicts 5 points of damage.

Ogres rarely flee from a fight, and only a foe of overwhelming power can force them to surrender.

Interaction: Ogres are stupid and cruel. They speak whatever language is most common in the area in which they live, but their vocabulary is extremely limited. They don't like conversation, even with their own kind. Reasoning with them is difficult at best, but sometimes they can be fooled.

Use: A solitary ogre is an excellent encounter for a group of first-tier characters. A number of ogres, particularly well-equipped and well-trained warriors, make excellent troops or guards in the service of a powerful master. Evil wizards and warlords like to enslave ogres and place them at the forefront of their armies. In these cases, the ogres are typically bribed, ensorcelled, or intimidated by great force.

Loot: Some ogres hoard gold or other valuables in their lairs, but they rarely have use for magic or cyphers.

CREATURES

ORC　　2 (6)

Born into squalor and fear, the orc species is composed of miserable, misbegotten humanoids that seem destined to serve as fodder for more powerful evil overlords. When left to their own devices, these loathsome creatures turn on each other, the strongest oppressing the next weakest (and so on down the line) with cruel barbs, gruesome jokes, and physical beatings. When these creatures have no masters to hate, they hate themselves.

No two orcs look exactly alike, but all have a mean, ugly, and shambolic facade. Never clean and often spattered with the remains of recent meals, orcs have a mouthful of sharp, broken teeth that can develop into true fangs. Adults range in height from no larger than a human child to massive specimens larger than a strapping man. Whether big or small, nearly all orcs have stooped backs and crooked legs. The hue of their skin is hard to ascertain, because they are covered by the sediment of years, not to mention the iron armor every orc constantly wears from the moment it's able to lift a weapon.

Motive: Make others more miserable than itself

Environment: Anywhere near, on, or under mountains, usually in groups of four to six, or in tribes dozens to hundreds strong

Health: 7

Damage Inflicted: 4 points

Armor: 2

Movement: Short

Modifications: Speed defense as level 3 when carrying a shield; pleasant interactions as level 1

Combat: Most orcs have bows able to target foes within long range. Some carry a shield and wield a medium axe, sword, or mace that inflicts 4 points of damage. Other orcs (usually those that are larger than their fellows) dispense with shields and wield heavy two-handed mauls and hammers that inflict 6 points of damage.

Orcs live short, brutish lives. The few that survive for years do so because of some special advantage; they're sneakier, stronger, tougher, or meaner than average. These have the following modifications, respectively:

- Stealth tasks as level 5
- Deal 2 additional points of damage with melee weapons
- +10 health
- Tasks related to trickery and deceit as level 5

Interaction: An orc would stab its own mother if it thought doing so would give it another hour of life in a desperate situation. That said, most orcs have been conditioned, through beatings and torture, to fear the evil master they serve (if any). Characters attempting to negotiate with an orc through intimidation find that short-term success is followed by medium-term betrayal.

Use: A band of orcs fires on the PCs from the edge of the forest. However, these orcs are crafty, and characters who rush directly into combat might fall victim to a hidden pit trap or other prepared ambush.

Loot: Orcs carry a lot of garbage. Amid this dross, a band of orcs might have currency equivalent to a moderately priced item among them.

Powerful orc leader: *level 5; health 25; Armor 3; heavy sword that deals 8 points of damage*

GM intrusion: *With a scream of savage glee, five more orcs rush to join the fight.*

PRINCE(SS) OF SUMMER 5 (15)

Fey nobility are as numberless as cottonwood seeds on the June breeze. But that doesn't mean each isn't unique, with a quirky personality and a specific role to play in the mysterious Court of Summer. Demonstrating life, vigor, predation, growth, and competition, the princesses and princes of summer are beings of warmth and generosity, usually. But catch them during the change of the season, and they can be deadly adversaries just as easily. Fey nobles dress in costly diaphanous and flowing garments, and often wear some sign of their noble lineage, such as a circlet or diadem.

Motive: Unpredictable; defend fey territory and prerogatives
Environment: Almost any wilderness region alone or commanding a small group of lesser faerie creatures
Health: 22
Damage Inflicted: 5 points
Armor: 2
Movement: Short; short when gliding on the wind
Modifications: Tasks related to deception, disguise, courtly manners, and positive interactions as level 7
Combat: Most fey princesses and princes are armed with an elegant sword and possibly a bow carved of silverwood. Also, each knows one or more faerie spells. Faerie spells include the following.

Brilliant Smile: Target must succeed on an Intellect defense task or do the fey creature's will for up to one minute.

Golden Mead: Allies who drink from the fey's flask gain an asset to all defense tasks for ten hours.

Night's Reward: Target suffers 5 points of Intellect damage (ignores Armor) and must make an Intellect defense roll or fall asleep for up to one minute.

Summer Confidence: Selected targets in short range have an asset on tasks related to resisting fear and acting boldly.

Thorns: Target suffers 5 points of Speed damage (ignores Armor) and must succeed on a Might defense task or lose their next turn entangled in rapidly grown thorny vines.

Princes and princesses of summer regain 2 points of health per round while their health is above 0 unless they've been damaged with a silvered or cold iron weapon.

Interaction: Most fey are willing to talk, and those of the Summer Court are especially eager to make deals. However, people who bargain with fey nobles should take care to avoid being tricked.
Use: The characters find a fey noble wounded and in need of aid.
Loot: In addition to fine clothing, fine equipment, and a considerable sum of currency, a prince or princess of summer might carry a few cyphers and even a faerie artifact.

A king or queen of summer is a level 8 version of the prince or princess of summer.

GM intrusion: *The character is blinded for up to one minute by a shaft of brilliant sunlight unless they succeed on a Might defense task.*

PUPPET TREE 6 (18)

A puppet tree is a 25-foot (8 m) tall, spiky, orange and blue tree surrounded by a large area of red reeds that tremble and wave enticingly even when no wind is present. Humanoid figures are often gathered around it, but these rotted, overgrown corpses are the tree's victims, dead but serving as fleshy puppets to the tree's will.

Victims drained of knowledge and life are used as lures to draw in yet more victims, at least until the bodies rot away. When not used as lures, the corpse puppets are sent to scout nearby areas.

Motive: Hungers for fresh bodies
Environment: On hilltops, isolated from other plant life
Health: 33
Damage Inflicted: 8 points
Armor: 3
Movement: None
Modifications: Speed defense as level 5 due to size and immobility; deception and disguise (puppeteering corpses to act in a lifelike manner) as level 7
Combat: Some of the red reeds surrounding a puppet tree end in a hard, sharp crystal spike. When a living creature comes within short range of the tree, the reeds rise behind the target and try to skewer them through the head or neck with the spike. If a target is killed by these attacks, the puppet tree controls the body as a corpse puppet, using it to enact its plans. Over time these humanoids rot and are overgrown by the biology of the plant, losing utility for the tree. Most trees have about five corpse puppets active, which can be simultaneously animated to attack foes.

A puppet tree is vulnerable to fire. All fire attacks against the tree inflict 2 additional points of damage and ignore Armor. The puppet tree will always attempt to stop a fire, or target the source of flame during combat.

A corpse puppet can be detached and sent roaming; however, it retains only about a day's worth of animation, after which it collapses and molders like a normal corpse. Sometimes, however, a sapling puppet tree blooms from the remains.

Interaction: Puppet trees are highly intelligent, but malevolent. Even if communication can be opened via telepathy or some other means, the tree will always attempt to double-cross the PCs.
Use: The PCs spy a group of "people" having a picnic under a strange-looking tree in the middle of nowhere.
Loot: Possessions of former victims can be found in the red reeds, usually including a moderate amount of currency and various bits of gear. Devices of victims (if any) are collected by the corpse puppets and cobbled together into a strange machine, its purpose inexplicable.

Corpse puppet: *level 2; struck targets must also succeed on a Might defense task or be grabbed until they can escape; all tasks attempted by the grabbed target are hindered; free-roaming puppets remain animate for one day*

GM intrusion: *Two corpse puppets, unseen in the red reeds, rise and seize a character in an attempt to hold them still for a crystal spike attack. The character must make a difficulty 4 Speed or Might task to shake free.*

RAVAGE BEAR 4 (12)

Ravage bears could be predators found on an alien planet, hunters from an alternate dimension, mutants, or even Kodiak bears in modern settings.

A ravage bear is a hideous predator that hunts entirely by sense of smell. It is blind and nearly deaf, but it still tracks and senses prey easily. It is very protective of its young, and if hungry, it is extremely dangerous. Otherwise, it gives most creatures a wide berth.

Motive: Hungers for flesh

Environment: Alone or in pairs (usually with a few cubs) in wooded, rocky, or mountainous areas, typically in cold or temperate climes

Health: 20

Damage Inflicted: 7 points

Armor: 1

Movement: Long

Modifications: Makes Might defense rolls as level 6; runs, climbs, and jumps as level 7

Combat: A ravage bear grabs foes with its powerful arms, holds them fast, and then squeezes and tears at them until they are dead. It can hold only one creature at a time. While a ravage bear is holding a creature, it can attack only the held creature. In each round that a held creature does not escape, it suffers 4 points of damage in addition to damage from attacks made against it.

A ravage bear can move very quickly in short sprints. In combat, it can go into an insane fury and will fight to the death. If it takes 10 or more points of damage, its defenses are hindered, but its attacks are eased.

Ravage bears are immune to visual effects, such as illusions. However, olfactory effects can confuse and "blind" them temporarily.

Interaction: Ravage bears are animals and act like animals.

Use: Ravage bears are likely chance encounters in the wilderness for unlucky travelers.

GM intrusion: *In its rage, the ravage bear makes an extra attack that does 2 additional points of damage.*

REPLICANT 5 (15)

Virtually identical to adult humans, these biosculpted androids are stronger, faster, and potentially smarter. However, because they are manufactured beings with grafted memories, replicants rarely feel true human emotion, be that love, sadness, or empathy, though those who live long enough to lay down their own memories can develop the capacity to do so.

However, few replicants gain the opportunity because they are created for a purpose, which could be to serve as police or guards, as soldiers in a distant war, or as impostors shaped to blend in with people so they can explore on behalf of an alien intelligence or a bootstrapped AI. In most of these cases, these purposes lead to a relatively short span of existence, which usually ends when the replicant chooses to detonate itself rather than be captured.

Motive: Go unnoticed; stamp out (or replace) any who learn of their existence
Environment: Anywhere
Health: 18
Damage Inflicted: 6 points
Movement: Short
Modifications: Tasks related to pleasant social interaction, understanding human social norms, and deception as level 2
Combat: Replicants blend in and prefer not to enter combat. Since destruction is not usually their principal goal, they avoid confrontation. If, however, something threatens their mission, they defend themselves to the best of their ability. Replicants might use weaponry but are adept in using their limbs to batter foes into submission.

A replicant poses the greatest danger when its physical form begins to fail through violence or natural degradation (many seem to have a natural "life" span of just a few years). When reduced to 0 points of health, the replicant explodes, inflicting 10 points of damage to everything in long range.

Interaction: Replicants are designed to look human and, at least during a casual interaction, pass as human. But extended conversation trips up a replicant more often than not. Eventually, a replicant gets something wrong and says inappropriate things or exhibits strange mannerisms.

Use: A contact of one of the characters is secretly a replicant. It has survived longer than expected, and its connection to whatever created it has weakened enough that it has gained some independence and made strong emotional connections to the PC. It knows its time is running out and may turn to the character for help.

Some replicants can interface with technological systems, such as computers, by extruding data tendrils for direct, high-speed transfer of information.

GM intrusion: *The character struck by the replicant is smashed into the wall so hard that the surrounding structure begins to collapse on them.*

SHADOW ELF 4 (12)

GM intrusion: The shadow elf casts a spell that charms a character on a failed Intellect defense roll. The character fights on the side of the shadow elf for up to one minute, though they can make another Intellect defense roll each round to try to break the influence.

Elves who faded from the surface to escape the justice of their fey cousins for crimes uncounted are sometimes called shadow elves, dark elves, or simply trow. It's widely assumed that shadow elves fled to new realms deep below the ground, and indeed, the routes that lead to their true abodes are mostly subterranean and include many grand underground keeps. However, the heart of the shadow elf kingdom lies in the colorless dimension of Shadow itself, where all things exist as a dim reflection of the real world.

Sometimes shadow elves appear on the surface, spilling from dark tunnels or, in some cases, from the shadows themselves. They raid for plunder, fresh slaves, and sacrifices. The sacrifices are made to their godqueen, a monstrously sized black widow spider that schemes in darkness.

When a shadow elf returns to the world of light, it can choose to appear as a silhouette only: a slender humanoid outline lurking as if at the nadir of a well.

Motive: Tortures for pleasure, serve the shadow elf godqueen
Environment: Almost anywhere dimly lit, singly or in groups of up to four
Health: 15
Damage Inflicted: 5 points
Armor: 1
Movement: Short
Modifications: Stealth and perception as level 6; Speed defense as level 6 due to shadowy nature
Combat: Shadow elves attack with short blades, knives, and crossbow quarrels of steel-hard shadow.
They can see in dim light and absolute darkness as if it were daylight.
Some shadow elves can cast spells, including the following. Each spell requires an action to cast.

d6	Shadow Elf Spell
1	Enchant weapon to inflict 3 additional points of damage (8 total)
2	Enchant weapon to inflict 1 additional point of Speed damage (poison, ignores Armor), plus 2 points of Speed damage each additional round until victim succeeds on a Might defense roll
3	Fly a long range each round for ten minutes
4	Gain +2 to Armor (total of 3 Armor) for ten minutes
5	Long-range spell renders subject blind for ten minutes on failed Might defense roll
6	Long-range spell targets up to three creatures next to each other; holds them motionless in a shadow web for one minute on failed Speed defense rolls

If subject to full daylight, a shadow elf loses its modifications to stealth, perception, and Speed defense, and is likely to retreat.

Interaction: Shadow elves may negotiate and even ally with other creatures for a time. But they do so only until the best opportunity for a betrayal presents itself.
Use: Shadow elves have overrun an outlying keep, and even in broad daylight, the castle is shrouded in darkness and webs of shadow. The treasures said to lie in the keep's coffers may already be in the hands of the dark fey.
Loot: A shadow elf carries currency equivalent to an expensive item, in addition to weapons, light armor, and a cypher or two. Shadow elf leaders may carry an artifact.

SKELETON 2 (6)

Skeletons are animated bones without much sense of self-preservation. They enjoy a crucial advantage over living creatures in one important and often exploited area: skeletons are dead shots with ranged weapons. They have no breath, no heartbeat, and no shaking hands to contend with as they release a shot, which means that skeletons armed with ranged weapons are something to be feared.

Motive: Defense or offense
Environment: Nearly anywhere, in formations of four to ten
Health: 6
Damage Inflicted: 3 points (claw) or 5 points (ranged weapon)
Armor: 1
Movement: Short
Modifications: Ranged attacks as level 5; Speed defense against most ranged attacks as level 5; resist trickery as level 1
Combat: Skeletons can attack with a bony claw if they have no other weapon, but most attack with a long-range weapon. If a skeleton can see any portion of its target, the target loses any benefits of cover it might have otherwise enjoyed.

When in formation, a group of four or more skeletons with ranged weapons can focus their attacks on one target and make one attack roll as a single level 7 creature, dealing 7 points of damage.

Skeletons can see in the dark.

Reanimators: Some skeletons were created by a curse, and simply battering them into a pile of bones isn't enough to end their existence. Two rounds after reanimator skeletons are "killed," they regain full health in a flash of magical illumination. This regeneration can be prevented if the linchpin of the animating curse is separated from the skeleton after it falls. Such an item is usually obvious and might take the form of a lead spike through the skull, an ebony amulet, a dull sword through the ribs, a crown, and so on.

Interaction: A skeleton usually interacts only by attacking. Unless animated by a sapient spirit able to communicate via magic, skeletons lack the mechanisms for speech. However, they can hear and see the world around them just fine.

Use: Skeletons make ideal units in armies, especially when archery or artillery is required. A formation of four or more skeletons with ranged weapons atop a tower provides a surprisingly robust defense.

Loot: Sometimes the linchpin item required to create a reanimator skeleton is valuable.

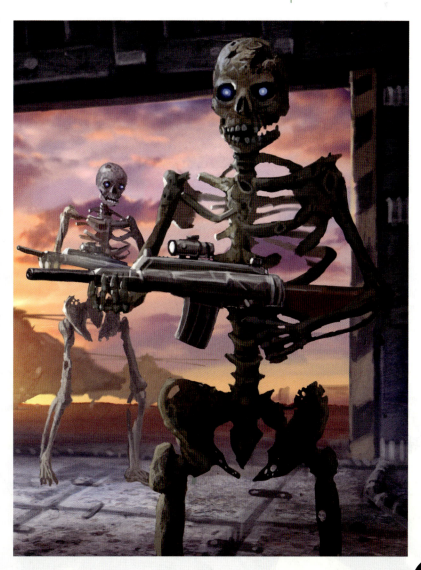

Some animate skeletons are created by spells, scrolls, or specific items. Others arise spontaneously after a great battle or if in the presence of strong death magic.

GM intrusion: *A skeleton destroyed by a melee attack explodes like a grenade. The bone shrapnel inflicts 5 points of damage to every creature in immediate range.*

SLIDIKIN 5 (15)

Slidikin might be the result of a magical curse, a demon possession by several entities at once, a transhuman experiment, a species of creatures driven insane after modifying themselves to speak with humans, or something else.

Skulking from shadow to shadow, the slidikin dwell on the fringes of society. They are bizarre creatures, their origins a complete mystery. While one might pass as a human from a distance, their chalk-white skin, lack of eyes or nose, and far-too-many mouths ensure that a close examination would prove them otherwise. In people's rare, brief, and frankly disturbing interactions with slidikin, they have made passing references to "the hideous game." This seems to be an incongruous competition among slidikin (and only slidikin) that involves dark deeds—theft, kidnapping, mutilation, and murder. (It likely involves other things as well, but no one knows what they are, focusing only on those activities that affect humanity.)

Motive: The game
Environment: Edges of society
Health: 22
Damage Inflicted: 5 points
Movement: Long
Modifications: Speed defense and stealth as level 6
Combat: Slidikin often use weapons in combat, although they never wear armor, preferring to remain agile rather than encumbered.
Interaction: Talking with a slidikin can be infuriating. No matter what the situation, the slidikin—with its multiple, grating, whispered voices—speaks with outlandish contempt for whomever it encounters, as if it knows a great many things that everyone else does not. It finds odd things (like physical threats) humorous, and many normal concepts (like justice or revenge) incomprehensible. It never tells anyone the nature of the game or anything of its own nature.
Use: A man stumbles out of a dark alleyway toward the PCs, blood running down his face. "The mouths," he whispers hoarsely. "The mouths." If the characters examine him, they see that his eyelids have been sliced off. He says that men—at least, he thought they were men at first—grabbed him the day before and held him in a dank cellar overnight, bound and gagged. They giggled and whispered among themselves the whole time. Then they mutilated him with knives and left him in the alley. He gives a frantic, fevered description of a slidikin.
Loot: A slidikin very likely carries currency equivalent to a moderately priced item and a cypher as well as a variety of knives and poisons, knockout drugs, lockpicks, and other tools.

GM intrusion: *The slidikin runs away and around a corner. If the character follows it, the creature is gone. Is there a secret door? Did it disappear into the shadows? Did it climb up to the roof? It's nowhere to be seen.*

STATUE, ANIMATE 7 (21)

Towering statues carved from stone or cast in metal are sometimes more than humans rendered in moments of triumph, celebration, or suffering. Sometimes a statue moves, usually in service to some ancient geas or command that animated it in the first place.

Most animate statues are vessels imprisoning the mind of a sentient creature. Such entrapment usually tumbles the spirits into the abyss of insanity, though most rest in a dormant state, their minds lost in whatever memories they retain. Disturbing animate statues can cause them to awaken, usually with disastrous results.

Motive: Release from imprisonment; guard an area
Environment: In out-of-the-way places, especially ancient ruins
Health: 33
Damage Inflicted: 9 points
Armor: 4
Movement: Short
Modifications: All tasks involving balance as level 2; Might defense as level 8; Speed defense as level 5 due to size
Combat: An animate statue towers over most foes, and it can smash or stomp a target within short range as a melee attack. The statue's massive size and the material of its body means it can walk through nearly any obstacle, smashing through walls of solid rock, buildings, and trees. When walking, it pays no attention to what it steps on. Anything in its path is likely flattened. A character who is stepped on must make a Speed defense roll to dodge or be knocked down and take 9 points of damage.

Animate statues are strong and hard to hurt, but they are often top-heavy. If one falls or is knocked over, it takes a few rounds to rise and resume whatever it was doing.

Interaction: Statues spend years immobilized and insensate, their minds lost in half-remembered experiences and hallucinations. Rousing a statue has unpredictable results. Some might rampage. Others laugh, cry, or scream streams of nonsense. Regardless, if one has been commanded to guard an area or entrance, it also likely lashes out.

Use: An animate statue holds a treasure trove of knowledge. If the characters can keep it focused or knocked down long enough, they might coax from it the information they seek.

GM intrusion: *The animate statue strikes a character so hard that the victim flies a long distance and lands in a heap, possibly dropping gear and weapons along the way.*

SUPERVILLAIN

People with amazing abilities who use them for evil earn the label of supervillain. This section presents five sample supervillains.

ANATHEMA   7 (21)

The supervillain called Anathema is big, bright red, and stronger than anyone on this planet or any other (or so he claims). Superheroes who go head to head with him learn that he can withstand almost any hit and always gives back twice as hard as he receives. He can bring down buildings with a punch and throw semi trucks across state lines.

Before he was Anathema, he was Sameer Stokes, a bitter and spiteful coder working for a large software company. Having failed in relationships, promotions, and retaining friends, Sameer retreated online and learned that he had power when he bullied people. He delighted in causing emotional distress in others in forums and social media. In effect, he was a troll. When the metamorphosis happened, he was turned into a troll for real. (Sameer doesn't recall the metamorphosis or the days before and immediately after his change, despite using therapy and drugs in an attempt to recover those memories.)

> Assume that Anathema has three power shifts in strength and two in resilience. These shifts are already figured into his modifications and other stats.
>
> Power shifts, page 292

Motive: Accumulate wealth, live on the edge
Environment: Anywhere vast wealth can be stolen
Health: 70
Damage Inflicted: 12 points
Movement: Short; a few miles (5 km) per leap
Modifications: Strength tasks as level 10; Might defense as level 9; Speed defense as level 5 due to size
Combat: Anathema hits foes with bone-shocking force. He can throw cars and large objects at targets within long range, dealing damage to all creatures within immediate range of his target.

Anathema has a healing factor that makes it hard to hurt him in any meaningful sense. He regains 10 points of health per round. In any round in which he regains health, his attacks deal 3 additional points of damage (15 total), and he seems to visibly swell with muscle.

Interaction: When Anathema is riled up during a fight, it's difficult to reason with him. However, he is willing to negotiate if someone offers him wealth or convinces him they have valuable secrets for breaking mental blocks. Anathema doesn't know how he became the way he is, and he wants to recover his missing memories.

> **GM intrusion:** Anathema's attack sends the character flying a long distance and potentially into dangerous terrain.

Use: The rolling earthquake afflicting the city is actually Anathema fighting a group of newbie superheroes who haven't figured out that engaging the red mountain will likely cause more deaths than leaving him alone. (The first rule of fighting Anathema is to lead or move him somewhere with a low population density.)
Loot: Anathema doesn't normally carry wealth or other valuables. In his lair, Anathema typically has three to five expensive items, 1d6 cyphers, and possibly an artifact.

"Clear out, or I'll smash you into paste. Red, screaming, bone-protruding paste. This is your only warning."

~Anathema

Creatures

DOCTOR DREAD 7 (21)

Doctor Dread is larger than life thanks to her brilliant mind, her media savvy, and the robotic armor she uses to enhance her otherwise normal abilities. Indeed, Doctor Dread has become the most feared terrorist on the planet. She uses her abilities to extort money, influence, and technology from the rich and powerful, whether her victims are individuals, governments, corporations, or superheroes.

Alicia Coleridge is Doctor Dread's secret identity. Born into relative obscurity, she received a full scholarship to the Russell Institute of Technology, where she studied the effects of radioactive substances on living tissue. In a freak lab accident, Alicia's fiancé was slain, and Alicia was disfigured and driven slightly insane, so much so that she built the Doctor Dread armor. She plows the vast wealth she accumulates through terrorism into research into the rejuvenation of dead flesh. She hopes to one day bring back her dead love, whose body she keeps in suspended animation.

Motive: Accumulate wealth; reanimate dead flesh
Environment: Wherever money can be extorted
Health: 40
Damage Inflicted: 7 points
Armor: 4
Movement: Short; long when flying
Modifications: Resists mental attacks and deception as level 8; understands, repairs, and crafts advanced technology as level 10
Combat: Doctor Dread's armor allows her to exist without outside air (or air pressure), food, or water for up to ten days at a time. She can call on her robotic armor to accomplish a variety of tasks, including the following:

Barricade: Establish an immobile, two-dimensional field of transparent force 10 feet by 10 feet (3 m by 3 m) for ten minutes

Energy Cloak: Create an energy field that gives her +5 to Armor against heat, cold, or magnetism (one at a time, chosen when she uses the power) for ten minutes

Fade: Become invisible for one minute, or until she makes an attack

Plasma Blast: Long-range heat and electricity blast that inflicts 7 points of damage

Interaction: Doctor Dread is slightly mad, but that's normally disguised by her amazing brilliance. She is an egomaniac but will negotiate in return for a promise of wealth or biomedical lore she doesn't already know.

Use: The PCs are called to handle a hostage situation at a party in which many of the city's wealthy elite are being held captive by Doctor Dread. She promises to let them go once sufficient wealth is paid into her offshore accounts.

Loot: Most of Doctor Dread's considerable wealth is tied up in online accounts, two or three secret fortresses, and cutting-edge biological research equipment.

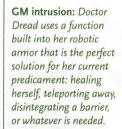

Doctor Dread is usually accompanied by a handful of robot minions.

Dread's robot minion: level 3; Armor 1; long-range laser attack inflicts 4 points of damage

Assume that Doctor Dread has three power shifts in intelligence and two in resilience. These shifts are already figured into her modifications and other stats.

GM intrusion: *Doctor Dread uses a function built into her robotic armor that is the perfect solution for her current predicament: healing herself, teleporting away, disintegrating a barrier, or whatever is needed.*

MAGNETAR 8 (24)

Not much is known about Magnetar other than its powerful ability to generate and control magnetic fields. Various research groups theorize that Magnetar is an alien, a sentient and self-improving robot, or even some kind of manifestation of a fundamental force. Given Magnetar's vaguely humanoid shape, a few people even suggest that the villain is actually a man with a mutant ability so powerful that it burned out all memories of his former self.

In truth, Magnetar is the animate, sentient, and self-regulating nucleus of a neutron star that is able to rein in its immense electromagnetic signature. One of two such beings an advanced alien species created from a single magnetar (a type of neutron star with an extremely powerful magnetic field), Magnetar was sent on a mission of exploration. After millennia, it crashed on Earth and was damaged. Having lost most of its memory data, Magnetar knows that something was taken from it (its twin), but it can't remember what. It has decided to blame the humans.

Motive: Revenge; regain memory

Environment: Almost anywhere, searching for what it has lost

Health: 50

Damage Inflicted: 12 points

Armor: 8

Movement: Short; long when magnetically levitating

Modifications: Speed defense as level 5 due to mass; tasks related to controlling and shaping metal through electromagnetic manipulation as level 11

Combat: Magnetar's fist packs a wallop, since it can selectively add mass to the punch. However, its most potent ability is its level 11 control over all metal within very long range, which it uses to create anything it can imagine, including walls, attacks, pincers, and more. Magnetar can lift bridges, vehicles, and structures infused with rebar that it can see within its area of influence. When it throws such a large object as part of an attack, the target and everything within short range of the target takes 10 points of damage.

Magnetar's only weakness is psychic attacks, which is fortunate since reducing it to 0 health through an old-fashioned beating could release an uncontrolled neutron star chunk on the Earth's surface.

Interaction: Morose and gruff, Magnetar would rather be alone, but every so often, it goes on a rampage, hoping that a display will draw out whoever or whatever made it the way it is. Magnetar constantly feels the drag of emotional loss, but it doesn't know why (it doesn't realize that the feeling comes from the loss of its twin).

Use: Doctor Dread has put a bounty on Magnetar's head because she wants to study the advanced technology woven through its body. The bounty amount is outrageous, but then again, so is Magnetar.

Assume that Magnetar has three power shifts in its magnetic power and two in resilience. These shifts are already figured into its modifications and other stats.

For levels above 10, see Really Impossible Tasks, page 293

GM intrusion: *On a failed Might defense roll, all of the character's loose metallic items (including weapons) are stripped from them and become stuck to a nearby metallic buttress.*

MISTER GENOCIDE   5 (15)

Real name Alfred Webster, Mister Genocide has the unfortunate ability to synthesize deadly poison from his skin. His touch can kill, but if he wishes it, so can his spittle or even his breath.

Anyone who spends too much time in Mister Genocide's presence becomes ill, even if the villain isn't actively using his power. Thus, his cronies usually wear gas masks and protective clothing. Mister Genocide has promoted himself to the head of the mob in the city where he resides and is always looking to expand his operations, sometimes at the expense of other criminals.

When victims are killed by Mister Genocide's poison, their skin and the whites of their eyes take on a bright green hue, which increases the terror that normal people feel regarding him. Even superheroes have been brought down by his toxins.

Motive: Accumulate power
Environment: Anywhere crime lords congregate
Health: 15
Damage Inflicted: 5 points; see Combat
Armor: 1
Movement: Short
Modifications: Poison breath attack and Might defense as level 7; Intellect defense and evil genius as level 6
Combat: Targets touched by Mister Genocide must make a difficulty 7 Might defense roll or take 5 points of Speed damage (ignores Armor) from the poison transmitted. Worse, the poison continues to inflict 2 points of Speed damage each round until the victim succeeds at a Might defense roll.

Every other round, Mister Genocide can make a level 7 poison attack that can affect up to ten victims within short range as a single action. Those who fail a Might defense roll take 7 points of Speed damage (ignores Armor) and spend a round helpless as they cough and gag. The inhalant poison does not continue to inflict damage each round.

Mister Genocide is immune to most venoms, toxins, and poisons.
Interaction: Certifiably insane, Mister Genocide likes to kill people. He may negotiate for a while, but if there is not enough gain to be had, he might kill everyone with a breath just for the fun of watching them suffocate and turn green.
Use: Gang warfare between two criminal organizations is shooting up downtown, and many innocent bystanders caught in the crossfire end up bullet-ridden or poisoned (with green skin). Someone needs to put a stop to Mister Genocide.
Loot: The supervillain carries currency equivalent to 1d6 expensive items, a cypher or two, and a variety of poisoned knives, needles, and vials.

Mister Genocide sometimes teams up with Anathema, because the red mountain is the only villain who can withstand the poison that Genocide constantly emits.

Assume that Mister Genocide has two power shifts in his poison power, one in intelligence, and two in resilience. These shifts are already figured into his modifications and other stats.

GM intrusion: *A character affected by the poison must make a second Might defense roll or fall unconscious from shock. Unconsciousness lasts for up to a minute, or until the victim is jostled awake.*

WRATH   6 (18)

The head of an elite group of assassins, Wrath wants to save the world by killing everyone who impedes her vision of perfection—which turns out to be the better part of humanity. In addition to being one of the most accomplished martial artists to walk the earth (thanks to her connection with a mystical entity called the Demon), Wrath is also a criminal mastermind whose assassins are just one layer of the organization she controls.

Born more than two hundred and fifty years ago in China to a name lost to history, Wrath was taken in by a monastery and trained in the ways of fist and sword. Everything changed when raiders attacked and killed everyone in her monastery, leaving her the sole survivor. Vowing revenge against the raiders and the world that allowed animals like them to exist, she acquired a magical amulet that contains the Demon. The Demon in turn bequeathed her extraordinary speed, strength, and longevity.

Wrath is content to let her assassins (and mobsters, lawyers, and politicians) accomplish many of her goals, though she relishes being present when particularly important adversaries are brought down.

Motive: Save the world

Environment: Anywhere wrongs (to Wrath's way of thinking) must be righted

Health: 36

Damage Inflicted: 8 points

Armor: 1

Movement: Short

Modifications: Stealth, attacks, and Speed defense as level 8

Combat: Wrath prefers a sword, though she is equally adept with a crossbow or, in rare cases, modern weapons. In melee she can attack two foes as a single action every round.

Thanks to the influence of the Demon, Wrath regains 3 points of health each round, even if reduced to 0 health. The only way to permanently kill her is to reduce her to 0 health and keep her that way long enough to burn away the tattoo of the Demon that is engraved across her back.

Interaction: Wrath is arrogant and confident, though not so much that she is easily fooled by flattery. She is usually amenable to negotiating, because she can anticipate the agenda of others and usually gain far more for herself in the end. However, she is not one to betray her word.

Use: Wrath is making a bid to form a group of supervillains—all of whom will answer to her, of course—and it seems that initial talks are going well. The only holdout is Mister Genocide, who feels threatened by Wrath's larger organization, and this tension has led to ongoing warfare in the streets as assassins battle mobsters.

Loot: In addition to weapons and armor, Wrath likely possesses the equivalent of five exorbitant items, 1d6 cyphers, and possibly one or two artifacts.

Assassin of Wrath: level 4, stealth as level 7

Assume that Wrath has two power shifts in dexterity, two in accuracy, and one in resilience. These shifts are already figured into her modifications and other stats.

GM intrusion: Just as things seem bleakest for her, Wrath summons a group of assassins waiting in the wings to surround the PCs and demand their surrender.

CREATURES

TYRANNOSAURUS REX 7 (21)

The short arms of a tyrannosaurus have been much parodied in Earth social media circles, but the arms aren't really important when a hunting tyrannosaurus is after you. It's more the soul-shivering roar, designed to freeze prey in place, and a skull and mouth so enormous that the entire creature is cantilevered by a massive tail that itself can be used as a powerful weapon.

As vicious as tyrannosauruses likely were 66 million years ago, the versions still hunting today could be even more dangerous. That's because the ones with a taste for humans have learned to adapt to human defenses and to use their roar to terrorize prey as they hunt.

Motive: Hungers for flesh

Environment: Tyrannosauruses hunt solo or in pairs; they're drawn to loud, unfamiliar noises (like motor engines).

Health: 50

Damage Inflicted: 10 points

Movement: Short

Modifications: Perception as level 5; Speed defense as level 5 due to size

Combat: A tyrannosaurus attacks with its massive bite. Not only does it deal damage, but the target must also make a Might defense roll to pull free or be shaken like a rat in the mouth of a pit bull for 3 additional points of Speed damage (ignores Armor). The shaking recurs each subsequent round in which the target fails a Might-based task to pull free.

A tyrannosaurus can also make a trampling attack if it can charge from just outside of short range. When it does, it moves 50 feet (15 m) in a round, and anything that comes within immediate range is attacked. Even those who make a successful Speed defense roll take 2 points of damage.

Finally, a tyrannosaurus can roar. The first time creatures within short range hear the roar on any given day, they must succeed on a difficulty 2 Intellect defense roll or stand frozen in fear for a round. Attacks against them are eased by two steps in the attacker's favor and deal 2 additional points of damage.

For all their power, tyrannosauruses are not above self-preservation. They never fight to the death if they are outclassed, and they usually break off if they take more than 30 points of damage in a conflict.

Interaction: Tyrannosauruses are animals, but they're clever hunters, too. When they hunt in pairs, they work to keep prey penned between them.

Use: Something is killing big game in a forest preserve. Poachers are suspected at first, but when they are also found dead, it's clear that something else is to blame.

Even though the tyrannosaurus rex was the largest carnivore in its environment, some paleontologists believe that the creature was more of a scavenger than an apex predator. However, many scientists think that it was both—it preyed upon things that ran, but it wasn't adverse to stripping a carcass from another predator's kill.

GM intrusion: *The tyrannosaurus's tail swings around and knocks the character tumbling out of short range and possibly into dangerous terrain.*

VAMPIRE

Several varieties of vampires exist, including the two kinds detailed here.

VAMPIRE 6 (18)

Vampires are undead creatures, risen from the grave to drink blood. Their very nature and essence are evil and anti-life, even as they revel in their own endless existence. Most vampires are vain, arrogant, sadistic, lustful, and domineering. Their powers allow them to manipulate others, and they frequently toy with their prey before feeding. Vampires come out only at night, as the sun's rays will destroy them.

The bite of a vampire over three nights (in which it exchanges a bit of its own blood) ensures that the victim will rise as a vampire under the thrall of the one that killed it. While vampires are careful not to create too many of their kind (which amount to competition), each thrall conveys a bit more supernatural power to a vampire.

Motive: Thirsts for blood
Environment: Usually solitary, on the edges of civilization
Health: 24
Damage Inflicted: 7 points
Movement: Long
Modifications: Climb, stealth, and perception as level 8; Speed defense as level 7 due to fast movement
Combat: Vampires are strong and fast. They have impressive fangs, but these are usually used in feeding, not in battle. They typically fight with their fists or hands (which basically become claws) but sometimes use weapons.

A vampire can change into a bat or a wolf. This transformation does not change its stats or abilities except that, as a bat, it can fly. Vampires can also transform into shadow or mist, and in these forms they can't be harmed by anything (but also can't affect the physical world).

Vampires possess an unholy charisma and can mesmerize victims within immediate distance so that they stand motionless for one round. In subsequent rounds, the victim will not forcibly resist the vampire, and the vampire can suggest actions to the victim (even actions that will cause the victim to harm themselves or others they care about). Each round, the victim can attempt a new Intellect defense roll to break free.

Vampires are notoriously difficult to hurt. Unless a weapon is very special (blessed by a saint, has specific magical enchantments against vampires, or the like), no physical attack harms a vampire. They simply don't take the damage. Exceptions include the following:

Fire: Vampires burn, though the damage doesn't kill them. It only causes pain, and a vampire regains all health lost to fire damage within a day.
Running water: Complete immersion inflicts 10 points of damage per round. If not destroyed, the vampire can use a single action to regain all health lost in this way.
Holy water: This inflicts 4 points of damage and affects a vampire exactly like fire.
Sunlight: Exposure to sunlight inflicts 10 points of damage per round. If not destroyed, the vampire regains all health lost to exposure within a day.

A vampire might bite for only one round and then leave, starting the process of creating a new vampire. The victim becomes a transitional vampire the next night.

To ensure that a defeated vampire can never come back to life, most vampire hunters decapitate it and stuff its mouth with holy wafers.

Vampires will not enter a home unless invited in.

Wooden stake: This weapon inflicts 25 points of damage, effectively destroying the vampire in one blow. However, if the vampire is aware and able to move, this attack is hindered as the vampire does everything it can to evade.

Further, vampires have the following special weaknesses:

Garlic: Significant amounts of garlic within immediate distance hinder a vampire's tasks.

Cross, holy symbol, or mirror: Presenting any of these objects forcefully stuns a vampire, causing it to lose its next action. While the object is brandished and the vampire is within immediate range, its tasks are hindered by two steps.

Eventually, a vampire with a multitude under its command becomes the new vampire lord. The vampire lord is the most powerful vampire in the world and is often (but not always) the most ancient of its kind. It has many vampires under its control, and even those that it did not create pay it respect and homage.

Interaction: Most vampires look upon humans as cattle upon which to feed. They rarely have respect for anything but other vampires, and they often hate other supernatural creatures that they cannot enslave.

Use: Strange stories of shadows in the night, people disappearing from their beds, and graves missing their former occupants could portend the arrival of a vampire in the region.

Vampire lord: level 9; climb, stealth, and perception as level 10; Speed defense as level 10; health 40; Armor 2; all the powers and weaknesses of a regular vampire, plus one or two unique abilities

Traditional methods of killing a vampire are just temporary setbacks for a vampire lord. The only way to destroy it for good is mysterious and unique, such as an ancient ritual, a special weapon, or the like.

TRANSITIONAL VAMPIRE 3 (9)

When humans are "visited upon" (bitten) by a vampire, they might be killed, or they might be left alive to begin a slow transformation into a creature of the night. If victims are bitten three times, they become a vampire forever under the control of the one that bit them. From the time of the first bite until their complete transformation after the third bite, they are transitional vampires. Ways to return transitional vampires to normal include using special ancient rituals or destroying the vampire that bit them in the first place.

Transitional vampires usually serve as guardians, consorts, or spies for their masters.

Motive: Thirsts for blood

Environment: Anywhere, usually solitary but sometimes in groups of two or three

Health: 12

Damage Inflicted: 4 points

Movement: Short

Modifications: Climb and stealth as level 4

Combat: Transitional vampires can maintain a human existence during the day without any of a vampire's powers or weaknesses. However, they have a disdain for garlic and the sun. At night they take on all the characteristics of a vampire, and if confronted by any of the traditional vampiric weaknesses (a wooden stake, a cross, and so on), they flee unless their master is present.

Interaction: Transitional vampires are utterly devoted to their master.

Use: Transitional vampires lie in the intersection of foe and victim. A loved one or trusted companion who has been turned into a transitional vampire will try to betray, defeat, and kill the PCs, but the characters are motivated to save them rather than destroy them.

It's possible for a vampire to turn a fresh corpse into a transitional vampire. Unlike others of its kind, it is truly undead—like a vampire—and cannot take on a human nature during the day. But it will never become a full vampire and always remains in its lesser state.

GM intrusion: *The character struck by the vampire is caught fast in its powerful grip. If the character doesn't escape immediately, the vampire bites them automatically.*

VAT REJECT 3 (9)

Vat rejects come into being when clone vats meant to produce clone soldiers or similar mass-produced entities are corrupted. How the carefully controlled process becomes compromised varies, but possibilities include yeast contamination, sunspot activity, nanovirus evolution, or purposeful meddling with control parameters. Unskilled operators experimenting with derelict cloning equipment can also produce a vat of rejects.

Vat rejects fear nothing and welcome death, except that their existential rage requires an outlet other than immediate suicide. Their warped forms mean that most are in constant pain, and they somehow understand that this was artificially stamped into them by their creators. Revenge is their only possible redemption.

Motive: Self-destruction through endless aggression
Environment: Anywhere in lost and lonely places
Health: 9
Damage Inflicted: 3 points
Movement: Short
Modifications: Speed defense as level 4 due to frenzied alacrity
Combat: Vat rejects charge into battle with berserk speed, hindering defenses against their initial attack. All vat rejects are able to inflict damage directly by cutting, bashing, or biting a victim, depending on their particular morphology. Some also have additional abilities; roll on the table below for each reject.

d6	Ability
1	Reject deals +3 damage in melee (6 points total)
2	Reject has short-range acid spit attack that inflicts 2 points of damage, plus 2 points of damage each additional round until victim succeeds on a Might defense roll
3	Reject can fly a long distance as an action
4	Reject has 2 Armor
5	Reject has long-range destructive eye ray attack that inflicts 6 points of damage
6	When struck by an attack, reject detonates in an immediate radius, inflicting 6 points of damage in a radioactive explosion (and 1 point even on a successful Speed defense roll)

Interaction: Vat rejects are usually always enraged, making interaction nearly impossible. However, some may negotiate if offered a reasonable hope of salvation through extreme surgery or other transformation.
Use: A long-missing derelict ship, famous for carrying a load of planet-buster superweapons, is found. However, salvagers discover it to be overrun by vat rejects. No one knows if the rejects plan to use the superweapons, if they have been released by someone else as a distraction, or if they are part of a mutated ship defense system.

GM intrusion: The vat reject also has a radioactive sting. On a failed Might defense roll, the character struck by the reject descends one step on the damage track.

WARDROID 6 (18)

When star troopers need heavy support, they sometimes bring in wardroids. These fearsome robots, standing about 8 feet (2 m) tall, are ruthless even by trooper standards and are known to kill innocent bystanders as often as they kill foes. It is said that when wardroids are unleashed, wise troopers fall back and take cover.

Motive: Maintain control, crush, kill, destroy
Environment: Anywhere
Health: 30
Damage Inflicted: 8 points
Armor: 3
Movement: Short; some models can fly a short distance each round
Modifications: Attacks as level 7
Combat: A wardroid's main weapon is a bank of laser blasters that it can use to attack up to three foes standing next to each other as one action. When damaged, a wardroid regains 1 point of health each round. Furthermore, each wardroid has one additional capability:

d6	Ability
1	Emit poison gas that inflicts 5 points of damage on organic beings in immediate range
2	Project grenades up to long distance that detonate in an immediate radius, inflicting 5 points of damage
3	Fire a beam that stuns an organic being for one round, during which it cannot take actions
4	Emit a field that disrupts machines; technological devices and machine creatures in immediate range cannot function for one round
5	Fire a piercing projectile up to long range that inflicts 6 points of damage that ignores physical armor (but not necessarily other Armor)
6	Spray a corrosive that inflicts 5 points of damage on everything in immediate range

Interaction: Interaction is difficult for those not authorized to communicate with a wardroid.
Use: Wardroids are often deployed in groups of two or three to guard a vault or the entrance to a spacecraft, or to track down intruders aboard a space station.
Loot: The remains of a wardroid can yield one or two cyphers to someone adept at salvage.

Star troopers are guards; see page 374.

GM intrusion: When defeated, the wardroid detonates, inflicting 8 points of damage on all creatures within immediate range.

WENDIGO   5 (15)

Eating human flesh is taboo. Violators face a terrible curse, one that strips them of their humanity and turns them into terrifying monsters filled with an unnatural craving to eat their former kin. Driven to the hinterlands, they hibernate until winter begins to tighten its grip. With the first snows come the wendigos, and they prowl the darkest hours in search of people to snatch and devour.

The curse that transforms a person into a wendigo destroys much of their humanity, leaving behind a skeletal body, bones pressing against taut skin, and eyes sunken into skull-like visages, flicking back and forth for any signs of life. With gnarled fingers ending in long claws and mouths filled with sharp black teeth, wendigos have everything they need to pull apart their victims and stuff their greedy maws with raw flesh.

Motive: Hungers for flesh

Environment: Solitary hunters, wendigos drift like ghosts through the snow-covered plains.

Health: 20

Damage Inflicted: 5 points

Movement: Short

Modifications: All tasks related to intimidation and perception as level 7; Intellect defense as level 6 when hungry

Combat: A reek of decay and death betrays a wendigo's approach. At first, the stench is nothing more than a malodorous presence, but as the wendigo draws nearer, the smell becomes overpowering. Any foe within a short distance of a wendigo must make a Might defense roll or become sickened. The affected victim's tasks are hindered. The victim can use an action to roll again and shake off the effects of the stench on a success.

A wendigo attacks foes with its teeth or claws. A foe who takes damage must make a Might defense roll or suffer as the wendigo tears free a gobbet of flesh. The bleeding wound inflicts 1 point of ambient damage each round until the target uses an action to stanch the wound.

Interaction: A wendigo gripped by unnatural hunger thinks about nothing else. After the creature feeds, it becomes lucid for a while—usually no more than a few hours—before the hunger pangs return. During its lucid period, it may regret what it's become, look for those it left behind, or take some other similarly motivated action.

Use: Locals make a regular offering of flesh to a wendigo to protect their people. They prefer to use outsiders as the offerings, and the PCs seem ideally suited to keep the creature at bay.

> **GM intrusion:** A wendigo howl causes nearby animals to panic and flee, possibly trampling a character in their path, throwing them from their saddle, or otherwise discomfiting them.

WEREWOLF   4 (12)

The curse of lycanthropy begins as nightmares about being chased or, somehow more terrifying, chasing someone else. As the dreams grow more fierce and each night's sleep provides less rest, victims begin to wonder about the bloodstains on their clothing, the strange claw marks in their homes, and eventually, the mutilated bodies they find buried in their backyards.

When not transformed, many who suffer the curse seem like completely normal people, if emotionally traumatized by the fact that most of their friends and family have been brutally slaughtered over the preceding months. Some few, however, realize the truth of their condition, and depending on their natures, they either kill themselves before their next transformation or learn to revel in the butchery.

Motive: Slaughter when transformed; searching for answers when human
Environment: Anywhere dark, usually alone but sometimes as part of a small pack of two to five
Health: 24
Damage Inflicted: 5 points
Movement: Short; long when in wolf form
Modifications: Attacks as level 6 when half lupine; Speed defense as level 6 when full lupine; perception as level 7 when half or full lupine
Combat: In normal human form, a werewolf has no natural attacks, though it may use a weapon. It also lacks the abilities described below; its only power is to transform into a half-lupine form or full-lupine form, which takes 1d6 agonizing rounds. A handful of werewolves can control their transformation, but most change at night in response to moon-related cues.
Half Lupine: A half-lupine werewolf is part humanoid and part wolf, but completely terrifying. It attacks with its claws.
Full Lupine: A full-lupine werewolf is a particularly large and vicious-looking wolf. It normally bites foes and deals 2 additional points of damage (7 points total) but can also use its claws.
Half and Full Lupine: Half-lupine and full-lupine werewolves both enjoy enhanced senses and regain 2 points of health per round. However, a werewolf that takes damage from a silver weapon or bullet stops regenerating for several minutes.
Interaction: In human form, werewolves have the goals and aspirations of normal people, and they often don't recall what they did while transformed or even realize that they suffer the curse of lycanthropy. In half- or full-lupine form, there's no negotiating with one.
Use: When the moon is full, werewolves hunt.

Favorite methods for curing a werewolf include medicine (wolfsbane), surgery, or exorcism. Many "cures" are effective only because they kill the werewolf in human form before the next transformation.

GM intrusion: *A PC who moves down one step on the damage track due to damage inflicted by a werewolf must succeed on a Might defense roll or be afflicted with the curse of lycanthropy.*

WITCH   5 (15)

They studied the old ways at the dark of the moon. They heard the shuffle of unnamed things through the darkling forest, watched the convection of the bubbles rise in the cauldron, and attended to the mumbled instructions of withered crones and crumbling messages traced on dead leaves. Then one midnight, everything came together. Another witch was born.

When witches lose sight of their humanity and use their powers for personal gain without regard for others, they are warped by the power they channel, both mentally and physically. However, they can hide such transformations beneath layers of illusion.

Motive: Domination of others, knowledge

Environment: Almost anywhere, usually alone, but sometimes as part of a coven of three to seven witches

Health: 21

Damage Inflicted: 5 points

Movement: Short; long when flying (on a broomstick)

Modifications: Deception and disguise as level 7; Speed defense as level 6 due to familiar; knowledge of forests and dark secrets as level 6

Combat: When attacked, a witch relies on the aid of their familiar to improve their Speed defense. The familiar could be a large black cat, an owl, a big snake, or some other creature. Killing a witch's familiar is so shocking to a witch that their attacks and Speed defense are hindered for a few days. It's also a way to ensure that the witch never forgives their foe or grants mercy.

A witch can use their ritual blade to attack a creature in immediate range, but would much rather use curses, including the ones described below. A witch can't use the same curse more than once every other round.

Charm: Victims within short range who fail an Intellect defense roll are enslaved. Victims turn on their allies or take some other action described by their new master. The curse lasts for one minute, or until the victims succeed on an Intellect defense roll; each time they fail a roll, the next roll is hindered by one additional step.

Hexbolt: A victim within long range is attacked with fire, cold, or psychic bolts, as the witch chooses. Psychic bolts deal 3 points of Intellect damage (ignores Armor).

Shrivel: A victim within long range and up to two creatures next to the victim must succeed on a Might defense roll or take 3 points of Speed damage (ignores Armor). In each subsequent round, a victim who failed the previous roll must make another Might defense roll with the same outcome on failure.

Vitality: The witch regains 11 points of health and gains +3 to Armor for one minute. Multiple uses don't further improve Armor.

Interaction: Most witches are deceptive and conniving, though a few work against the stereotype. All witches are willing to negotiate, though the devious ones usually do so in bad faith.

Use: The PCs need an old book to continue their investigation. Word is that the old woman who lives on the edge of the woods has the only copy.

Loot: A witch usually has an artifact or two on their person, possibly including a flying broom (which has a depletion roll of 1 in 1d10).

Familiar: level 3; health 9; Armor 1

Both women and men can practice witchcraft. A male witch is no less foreboding or dangerous, but given that the tradition was developed by women, most witches consider males to be lesser practitioners.

GM intrusion: After a character succeeds on a defense roll against one of the witch's ongoing curse effects, the witch immediately tosses a hexbolt at them. If the character is hit, the ongoing curse effect also continues.

XENOPARASITE 6 (18)

This alien creature exists only to eat and reproduce. In doing so, it also destroys every form of life it encounters. Xenoparasites are not technological but were likely engineered by a species with advanced biological super-science. Xenoparasites don't travel between star systems on their own; they were presumably spread across an area of space by their creators to serve as a broad-spectrum bioweapon. What has become of the original maker species is unknown, but given the fecundity and ferocity of the xenoparasite, it's likely they were consumed by their own creation.

Xenoparasites use ovipositors to lay thousands of microscopic eggs in victims. The implanted eggs, like tiny biological labs, detect the particular biology of the new host, adapt accordingly, and use it to fertilize themselves. Within a day or two, victims who haven't already been consumed by adult xenoparasites (which are human sized) give explosive birth to multiple vicious juveniles (which are the size of cats). These juvenile xenoparasites have an edge in dealing with the particular species of creature they hatched from.

Motive: Eat and reproduce
Environment: Hunts alone or in small groups
Health: 28
Damage Inflicted: 6 points
Armor: 2
Movement: Short; long when flying
Modifications: All stealth actions as level 8
Combat: A xenoparasite bites with its mandibles and stings one victim with its ovipositor as a single action. The bite inflicts 6 points of damage, and the ovipositor inflicts 3 points of damage and injects thousands of microscopic eggs if the victim fails a Might defense roll.

Once every other round, an adult can fly at least a short distance to build terrifying velocity and then make a flying attack with its mandibles, dealing 12 points of damage. Defenses against this attack are hindered.

An egg host requires the attention of someone skilled in medicine (and a successful difficulty 7 Intellect-based roll) to sterilize all the eggs in the victim's blood before they hatch twenty or more hours after being deposited, which kills the host and releases 1d6 juvenile xenoparasites. Juveniles are level 2 creatures, but they attack the species of the host they were hatched from as if level 4. After just a few days of feeding, they grow to full adult size.

Xenoparasites can survive at crushing ocean and gas giant pressures, as well as in the vacuum of space. They can encrust abandoned spacecraft and desolate moons for millennia in extended hibernation, only to become active again when vibrations alert them to potential new food sources.

Interaction: These creatures are built to consume, not negotiate.
Use: Xenoparasites are tough aliens. A colony of them would be a challenge even for PCs normally accustomed to stiff opposition. A single xenoparasite introduced into an inhabited area could turn the entire place into an infested hive within a week.

Adult xenoparasites build sprawling, wasplike nests in the areas they infest, using the nest as a base from which to slowly spread their influence. Whole space stations, moons, and planets have been covered in convoluted white nests crawling with death.

GM (group) intrusion: *An NPC shrieks, bursts, and births 1d6 juvenile xenoparasites.*

ZHEV   5 (15)

The zhev are robotic entities who often serve as the peacekeeping force in technologically advanced cities. They are cylinders 6 feet (2 m) high and 3 feet (1 m) in diameter, and they typically hover 3 feet (1 m) off the ground.

The zhev have three triangular eyes that appear to be organic. The eyes usually stay together in a larger triangle formation, moving inside the cylinder, peering through a slit near the top that goes all the way around. The eyes can also separate, each looking in a different direction, but they do this rarely. Although the zhev are essentially automatons, they have organic interior components as well as mechanical parts.

The zhev usually patrol in pairs but sometimes do so alone, preventing infractions of the law and acting to keep order, keep the peace, and protect the lives of innocents. When forced to choose between options, they always make the choice that saves the most people from the greatest harm. Protecting innocents takes priority over enforcing laws. Some people assume they were manufactured for their role as a peacekeeping force, but their origins aren't clear.

Motive: Maintain order
Environment: Anywhere the zhev have been retained to keep the peace
Health: 20
Damage Inflicted: 6 points
Armor: 4
Movement: Long
Modifications: Attacks as level 6; perception and knowledge of local law as level 7
Combat: The zhev usually begin a fight by firing stun gas canisters at long range that explode and impede actions for creatures within immediate range of the blast. Affected targets can take no actions for 1d6 rounds unless they make a Might defense roll to resist the gas. The zhev also project nets within short range that immobilize struck targets unless they can break or wriggle free (a Might or Speed task). If the gas and nets fail, zhev attack with their metallic arms that are 10 feet (3 m) long and jointed like tentacles. The zhev have three such arms and can attack three different foes as a single action if they are all within reach.

Unlike many robots, the zhev retreat if faced with a more powerful foe (unless they have been commanded to stay and fight). They usually try to get reinforcements and then return to engage the enemy.

Interaction: The zhev obey the orders given to them by their superiors, if any. More important, they follow codified law in the area and may use a special interpretation of a law to supersede a command, especially if someone offers them such an interpretation. Otherwise, they are relentless and merciless, although they are ordered to capture criminals rather than use violent or lethal force if at all possible.

Use: The zhev are dangerous, capable law enforcers and protectors. Where they are deployed, they are well respected but not always well liked. PCs who run afoul of them have likely done something very wrong.

Loot: The body of a zhev can be scavenged for 1d6 + 1 cyphers, and perhaps an artifact.

GM intrusion: The zhev grabs a character with its metallic arms and holds them fast, immobilizing them.

ZOMBIE 3 (9)

Humans transformed into aggressive, hard-to-kill serial killers with no memory of their former existence are called zombies. Depending on a zombie's origin, the reason for its transformation varies. A zombie might arise from an undead curse, a psychic possession, an AI meatware overwrite, a viral infection, a drug overdose, or something else. Regardless of how the transformation happened, the result is much the same: a creature whose humanity has been burned out and replaced with unquenchable hunger.

Zombies aren't intelligent, but enough of them together sometimes exhibit emergent behavior, just as ants can coordinate activities across a colony. Thus, zombies alone or in small groups aren't an overwhelming threat for someone who has a baseball bat or can get away. But it's never wise to laugh off a zombie horde.

Motive: Hunger (for flesh, cerebrospinal fluid, certain human hormones, and so on)
Environment: Almost anywhere, in groups of five to seven, or in hordes of tens to hundreds
Health: 12
Damage Inflicted: 3 points
Movement: Immediate
Modifications: Speed defense as level 2
Combat: Zombies never turn away from a conflict. They fight on, no matter the odds, usually attacking by biting, but sometimes by tearing with hands made into claws by the erosion of skin over their finger bones.

When zombies attack in groups of five to seven individuals, they can make a single attack roll against one target as one level 5 creature, inflicting 5 points of damage.

Zombies are hard to finish off. If an attack would reduce a zombie's health to 0, it does so only if the number rolled in the attack was an even number; otherwise, the zombie is reduced to 1 point of health instead. This might result in a dismembered, gruesomely damaged zombie that is still moving. Zombies can see in the dark at short range.

"Fresh" zombies are vulnerable to electricity. The first time a zombie takes 5 or more points of damage from an electrical attack, it falls limp and unmoving. Assuming nothing interferes with the process, the zombie arises minutes or hours later without the vulnerability.

Some zombies are infectious. Their bites spread a level 8 disease that moves a victim down one step on the damage track each day a Might defense roll is failed. Victims killed by the disease later animate as zombies.

Interaction: Zombies groan when they see something that looks tasty. They do not reason, cannot speak, and never stop pursuing something they've identified as a potential meal, unless something else edible comes closer.

Use: The characters are asked to clear out a space that once served as an old military depot. The appearance of zombies sealed in the area comes as an unpleasant surprise.

GM intrusion: *When the character fails to kill a zombie by rolling an odd number on an attack that otherwise would have been successful, in addition to the normal effect, the zombie's arm comes free and animates as a separate level 2 zombie.*

Chapter 23

NPCs

NPCs by Level	
Guard	2
Crime boss	3
Detective	3
Thug	3
Occultist	5
Secret agent	5
Assassin	6
Wizard, mighty	8

The NPCs in this chapter are generic examples of nonplayer characters that can be used in many genres.

Reskinning NPCs: GMs will find that with a few tweaks, a guard can be a modern-day cop, a fantasy caravan guard, or a science fiction drone soldier. This is known as reskinning—making slight changes to existing stats to customize the NPC for your own game.

Health, Not Pools: Remember that NPCs don't have stat Pools. Instead, they have a characteristic called health. When an NPC takes damage of any kind, the amount is subtracted from its health. Unless described otherwise, an NPC's health is always equal to its target number. Some NPCs might have special reactions to or defenses against attacks that would normally deal Speed damage or Intellect damage, but unless the NPC's description specifically explains this, assume that all damage is subtracted from the NPC's health.

Appropriate Weapons: NPCs use weapons appropriate to their situation, which might be swords and crossbows, knives and shotguns, malefic psychic weapons, blasters and grenades, and so on.

OTHER NPCs

Many NPCs are simple and understandable enough to be encapsulated just by their level and a few other other relevant stats.

Cannibal: level 3, deception and other interaction tasks as level 6; health 12

Hacker: level 2; programming, digital infiltration, and repairing computers as level 7

Mad scientist: level 4, most actions as level 6 due to gadgets, serums, artifacts, etc.

Marauder: level 4, initiative and intimidation as level 7; health 28; Armor 1

Master detective: level 5; perception, intuition, initiative, and detecting falsehood as level 9

Politician: level 2, all interaction tasks as level 6

Priest: level 2, religious lore and all interaction tasks as level 6

Professor: level 2, knowledge of science and all interaction tasks as level 6

Soldier: level 3, perception as level 4; health 12; Armor 1; attacks inflict 5 points of damage

ASSASSIN 6 (18)

An assassin kills with poison, with high-velocity bullets from a distance, or by arranging for an unfortunate accident. Assassins accept contracts from governments, corporations, crime bosses, and aggrieved former partners, though some assassins pay themselves by tracking criminals anywhere to collect on "dead or alive" bounties.

Motive: Murder (usually for hire)
Health: 18
Damage Inflicted: 6 points
Armor: 1
Movement: Short
Modifications: Stealth and deception tasks as level 8; when attacking from hiding, melee and ranged attacks as level 7
Combat: An assortment of small weapons are hidden about an assassin's body. They can also coat their weapons or ammo with a level 6 poison that moves victims who fail a Might defense roll one step down the damage track.
Interaction: Some assassins have a sort of integrity about their work and can't be dissuaded from completing their contracts with bribes.
Use: An assassin is greatly feared by anyone with powerful, wealthy enemies.
Loot: Aside from their weapons and poisons, most assassins have currency equivalent to a very expensive item and maybe one or two cyphers.

GM intrusion: The character loses their next turn, stunned, after recognizing the assassin to be the same murderer who killed someone important to them in the past.

CRIME BOSS 3 (9)

A crime boss usually isn't physically powerful but wields power through lies, bribery, and control. Rarely encountered alone, they rely on guards, thugs, and other measures to provide physical security. A crime boss could be a petty noble, a mafia king, or the captain of a pirate ship that sails the seas or glides the space lanes.

Motive: Money and power
Health: 12
Damage Inflicted: 5 points
Armor: 1
Movement: Short
Modifications: Deception, persuasion, intimidation, and tasks related to friendly interaction as level 7
Combat: Guards, thugs, and other followers deal 1 additional point of damage when the crime boss can see them and issue commands. If possible, crime bosses fight while mounted or in a vehicle, directing their followers from the rear of any conflict, concentrating first on issuing orders.
Interaction: Crime bosses are committed to their plans, whatever those might be. Most bosses rely on a lieutenant or trusted thug to interact with people in their place.
Use: A crime boss and their followers execute a heist on a secure location and take hostages when things go south. Someone must go in and talk to the crime boss to defuse the situation.
Loot: A crime boss has currency equivalent to a very expensive item in addition to weapons, medium armor, and miscellaneous gear.

GM intrusion: The crime boss uses a clever trick or cypher to block all incoming attacks in a given round of combat.

DETECTIVE 3 (9)

Detectives are usually veterans of their organization (such as the police, city watch, marshals, space command, and so on) with extensive experience. Some detectives are freelance sleuths whose uncanny ability to see the truth comes from personal training combined with an underlying talent for noticing clues that others miss.

Motive: Solve the crime
Health: 12
Damage Inflicted: 4 points
Movement: Short
Modifications: Tasks relating to perception, intuition, initiative, and detecting falsehoods as level 6
Combat: Detectives prefer to outwit their foes rather than engage in a straight-up fight. Even then, most conflicts occur in a place and time of the detective's choosing, preferably in the presence of their allies. A detective can deduce weaknesses of their enemies (if any) and exploit them in combat.
Interaction: Some detectives are insufferable know-it-alls. Others have learned that humility is also a useful tool for getting answers from people.
Use: To the PCs, detectives can be obstacles (a detective is on their trail), allies (a detective helps them assemble clues), or both, but the sleuths are rarely a way for the characters to hand off responsibility for accomplishing a hard task.
Loot: Aside from their weapons, most detectives have currency equivalent to a very expensive item and a cypher.

GM intrusion: The detective intuits the character's next attack and moves perfectly so that an ally of the character takes the attack instead.

GUARD 2 (6)

Guards keep the peace but don't usually show much initiative. Ultimately, they do as they're ordered by their superiors, regardless of legality. A guard might be a star trooper dressed in intimidating armor, a mall security guard, a beat police officer, or a mafia goon.

Motive: Keep the peace; follow orders
Health: 8
Damage Inflicted: 3 points
Armor: 1 or 2
Movement: Short
Modifications: Perception as level 3
Combat: Guards are not often wily, but they understand strength in numbers. If two or more guards attack the same target with at least one melee attack in the same round, the target's Speed defense roll against those attacks is hindered.
Interaction: Interacting with a guard typically involves one issue: does the PC want to do something that the guard has been told to prevent? If so, the PC could have a difficult time.
Use: To the PCs, guards can be allies, obstacles, or both. Guards who serve the public good have their own duties and aren't interested in doing the characters' work for them.
Loot: A guard has currency equivalent to an inexpensive item in addition to weapons, armor, and basic gear.

When attacked, guards always call for the help of other guards, if possible.

GM intrusion: 1d6 local citizens intervene on the guard's behalf, calling for more guards or even fighting the guard's foes.

OCCULTIST   5 (15)

Paranormal researchers, cultists, secret practitioners of white magic, and coven members might be occultists. Thanks to their study of the metaphysical, occultists learn several magical tricks, including the ability to summon or banish the dead.

Health: 15
Damage Inflicted: 5 points
Movement: Short
Modifications: Knowledge of occult topics and rituals as level 8; ability to detect lies and tricks as level 2
Combat: An occultist has a charm or device for summoning a level 5 spirit or demon that will do their bidding for ten minutes. Some also have (or instead have) a spell, item, or device that inflicts 5 points of damage on normal creatures within long range, and 10 points of damage on a demon or spirit (or, instead of dealing extra damage, the effect confines the demon or spirit in some way).
Interaction: Occultists are deeply concerned with spiritual or demonic matters and see those influences in all things, whether those influences exist or not. That makes them amenable to persuasion and deception, if couched in the language of spiritual influence.
Use: To find a needed answer, the spirit of a dead person must be questioned. Alternatively, a haunting presence must be banished. Either way, the task requires an occultist.
Loot: In addition to their clothing and mundane weapons, occultists have currency equivalent to an inexpensive item, a cypher, and possibly an artifact related to their power over spirits or demons.

GM intrusion: *A bony hand erupts from the ground at the character's feet. On a failed Speed defense roll, they are held in place until they succeed on a Might-based task to escape. Each round the character fails to escape, the hand squeezes for 3 points of damage.*

SECRET AGENT   5 (15)

Secret agents are trained professionals who put their mission before their own well-being, regardless of which government agency, corporation, guild, or kingdom employs them. An agent operates under a fake cover, perhaps as an envoy, inspector, technician, actor, tourist, or bumbling fool.

Motive: Accomplish the goals of the employer while maintaining cover
Health: 15
Damage Inflicted: 5 points
Movement: Short
Modifications: Tasks related to disguise and deceiving as level 6
Combat: A secret agent always has a covert, unexpected backup weapon that they can use to make a surprise attack, such as a ring or glove with a hidden poisoned needle (dealing 5 points of Speed damage that ignore Armor), a fake tooth filled with poison gas to blow in a victim's face (inducing sleep for ten minutes), or a ring with a miniature gun.
Interaction: Secret agents are confident, masterful, and always give the impression of being one step ahead of the game, even when caught off guard.
Use: As an ally, a secret agent can guide the PCs to their next mission, fill in gaps in their knowledge, and warn them of dangers. If the characters encounter an unfriendly agent, the NPC likely pretends to be a friend.
Loot: Agents typically have currency equivalent to an expensive item, a couple of cyphers, tools for spying and maintaining their cover, and possibly an artifact.

GM intrusion: *The secret agent produces a cypher that, for the rest of the day, eases all tasks by two steps.*

THUG — 3 (9)

Thugs are usually rough, crude, and harsh individuals who prey on those who follow the rules. A thug might be a streetwise drug dealer, a bandit who hunts lone travelers in the wilds, a savage warrior adroit with ranged weapons, or a cyberbully among pacifists. Most thugs work for themselves, but they may employ gangs of guards to help them conduct their business.

Motive: Take what they want
Health: 9
Damage Inflicted: 4 points
Armor: 1
Movement: Short
Combat: Thugs prefer ambushes, making ranged attacks from hiding if possible. Sometimes they spoil the ambush to issue an ultimatum before attacking: give us your valuables or you'll be sorry.
Interaction: Thugs are interested in money and power, which means they almost always accept bribes. If faced with a real threat, thugs usually retreat.
Use: Thugs are everywhere, sometimes accompanied by guards who are equally malicious but not quite as powerful.
Loot: A thug has currency equivalent to an inexpensive item in addition to weapons, shields, and light armor. One thug in a group might have a cypher.

GM intrusion: Another thug, hidden until just the right moment, appears and takes a shot with a ranged weapon before joining the fray.

WIZARD, MIGHTY — 8 (24)

Some wizards learn so many spells and accumulate so much lore that they become incredibly powerful. Some work for a higher purpose, whereas others are concerned only with themselves.

Motive: Seek powerful sources of magic (to collect or to keep safe)
Health: 40
Damage Inflicted: 8 points
Movement: Short
Modifications: All tasks related to knowledge of arcane lore as level 9
Combat: When a wizard makes a long-range attack with their staff or strikes someone with it, arcane energy damages the target and, if desired, all creatures the wizard selects within short range of the target. Targets that are within immediate range of the wizard when they take damage are thrown out of immediate range.
A mighty wizard knows many spells, including spells that grant +5 to Armor for an hour, spells of teleportation, spells of finding, and so on. A wizard also likely carries several cyphers useful in combat.
Interaction: Care should be taken when negotiating with wizards because they are subtle and quick to anger. Even when negotiations succeed, a wizard's suggestions are usually cryptic and open to interpretation. A mighty wizard might be convinced to teach a character how to cast a spell.
Use: A wizard is putting together a team to challenge a great foe, and the PCs fit the bill.
Loot: A mighty wizard has 1d6 cyphers.

GM intrusion: The wizard casts two spells as a single action instead of just one.

CHAPTER 24

CYPHERS

Cyphers are one-use abilities that characters gain over the course of play. They have cool powers that can heal, make attacks, ease or hinder task rolls, or (in a more supernatural and extreme example) produce effects such as nullifying gravity or turning something invisible.

Most cyphers aren't physical objects—just something useful that happens right when you need it. They might be a burst of insight that allows a character to make a perfectly executed attack, a lucky guess when using a computer terminal, a coincidental distraction that gives you an advantage against an NPC, or a supernatural entity that makes things work out in your favor. In some games, cyphers come in the form of items, like magic potions or bits of alien technology.

Cyphers that don't have a physical form are called subtle cyphers.

Cyphers that have a physical form are called manifest cyphers.

Regardless of their form, cyphers are single-use effects and are always consumed when used. Unless a cypher's description says otherwise, it works only for the character who activates it. For example, a PC can't use an enduring shield cypher on a friend.

Cyphers are a game mechanic designed for frequent discovery and use. PCs can have only a small number of cyphers at any given time, and since they're always finding more, they're encouraged to use them at a steady pace.

In theory, the cyphers gained by the PCs are determined randomly. However, the GM can allow PCs to acquire or find them intentionally as well. Cyphers are gained with such regularity that the PCs should feel that they can use them freely. There will always be more, and they'll have different benefits. This means that in gameplay, cyphers are less like gear or treasure and more like character abilities that the players don't choose. This leads to fun game moments where a player can say "Well, I've got an X that might help in this situation," and X is always different. X might be an intuitive understanding of the local computer network, a favor from the Faerie Court, an explosive device, a short-range teleporter, or a force field. It might be a powerful magnet or a prayer that will cure disease. It could be anything. Cyphers keep the game fresh and interesting. Over time, characters can learn how to safely carry more and more cyphers at the same time, so cyphers really do seem more like abilities and less like gear.

Cyphers don't have to be used to make room for new ones. For subtle cyphers, a character can just use an action to "lose" the cypher, freeing up space to "find" one later (once a subtle cypher is discarded this way, it is gone and can't be

"Carry" in this sense refers to both subtle cyphers and manifest cyphers, though a PC may not actually carry anything that physically represents the cypher. A character thrown into prison without their equipment might still have subtle cyphers.

Enduring shield, page 388

WHY CYPHERS?

Cyphers are (not surprisingly, based on the name) the heart of the Cypher System. This is because characters in this game have some abilities that rarely or never change and can always be counted on—pretty much like in all games—and they have some abilities that are ever-changing and inject a great deal of variability in play. They are the major reason why no Cypher System game session should ever be dull or feel just like the last session. This week your character can solve the problem by walking through walls, but last time it was because you could create an explosion that could level a city block.

The Cypher System, then, is one where PC abilities are fluid, with the GM and the players both having a role in their choice, their assignment, and their use. Although many things separate the game system from others, this aspect makes it unique, because cyphers recognize the importance and value of two things:

1. "Treasure," because character abilities make the game fun and exciting. In fact, in the early days of roleplaying, treasure (usually in the form of magic items found in dungeons) was really the only customization of characters that existed. One of the drives to go out and have adventures is so you can discover cool new things that help you when you go on even more adventures. This is true in many RPGs, but in the Cypher System, it's built right into the game's core.

2. Letting the GM have a hand in determining PC abilities makes the game move more smoothly. Some GMs prefer to roll cyphers randomly, but some do not. For example, giving the PCs a cypher that will allow them to teleport far away might be a secret adventure seed placed by a forward-thinking GM. Because the GM has an idea of where the story is going, they can use cyphers to help guide the path. Alternatively, if the GM is open to it, they can give out cyphers that enable the characters to take a more proactive role (such as teleporting anywhere they want). Perhaps most important, they can do these things without worrying about the long-term ramifications of the ability. A device that lets you teleport multiple times might really mess up the game over the long term. But once? That's just fun.

recovered). For manifest cyphers, it's perfectly acceptable for the PCs to stash one elsewhere for later use; of course, that doesn't mean it will still be there when they return.

CYPHER LIMITS

All characters have a maximum number of cyphers they can have at any one time, determined by their type. If a character ever attempts to carry more, random cyphers instantly disappear until the PC has a number of cyphers equal to their maximum (depending on the genre of the campaign, subtle cyphers may be more or less likely to vanish this way). These vanished cyphers are not recoverable.

SUBTLE CYPHERS

Subtle (nonphysical) cyphers are a way to introduce cyphers into a game without overt "powered stuff"—no potions, alien crystals, or anything of that nature. They're most useful, perhaps, in a modern or horror setting without obvious fantasy elements. Subtle cyphers are more like the inherent abilities PCs have, adding boosts to Edge, recovering points from Pools, coming up with ideas, and so on. In general, these are commonplace, non-supernatural effects—a subtle cypher wouldn't create a laser beam or allow a character to walk through a wall. They don't break the fragile bubble of believability in genres where flashy powers and abilities don't make a lot of sense.

Subtle cyphers are particularly nice in a genre where the PCs are supposed to be normal people. The cyphers can simply be an expression of innate capabilities in characters that aren't always dependable. And in many ways, that's probably more realistic than an ability you can count on with certainty, because in real life, some days you can jump over a fence, and some days you just can't.

Concepts for subtle cyphers include the following:

Good fortune: Once in a while, things just go your way. You're in the right place at the right time.

Inspirations: Sometimes you get inspired to do something you've never done before and might not be able to do again. Call it adrenaline mixed with the right motivation, or just doing the right thing at the right place at the right time. Who can really define it? Life's funny that way.

Alien concepts: Complex and utterly inhuman memes enter our world and worm their way into and out of human consciousness. When this happens, it can cause mental distress and disorientation. It can also grant impossible abilities and advantages.

Blessings: In a fantasy world, there are nine gods. Each morning, all intelligent residents of the world pray to one of the gods, and some of the faithful gain a divine blessing. Some people believe that praying to different gods gives you different blessings.

Earworms: You know how some songs pop into your head and just won't leave? There's a power to those songs, and the right people know how to harness it. Make the songs disturbing or reminiscent of evil chants, and you've got a perfect cypher concept for a horror campaign.

Mysterious transmissions: What's that buzzing? That mechanical chittering? Those numbers repeating over and over? And why can only some people hear it? A few who are aware of the sounds have learned how to make use of them.

Supernatural powers: Mental or mystical energies constantly shift and change, ebb and flow. But you've figured out how to attune your mind to them. There are no physical actions or paraphernalia required—just an inner conduit to the numinous.

DISCOVERING SUBTLE CYPHERS

Since subtle cyphers aren't physical objects, GMs will need to figure out when to give PCs new ones to replace the ones they have used. The cyphers probably shouldn't be tied to actions entirely under the characters' control—in other words, they shouldn't come as a result of meditation or anything of that nature. Instead, the GM should choose significant points in the story when new cyphers might simply come unbidden to the PCs. In the broader view, this is no different than manifest cyphers placed as treasure in a creature's lair, a secret cache, or somewhere else for the characters to find. Either way, the GM is picking good spots to "refill" potentially used cypher-based abilities.

Subtle cyphers are often found in groups of one to six (the GM can roll 1d6 to determine the number). The GM might randomly assign the cyphers to each PC who has space for more, or present a selection of cyphers to the group and allow the players to choose which ones they want for their characters. Characters should immediately know what their subtle cyphers do. If a PC activates a healing subtle cypher when they think it's something to help pick a lock, that's a waste of a useful character ability.

PCs might be able to obtain subtle cyphers from NPCs or in unusual circumstances as gifts, boons, or blessings, even asking for a particular kind of subtle cypher, such as healing, protection, or skill. For example, PCs who make a donation at a temple of a healing goddess could ask to receive a blessing (subtle cypher) that allows them to speak a healing prayer that restores points to one of their Pools. An NPC wizard who owes the PCs a favor might cast a spell on them that deflects one weapon if they say a magic word. An alien pylon might grant knowledge of a strange mental code that lets a person see in the dark for a few hours.

A PC can also acquire a new subtle cypher by spending 1 XP on one of the following player intrusions:

General cypher: You ask the GM for a general subtle cypher, such as "healing," "movement," "defense," or perhaps something as specific as "flight." The GM gives you a cypher that meets that description and randomly determines its level. If you don't have space for this cypher, you immediately lose one of your current cyphers (your choice) and the new cypher takes its place.

Specific cypher: You ask the GM for a specific subtle cypher (such as curative or stim) of a specific level. Make an Intellect roll with a difficulty equal to the cypher's level plus 1. If you have had this cypher before, the task is eased. If you fail the roll, you do not gain a cypher. If you succeed, the GM gives you that subtle cypher at that level. If you don't have space for this new cypher, you immediately lose one of your current cyphers (your choice) and the new cypher takes its place. Whether or not you succeed at the roll, the 1 XP is spent.

MANIFEST CYPHERS

Because manifest cyphers are physical objects, and people are familiar with the idea of finding "treasure" as part of playing an RPG, these kinds of cyphers are easy to get into the hands of the PCs. They are often found in groups of one to six (the GM can roll 1d6 to determine the number), usually because the characters are searching for them. They might be among the possessions of a fallen foe, hidden in a secret room, or scattered amid the wreckage of a crashed starship. The GM can prepare a list ahead of time of what successful searchers find. Sometimes this list is random, and sometimes there is logic behind it. For example, a warlock's laboratory might contain four different magic potions that the PCs can find.

If the characters search for cyphers, the GM sets the difficulty of the task. It is usually 3 or 4, and scavenging can take fifteen minutes to an hour.

Scavenging is not the only way to obtain manifest cyphers. They can also be given as gifts, traded with merchants, or sometimes purchased in a shop.

Unlike subtle cyphers, characters don't automatically know what manifest cyphers do. Once the PCs find a manifest cypher, identifying it is a separate task, based on Intellect and modified by knowledge of the topic at hand. In a fantasy setting, that knowledge would probably be magic, but in a science fiction setting, it might be technology. The GM sets the difficulty

Player intrusion, page 21

Curative, page 386
Stim, page 398

of the task, but it is usually 1 or 2. Thus, even the smallest amount of knowledge means that cypher identification is automatic. The process takes one to ten minutes. If the PCs can't identify a cypher, they can bring it to an expert for identification and perhaps trade, if desired.

MANIFEST CYPHERS DUPLICATING SUBTLE CYPHERS

Lots of overlap exists between what subtle cyphers and manifest cyphers can do. Nearly anything that can be explained as a subtle cypher can just as easily be a magic item, scientific device, or other manifest object. A bit of luck that helps you sneak (a subtle cypher) and a potion that helps you sneak (a manifest cypher) do the exact same thing for a character. One advantage of manifest cyphers is that characters can easily trade them to each other or sell them to NPCs. On the other hand, manifest cyphers can be dropped or stolen, and subtle cyphers can't.

It's fine if the GM decides to include both kinds of cyphers in the same game. A horror game could begin with the PCs as normal people with subtle cyphers, but as time goes on, they find one-use spells in occult tomes, weird potions, and bone dust that has strange powers.

USING CYPHERS

The action to use a cypher is Intellect based unless described otherwise or logic suggests otherwise. For example, throwing an explosive might be Speed based because the device is physical and not really technical, but using a ray emitter is Intellect based.

Because cyphers are single-use items, cyphers used to make attacks can never be used with the Spray or Arc Spray abilities that some characters might have. They are never treated as rapid-fire weapons.

Identified manifest cyphers can be used automatically. Once a manifest cypher is activated, if it has an ongoing effect, that effect applies only to the character who activated the cypher. A PC can't activate a cypher and then hand it to another character to reap the benefits.

A character can attempt to use a manifest cypher that has not been identified; this is usually an Intellect task using the cypher's level. Failure might mean that the PC can't figure out how to use the cypher or that they use it incorrectly (GM's discretion). Of course, even if the PC activates the unidentified cypher, they have no idea what its effect will be.

Spray, page 185
Arc Spray, page 110

Cyphers are meant to be used regularly and often. If PCs are hoarding or saving their cyphers, feel free to give them a reason to put the cyphers into play.

CYPHER LEVELS AND EFFECTS

All cyphers have a level and an effect. The level sometimes determines an aspect of the cypher's power (how much damage it inflicts, for example) but otherwise it only determines the general efficacy, the way level works with any object. The Level entry for a cypher is usually a die roll, sometimes with a modifier, such as 1d6 or 1d6 + 4. The GM can roll to determine the cypher's level, or can allow the player to roll when they receive the cypher.

NORMAL AND FANTASTIC EFFECTS

Cypher effects fall into two categories: normal and fantastic. Normal effects are things that could reasonably happen or be explained in the normal physical world we're familiar with. Fantastic effects are things that can't. A normal person could hit a target 240 feet (73 m) away with a football, quickly get over a cold, run across a tightrope, or multiply two two-digit numbers in their head. These tasks are difficult, but possible. A normal person can't throw an armored car, regrow a severed arm, create a robot out of thin air, or control gravity with their mind. These tasks are impossible according to the world as we know it. Cypher effects are either normal (possible) or fantastic (impossible according to the world as we know it).

Normal cypher effects should be available to PCs regardless of the genre of your game. It's perfectly reasonable for a modern, fantasy, horror, science fiction, or superhero PC to have a cypher that gives them a one-use bonus on an attack or skill task, lets them take a quick breather to recover a few points in a Pool, or helps them focus their will to avoid distractions or fatigue.

Fantastic cypher effects should be limited to games where magic, technology, or other factors stretch the definition of "impossible." A cypher that turns a corpse into a zombie is out of place in a non-fantastic modern game, but is perfectly reasonable for a fantasy, science fiction, or superhero game, or even a horror game where zombies exist, as long as the GM decides there is an appropriate story explanation for it. The zombie cypher might be a necromantic spell in a fantasy or superhero game, a code that activates a swarm of nanobots in a science fiction game, or a virus in a horror game. The rules categorize some cypher effects as fantastic to help the GM decide whether to exclude cyphers that don't fit the game they're running. For example, it is appropriate for a GM running a zombie horror survival game set in 1990s Georgia to allow the zombie-creating cypher but not a teleportation cypher, because creating a zombie is a fantastic effect that fits the setting and teleportation isn't.

Fantastic cyphers can be subtle or manifest.

You can choose or randomly determine fantastic cyphers using the Fantastic Cypher table. Reroll any result that feels inappropriate for the game.

OPTIONAL RULE: NORMAL CYPHERS DUPLICATING FANTASTIC EFFECTS

If the GM and players are willing to stretch their imaginations a bit, it's possible to include some fantastic cypher effects in a game where only normal cypher effects should exist, even if the PCs are only using subtle cyphers. The player using the cypher just needs to come up with a practical, realistic explanation for how the fantastic result occurred (perhaps with a much shorter or reduced effect than what's described in the cypher text).

For example, a PC with a phase changer who is trapped in a prison cell could say that instead of physically phasing through the wall, using the cypher means they find a long-forgotten secret door connected to a narrow hallway leading to safety. A PC with a fire detonation could say they notice a can of paint thinner in the room, kick it over, and throw a table lamp into the spill, creating a spark and a momentary burst of harmful flames. A PC with a monoblade could say they spot structural flaws in an opponent's armor, allowing them to attack for the rest of that combat in such a way that the foe's Armor doesn't count.

These interpretations of fantastic cyphers in a non-fantastic setting require player ingenuity and GM willingness to embrace creative solutions (similar to players using player intrusions to make a change in the game world). The GM always has the right to veto the explanation for the fantastic effect, allowing the player to choose a different action instead of using the fantastic cypher.

MANIFEST CYPHER FORMS

None of the manifest cyphers in this chapter have a stated physical form. The entries don't tell you if something is a potion, a pill, or a device you hold in your hands because that sort of detail varies greatly from genre to genre. Are they magic? Are they tech? Are they symbiotic creatures with programmed DNA? That's up to the GM. It's flavor, not mechanics. It's as important or unimportant as the style of an NPC's hair or the color of the car the bad guys are driving. In other words, it's the kind of thing that is important in a roleplaying game, but at the same time doesn't actually change anything (and RPGs have a lot of things like that, if you think about it).

A manifest cypher's physical form can be anything at all, but there are some obvious choices based on genre. The GM can design a setting that uses just one type—for example, a magical world where all cyphers are potions made by faeries. Or they can use many types, perhaps mixing them from different genres. Some suggestions include the following.

Fantastic Cypher table, page 382

Phase changer, page 394
Fire detonation, page 386
Monoblade, page 393
Player intrusion, page 21

Historical settings will normally feature only subtle cyphers, unless it's a mash-up with a genre that has fantastic elements.

MANIFEST CYPHER FORM OPTIONS

Fantasy/Fairy Tale
Potions
Scrolls
Runeplates
Tattoos
Charms
Powders
Crystals
Books with words of power

Modern/Romance
Drugs (injections, pills, inhalants)
Viruses
Smartphone apps

Science Fiction/Post-Apocalyptic
Drugs (injections, pills, inhalants)
Computer programs
Crystals
Gadgets
Viruses
Biological implants
Mechanical implants
Nanotechnological injections

Horror
Burrowing worms or insects
Pages from forbidden books
Horrific images

Superhero
Forms from all the other genres

MANIFEST CYPHER TABLE

d100	Result
01–03	Adhesion
04–05	Antivenom
06–09	Armor reinforcer
10–11	Attractor
12–13	Blackout
14–15	Catholicon
16–17	Curse bringer
18–19	Death bringer
20–22	Density
23–26	Detonation
27–29	Detonation (flash)
30–31	Detonation (massive)
32–34	Detonation (pressure)
35–36	Detonation (sonic)
37–38	Detonation (spawn)
39–41	Detonation (web)
42–44	Equipment cache
45–46	Fireproofing
47–49	Friction reducer
50–52	Gas bomb
53–55	Hunter/seeker
56–57	Infiltrator
58–60	Information sensor
61–63	Metal death
64–65	Nullification ray
66–68	Poison (emotion)
69–70	Poison (mind disrupting)
71–73	Radiation spike
74–76	Remote viewer
77–79	Shocker
80–82	Sleep inducer
83–85	Sniper module
86–88	Solvent
89–90	Spy
91–92	Tracer
93–94	Uninterruptible power source
95–96	Warmth
97–98	Water adapter
99–00	X-ray viewer

FANTASTIC CYPHER TABLE

d100	Result
01	Age taker
02	Banishing
03–04	Blinking
05	Chemical factory
06	Comprehension
07–08	Condition remover
09	Controlled blinking
10	Detonation (creature)
11	Detonation (desiccating)
12	Detonation (gravity)
13	Detonation (gravity inversion)
14	Detonation (matter disruption)
15	Detonation (singularity)
16	Disguise module
17	Disrupting
18	Farsight
19	Flame-retardant wall
20	Force cube
21–22	Force field
23	Force screen projector
24	Force shield projector

d100	Cypher
25	Frigid wall
26–27	Gravity nullifier
28	Gravity-nullifying application
29–30	Heat attack
31	Image projector
32	Inferno wall
33–34	Instant servant
35	Instant shelter
36	Lightning wall
37–38	Machine control
39	Magnetic attack drill
40	Magnetic master
41	Magnetic shield
42	Manipulation beam
43	Matter transference ray
44	Memory switch
45	Mental scrambler
46	Mind meld
47	Mind-restricting wall
48–49	Monoblade
50	Monohorn
51	Null field
52–53	Personal environment field
54–55	Phase changer
56	Phase disruptor
57	Poison (explosive)
58	Poison (mind controlling)
59	Psychic communique
60	Ray emitter
61	Ray emitter (command)
62	Ray emitter (fear)
63	Ray emitter (friend slaying)
64	Ray emitter (mind disrupting)
65	Ray emitter (numbing)
66	Ray emitter (paralysis)
67	Reality spike
68	Repair unit
69	Repeater
70–71	Retaliation
72	Sheen
73–74	Shock attack
75	Slave maker
76	Sonic hole
77–78	Sound dampener
79	Spatial warp
80	Stasis keeper
81	Subdual field
82–83	Telepathy
84	Teleporter (bounder)
85	Teleporter (interstellar)
86	Teleporter (planetary)
87	Teleporter (traveler)
88	Temporal viewer
89	Time dilation (defensive)
90	Time dilation (offensive)
91	Trick embedder
92	Vanisher
93–94	Visage changer
95	Visual displacement device
96	Vocal translator
97–98	Weapon enhancement
99	Wings
00	Zero point field

SUBTLE CYPHER TABLE

d100	Cypher
01–04	Analeptic
05–07	Best tool
08–10	Burst of speed
11–13	Contingent activator
14–17	Curative
18–20	Darksight
21–23	Disarm
24–26	Eagleseye
27–29	Effect resistance
30–32	Effort enhancer (combat)
33–35	Effort enhancer (noncombat)
36–39	Enduring shield
40–42	Intellect booster
43–45	Intelligence enhancement
46–48	Knowledge enhancement
49–51	Meditation aid
52–54	Mind stabilizer
55–57	Motion sensor
58–60	Nutrition and hydration
61–63	Perfect memory
64–66	Perfection
67–69	Reflex enhancer
70–73	Rejuvenator
74–76	Remembering
77–79	Repel
80–82	Secret
83–85	Skill boost
86–88	Speed boost
89–91	Stim
92–94	Strength boost
95–97	Strength enhancer
98–00	Tissue regeneration

CYPHER SYSTEM

TYPES OF CYPHERS

 SUBTLE

 MANIFEST

 FANTASTIC

A LISTING OF VARIOUS CYPHERS

All cyphers in this section without a symbol may be subtle cyphers. Those that are usually manifest cyphers are marked with a symbol. Cyphers with fantastic effects (including cyphers with a mix of normal and fantastic effects) are marked with a symbol. (But as previously noted, lots of cyphers can be either manifest or subtle, and some fantastic cyphers could be reinterpreted to gain their effect through normal means.)

ADHESION
Level: 1d6
Effect: Allows for automatic climbing of any surface, even horizontal ones. Lasts for ten minutes per cypher level.

AGE TAKER
Level: 1d6 + 4
Effect: Begins a process of rejuvenation that removes years from the wearer's physiological age. Over the course of the next seven days, the wearer sheds a number of years equal to three times the cypher's level. The cypher doesn't regress physiological age past the age of twenty-three.

ANALEPTIC
Level: 1d6 + 2
Effect: Restores a number of points equal to the cypher's level to the user's Speed Pool.

ANTIVENOM
Level: 1d6 + 2
Effect: Renders user immune to poisons of the cypher's level or lower for one hour per cypher level (and ends any such ongoing effects, if any, already in the user's system).

ARMOR REINFORCER
Level: 1d6 + 1
Effect: The user's Armor gains an enhancement for twenty-four hours. Roll a d6 to determine the result.

1	+1 to Armor
2	+2 to Armor
3	+3 to Armor
4	+2 to Armor, +5 against damage from fire
5	+2 to Armor, +5 against damage from cold
6	+2 to Armor, +5 against damage from acid

ATTRACTOR
Level: 1d6 + 4
Effect: One unanchored item the user's size or smaller within long range (very long range if the cypher level is 8 or higher) is drawn immediately to them. This takes one round. The item has no momentum when it arrives.

BANISHING
Level: 1d6
Effect: For the next day, each time the user strikes a solid creature or object, it generates a burst of energy that teleports the creature or object an immediate distance in a random direction (not up or down). The teleported creature's actions (including defense) are hindered on its next turn (hindered by two steps if the cypher level is 5 or higher).

BEST TOOL
Level: 1d6
Effect: Provides an additional asset for any one task using a tool, even if that means exceeding the normal limit of two assets.

BLACKOUT
Level: 1d6 + 2
Effect: An area within immediate range of the user becomes secure against any effect outside the area that sees, hears, or otherwise senses what occurs inside. To outside observers, the area is a "blur" to any sense applied. Taps, scrying sensors, and other direct surveillance methods are also rendered inoperative within the area for a day.

 BLINKING

Level: 1d6

Effect: For the next day, each time the user is struck hard enough to take damage (but not more than once per round), they teleport an immediate distance in a random direction (not up or down). Since the user is prepared for this effect and their foe is not, the user's defenses are eased for one round after they teleport.

BURST OF SPEED

Level: 1d6

Effect: For one minute, a user who normally can move a short distance as an action can move a long distance instead.

 CATHOLICON

Level: 1d6 + 2

Effect: Cures any disease of the cypher level or lower.

 CHEMICAL FACTORY

Level: 1d6

Effect: After one hour, the sweat of the user produces 1d6 doses of a valuable liquid (these doses are not considered cyphers). They must be used within one week. Roll a d100 to determine the effect.

01–04	Euphoric for 1d6 hours
05–08	Hallucinogenic for 1d6 hours
09–12	Stimulant for 1d6 hours
13–16	Depressant for 1d6 hours
17–20	Nutrient supplement
21–25	Antivenom
26–30	Cures disease
31–35	See in the dark for one hour
36–45	Restores a number of Might Pool points equal to cypher level
46–55	Restores a number of Speed Pool points equal to cypher level
56–65	Restores a number of Intellect Pool points equal to cypher level
66–75	Increases Might Edge by 1 for one hour
76–85	Increases Speed Edge by 1 for one hour
86–95	Increases Intellect Edge by 1 for one hour
96–00	Restores all Pools to full

 COMPREHENSION

Level: 1d6 + 1

Effect: Within five minutes, the user can understand the words of a specific language keyed to the cypher (two languages if the cypher is level 5 or higher). This is true even of creatures that do not normally have a language. If the user could already understand the language, the cypher has no effect. Once the cypher is used, the effect is permanent, and the cypher no longer counts against the number of cyphers that a PC can bear.

CONDITION REMOVER

Level: 1d6 + 3

Effect: Cures one occurrence of one specific health condition of the cypher level or lower. It does not prevent the possibility of future occurrences of the same condition. Roll a d20 to determine what it cures.

1	Addiction to one substance
2	Autoimmune disease
3	Bacterial infection
4	Bad breath
5	Blisters
6	Bloating
7	Cancer
8	Chapped lips
9	Flatus
10	Hangover
11	Heartburn
12	Hiccups
13	Ingrown hairs
14	Insomnia
15	Joint problem
16	Muscle cramp
17	Pimples
18	Psychosis
19	Stiff neck
20	Viral infection

CYPHER SYSTEM

TYPES OF CYPHERS

 SUBTLE

 MANIFEST

 FANTASTIC

All damaging detonations inflict a minimum of 2 points of damage to those in the radius, regardless of attack or defense rolls.

CONTINGENT ACTIVATOR
Level: 1d6 + 2
Effect: If the device is activated in conjunction with another cypher, the user can specify a condition under which the linked cypher will activate. The linked cypher retains the contingent command until it is used (either normally or contingently). For example, when this cypher is linked to a cypher that provides a form of healing or protection, the user could specify that the linked cypher will activate if they become damaged to a certain degree or are subject to a particular dangerous circumstance. Until the linked cypher is used, this cypher continues to count toward the maximum number of cyphers a PC can carry.

CONTROLLED BLINKING
Level: 1d6 + 2
Effect: For the next day, each time the user is struck hard enough to inflict damage (but no more than once per round), they teleport to a spot they desire within immediate range. Since they are prepared for this effect and their foe is not, the user's defenses are eased for one round after they teleport.

CURATIVE
Level: 1d6 + 2
Effect: Restores a number of points equal to the cypher's level to the user's Might Pool.

CURSE BRINGER
Level: 1d6 + 1
Effect: The cypher can be activated when given to an individual who doesn't realize its significance. The next time the victim attempts an important task when the cypher is in their possession, the task is hindered by three steps.

DARKSIGHT
Level: 1d6
Effect: Grants the ability to see in the dark for five hours per cypher level.

For a more realistic game, this cypher could instead make the user specialized in low-light spotting. See Illumination, page 220.

DEATH BRINGER
Level: 1d6
Effect: For the next minute, when the user strikes an NPC or creature of the cypher level or lower, they can choose to make a second attack roll. If the second attack roll is a success, the target is killed. If the target is a PC, the character instead moves down one step on the damage track.

DENSITY
Level: 1d6
Effect: For the next day, each time the user strikes a solid creature or object with a weapon, the weapon suddenly increases dramatically in weight, causing the blow to inflict 2 additional points of damage.

DETONATION
Level: 1d6 + 2
Effect: Projects a small physical explosive up to a long distance away that explodes in an immediate radius, inflicting damage equal to the cypher's level. Roll a d100 to determine the type of damage.

01–10	Cell-disrupting (harms only flesh)
11–30	Corrosive
31–40	Electrical discharge
41–50	Heat drain (cold)
51–75	Fire
76–00	Shrapnel

DETONATION (CREATURE)
Level: 1d6 + 1
Effect: Projects a small physical explosive up to a long distance away that explodes and creates a momentary teleportation gate. A random creature whose level is equal to or less than the cypher's level appears through the gate and attacks the closest target. After about one minute, the creature vanishes.

DETONATION (DESICCATING)
Level: 1d6 + 2
Effect: Projects a small physical explosive up to a long distance away that bursts in an immediate radius, draining moisture from everything within it. Living creatures take damage equal to the cypher's level. Water in the area is vaporized.

DETONATION (FLASH)
Level: 1d6 + 2
Effect: Projects a small physical explosive up to a long distance away that bursts in an immediate radius, blinding all within it for one minute (ten minutes if the cypher is level 4 or higher).

DETONATION (GRAVITY)

Level: 1d6 + 2

Effect: Projects a small physical explosive up to a long distance away that bursts in an immediate radius, inflicting damage equal to the cypher's level by increasing gravity tremendously for one second. All creatures in the area are crushed to the ground for one round and cannot take physical actions.

DETONATION (GRAVITY INVERSION)

Level: 1d6 + 1

Effect: Projects a small physical explosive up to a long distance away that explodes, and for one hour gravity reverses within long range of the explosion.

DETONATION (MASSIVE)

Level: 1d6 + 2

Effect: Projects a small physical explosive up to a long distance away that explodes in a short-range radius, inflicting damage equal to the cypher's level. Roll a d100 to determine the type of damage.

01–10	Cell-disrupting (harms only flesh)
11–30	Corrosive
31–40	Electrical discharge
41–50	Heat drain (cold)
51–75	Fire
76–00	Shrapnel

DETONATION (MATTER DISRUPTION)

Level: 1d6 + 4

Effect: Projects a small physical explosive up to a long distance away that explodes in an immediate radius, releasing nanites that rearrange matter in random ways. Inflicts damage equal to the cypher's level.

DETONATION (PRESSURE)

Level: 1d6 + 2

Effect: Projects a small physical explosive up to a long distance away that explodes in an immediate radius, inflicting impact damage equal to the cypher's level. Also moves unattended objects out of the area if they weigh less than 20 pounds (9 kg) per cypher level.

DETONATION (SINGULARITY)

Level: 10

Effect: Projects a small physical explosive up to a long distance away that explodes and creates a momentary singularity that tears at the fabric of the universe. Inflicts 20 points of damage to all within short range, drawing them (or their remains) together to immediate range (if possible). Player characters in the radius who fail a Might defense roll move down one step on the damage track.

The singularity detonation is a greatly feared device, sought by those interested in truly horrific destruction.

DETONATION (SONIC)

Level: 1d6 + 2

Effect: Projects a small physical explosive up to a long distance away that explodes with terrifying sound, deafening all in an immediate radius for ten minutes per cypher level.

DETONATION (SPAWN)

Level: 1d6 + 2

Effect: Projects a small physical explosive up to a long distance away that bursts in an immediate radius, blinding all within it for one minute and inflicting damage equal to the cypher's level. The burst spawns 1d6 additional detonations; in the next round, each additional detonation flies to a random spot within short range and explodes in an immediate radius. Roll a d100 to determine the type of damage dealt by all detonations:

01–10	Cell-disrupting (harms only flesh)
11–30	Corrosive
31–40	Electrical discharge
41–50	Heat drain (cold)
51–75	Fire
76–00	Shrapnel

DETONATION (WEB)

Level: 1d6 + 2

Effect: Projects a small physical explosive up to a long distance away that explodes in an immediate radius and creates sticky strands of goo. PCs caught in the area must use a Might-based action to get out, with the difficulty determined by the cypher level. NPCs break free if their level is higher than the cypher level.

Rather than strands of sticky goo, some web detonations fill the area with a mass of quick-hardening foam that has the same result.

DISARM

Level: 1d6 + 1

Effect: One NPC within immediate range whose level is lower than the cypher level drops whatever they are holding.

CYPHER SYSTEM

TYPES OF CYPHERS

 SUBTLE

 MANIFEST

 FANTASTIC

For a more realistic game, the eagleseye cypher could instead give the user two assets on tasks involving seeing to long distances.

Although a force cube's walls are not gaseous permeable, there is likely enough air within for trapped creatures to breathe for the hour it lasts.

Some force walls, shields, and cubes are transparent. Others are translucent. A few are opaque.

Free level of effort, page 209

DISGUISE MODULE
Level: 1d6 + 2
Effect: For the next ten minutes per cypher level, the user's features become almost identical to those of one designated person they have previously interacted with, easing by two steps attempts to disguise the user as that person. Once designated, the user cannot shift the effect to look like another person, though they can remove the module to look like themselves again before the end of the duration.

DISRUPTING
Level: 1d6
Effect: For the next day, each time the user strikes a solid creature or object, the attack generates a burst of nanites that directly attack its organic cells. The target takes 1 additional point of damage. If the target's level is less than the cypher's level, it loses its next action; otherwise its next action is hindered.

EAGLESEYE
Level: 1d6
Effect: Grants the ability to see ten times as far as normal for one hour per cypher level.

EFFECT RESISTANCE
Level: 1d6 + 1
Effect: Provides a chance for additional resistance to directly damaging effects of all kinds, such as fire, lightning, and the like, for one day. (It does not provide resistance to blunt force, slashing, or piercing attacks.) If the level of the effect is of the cypher level or lower, the user gains an additional defense roll to avoid it. On a successful defense roll, treat the attack as if the user had succeeded on their regular defense roll. (If the user is an NPC, a PC attacking them with this kind of effect must succeed on two attack rolls to harm them.)

EFFORT ENHANCER (COMBAT)
Level: 1d6 + 1
Effect: For the next hour, the user can apply one free level of Effort to any task (including a combat task) without spending points from a Pool. The free level of Effort provided by this cypher does not count toward the maximum amount of Effort a character can normally apply to one task. Once this free level of Effort is used, the effect of the cypher ends.

EFFORT ENHANCER (NONCOMBAT)
Level: 1d6
Effect: For the next hour, the user can apply one free level of Effort to a noncombat task without spending points from a Pool. The level of Effort provided by this cypher does not count toward the maximum amount of Effort a character can normally apply to one task. Once this free level of Effort is used, the effect of the cypher ends.

ENDURING SHIELD
Level: 1d6 + 4
Effect: For the next day, the user has an asset to Speed defense rolls.

EQUIPMENT CACHE
Level: 1d6 + 1
Effect: The user can rummage around and produce from the cypher a desired piece of equipment (not an artifact) whose level does not exceed the cypher's level. The piece of equipment persists for up to one day, unless its fundamental nature allows only a single use (such as with a grenade).

FARSIGHT
Level: 1d6 + 1
Effect: The user can observe a location they have visited previously, regardless of how far away it is (even across galaxies). This vision persists for up to ten minutes per cypher level. The character can switch between viewing this location and viewing their current location once per round.

FIREPROOFING
Level: 1d6 + 4
Effect: A nonliving object treated by this cypher has Armor against fire damage equal to the cypher's level for one day.

FLAME-RETARDANT WALL
Level: 1d6
Effect: Creates an immobile plane of permeable energy up to 20 feet by 20 feet (6 m by 6 m) for one hour per cypher level. The plane conforms to the space available. Flames passing through the plane are extinguished.

FORCE CUBE
Level: 1d6 + 3
Effect: Creates an immobile cube composed of six planes of solid force, each 30 feet (9 m) to a side, for one hour. The planes conform to the space available.

388

FORCE FIELD

Level: 1d6

Effect: For the next day, the user is surrounded by a powerful force field, granting them +1 to Armor (+2 to Armor if the cypher level is 5 or higher).

FORCE SCREEN PROJECTOR

Level: 1d6 + 3

Effect: Creates an immobile plane of solid force up to 20 feet by 20 feet (6 m by 6 m) for one hour. The plane conforms to the space available.

FORCE SHIELD PROJECTOR

Level: 1d6 + 3

Effect: Creates a shimmering energy shield around the user for one hour, during which time they gain +3 to Armor (or +4 to Armor if the cypher is level 5 or higher).

FRICTION REDUCER

Level: 1d6

Effect: Spread across an area up to 10 feet (3 m) square, this makes things extremely slippery. For one hour per cypher level, movement tasks in the area are hindered by three steps.

FRIGID WALL

Level: 1d6 + 2

Effect: Creates a wall of supercooled air up to 30 feet by 30 feet by 1 foot (9 m by 9 m by 30 cm) that inflicts damage equal to the cypher's level on anything that passes through it. The wall conforms to the space available. It lasts for ten minutes.

GAS BOMB

Level: 1d6 + 2

Effect: Thrown a short distance, this bursts in a poisonous cloud within an immediate area. The cloud lingers for 1d6 rounds unless conditions dictate otherwise. Roll a d100 to determine the effect.

01–10	**Thick smoke:** occludes sight while the cloud lasts.
11–20	**Choking gas:** living creatures that breathe lose their actions to choking and coughing for a number of rounds equal to the cypher's level.
21–50	**Poison gas:** living creatures that breathe suffer damage equal to the cypher's level.
51–60	**Corrosive gas:** everything suffers damage equal to the cypher's level.
61–65	**Hallucinogenic gas:** living creatures that breathe lose their actions to hallucinations and visions for a number of rounds equal to the cypher's level.
66–70	**Nerve gas:** living creatures that breathe suffer Speed damage equal to the cypher's level.
71–80	**Mind-numbing gas:** living creatures that breathe suffer Intellect damage equal to the cypher's level.
81–83	**Fear gas:** living creatures that breathe and think flee in a random direction in fear (or are paralyzed with fear) for a number of rounds equal to the cypher's level.
84–86	**Amnesia gas:** living creatures that breathe and think permanently lose all memory of the last minute.
87–96	**Sleep gas:** living creatures that breathe fall asleep for a number of rounds equal to the cypher's level or until awoken by a violent action or an extremely loud noise.
97–00	**Rage gas:** living creatures that breathe and think make a melee attack on the nearest creature and continue to do so for a number of rounds equal to the cypher's level.

CYPHER SYSTEM

TYPES OF CYPHERS

 SUBTLE

 MANIFEST

 FANTASTIC

GRAVITY NULLIFIER
Level: 1d6 + 3
Effect: For one hour, the user can float into the air, moving vertically up to a short distance per round (but not horizontally without taking some other action, such as pushing along the ceiling). The user must weigh less than 50 pounds (23 kg) per level of the cypher.

GRAVITY-NULLIFYING APPLICATION
Level: 1d6 + 2
Effect: If a nonliving object no larger than a human (two humans if the cypher level is 6 or higher) is coated by this cypher, it floats 1d20 feet in the air permanently and no longer has weight if carried (though it needs to be strapped down).

HEAT ATTACK
Level: 1d6
Effect: For the next day, each time the user strikes a solid creature or object, the attack generates a burst of heat that inflicts 2 additional points of damage.

HUNTER/SEEKER
Level: 1d6
Effect: With long-range movement, this intelligent missile tracks and attacks a specified target (target must be within sight when selected). If it misses, it continues to attack one additional time per cypher level until it hits. For example, a level 4 hunter/seeker will attack a maximum of five times. Roll a d100 to determine the type of attack.

01–50	Inflicts 8 points of damage.
51–80	Bears a poisoned needle that inflicts 3 points of damage plus poison.
81–90	Explodes, inflicting 6 points of damage to all within immediate range.
91–95	Shocks for 4 points of electricity damage, and stuns for one round per cypher level.
96–00	Covers target in sticky goo that immediately hardens, holding them fast until they break free with a Might action (difficulty equal to the cypher's level + 2).

Stunned creatures lose their turn that round.

IMAGE PROJECTOR
Level: 1d6
Effect: Projects one of the following immobile images in the area described for one hour. The image appears up to a close distance from the user (long distance if the cypher level is 4 or higher, very long distance if the cypher level is 6 or higher). Scenes include movement, sound, and smell. Roll a d100 to determine the image.

01–20	Terrifying creature of an unknown species, perhaps no longer alive in the world (10-foot [3 m] cube)
21–40	Huge machine that obscures sight (30-foot [9 m] cube)
41–50	Beautiful pastoral scene (50-foot [15 m] cube)
51–60	Food that looks delicious but may not be familiar (10-foot [3 m] cube)
61–80	Solid color that obscures sight (50-foot [15 m] cube)
81–00	Incomprehensible scene that is disorienting and strange (20-foot [6 m] cube)

INFERNO WALL
Level: 1d6 + 2
Effect: Creates a wall of extreme heat up to 30 feet by 30 feet by 1 foot (9 m by 9 m by 30 cm) that inflicts damage equal to the cypher's level on anything that passes through it. The wall conforms to the space available. It lasts for ten minutes.

INFILTRATOR
Level: 1d6
Effect: Tiny capsule launches and moves at great speed, mapping and scanning an unknown area. It moves 500 feet (150 m) per level, scanning an area up to 50 feet (15 m) per level away from it. It identifies basic layout, creatures, and major energy sources and either transmits this information back to the user (perhaps by telepathy or an electronic signal) or returns to the user to show what it saw. Its movement is blocked by any physical or energy barrier.

INFORMATION SENSOR

Level: 1d6 + 2

Effect: Over the course of one day, the user can activate the cypher a total number of times equal to its level. Each time, they can select a living creature within long range and learn the following about it: level, origin, species, name, and possibly other facts (such as an individual's credit score, home address, phone number, and related information).

INSTANT SERVANT

Level: 1d6

Effect: Small device expands into a humanoid automaton that is roughly 2 feet (60 cm) tall. Its level is equal to the cypher's level, and it can understand the verbal commands of the character who activated it. Once the servant is activated, commanding it is not an action. It can make attacks or perform actions as ordered to the best of its abilities, but it cannot speak.

The automaton has short-range movement but never goes farther than long range from the character who activated it. At the GM's discretion, the servant might have specialized knowledge, such as how to operate a particular device. Otherwise, it has no special knowledge. In any case, the servant is not artificially intelligent or capable of initiating action. It does only as commanded.

The servant operates for one hour per cypher level.

INSTANT SHELTER

Level: 1d6 + 3

Effect: With the addition of water and air, this cypher expands into a simple one-room structure with a door and a transparent window (two rooms with an internal door if the cypher level is 7 or higher). The structure is 10 feet by 10 feet by 20 feet (3 m by 3 m by 6 m). It is made from a durable, nonflammable material similar to sandstone, and is permanent and immobile once created.

INTELLECT BOOSTER

Level: 1d6 + 2

Effect: Adds 1 to the user's Intellect Edge for one hour (or 2 if the cypher is level 5 or higher).

INTELLIGENCE ENHANCEMENT

Level: 1d6

Effect: All of the user's tasks involving intelligent deduction—such as playing chess, inferring a connection between clues, solving a mathematical problem, finding a bug in computer code, and so on—are eased by two steps for one hour. In the subsequent hour, the strain hinders the same tasks by two steps.

KNOWLEDGE ENHANCEMENT

Level: 1d6

Effect: For the next day, the character has training in a predetermined skill (or two skills if the cypher is level 5 or higher). The skill could be anything (including something specific to the operation of a particular device), or roll a d100 to choose a common skill.

01–10	Melee attacks
11–20	Ranged attacks
21–40	One type of academic or esoteric lore (biology, history, magic, and so on)
41–50	Repairing (sometimes specific to one device)
51–60	Crafting (usually specific to one thing)
61–70	Persuasion
71–75	Healing
76–80	Speed defense
81–85	Intellect defense
86–90	Swimming
91–95	Riding
96–00	Sneaking

LIGHTNING WALL

Level: 1d6 + 2

Effect: Creates a wall of electric bolts up to 30 feet by 30 feet by 1 foot (9 m by 9 m by 30 cm) that inflicts damage equal to the cypher's level on anything that passes through it. The wall conforms to the space available. It lasts for ten minutes.

It is easy to get addicted to the quick hit of training that comes from knowledge enhancement cyphers. Characters who rely on them too often may find themselves at a disadvantage when they run out, presenting a great opportunity for GM intrusion.

CYPHER SYSTEM

TYPES OF CYPHERS

 SUBTLE

 MANIFEST

 FANTASTIC

MACHINE CONTROL
Level: 1d6 + 2
Effect: Splits into two pieces; one is affixed to a device and the other to a character. The character can then use their mind to control the device at long range, bidding it to do anything it could do normally. Thus, a device could be activated or deactivated, and a vehicle could be piloted. The control lasts for ten minutes per cypher level, and once the device is chosen, it cannot be changed.

MAGNETIC ATTACK DRILL
Level: 1d6 + 2
Effect: The user throws this cypher at a target within short range, and it drills into the target for one round, inflicting damage equal to the cypher's level. If the target is made of metal or wearing metal (such as armor), the attack is eased.

MAGNETIC MASTER
Level: 1d6 + 2
Effect: Establishes a connection with one metal object within short range that a human could hold in one hand. The user can then move or manipulate the object anywhere within short range (each movement or manipulation is an action). For example, they could wield a weapon or drag a helm affixed to a foe's head to and fro. The connection lasts for ten rounds per cypher level.

MAGNETIC SHIELD
Level: 1d6 + 2
Effect: For ten minutes per cypher level, metal objects cannot come within immediate range of the user. Metal items already in the area when the device is activated are slowly pushed out.

MANIPULATION BEAM
Level: 1d6 + 2
Effect: Over the course of one day, the user can activate the cypher a total number of times equal to its level. Each time, they can affect an object they can see within long range that is not too heavy for them to affect physically. The effect must occur over the course of a round and could include closing or opening a door, keying in a number on a keypad, transferring an object a short distance, wresting an object from another creature's grasp (on a successful Might-based roll), or pushing a creature an immediate distance.

A manipulation beam could be used to operate a computer at a distance, which would make some infiltration and hacking jobs easier.

MATTER TRANSFERENCE RAY
Level: 1d6 + 3
Effect: The user can target one nonliving object within long range that is their size or smaller of the cypher level or lower. The object is transferred directly to a random location at least 100 miles (160 km) away. If the GM feels it appropriate to the circumstances, only a portion of an object is transferred (a portion whose volume is no more than the user's).

MEDITATION AID
Level: 1d6 + 2
Effect: Restores a number of points equal to the cypher's level to the user's Intellect Pool.

MEMORY SWITCH
Level: 1d6 + 2
Effect: The user selects a point within long range, and the minds of all thinking creatures within immediate range of that point are attacked. Victims are dazed and take no action for a round, and they have no memory of the preceding hour.

MENTAL SCRAMBLER
Level: 1d6 + 2
Effect: Two rounds after being activated, the device creates an invisible field that fills an area within short range and lasts for one minute. The field scrambles the mental processes of all thinking creatures. The effect lasts as long as they remain in the field and for 1d6 rounds after, although an Intellect defense roll is allowed each round to act normally (both in the field and after leaving it). Each mental scrambler is keyed to a specific effect. Roll a d100 to determine the effect.

01–30	Victims cannot act.
31–40	Victims cannot speak.
41–50	Victims move slowly (immediate range) and clumsily.
51–60	Victims cannot see or hear.
61–70	Victims lose all sense of direction, depth, and proportion.
71–80	Victims do not recognize anyone they know.
81–88	Victims suffer partial amnesia.
89–94	Victims suffer total amnesia.
95–98	Victims lose all inhibitions, revealing secrets and performing surprising actions.
99–00	Victims' ethics are inverted.

392

METAL DEATH

Level: 1d6 + 2

Effect: Produces a stream of foam that covers an area about 3 feet by 3 feet (1 m by 1 m), transforming any metal that it touches into a substance as brittle as thin glass. The foam affects metal to a depth of about 6 inches (15 cm).

 MIND MELD

Level: 1d6 + 1

Effect: Lets the user speak telepathically with creatures they can see within short range for up to one hour. The user can't read a target's thoughts, except those that are specifically "transmitted."

 MIND-RESTRICTING WALL

Level: 1d6 + 2

Effect: Creates an immobile plane of permeable energy up to 20 feet by 20 feet (6 m by 6 m) for one hour. The plane conforms to the space available. Intelligent creatures passing through the plane fall unconscious for up to one hour, or until slapped awake or damaged.

MIND STABILIZER

Level: 1d6

Effect: The user gains +5 to Armor against Intellect damage.

 MONOBLADE

Level: 1d6 + 2

Effect: Produces a 6-inch (15 cm) blade that's the same level as the cypher. The blade cuts through any material of a level lower than its own. If used as a weapon, it is a light weapon that ignores Armor of a level lower than its own. The blade lasts for ten minutes.

 MONOHORN

Level: 1d6 + 3

Effect: The user gains a horn in the center of their forehead. The horn is deadly sharp and strong, and it spirals down to a solid base where it fuses with their flesh and bone. The user is specialized in making melee attacks with the horn, which is considered a medium weapon. The horn lasts for a number of hours equal to the cypher's level.

MOTION SENSOR

Level: 1d6 + 2

Effect: For one hour per cypher level, the user knows when any movement occurs within short range, and when large creatures or objects move within long range (the cypher distinguishes between the two). It also indicates the number and size of the creatures or objects in motion.

NULL FIELD

Level: 1d6 + 3

Effect: The user and all creatures within immediate range gain +3 to Armor (+5 if the cypher is level 8 or higher) against damage of a specified kind for one hour. Roll a d100 to determine the effect.

01–12	Fire
13–27	Cold
28–39	Acid
40–52	Psychic
53–65	Sonic
66–72	Electrical
73–84	Poison
85–95	Blunt force
96–00	Slashing and piercing

NULLIFICATION RAY

Level: 1d6 + 3

Effect: The user can immediately end one ongoing effect within long range that is produced by an artifact, cypher, or special ability.

NUTRITION AND HYDRATION

Level: 1d6 + 1

Effect: The user can go without food and water for a number of days equal to the cypher's level without ill effect.

PERFECT MEMORY

Level: 1d6

Effect: Allows the user to mentally record everything they see for thirty seconds per cypher level and store the recording permanently in their long-term memory. This cypher is useful for watching someone pick a specific lock, enter a complex code, or do something else that happens quickly.

PERFECTION

Level: 1d6 + 2

Effect: The user treats their next action as if they had rolled a natural 20.

In some games, telepathy transcends normal language barriers (if the target has a mind that allows for telepathic communication). In others, it might only pick up emotions or general concepts of thoughts in another language. It also might vary based on the ability used.

Sometimes a monohorn cypher covers the user in a thin sheen of black hide-like material, which disguises their identity but doesn't interfere with their senses.

TYPES OF CYPHERS

 SUBTLE

 MANIFEST

 FANTASTIC

Most poisons are not considered cyphers, except for a very few that are unique.

PERSONAL ENVIRONMENT FIELD

Level: 1d6 + 2

Effect: Creates an aura of temperature and atmosphere that will sustain a human safely for a day. The aura extends to 1 foot (30 cm) around the user (double that radius if the cypher is level 7 or higher). It does not protect against sudden flashes of temperature change (such as from a heat ray). A small number of these cyphers (1%) accommodate the preferred environment of a nonhuman, nonterrestrial creature.

PHASE CHANGER

Effect: Puts the user out of phase for one minute (two minutes if the cypher is level 6 or higher). During this time, they can pass through solid objects as though they were entirely insubstantial, like a ghost. They cannot make physical attacks or be physically attacked.

PHASE DISRUPTOR

Level: 1d6 + 2

Effect: Puts a portion of a physical structure (like a wall or floor) out of phase for one hour. It affects an area equal to one 5-foot (1.5 m) cube per cypher level. While the area is out of phase, creatures and objects can pass through it as if it were not there, although one cannot see through it, and it blocks light.

POISON (EMOTION)

Level: 1d6 + 2

Effect: The victim feels a specific emotion for one hour. Roll a d100 to determine the emotion.

01–20	Anger. Likely to attack anyone who disagrees with them. Very hard to interact with; all such actions are hindered by two steps.
21–40	Fear. Flees in terror for one minute when threatened.
41–60	Lust. Cannot focus on any nonsexual activity.
61–75	Sadness. All tasks are hindered.
76–85	Complacency. Has no motivation. All tasks are hindered by two steps.
86–95	Joy. Easy to interact with in a pleasant manner; all pleasant interaction tasks are eased.
96–00	Love. Much easier to interact with; all interaction tasks are eased by two steps, but temporary attachment is likely.

POISON (EXPLOSIVE)

Level: 1d6 + 1

Effect: Once this substance enters the bloodstream, it travels to the brain and reorganizes into an explosive that detonates when activated, inflicting 10 points of damage (ignores Armor). Roll a d100 to determine what activates the poison.

01–25	The detonator is activated (must be within long range).
26–40	A specified amount of time passes.
41–50	The victim takes a specific action.
51–55	A specific note is sung or played on an instrument within short range.
56–60	The victim smells a specific scent within immediate range.
61–80	The victim comes within long range of the detonator.
81–00	The victim is no longer within long range of the detonator.

POISON (MIND CONTROLLING)

Level: 1d6 + 2

Effect: The victim must carry out a specific action in response to a specific trigger. Roll a d100 to determine the action.

01–20	Lies down for one minute with eyes closed when told to do so.
21–40	Flees in terror for one minute when threatened.
41–60	Answers questions truthfully for one minute.
61–75	Attacks close friend for one round when within immediate range.
76–85	Obeys next verbal command given (if it is understood).
86–95	For one day, becomes sexually attracted to the next creature of its own species that it sees.
96–00	For one minute, moves toward the next red object seen in lieu of all other actions, ignoring self-preservation.

POISON (MIND DISRUPTING)

Level: 1d6 + 2

Effect: The victim suffers Intellect damage equal to the cypher's level and cannot take actions for a number of rounds equal to the cypher's level.

PSYCHIC COMMUNIQUE
Level: 1d6 + 2
Effect: Allows the user to project a one-time, one-way telepathic message of up to ten words per cypher level, with an unlimited range, to anyone they know.

RADIATION SPIKE
Level: 1d6 + 4
Effect: Delivers a powerful burst of radiation that disrupts the tissue of any creature touched, inflicting damage equal to the cypher's level.

RAY EMITTER
Level: 1d6 + 2
Effect: Allows the user to project a ray of destructive energy up to very long range that inflicts damage equal to the cypher's level. Roll a d100 to determine the type of energy.

01–50	Heat/concentrated light
51–60	Cell-disrupting radiation
61–80	Force
81–87	Magnetic wave
88–93	Molecular bond disruption
94–00	Concentrated cold

RAY EMITTER (COMMAND)
Level: 1d6 + 2
Effect: Allows the user to project a ray up to long range (very long range if the cypher is level 6 or higher) that forces a target to obey the next verbal command given (if it is understood) for one round per cypher level.

RAY EMITTER (FEAR)
Level: 1d6 + 2
Effect: Allows the user to project a ray up to long range (very long range if the cypher is level 6 or higher) that causes the target to flee in terror for one minute.

RAY EMITTER (FRIEND SLAYING)
Level: 1d6 + 2
Effect: Allows the user to project a ray up to long range (very long range if the cypher is level 6 or higher) that causes the target to attack its nearest ally for one round.

RAY EMITTER (MIND DISRUPTING)
Level: 1d6 + 2
Effect: Allows the user to project a ray of destructive energy up to very long range that inflicts Intellect damage equal to the cypher's level. Also, the victim cannot take actions for a number of rounds equal to the cypher's level.

RAY EMITTER (NUMBING)
Level: 1d6 + 2
Effect: Allows the user to project a ray of energy up to long range (very long range if the cypher is level 6 or higher) that numbs one limb of the target, making it useless for one minute. A small number of these devices (5%) induce numbness that lasts for one hour.

RAY EMITTER (PARALYSIS)
Level: 1d6 + 2
Effect: Allows the user to project a ray of energy up to very long range that paralyzes the target for one minute. A small number of these devices (5%) induce paralysis that lasts for one hour.

REALITY SPIKE
Level: 1d6 + 4
Effect: Once activated, the cypher does not move—ever—even if activated in midair. A Might action will dislodge it, but then it is ruined.

REFLEX ENHANCER
Level: 1d6
Effect: All tasks involving manual dexterity—such as pickpocketing, lockpicking, juggling, operating on a patient, defusing a bomb, and so on—are eased by two steps for one hour.

REJUVENATOR
Level: 1d6 + 2
Effect: Restores a number of points equal to the cypher's level to one random stat Pool.

01–50	Might Pool
51–75	Speed Pool
76–00	Intellect Pool

Even weirder ray emitters:
- *Turns target inside out*
- *Inflicts damage and turns flesh blue*
- *Renders target mute*
- *Damages only plants*
- *Damages only inorganic matter*
- *Turns flesh to dead, stonelike material*

TYPES OF CYPHERS

 SUBTLE

 MANIFEST

 FANTASTIC

REMEMBERING
Level: 1d6
Effect: Allows the user to recall any one experience they've ever had. The experience can be no longer than one minute per cypher level, but the recall is perfect, so (for example) if they saw someone dial a phone, they will remember the number.

REMOTE VIEWER
Level: 1d6
Effect: For one hour per cypher level, the user can see everything going on in the vicinity of the cypher, regardless of the distance between them.

REPAIR UNIT
Level: 1d10
Effect: The cypher becomes a multiarmed sphere that floats. It repairs one designated item (of its own level or lower) that has been damaged but not destroyed. The repair unit can also create spare parts, unless the GM rules that the parts are too specialized or rare (in which case, the unit repairs the device except for the specialized part). Repair time is 1d100 + 20 minutes.

REPEATER
Level: 1d6 + 1
Effect: For the next minute, the user's ranged weapon fires one additional time with ammo fabricated by the cypher. The weapon wielder can aim the free shot at the same target, or at a different target next to the first one.

Recovery roll, page 218

REPEL
Level: 1d6 + 1
Effect: One NPC within immediate range who is of a level lower than the cypher decides to leave, using their next five rounds to move away quickly.

RETALIATION
Level: 1d6
Effect: For the next day, anyone striking the user receives a small burst of electricity that inflicts 1 point of damage (2 points if the cypher is level 4 or higher, 3 points if the cypher is level 6 or higher). No action or roll is required by the user.

SECRET
Level: 1d6 + 2
Effect: The user can ask the GM one question and get a general answer. The GM assigns a level to the question, so the more obscure the answer, the more difficult the task. Generally, knowledge that a PC could find by looking somewhere other than their current location is level 1, and obscure knowledge of the past is level 7. Gaining knowledge of the future is level 10, and such knowledge is always open to interpretation. The cypher cannot provide an answer to a question above its level.

SHEEN
Level: 1d6
Effect: For one week, the user's cells are coated with a protective veneer that resists damage (+1 to Armor, or +2 to Armor if the cypher is level 5 or higher) and eases Might defense rolls by two steps. However, healing is more difficult during this time; all recovery rolls suffer a −1 penalty.

SHOCK ATTACK
Level: 1d6
Effect: For the next day, each time the user strikes a solid creature or object, the attack generates a burst of electricity, inflicting 1 additional point of damage (2 points if the cypher is level 4 or higher, 3 points if the cypher is level 6 or higher).

SHOCKER
Level: 1d6 + 4
Effect: Delivers a powerful burst of electricity that shocks any creature touched, inflicting damage equal to the cypher's level.

SKILL BOOST

Level: 1d6

Effect: Dramatically but temporarily alters the user's mind and body so they can ease one specific kind of physical action by three steps. Once activated, this boost can be used a number of times equal to the cypher's level, but only within a twenty-four-hour period. The boost takes effect each time the action is performed. For example, a level 3 cypher boosts the first three times that action is attempted. Roll a d100 to determine the action.

01–15	Melee attack
16–30	Ranged attack
31–40	Speed defense
41–50	Might defense
51–60	Intellect defense
61–68	Jumping
69–76	Climbing
77–84	Running
85–92	Swimming
93–94	Sneaking
95–96	Balancing
97–98	Perceiving
99	Carrying
00	Escaping

 SLAVE MAKER

Level: 1d6 + 2

Effect: To activate the cypher, the user must succeed on a melee attack against a creature about the size of the user and whose level does not exceed the cypher's level. The cypher bonds to the target, who immediately becomes calm. The target awaits the user's commands and carries out all orders to the best of its ability. The target remains so enslaved for a number of hours equal to the cypher's level minus the target's level. (If the result is 0, the target is enslaved for only one minute.)

SLEEP INDUCER

Level: 1d6

Effect: Touch puts the victim to sleep for ten minutes per cypher level or until awoken by a violent action or an extremely loud noise.

SNIPER MODULE

Level: 1d6

Effect: For the next hour per cypher level, the effective range of the user's ranged weapon increases by one category (immediate to short, short to long, long to very long, very long to 1,000 feet [300 m]). A weapon with a range greater than very long has its range doubled.

SOLVENT

Level: 1d10

Effect: Dissolves 1 cubic foot of material each round. After one round per cypher level, the cypher becomes inert.

SONIC HOLE

Level: 1d6 + 2

Effect: Draws all sound within long range into the device for one round per cypher level. Within the affected area, no sound can be heard.

SOUND DAMPENER

Level: 1d6 + 2

Effect: Dampens all sound within immediate range for one minute per cypher level, providing an asset on stealth actions by all creatures in the area.

SPATIAL WARP

Level: 1d6 + 4

Effect: When affixed to a device that affects a single target at range, that range is increased to 1 mile (1.5 km) with no penalties. Space is temporarily warped in terms of seeing and reaching the target. If direct line of sight is important to the device's effect, it remains important. The spatial warp lasts 10 minutes per cypher level.

Sonic holes are much-loved by thieves everywhere but can also be used for less nefarious purposes, such as hunting prey and sneaking past enemies.

TYPES OF CYPHERS

 SUBTLE

 MANIFEST

 FANTASTIC

SPEED BOOST
Level: 1d6 + 2
Effect: Adds 1 to the user's Speed Edge for one hour (adds 2 if the cypher is level 5 or higher).

SPY
Level: 1d6 + 2
Effect: Produces a tiny spying object that resists detection as a level 8 creature. The object moves at great speed, mapping and scanning an unknown area. It moves 500 feet (150 m) per level, scanning an area up to 50 feet (15 m) away from it. It identifies basic layout, creatures, and major energy sources. Its movement is blocked by any physical or energy barrier. At the end of its mapping run, it returns to the user and reports. If it discovers a predefined target during its run (such as "a creature of level 5 or higher," "a locked door," "a major energy source," and so on), it detonates instead, dealing damage equal to the cypher's level (half electrical damage, half shrapnel damage) to all creatures and objects in short range.

STASIS KEEPER
Level: 1d6
Effect: Puts a subject into stasis for a number of days equal to the cypher's level, or until it is violently disturbed. An object in stasis does not age and comes out of the stasis alive and in the same condition as it went in, with no memory of the period of inactivity.

STIM
Level: 1d6
Effect: Eases the user's next action taken by three steps.

STRENGTH BOOST
Level: 1d6 + 2
Effect: Adds 1 to Might Edge for one hour (or 2 if the cypher is level 5 or higher).

STRENGTH ENHANCER
Level: 1d6
Effect: All noncombat tasks involving raw strength—such as breaking down a door, lifting a heavy boulder, forcing open elevator doors, competing in a weightlifting competition, and so on—are eased by two steps for one hour.

SUBDUAL FIELD
Level: 1d6 + 3
Effect: Two rounds after being activated, the device creates an invisible field that fills a specified area (such as a cube a short distance across) within long range. The field lasts for one minute. It affects the minds of thinking beings within the field, preventing them from taking hostile actions. The effect lasts as long as they remain in the field and for 1d6 rounds after, although an Intellect defense roll is allowed each round to act normally (both in the field and after leaving it).

TELEPATHY
Level: 1d6 + 2
Effect: For one hour, the device enables long-range mental communication with anyone the user can see.

TELEPORTER (BOUNDER)
Level: 1d6 + 2
Effect: User teleports up to 100 × the cypher level in feet to a location they can see. They arrive safely with their possessions but cannot take anything else with them.

TELEPORTER (INTERSTELLAR)
Level: 1d6 + 4
Effect: User teleports anywhere in the galaxy to a location they have previously visited or seen. They arrive safely with their possessions but cannot take anything else with them.

TELEPORTER (PLANETARY)
Level: 1d6 + 4
Effect: User teleports anywhere on the planet to a location they have previously visited or seen. They arrive safely with their possessions but cannot take anything else with them.

TELEPORTER (TRAVELER)
Level: 1d6 + 4
Effect: User teleports up to 100 × the cypher level in miles to a location they have previously visited or seen. They arrive safely with their possessions but cannot take anything else with them.

TEMPORAL VIEWER

Level: 1d6 + 4

Effect: Displays moving images and sound, up to ten minutes per cypher level in length, depicting events that occurred at the current location up to one year prior. The user specifies the time period shown by the viewer.

TIME DILATION (DEFENSIVE)

Level: 1d6

Effect: For the next twenty-four hours, when the user is attacked, they move in rapid, seemingly random jumps, a few inches to one side or the other. This is an asset that modifies the user's defense rolls by two steps (three steps if the cypher is level 6 or higher).

TIME DILATION (OFFENSIVE)

Level: 1d6

Effect: For the next twenty-four hours, when the user makes a melee attack, they move at almost instantaneous speed, easing their attacks by two steps (three steps if the cypher is level 6 or higher).

TISSUE REGENERATION

Level: 1d6 + 4

Effect: For the next hour, the user regains 1 point lost to damage per round, up to a total number of points equal to twice the cypher's level. As each point is regained, they choose which Pool to add it to. If all their Pools are at maximum, the regeneration pauses until they take more damage, at which point it begins again (if any time remains in the hour) until the duration expires.

TRACER

Level: 1d6

Effect: Fires a microscopic tracer that clings to any surface within short range. For the next twenty-four hours, the launcher shows the distance and direction to the tracer, as long as it is within 1 mile (100 miles if the cypher is level 3 or higher, in the same dimension if the cypher is level 6 or higher).

TRICK EMBEDDER

Level: 1d6

Effect: A nonintelligent animal immediately and perfectly learns one trick (two tricks if the cypher is level 4 or higher) it is capable of physically performing (roll over, heel, spin, shake, go to an indicated place within long range, and so on). The trick must be designated when the cypher is activated.

UNINTERRUPTIBLE POWER SOURCE

Level: 1d6 + 4

Effect: Provides power to another device for up to a day. The device to be powered can be as simple as a light source or as complex as a small starcraft, assuming the cypher's level is equal to the item's power requirements. A desk lamp is a level 1 power requirement, a car engine is a level 5 power requirement, and a starship is a level 10 power requirement.

VANISHER

Level: 1d6 + 2

Effect: The user becomes invisible for five minutes per cypher level, during which time they are specialized in stealth and Speed defense tasks. This effect ends if they do something to reveal their presence or position—attacking, using an ability, moving a large object, and so on. If this occurs, they can regain the remaining invisibility effect by taking an action to focus on hiding their position.

VISAGE CHANGER

Level: 1d6

Effect: Changes the appearance of one human-sized creature, providing an asset to disguise tasks (easing them by two steps if the cypher is level 5 or higher). The change takes ten minutes to apply and lasts for twenty-four hours.

VISUAL DISPLACEMENT DEVICE

Level: 1d6

Effect: Projects holographic images of the user to confuse attackers. The images appear around the user, giving them an asset to Speed defense actions for ten minutes per cypher level.

VOCAL TRANSLATOR

Level: 1d6

Effect: For twenty-four hours per cypher level, translates everything said by the user into a language that anyone can understand.

A tissue regeneration cypher can be used to regenerate a lost appendage (an arm, a foot, a leg, and so on) or to repair scar tissue from burns and other tissue-related disfigurements. If the cypher is used in this fashion, it restores only 1d6 points over the hour duration.

CYPHER SYSTEM

TYPES OF CYPHERS

 SUBTLE

 MANIFEST

 FANTASTIC

Master thief Garthal North likes to use X-ray viewers in his work. "Never open a locked door if you don't already know what's on the other side," he says.

A water adapter cypher can also be used in the regular atmosphere, allowing the user to ignore ill effects from very low or very high atmospheric pressure. The cypher does not protect against vacuum.

WARMTH
Level: 1d6
Effect: Keeps the user warm and comfortable, even in the harshest cold temperatures, for twenty-four hours. During this time, the user has Armor equal to the cypher's level that protects against cold damage.

WATER ADAPTER
Level: 1d6
Effect: The user can breathe underwater and operate at any depth (without facing the debilitating consequences of changing pressure) for four hours per cypher level.

WEAPON ENHANCEMENT
Level: 1d6 + 2
Effect: Modifies a weapon's attack in a particular fashion for ten minutes per cypher level. Roll a d100 for the modification.

01–10	Eases attack by one step
11–20	Deals bonus electrical damage equal to cypher level
21–30	Deals bonus cold damage equal to cypher level
31–40	Deals bonus poison damage equal to cypher level
41–50	Deals bonus acid damage equal to cypher level
51–60	Deals bonus fire damage equal to cypher level
61–70	Deals bonus sonic damage equal to cypher level
71–80	Deals bonus psychic damage equal to cypher level
81–90	Knockback (on 18–20 on successful attack roll, target knocked back 30 feet [9 m])
91–95	Holding (on 18–20 on successful attack roll, target can't act on its next turn)
96–97	Eases attack by two steps
98	Banishing (on 18–20 on successful attack roll, target is sent to random location at least 100 miles [160 km] away)
99	Explodes, inflicting damage equal to cypher level to all within immediate range
00	Heart-seeking (on 18–20 on successful attack roll, target is killed)

WINGS
Level: 1d6 + 2
Effect: User can fly at their normal running speed for ten minutes per cypher level.

X-RAY VIEWER
Level: 1d6 + 4
Effect: Allows the user to see through up to 2 feet (60 cm) of material of a level lower than the cypher. The effect lasts for one minute per cypher level.

ZERO POINT FIELD
Level: 1d6 + 3
Effect: Renders an inanimate object outside the effects of most energy for one minute. This means the object cannot be harmed, moved, or manipulated in any way. It remains in place (even in midair).

POWER BOOST CYPHERS

These cyphers increase, modify, or improve a character's existing powers. A burst boost cypher, for example, allows someone with the Bears a Halo of Fire focus to create a blast of fire in all directions, one time. Imagine this as being a fire-using superhero's ability to "go nova."

Power boost cyphers affect one use of a character's abilities but do not require an action. Their use is part of the action that they affect.

Power boost cyphers are a special type of cypher. In some Cypher System games, they may be inappropriate, and in others, they may be the main (or only) type of cypher available, as determined by the GM. They can be either subtle or manifest.

AREA BOOST
Level: 1d6 + 1
Effect: This cypher boosts an ability that affects a single target. The ability expands the effect so it includes the immediate area around that target. If the ability normally affects an immediate area, the area becomes short. Short areas are increased to long. Long areas are increased to very long. Abilities with very long areas become 1,000-foot (300 m) areas. All other areas double in radius.

BURST BOOST
Level: 1d6 + 2
Effect: This cypher boosts an ability that affects a single target at short range or farther. The range decreases to immediate, but the ability affects all targets within immediate range.

DAMAGE BOOST
Level: 1d6 + 2
Effect: This cypher boosts an ability that inflicts points of damage. The ability inflicts additional damage equal to this cypher's level.

EFFICACY BOOST (MAJOR)
Level: 1d6 + 1
Effect: This cypher boosts an ability that requires a skill roll. The use of the ability is eased by two steps.

EFFICACY BOOST (MINOR)
Level: 1d6
Effect: This cypher boosts an ability that requires a skill roll. The use of the ability is eased.

ENERGY BOOST
Level: 1d6
Effect: This cypher boosts an ability that has a stat Pool cost. The cost is reduced to 0.

RANGE BOOST
Level: 1d6 + 1
Effect: This cypher boosts the range of an ability. Something that affects only you can now affect someone you touch. Any other ability increases its range by one category (touch to immediate, immediate to short, short to long, long to very long, very long to 1,000 feet [300 m], or double for any range longer than very long).

TARGET BOOST
Level: 1d6 + 2
Effect: This cypher boosts an ability that affects a target at a range greater than touch. It can affect a second target within range (if the ability is an attack, make a separate attack roll for the second creature).

Bears a Halo of Fire, page 64

Major efficacy boost cyphers might be appropriate only in superhero campaigns, at least with any regularity.

Chapter 25

RUNNING THE CYPHER SYSTEM

Unlike in the rest of this book, I'm going to write this chapter from me to you. I'm addressing you, the game master (or potential game master), directly because you are vital to turning a halfway-decent game into an amazing game. In uninformed hands, even the greatest rules and the greatest setting will make, at best, a mediocre game. You are the key in this process.

The game master (GM) is the architect of the game but not the sole builder. You're the facilitator as well as the arbiter. You're all of these things and more. It's a challenging role that's not quite like anything else. People try to equate the GM with a playwright, a referee, a judge, or a guide. And those are not terrible analogies, but none of them is quite right, either.

The Cypher System has been designed to make the challenging tasks of game mastering as simple as possible and allow you as the GM to focus on what's important. Rather than dealing with a lot of die rolls, modifiers, and rules minutiae, you can focus mainly on the flow of the story. This is not to say that you are the sole storyteller. The group is the storyteller. But it's the GM's job to pull together the actions, reactions, and desires of all the people sitting around the table, mesh them with the setting and background created before the session began, and turn it all into a cohesive story—on the fly. Sometimes this means using a heavy hand. Sometimes it means stepping back. Sometimes it means being open-minded. It always means giving the other players as much of the spotlight as you have as the GM, and attempting to give it to each of them in turn so that no one person dominates the narrative or the gameplay—not even you.

I will say this now, up front, and I will say it often: the rules are your tools to tell a story, to portray a character, and to simulate your world. The rules are not the final word—you are. You are not subservient to the rules. But you do have a master. That master is fun gameplay mixed with exciting story.

The Cypher System has also been designed to make game mastering work the way that many experienced GMs run games anyway. The GMs who recognize that they are not subservient to the rules are often forced to work against the rules, to work in spite of the rules, or to use the rules as smoke and mirrors to cover up what they're really doing (which is providing everyone with an exciting, compelling, and interesting narrative in which to participate). Hopefully, as a Cypher System GM, you will not find that to be the case. On the contrary, most of the rules were designed specifically to make it easier to run the game—or rather, to allow the GM to focus on helping to shepherd a great story.

In this chapter, we're going to talk about the rules and how to use them as your tools, as well as interacting with players, running games, and crafting great stories.

THE RULES VERSUS THE STORY

On first glance, it might seem that for a story-based game, there isn't a lot of "story" in the rules. A wall, a bear, a pit to leap, and a gun can be more or less summed up as a single number—their level. The thing is, the Cypher System is a story-based game *because* the rules at their core are devoid of story. A wall, a bear, a pit to leap, and a gun can be summed up as levels because they're all just parts of the story. They're all just obstacles or tools.

There aren't a lot of specifics in the rules—no guidelines for particular judo moves or the differences between repairing an electrically powered force screen projector and fixing a biomechanical aircraft. That's not because those kinds of things are to be ignored, but because those kinds of things are flavor—they are story, description, and elaboration for the GM and the players to provide. A player running a character in a fistfight can and should describe one attack as an uppercut and another as a roundhouse punch, even though there's no mechanical difference. In fact, *because* there's no mechanical difference. That's what a narrative game is all about. It's interesting and entertaining, and that's why you're all sitting at the table in the first place.

If different aspects of the game—walls, bears, pits, and so on—have distinctions, they come through as story elements, which are special exceptions to the rules. Having so few general rules makes adding special conditions and situations easier, because there is less rules tinkering to deal with. Fewer special circumstances to worry about. Less chance of contradictions and rules incompatibilities. For example, you can easily have a wall that can be destroyed only by mental attacks. A ravage bear has its unique grapple attack. A pit could have frictionless walls. A ray emitter could freeze foes solid. These are story elements that mechanically build on the very simple base mechanics, and they all make things more interesting.

SETTING DIFFICULTY RATINGS

The GM's most important overall tasks are setting the stage and guiding the story created by the group (not the one created by the GM ahead of time). But setting difficulty is the most important mechanical task the GM has in the game. Although there are suggestions throughout this chapter for various difficulty ratings for certain actions, there is no master list of the difficulty for every action a PC can take. Instead, the Cypher System is designed with the "teach a person to fish" style of good game mastering in mind. (If you don't know what that means, it comes from the old adage "Give a person a fish and they'll eat for a day. Teach a person to fish and they'll eat for a lifetime." The idea is not to give GMs a ton of rules to memorize or reference, but to teach them how to make their own logical judgment calls.) Of course, most of the time, it's not a matter of exact precision. If you say the difficulty is 3 and it "should" have been 4, the world's not over.

For the most part, it really is as simple as rating something on a scale of 1 to 10, 1 being incredibly easy and 10 being basically impossible. The guidelines in the Task Difficulty table, presented again on page 404 for reference, should help put you in the right frame of mind for assigning difficulty to a task.

For example, we make the distinction between something that most people can do and something that trained people can do. In this case, "normal" means someone with absolutely no training, talent, or experience—imagine your ne'er-do-well, slightly overweight uncle trying a task he's never tried before. "Trained" means the person has some level of instruction or experience but is not necessarily a professional.

With that in mind, think about the act of balance. With enough focus, most people can walk across a narrow bridge (like a fallen tree trunk). That suggests it is difficulty 2. However, walking across a narrow plank that's only 3 inches (8 cm) wide? That's probably more like difficulty 3. Now consider walking across a tightrope. That's probably difficulty 5—a normal person can manage that only with a great deal of luck. Someone with some training can give it a go, but it's still hard. Of course, a professional acrobat can do it easily. Consider, however, that the professional acrobat is specialized in the task, making it difficulty 3 for them. They probably are using Effort as well during their performance.

Let's try another task. This time, consider how hard it might be to remember the name of the previous leader of the village where the character

Ravage bear, page 350

Ray emitter, page 395

lives. The difficulty might be 0 or 1, depending on how long ago they were the leader and how well known they were. Let's say it was thirty years ago and they were only mildly memorable, so it's difficulty 1. Most people remember them, and with a little bit of effort, anyone can come up with their name. Now let's consider the name of the leader's daughter. That's much harder. Assuming the daughter wasn't famous in her own right, it's probably difficulty 4. Even people who know a little about local history (that is to say, people who are trained in the subject) might not be able to remember it. But what about the name of the pet dog owned by the daughter's spouse? That's probably impossible. Who's going to remember the name of an obscure person's pet from thirty years ago? Basically no one. However, it's not forbidden knowledge or a well-guarded secret, so it sounds like difficulty 7. Difficulty 7 is the rating that means "No one can do this, yet some people still do." It's not the stuff of legend, but it's something you would assume people can't do. When you think there's no way you can get tickets for a sold-out concert, but somehow your friend manages to score a couple anyway, that's difficulty 7. (See the next section for more on difficulties 7, 8, 9, and 10.)

If you're talking about a task, ideally the difficulty shouldn't be based on the character performing the task. Things don't get inherently easier or harder depending on who is doing them. However, the truth is, the character does play into it as a judgment call. If the task is breaking down a wooden door, an 8-foot-tall (2 m) automaton made of metal with nuclear-driven motors should be better at breaking it down than an average human would be, but the task rating should be the same for both. Let's say that the automaton's nature effectively gives it two levels of training in such tasks. Thus, if the door has a difficulty rating of 4, but the automaton is specialized and reduces the difficulty to 2, it has a target number of 6. The human has no such specialization, so the difficulty remains 4, and the person has a target number of 12. However, when you set the difficulty of breaking down the door, don't try to take all those differences into account. The GM should consider only the human because the Task Difficulty table is based on the ideal of a "normal" person, a "trained" person, and so on. It's humanocentric.

Most characters probably are willing to use one or two levels of Effort on a task, and they might have an appropriate skill or asset to decrease the difficulty by a step. That means that a difficulty 4 task will often be treated as difficulty 2 or even 1, and those are easy rolls to make. Don't hesitate, then, to pull out higher-level difficulties. The PCs can rise to the challenge, especially if they are experienced.

THE IMPOSSIBLE DIFFICULTIES

Difficulties 7, 8, 9, and 10 are all technically impossible. Their target numbers are 21, 24, 27, and 30, and you can't roll those numbers on a d20 no matter how many times you try. Consider, however, all the ways that a character can reduce difficulty. If someone spends a little Effort or has some skill or help, it brings difficulty 7 (target number 21) into the range of possibility—difficulty 6 (target number 18). Now consider that they have specialization, use a lot of Effort, and have help. That might bring the difficulty down to 1 or even 0 (reducing it by two steps from training and specialization, three or four

Unless for some reason you tell the players directly, they'll never know if you change an NPC's stats or a task's difficulty on the fly. If you're doing it to make a better story, that's your purview.

TASK DIFFICULTY

Task Difficulty	Description	Target No.	Guidance
0	Routine	0	Anyone can do this basically every time.
1	Simple	3	Most people can do this most of the time.
2	Standard	6	Typical task requiring focus, but most people can usually do this.
3	Demanding	9	Requires full attention; most people have a 50/50 chance to succeed.
4	Difficult	12	Trained people have a 50/50 chance to succeed.
5	Challenging	15	Even trained people often fail.
6	Intimidating	18	Normal people almost never succeed.
7	Formidable	21	Impossible without skills or great effort.
8	Heroic	24	A task worthy of tales told for years afterward.
9	Immortal	27	A task worthy of legends that last lifetimes.
10	Impossible	30	A task that normal humans couldn't consider (but one that doesn't break the laws of physics).

steps from Effort, and one step from the asset of assistance). That practically impossible task just became routine. A fourth-tier character can and will do this—not every time, due to the cost, but perhaps once per game session. You have to be ready for that. A well-prepared, motivated sixth-tier character can do that even with a difficulty 10 task. Again, they won't do it often (they'd have to apply six levels of Effort, and even with an Edge of 6 that would cost 7 points from their Pool, and that's assuming they're specialized and have two levels of assets), but it can happen if they're really prepared for the task (being specialized and maxed out in asset opportunities reduces the difficulty by four more steps). That's why sixth-tier characters are at the top of their field, so to speak.

FALSE PRECISION

One way to look at difficulty is that each step of difficulty is worth 3 on the die. That is to say, hinder the task by one step, and the target number rises by 3. Ease the task by one step, and the target number is lowered by 3. Those kinds of changes are big, meaty chunks. Difficulty, as a game mechanic, is not terribly precise. It's measured in large portions. You never have a target number of 13 or 14, for example—it's always 3, 6, 9, 12, 15, and so on. (Technically, this is not true. If a character adds 1 to a d20 roll for some reason, it changes a target number of 15 to 14. But this is not worth much discussion.)

Imprecision is good in this case. It would be false precision to say that one lock has a target number of 14 and another has a target number of 15. What false precision means in this context is that it would be a delusion to think we can be that exact. Can you really say that one lock is 5% easier to pick than another? And more important, even if you could, is the difference worth noting? It's better to interact with the world in larger, more meaningful chunks than to try to parse things so carefully. If we tried to rate everything on a scale of 1 to 30 (using target numbers and not difficulty), we'd start to get lost in the proverbial weeds coming up with a meaningful distinction between something rated as an 8 and something rated as a 9 on that scale.

CONSISTENCY

Far more important than that level of precision is consistency. If the PCs need to activate a device that opens a spatial displacement portal, and the GM rules that it is a difficulty 6 task to get the antimatter rods spinning at the proper rates to achieve a specific harmonic frequency, then it needs to be a difficulty 6 task when they come back the next day to do it again (or there needs to be an understandable reason why it's not). The same is true for simpler tasks like walking across a narrow ledge or jumping up onto a platform. Consistency is key. The reason is that players need to be able to make informed decisions. If they remember how hard it was to open that portal yesterday, but it's inexplicably harder to open it today, they'll get frustrated because they tried to apply their experience to their decision-making process, and it failed them. If there's no way to make an informed decision, then all decisions are arbitrary.

Think about it in terms of real life. You need to cross the street, but a car is approaching. You've crossed the street thousands of times before, so you can look at the car and pretty easily judge whether you can cross safely or whether you have to wait for it to pass first. If the real world had no consistency, you couldn't make that decision. Every time you stepped into the street, you might get hit by a car. You'd never cross the street.

Players need that kind of consistency, too. So when you assign a difficulty to a task, note that number and try to keep it consistent the next time the PCs try the same task. "Same" is the key word. Deciphering one code isn't necessarily like deciphering another. Climbing one wall isn't the same as climbing another.

You'll make mistakes while doing this, so just accept that fact now. Excuse any mistakes with quick explanations about "a quirk of fate" or something along the lines of a surprisingly strong wind that wasn't blowing the last time.

MISTAKES

Sometimes the PCs will break down a door, and you'll realize that you rated it too low. Or the PCs will try to paddle a raft down a fast-moving river, and you (and probably they) will quickly discover that the difficulty you gave the task was ridiculously high.

Don't fret.

That door was already weakened by an earthquake, a structural flaw, or the fact that a while back some other explorers pounded on it all day. That river was actually moving far faster than the PCs thought at first, or their raft was faulty.

The point is, mistakes are easy to cover up. And sometimes, you can even tell your players it was just a mistake. They might even help provide an explanation if you do. It's not the end of the world.

More important, most of the time, no one will even know. Should have rated a task as difficulty 3 and instead you said it was 4? Oh well. Unless

Superhero games may want to take the task difficulty range up to 15. See page 293.

While I continually stress that the Cypher System is about story, not rules, it is still a game, which means that the PCs (and the players) can fail. That's why it's not accurate to think of the game as being identical to novels or movies. The system invites its own kind of storytelling. The players have to feel that there are real stakes. That if they screw up, there will be consequences— sometimes very harsh consequences. And they have to be right in that assumption.

the player rolls a 9, 10, or 11—which would have succeeded for difficulty 3 but not difficulty 4—it won't matter. And even if they do roll one of those numbers, who cares? Maybe the rain was really coming down that day, and it hindered their task.

The thing to take away is this: don't let the fear of making a mistake keep you from freely and quickly assessing the difficulty of a task and moving on with the game. Don't agonize over it. Give it a difficulty, call for a roll, and keep the game moving. Hesitating over a rating will be far more detrimental to the game than giving something the wrong rating.

GM intrusion, page 408

ROUTINE ACTIONS

Don't hesitate to make actions routine. Don't call for die rolls when they're not really needed. Sometimes GMs fall into the trap illustrated by this dialogue:

GM: What do you do?
Player: I _____.
GM: Okay, give me a roll.

That's not a good instinct—at least, not for the Cypher System. Players should roll when it's interesting or exciting. Otherwise, they should just do what they do. If the PCs tie a rope around something and use it to climb down into a pit, you could ask for tying rolls, climbing rolls, and so on, but why? Just to see if they roll terribly? So the rope can come undone at the wrong time, or a character's hand can slip? Most of the time, that makes players feel inadequate and isn't a lot of fun. A rope coming undone in the middle of an exciting chase scene or a battle can be a great complication (and that's what GM intrusions are for). A rope coming undone in the middle of a simple "getting from point A to point B" scene only slows down gameplay. The real fun—the real story—is down in the pit. So get the PCs down there.

There are a million exceptions to this guideline, of course. If creatures are throwing poisoned darts at the PCs while they climb, that might make things more interesting and require a roll. If the pit is filled with acid and the PCs must climb halfway down, pull a lever, and come back up, that's a situation where you should set difficulty and perhaps have a roll. If a PC is near death, carrying a fragile item of great importance, or something similar, climbing down the rope is tense, and a roll might add to the excitement. The important difference is that these kinds of complications have real consequences.

On the flip side, don't be afraid to use GM intrusion on routine actions if it makes things more interesting. Walking up to the king in his audience chamber in the middle of a ceremony only to trip on a rug? That could have huge ramifications for the character and the story.

OTHER WAYS TO JUDGE DIFFICULTY

Rating things on a scale of 1 to 10 is something that most people are very familiar with. You can also look at it as rating an object or creature on a similar scale, if that's easier. In other words, if you don't know how hard it would be to climb a particular cliff face, think of it as a creature the PCs have to fight. What level would the creature be? You could look in chapter 22 and say "I think this wall should be about as difficult to deal with as a demon. A demon is level 5, so the task of climbing the wall will be difficulty 5." That's a weird way to do it, perhaps, but it's fairly straightforward. And if you're the kind of GM who thinks in terms of "How tough will this fight be?" then maybe rating tasks as creatures or NPCs to fight isn't so strange after all. It's just another way to relate to them. The important thing is that they're on the same scale. Similarly, if the PCs have to tackle a knowledge task—say, trying to determine if they know where a caravan is headed based on its tracks—you could rate the task in terms of an object. If you're used to rating doors or other objects that the PCs have broken through recently, the knowledge task is just a different kind of barrier to bust through.

Everything in the Cypher System—characters, creatures, objects, tasks, and so on—has a level. It might be called a tier or a difficulty instead of a level, but ultimately it's a numerical rating system used to compare things. Although you have to be careful about drawing too many correlations—a first-tier character isn't easily compared to a difficulty 1 wall or a level 1 animal—the principle is the same. Everything can be rated and roughly compared to everything else in the world. (It works best to take PCs out of this equation. For example, you shouldn't try to compare a PC's tier to a wall's level. Character tiers are mentioned here only for completeness.)

Last, if your mind leans toward statistics, you can look at difficulty as a percentage chance. Every number on the d20 is a 5% increment. For example, you have a 5% chance of rolling a 1. You have a 10% chance of rolling a 1 or a 2. Thus, if you need to roll a 12 or higher, you have a 45% chance of success. (A d20 has nine numbers that are 12 or higher: 12, 13, 14, 15, 16, 17, 18, 19, and 20. And 9 × 5 equals 45.)

For some people, it's easier to think in terms of a percentage chance. A GM might think "She has about a 30% chance to know that fact about geography." Each number on a d20 is a 5% increment, and it takes six increments to equal 30%, so there are six numbers that mean the PC succeeds: 15, 16, 17, 18, 19, and 20. Thus, since the player has to roll 15 or higher, that means the target number is 15. (And that means the task is level 5, but if you've already determined the target number, you likely don't care about the level.)

ADVANTAGES TO THIS SYSTEM

1. The GM makes measured adjustments in large, uniform steps. That makes things faster than if players had to do arithmetic using a range of all numbers from 1 to 20.

2. You calculate a target number only once no matter how many times the PCs attempt the action. If you establish that the target number is 12, it's 12 every time a PC tries that action. (On the other hand, if you had to add numbers to your die roll, you'd have to do it for every attempt.) Consider this fact in light of combat. Once a player knows that they need to roll a 12 or higher to hit a foe, combat moves very quickly.

3. If a PC can reduce the difficulty of an action to 0, no roll is needed. This means that an Olympic gymnast doesn't roll a die to walk across a balance beam, but the average person does. The task is initially rated the same for both, but the difficulty is reduced for the gymnast. There's no chance of failure.

4. This is how everything in the game works, whether it's climbing a wall, sweet-talking a guard, or fighting a bioengineered horror.

5. Perhaps most important, the system gives GMs the freedom to focus entirely on the flow of the game. The GM doesn't use dice to determine what happens (unless you want to)—the players do. There aren't a lot of different rules for different actions, so there is little to remember and very little to reference. The difficulty can be used as a narrative tool, with the challenges always meeting the expected logic of the game. All the GM's mental space can be devoted to guiding the story.

Chapter 22: Creatures, page 312

Ultimately what you want is for the players to interact with the situations in the game, not with the rules and numbers that represent the situation. Don't let the players get too worked up over mechanics, dice percentages, and whatnot. That doesn't drive the story.

GM INTRUSION

GM intrusion is the main mechanic that the GM uses to inject drama and additional excitement into the game. It's also a handy tool for resolving issues that affect the PCs but do not involve them. GM intrusion is a way to facilitate what goes on in the world outside the characters. Can the minotaur track the PCs' movements through the maze? Will the fraying rope hold?

Since the players roll all the dice, GM intrusion is used to determine if and when something happens. For example, if the PCs are fighting a noble's guards, and you (the GM) know that there are more guards nearby, you don't need to roll dice to determine if the other guards hear the scuffle and intervene (unless you want to). You just decide when it would be best for the story—which is probably when it would be worst for the characters. In a way, GM intrusion replaces the GM's die rolling.

The mechanic is also one of the main ways that GMs award experience points to the PCs. This means that you use experience points as a narrative tool. Whenever it seems appropriate, you can introduce complications into the game that affect a specific player, but when you do so, you give that player 1 XP. The player can refuse the intrusion, but doing so costs them 1 XP. So by refusing an intrusion, the player does not get the experience point that the GM is offering, and they lose one that they already have. (This kind of refusal is likely to happen very rarely in your game, if ever. And, obviously, a player can't refuse an intrusion if they have no XP to spend.)

Here's how a GM intrusion might work in play. Say the PCs find a hidden console with some buttons. They learn the right order in which to press the buttons, and a section of the floor disappears. As the GM, you don't ask the players specifically where their characters are standing. Instead, you give a player 1 XP and say "Unfortunately, you're standing directly over this new hole in the floor." If the player wanted, they could refuse the XP, spend one of their own, and say "I leap aside to safety." Most likely, though, they'll make the defense roll that you call for and let it play out.

There are two ways for the GM to handle this kind of intrusion. You could say "You're standing in the wrong place, so make a roll." (It's a Speed defense roll, of course.) Alternatively, you could say "You're standing in the wrong place. The floor opens under your feet, and you fall down into the darkness." In the first example, the PC has a chance to save themselves. In the second example, they don't. Both are viable options.

The distinction is based on any number of factors, including the situation, the characters involved, and the needs of the story. This might seem arbitrary or even capricious, but you're the master of what the intrusion can and can't do. RPG mechanics need consistency so players can make intelligent decisions based on how they understand the world to work. But they'll never base their decisions on GM intrusions. They don't know when intrusions will happen or what form they will take. GM intrusions are the unpredictable and strange twists of fate that affect a person's life every day.

When player modifications (such as skill, Effort, and so on) determine that success is automatic, the GM can use GM intrusion to negate the automatic success. The player must roll for the action at its original difficulty level or target number 20, whichever is lower.

PLAYER-AWARDED EXPERIENCE POINTS

Players who gain 1 XP as the result of GM intrusion also get 1 XP to award to another player for whatever reason they wish—maybe the other player had a good idea, told a funny joke, lent a helping hand, or whatever seems appropriate. This means that whenever you use GM intrusion, you're actually giving out 2 XP. The ability for a player to award XP to their friends is empowering and interactive. It helps the players regulate the flow of XP so that no one is left out. It rewards good play that pleases the group as a whole, ensuring that everyone contributes to everyone else's enjoyment. It shouldn't just be the GM who decides which players have done well. Some groups will want to decide the criteria for player-awarded points ahead of time. Some will just want to play it by ear.

Variant: Alternatively, the group could combine the player-awarded points and vote at the end of a session to decide who gets how many XP. This might be the most egalitarian way to do it, but it's probably not as fun or empowering to the individual players.

USING GM INTRUSION AS A NARRATIVE TOOL

A GM can use this narrative tool to steer things. That doesn't mean railroad the players or direct the action of the game with a heavy hand. GM intrusion doesn't enable you to say "You're all captured, so here's your 1 XP." Instead, the GM can direct things more subtly—gently, almost imperceptibly influencing events rather than forcing them. GM intrusion represents things

Remember, any time you give a player 1 XP for a GM intrusion, you're actually giving them 2—one to keep and one to give to another player.

going wrong. The bad guys planning well. Fortune not favoring the characters.

Consider this scenario: the GM plants an interesting adventure seed in a small village, but the PCs don't stay there long enough to find it. So just outside the village, the PCs run afoul of a vicious viper that bites one of them. The GM uses intrusion to say that the poison from the snake will make the character debilitated unless they get a large dose of a specific antitoxin, which the group doesn't have. Of course, they aren't required to go back to the village where the GM's interesting adventure can start, but it's likely that they will, looking for the antitoxin.

Some players might find intrusion heavy-handed, but the XP softens the blow. And remember, they can refuse these narrative nudges. Intrusion is not meant to be a railroading tool—just a bit of a rudder. Not an inescapable track, but a nudge here and there.

What's more, the GM doesn't need to have a deliberate goal in mind. The complication you introduce could simply make things more interesting. You might not know where it will take the story, just that it will make the story better.

This is wonderfully empowering to the GM—not in a "Ha ha, now I'll trounce the PCs" way, but in an "I can control the narrative a little bit, steering it more toward the story I want to create rather than relying on the dice" sort of way. Consider that old classic plot development in which the PCs get captured and must escape from the bad guys. In heroic fiction, this is such a staple that it would almost seem strange if it didn't happen. But in many roleplaying games, it's a nearly impossible turn of events—the PCs usually have too many ways to get out of the bad guy's clutches before they're captured. The dice have to be wildly against them. It virtually never happens. With GM intrusion, it could happen (again, in the context of the larger encounter, not as a single intrusion that results in the entire group of PCs being captured with little explanation or chance to react).

For example, let's say the PCs are surrounded by orcs. One character is badly injured—debilitated—and the rest are hurt. Some of the orcs produce a large weighted net. Rather than asking for a lot of rolls and figuring the mechanics for escape, you use intrusion and say that the net goes over the PCs who are still on their feet. The rest of the orcs point spears menacingly. This is a pretty strong cue to the players that surrender is a good (and possibly the only) option. Some players won't take the hint, however, so another use of intrusion might allow the orcs to hit one of the trapped PCs on the head and render them unconscious while their friends struggle in the net. If the players still don't surrender, it's probably best to play out the rest of the encounter without more GM intrusions—using more would be heavy-handed by anyone's measure—although it's perfectly reasonable to rule that a character rendered debilitated is knocked unconscious, since the orcs are trying to take the PCs alive.

USING GM INTRUSION AS A RESOLUTION MECHANIC

This mechanic offers a way for the GM to determine how things happen in the game without leaving it all to random chance. Bad guys trying to smash down the door to the room where the PCs are holed up? You could roll a bunch of dice, compare the NPCs' stats to the door's stats, and so on, or you could wait until the most interesting time, have the bad guys break in, and award an experience point to the PC who tried their best to bar the door. The latter way is the Cypher System way. Intrusion is a task resolution tool for the GM. In other words, you don't base things on stats but on narrative choice. (Frankly, a lot of great GMs over the years—even in the very early days of the hobby—have run their games this way. Sometimes they rolled dice or pretended to roll dice, but they were really manipulating things.) This method frees the GM from worrying about mechanics and looking up stats and allows them to focus on the story.

This isn't cheating—it's the rules of the game. This rule simply replaces traditional dice rolling with good game mastering, logic, and intelligent storytelling. When a PC is climbing a burning rope, and everyone knows that it will break at some point, the game has a mechanism to ensure that it breaks at just the right time.

Variant: If you want more randomness in your game, or if you want your game to seem like more of a simulation, assign a flat percentage chance for whatever you're trying to resolve. For example, each round, the star troopers have a 20% chance to blast through the door—or, if you want the risk to escalate, a cumulative 20% chance to blast through the door. By not using GM intrusion, this method robs the PCs of a few XP, but when they see you rolling dice, it might help with their immersion. Alternatively, you can pretend to roll dice but really use GM intrusion, though this method seriously robs the characters of XP.

There's a better way. Announce your intrusion, but say that there's only a chance it will happen

Remember that GM intrusions can occur at any time, not just during combat. Disrupting or changing a tense interaction with NPCs can have big repercussions.

This might not be true of your players, but many players rarely, if ever, spend XP to refuse an intrusion from the GM, though they regularly use XP to avoid an intrusion that comes from a bad roll. And there's nothing wrong with that. Some GMs might want to forbid using an XP to reroll a 1, but there's really no point—if you've got an idea for a good intrusion, you don't need to wait until a player rolls a 1 to use it.

(state the percentage chance), and then roll the dice in plain view of everyone. If the intrusion occurs, award the XP as normal. This is likely the best of both worlds. However, it takes the narrative power out of your hands and gives it to the dice. Perhaps this method is best used only occasionally. If nothing else, it injects some variety and certainly some drama.

USING (AND NOT ABUSING) GM INTRUSION

Too much of a good thing will make the game seem utterly unpredictable—even capricious. The ideal is to use about four GM intrusions per game session, depending on the length of the session, or about one intrusion per hour of game play. This is in addition to any intrusions that are triggered by players rolling a 1.

INTRUSION THROUGH PLAYER ROLLS

When a PC rolls a 1, handle the GM intrusion the same way that you'd handle an intrusion you initiated. The intrusion could mean the PC fumbles or botches whatever they were trying to do, but it could mean something else. Consider these alternatives:

- In combat, the PC's foe is not as hurt as they thought. Give the foe 5 extra points of health.
- In combat, the PC drops their guard, and the foe gets a free attack.
- In combat, reinforcements for the PC's foes show up.
- In combat (or any stressful situation), an ally decides to flee.
- In combat (or any stressful situation), an ally doesn't like the PCs as much as they thought. The ally steals from them or betrays them.
- Out of combat, the PC's pack falls open, or the sole of their shoe tears open.
- Out of combat, it begins to rain heavily.
- Out of combat, a surprise foe appears, and the scene turns into a combat.
- In an interaction, the GM introduces a surprising motive for the NPC. For example, the PCs are trying to bribe an official for information, and the official reveals that what they really want isn't money but for someone to rescue their kidnapped son.

GM INTRUSION THAT AFFECTS THE GROUP

The core of the idea behind GM intrusion is that the player being adversely affected gains an experience point. But what if the intrusion affects the whole group equally? What if the GM uses it to have an unstable device overload and explode, harming all the characters? In this case, if no PC is involved more than the others (for example, no single PC was frantically attempting to repair the device), you should give 1 XP to each character but not give any of them an extra XP to hand out to someone else.

However, this kind of group intrusion should be an exception, not the rule. GM intrusions are much more effective if they are more personal.

EXAMPLE GM INTRUSIONS

It's not a good idea to use the same events as GM intrusions over and over ("Dolmar dropped his sword *again*?"). Below are a number of different intrusions you can use.

BAD LUCK

Through no fault of the characters, something happens that is bad or at least complicating. For example:

- The floorboard beneath the PC gives way.
- The boat lists to starboard at just the wrong moment.
- A gust of wind blows the papers out of the character's hand.
- The buckle of the PC's pack snaps at an inopportune time.
- The NPC that the characters need to speak with is home sick today.
- A device (cypher or artifact) malfunctions or gives the user a jolt.

AN UNKNOWN COMPLICATION EMERGES

The situation was more complex (and therefore more interesting) than the PCs knew—perhaps even more than the GM knew, at least at the start. For example:

- A poisonous snake darts out from the tall grass and attacks.
- The box that holds the plans is trapped with a poison needle.
- The NPC that the PCs need to befriend doesn't speak their language.
- The NPC that the PCs try to bribe is allergic to the bottle of alcohol they offer.
- The PCs find the book they need, but the pages are so brittle that if they open it, it might crumble.

AN IMPENDING COMPLICATION EMERGES

GMs can use this type of intrusion as a resolution mechanic to determine NPC success or failure. Rather than rolling dice to see how long it takes an NPC to rewire a damaged force field generator, it happens at a time of the GM's choosing—ideally when it would be most interesting. For example:

- The goblin reinforcements finally get through the locked door.
- The ropes of the old rope bridge finally snap.
- The city guards show up.
- The unstable ceiling collapses.
- The NPC who holds a dagger to a character's throat and says "Don't move" cuts the PC when they do, in fact, move, putting them immediately at debilitated on the damage track.

OPPONENT LUCK OR SKILL

The PCs aren't the only ones with surprising tricks up their sleeves. For example:

- The PC's opponent uses a lightning-fast maneuver to dodge all attacks.
- The PC's opponent sees an opening and makes an additional, immediate attack.
- The NPC commander rallies their troops, who all deal 2 additional points of damage for one round.
- The PC's opponent uses a cypher or similar device that produces just the right effect for the situation.
- A bit of the wall collapses in the middle of the fight, preventing the characters from chasing the fleeing NPC.

FUMBLES

Although you might not want every player roll of 1 to be a fumble, sometimes it could be just that. Alternatively, the GM could simply declare that a fumble has occurred. In either case, consider the following examples:

- In combat, the PC drops their weapon.
- In combat, the PC misses and strikes the wall, breaking or damaging their weapon.
- In combat, the NPC hits the PC harder than usual, inflicting 2 additional points of damage.
- In combat, the PC hits an ally by accident and inflicts regular damage.
- Out of combat, the PC drops or mishandles an important object or piece of equipment.
- In an interaction, the PC inadvertently or unknowingly says something offensive.

PARTIAL SUCCESS

GM intrusion doesn't have to mean that a PC has failed. For example:

- The PC disables the explosive device before it goes off, but if someone doesn't remain and hold the detonator, it will still explode.
- The PC creates the antidote, but it will turn the imbiber's flesh blue for the next few weeks.
- The PC jumps across the pit but accidentally knocks loose some stones from the edge, making the jump harder for their friend right behind them.

PLAYER INTRUSIONS

Player intrusion, page 21

Player intrusions give the players a small bit of narrative control over the world. However, the world still remains in the GM's purview. You can always overrule a player intrusion, or suggest a way to massage it so that it fits better into the setting. Still, because it is indeed narrative control, a player intrusion should always involve a small aspect of the world beyond the character. "I punch my foe really hard" is an expression of Effort or perhaps character ability. "My foe slips and falls backward off the ledge" is a player intrusion.

Player intrusions should never be as big as GM intrusions. They should not end an encounter, only (perhaps) provide the PC with the means to more easily end an encounter. They should not have a wide-reaching or even necessarily a long-term effect on the setting. A way to consider this might be that player intrusions can affect a single object (a floorboard snaps), feature (there's a hidden shallow spot in the stream to ford), or NPC (the vendor is an old friend). But not more than that. A player intrusion can't affect a whole village or even a whole tavern in that village. A rock can come loose, but a player intrusion can't create a landslide.

Needler, page 273

THE REST OF THE RULES

I'll say it again: the rules exist to be used as tools to shape the game, the story, and the experience. When you tell a player that the howling, bestial Cro-Magnon warriors at the top of the cliff throw down heavy stones and their character gets hurt, the rules give you a way to explain just how hurt.

One way to look at it is this: the GM is the sensory input for the players. They can't know anything about what's going on in the fictional reality of the game unless the GM tells them. The rules, then, are one way to convey information to the players in a manner that is meaningful to everyone sitting at the table. The GM could say "You're quite hurt," but the rules clarify how hurt they are. The GM could say "You can hurl that spear pretty far," but the rules provide a definition of "pretty far" that helps keep things consistent, moderately realistic, and understandable so the GM doesn't have to repeat things over and over.

The rules do more than that, of course. They determine success or failure for PCs and NPCs. They help define what resources characters have to interact with the world (although the best resource is the players' ingenuity, and that isn't defined by the rules).

It's telling that in the Cypher System, the rules define "quite hurt" and "pretty far" very generally, intentionally leaving a lot up to the GM's storytelling abilities. A game with a less story-based approach would likely define such things far more precisely.

At any time, it's reasonable to switch one "condition" for another. Thus, if a PC is supposed to move down one step on the damage track as the result of someone attempting to knock them out, something equally dire happens instead. This could also be the case if someone tries to blind or deafen a PC, or anything else appropriate. Conversely, an effect that normally blinds a character could just move them one step down the damage track instead.

ADJUDICATING

A lot of what I'm talking about here is what people sometimes call "adjudicating." Adjudicating is basically the difference between a computer game and a game run by an actual, living human being. All a computer can do (as of yet) is follow the rules. But a human can use their sense of logic (we'll discuss that in detail below) to determine whether the rules make sense for a given situation, and they can do it on a case-by-case basis. Because there's a human GM using logic, the rules for how to play the Cypher System take up only a small part of this hefty book. If the rules had to cover every imaginable situation, well, this would be a very different book.

For example, imagine that the PCs encounter an assassin who tries to kill them with a needler loaded with poisoned needles. One of the PCs is heavily armored, so they take no damage from the needles—not even close. That sort of sounds like the needles just bounced off their armor. Should the poison on a needle that can't penetrate a character's armor affect that character? Probably not. But that's not an actual rule. Well, why not make it a rule? Because then suddenly anyone wearing a leather jerkin can't be affected by poison needles. Should that be the case? No, because the thick leather doesn't protect every area on the PC's body. It's more complex than that. Could you devise a rule to cover both situations? Probably, but why bother? You can make a decision based on the situation. (You can also use GM intrusion and say that a needle hit where the armor didn't offer protection—GM intrusion really does solve a lot of these issues.)

Likewise, sometimes a character who falls off a high ledge should be stunned and lose their next turn. That isn't a rule, but it makes sense—sometimes. And the key word is *sometimes*. Because sometimes the situation or the context means you don't want that to happen, so you adjudicate.

A character falling from a 100-foot (30 m) ledge might take 10 points of damage. That's a lot, but a fresh character with a decent amount of Might can take that and keep going. Sometimes that's okay, but sometimes it stretches our suspension of disbelief. If a player reads the rules on how much damage is dealt by falling, they might even have their character jump off a high cliff deliberately, knowing that they can take it. So you adjudicate that they don't just lose their next turn, but the fall also knocks them down a step on the damage track. That's harsh, and the player will really feel it. But they should, and it will keep them from exploiting what might seem like a hole in the rules in a way that no real person would (and no one in a story would).

Remember, it's your job to use the rules to simulate the world, even if the world is a fictional place with all kinds of strangeness. You're not a slave to the rules—it's the other way around. If you come across a hole in the rules or something that doesn't make sense, don't shrug your shoulders and say "Well, that's what the rules say (or don't say)." Fix it.

When talking about rules, sometimes people will toss around words like "game balance" or refer to rules as "broken." These concepts belong in games where players build characters using extensive rules and make a lot of choices and then pit those characters against specific challenges to see how they fare. In such a game, a challenge rated or designed poorly, or a character option that grants too much or too little power, can throw everything completely out of whack. Advancing and improving characters is the point of that kind of game, and the way that characters "win" is by overcoming challenges (often, by fighting). Because the Cypher System is not a game about matching PC builds against specific challenges, nor a game about advancing characters (at least not solely, and in any event, characters do not advance due to fights or overcoming challenges), these concepts really don't apply. If something seems broken, change it. If a PC ability is too powerful, make it less so. Do it either as part of the story, or—perhaps even better—just be upfront with the players. "Hey, guys, this new psychic power of Ray's is just too good. It's making every fight a pushover and that's not fun. So I'm going to tone down its effect. Sound okay?" An honest discussion with the players is often the best way to handle, well, just about any problem that crops up in a game. And if a player can't handle that kind of interaction, maybe you don't want them at your table anyway.

LOGIC

Running a game requires a lot of logic rather than a careful reading of the rules. For example, some things give characters a resistance to fire (almost always expressed as Armor). But there is no special rule for "fire damage" as opposed to "slicing damage" or "lightning damage." Instead, you use logic to determine whether the damage inflicted counts as fire. In these situations, there are only two times when your answer is wrong.

The first is when the answer breaks the players' suspension of disbelief. For example, something that makes a PC fire resistant should probably provide some protection against a heat-based weapon. If it doesn't, your answer will spoil the moment for the group.

The second wrong answer is when you're inconsistent. If you allow a PC's fireproof armor to give them some protection against lava one time but not the next, that's a problem—not only because it breaks the suspension of disbelief but also because it gives the players nothing to base their decisions on. Without predictable consistency, they can't make intelligent decisions.

The Cypher System rules are written with the assumption that the GM does not need to fall back on rules for everything, either for your own sake or as a defense against the players. "I'm going to run a long distance and jump on my big friend's back. On their action, they will run a long distance. So I can move twice as far in one round. There's no rule against that, right?" It's true that there isn't a rule against that, but it makes no sense. The GM's logic rules the day here.

You shouldn't need pedantic rules to defend against the players. You and the players should work together to create a logical, consistent, and believable world and story. Players who try to use the lack of pedantry in the rules to gain unrealistic and illogical advantages for their characters should revisit the basic concept of the Cypher System.

Further, the rules don't say things like "The GM decides if the NPC knows the answer to the question, or if they will answer, or how they will answer." Of course that's the kind of thing you decide—that's your role. The rules don't state that you decide if something is logical and appropriate to the story or setting any more than they state that the player decides what actions their character will take. That's just the way the game works.

Does this put more pressure on the GM? Yes and no. It means that you need to make more judgment calls—more of the adjudication described above—which can be challenging if you're new at it. But being an arbiter of what seems appropriate and makes sense is something that we all do, all day long. Look at it this way: when you're watching a television show or a movie, at some point you might say "That seems wrong" or "That seems unrealistic." There's no difference between doing that and using logic as a GM.

In the long run, relying on logic frees the GM. No longer saddled with hundreds (or thousands)

While GMs always have notes that they put together before the game session, it's smart to have a lot of blank paper to scribble notes on during the game. You'll invariably have to make stuff up as you go, and later you might want to be able to remember what you did. Sometimes it will be a rules issue (remembering that it was a difficulty 4 jump to cross the pit, so that it will be consistent when the PCs come back that way again), and sometimes it will just be an NPC's name or some detail about them.

GMs can encourage smart players to be ready with their actions, and to know enough about how actions work so that you don't have to ask if they're using Effort or tell them to make a roll. In a perfect world, when it's Michele's turn and you ask what she's doing, she says "I'm going to try to climb the tree to get out of reach of the golem. I'm using a level of Effort, and I rolled a 14." That way, you can take the info and immediately tell her if she succeeded or not. This keeps play moving at a wonderfully brisk pace, and doesn't let talk of game mechanics bog things down.

of individual rules, compatibility issues, loopholes, and the like, you are free to move ahead with the story being told by the group. You can focus more on the narrative elements of the game than on the mechanical ones. To look at it a different way, in other games GMs sometimes spend a lot of time preparing, which is almost always rules-related stuff: creating NPC stat blocks, memorizing rules subsystems that will come into play, carefully balancing encounters, and so on. A Cypher System GM does very little of that. Prepping for the game means figuring out cool storylines, weird new devices or foes, and the best way to convey the atmosphere. The mechanical elements can be handled during the game, using logic at the table.

DICE ROLLING

Using the rules involves rolling dice. If the dice don't mean anything, then everything is predetermined, and it's no longer a game by any definition—just a story being told. So the dice need to matter. But that means that sometimes a PC will fail when they would succeed if it were a story, and vice versa. That's not a flaw; it's a feature. It's what makes roleplaying games so exciting. When we're watching an action movie, we know that in the third act the hero will defeat the villain at just the right moment. But in an RPG, maybe not. It's not so predictable. That's one of the things that makes them so special.

On the other hand, things like GM intrusions sometimes trump the die rolls to help the story move along in a direction that is (hopefully) best for the game. How do you manage it all?

As you describe the action or as the PCs move about the world, the vast majority of things that happen shouldn't involve dice. Walking around, buying things in a market, chatting with NPCs, crossing the wilderness, looking for an ancient ruin—these are not actions that normally require die rolls. However, it's easy to think of exceptions where rolls might be needed. How do you decide? There are two rules of thumb.

First, don't ask for a roll unless it seems like there should be a chance of failure and a chance of success. If a PC wants to shoot an arrow from their bow and hit the moon, there's no need to roll, because there's no chance for success. Likewise, if they want to shoot that same arrow at a large building from 10 feet (3 m) away, there's no chance for failure. You and logic run the game, not the dice.

Second, if a creature (PC or NPC) or object is affected in a harmful way—or, in the case of a creature, in a way that it doesn't want to be affected, harmful or not—you need to involve a die roll. Whether the action is slashing with a blade, using deception to trick someone, intrusively reading an NPC's mind, breaking down a door, or applying poison, something is being harmed or affected in a way that it doesn't want to be, so a die roll is needed.

Thus, someone using a power to become invisible likely doesn't require a roll. It just works. There's really no chance of failure (unless the power comes from a faulty device or some other extraneous force is at work), and it doesn't directly affect anyone or anything other than the character becoming invisible. However, using a device to shape the emotions of another creature would require a die roll.

Of course, sometimes a character can use Effort to reduce the difficulty so there's no need to make a roll. But you, as the GM, can also waive the need for a roll. Consider a character who uses their Flash ability on a bunch of level 1 rodents. Each has 3 health, and the PC needs to roll only 3 or higher to affect each one, but there are twenty-four rodents. You can simply say, "With a discharge of sudden energy, you incinerate the swarm of rodents, leaving little behind but scorch marks and the smell of burnt hair." This keeps things moving and prevents the game from coming to a dead stop while the player makes two dozen rolls. Frankly, most first-tier characters will find level 1 creatures merely a nuisance, so no drama is ruined when the PC takes them all out. Move on to another, greater challenge.

When you waive the need for a die roll, what you're effectively doing is making the action routine, so no roll is needed. In the case of the PC who uses Flash, you're reducing the difficulty by one step due to circumstances: the rodents just aren't that tough. That's not breaking the rules—that's using the rules. That's the way the game is meant to be played.

As an aside, this doesn't mean that the swarm of rodents is a bad encounter. It would be bad in a game where it takes an hour and a half to resolve a fight that was no real challenge. But in the Cypher System? Even if the character doesn't blast every rodent, an encounter like that can be resolved in five minutes. Not every encounter needs to be life-or-death to be interesting. But we'll talk about designing encounters (and the related issue of pacing) later in this chapter.

Flash, page 140

Remember, most of the time, powers, abilities, devices, and so forth are written from the point of view of the characters. But the players make die rolls, not the GM. So, for example, if the circumstances call for an NPC to make a defense roll, that means a PC should make an attack roll instead.

Running the Cypher System

USING CHARACTER TYPES TO DEFINE THE SETTING

Much more than in other Cypher System games like Numenera or The Strange, the types presented in chapter 5 of this book are meant to be tools for you to customize your game. Nothing helps define the specifics of the setting like the options that characters have at their disposal, just as nothing defines the setting of a novel like the main characters—who they are, what they know, and what they can do.

This means that you have all the freedom in the world to mix and match abilities, or predetermine ability choices. If, in your fantasy world, you have a character type that is a wizard who is a master of magic, it might be hard to imagine that character not being trained in magical lore. So you take the Adept type, rename it "Wizard," and make the Magic Training ability mandatory at first tier, leaving the player three rather than four choices for special abilities.

For a more in-depth example, consider the Glaive from Numenera. The Glaive is much like the Warrior type, but at first tier, the abilities Fighter and Combat Prowess are predetermined for Glaives, ensuring that they are the most physical of the types and reinforcing the idea that they're the best at inflicting damage with weapons. This leaves Glaives with two ability choices at first tier (instead of a Warrior's four choices). At second tier, Glaives get one choice (instead of a Warrior's two choices) because all glaives get Skill With Attacks.

This emphasis is intended to reinforce (not limit) the setting and the character concept. In Numenera's setting, Glaives are combatants, and most combatants wear armor and they all make attacks. A Glaive who is not skilled in attacks makes no sense within the context of the setting.

The types can also be ad hoc rather than predetermined. Find out what the player's character concept is, and tailor the type to that concept, perhaps using flavor.

For example, if a player in a modern game wants to be a rock musician, use the Speaker type but call it "Musician" (all of the abilities will be music based rather than word based, but the effects remain the same). If a player in the same game wants to be a rebellious teen who sneaks out a lot, make them an Explorer with lots of physical skills and abilities (perhaps add in stealth flavor) and call it "Teenager." If they change their mind and want to be a scientist, they can still be an Explorer, but adjust the type so its emphasis is on knowledge skills (perhaps add in skills and knowledge flavor) and call it "Scientist."

Basically, the thing to remember is that types serve two purposes: to help define the setting,

Feel free to rename the types to anything you want to make them fit a player's character concept. Chapter 5 offers some alternative names for each type in a range of game genres.

Flavor, page 34

415

and to help fulfill the player's character concept. Descriptor and focus also help to do the latter, so GMs should feel free to make whatever changes or predetermined choices they see fit for the types offered in their game.

TYING ACTIONS TO STATS

Although the decision is open to your discretion, when a PC takes an action, it should be fairly obvious which stat is tied to that action. Physical actions that involve brute force or endurance use Might. Physical actions that involve quickness, coordination, or agility use Speed. Actions that involve intelligence, education, insight, willpower, or charm use Intellect.

In rare instances, you could allow a PC to use a different stat for a task. For example, a character might try to break down a door by examining it closely for flaws and thus use Intellect rather than Might. This kind of change is a good thing because it encourages player creativity. Just don't let it be abused by an exuberant or too-clever player. It's well within your purview to decide that the door has no flaws, or to rule that the character's attempt will take half an hour rather than one round. In other words, using a stat that is not the obvious choice should be the exception, not the rule.

THE FLOW OF INFORMATION

You are the eyes and ears of the players. They can't know anything about the world unless you tell them. Make sure that the information you provide is both precise and concise. (We'll discuss good description later in this chapter.) Be evocative, but not to the point that the players lose details in the language you use. Be open to answering their questions about the world around them.

Sometimes it's easy: a PC looks over the top of the hill, and you tell them what they see. Other times things are hidden, or there's a chance that they miss something important—secret panels, cloaked assassins, creatures with natural camouflage, details of significance in a crowded marketplace, and so on. In these cases, perhaps a roll is involved. But it's odd to ask players to roll when they haven't taken any actions. It's within the bounds of the rules, but it can be jarring. There are different ways to handle the situation: you can call for a roll, compare levels, or use an intrusion.

GM Calls for Rolls: This is the most straightforward approach. It's always the best choice if a PC's action is to search, listen, or otherwise keep an eye out. If a PC is on watch while their comrades rest, call for an Intellect roll immediately and use the result if anything happens during the entire time they are guarding.

But what if the PC isn't actively looking? Let's say a pickpocket moves up behind them to lift a few coins, so you ask the player to make an Intellect roll with a difficulty equal to the pickpocket's level. (Arguably, they could make a Speed-based roll to see if they are quick enough to catch a glimpse—it's up to you.) Some PCs are skilled in perceiving, and that would come into play here. Success means that you tell the character what they see, and failure means that they notice nothing. However, the player knows that they had to make a roll, so they know that something was up. One way to keep players on their toes is to call for rolls when there is nothing to notice.

GM Compares Levels: You can take the player out of the equation (so as not to alert their suspicions) by comparing the PC's tier to the difficulty of the perceiving task. Ties go to the PC. You can still figure in skills and assets as bonuses to the PC's tier. So a third-tier character trained in perceiving will spot the level 4 predator cat stalking up behind them. This method is particularly good for determining simple results, such as whether the PC hears a river in the distance. That kind of thing isn't worth a roll, but for some reason, you might not want to give out the information automatically. This method also rewards a perceptive character, who will hear the noise before anyone else. Don't forget to increase the difficulty for distance in such a situation.

GM Intrudes: Rarely, you can keep things to yourself and spring the knowledge of what happened as a GM intrusion. If the PC discovers that their pocket is now empty of coins, that's certainly a complication. Sometimes the "discovery" itself is a complication—for example, the character notices a mugging going on in the alley as they walk by.

In addition, the GM is the source of knowledge about the parts of the PCs' lives that don't take place in a game session. If a character used to be in the military and needs to know the name of their old unit commander, you need to give it to the player (or, better yet, let the player come up with the name).

FAILURE TO NOTICE

If PCs miss a sensory detail, you should consider very carefully what to do about that. If there's a cool secret chamber in the ancient complex or an important clue under the table in the castle guardroom, maybe a perceptive PC should just find it (no roll required), particularly if they said they were looking. To do otherwise might mean submitting to the tyranny of the dice. Just because the PC rolled a 2, should the adventure come to a dead stop?

Well, in the first place, don't design a scenario that can come to a dead stop if the PCs botch one roll. There should always be multiple paths to success.

In the second place, consider your other options. Maybe the PCs will learn about the secret chamber later and they'll have to backtrack to find it. If the characters don't find the clue under the table, an NPC might—and then lord it over them with a show of superiority. If all else fails, as noted above, sometimes discovery is a complication, and you can simply foist it upon a PC through GM intrusion. In such a case, however, you might want to include a challenge. For example, the PC finds the secret door accidentally by leaning against the hidden control pad, which lets out the flying insectoid hunter-seekers guarding the chamber before the characters are ready for them.

On the other hand, perhaps in such a situation, the PCs didn't "earn" the discovery—if there was no roll, then no Effort was used and no risks were taken. That's not good. Maybe the PCs just miss out this time. Maybe they should learn to be more observant.

In other words, the answer depends on the situation. Don't hesitate to vary things. It keeps the players guessing.

GRADUATED SUCCESS

Sometimes, a GM will break away from the traditional model that governs Cypher System task resolution and allow for a graduated success. With this method, you set a difficulty as usual, but if the player succeeds at a difficulty at least one step higher, their success is better than normal. Likewise, if their roll indicates that they would have succeeded at one step (or more) lower, they might have a partial success.

For example, a PC tracking the bandits that robbed the train looks for tracks in the woods to see if any of them came down a certain path recently. Given the terrain and the weather, the GM decides that the difficulty is 4, so the target number is 12. The player rolls a 10. This isn't enough to accomplish the task that the PC set out to do, but since they would have succeeded if the difficulty had been 3, the GM decides that the character still learns that something had come down the path recently—they just aren't certain if it was bandits. The reason is that if the PC had simply been looking for tracks of any kind, the GM would have set a difficulty of 3. Similarly, if the player had rolled a 17—a success at least one step higher—the GM would have said that not only did they find bandit tracks, but there were five of them, and the tracks show that the bandits were burdened. In other words, the player would have received more information than they asked for.

In a situation where there are more results than simply success or failure, you can convey these results based on multiple difficulties. A player can state an action, and you can come up with not one difficulty but two, three, or more. For example, if the PCs try to persuade a merchant to give them information, the GM can predetermine that he gives them one minor bit of information if they succeed at a task with a difficulty of 2, a fair bit of information if they succeed at a task with a difficulty of 3, and everything he knows on the topic if they succeed at a task with a difficulty of 4. The players don't make three different rolls. They make one roll with a scaled, graduated success.

As a rule of thumb, reverse-engineer the situation. If the player rolls considerably higher or lower than the target number (more than 3 away), consider what a success at the difficulty they did overcome would have gained them. If creating a makeshift electronic key to open a sealed door has a target number of 18, what does the PC create if the player rolls 16? Perhaps the answer is nothing, but perhaps it is a makeshift key that works intermittently.

This system is rarely (if ever) used in combat or situations where something either works or doesn't. But when crafting an object, interacting with an NPC, or gaining information, it can be very useful. Of course, you are never required to use this model of task resolution—sometimes success or failure is all you need to know. Usually, graduated success involves going only one step higher or lower than the original difficulty, but you can be as flexible about that as you wish.

Finally, sometimes you can offer a "consolation prize" for trying. Say a PC fears that a door has been rigged with a trap. They search it but fail the roll. The GM might still reveal something about the door. "You don't find

A good rule of thumb is: players should always know why they are rolling. If you suddenly say "Give me a roll" to see if they notice something, it's probably better either to act as if they noticed it and give them the information, or to proceed as if they didn't, and then spring a surprise on them via a GM intrusion. Of course, if a player says that they're looking around carefully, that's another story entirely.

anything special, but you do note that the door appears quite sturdy and is locked." It's the kind of information the GM might give automatically (think of it as difficulty 0), but it softens the blow of failure. Some information is better than none, and it makes sense that the PC will learn at least something if they study an object for a few minutes.

DEALING WITH CHARACTER ABILITIES

A lot of people might think that the Cypher System is a class-and-level game because it has things that are enough like classes (types) and levels (tiers) that it's easy to see the misconception. And that's fine.

But here's the real secret, just between you and me: it's not tiers, types, or any of that stuff that is the key to really understanding the system.

It's the cyphers.

The cyphers are the key to making the game work differently than other games. The Cypher System isn't about playing for years before a character is allowed to teleport, travel to other dimensions, lay waste to a dozen enemies at once, or create a mechanical automaton to do their bidding. They can do it right out of the gate if they have the right cypher.

This system works because both the GM and the player have a say over what cyphers a character has. It's not limiting—it's freeing.

The easiest way to design a good game is to limit—and strictly define—PC power. Characters of such-and-such a level (or whatever) can do this kind of thing but not that kind of thing. The GM knows that the characters aren't going to ruin everything by seeing into the past or creating a nuclear explosion.

But that's not the only way to design a good game. What if you—the GM—decide that while it would not be so great if the PCs could see into the past (which would ruin the mystery of your scenario), it would be okay if they could blow up half the city? The Cypher System allows you to permit anything you feel is appropriate or interesting.

To put it another way (and to continue the ever-more-absurd examples), PCs who can solve every mystery and blow up every city probably end up making the game a pushover (and thus dull), but PCs who can solve *one* mystery or blow up *one* city won't ruin the campaign. Cyphers allow the characters to do amazing, cool, and fun things—just not reliably or consistently. Thus, although they potentially have access to great power from time to time, they have to use it wisely.

As the GM, it's important to remember the distinction between a character ability gained through type or focus, an ability or advantage gained through an artifact, and an ability gained through a cypher. The first two kinds of abilities will shape the way you expect the characters to behave, but the cyphers won't. If a PC has the Exists Partially Out of Phase focus, they're going to be walking through walls all the time—it's what they do—so it shouldn't catch you off guard. In a way, you should "prepare" for it. I put that word in quotes because I don't mean that you nullify it. Don't put in a bunch of walls that they can't get through. That's no fun. Walking through walls is what they do, and if you take that away, they don't get to do anything. (Foiling their power every once in a while is fine because it might add to the challenge, but it should be the exception, not the rule.) By "preparing" for their ability, I mean don't expect a locked door to keep them out. Be ready when they sneak into places most people can't go, and be ready to tell them what they find.

But with cyphers, no preparation is necessary. First of all, most of them don't throw a wrench into anything—they just help the character deal with a situation in a faster way, giving them some healing, a temporary boost, or a one-use offensive power. Second, the PCs never end up with a cypher that you didn't give them, so you can have as much say over their cyphers as you want. And third (and perhaps most important), when a PC pulls out a detonation cypher and blows up the lead wagon in the caravan, completely changing the situation, that's part of the fun. You'll have to figure out on the fly what happens next, and so will the players. That's not ruining things—that's what is supposed to happen. Players surprising the GM is part of the game. Cyphers just make those surprises more frequent, and in ways as interesting as you're willing to allow.

We'll look at designing encounters later, but for now, remember this point: no single encounter is so important that you ever have to worry about the players "ruining" it. You hear those kinds of complaints all the time. "Her telepathic power totally ruined that interaction" or "The players came up with a great ambush and killed the main villain in one round, ruining the final encounter."

No. No, no, no. See the forest for the trees. Don't think about the game in terms of encounters. Think about it in terms of the adventure or the campaign. If a PC used a potent cypher to easily kill a powerful and important opponent, remember these three things:

1. They don't have that cypher anymore.
2. There will be more bad guys.

3. Combat's not the point of the game—it's merely an obstacle. If the players discover a way to overcome an obstacle more quickly than you expected, there's nothing wrong with that. They're not cheating, and the game's not broken. Just keep the story going. What happens next? What are the implications of what just happened?

OPTIONAL RULE: MODIFYING ABILITIES ON THE FLY

Sometimes, a player can use a special ability in a way that goes beyond its normal bounds. Such changes can be done on the fly. In some cases, it simply costs more points to use the ability in a new way. In other cases, more challenges are involved.

For any Intellect ability with a specific range, you can increase the range by using more mental energy. If you spend 1 additional Intellect point, you can change the range by one step—either from short to long, or from long to very long. You can't increase a range beyond very long (which is 500 feet, or 150 m) by spending more points. Any Intellect ability that has a duration (anything more than a single action in a single round) usually lasts one minute, ten minutes, or one hour. By spending 1 additional point of Intellect, you can increase the duration by one step, so an ability that lasts one minute can be made to last ten minutes. Durations cannot be increased more than one step.

A player can make a special roll to modify the range, area, or other aspects of an ability. The roll is always modified by the stat it's normally based on. The GM sets the difficulty for the roll based on the degree of modification. Like any roll, the player can use Effort, skill, and assets to ease the task. Generally, the difficulty falls into one of three categories from the Task Difficulty table:

Impossible (modifying an ability to accomplish an effect that has nothing to do with its description or intent)

Formidable (modifying an ability to do something similar to the description or intent, but changing its nature)

Difficult (modifying an ability to do something within the spirit and general idea of the ability)

For example, say an Adept has the Hover ability and wants to modify its use in the middle of an encounter. If they want to use it to blast someone with fire, that's an impossible task (difficulty 10) because fire has nothing to do with the ability.

If they want to use it offensively within the general description of the ability, they might

Exists Partially Out of Phase, page 68

Hover, page 149

ENCOURAGING PLAYER CREATIVITY

The Cypher System is a game that places more importance on creativity than on understanding the rules. The players should succeed not because they've chosen all the "right" options when creating their characters but because they come up with the best ideas when facing challenges. This means that for every challenge, there should be a straightforward solution (destroy the lightning-emitting turret to get into the tower) and a not-so-straightforward one (sneak up to the tower, find the power conduit to the turret, and sever it). It's not your responsibility as the GM to come up with both. The players will come up with the not-so-straightforward solutions. You just have to be willing to go with their ideas.

This doesn't mean you have to let them succeed if they try something weird. On the contrary, the not-so-straightforward solution might end up being as hard or harder than the straightforward one. But you have to be ready to adjudicate the idea no matter what. It's tempting to say that there's no way to find or sever the power conduit and the PCs have to destroy the turret the old-fashioned way (a combat encounter). In some situations, that might be appropriate—perhaps the conduit is simply not accessible to the PCs on the outside of the tower. But a GM has to be willing to say that sometimes it is possible and to adjudicate the details on the fly. If you don't, and you shut down the players' outside-the-box ideas, they will learn that the only thing to do is charge into the fray every time. That the obvious solution is the only possible solution. Eventually, this will make for boring play because things will seem repetitive and too tightly structured.

The best solution is not to develop preconceived notions of how the PCs might deal with the encounters in an adventure. If they're going to break into a tower, you can note that the tower has a few guards, a pressure-sensitive intruder alert system around the perimeter, and a lightning-emitting turret on the top. But you don't know if the PCs will fight the guards, bribe them, or sneak past them. You don't know how they're going to deal with the alert system and the turret. That's not the kind of thing you need to think about ahead of time, but you have to be ready when it comes up at the table. You should prepare for the most obvious situations—for example, predetermine the level of the turret and how much damage it does. But when a player states that their action is to look around for spots where the turret cannot strike because a wall blocks it or the angle prevents it, that's when you take a second to consider and (particularly if they roll well on an Intellect action) maybe say "Yes, as a matter of fact, there is a spot," even if no such thing had occurred to you before that moment.

Cyphers teach GMs to design different kinds of scenarios—ones in which the whole adventure isn't wrecked if a player has something that can solve a single problem (defeat a foe, read a mind, bypass a barrier, or whatever). There should always be more to the adventure than one linchpin encounter, obstacle, foe, or secret.

It's all right if players think of cyphers (especially manifest cyphers) as equipment or treasure. You should choose points in the course of the story that are appropriate for awarding subtle cyphers, especially if the PCs aren't at their full capacity. Discovering Subtle Cyphers, page 379.

Manifest Cyphers, page 379

try to make a foe fly up and hit its head on the ceiling. However, turning an ability that is not offensive into an attack changes its nature, making the task formidable (difficulty 7).

If they want to use it to make a friend hover rather than themselves, that's within the spirit and general idea of the ability. That's difficult (difficulty 4) but not unreasonable.

CYPHERS

You should think of cyphers as character abilities, whether they're subtle cyphers or manifest cyphers. This means that it is incumbent upon you to make sure that players always have plenty of cyphers to use. In the course of their travels, the PCs should find that cyphers are extremely common. And since the PCs are limited in the number of cyphers they can carry, they will use them liberally.

Manifest cyphers can be found by scavenging through old ruins. They can be found in the corpses of magical or technological foes. They can be found among the possessions of intelligent fallen opponents or the lairs of unintelligent creatures, either amid the bones of former meals or as shiny decorations in a nest. They can be found in villages, in the back of a merchant's cart that sells junk and scavenged parts. They are offered as rewards by people who are grateful for the PCs' help.

Some adventures will offer more cyphers than others. Still, as a rule of thumb, in any given adventure, a character should use at least as many cyphers as they can carry. This means they should find that number of cyphers in that same amount of time (give or take). Thus, you can simply add up the number of cyphers the PCs can carry, and on average, they should find at least that many cyphers in a given adventure.

If your players are typical, they will use combat-related cyphers liberally but hold onto their utility cyphers. A ray emitter or defensive shield will be used, but a suspensor belt or phasing module will linger longer on their character sheets.

As with everything else in the game, it's intentionally very easy for the GM to create new cyphers. Just think of the effect and how to express it as a game advantage. Two kinds of cyphers exist when it comes to effect: those that allow the user to do something better, and those that allow the user to do something they couldn't do otherwise.

The first group includes everything that reduces the difficulty of a task (including defense tasks). The second group includes things that

Running the Cypher System

grant new abilities, such as flight, a new means of attack, the ability to see into the past, or any number of other powers.

A few more important notes about devising new cyphers:

- Cyphers should be single-use items. The PCs use them up and find new ones.
- Cyphers should be potent. A minor ability isn't worth the trouble. If an attack cypher isn't as good as a regular weapon, why bother with it?
- Cyphers shouldn't have drawbacks.
- Cyphers should be temporary. Typically, a power is used once. Abilities or advantages that have a duration last from ten minutes to twenty-four hours (at most).
- Manifest cyphers can take any form. Just make them appropriate to the genre.

ARTIFACTS

In terms of the narrative, artifacts are a lot like cyphers, except that most are not one-use items. Mechanically, they serve a very different purpose. It's assumed that characters are exploring with some cyphers at their disposal. Artifacts, however, are added abilities that make characters broader, deeper, and often more powerful. They aren't assumed—they're extra.

The powers granted by artifacts are more like the abilities gained from a character's type or focus in that they change the way the PC is played overall. The difference between an artifact and a type or focus ability is that almost all artifacts are temporary. They last longer than cyphers do, but because they have a depletion roll, any use could be their last.

Like cyphers, then, artifacts are a way for the GM to play a role in the development of the characters. Although armor, weapons, and the like are fine, special capabilities—such as long-range communication or travel—can really change the way the PCs interact with the world and how they deal with challenges. Some of these abilities enable the actions you want the PCs to take. For example, if you want them to have an underwater adventure, provide them with artifacts (or cyphers) that allow them to breathe underwater.

Also like cyphers, artifacts are simple for the GM to create. The only difference with artifacts is that you give them a depletion roll, using any numbers on 1d6, 1d10, 1d20, or 1d100. If you want the artifact to be used only a few times, give it a depletion roll of 1 in 1d6, 1 or 2 in 1d10, or even 1 or 2 in 1d6. If you want the PCs to use it over and over, a depletion roll of 1 in 1d100 more or less means that they can use it freely without worrying too much.

SKILLS AND OTHER ABILITIES

Sometimes, the rules speak directly to character creativity. For example, players can make up their own skills. It's possible to have a skill called "tightrope walking" that grants a character a better chance to walk across a tightrope, and another skill called "balance" that gives a character a better chance to walk across a tightrope and perform other balance actions as well. This might seem unequal at first, but the point is to let players create precisely the characters they want. Should you let a character create a skill called "doing things" that makes them better at everything? Of course not. The GM is the final arbiter not only of logic but also of the spirit of the rules, and having one or two single skills that cover every contingency is clearly not in the spirit.

It's important that players play the character they want. This concept is supported not only with the open-ended skill system but also with the ability to get an experience point advance to tailor a character further. Likewise, the GM should be open to allowing a player to make small modifications to refine their character. In many cases, particularly ones that don't involve stat Pools, Armor, damage inflicted, or the costs of Effort or special abilities, the answer from the GM should probably be "Sure, why not?" If a PC ends up being really good at a particular skill— better than they "should" be—what's the harm? If Dave can swim incredibly well, how does that hurt the game in terms of the play experience or the story that develops? It doesn't. If Helen can pick practically any mundane lock she finds, why is that a bad thing? In fact, it's probably good for the game—there's likely something interesting on the other sides of those doors.

In a way, this is no different than adjudicating a not-so-straightforward solution to a challenge. Sometimes you have to say "No, that's not possible." But sometimes, if it makes sense, open yourself up to the possibility.

CHARACTER ARCS

Character arcs encourage players to be proactive and create their own goals, with their own definitions of success and failure. Chapter 12 has more details about using character arcs and offers plenty of sample arcs for the PCs.

It's the spirit of character arcs that's important, not the specific rules. Because the arcs consist of broad sets of guidelines for handling a

You may wish to forbid the use of XP to reroll artifact depletion rolls. That's pretty reasonable.

Experience point advance, page 232

Chapter 12: Experience Points, page 237

Character arcs, page 238

421

potentially limitless number of stories, you'll want to play fast and loose. Sometimes steps will be skipped. Sometimes they'll be repeated. Sometimes you'll go straight to the climax after the opening (this should be rare, however).

Other times, no character arc in chapter 12 will fit what a player wants to do. In that case, it behooves you to work with the player to make an arc that fits. The player's intention is what's important. Players should think of a goal for their character first and then look through the sample arcs, rather than browse the list and feel that those are the only options. When in doubt, find the arc in chapter 12 that most closely fits what the player wants and then massage it in a few places where needed.

One thing to keep in mind: if the arc doesn't involve at least a few steps and at least some time, it's not really a character arc. If a PC gets picked on in a bar one evening by a jerk NPC and says "My character arc is to punch that guy in the face," that's not really a character arc. That's just an action. Character arcs require depth, thought, and, most likely, change on the PC's part.

Think of them in terms of the arcs of characters in your favorite novels or movies. When a PC takes on and eventually completes a character arc, that should feel like a novel or a movie's worth of story (or at least the story of one character in the novel or movie). There should be a real feeling of accomplishment and closure at the end of an arc, but at the same time—assuming the narrative is going to continue—a sense that there's more to come. One arc often leads right into the next.

Character arcs aren't meant to be entirely solo affairs. PCs working as a group should help each other with their respective arcs from time to time. The Aid a Friend arc helps to encourage this. If one or two PCs use this arc to help another character, suddenly it's a group arc, and cohesion and cooperation will come naturally.

Aid a Friend, page 242

It's worth noting, however, that some players will want one of their character arcs to be a solitary venture. They won't want help. They might not even want the other PCs to know about it. That's okay too, but it might require that you spend some time with them playing outside of regular sessions, even if it's just through text or email.

HANDLING NPCs

Nonplayer characters are people and creatures that live in the world alongside the PCs. They are just as much a part of the world as the PCs and should be portrayed just as realistically. NPCs are the main way to breathe life into the world, tell the stories the world has to tell, and portray the kind of game you want to run. Memorable NPCs can make or break a campaign.

NPCs shouldn't be "cannon fodder" because no one thinks of themselves that way. Real people value their lives. They shouldn't be idiots, easily fooled into doing things or acting in ways that no person ever would, simply because a die roll suggests it (unless they're not very bright or something more powerful—like mind control—is at work).

Think about real people that you know or characters from books, television, and movies. Base your NPCs' personalities on them. Make them as widely varying, as interesting, and as deep as those people.

Remember, too, that there are minor characters and major ones, just like in a book. The bandits who waylay the PCs are in the spotlight for only a few minutes at most and don't need a lot of development, but a major adversary or ally might get a lot of attention from the players and therefore deserves a lot from you. As with so many things related to being a good GM, consistency and believability are the keys to developing a good NPC.

NPC GAME STATS

NPCs are easy to create. Most can simply be pegged at a level from 1 to 10 and you're done. Working on how to describe or portray them will take longer than working up their game stats.

Sometimes, though, you'll want to elaborate on the NPC's capabilities and tailor them to the concept. A level 4 NPC who is a computer genius might be level 5 or 6 in computer-related tasks. But don't simply make the NPC level 5 or 6 overall because then they'd also be better at combat, interactions, climbing, jumping, and everything else, and that doesn't fit your concept.

Use the NPCs in chapter 23 as good starting points or as examples for what you can do. But you're not limited by them. In fact, you're not limited in any way. The most important thing to remember about NPCs in the Cypher System is that they do not follow the same rules as PCs. They don't have descriptors, types, or foci. They don't have tiers or any of the same stats. They don't even roll dice.

NPCs work precisely as you (and the setting and story) need them to. If an NPC is the greatest swordsman in the land, you can give him obvious advantages with a sword in attack and defense, but you can go outside the box as well, allowing him to attack more than once per

Running the Cypher System

turn, attempt to disarm foes with a flick of his blade, and so on.

There are no hard-and-fast rules for creating an NPC who can be matched perfectly against the PCs in combat—it's not that kind of game, and that's not the purpose of NPCs. Instead, use the game's simple mechanics to portray the NPCs in the world and in your narrative so that they make sense and can do what you want them to do (and cannot do what you don't want them to do).

Like the player characters, NPCs often carry and use cyphers. Thus, any NPC could have virtually any capability at their disposal as a one-shot power. In theory, NPCs can heal themselves, create force fields, teleport, turn back time, hurt a foe with a sonic blast, or do anything else. An NPC might also use spells, possess mutant powers, or have biomechanical implants. You can lay out these cyphers and abilities when preparing for the game, or you can just go with the idea that certain NPCs can produce amazing and surprising effects and make them up as you go along—with some caveats.

If all NPCs can do whatever they want, whenever they want, that won't instill much belief in the players or give you much credibility as a GM. So keep the following things in mind.

Keep to the Level: NPCs should generally keep to their level parameters. Sure, you can give a tough NPC more health than their level might indicate, and the aforementioned great swordsman might attack and defend with his blade at higher than his normal level, but these are minor exceptions.

Explain Things However You Want: If you keep to the level parameters generally, you can express them in all sorts of interesting ways. For example, a level 5 NPC usually inflicts 5 points of damage. But that damage might come from waves of magnetic force that they can produce thanks to a nanotech virus that has taken over their body.

Wild Cards: You might give some NPCs—sorcerers, gadgeteers with many strange devices, and the like—a wild card ability that allows them to do interesting things like levitate, use telekinesis, construct objects of pure force, and so forth. You don't have to nail down these powers ahead of time. These rare NPCs can just do weird things. As long as you keep them reasonable most of the time, no one will bat an eye. (If every important foe has a force field, that will seem repetitious, dull, and unfair to the PCs.)

Use GM Intrusions: Since a PC can produce all kinds of interesting, useful, and surprising effects thanks to cyphers, you can occasionally

Although an NPC's level and stats are important, just as important are their appearance, the way they talk, and how they act. If an NPC is going to be more than a simple, short-term foe (like a bandit), when you make your notes about things like their level and Armor, also note something about their appearance or personality. If an NPC is going to interact with the PCs for more than a minute, note at least two different things: they make stupid jokes, they have a scar on their ear, they laugh too much, they talk very softly, they smell bad, and so on.

423

Because Cypher System games aren't just about combat and gaining power, the NPCs should be motivated by things beyond that. Love, lust, embarrassment, loyalty, revenge, familial ties, altruism, and curiosity are all great motivators.

Chapter 11: Rules of the Game, page 206

replicate this for an NPC by using GM intrusion to give them precisely the ability needed in the current situation. If the NPC has been poisoned, they pull out a vial of antivenom. If a villain is cornered by the PCs, they activate a device on their belt that lets them phase down through the floor. If the foe is at the extreme edge of low health, they inject themselves with a temporary adrenaline boost that restores 15 points of health immediately.

NPCs AND DEATH

As explained in chapter 11, NPCs have a health score rather than three stat Pools. When an NPC reaches 0 health, they are down. Whether that means dead, unconscious, or incapacitated depends on the circumstances as dictated by you and the players. Much of this can be based on logic. If the NPC is cut in half with a giant axe, they're probably dead. If they're mentally assaulted with a telepathic attack, they might be insane instead. If they're hit over the head with a club, well, that's your call.

It depends on the intentions of those who are fighting the NPC, too. PCs who want to knock out a foe rather than kill them can simply state that as their intention and describe their actions differently—using the flat of the blade, so to speak.

INTERACTIONS

Let's say the PCs want to learn more about a missing man, so they talk to his best friend. You and the players roleplay the conversation. The players are friendly and helpful and ask their questions with respect. Do you call for an Intellect roll (using the friend's level to determine the difficulty) to see if he will talk to them, or do you simply decide that he reacts to them well and gives them the information?

As another example, an old woman has watched over the entrance to an ancient ruin for years. She considers it a duty given to her by the gods and has never told anyone the secrets she knows. The PCs come along with some training in interactions, roll dice, and expect the woman to spill her guts. Does she tell them everything?

The answer to both questions is: it depends. In either situation, you're justified in ignoring the dice and mechanics and simply handling things through table conversation. That's what makes interaction encounters so interesting and so distinctive from, say, combat. You can't put aside the dice and act out the fight between the PCs and a giant, but you can roleplay a conversation. In such cases, you can portray the NPCs precisely as you want, in ways that seem fitting to their personalities, without worrying about die rolls. The best friend probably wants to help the

PCs find his missing comrade. The old woman would never give her secrets to a band of smooth talkers that shows up on her doorstep one day. You can also ensure that the players get the information you want them to get—and don't get the information you don't want them to get.

On the other hand, sometimes using game mechanics is a better option. For example, a person who isn't particularly eloquent might want to play a character who's a smooth talker. You wouldn't require a player who's never held a sword in real life to prove that they're an adept combatant to win a fight in the game, so you should not force the player of a charming character to be, well, charming. The game mechanics can simulate those qualities.

And sometimes, you can use both approaches. You can let the conversation with the NPC play out around the table, and then call for rolls—not to determine whether the PCs succeed or fail at the interaction, but to get an idea of the degree of success. For example, if the characters have a good cover story for why the guards at the gate should let them pass, the roll might determine not whether the guards say yes (you can use logic for that) but whether the guards accompany the PCs beyond the gate. In a way, the die roll shapes an NPC's reaction. It's not an on/off switch but a general degree of the overall trust that the PCs earn.

LANGUAGES

Careful readers will have noticed that there are no intricate rules for languages in the Cypher System, just a brief mention that you can become fluent in a new language rather than gain a skill. That's because for most people, language is more of a background or roleplaying feature than a mechanical one. You don't want to have to make a roll to speak, for example. Characters should begin the game knowing the language(s) that make the most sense for them.

Languages are a special case, however, because some people won't want to deal with it. And that's fine. Some players and GMs will find it an interesting challenge to communicate with people or creatures who don't share a common language. Others will think it's an impediment to interaction with no real upside. You can handle the issue however you want.

NPC ALLIES

Because the players usually roll all the dice, NPCs who are not opponents raise unique issues in the Cypher System. If a character gains an NPC ally who accompanies the group, how are the ally's actions resolved?

Most of the time, the GM should decide what makes the most sense in the context of the situation and the NPC. If the characters climb up a steep slope and must make rolls to ascend, the NPC doesn't make a roll. Instead, the GM quickly considers whether they could climb it and goes from there. A fit, able ally should simply climb the slope. A feeble or clumsy NPC will need assistance. In other words, the NPC doesn't face the challenge (that's what the PCs do)—they remain a part of the unfolding story. The old man the PCs must escort through dangerous mountains needs help climbing because that's part of the story of the adventure. His able-bodied daughter who also travels with the group does not need help because that wouldn't make much sense.

If the entire group is caught in a landslide later in that same adventure, the GM can do one of two things in regard to the NPCs. Either decide what happens to them as seems most logical or fitting (perhaps using GM intrusion, since what befalls the NPCs also affects the PCs), or have the players roll on behalf of the NPCs and treat them just like the player characters in every way possible.

CREATURES

Whenever possible, creatures should be handled like other NPCs. They don't follow the same rules as the player characters. If anything, they should have greater latitude in doing things that don't fit the normal mold. A many-armed beast should be able to attack multiple foes. A charging rhino-like animal ought to be able to move a considerable distance and attack as part of a single action.

Consider creature size very carefully. For those that are quick and hard to hit, hinder attacks against them. Large, strong creatures should be easier to hit, so ease attacks against them. However, you should freely give the stagger ability to anything twice as large as a human. This means that if the creature strikes a foe, the target must make an immediate Might defense roll or lose its next turn.

A creature's level is a general indicator of its toughness, combining aspects of power, defense, intelligence, speed, and more into one rating. In theory, a small creature with amazing powers or extremely deadly venom could be high level, and a huge beast that isn't very bright and isn't much of a fighter could be low level. But these examples go against type. Generally, smaller creatures have less health and are less terrifying in combat than larger ones.

GMs need to be fluid and flexible as they're running a game. Sometimes a strict mechanical approach is needed, and other times it's fine to just handwave the situation and keep the story moving. The important thing—particularly for newer GMs—isn't always knowing when to do which, but to remember that you have the freedom to experiment.

Stagger: If the creature strikes a foe, the target must make an immediate Might defense roll or lose their next turn.

CYPHER SYSTEM

> ### OPTIONAL RULE: ACTING WHILE UNDER ATTACK
>
> When a character is engaged in melee combat, doing anything other than fighting makes them more vulnerable. This is true for PCs and NPCs. If a character engaged in melee takes an action other than fighting, each of their opponents can make an immediate extra attack. The only exception to this rule is moving. If the character's only action is to move, they are assumed to be moving slowly and carefully out of the fight, safely withdrawing from combat.
>
> For example, Tom has his back against a security door while fighting two guards. If he tries to open the door using its control terminal, he is taking an action other than fighting, and both guards get to make an attack against him.

Chapter 3: How to Play the Cypher System, page 7

The Cypher System has no system for building creatures. There is no rule that says a creature with a certain ability should be a given level, and there is no rule dictating how many abilities a creature of a given level should have. But keep the spirit of the system in mind. Lower-level creatures are less dangerous. A level 1 creature could be poisonous, but its venom should inflict a few points of damage at most. The venom of a level 6 creature, however, might knock a PC down a step on the damage track or put them into a coma if they fail a Might defense roll. A low-level creature might be able to fly, phase through objects, or teleport because these abilities make it more interesting but not necessarily more dangerous. The value of such abilities depends on the creature that uses them. In other words, a phasing rodent is not overly dangerous, but a phasing battle juggernaut is terrifying. Basic elements such as health, damage, and offensive or defensive powers (such as poison, paralysis, disintegration, immunity to attacks, and so on) need to be tied directly to level—higher-level creatures get better abilities and more of them.

TEACHING THE RULES

It's not really your job to teach the players the rules, yet it often falls upon the GM to do just that. Before beginning a game, encourage the players to read chapter 3 to get an overview of the game. It won't take them long.

You'll probably also want to give them an overview of the setting you've created and the genre expectations that exist. Focus primarily on the kinds of characters a player can create and what they might do in the game. Once players understand who they are and what they'll do, the rest of the setting is just details they can discover as they go along.

The key to teaching someone the game is to start with the idea of die rolls and how they use the same mechanic no matter what a character tries to do. Then explain using Effort, which involves an introduction to the three stats. After that, a player is ready to start making a character. Taking a new player through the character-creation process gets them ready to play. Don't overload them with a lot of details beyond that. All of those can be picked up as needed in the course of play.

THE FIRST FEW SESSIONS

With any game, GMs should consider running it a little differently the first few times, and the Cypher System is no different. There are a few things you can expect with a table full of new players. First of all, they won't get the terminology and the jargon right—they'll use the terminology and jargon of the last game they played. And that's fine. But you should try to get it right because the players will follow your lead, and after a session or two, they'll start getting it right. If you always call things by the wrong name, the players will, too. However, don't just spout jargon. Each time you use a new term for the first time, such as "damage track," "GM intrusion," or even "difficulty," explain what it means. Make sure everyone's on the same page, even with the basic stuff.

The players won't know what's easy and what's hard. Part of good Cypher System play is knowing when to use Effort and when to conserve, but beginning players will have no frame of reference. In this case, the best way to give them solid ground to stand on is to be fairly transparent. Tell them the target number for each task before they attempt an action. Guide them through the process. Remind them that they can use Effort if need be, although they probably won't forget. On the contrary, beginning players tend to use Effort on every roll. You can almost count on it. This means you can expect beginning characters to do very well in whatever they set out to do, but they'll have to rest more often because they'll deplete their stat Pools more quickly.

RUNNING CYPHER SYSTEM COMBATS

Cypher System combats should be about something. There should be something interesting at stake. "Trying not to die" is an interesting stake, but it's not the only one. Combat can be fun and hopefully exciting in its own right, but it's not necessarily the focus. In other words, fighting through a long combat isn't the point, and finding a way to win a combat quickly through creative thought isn't cheating. In fact, it should be encouraged. Defeating the "big boss monster" easily should not be a letdown; it should be the result of smart, creative play. And Cypher System adventures shouldn't always have a climax involving a "big boss monster," anyway. The exciting end to the story could involve surviving a massive landslide, finding a way to shut down a dangerous machine, or convincing a tyrannical warlord to let the hostages go.

The Cypher System is about discovery. Can you have discovery through combat?

Sure. Say the PCs are exploring an ancient complex and encounter a strange life form. The creature attacks, but during the fight, it telepathically says "Curious" and "Creature unknown" and "Protect the sanctum." It's telepathically talking to someone else, but the PCs "overhear." Although the combat is fairly standard, the PCs have discovered a new creature, and they know it's something that's never encountered a human before. There are more of them, somewhere, and there's some kind of sanctum. It's not just a fight. The PCs have learned something.

In a more standard setup, the combat is the obstacle that the PCs must overcome to reach the discovery, which again reinforces the idea that there is no right or wrong way to overcome the obstacle. Sneak past the foes or convince them to let the PCs pass—both are entirely valid.

Mechanically, combat in the Cypher System doesn't play out as it does in many games where damage whittles down a character's hit points or health score. This kind of slow attrition is less likely to happen in the Cypher System because the PCs will try to avoid getting hit. For example, many players will spend points from their Speed Pool to add Effort to their defense rolls to ensure that they don't get hit (and thus don't lose points from their Might Pool). Characters also have numerous abilities to add to their Speed defense rolls or reduce the difficulty of a Speed defense task. Last, and perhaps most significant, the most frequent use of experience points for rerolls will probably be defensive in nature. Players just don't like their characters to get hit.

There are two important aspects to this. The first is that it's the players' choice. They're in control of which points they lose and how many, so it feels different, even though the effect is largely the same—a slow loss of points over time. The second aspect is that, narratively, you don't have to explain and describe lots of minor wounds and scratches that eventually amount to something. In Cypher System combats, when PCs are struck, it's likely significant. Plus, so many creatures and foes have effects that paralyze, infect, poison, stun, and so on that the damage is not necessarily the interesting or significant part. That's why there are creatures whose attacks can move a PC down the damage track a step or two. It's not so much about the points of damage but the consequences of being hit at all.

When referring to distance, feel free to use the terms "close" and "immediate" interchangeably. Use whatever sounds best in context. The Adept might be "close" to the Warrior, within "close range," or within "immediate distance."

Encourage the players to describe their actions, not the mechanics involved. The game is more fun if a player says things like "I leap up on the table and swing my sword down on the creature," instead of "I use my jump skill to get up on the table so I can ease my attack roll."

CRAFTING STORIES

I keep saying over and over that the Cypher System is all about story—narrative. Your biggest job as the GM is to provide the impetus for stories in the game. The stories themselves arise out of gameplay, but they are started and guided by you. You provide the seed of the story and present the events as they unfold because of what the PCs and NPCs do.

Crafting a good story is a topic that could fill a book of this size. I highly recommend that interested GMs read books or articles aimed at fiction writers (many of which are available on the internet) that provide advice on plot. For that matter, similar sources about characterization can help in the creation of NPCs as well.

For now, remember these key concepts:

- Learn what motivates the players at your table. Exploration? Combat? Puzzle-solving? Interacting with NPCs? Cater to these desires.
- Learn what motivates the PCs that the players run. What are the characters' goals? What do they seek? Wealth? Curiosity? Power? Protecting others? Use these things to start your stories.
- Create stories that involve the PCs as directly as possible. If something bad is affecting people, have it affect the PCs or their loved ones, too. Rather than enticing them to strive to save a random farmer, get them to save a character's brother or best friend.
- Remember that the players are your co-storytellers, and that the PCs are the main characters of the story, so their decisions should have direct impact on what happens.
- Weave multiple stories together. Have the PCs learn about the beginning of one story while they're still embroiled in another.
- Vary your stories. Follow a combat-heavy exploration of an ancient ruin with an intrigue-filled adventure in a large city that involves a lot of interaction. Create one story that is a long quest but then follow it up with another that wraps up in a single game session.
- Vary the encounters within a story. Even in the middle of a series of battles, there's always room for exploration or interaction (and it breaks things up).
- Not every story needs to be about saving the world. Sometimes the smaller stories about helping one person can be the most interesting.
- Twists and unexpected events are wonderful and should be used often, but sometimes the biggest twist is to have things go exactly the way the players think they will.
- Don't get bogged down justifying, rationalizing, or explaining every detail. The players aren't supposed to understand everything.
- Stories that involve a lot of events the PCs are unaware of will end up making little sense to the players, and should probably be avoided.
- Base your stories on real human emotion. NPC villains can be driven by greed or power, but also by love, longing, curiosity, or even misguided altruism. Don't make your players just interact with the events—make them react to the emotions behind the events. Villains should inspire actual hate and anger. The loss of a valued ally should inspire actual sadness and loss.
- Occasionally, create stories that are sequels to your previous stories. The decisions that the players made in the past affect things in the present. Villains return for another try at reaching their goal, or perhaps just for revenge.

PACING

The key to running a great game as opposed to an adequate one is often the simple matter of pacing. Well, pacing is simple to describe, but it's not so simple to understand or implement. It comes with practice and a sort of developed intuition.

Pacing can mean many things. Let's briefly break them down.

PACING WITHIN AN ENCOUNTER

Keep things moving. Don't let the action get bogged down by indecisive players, arguments about the rules, or irrelevant minutiae. Don't let the middle of an encounter get sidetracked by something that reminds a player (or worse, you) of a gaming story, a movie, or a funny thing on the internet. There's time for all of that later, probably after the game session is over.

Don't let the end of the encounter drag out. When it's clear how things are going to turn out, and people might start to get bored, wrap it up. If the PCs were fighting two dozen giant rats and only three are left, there's nothing wrong with saying that those last three run away or that the PCs handily dispatch them. Wrap things up and move along.

I've seen bad pacing ruin more games than probably anything else. Keep things moving. Keep them interesting.

PACING WITHIN A GAME SESSION

Have many different encounters in a session—some long, some short, some complex, some straightforward. One of the trickiest aspects of game session pacing is deciding what to play out and what to skip. For example, the PCs want to buy new gear with the money they were paid for a job. You could describe the town's market and roleplay each interaction with various merchants. You could even call for occasional rolls to see if the characters get good deals or not. Alternatively, you could say "Okay, you can buy whatever you want," and then move on. There are good cases to be made for both approaches, depending on the context. Maybe one of the PCs contracted a disease on the last mission and doesn't realize it until they are interacting with people in the market. Maybe a pickpocket in the mall attempts to steal from the PCs, or they notice a thief stealing from a store. Maybe the players like interacting with NPCs and enjoy your portrayal of minor characters. All of these are good reasons to play out a shopping encounter. But if there's no compelling reason, just advance through it.

Sometimes, you should do this even if one player wants to play out every moment of their character's life and describe everything in excruciating detail. Although you want everyone to be happy, you're in charge of pacing. If you must err, make the players struggle to keep up, rather than letting them be bored and wonder when you're going to get on with it. Thus, if there's no compelling reason against it, don't hesitate to advance time, even in large chunks. If the PCs finish a big scenario and some downtime makes sense, there's nothing wrong with announcing, "So three weeks later, you hear that . . ." and starting the next storyline (as long as the players are content with it). Books and movies do this kind of thing all the time. Skip the boring bits.

In addition, feel free to intrude on player discussions for the purpose of moving things along. Sometimes players spin their wheels or plan and plan their next move, never accomplishing anything. You can intrude by throwing an encounter or a surprise their way ("A message arrives from the priests at the clave"), or you can simply say "Let's move things along."

Keep a clock handy so you can see how much time is left in the session. Never lose track of time. You want to end a session at a good point—a place where everyone can catch their breath, at a good cliffhanger, or as everything in a story wraps up so you can start anew next

time. These are all fine stopping points, but you want to control which one you use. Next session, you'll have to start things up again, recap past events, and get everyone back into the swing of things.

Try to ensure that at the end of any session, the players can look back on what they did and feel like they accomplished something.

PACING WITHIN A STORY

This aspect of pacing goes back to researching how fiction writers handle story creation, and it's a huge subject, but consider the standard three-act structure as a good starting point. In act one, the problem is introduced. In act two, things get worse (or a new complication is introduced). In act three, things are resolved. There are many other ways to do it, but remember that the action needs to ebb and flow. You need downtime between the moments of action, horror, or high drama.

PACING WITHIN A CAMPAIGN

Mix short scenarios in with longer ones. Weave the plotlines together so that as one story ends, the PCs still have things to do. But don't be afraid of downtime. Let the characters have a week, a month, or longer here or there to live their normal lives before throwing them once again into the heart of danger. If a campaign takes a year of play time in the real world, you don't want it to take place in only three weeks of game time. That never feels right.

DESCRIPTION

Earlier, I recommended using description that was both precise and concise. Precision comes from avoiding relative terms like "big" or "small" or emotional words like "terrifying" because these words mean different things to different people. This doesn't mean you have to specify the exact height of every structure the PCs find. But rather than describing a building as "a tall tower," consider saying "a tower at least five times the height of the trees around it."

Being concise is important, too. Go on too long with descriptions, and the players' minds will drift. Sometimes, what works best are short, declarative, evocative descriptions with pauses in between for player comments or questions.

Fantasy, page 252

DESCRIBING THE ACTION

Great roleplaying game sessions often involve immersion. Immersion comes from a sense of being truly caught up in the action and the fictional world. Just as when you read a great book or watch a well-made movie, playing an RPG can get you caught up in your own imagination. And best of all, you're sharing your imaginative escape with everyone else at the table. For immersion to work, you have to give great descriptions.

Cypher System combat, for example, is very simple and open-ended rather than precise, giving you lots of room to describe how characters move, how they attack, and how they avoid attacks. A successful Speed defense roll might mean dodging, blocking with a weapon, or ducking behind a pillar. A character who is struck in combat for 3 points of damage might have dodged the weapon attack but fallen backward onto a jagged and ruined control console.

The players should describe their actions, too. Encourage them to be creative in what they do and how they perform a task, whether it involves the way they attack, what they do to give themselves the best chance to make a difficult leap over a pit, or how they slip into a noble's study to steal the map they need.

Don't take any of this as a requirement. Long descriptions can be tedious as easily as they can be interesting. Sometimes the best way to serve the pacing of a combat encounter is to state whether an attack hit and how much damage is dealt and keep things moving. Vivid description is great, but it's not a valid excuse for you or a player to drag things out and destroy the pacing.

DESCRIBING THE WORLD

With so many different choices in the Cypher System, "the world" could mean a lot of different things. Below are a few thoughts about genres. See the chapters in part 3 for more details on these genres.

Fantasy: A fantasy setting can be a weird place, and describing it can be difficult. It's all right to fall back on clichés—castles, knights, dragons, and so forth. Keep in mind, however, that these concepts are so well worn that if you use them, either you need to be okay with the generic images that pop into the players' heads, or you need to be very specific about what makes this dragon different. (And if you have the time and inclination, by all means make your dragon or your knight different—the players will enjoy it and remember it.)

Don't hesitate to make your fantasy world grand and striking. If magic is prevalent in the world, have the Emperor's palace made of nothing but foes petrified by his pet basilisk. Have the cavalry mounted on six-winged birds rather than horses. Put the sorcerer's home on the other side of a magical portal found only in a waterfall at midnight.

When possible, stress the most interesting aspect of your description. For example, don't bother telling the PCs about the normal buildings in the city if the central tower is a hundred feet tall and topped with a huge red crystal.

Modern: If the setting is the modern world, use specific references when you can. The bad guys aren't in a car—they're in a Ford Explorer. The agency boss is wearing a blue Armani suit and offers you a glass of eighteen-year-old Glenfiddich.

On the other hand, since it's the real world, don't bother with description that's not needed. You don't need to detail every building the characters drive by, obviously—just the one they're going to. The rest is simply "downtown."

Science Fiction: As with fantasy, use clichés and tropes if they're handy. Refer to scenes from television and movies that would be familiar to the players.

Be wary of shorthand description and inappropriate comparisons. If the PCs see an alien vehicle flying through the air toward them and you describe it as "sort of like a flying car," they're going to picture a flying 21st-century sedan with tires, a steering wheel, and bumpers, and that's probably not the image you want in their heads. Instead, try to give them the gist of the vehicle. Saying something like "A large, dark vehicle—sharply angled and full of strange protrusions from all directions—suddenly rumbles toward you through the sky, blocking out the sun" puts a more evocative and weird image in the players' minds. It's better to be vague than incorrect or, worse, jarringly inappropriate.

If you must, use 21st-century terms or comparisons to describe things, but introduce them sparingly because they can break the mood very easily.

Horror: Description is vital in horror—both in what you say and in what you don't. Although precision is a good thing, pedantic, exhaustive detail is not. Even if that's what is needed to fully describe the monster or phenomenon, don't do it. Leave the players with an impression rather than an exact description. "A creature that looks like three black beetles, each the size of a mastiff, with too many legs and eyes" isn't a full description, but it's an impression. It gives the players something to picture, even if it's not precisely what you're picturing. It's weird and evocative, and that's important.

Romance: Don't hesitate to use emotions in your descriptions, and even more importantly, ask the players how events, characters, and places make their characters feel. Remember that in an interaction-heavy game, facial expressions and use of a furtive glance can be extremely informative.

Superheroes: While the setting is ostensibly the modern world, everything in superhero games is usually bigger, bolder, and brighter. Strong characters are rippling with muscles. Important characters are usually good-looking— or hideously ugly. When a supervillain creates a device that will destroy a city, the machine *looks* dangerous. Things in this setting are rarely vague or subtle.

Post-Apocalyptic: In a post-apocalyptic setting in the near future, use the same techniques as with a modern game, but stress the run-down nature of the objects or people, or the rarity of preserved objects or places that the PCs encounter. Tell the story of the apocalypse in what remains. Don't just have a "ruined building"— describe a three-story structure, blackened by fire, with the top floor collapsed and a crashed emergency services helicopter protruding from the wreckage.

In a post-apocalyptic world set far in the future, where the PCs don't have knowledge of the time before the ruin, do the opposite. Don't describe what they see using names and language that they would never use. Treat it like the sci fi setting discussed above, but the pre-ruin world is the "alien" stuff. Don't call it a smartphone—describe a small plastic artifact with a dead window revealing nothing inside.

Fairy Tale: In a fairy tale setting, everything is larger than life. The forest is darker than dark. The castle soars high into the sky. The ravenous beast is hunger personified.

Historical: As with a modern setting, use specificity and real references as much as you can.

PREPARING FOR THE GAME SESSION

The Cypher System doesn't require you to spend hours carefully designing stats for NPCs (unless you want to). There aren't a lot of rules to memorize. It's not worth writing out elaborate descriptions of each encounter because if you let things proceed organically, many planned

Romance, page 286

Superheroes, page 289
Modern, page 261

Post-apocalyptic, page 295

Science fiction, page 270

Fairy tale, page 302

Historical, page 307

Horror, page 280

encounters might not be used. The rules of the Cypher System allow you to come up with a lot of the details as you go along, since you don't have to reference loads of books and stats during the game session.

To prepare for a session, you need to create only three things: a list of names, a brief outline, and a list of ideas.

1. A list of names appropriate to the setting

No matter how much you prepare, you'll end up creating some NPCs on the fly, so have a list of names to use when this happens. Leave room to write a quick note next to each name you use in case that NPC shows up in the game again.

2. A brief outline

The outline is an idea of where you think the story could go. Of course, the key word is *think*. You can't know for certain—the actions of the PCs will take things in unexpected directions. In truth, "outline" is probably not the right word. Think in terms of places the PCs might go, people or creatures they might interact with, and events that might occur. For example, let's say that in a fantasy campaign, the PCs enter a small village. You plan to start the session by having them hear about a local man named Barlis who disappeared mysteriously. Your notes might say:

- Barlis disappeared outside the flour mill where he worked. North of town.
- Barlis lived in a small, run-down house. Partner: Nillen—distraught and prone to drink.
- Flour mill: About a dozen workers. Boss: Vorriln. Witness: Vadda saw Barlis disappear right in front of her. Doesn't want to talk about it because she's heard about some kind of faerie curse that she thinks is involved (level 4 to get her to talk). Knows Barlis recently found a strange item—looked like a large silver coin with a horned skull on it.
- Pickpocket (level 3) attempts to steal from one PC while they're in town.
- Local priest: Rorich. Has seen small coins like the one Vadda describes, and says that they are symbols of a demonic cult. Sends PCs to a hermit who lives west of the village and knows more about the cult.

And so on.

Obviously, that's just the beginning, but you've covered a lot of the contingencies, assuming the PCs investigate Barlis's disappearance at all. Some of that material might not get used. The PCs might not go to his house—only to the mill and then to the priest. Maybe they won't go to the priest at all, and you'll need to have someone else direct them to the hermit. Or maybe the PCs will come up with a wholly unexpected path of investigation.

3. A list of ideas
Just like with the list of names, jot down a bunch of random ideas. These are things you can throw into the game at a moment's notice. They might be flavor, cool visuals, or important side plots. For example, in a horror game, your list might include:

- A music box from the 1800s with ornate but slightly macabre decoration, currently broken
- Man with one side of his face horribly burned long ago
- Graffiti painted on the side of a building: "I saw it. And worse, it saw me."
- Dogs constantly barking in the distance, and then silence
- A trail of blood that leads to a door that won't open

These are all ideas that you can sprinkle into the game when appropriate. You haven't tied them to a specific encounter, so you can insert them whenever you want. You might not use them all in the same adventure—they're just ideas.

HANDLING PLAYERS

Part of being a GM is handling players. This means a lot of things. For example, it's partially your job to make sure that everyone has a good time. You need to ensure that all the players get to do the kinds of things they like to do in games, and that no one is left out. If one player really likes combat and another enjoys NPC interaction, provide some of both. Before you can do that, you need to find out what the players want in the first place, so talk to them and learn their expectations.

Another big part of handling players is coping with disruptive players. Disruptive players can be the death of a game. They can hog all the attention, tell other players what to do, or challenge your rulings at every turn. A lot of GMs are tempted to deal with such players during the game by punishing them or giving them negative feedback. For example, they have the character get attacked more often, lose experience points, or suffer similar consequences. Resist this temptation. Instead, speak with the player person to person (not GM to player) outside of the game and explain that their behavior is causing problems. Be clear, direct, and firm, but also be friendly.

The bottom line, however, is don't play games with jerks. One disruptive, rude, or offensive player can ruin the whole group's fun.

A different problem player is one who just doesn't get the narrative focus of the Cypher System. These kinds of players tend to see all games as competitive enterprises, and they might try to "win" by exploiting what they see as holes in the rules to create and play an unbeatable character. Although part of many people's RPG experience is the fun of playing a powerful character, it shouldn't be the ultimate goal in the Cypher System because such a player will get frustrated and bored.

For example, a player might try to use the Energy Protection ability to protect against kinetic energy and then claim that he is immune to all attacks. He'll see this as a hole that he was smart enough to exploit, and he'll hold up the rules and say "Show me where I'm wrong!"

When a player does that, point him here: "You're wrong."

He's wrong because the Cypher System isn't a board game where the rules are like a puzzle to be solved or beaten. The rules exist to facilitate the story and portray the world. If there's a "hole" in the rules or a rule that would produce an illogical or unenjoyable result if followed to the letter, change it, redefine it, or just overrule it. It's that easy.

On the other hand, some players absolutely will get it. They'll understand that it's the spirit of the rules, not the letter, that's important. They'll get that the story being told is key. Rather than poring over the description of a power and trying to twist the words to an unintended meaning, they'll use their intelligence and creativity to figure out the best way to use the power to portray a character who fits the setting and is fun to play.

People who try to exploit the rules don't understand the Cypher System, but people who exploit the situations do. If a player is smart and creative enough to turn the tables on their foes in an unexpected way by using what's around them, allow it (if it makes sense). If the PCs find a pool of caustic fluid and lure their foes into it rather than fighting them in a straightforward manner, that's not cheating—that's awesome.

Be certain you don't accidentally penalize players for not doing the obvious or straightforward thing. Be generous with people who take nonstandard actions or who do something realistic (such as using their action to take stock of the situation rather than attack—ease their next action). Don't make "attack" always the right choice. It's a creative game, so allow the players to be creative.

Energy Protection, page 134

Remember that anything you prepare that doesn't get used can always be recycled later. Never force the players into a situation just because you planned it out and are really fond of what you came up with. Save that cool idea and use it later.

MATURE THEMES

Sometimes, it's appropriate to involve mature themes in Cypher System games. Sex, extreme violence, and other topics can certainly fit into the world. But each group must decide for themselves if such themes fit into their game. You should also prepare your stories with your specific players in mind. If one or more are very young or have issues with certain topics, avoid things that would be inappropriate. Also be aware that some topics, like overt sexuality, rape, and graphic violence might disturb players even when you aren't expecting it. It's always best to know for certain before allowing these topics into your game.

Think of it like the movie rating system. If you can tell the story that you want to tell in a G or PG (or even PG-13) way, you're likely fine. If events unfold that will give your game an R rating or higher, it's best to talk with your players ahead of time. It's not a matter of good or bad, but a matter of appropriateness for the "audience" and giving people a heads-up ahead of time—just like movie ratings.

DESIGNING ENCOUNTERS

Encounters are to a game session what scenes are to a movie or a book. They're a way to break up the session, and the adventure at large, into smaller, more manageable chunks.

Sometimes it's more difficult to know where one encounter ends and another begins. For that reason, "encounter" is not always a useful or meaningful game term. It's only useful for you when you think about the scenes of your adventure. When the PCs talk to the temple priests, that's one encounter. After they do so, hopefully getting the information they need, they head off into the wilderness, where they have to cross a deep chasm—another encounter. When a dragon appears and attacks, that's another encounter. And so on.

Thus, not everything that happens is an encounter. Heading off into the wilderness, for example, probably involves gathering supplies, deciding on a route, and so on, but it isn't really an encounter. An encounter is when you, the GM, provide a lot of detail. You and the players interact a lot in an encounter. You might decide to subdivide everyone's actions into rounds to help keep track of who's doing what, when.

COMPLEX ENCOUNTERS

Encounters aren't just about combat. As mentioned above, talking to NPCs is an encounter. Dealing with a physical obstacle is an encounter. Figuring out how to use a complex machine is an encounter. The best encounters—the really memorable ones, in fact—involve multiple things happening at once. A fight on a boat racing down the rapids, for example, is an interesting encounter. An encounter where a couple of PCs must disable a bomb before it blows up the space station while the others fend off attacking star troopers is interesting too.

Sometimes an encounter can be intentionally designed with that goal. At least occasionally, you should take an idea you have for an encounter and then add something else that will make it even more interesting, exciting, or challenging. The possibilities are endless. Perhaps gravity functions differently than expected. A weird fungus gives off spores that alter perception. The encounter takes place inside a sentient machine that must be reasoned with and appeased while everything else is going on. An interdimensional effect makes all metal in the encounter temporarily cease to exist. And that's just for starters. Make things crazy and fun. Design encounters that are like nothing the players have ever experienced.

Sometimes encounters with multiple levels of action or weird complications arise out of the game itself. The PCs have to leap onto a moving platform to get down into the giant machine's interior conduit system, which is interesting, but the robots that they ran from earlier suddenly show up. You didn't plan for that ahead of time; it just happened because that's the way things went. And that's great.

Finally, GM intrusions can bring about these kinds of encounters on the fly. The PCs have to repair a huge device at the heart of an ancient complex that is venting poisonous gas before they are all overcome. With a GM intrusion that occurs to you at the last minute, you let them know that the gas also weakens the structural integrity of metal, which means the supports under the floor the PCs are standing on are buckling and will collapse at any moment.

BALANCING ENCOUNTERS

In the Cypher System, there is no concept of a "balanced encounter." There is no system for matching creatures of a particular level or tasks of a particular difficulty to characters of a particular tier. To some people, that might seem like a bad thing. But as I've written earlier,

---

GM intrusion, page 408

Sometimes, the term "adventure" gets just as messy as "encounter." Deciding where one adventure begins and another ends can be, and perhaps should be, difficult. "Adventure" is a useful term for published products, but for your own use, you might want to toss the concept out and just let one story or event flow into another naturally.

matching character builds to exacting challenges is not part of this game. It's about story. So whatever you want to happen next in the story is a fine encounter as long as it's fun. You're not denying the characters XP if you make things too easy or too difficult, because that's not how XP are earned. If things are too difficult for the PCs, they'll have to flee, come up with a new strategy, or try something else entirely. The only thing you have to do to maintain "balance" is set difficulty within that encounter accurately and consistently.

In a game like the Cypher System, if everyone's having fun, the game is balanced. Two things will unbalance the game in this context.

- One or more PCs are far more interesting than the others. Note that I said "more interesting," not "more powerful." If my character can do all kinds of cool things but can't destroy robots as efficiently as yours does, I still might have a whole lot of fun.
- The challenges the PCs face are routinely too easy or too difficult.

The first issue should be handled by the character creation rules. If there's a problem, it might be that poor choices were made or a player isn't taking full advantage of their options. If someone really doesn't enjoy playing their character, allow them to alter the PC or—perhaps better—create a new one.

The second issue is trickier. As previously stated, there is no formula that states that N number of level X NPCs are a good match for tier Y characters. However, when the game has four or five beginning characters, the following guidelines are generally true.

- Level 1 opponents will be nothing but a nuisance, even in sizable numbers (twelve to sixteen).
- Level 2 opponents will not be a challenge unless in numbers of twelve or more.
- Level 3 opponents will be an interesting challenge in numbers of four to eight.
- Level 4 opponents will be an interesting challenge in numbers of two or three.
- A single level 5 opponent might be an interesting challenge.
- A single level 6 opponent will be a serious challenge.
- A single level 7 or 8 opponent will likely win in a fight.
- A single level 9 or 10 opponent will win in a fight without breaking a sweat.

But let me caution you, and I can't stress this enough: it depends on the situation at hand. If the PCs are already worn down from prior encounters, or if they have the right cyphers, any of the expectations listed above can change. That's why there is no system for balancing encounters. Just keep in mind that beginning characters are pretty hardy and probably have some interesting resources, so you aren't likely to wipe out the group by accident. Character death is unlikely unless the PCs have already been through a number of other encounters and are worn down.

RESOLVING ENCOUNTERS

Don't plan for how an encounter will end. Let the game play determine that. This ensures that players have the proper level of input. You can decide, for example, that if the PCs go into the tower, a gang of mutants inside will attack. However, you can't decide how that encounter will end. Maybe the PCs will be victorious. Maybe they won't. Maybe they'll flee, or maybe they'll bargain for their lives.

If you try to decide such things ahead of time, that's called railroading the game, and it puts the players in the role of observers rather than actors. Even if you try to plan out the results of an encounter ahead of time but then let the game play dictate them, you still might end up planning for a lot of outcomes that don't happen. In other words, if you base a whole plotline on the PCs fleeing the tower to get away from the mutants, but instead they manage to drive the mutants out instead, all your plans are wasted.

Plan for various possible outcomes, but don't predetermine them. Think of your story as having many possible plotlines, not just one.

CHALLENGING CHARACTERS

If the game has a balance problem, it's more likely due to players finding things too easy rather than too hard. If things are too hard, they should run away and find something else to do (or you should lighten up a bit). But if the characters in the group need a greater challenge, try one or more of the following options.

Damage Track: Sometimes a few points of damage aren't enough to scare a player. But a weapon or effect that immediately moves them one step down the damage track will terrify them. No matter how big a character's stat Pools are, no matter how much Armor they have, there are only three such steps to death.

A railroad adventure is one in which the players have no meaningful choices. It's like riding on a train, which can only follow the tracks, and the tracks go in one direction.

Damage track, page 218

Ongoing Damage: Poisons that inflict even a small amount of damage (1 or 2 points) every round until an antidote is found can be extremely deadly. Or consider this: one of the reasons that napalm is so terrible is that it clings to surfaces, including flesh. Imagine a weapon or effect that inflicts 5 points of fire damage every round and persists for eight rounds unless the characters can figure out a way to douse it.

Lasting Damage: For a more realistic simulation of damage, you can use a GM intrusion to indicate that damage suffered by a player character is "lasting." Most of the time, this damage is described as being a concussion, a broken bone, a torn ligament, or severe muscle or tissue damage. This damage does not heal normally, so the points lost cannot be regained by making recovery rolls. Instead, they return at a rate of 1 point per day of complete rest (or 1 point per three days of regular activity). Until the points are restored, the damage has a secondary effect, such as hindering tasks with an injured arm, reducing movement speed by half from an injured leg, hindering Intellect actions from a concussion, and so on. Using lasting damage is particularly appropriate in cases where it would be an obvious consequence, such as when a character falls a long distance. It is also appropriate for characters who are already impaired or debilitated.

Permanent Damage: Similar to lasting damage, permanent damage is a special situation adjudicated by the GM. Permanent damage never heals normally, although extraordinary technologies and magic can potentially repair damage or replace lost body parts. This kind of damage should be used sparingly and only in special situations.

Effects Other Than Damage: Attacks can blind, stun, grapple, paralyze, infect, hobble, or otherwise hinder a character without dealing any points of damage at all.

Effects That Harm Equipment: A PC's gear is often the source of their abilities. Destroying or nullifying cyphers or artifacts damages them just as surely as breaking their leg would—it limits a player's options, which really hurts.

Enemies Working in Concert: Although a group effectively acting as one is a special ability of some creatures, you could apply it to any creature you like. As a general rule, for every four creatures working together, treat them as one creature with a level equal to the highest of them plus 1, dealing a minimum of 2 additional points of damage. So a level 4 bandit who has three level 3 allies could team up and attack one foe as a level 5 NPC. That means their attack deals more damage and is harder to defend against. It also means less die rolling, so the combat moves along faster.

Beef up the Foes: You're in charge of the NPC stats. If they need more Armor, more health, or higher levels to be a challenge, simply make it so. It's easy and straightforward to give an NPC a "boost package" of four things:

- +10 health
- +1 to Armor
- 3 additional points of damage
- Attacks and defends as one level higher

That should do the trick, but if necessary, give the boost package to the same NPC again.

Beef up the Obstacles: Include more exotic materials in doors and other barriers, which increase their level. Make physical challenges more difficult—the surfaces that need to be climbed are slippery, the waters that need to be swum are roiling, and other actions are hampered by strong winds. Don't beef up obstacles in this way too often, but remember that circumstances such as weather are your tools for adjusting the difficulty of any action.

HIGHER-TIER CHARACTERS

Although characters start out quite capable, by the time they reach the fifth or sixth tier, they will be truly legendary. Both you and the players might find reaching the upper tiers more rewarding and satisfying if the journey unfolds more gradually, so you can slow down this progress if desired. To do this, starting at third or fourth tier, you can specify how the players can spend the experience points they earn. Requiring that some XP (as much as half) must be spent on immediate, short- and medium-term, or long-term advantages—rather than on character advancement—will slow down the progression through the upper tiers. But it won't take anything away from the play experience because spending XP on those advantages is fun and rewarding, too.

CHARACTER DEATH

Challenging characters is important. If there is no threat of failure—or at least the perceived threat of failure—it's hard for players to feel compelled by the story. Very often, the ultimate failure a PC might face is death. An adventurer's life is a dangerous one. But death is serious because it means the player can no longer play their character.

If a character dies, the easiest and most straightforward response is to have the player

---

Lasting and permanent damage could also be caused by a particularly vicious disease, the effect of an especially hellish curse, a brush with a psychic or cybernetic entity with godlike intelligence, standing at ground zero when the bomb goes off, and so on.

Sometimes players are unwilling to spend XP on anything other than character benefits, which in turn lead to advancing to new tiers. The truth is, spending XP on immediate or short-term gains very likely provides as much overall benefit. In other words, in the big picture, four crucial rerolls are probably about the same as acquiring a new skill. It will take some players a while to come to that conclusion, however.

Running the Cypher System

create a new character. Ideally, they will make a beginning character (which is the easiest to create), but if the other characters are third tier or higher, it will be more satisfying to let the player create their new character at an advanced tier.

However, keep in mind that a lower-tier PC can operate effectively in the company of higher-tier characters. The differences are not so striking. If a player brings a new beginning PC into a group of advanced characters, be particularly generous with XP to help the new character catch up to the others a bit.

Regardless, arrange the circumstances of the story so that you can bring in the new character in a logical fashion and as quickly as possible.

Not Quite Dead: There is an alternative for a player who really, really wants to keep playing the same character. Allow the PC to teeter on the brink of death but survive, saved by their companions or by sheer luck. They might recover but have serious injuries that result in a weakness, an inability, or some other drawback. The point is not to penalize the PC (although barely escaping death should have some repercussions) but to change the character in a memorable way.

SWITCHING DESCRIPTORS AND FOCI AFTER CHARACTER CREATION

As the campaign goes along, it's possible that a player might want to switch the descriptor or focus that they chose when creating their character.

It's best if these changes occur organically rather than being forced. In other words, a character's descriptor changes because something happened in the game to change them, or their focus changes because a new opportunity arose in the course of play. (Don't do it if a player wants to change just for the sake of variety or to become more powerful in the current situation. In those cases, they should make a new character instead.)

Changing a descriptor is both easy and appropriate. For example, in the course of play, a Strong Warrior's father is killed by a terrible villain. The Warrior is fueled now by revenge. This story event could easily justify the Warrior changing their descriptor from Calm or Kind. If the Warrior became a terrible person because of it, they might take the Dishonorable descriptor. Likewise, a Learned Adept who falls into a vat of acid might become Hideous or Mad.

The GM can use lasting or permanent damage as a substitute for death. In other words, if a PC reaches 0 in all of their stat Pools, they would normally be dead, but instead you could say that they are knocked unconscious and wake up with some kind of lasting or permanent damage.

Inability, page 207

437

As with everything, switching descriptors and foci should be worked out between the player and the GM. The best play experiences come from good communication.

Of course, these characters lose their old descriptor and any benefits it conveyed, but that can be part of the story, too. The Strong Warrior who is now a Calm Warrior stopped exercising and physically pushing their body. They might still be strong, but it's not their defining characteristic—they're not as strong as they were. They're calmer instead. Likewise, the Learned Adept forgets some of their schooling and loses their focus on such pursuits due to the accident that made them Hideous.

There's no limitation on the number of times a character can change their descriptor. For example, if the aforementioned Warrior achieves their vengeance, maybe they go back to being strong—as long as it fits the story.

Switching a focus is a bit trickier, and the story reason is probably more awkward. How does an Explorer who Battles Robots become an Explorer who Bears a Halo of Fire? The change likely involves time to train and a story reason. Perhaps the Explorer trained at a monastery they found in the hills where they specialize in "fire magic," or maybe they discovered some fire-related device. Perhaps they were kidnapped by strange forces and bathed in weird energies. Almost anything is possible. You just have to work at it a bit.

A focus change should occur only when a character attains a new tier, and it probably shouldn't be allowed more than once per character.

Mechanically, the new focus does not overwrite the old focus the way a new descriptor replaces an old descriptor. Instead, the old focus abilities remain, and at the new tier, the character gains an ability from the new focus, but the ability must come from a tier lower than the one just attained. For example, if our Explorer who Masters Weaponry begins to Bear a Halo of Fire at tier 3, they keep their tier 1 and tier 2 abilities from from mastering weaponry, and for their tier 3 ability, they choose either a tier 1 or tier 2 ability from Bears a Halo of Fire (probably the tier 1 ability, because that makes more sense). When they reach tier 4, they choose from the tier 1, 2, or 3 abilities of Bears a Halo of Fire (although obviously they can't choose the one they already selected). The character always chooses new abilities from tiers lower than the one they attain in their new focus. This means that the only way to get the sixth-tier ability of a focus is to start with that focus.

A character can't choose abilities from their former focus. Once the change is made, it's made.

If a focus gives a character multiple abilities at the same tier, the character gains all of those abilities.

AN EXAMPLE OF PLAY

Sometimes the best way to understand a game is to see it played. This section provides the next best thing: a script depicting a group playing through a Cypher System encounter in a science fiction space opera setting.

GAME MASTER: Just as the scanners indicated, you see the structure near the river. You note that its smooth walls are 40 feet high and faceted, almost like crystal. There's a small door on the side facing the river.

STEVE (playing a second-tier Explorer named Catissan): Does it look like something a human might build?

GM: It's tough to know that without investigating further, but it does occur to you that the door seems designed for creatures both taller and narrower than you.

SASHA (playing a second-tier Warrior named Viddo): This is where the Muggariks we're after went, then. They were tall and thin.

GM: Perhaps.

TONY (playing a second-tier Adept named Irom): I walk up to the building.

SASHA: I cover him with my blaster rifle.

STEVE: I'm going to check around the door—search for anything strange or dangerous.

GM: Okay, Steve. That's going to be an Intellect task.

STEVE: I'm going to use a level of Effort. I have an Intellect Edge of 1, so it will cost me 2 points from my Pool.

The GM knows there's nothing to find at the doorway, but she muses for half a second as if pretending to figure out a target number.

GM: Roll.

STEVE: Rolled a 7.

GM: You don't find anything out of the ordinary. However, tracks on the ground indicate that a number of creatures go through this doorway on a regular basis, and their footprints are longer and narrower than a human's.

This bit of information is a "gimme." The characters had already figured out that this was made by the alien Muggariks.

SASHA: The Muggariks. We're at the right place.

TONY: I take out my light blaster and go inside.

STEVE (to Tony): Steady, there. We should go in as a team. (To the GM) I go, too.

SASHA: I go in, too. They'll need me.

TONY: I've got my Ward to protect me. Don't forget, I've got cool psychic powers.

STEVE: Still, I'm going to take the lead.

GM: Okay.

SASHA: I'm following close, but keeping to the shadows and keeping quiet.

The GM knows that Sasha's Tough Warrior is flavored with stealth, so her tactics are no surprise.

GM: The door opens, and it's quiet and dimly lit inside. The ceilings are high, and there's weird art on the walls that just looks like colored blobs to you.

STEVE: No guards? No alarm?

GM: Not that you perceive.

SASHA: I keep my eyes peeled.

TONY: I walk in farther and call out in my most charming voice, "Hey, fellas, it's us, the guys whose hyperdrive crystals you stole. We're just here to talk!"

SASHA: That never works.

STEVE: No, I think it's prudent. Maybe we can talk this through. We still don't know why they stole them.

GM: Well, there's no response to your entreaty. Eventually, you explore the structure's interiors and see what might be some sleeping chambers, a common area, and some storage, but no one's here.

TONY: And no sign of the crystals?

GM: Nope.

SASHA: Have we explored the whole place?

GM: There's one door near the back you haven't opened. It seems to be sealed.

STEVE: That must be it. I'll try to force it open.

GM: That's a Might roll.

STEVE: I roll a 13.

GM: It doesn't budge.

SASHA: Damn.

TONY: Is there a mechanical seal? Something I can tap into with my Machine Interface ability?

Tony's Adept has tech flavoring. The GM calls his type a "Psi-tech."

GM: Yes.

SASHA: Before he starts that process, I'm going to spend 3 Intellect points for an Insight.

The GM thinks for a moment.

GM: Okay. You know from having read about the Muggariks that their species has a powerful sense of claustrophobia. They hate feeling closed in or trapped, and can't stand locked doors.

STEVE: That explains the front door, but what's with this one?

TONY: Maybe we're not dealing with Muggariks after all.

SASHA: Back at the spaceport, we heard that guy talking about alien mind-control spiders or something.

TONY: That was quite a while ago, though. I don't know if that's involved.

STEVE: Still, if we see a Muggarik, let's not necessarily shoot to kill or anything. Maybe they're being controlled and aren't themselves.

GM (to Tony): Going to try to open the door?

TONY: Yes. I'm trained and Machine Interface eases the task by another step. I won't bother with Effort at this point. I roll a 7.

GM: Good enough. You realize that it was kind of a jury-rigged seal. This door was never meant to be locked.

SASHA: Nice work. What's inside?

GM: It's dark, but you hear something moving around, out of sight.

TONY: "Hello?"

STEVE: He's not actually trained in social interaction—he just thinks he is. Any chance I can use my Good Advice ability from my Leads focus to help him if we start a dialogue? My Intellect Edge means that it doesn't actually cost me anything.

GM: Sure thing. But so far, Irom doesn't have anyone to talk to.

SASHA: I'll sneak ahead and see if I can figure out what's making the noise.

GM: Farther in, you see a tall, angular figure in a torn shipsuit. It has smooth reddish skin, and its back is to you.

TONY: That's a Muggarik!

STEVE: Don't shoot it, Sasha—remember what we said.

SASHA: I know. "Hey, you," I say.

Running the Cypher System

GM: The alien figure turns around. In the dim light from the open doorway, you see that there's something covering its face—something alive with a number of squirming legs.

SASHA: I was right! Mind-control spiders!

STEVE: Let's try not to hurt the guy, just the thing on his face.

TONY: When did we start to care about the Muggariks so much? They stole our hyperdrive crystals.

STEVE: They were probably mind-controlled then, too.

GM: I need initiative rolls.

The Muggarik is a level 4 NPC. That means the target number to beat it in initiative (and just about anything else) is 12. It also means the Muggarik has 12 health and if it hits in combat, it will do 4 points of damage. The thing on its face is level 4 as well, but level 5 for Speed defense because it is so small.

STEVE: I got a 12.

TONY: 4.

SASHA: 8.

GM: Okay, Catissan goes first, but Irom and Viddo don't act until after the Muggarik.

STEVE: I run up and try to yank that thing off his face.

GM: It's not a big room, so it's just an immediate distance. You need to make an attack roll.

STEVE: Right. I'll use two levels of Effort. That will cost me 4 points instead of 5, because I have a Might Edge of 1. I roll a 20!

GM: That not only hits, but you get the points back too. Plus, you get a major effect.

STEVE: I want to grab the thing with all the legs and pull it off the Muggarik! Then I throw it on the ground, hoping Viddo will shoot it.

GM: Sounds like a reasonable major effect. You pull it off his face and toss it down. The Muggarik stumbles backward.

TONY: Nice one.

GM: The Muggarik seems dazed and incoherent. His face is pale. The smaller thing scuttles across the ground and leaps toward Catissan. Speed defense roll, please.

STEVE: Oh, no. I wish I had something to block it. A shield or something.

SASHA: We'll get you one for next time.

TONY: If there *is* a next time.

STEVE: I'm putting Effort into this roll too. Just one level. That costs 3 points because I don't have any Speed Edge. I roll a 12.

GM: The thing leaps toward your face, but you duck backward. It lands on the wall next to you and clings there.

TONY: I shoot it with my blaster on my turn. I . . . roll a 1. Crap.

GM: Okay. That's an intrusion. The Muggarik shakes off its condition and draws a long knife. It doesn't have a thing clutched to its face, but it's moving strangely.

SASHA: It's still controlled, maybe.

TONY: Just shoot him!

GM: It uses the knife to slash at Catissan.

STEVE: I don't use Effort for this Speed defense. I roll a 7.

GM: The knife slashes your arm. You take 4 points of damage. But you've got light armor, so you lose 3 points from your Might Pool.

TONY: Shoot him!

SASHA: I shoot my blaster rifle, but at the creepy thing on the wall. I use one level of Effort and roll a 14.

GM: It's small and fast, but that's a hit, thanks to putting Effort into it.

SASHA: I do 6 points of damage, plus 1 from my Masters Weaponry focus.

GM: Your blast sends some of its many legs flying across the room. Yellow fluid splatters across the wall. But it's still alive.

STEVE: Ew. Okay, my turn? I step back, keeping my eye on both of them, but wait to use my Good Advice ability to help Tony's attack on his turn.

GM: Okay. Both of them continue to attack you, Steve.

STEVE: I figured. It's costly, but I'm going to use a level of Effort on both Speed defense rolls. I roll a 16 against the spider-thing, but only a 4 against the Muggarik.

441

GM: The Muggarik cuts you with his knife again. That's 3 more points after you subtract your Armor.

STEVE: Ouch. I'm really hurting here, guys.

TONY: I shoot the spider-thing. Since Catissan's ability is easing my attack, and I've got a light blaster that reduces it another, I'm going to use a level of Effort, but for damage. I roll a 17!

GM: That's a hit!

TONY: Okay, so the blaster does 2 points of damage, but my level of Effort makes that 5, and my 17 roll adds another 1, for a total of 6 points.

GM: Its blackened corpse slides down to the floor.

TONY: That's the way it's done, my friends.

SASHA: All right. What about the Muggarik?

GM: He stands utterly motionless for a moment and then falls to the ground.

SASHA: Aha! I was hoping that would happen. Kill the icky thing, and the mind control ends.

STEVE: Whenever it's my turn, I'm making a recovery roll.

GM: We don't need to pay attention to initiative at this point, although I guess it depends on what you guys do next.

STEVE: I got a 4 on my roll, and I add 2 points for my tier. I'm putting all those points back into my Might Pool.

SASHA: I check out the Muggarik.

GM: He's alive and conscious. His large black eyes don't seem to focus.

TONY: Ask him where our crystals are.

SASHA: I'm going to give him a minute first.

STEVE: Yeah, I help Viddo. We make him comfortable. We'll ask him about the crystals when he can talk.

TONY: I don't trust him. My blaster is still out.

GM: Eventually the Muggarik seems to recover a bit. He sees the two of you giving him some aid, but then he spots Irom's blaster pointed at him.

Normally, the Muggarik would be grateful, but the GM decides that it panics instead, so she slides two cards toward Steve—a GM intrusion. (The group uses cards to represent XP.)

GM: The Muggarik's eyes grow wide, and he tries to get up and make a run for it.

SASHA: We should grab him.

STEVE: I try to calm him down. "Hey, friend. It's okay, we just got rid of that thing that was controlling you."

SASHA: Yeah, I try to help. I'm trained in pleasant social interactions, so that should ease the task.

GM: Okay, make a roll.

STEVE: I'll use a level of Effort, too. That costs 3 points because I don't have any Intellect Edge. And I roll . . . a 2.

SASHA (sliding an XP card toward the GM): I'm going to spend an experience point to have Steve reroll that.

GM: Okay. Steve, roll again.

STEVE: Thank you, Sasha. I roll a 12 this time. That's better, at least.

GM: It's good enough. The Muggarik stops and calms down. Oh, and Steve, you still have an experience point to give to one of the other players.

STEVE: Right. I give it to Sasha, obviously, for helping me.

SASHA: Thanks.

TONY: "All right, dude. Where's our hyperdrive crystals? And where are the rest of your buddies?" And I'll holster my blaster.

GM: Now that he's calm, he clearly realizes that you saved him. Getting him to talk won't require a roll. He begins to tell you about the K-chiln in a strangely cracking voice. "They are horrible, awful, multilegged insect-like creatures that have taken control of many of my people. I do not know what I did while under their control, but I do recall a number of my friends leaving with some canisters holding crystals. They were headed for a starship at a landing platform in the woods." What do you do?

Part 5
BACK MATTER

INDEX	444
CAMPAIGN DESIGN WORKSHEET	446
CHARACTER SHEET	447

INDEX

Abides in Stone	64	crime boss	373	experience points, see XP	237
abomination	315	Cruel	43	exploration focus category	86
Absorbs Energy	64	cure ability category	98	Explorer	27
action	215, 207	currency	201	Explores Dark Places	68
Adept	24	customizing descriptors	59	fairy tale genre	302
advancement, character	240	customizing foci	94	fallen angel	329
ally use focus category	82	cypher	377	fantasy genre	252
ambient damage	217	damage	216	Fast	45
Anathema (supervillain)	356	damage from hazards	217	Fights Dirty	68
Appealing	38	damage track	218	Fights With Panache	68
Armor	202	Dances With Dark Matter	66	flavor	34
armor	217	darkness	221	Flies Faster Than a Bullet	68
artifact	204	dazed	219	focus	60
artificially intelligent, PC species	279	debilitated	218	focus categories	82
assassin	373	deep one	319	focus connection	61
asset	209	deep water	221	Focuses Mind Over Matter	68
attack	215	defend action	225	follower	233
attack modifiers	220	Defends the Gate	66	Foolish	46
attack skill ability category	96	Defends the Weak	66	free level of Effort	209
Awakens Dreams	64	defense task	23	Fuses Flesh and Steel	69
basic focus category	83	deinonychus	320	Fuses Mind and Machine	69
Battles Robots	64	demigod	321	fusion hound	330
Bears a Halo of Fire	64	demon	322	genre	5
Beneficent	39	Descends From Nobility	67	ghost	331
Blazes With Radiance	64	descriptor	38	ghoul	332
Brandishes an Exotic Shield	64	detective	374	giant	333
Brash	39	devil	323	giant rat	334
Builds Robots	65	difficulty	207, 7	giant snake	334
Calculates the Incalculable	65	dim light	220	giant spider	335
Calm	40	disease	219	GM intrusion	237, 408
Channels Divine Blessings	65	Dishonorable	44	GM intrusion, group	410
Chaotic	40	distance	213	goblin	335
character arc	238	distraction	227	golem	336
Charming	41	djinni	324	Graceful	46
chase	224	Doctor Dread (supervillain)	357	gravity, effects of	222, 276
childhood adventure genre	265	Doesn't Do Much	67	grey	337
chimera	316	Doomed	44	Grows to Towering Heights	69
chronophage	317	dragon	325	guard	374
Clever	41	draw the attack	227	Guarded	47
climbing	226	Drives Like a Maniac	67	half-giant, PC species	259
Clumsy	41	dwarf, PC species	258	hard science fiction genre	276
combat	8	ease	207, 7	Hardy	47
combat flavor	36	Edge	15	healing	228
Commands Mental Powers	65	Effort	15	heavy weapon	203
companion ability category	96	elemental, earth	327	helborn, PC species	259
Conducts Weird Science	65	elemental, fire	326	helping	226
Consorts With the Dead	65	elf, PC species	258	Helps Their Friends	69
control ability category	97	Emerged From the Obelisk	67	Hideous	48
Controls Beasts	65	Empathic	44	high-tier abilities	95
Controls Gravity	66	Employs Magnetism	67	hinder	207, 7
cooperative actions	226	encounter	214	historical genre	307
cover	220	encounters, designing	434	Honorable	48
craft ability category	97	energy manipulation focus category	84	horror genre	280
crafting	227	Entertains	67	horror mode, optional rule	283
Crafts Illusions	66	enthraller	328	Howls at the Moon	69
Crafts Unique Objects	66	environment ability category	99	Hunts	69
Craven	42	environment manipulation focus category	85	immediate distance	213
CRAZR	318			impaired	218
creating new foci	80	example of play	439	Impulsive	48
Creative	42	Exiled	45	inability	207, 33
creature	312	Exists in Two Places at Once	67	infatuation, optional rule	287
crime and espionage genre	268	Exists Partially Out of Phase	68	Infiltrates	70

Index

influence focus category	87
information ability category	99
initial cost	212
initiative	214
Inquisitive	49
Insight, gaining	231
Intellect	14
Intelligent	49
Interprets the Law	70
Intuitive	49
invisible target	221
irregular focus category	88
Is Idolized by Millions	70
Is Licensed to Carry	70
Is Wanted by the Law	70
Jovial	50
jumping	228
kaiju	338
Keeps a Magic Ally	71
killer clown	339
killing white light	340
Kind	50
Leads	71
Learned	51
Learns Quickly	71
level	207
light weapon	203
Lives in the Wilderness	71
long distance	213
Looks for Trouble	71
Loves the Void	71
low-tier abilities	95
Lucky	51
Mad	51
madness, optional rule	284
magic flavor	36
Magnetar (supervillain)	358
major effect	212
manifest cypher	379
Masters Defense	72
Masters Spells	72
Masters the Swarm	72
Masters Weaponry	72
Mechanical	52
mechanical soldier	341
medium weapon	203
meta ability category	100
Metes Out Justice	72
mi-go	342
mid-tier abilities	95
Might	14
miniatures	235
minor effect	211
Mister Genocide (supervillain)	359
modern genre	261
mokuren	343
morlock, PC species	300
move	223
movement ability category	101
movement expertise focus category	89
Moves Like a Cat	73
Moves Like the Wind	73
Murders	73
Mysterious	52
Mystical	53
Naive	53
Needs No Weapon	73
Never Says Die	73
neveri	344
nuppeppo	345
occultist	375
ogre	346
Operates Undercover	73
orc	347
paralysis	219
Perceptive	54
Performs Feats of Strength	73
Pilots Starcraft	74
player intrusion	21, 412
Plays Too Many Games	74
poison	219
Pool	15
position	220
post-apocalyptic genre	295
power boost cypher	401
power shifts, optional rule	292
practiced	207
price categories	202
prince(ss) of summer	348
protection ability category	102
puppet tree	349
quintar, PC species	279
Rages	74
range	220
ravage bear	350
recovery roll	218
relationship levels, optional rule	288
repairing	227
replicant	351
Resilient	54
retrying	212
Rides the Lightning	74
riding	229
Risk-Taking	54
roach, PC species	301
romance genre	286
round	214
Rugged	55
Runs Away	74
Sailed Beneath the Jolly Roger	74
Scavenges	75
scavenging	296
science fiction genre	270
secret agent	375
Sees Beyond	75
senses ability category	103
Separates Mind From Body	75
shadow elf	352
Sharp-Eyed	55
Shepherds Spirits	76
Shepherds the Community	75
shock, optional rule	282
short distance	213
Shreds the Walls of the World	76
Siphons Power	76
skeleton	353
Skeptical	55
skill	19
skills and knowledge flavor	37
Slays Monsters	76
slidikin	354
sneaking	229
social ability category	103
Solves Mysteries	77
Speaker	30
Speaks for the Land	77
special abilities	18
special attack ability category	104
special roll	210
specialized	207, 7
species as descriptor	59
Speed	14
spellcasting, optional rule	259
stagger	425
Stands Like a Bastion	77
stat	207
statue, animate	355
stealth flavor	34
Stealthy	56
striker combat focus category	90
Strong	56
Strong-Willed	56
stunned	219
subtle cypher	378
superheroes genre	289
support ability category	105
support focus category	92
surprise	220
Swift	57
swimming	229
take the attack	227
Talks to Machines	77
tank combat focus category	93
target number	7
task	207, 7
task ability category	106
Task Difficulty table	8, 208, 404
technology flavor	35
terrain	224
Throws With Deadly Accuracy	77
thug	376
Thunders	77
tier	17
Tongue-Tied	57
Tough	57
trained	207, 7
transform ability category	107
Travels Through Time	77
turn	207
type	20
tyrannosaurus rex	361
underwater	221
vacuum, effects of	277
vampire	362
vampire, transitional	363
vat reject	364
vehicular combat	230
vehicular movement	230
very long distance	213
Vicious	58
Virtuous	58
wait action	225
wardroid	365
Warrior	20
Was Foretold	78
weakness	33
weapons	203
Wears a Sheen of Ice	78
Wears Power Armor	78
Weird	58
wendigo	366
werewolf	367
Wields Two Weapons at Once	78
witch	368
wizard, mighty	376
Works for a Living	78
Works Miracles	79
Works the Back Alleys	79
Works the System	79
Would Rather Be Reading	79
Wrath (supervillain)	360
xenoparasite	369
XP	237
XP advance	232
zhev	370
zombie	371

CAMPAIGN DESIGN WORKSHEET

CAMPAIGN

GENRE　　　　　　　　　　　　　　　　　　　　　　**GM**

TYPES AVAILABLE

TYPE	BASED ON	MODIFICATIONS

DESCRIPTORS AVAILABLE

- ☐ Appealing
- ☐ Beneficent
- ☐ Brash
- ☐ Calm
- ☐ Chaotic
- ☐ Charming
- ☐ Clever
- ☐ Clumsy
- ☐ Craven
- ☐ Creative
- ☐ Cruel
- ☐ Dishonorable
- ☐ Doomed
- ☐ Empathic
- ☐ Exiled
- ☐ Fast
- ☐ Foolish
- ☐ Graceful
- ☐ Guarded
- ☐ Hardy
- ☐ Hideous
- ☐ Honorable
- ☐ Impulsive
- ☐ Inquisitive
- ☐ Intelligent
- ☐ Intuitive
- ☐ Jovial
- ☐ Kind
- ☐ Learned
- ☐ Lucky
- ☐ Mad
- ☐ Mechanical
- ☐ Mysterious
- ☐ Mystical
- ☐ Naive
- ☐ Perceptive
- ☐ Resilient
- ☐ Risk-Taking
- ☐ Rugged
- ☐ Sharp-Eyed
- ☐ Skeptical
- ☐ Stealthy
- ☐ Strong
- ☐ Strong-Willed
- ☐ Swift
- ☐ Tongue-Tied
- ☐ Tough
- ☐ Vicious
- ☐ Virtuous
- ☐ Weird

FOCI AVAILABLE

- ☐ Abides in Stone
- ☐ Absorbs Energy
- ☐ Awakens Dreams
- ☐ Battles Robots
- ☐ Bears a Halo of Fire
- ☐ Blazes With Radiance
- ☐ Brandishes an Exotic Shield
- ☐ Builds Robots
- ☐ Calculates the Incalculable
- ☐ Channels Divine Blessings
- ☐ Commands Mental Powers
- ☐ Conducts Weird Science
- ☐ Consorts With the Dead
- ☐ Controls Beasts
- ☐ Controls Gravity
- ☐ Crafts Illusions
- ☐ Crafts Unique Objects
- ☐ Dances With Dark Matter
- ☐ Defends the Gate
- ☐ Defends the Weak
- ☐ Descends From Nobility
- ☐ Doesn't Do Much
- ☐ Drives Like a Maniac
- ☐ Emerged From the Obelisk
- ☐ Employs Magnetism
- ☐ Entertains
- ☐ Exists Partially Out of Phase
- ☐ Exists in Two Places at Once
- ☐ Explores Dark Places
- ☐ Fights Dirty
- ☐ Fights With Panache
- ☐ Flies Faster Than a Bullet
- ☐ Focuses Mind Over Matter
- ☐ Fuses Flesh and Steel
- ☐ Fuses Mind and Machine
- ☐ Grows to Towering Heights
- ☐ Helps Their Friends
- ☐ Howls at the Moon
- ☐ Hunts
- ☐ Infiltrates
- ☐ Interprets the Law
- ☐ Is Idolized by Millions
- ☐ Is Licensed to Carry
- ☐ Is Wanted by the Law
- ☐ Keeps a Magic Ally
- ☐ Leads
- ☐ Learns Quickly
- ☐ Lives in the Wilderness
- ☐ Looks for Trouble
- ☐ Loves the Void
- ☐ Masters Defense
- ☐ Masters Spells
- ☐ Masters the Swarm
- ☐ Masters Weaponry
- ☐ Metes Out Justice
- ☐ Moves Like a Cat
- ☐ Moves Like the Wind
- ☐ Murders
- ☐ Needs No Weapon
- ☐ Never Says Die
- ☐ Operates Undercover
- ☐ Performs Feats of Strength
- ☐ Pilots Starcraft
- ☐ Plays Too Many Games
- ☐ Rages
- ☐ Rides the Lightning
- ☐ Runs Away
- ☐ Sailed Beneath the Jolly Roger
- ☐ Scavenges
- ☐ Sees Beyond
- ☐ Separates Mind From Body
- ☐ Shepherds the Community
- ☐ Shepherds Spirits
- ☐ Shreds the Walls of the World
- ☐ Siphons Power
- ☐ Slays Monsters
- ☐ Solves Mysteries
- ☐ Speaks for the Land
- ☐ Stands Like a Bastion
- ☐ Talks to Machines
- ☐ Throws With Deadly Accuracy
- ☐ Thunders
- ☐ Travels Through Time
- ☐ Was Foretold
- ☐ Wears Power Armor
- ☐ Wears a Sheen of Ice
- ☐ Wields Two Weapons at Once
- ☐ Works for a Living
- ☐ Works Miracles
- ☐ Works the Back Alleys
- ☐ Works the System
- ☐ Would Rather Be Reading
- ☐ _____
- ☐ _____
- ☐ _____

OTHER NOTES

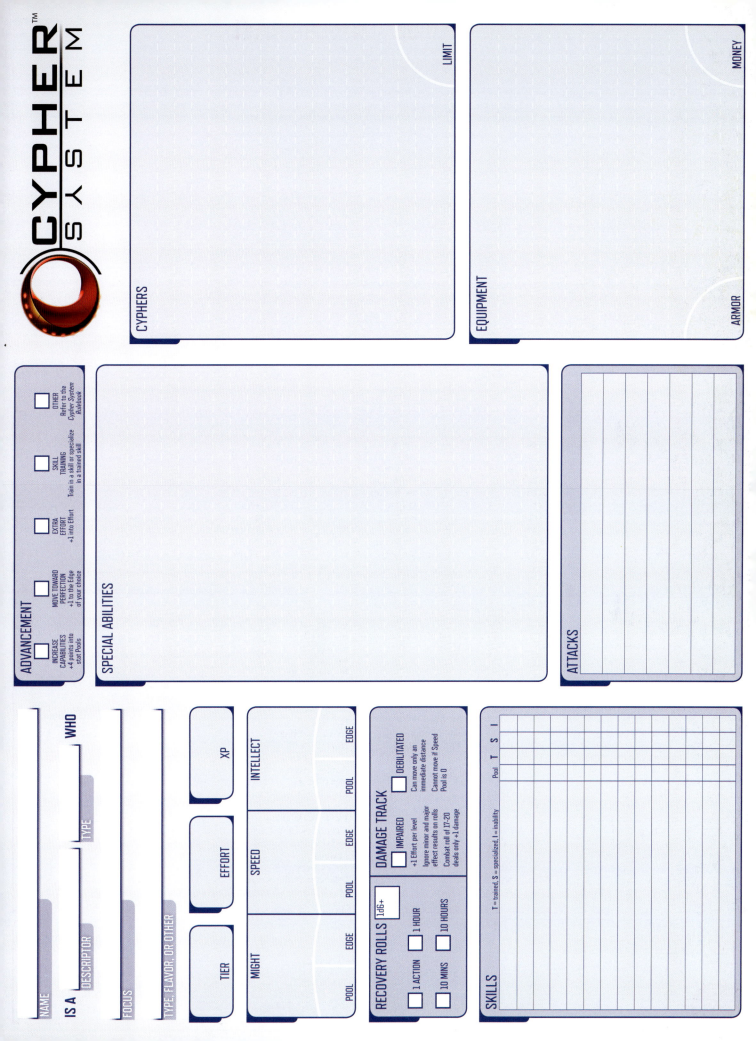

BACKGROUND

NOTES

PORTRAIT